Extremist Mindsets
and Strategies

Extremist Mindsets and Strategies

S. Clara Kim

McFarland & Company, Inc., Publishers
Jefferson, North Carolina

Library of Congress Cataloguing-in-Publication Data

Names: Kim, S. Clara, author.
Title: Extremist mindsets and strategies / S. Clara Kim.
Description: Jefferson, North Carolina : McFarland & Company, Inc.,
    Publishers, 2021. | Includes bibliographical references and index.
Identifiers: LCCN 2020058333 | ISBN 9781476679204
    (paperback : acid free paper) ♾
    ISBN 9781476642536 (ebook)
Subjects: LCSH: Radicalism. | Right-wing extremists.
Classification: LCC HN49.R33 K556 2021 | DDC 303.48/4—dc23
LC record available at https://lccn.loc.gov/2020058333

British Library cataloguing data are available
**ISBN (print) 978-1-4766-7920-4
ISBN (ebook) 978-1-4766-4253-6**

© 2021 S. Clara Kim. All rights reserved

*No part of this book may be reproduced or transmitted in any form
or by any means, electronic or mechanical, including photocopying
or recording, or by any information storage and retrieval system,
without permission in writing from the publisher.*

Front cover image © 2021 Nosyrevy/arloo/Shutterstock

Printed in the United States of America

*McFarland & Company, Inc., Publishers
  Box 611, Jefferson, North Carolina 28640
  www.mcfarlandpub.com*

To all the victims of
extremist aggressions and injustices

Table of Contents

Preface   1
Introduction   5

1. Extremist Cultural Mindsets on a Group Level   30
2. Extremist Cultural Mindsets on a Personal Level   60
3. Extremist Strategies of Pivoting Group Identities   98
4. Extremist Strategies Designed to Enhance Group Power   145
5. Typical Goals of Extremist Groups   175
6. Factors That Facilitate the Rise of Extremist Groups   200
7. Deterring Extremist Group Aggressions   240

Conclusion   293
Chapter Notes   295
Bibliography   357
Index   383

Preface

Most existing studies of extremism and extremist groups focus on specific groups or categories of groups, such as ethno-nationalist, racist, religious or sectarian, militia, far-right reactionaries, far-left radicals, rebel groups, gangs, or criminal syndicates. I present a more generalized and synthesized analysis of extremisms across the spectrum by delving into their commonly shared cultural mindsets and strategies, based on an assumption that *any* group, collectivity, organization, or movement, irrespective of differences in religion, civilization, race, ethnicity, ideology, or nationality, *can* turn extremist when members feel that their group's security, honor, status, interest, or privilege is under threat.

Previous studies of extremist groups have been attentive to deviant, criminal, unconventional, or "fringe" groups with pejorative reputations, such as Islamist/jihadist terror groups, rebel and revolutionary groups, militias and hate groups, gangs, criminal cartels, and exotic religious cults. I maintain that extremist mindsets and strategies are not distinctively unique to groups already labeled as terrorist, unconventional, or deviant "fringe" groups, nor do they exist only in cultures of the "less-civilized" societies and "backward" communities. Even in the most modernized and advanced Western societies, members of various legitimate and conventional groups and organizations regularly display some of the extremist mindsets and deploy extremist strategies to further their group-centric interests and agendas, disregarding the welfare and rights of others. I expose the traces of extremist attributes and aptitudes that persist in various conventional and legitimate groups and organizations in modern societies, such as in political parties, military, police, prisons, religious groups, corporations, interest groups, activist groups, nation-states, fraternities, and athletic teams. By recognizing the extremist tendencies and proclivities that exist among and around us, I hope more people will begin to question the common myths, stereotypes, and assumptions that extremists are "uncivilized" and "barbaric" "evil-doers" who are fundamentally different from the "righteous" and "civilized" who do good.

Most resistant extremist groups (and some redemptive and reactionary groups) surface because powerful groups use extremist measures to maximize their group-centric interests by unfairly taking advantage of powerless groups of people ("dominant extremism"). In response, the mistreated groups of people also use extremist means to rebel against the dominant extremisms that engender systemic unfairness, injustice, and extreme inequalities, demanding equal rights and a share of the benefits. The dominant groups, instead of sharing power and wealth, label the resistant groups as "extremists/terrorists," "radicals," and "agitators," and deploy repressive campaigns to oppress them, crushing their aspirations for reform. History is awash with such struggles between the dominant and privileged versus subordinate and marginalized groups of people—e.g., slaves fought against the system of slavery to be liberated; colonized against the colonizers; exploited workers against the capitalists; women against male domination; and persecuted and discriminated minority groups, whether religious, racial, ethnic, or sexual orientation, against the dominant majority groups. Systemic police killings and abuse of criminal suspects with impunity lead to riots and mob violence by the wronged and their sympathizers, and extreme and prolonged economic injustice and inequality elicit the rise of populist revolts. In the same way, when powerful nations and multinational corporations plunder natural resources, harm the environment, exploit cheap labor in less developed nations, and get away with their malfeasance by propping up corrupt dictators who brutally suppress their own people's democratic aspirations, anti–West sentiments and extremist aggressions are bound to ensue.

Therefore, in order to deter resistant extremisms from evolving we must prevent dominant extremisms from developing. The study of extremist aggressions must include an understanding of the mutually causative dynamics between the dominant and resistant extremisms—how they provoke and inflame each other—and counter-extremist measures should focus upon resolving the root causes of the grievances and indignation that resistant group members harbor against dominant groups. The most ideal approach to deterring extremist aggressions in any given society would be curtailing the likely causes of both dominant and resistant extremisms by improving the general security, justice, and fairness for *all* groups of people. I discuss some of the structural, cultural, and strategic changes that can assist the process. In our interconnected modern world, economic and political injustices spread globally, spurring extremist/terror groups to globalize, also. Unless the world can tame and restrain both dominant and resistant extremisms concurrently, reconciling their clashing interests and demands in mutually beneficial and respectful ways with the help of international organizations, anti–West extremism will not subside. The hardline, militarized counterterrorism measures aimed at "crushing" and "annihilating" extremist/terrorist groups will only validate their causes and intensify their wrath toward the West, and pose graver threats to humanity, possibly armed with weapons of mass destruction, as cycles of fear, outrage, and violence escalate, spiraling out of control.

Introduction

Extremist groups and acts have existed throughout history, more frequently in the pre-modern era than in modern societies. Scholars have documented that deaths from violent conflicts (e.g., wars, intergroup collisions, inter-personal violence, and terrorist attacks), whether for political, religious, racial, ethnic, or ideological motives, have declined drastically in modern era, especially since the end of the Cold War.[1] Perhaps for this reason, the 9/11 terrorist attacks on the New York World Trade Center and Pentagon in 2001 were particularly alarming to Westerners, and renewed their attention to and fear of extremist groups, which was compounded by fears of proliferating weapons of mass destruction. Since the 9/11 attacks, Islamist/jihadist groups have become the archetype of extremist groups, and extremism has become virtually synonymous with terrorism. Studies of extremism shifted their attention to terrorist groups with Islamist/jihadist ties in lieu of the usual extremist groups of the past—e.g., ethno-nationalist, far-left, far-right, rebel, revolutionary, militia, racist, and anti–Semitic, and other hate groups.

Contrary to the evolving trend, I maintain that extremism can occur in any group in any society where people band together and try to achieve their group-centric goals, disregarding the welfare and rights of others, irrespective of culture, civilization, race, ethnicity, religion, class, and ideology. The groups can be small or large, dominant or subordinate, privileged or underprivileged, majority or minority, legitimate or illegitimate, left or right, and change-seeking or change-resisting. As long as the group members act upon extremist mindsets and deploy extremist strategies to achieve their extremist goals supported by extremist ideologies, they are extremist groups and participants become extremists.

The sources of group identities can be biological (e.g., race, sex, family, kinship), birthright-based (e.g., castes, slaves, monarchs, aristocrats), religious, sectarian, cultural, regional, national, civilizational, multinational, ideological (e.g., right/left, class-oriented), or political (e.g., interest groups, political parties, nation-states, or rebel or paramilitary groups). They can also be organizational (e.g., police, prison, military, corporations, criminal syndicates, fraternities), agenda-related (e.g., pro-environmental, anti-abortion, pro-gun rights, anti-war, pro-labor unions), situational (e.g., street gangs, vigilante mobs, protesting rioters), or privileged status groups. However, being "groupish" or "groupistic," such as having a strong sense of belonging and emotional attachment to a group with a "buddy-buddy" type of camaraderie and love for the group (e.g., patriotism), even feeling proud of group identity alone is not extremism.

Groups become extremists when members capitalize on the "groupish" human emotions, and try to exploit them to seek group empowerment, either to dominate others or to resist domination, by *violating* other people's rights, lives, and welfare.

Typically, groups become extremists when members try to maximize their group-centric interests at any costs and by any means—e.g., ignoring rules, laws, ethics, morality, fairness, and justice; violating or denying interests or rights of other groups of people—while refusing to negotiate, compromise, share powers, and reconcile colliding interests between sparring groups. Their extremist acts can be organized (e.g., state-sponsored terrorism, foreign invasion, war crimes) or spontaneous (e.g., vigilante mob violence, violent protests), legal or illegal, violent or non-violent.

Non-violent extremist acts, even if they are legal, can be just as devastating and harmful to a large number of people as violent acts are, although they may not be as instantaneously and spectacularly destructive and lethal as terrorist acts are. They occur when a group of people tries to enrich or empower themselves and further their political and economic benefits by taking advantage of other groups of people in systematically unjust and unfair ways and means.

History is awash with extremely unjust political, economic, and social systems and policies that were implemented for the benefit of one group at the expense of another, even though they may not be physically violent, such as slavery, apartheid, caste systems, patriarchy, polygyny, colonialism, imperialism, autocracy, unfettered capitalism, and other discriminatory and abusive policies and practices. In such cases, the dominant groups use extremist ideologies (e.g., nationalism, racism, ethnocentrism, sexism, fascism, Nazism, social Darwinism, communism, free-market fundamentalism) to support, justify, normalize, and legitimize the extremely unfair and unjust actions, norms, and policies from which they benefit unilaterally. For instance, the history-long practice of patriarchy has yielded brutally abusive and unjust treatments of women for centuries that were justified by sexist ideologies and sanctioned by religious and political institutions.

Powerless minority groups of all categories—e.g., race, ethnicity, religion, caste, region, and sexual orientation—have endured devastating consequences of discrimination and maltreatment at the hands of the dominant majority groups. This unabashedly exploitive and unfettered capitalism, pushed for by ruthlessly pro-business economic elites and corporations, and justified by the ideology of free-market fundamentalism, supply-side theories, and economic neoliberalism, has yielded immense human suffering, injustices, and unfair inequalities on a mass scale.

Extremism is not limited to actions (e.g., hate crimes, war crimes, genocides), tactics (e.g., terrorism, political obstructionism), or unfair and unjust economic and political policies implemented for the benefit of one group at the expense of another group. It can also be ideologies (e.g., racism, sexism, ethno-nationalism, far-right or far-left conservatism or liberalism, radicalized communism, Islamism, religious and free-market fundamentalism); attitudes and mindsets (e.g., extreme prejudice, intense hatred, fanaticism, paranoiac fears, and extreme rigidity and intransigency), and beliefs (e.g., fundamentalism, ideological dogmatism, unconventional and exotic cultic beliefs).

Not every group with outlandish beliefs and activities, however, becomes extremist, unless the group infringes upon the rights and welfare of people, whether victims are its own members or outsiders. Simply "being different" or "acting differently," no matter how bizarre it may be, does not warrant extremism, unless groups *violate* people's basic rights and welfare, including members of their own group (e.g., ideological indoctrination, financial extortion through deception, encouraged suicide bombings, coerced membership and entrapment, sacrifice, isolation, sex, crime, unpaid labor, sexual and physical abuse of children). Most hate groups (e.g., racist, sexist, misogynist, anti-gay, anti–Semitic, anti-immigrant, xenophobic, homophobic) can be considered extremist groups even when they do not engage in unfair acts of discrimination or terrorizing acts of violence, *if* the targeted groups of people feel intimidated and threatened by their hate-filled prejudicial beliefs and attitudes.

At the same time, when groups of people commit extremist/terrorist acts to promote their beliefs and agendas, even if their beliefs and agendas may not be discriminatory or pose threats to others, they will be regarded as extremist groups. Seeking justice through unjust means—e.g., by violating innocent people's welfare, rights, and lives—is just as extreme as inflicting injustice against others, even if the goal is to "right the wrong" or "send a political message." Some anti-war, anti-nuke, anti-racist, anti-fascist, socialist, communist, animal rights, and environmental groups and activists have taken up violent means and terrorist acts to promote their agendas.

By the same reasoning, religious fundamentalist groups can be extremists if they rationalize mistreatment of women, demand unwarranted sacrifice of human lives, or deny equal rights of homosexuals and people of different religious beliefs, using their beliefs as justification for their discriminatory actions. Catholic churches' beliefs and creeds may not be extremist, but when they systematically engage in covering up pedophile priests to protect the reputation of the church, thus allowing more children to be sexually abused, they become extremist groups because their group-centric acts violate the rights and welfare of children.

Likewise, some groups can be extremists in their beliefs and ideologies only, but not in actions and strategies ("extremism in beliefs"), and others can be extremists in their actions and strategies only, but not in their beliefs and ideologies ("extremism in actions"). Within this framework of extremism, we can infer that not all extremist acts and groups are violent and terroristic, although most terrorist acts and groups are extremist acts and groups.

Equating extremism with terrorism and studying extremism with exclusive focus on terrorist groups and acts will confound and distort understanding of extremism and extremist groups. We need to decouple extremism from terrorism, and regard terrorism as one of the tactical means *some* extremist groups deploy.

As with all forms of deviances, defining extremism is challenging because people disagree over what constitutes extremism and criteria for being "extreme." In most cases, the definition of extremism is relative and "in the eye of the beholder"—i.e., what one group considers extremism may not be deemed as extremism by another group. One group's "terrorists" can be another group's "freedom fighters" and "martyrs," and one group's "freedom of economic activity" can be another group's economic "oppression and exploitation." Most people in the Western world consider the Burmese military's brutal massacres, destruction of villages, and expulsion of ethnic minority Rohingya people as "ethnic cleansing"; whereas, the government and military of Myanmar call it a "clean-up operation of terrorist groups."[2]

The majority of Westerners would judge the use of chemical weapons and indiscriminate bombings of civilian infrastructures of Sunni enclaves by Syria's Assad regime as "war crimes"; yet, the regime says it is trying to "liberate the area from terrorists."[3] The "White Helmets" are civilian volunteer rescuers in Syria formed in rebel-held areas during the civil war, because the Syrian government does not provide rescue operation forces.

They risk their lives rescuing anyone who is injured by the Assad regime's indiscriminate bombings, and help them to evacuate and find shelter. They are hailed as heroes and were nominated for the Nobel Peace Prize in 2016 for saving over 100,000 Syrian civilian lives.

Yet, the Syrian government and Russian allies consider them "terrorists" and "criminals," systematically hunted them down and killed them, and prohibited them from leaving Syria because they are key witnesses to the regime's war crimes.[4] Many people in the Western world considers North Korea and Iran as extremist "rogue" nations for pursuing nuclear weapons.

In contrast, North Korea and Iran regard acquiring nuclear weapons as a vital means of survival and defense against the aggressive, "imperialist" regime of the U.S. that threatens them with nuclear weapons and infringes upon their national sovereignty.

Most extremists probably do not consider themselves as extremists; rather, they justify and normalize their extreme acts as necessary, legitimate, or "the only possible way" available to achieve their "righteous" goals.

For this reason, the tactics and ideologies of *both* extremist/terrorist groups and counter-extremist/terrorist responses have been extreme throughout history—i.e., they committed equally violent and terrorizing acts—and both sides believe that they are pursuing "just and noble causes" that warrant violence and human sacrifice. Both communist and anti-communist groups and actions were brutal and extreme during the Cold War era, and both the 9/11 terrorist attacks and the West's counter-terrorist efforts (e.g., "war against terrorism") have been violent, destructive, and "terrorizing" to many people.

During the women's suffrage movement, both "suffs" (suffrage supporters) and "antis" (anti-suffrage protesters) engaged in violent acts claiming to be "righteous"[5]; during the Civil Rights movement era in the 1960s, both pro- and anti–Civil Rights protesters were destructive and fierce[6]; both anti-war and anti-anti-war protesters committed violence during the Vietnam War.[7] Pro-union and anti-union, far-left and far-right political activists, populists, and protesters have been violent and extreme,[8] as have Islamist and anti–Islam extremists in Europe (e.g., English Defense League, Darren Osborne, Alexandre Bissonnette).[9] Some anti-racist and anti-fascist groups and protests in the U.S. (e.g., some of the "Black Lives Matter" protesters, race rioters, and Antifa) have been violent and destructive at times. They also try to impose their beliefs and values upon others, and denounce other groups with a tone of moral superiority that justifies and condones violence.[10]

Even when people generally agree, the definition of extremism can vary over time, places, and situations. Throughout history, people routinely tolerated and approved even the most apparently atrocious acts, including mass murders and genocides, especially during war, and even glorified them and rewarded offenders with awards and recognitions. People in the past considered slavery, caste systems, monarchism, polygyny, child labor, child abuse, and subjugation of women as normal, traditional, and acceptable acts, and some still do in countless repressively traditional areas around the world.

Depending on what most people deem to be "mainstream," "ordinary," or "conventional" in a given society, the "extreme" positions can also vary dramatically. For instance, what the majority of Americans consider religious fundamentalism and extreme sexism would be quite normal and conventional in Afghanistan and Pakistan. Most Americans probably believe that imposing the death penalty for apostasy and blasphemy and mandating women to cover head-to-toe are extremist policies in violation of basic human rights of people, although they are perfectly legitimate and widely accepted norms in numerous Muslim nations. On the other hand, most Afghans would consider same-sex marriage and allowing women to bare their body and hair in public places to be extremist policies in violation of their traditional religious values.

Extremism is always a matter of degree—i.e., there is no dichotomy of clearly distinguishable "extremists" and "non-extremists." Some people are more extremist than others in a given situation and location, and some groups rely on more extremist beliefs and strategies than other groups do.

Groups are more likely to be labeled as extremist when their extremist qualities become more pronounced and pervasive compared to other "reference" groups—e.g., they violate or impinge upon others' rights, interests, and existence to achieve their group-centric goals—although not every group that violates others' rights and interests is labeled or perceived to be an extremist group. In general, the powerless minorities and underdog groups are more likely to be labeled as extremist and terrorist groups than the majority and powerful groups are when they commit equally extremist acts.[11]

Contrary to widely held beliefs, I maintain that extremism is not a phenomenon exclusive to deviant, criminal, unconventional, "fringe," or outcast groups and organizations (e.g., gangs, criminal cartels, rebel or revolutionary forces, terrorist groups, racist organizations, far-right/left political groups, and exotic cults). Although they may not be as physically and brazenly violent and threatening as terrorist acts are, some components of extremist proclivities and strategies are discernible in a salvo of legitimate and conventional groups and organizations in modern societies, such as in political parties, religious institutions, nation-states, repressive regimes, corporations, status groups, labor unions, military, police, prisons, fraternities, and sports teams.

For instance, partisan politics in America have been replete with extremist inclinations. Political campaigns are brimming with "enemization and demonization" and character assassination strategies designed to vilify and crush opponents—e.g., defamatory and slanderous smear tactics, spreading of false rumors, misinformation, and misrepresentations of facts—as they consider the end goal of winning elections as justification for the use of extremist means, heedless of ethical concerns and public interests. Even after elections, parties engage in tit-for-tat, retaliatory "obstructionism," refusing to negotiate and compromise, causing partisan gridlocks and congressional paralyses, ignoring welfare of the public, even with high political cost to the obstructing party.[12] The rancorous partisan politics in Washington, D.C., has spilled over into the mainstream in recent years, spurring a dramatic upsurge in "affective polarization" of the American electorate with "fear and loathing" across party lines.[13]

Considering these conceptual complexities of extremism, I restrict discussion of extremism in this monograph to group- or identity-based and ideologically- or politically-motivated extremisms—i.e., a group of people, who share the same identity or interests, trying to promote their group-centric agendas or maximize group-centric interests by taking advantage of or infringing upon other people's rights, interests, and lives. They do not hesitate to carry out extremely unfair and unjust actions that harm other groups of people, while refusing to negotiate compromises, share powers, or reconcile differences and conflicting interests. I analyze the cultural mindsets of people who act in extremist ways in a concerted effort to promote their group-centric interests and agendas, as leaders, followers, participants, supporters, sympathizers, propagandists, or financiers.

Extremism in this manuscript is not limited to behaviors, actions, and beliefs, but also includes coordinated policies and institutionalized systems that are designed to maximize group-centric interests by taking advantage of other people's lives, rights, and welfare. Examples of such extremism include state-organized or state-sponsored extremist acts, such as foreign invasion, occupation, political purging by dictatorial regimes, massacres, ethnic cleansings, genocides, and other war crimes; political, economic, and legal systems that are inherently favorable to one group of people at the expense of another group of people (e.g., slavery, patriarchy, aristocracy, caste systems, colonialism, and discrimination based on race, ethnicity, nationality, sexuality, socio-economic status); and similarly unfair and exploitive economic practices of multinational corporations and globalized economic elites.

This classification of extremists includes *individual* actors who commit extremist/terrorist acts alone on behalf of or representing a group, or inspired by group-centric ideologies and propagandas, such as so-called "lone-wolf" terrorists.

On the other hand, it excludes individuals who commit extremist acts alone *without* group-based ideological affiliation, such as sociopathic, psychopathic, and egocentric acts of violence, abuse, and exploitation motivated by *personal* greed, vendetta, pleasure, or mental illness, *unless* they commit such acts by capitalizing on group- and identity-related agendas or ideologies. For instance, group leaders who *use* group-centric, extremist causes and ideologies (e.g., racist, anti-immigrant, anti–Semitic, nationalistic) and stir-up people's emotions of fear and hatred, only to garner political support for themselves and satisfy their own selfish interests of amassing power, wealth, or fame, whether political or religious, by pitting groups against one another and inciting loathing and violence (e.g., "identitarian" demagogues), are included in the analysis, even though their goal may be achieving personal gains.

Depending on the goals and causes, there can be numerous types of extremist groups. Most extremist groups converge on roughly five main categories, although they are not always mutually exclusive or exhaustive. Some groups become extremists as they try to dominate and subjugate other groups or monopolize resources using extreme measures, which I call "dominant extremism."

Group members band together and try to maintain the status quo from which they benefit, or further their collective interests by exploiting subordinate groups. These groups become aggressively extreme when subjugated groups challenge their privileged status and demand equal status and rights. Monarchs and aristocrats fiercely fought against democratizing demands for centuries to secure their dominant status, and colonizers brutally suppressed independence movements by the colonized.

Throughout history, men have systematically subjugated women using extremely abusive policies disguised as "traditions" and "natural social order"; white supremacists tried to maintain superior status over non-whites using violent means and discriminatory tactics and ideologies, and countless right-wing, anti-immigrant, nativist groups tried to shield their superior or majority status and privilege by suppressing minority groups' access to equal rights and benefits. Some powerful nations have tried to maximize their national self-interest by taking advantage of the less-powerful nations and their people, politically and economically; some corporations have sought to maximize profit by hurting consumers, violating workers' rights and safety, and damaging the environment. Their acts are just as "extreme" and adverse as the rebel and resistant groups committing violent acts to send political messages by hurting vulnerable people.

On the other hand, there are groups whose goal is to *resist* domination and subjugation by other groups using extremist measures—"resistant extremism." Scores of subjugated, persecuted, oppressed, discriminated, or marginalized groups of people have banded together and demanded equal rights and access to power and resources using extremist measures, especially when legal and legitimate means of achieving equal rights are nonexistent or systematically obstructed.

Revolutionary movements by the marginalized, independence movements by the occupied, insurgency and rebel groups, labor unions, anti-establishment populist movements of the left and right, and equal rights movements by discriminated and stigmatized minorities have potential to become extremist when they resort to violent and destructive means of resistance and confrontation, causing harm to people and destruction of social order.

At times, groups with comparable power and status engage in extremist actions in their effort to seek hegemonic dominance and monopolize resources—"competitive extremist groups." Throughout history, incessant power-struggles have existed between a plethora of competitive groups, whether they were families, tribes, gangs, criminal cartels, political parties, ethnic groups, or nation states violently pursuing political and economic dominance and territorial expansion, or assorted religious, sectarian (e.g., Christians vs. Muslims; Catholics vs. Protestants; Sunnis vs. Shiites), and ideological groups of similar power (e.g., communist vs. anti-communist, left vs. right, conservative vs. liberal).

In "redemptive extremist groups," members commit extremist acts driven by "moralistic" aspirations of "saving the world" from whatever source they perceive to be "evil," unjust, or threatening, even when they are not directly affected by the "evil" or unjust acts and threats. The sources of the "evil" can be diverse, such as abortion, homosexuality, wars, nuclear weapons, animal abuse, environmental damage, the West, "evil empires," capitalism, communism, fascism, police, corrupt and abusive corporations, "big banks," and the government. In such groups, extremist acts become "righteous" acts members commit with a profound sense of indignation and "moralistic" duty and mission to protect the groups of people afflicted by the "evil" sources.[14]

Some groups become extremist and hostile toward outsiders out of an overriding aspiration to defend and maintain the group's identity, traditions, beliefs, and cultural distinction, which are often called "reactionary" or "change-resisting" extremist groups.

There are numerous traditional, socially- and culturally-conservative, and religiously fundamentalist groups that fear and resist modernizing, liberalizing, and secularizing trends and belligerently defend their group's dogmas, beliefs, and traditions. These groups can become extremists when they revile provocatively, attack violently, discriminate against, or deny rights of people who challenge or do not abide by their "orthodox" or "group-sanctioned" versions of beliefs, dogmas, creeds, and lifestyles (e.g., non-believers, infidels, heretics, atheists, homosexuals, non-conformists, and "traitors" of their beliefs).

These groups try to uphold the status-quo resisting changes, if not wishing to return to the "good-old days" of the past, or "undo modernity," fearing that their group's identity, tradition, and distinctiveness may disappear, whether they are religious, cultural, racial, ethnic, national, or regional ("fear of extinction"). Scholars have discussed that the ascent of anti–West and anti-globalization extremisms in the Arab and Muslim world is a form of "reactionary backlash" against the West's hegemonic cultural sway, technology, and modernization,[15] combined with their resentment against their secularizing trend.[16] Instead, they strive for "indigenization," "re-tribalization," and "re–Islamization" of the Middle East.[17] As Calhoun[18] discusses, tradition can be an essential source *and* resource for radicalization for these reactionary extremist groups. The globalizing and "heterogenizing" trends of the modern world have been an unsettling experience for the identity-bound traditionalists around the world.

As more people migrate, mix, mingle, and switch identities, it is becoming increasingly problematic for them to define and maintain their traditional identities and culture.[19] Fearing "extinction," they burrow in and hunker down deeper into their core identities and traditions (e.g., "bunker mentality"), becoming hostile toward "out-groups" and anyone who challenges or violates their traditions.

These classifications are Weberian "ideal types" presented solely for the purpose of discussing extremism in this monograph, and not intended for academic recognition. In addition, these types are not always mutually exclusive—i.e., some groups have of more than one cause or goal. For instance, Islamist/jihadist groups can be "resistant extremist groups" because they struggle to fight against the hegemonic dominance of the West; "reactionary extremist groups" because they endeavor to preserve Islamic identity, tradition, and ideological purity, rejecting changes and repudiating modern values; and "redemptive" in a sense that they try to "save the world" from "evil empires" of the West. Christian fundamentalist and nationalist groups in America can be "dominant extremist groups" because they, as numeric majorities, strive to maintain Christian heritage as the dominant tradition in America, as well as "reactionary extremist groups" for trying to preserve traditional religious beliefs renouncing secularization trends.

Assortments of "resistant extremist groups" are inspired by redemptive aspirations, also. The Communist movement, for instance, was a "resistant" extremism fighting against the wealthy and powerful capitalist class, but also a "redemptive," because revolutionaries believed in "saving the world" from the "evil" capitalism and concomitant injustices. Similarly, the Weathermen of the 1960s (radical left-wing group) would be both a "resistant" extremist group for targeting the wealthy and powerful and "redemptive" for aspiring to "save" the poor and underprivileged from the "evils" committed by the wealthy and powerful.

After the 9/11 terrorist attacks in 2001, some scholars and commentators reintroduced the popular projection that the world was going to be divided along the cultural fault lines of civilizations or religions, or between the Western vs. non–Western hemispheres (e.g., Huntington's "clash of civilizations"), replacing the class-based ideological clashes that plagued the world during the Cold War era. On the other hand, others doubted the salience of cultural and civilizational divide on the global level, and regarded the prediction largely as a misrepresented or misinterpreted overgeneralization.[20]

Rather than "clash of civilizations," the general trend seems to shed light on the emerging chasm *within* the Muslim world between the growing number of moderate modernists and secularists on one side and traditional Islamists and fundamentalist on the other side (called "culture clash within the Islamic world").[21] The prevailing values most modernized, moderate Muslims espouse appear to be quite similar to the values most Western modernites hold, regardless of nationality, race, ethnicity, and civilization—e.g., *individual* rights, liberty, autonomy, equality, basic human rights, and pursuance of personal happiness, comfort, achievement, and success.

The predominant values extremist hardliners, fundamentalists, and traditionalists hold are also comparatively analogous, irrespective of religion, nationality, race, ethnicity, and civilization—e.g., the *group's* security, power, dominance, honor, glory, and pride.

The Western world had undergone historic transformation from the group-bound traditionalism and fundamentalism to individualizing modern values earlier in history, which, albeit through tumultuous melees and bloodsheds, resulted in a dramatically reduced number, size, and vigor of extremist groups, whether they were political, religious, racial, ethnic, or ideological in origin.

As the Muslim world undergoes similar transformation, the feud between the moderate modernizing and extremely fundamentalist Muslims will continue to beleaguer their societies, and affect broader, interconnected geopolitics. Already, there are sizable and growing numbers of moderate, secularized, and modernized Muslims who condemn terrorist violence by Islamist/jihadist extremist groups just as vehemently as non–Muslim Westerners do, and they fear Islamist/jihadist extremism as much as Westerners do. Scores of moderate Muslims in Europe report the hardships of having to combat against their own radicalized extremists who vilify and assault them for "lacking loyalty," while battling against the West's stereotype of them as "terrorists." Some moderate Muslim leaders in Europe fear the threats from the hardline Muslims to such an extent that they need bodyguards.[22]

The 9/11 terrorist attacks and the subsequent counterterrorist responses by the Western world seem to have exposed the divergent and opposing values between the moderates and extremists in the U.S. as well. We observed the rise of conservative fundamentalist Christians who advocated that America, as a Christian nation, must unite and fight against the Islamists and Muslims.[23] We witnessed how some politicians tried to place America's values and morals on the higher ground to justify aggressively militant counterterrorist responses against terrorist groups and nations that harbor them.

On the other hand, moderate Americans expressed grave apprehension over the upsurge of (what they see as) irrational and over-zealous nationalism, anti-immigrant nativism, right-wing, populist authoritarianism and militarism, in the name of counterterrorism and national security (the "War against Terrorism"). Some Americans were "shocked and appalled" by how cruel and uncivilized some of their fellow Americans could be over the prisoner abuse incidences (e.g., in Abu Ghraib, Bagram, and the Guantanamo Bay detention center) and unjustified killings and rapes of civilians by U.S. soldiers and contractors in Iraq and Afghanistan. On the other hand, others were equally "shocked and appalled" by how some of their fellow Americans could be so "anti–American" and "unpatriotic," rebuking the U.S. military and government for trying to protect America.[24]

Moderates and extremists have existed and collided in every society throughout history with varying intensity—e.g., more extremists in traditional societies and communities, and more moderates in modernizing societies and communities. In the pre-modern era, most people, leaders and followers alike, were hardline, "groupish" and "tribalistic" extremists collectively endeavoring to secure their group-centric interests, whether they were survival, domination, resistance, or simply honor and pride.

People commonly revered extremists and glorified extremist acts of fighting and dying for the group with violent means, without much concern for the innocent victims of extremist acts in the process. In modern societies, people are becoming more reluctant to adopt or support extreme, violent, and unjust means of achieving any group-centric goals in violation of individual rights. Indiscriminate killings of a large number of civilians, torturing, raping, dismembering, and burning down villages, for instance, regardless of whether victims are enemies, terrorists, criminals, or prisoners, inexorably evoke moral opprobrium and condemnation from the moderate modernites.

Whichever group is engaged in extremist acts will eventually lose allies and sympathizers, which is a high price to pay in the end. In modern, democratic societies, therefore, terrorist operations inescapably contain the seeds of their own demise, because they offend the majority of the population. Without the majority's support, extremist campaigns are unlikely to succeed in democratic societies.[25]

As societies modernize, the fault lines of cultural chasm seem to be shifting—from identity-based intergroup feuds to those between the extremists and moderates of various groups, identities, ideologies, beliefs, and policy issues. These changes are reshaping and redefining contentious political and social discourse concerning a multitude of issues, both domestic and global.

In the domestic arena, open-minded moderates and hardline extremists quarrel over such wedge issues as the role of the government, religion, law enforcement, criminal justice policies, public assistance to the needy, and rights of the convicted, minorities, women, and homosexuals. Regarding foreign policies, they dispute over issues of war, foreign invasion, torture, military intervention and expenditures, political interference in foreign countries, and economic globalization. The so-called "culture wars" and "battle of ideas" generally mirror the opposing values between the group-bound extremists—e.g., "groupish" and "tribalistic" traditionalists and fundamentalists who fiercely defend their parochial views, identities, and group-centric interests such as ethno-nationalists, nativists, racists, sexists, anti-gay, religious and free-market fundamentalists—on one side, and more moderate, modernized individualists and humanists with cosmopolitan and universalistic views on the other.

Scholars have noted the shifting of fault lines within religious communities and political parties in America in recent decades. A growing number of Americans are realigning their religious affiliations from the denominational differences (e.g., Protestants vs. Catholics) toward extreme fundamentalist vs. moderate modernist. The progressive circle within Protestantism, Catholicism, and Judaism expresses virtually identical ideological concerns and interests, and the extremists and orthodox within each of these traditions displays nearly indistinguishable attributes—e.g., defense of fundamentalist and traditionalist dogmas and anxiety over change.[26]

In politics, there has been mounting intra-party discord *within* both the Republican and Democratic parties between the moderates (or the "established") and the extremist (or the "anti-establishment" populists), which became viscerally evident during the 2016 presidential campaign that bestowed power to the "anti-establishment" Trump presidency. During his reign, the Republican Party continued to face rancorous infighting between the two camps over a variety of social and political issues—e.g., attempts to repeal Obamacare, immigration, free trade, and tariffs.[27] In Europe, the center-right and center-left establishment parties have been working together, either unofficially or in a grand coalition, to battle against the rising threats from far-right extremist parties.[28]

The proportions of moderates and extremists in a given society seem to fluctuate depending on political and economic situations and unfolding events. As "intergroup threat theories"[29] suggest, under threats from external sources, whether political, military, cultural, economic, or resource-related, hardline extremist forces gain ground over moderate forces, activating more aggressively authoritarian mindsets among people and greater support for authoritarian leadership.[30] We observed how a substantial number of Americans reverted to extremist mindsets after the 9/11 terrorist attacks and endorsed hardline militaristic counterterrorist policies and authoritarian leadership (e.g., supporting the Iraq and Afghan wars, torture, and limitation of civil liberties and anti–Muslim sentiments).[31] With collaborating allies, America invaded a nation (Iraq) that "had nothing to do with 9/11," as the 9/11 Commission concluded and President Bush admitted,[32] and wreaked havoc with mass destruction and chaos that resulted in extensive civilian casualties.[33] The U.S. government and military detained thousands of terror suspects without due process and denied their right to habeas corpus. They sent some of the detainees to other nations ("extraordinary rendition" or "black sites") to be subjected to "enhanced interrogation techniques" in violation of international rules of engagement.[34]

By the same logic, we should be able to understand how Muslims' views of the West altered following the U.S.-led invasion of Iraq and a handful of ill-fated foibles and mishaps that followed the invasion. Muslims around the world, particularly the Sunnis, perceived the invasion as a painfully threatening and humiliating experience, and solidified their support for the Islamist/jihadist extremist groups.[35]

The Iraq War and subsequent fall of Saddam Hussein also prompted other "rogue" nations with tyrannical regimes, such as North Korea and

Iran, to pursue nuclear weapons fearing U.S. aggression and its policy of "regime change."[36]

Extremist aggressions tend to beget extremist responses. Rise of chauvinistic hostility in one group poses a security threat to the targeted group, which also turns to chauvinism to defend itself. Each side becomes a threat to the other, generating a vicious cycle of escalating fear, suspicion, and enmity, resulting in "securities dilemma."[37]

Violently radicalized communist movements with aggressively expansionistic territorial ambition galvanized the rise of hardline, militant, repressive anti-communist authoritarian regimes and policies around the world during the Cold War era, effecting immeasurably tragic consequences of human sacrifice, suffering, and destruction. Similarly, the 9/11 terrorist attacks in 2001 ignited equally terrorizing counterterrorist belligerence by the American government and military, with wide-ranging endorsement of the American people.

Military aggression and terrorist attacks are not the only sources that foment extremist responses. Extremely unfair and unjust systems and policies that serve interests of one group at the expense of another—whether they are political, economic, or social—can also prompt extremist reactions and aggression among the afflicted groups of people. History is brimming with examples of how slavery, apartheid, caste systems, patriarchy, monarchy, repressive autocracy, colonialism, imperialism, unregulated capitalism, and discrimination against minority groups has begotten an assortment of revolutionary, rebel, resistance, and protest groups and movements with extremist means revolting against the extremely unfair and unjust systems and policies.

As group psychologists discuss, every group provides a space and arena where actions and interactions take place, and in so doing, constructs a distinctive, idiosyncratic culture, called "idioculture"—i.e., a system of beliefs and customs members commonly adhere to.[38] Yet, there is a segment of overlapping commonalities *among* "idiocultures" that are patently similar.[39]

Such commonalities appear to be apparent among varieties of extremist groups across the spectrum. Specific goals, cultural practices, and artifacts may vary, but there are certain *patterns* of cultural mindsets and strategic actions that are consistently and predictably analogous, irrespective of differences in race, ethnicity, religion, region, nationality, ideology, culture, and civilization. Studies have ascertained strikingly parallel extremist analogies and strategies among various revolutionary groups, religious movements, and totalitarian regimes (e.g., use of symbols, rituals, myths, dogmas, ideologies, authoritarian leadership).[40] There are remarkable similarities both in ideologies and messaging strategies (e.g., fear of extinction, use of fear-mongering conspiracy theories, victimhood mentality) between Islamist/jihadist and white supremacist, nationalist and Neo-Nazi groups (e.g., Odinism) to such an extent that one may wonder whether they adopt ideas from each other.[41] Scholars and journalists observed notable ideological resemblances and membership overlaps between America's religious fundamentalism and ethno-nationalism,[42] far-right authoritarianism,[43] right-wing militia and racist groups,[44] and gun-right activism.[45]

Bjørgo[46] also documented ideological and doctrinal integration and amalgamation of right-wing extremism and conservative, fundamentalist religious traditions in diverse parts of the world, including Eastern and Southern Europe, South Africa, and Japan.

Individuals who follow extremist beliefs and ideologies with one issue tend to be extremists with other, related issues, also. For instance, militantly racist people in America and Europe tend to be anti–Semitic, militantly nationalistic, xenophobic, anti-communist, anti-socialist, anti-liberalism, and authoritarian[47]; they tend to be sexists, misogynists, anti-immigrant nativists, anti-gay, anti-transgender, anti-government (e.g., militia groups), gun-rights activists, anti-intellectual, anti-science, and anti-media in the U.S.[48] The majority of America's white Christian fundamentalists and evangelicals (77 percent) espouse anti–Muslim, anti-immigrant, and white-majority nativism (white nationalism), and support President Trump's policy of curbing Muslim immigration much more than other religious or racial groups.[49]

Nazis hated and killed not just Jews, but also communists, homosexuals, the disabled, and Roma people ("Gypsies")[50]; white nationalist groups, such as Atomwaffen, hate Jews and gays, as well as racial/ethnic minorities,[51] and frequently post sexist and misogynist comments online.[52] Scholars reported a substantial overlap among Europeans who are politically far-right, aggressively anti-immigrant, anti-Islam ("Islamophobic"), anti–Semitic, anti–EU, anti-globalization, and nationalistic.[53]

Scholars also observed that group movements tend to "feed upon each other" or "spin off" from one another (e.g., "inter-movement spillover" effects)[54], and many movements have evolved out of preexisting groups and movements.[55] For instance, Xu[56] revealed that the Communist Party in China recruited its members from an assortment of existing protest groups (called "block recruitments"), and scores of people who joined the Party during the revolutionary era did so *before* "converting" to communism ("belonging before believing"). Helfstein[57] ascertained that the "ideological affinity" among extremists often develops *after* establishing social ties with "like-minded" groups of people, especially during the early stages of the radicalization process. It appears that some people have a predilection for or predisposition toward extremism more than others because of certain mindsets and worldviews they embrace as "extremist cultural frames."[58]

Extremism usually manifests itself through actions. However, behind all extremist deeds, there are extremist beliefs, ideologies, and mindsets that prod and justify extremist acts, working as "cultural frames." Like most -isms, extremism is socially produced out of specific cultural contexts that exhort radicalization and justify aggression and injustice. It is this extremist cultural context that shapes people's ways of thinking, behaving, living, and dying, and out of this cultural context, "culturally-inscribed" extremist motives arise.[59]

Without the extremist cultural context, grievances and indignations do not transform into extremist/terrorist movements and actions. In fact, there are always more grievances than guerrillas, revolutionaries, and terrorists, because not every persecuted group, even when subjected to genocides, turns to extremist resistance efforts. When grievances foment terrorist acts, there is a "cultural catalyst—the coupling of the vivid collective memory of injustice with traditional and valued paradigms for action, paradigms embodied in projective narratives."[60] When culturally "framed" extremist ideas and beliefs are effectively projected to contentious group movements, they become persuasive narratives and justifications that can energize and mobilize political actions.[61] Understanding extremism and extremist groups, therefore, requires analyzing the extremist "cultural frames" that can activate extremist actions and reactions. I focus on two interconnected and mutually reinforcing dimensions of "cultural frames" that inspire and actuate extremist acts—extremist cultural mindsets and strategies.

Studies of group movements in the 1970s through the 1990s focused mainly on the *strategic* and *tactical* aspects (e.g., resource mobilization, organizational, political process and opportunity theories, and social performance theories). They often neglected the *cultural* dimensions (e.g., role of the collectively shared mindsets, beliefs, values, and commonly embraced ways of thinking) that predispose and activate people's passions into actions.[62]

Since the 2000s, there has been a nascent resurgence of "cultural turn,"[63] with a renewed interest in and emphasis on the role of culture effecting group movements and contentious feuds. As Moon[64] suggests, all social movements try to negotiate the tension between effective strategies *and* sincerely held principles and worldviews. Studying one without the other would be not only incomplete but also ineffectual.

By linking the underlying *cultural* propensities (e.g., mindsets, "habitus" or "frames") *with* strategic actions (e.g., processes, mechanisms, and mobilization efforts), I hope to explain why people respond *differently* to the same aggrieving and threatening situations, triggering events, and mobilization efforts, an aspect "event- and opportunity-focused" or "process- and mechanism-oriented" theories of group movements often overlook. Some people are more likely to be inspired, mobilized, or radicalized by extremist leaders, ideologies, and movements than others are ("elective affinity")[65] and more prone to using extremist strategies than others are.

After the 9/11 terrorist attacks, some Americans wanted to wage wars in response, while others did not; some became anti–Islamic, but others did not. Not everyone who is deprived, disaffected, mistreated, aggrieved, and humiliated radicalizes or joins terrorist groups, even with the same triggering events and opportunities offered. We need to scrutinize what underlying proclivities predispose *some* people to radicalize and join extremist groups, movements, and activisms, while others shy away, in conjunction with analyses of situational events, opportunities, and mobilization processes.

In Chapters 1 and 2, I elaborate on extremist cultural mindsets that prime some people to become more susceptible to extremist ideologies and acts than others—group-focused mindsets in Chapter 1, followed by personal and psychological predispositions in Chapter 2. I present these extremist cultural mindsets as a part of extremist "cultural frames" people acquire through socialization processes shaped by cultural and social environments or cultivated by extremist leaders and influencers. Once acquired, they tend to shape and guide people's ways of perceiving the world and selecting choices of action.

One of the most distinctive mindsets extremists express is the dichotomous worldview consisting of "us vs. them" portrayed as "good-doers vs. evil-doers." Extremists seek power by portraying themselves as "good-doers" with a morally "righteous" sense of "superiority," which they defend fiercely against any sources of challenge to their superiority. Subsequently, they become hostile toward "evil" and "inferior" outsiders, traitors, and anyone who challenges their "superiority" and offends their pride and honor associated with it. With a strong sense of group-based pride and righteousness, such people become exceedingly preoccupied with group identities and in- and out-group distinctions and boundaries, and they prefer to connect and bond with those with kindred identities while disavowing others with dissimilar identities ("homophily"). They stress in-group unity and solidarity as a source of group power, which, they believe, comes from sustaining uniformity in culture and conformity to group-prescribed norms, beliefs, and traditions. To maintain uniformity, they firmly adhere to existing group traditions, beliefs, ideologies, and the status quo without questioning, and resist changes and resent challenges, especially in reactionary extremist groups. In so doing, they become intolerant and resentful of differences, deviances, and diversities, and inimical toward outsiders who do not share the same identity.

In such group-focused and group-dominated cultures, members believe that their *group* is more important and valuable than individuals; individuals exist for the benefit of the group; thus, individuals' rights and lives can be easily sacrificed for the benefit of the group. Groups gain inordinate power over individuals, and group leaders expect members' total devotion to the group with utmost loyalty, duty, and sacrifice for the group.

Out of loyalty, members offer unconditional approval, protection, and patronage to in-group members, while subjecting outsiders to unwarranted suspicion, prejudice, and discrimination. With such a group-focused perspective, they regard each individual as representation of the whole group to which one belongs. When one or a few of the out-group members offend or harm one or a few of their group members, therefore, all out-group members become "guilty by association," and can be shamed and punished—a justification for collective punishments and terrorist attacks against innocent civilians. Their intense aversion toward out-group extends to everything and anything that is "associated with," "symbolizes," or "reminds them of" the group they hate, which they reject *en mass* regardless of merit or benefits ("collective rejection").

In Chapter 2, I discuss extremist mindsets on the personal and psychological level. Extremist groups are particularly alluring to people with a compelling desire to belong and be accepted by peers for security and comfort. In order to guarantee acceptance, they become loyal to the group, and out of that loyalty, they willingly sacrifice their personal interests for the honor and glory of the group. Most extremist acts are motivated by members' desire to defend the group's honor and avoid shame. People who value honor and are sensitive to shame are, thus, more prone to extremist acts and likely to join extremist groups with a vindictive desire to avenge against shameful affronts. Consumed by an exigent sense of defending the group's honor, they tend to overreact to confrontational situations and humiliating slights with brute force and justify the use of violence either to restore the group's honor ("retaliatory justice") or to scare off potential offenders ("preemptive strikes").

Extremists consider strong and unwavering convictions as a source of power and strength; thus, they tend to uphold group-prescribed beliefs and group-centric ideologies with absolute conviction and blind certitude, refusing to negotiate and compromise colliding interests and reconcile differences. When people join extremist groups or commit extremist acts, they are often goaded by an intense sense of fear, whether of rejection, group extinction, humiliation, change, or losing power, status, and superiority.

Those who are "hyper-sensitive to threats"—i.e., those who believe that the world is an inherently dangerous and threatening place—are, therefore, more likely to join extremist groups, compared to people who believe they are in a safe and secure place.[66] Absorbed by fear and feeling insecure, such people are more likely to seek group-rendered security and protection.

Extremism is more common among peoples with an "end-justifies-the-means" mindset. When such mindsets are applied to groups, they believe that the end goal of achieving group-centric interests always justifies use of any means possible or available, regardless of the law, justice, ethics, or morality. The "end-justifies-the-means" mindset emanates from a "zero-sum" view of the world—the belief that one group's interests can be secured only at the expense of other groups' interests, and one group's advances can be achieved only by thwarting other groups' advances. In order to survive, thus, people must always win by annihilating competitors and detractors, not by cooperating and collaborating.

Extremism thrives in authoritarian cultures where people are obsessed with and hypersensitive to power and the hierarchy of statuses, whether they are of individuals or groups. In such environments, people enjoy exercising power over their inferiors, although they tend to be subservient to the superiors.

Extremists tend to seek, admire, and blindly follow strong, authoritarian leaders, whom they fantasize to be heroic and messianic "saviors" with an uncanny ability to perform miracles, protect them from enemies, and restore law and order they perceive to be in disarray. Consumed by their own yearning for and idealization of such leaders, they become easy prey for authoritarian dictators and their ideological propaganda and utopian vision of the future. Extremism appeals to emotionally excitable and obsessive people who seek psychological gratification from pursuing "higher" or "nobler" causes and meanings in life, and from experiencing *group power* through collective rituals, mass gatherings and movements, and, in extreme cases, communal acts of violence.

In Chapters 3 and 4, I discuss some of the common strategies extremist group leaders and followers use to attain their group-centric goals—strategies of pivoting and cultivating group identities in Chapter 3, followed by strategies of enhancing group power in Chapter 4. Extremist group leaders use group identities as a mobilization tool and source of power. They construct new identities or invoke existing ones to be used for their extremist causes, and nurture and pivot them by accentuating and magnifying intergroup differences. They appeal to in-group unity and solidarity by enforcing cultural uniformity and ideological purity with repressive sanctions against deviators and nonconformists. Depending on their goals, some groups exclude outsiders to monopolize resources and maintain group boundaries; some try to include more members to expand group boundaries and power-base, and trap members within by prohibiting them from leaving the group or mixing with outsiders ("boundary maintenance").

Extremist group leaders try to cultivate a sense of "moral superiority" and "group-righteousness" in the consciousness of their followers to elevate the status of their own group above others, and formulate and propagate group-centric ideologies to justify their superior status and mistreatment of "inferior" groups of people. They identify and demonize enemy groups, exaggerate threats from enemy groups to shore up in-group solidarity, and vilify enemy groups to justify mistreatment of and violence against them. They denigrate out-groups with derogatory labels and stereotypes to downgrade the out-group's status and elevate their own, and blame, shame, and accuse them for all of their troubles and misfortunes to dodge blame and responsibilities (e.g., scapegoating).

In Chapter 4, I discuss strategies extremist leaders use to enhance group power, and empower themselves in the process. Extremist group leaders' primary goal is to produce and mobilize as many loyal and devoted followers as possible who would willingly sacrifice their personal interests for their group-centric causes and interests. Leaders appeal to and invoke human emotions to suppress rational thinking processes; encourage sacrifice for the group; and invoke collective sentiments of solidarity to inspire courage and bravery needed to defend the group. They use collective rituals that can generate awe-inspiring experiences of "we-ness" and "greatness" to conjure up a sense of group unity, solidarity, and collective power, and in the process, create supra-human images of themselves as a spiritual symbol of the group. They identify or create objects, signs, and images that symbolize the group, inspire solidarity, demark boundaries, and imbue loyalty to the group on their behalf. They offer a grossly simplified, grandiose utopian vision of the world with simplified solution options to all the complicated world problems that appeal to their followers, using simple, emotionally-charged, and attention-grabbing slogans and catchphrases that stir up human emotions. Extremist leaders use authoritarian means to monopolize the power, loyalty, and trust of their followers, as well as to command, control, and manipulate their followers. They reign in terror to discourage disobedience, dissent, and desertion, and viciously attack and purge competing authority sources and critics (e.g., media, scientists, scholars, and intellectuals), while keeping their followers enchanted with a grandiose vision of a utopian future only *they* can deliver. They are quick to react to confrontational situations with hardline approaches and militarized aggression, and inclined to flaunt their military or physical prowess and brutalities, hoping to "out-fear" enemies as preventive measures. When punishing or avenging enemy groups, they attack the whole out-group indiscriminately for the wrongdoings of one or a few members of the group to maximize the terrorizing and "deterrence" effects of their actions ("collective punishment").

While expounding upon these extremist mindsets and strategies, I hope to shed some light on the mechanisms and processes that transform ordinary individuals into irrational fanatics and zealots of extremist causes, to such an extent that they eagerly commit atrocities against other humans without guilt or contrition, or sacrifice their lives to defend their group's honor and glory. I also hope to expose some of the symbiotic *and* exploitive relationships and dynamics that exist between leaders and followers of extremist groups.

In Chapter 5, I discuss some of the common goals of extremist groups. Most extremist groups are motivated by a combination of a few, generalizable goals. These consist of seeking group empowerment for domination of other groups or resisting domination and elevating the group's position in the social hierarchy of statuses above others by claiming superiority or debasing other groups.

In some groups, the goals are seeking redemption from what members perceive to be the sources of "evil" and injustice; establishing a collective defense of the group's existence, identity, culture and interests; pooling resources to provide collective support and maintain a patronage system; and building a self-contained, insulated, autonomous entity, independent from external pressures. Some groups' primary goal is to expand their territory and membership by being more inclusive of outsiders ("expansionism"); others try to monopolize power, resources, and rewards by excluding others' access to their group. Some groups are formed to create alternative opportunities for empowerment, advancement, and belonging which they cannot achieve through legitimate means (e.g., gangs, criminal cartels, rebel and revolutionary groups, and some cults). Regardless of what members try to achieve, once a group is organized, every extremist group's chief goal becomes the group's survival.

In Chapter 6, I discuss some of the social and environmental factors that facilitate the rise of extremist groups. Typically, people radicalize and groups become extremist when they face threats to their existential security, whether real or perceived. The threats can be from external or internal sources.

When people feel threatened by *external* sources (e.g., out-groups or enemies), nested subgroups merge and people band together to form a "collective defense mechanism." On the other hand, when people face *internal* crises threatening their existential security (e.g., economic hard times, extreme inequality and injustice, "failed states" due to systemic failure and corruption), people "hunker down" to the core, most immediate identity circles which they can trust the most. As a consequence, nested subgroups splinter and "parochialize" (or "tribalize") spurring intragroup fracases (e.g., "bunker mentality").[67] In both cases—external and internal sources of threats—collectively perceived *fear* is the primary impetus for radicalization, whether they are fears of group extinction, change, deprivation, or losing power, status and honor. When such a collective sense of fear is hyped into anger and loathing toward whichever out-group is scapegoated by demagoguing extremist leaders, people become emotionally charged to embrace extremist ideologies and support extremist acts. Acute, group-felt trauma, humiliation, grievances and other collectively experienced fate-sharing events can also trigger extremist responses, as can extreme inequalities and injustices created by dominant extremisms. Some people radicalize out of a profound sense of indignation over how their "fellow humans" or "some of their-own" are unjustly mistreated, abused, and persecuted at the hands of the powerful oppressors, even though they are not directly victimized by the abusive acts ("sympathetic indignation").

Resistance groups are more likely to adopt extremist acts of resistance when legitimate means of seeking reforms are blocked or absent. Geographic or cultural isolation and insulation that restrict exposure to the outside world and different perspectives can reinforce group-centric worldviews that endorse extremism.

None of these factors and conditions alone would be enough to elicit extremist groups and movements without an organizational leadership which capitalizes on people's fears, anger, and grievances and effectively mobilizes people and resources to foment group- or identity-based movements and activisms (e.g., resource mobilization theories)[68] using extremist strategies.

In the final chapter, I offer a few suggestions that can forestall or mitigate extremist aggressions on structural, cultural, and strategic dimensions. Group-based extremisms flourish with increasing threats to groups' security, interests, pride, or honor, and wane when such threats dissipate. Promoting policies that can improve general existential security for *all* groups in a fairly balanced manner, thus, can abate group-felt grievances and indignations, and consequently, moderate extremisms of both dominance and resistance.

On the structural level, instituting fairness and equal justice in political, economic, social, and legal systems will curtail the rise of extremism by mitigating the root causes of it. As the world's economy globalizes, such efforts must be globalized, also. Every nation, large or small, powerful or powerless, must cooperate to achieve and maintain a fair, equitable, and balanced growth through economic cooperation and political power-sharing, following the international rule of law under the purview of international organizations (e.g., "global governance").[69]

On the cultural level, I propose nurturing a cultural ethos of pragmatic centrism, humanistic individualism, and communitarian spirit (e.g., seeking collective and balanced interests for all groups and individuals involved) extended to the global community of humanity. We need to encourage people to recognize the inexorably interdependent and "shared-fate" aspects of the global economy and community, and the importance of compromising and balancing personal vs. group interests, as well as group vs. humanity interests. With mounting threats of terrorism and the proliferation of weapons of mass destruction, the cost of maximizing group-centric interests by a few powerful nations, infringing upon the interests and rights of less-powerful nations and groups, can be ominous to humankind.

On the strategic level, I stress the importance of de-escalating intergroup contentions by restraining extremist urges to counter extremist threats. Instead, I advocate empowering the moderates while remedying the root causes of the grievances extremist groups harbor. The hardline, militaristic counter-extremist/terrorist measures with bellicose rhetoric and intimidation tactics intended to "scare off" extremist groups will only validate their extremist causes and alienate moderates. Extremism is usually a *symptom* of threatening or aggrieving socio-political circumstances, just as gang proliferation is a symptom of societal ills. Resistant extremisms arise in response to repressive and unjust policies and practices advanced by the dominant extremist groups, and dominant extremisms thrive under extremely unfair and unjust social systems that ignore rule of law and allow corruption and exploitation of the less powerful groups to flourish. Under such systems, the powerful and dominant groups can take advantage of the powerless and vulnerable with impunity, fomenting widely shared grievances and resentments on the part of the powerless and vulnerable groups, brooding for extremist rebellion.

Curbing dominant extremisms with fairer and more just social systems, power-sharing, and rule of law, therefore, will be the surest way to deter the rise of resistant extremisms.

Too often, people overlook the *symptomatic* aspects of resistant extremisms, and instead dramatize the "evilness" of extremist acts with one-sided blame targeted at extremist groups as "terrorist groups," "instigators of the problem" and "sources of threat." Fighting resistant extremisms by ignoring the initial root causes of the resistant extremism will never placate extremist threats: instead, it will only validate the extremist causes, inflame their hostility, and trap both sides in a vicious and escalating cycle of violence and destruction, causing much harm and misery for masses of people.

What most resistant (and some reactionary and redemptive) extremist groups demand is to be treated with respect, dignity, and fairness. Their desire to be treated with respect and dignity is so overpowering that they willingly risk and sacrifice anything, including their lives, to obtain it, and resort to violence to reclaim the dignity and restore the honor of their group. Hardline extremist threats and counterattacks designed to humiliate and annihilate them will only inflate their indignation and rage, seething for graver revenge, not deflate them.

These suggestions may sound like improbably idealistic fantasies or hollowly pretentious platitudes to some people. Nevertheless, in the broad historical spectrum, the world has achieved substantial progress toward these goals, improved people's existential securities, and tamed extremisms and violent conflicts of all kinds, as well as improved social injustices and human sufferings associated with them, albeit with periodic setbacks.[70] I offer these suggestions hoping that we can continue to achieve progress, even expedite it, while averting relapses and reversions.

♦♦ 1 ♦♦

Extremist Cultural Mindsets on a Group Level

Although groups' ideologies and goals may vary, there are similar worldviews, beliefs, attitudes, and mindsets extremist group members embrace, irrespective of differences in religion, nationality, race, ethnicity, culture, or civilization. In this chapter, I discuss some of the commonly shared cultural mindsets and attributes that predispose people to extremist ideologies, actions, groups, and causes. It is important to note that not every extremist displays all of the traits I discuss here. Most exhibit some combination of these qualities, and some demonstrate more of them in higher frequency and intensity than others do. Furthermore, not everyone or every group with these attributes commits violent, extremist acts: Those with more attributes in greater potency are more likely to commit violent acts, compared to those with fewer and in lesser degree. In general, groups and people become extremists when these attributes are markedly pronounced, excessive, and pervasive, compared to others.

Dichotomous Worldview of "Us vs. Them"

One of the most distinctive commonalities of extremists is that they embrace a clearly defined, dichotomous, "us vs. them" and "insiders vs. outsiders" worldview, portrayed as "good-doers vs. evil-doers" and "right-thinkers vs. wrong-thinkers." Groups are either "allies or enemies" and people are either "with us or against us." Everyone must take a side by pledging allegiance and displaying loyalty to the in-group, and disavowing out-groups, as individuals cannot be between the two sides. "Who one is" is defined by "who one is not,"[1] and even more markedly, "who one *hates*" delineates "who one is."[2] For instance, people are either believers or non-believers, Muslims or infidels, Jews or gentiles, liberals or conservatives, right or left, Republicans or Democrats, pro–America or anti–America, whites or non-whites, civilized or uncivilized, the oppressors or the oppressed, pro-life or pro-choice, pro-business or pro-labor, the "haves" or "have-nots," or the "deserving" and "desirable" or "undeserving" and "undesirable." With such a dichotomous worldview, extremists have difficulty accepting, understanding, or cooperating with "others" or "outsiders," and become unable to tolerate "lukewarm" moderates and those with "in-between" statuses or mixed identities they view as traitors, and defectors.

Al-Zarqawi, the al-Qaeda insurgent leader in Iraq until he was killed by a U.S. air strike in 2006, said to his followers: "Either you are with me or you are an enemy; there is no gray area."[3] The prime goal of ISIS/Daesh, according to its website, is to eradicate "nonbelievers" and "gray zones" where "true-believers" and "nonbelievers" are mixed, such as in Europe and America.[4] The "believers vs. nonbelievers" dichotomy persists among a sizable portion of Americans, also. Edgell et al.[5] discovered that, despite the attenuating salience of divisions among religious denominations, the boundary between believers and nonbelievers remains prominent, and believers' prejudice against nonbelievers remains stubbornly resolute in the U.S. The majority of Americans are less likely to accept atheists, publicly and privately, or trust them, than a litany of other minority groups—e.g., racial, ethnic, religious, sex or gender-related.

The "us vs. them" mindset is pervasive in American politics and political worldviews, as well. After the 9/11 terrorist attacks in 2001, countless Americans reverted to such "us vs. them" and "good vs. evil" dualism, effecting a surge of anti–Islam/Muslim sentiments and support for hardline counterterrorism policies.[6] President Bush said, "every nation must make a decision: either you are with us or with the terrorists."[7] In 2017, Trump-appointed American ambassador to the United Nations, Nikki R. Haley, addressed the United Nations saying that the U.S. "will have the backs of our allies and make sure our allies have our back as well." "For those who don't have our back," she added, "we're taking names, and we will make points to respond to that accordingly."[8] U.S. partisan politics are replete with "us vs. them" extremism and vitriolic partisan attacks—e.g., "enemization and demonization" strategy, tit-for-tat, retaliatory congressional obstructionism, and purging of the moderates ("Blue Dogs" and "RINOs"). Such "us vs. them" partisan politics in Congress have grown more pernicious and polarizing in the last few decades, spilling over to the general population.[9]

Dichotomously Simplified Worldviews

When people see the world with "us vs. them" dichotomy, they tend to scale down and reconfigure all the complex world events to make them fit into their grossly simplified and dichotomous worldviews, ignoring the overlapping, context-bound, complex, or situational contingencies and variances. They tend to believe that all the world's events and problems have clearly discernable, "black-or-white," and "all-or-nothing" causes with absolutely "right-or-wrong" answers and "good-or-bad" solution options. For instance, extreme Islamists/jihadists may believe that all of their problems are fallout from Western imperialism and political meddling, and thus can be resolved only by vanquishing the Western "infidels." Meanwhile, the Western counterterrorist hardliners may believe that the West will be safe only if they can "root out" all the Islamist/jihadi terrorists. Extreme religious fundamentalists may believe that their God will solve all of the world's problems; whereas, extreme atheists may assume that religion is the source of all the world's conflicts. Extreme, far-right, political and economic conservatives may believe that "big government" is the source of all the problems in society; extremists on the opposite, far-left spectrum may believe that strong government is the solution to all societal problems. Extreme gun control proponents may consider guns as the source of all the violence in America; whereas, extreme gun-rights advocates may argue that "more guns, not less" (in the hands of the "good guys") is the only solution to all violent crime. Extremist hardline "defense hawks" may believe that we can solve all geopolitical problems by building the world's largest and mightiest military forces; whereas, extremely dovish peace-activists may argue that all the world's problems are caused by America's jingoistic militarism bullying around the world and menacing the world's peace.

Hatred Toward Moderates and People with Ambiguous or Mixed Identities

As "us vs. them" mindsets deepen, group identities, loyalties, and ideological purity become preeminent in people's mindsets. People shun middle ground or neutral positions and abhor mixed- or inter-group relations and "in-between" statuses, such as half-hearted or lukewarm moderates, independent thinkers, vacillators, inter-faith couples, and mixed-race people. Throughout history, countless groups of people around the world have mistreated or looked down upon mixed-race people, and considered them "outcasts," bestowing statuses lower than any one of their parents.[10] Prejudice and discrimination against persons with ambiguous, non-binary identities, such as the transgendered, transvestites, homosexuals, and hermaphrodites have persisted throughout history in various places around the world. Even in modern times, a number of nations prohibit homosexuality with threats of the death penalty. Most recently in 2019, Brunei enacted laws criminalizing gay sex punishable by stoning offenders to death.[11] In the U.S., twelve transgender women were murdered between January and July of 2019,[12] including a Dallas transgender woman, Muhlaysia Booka, who was brutally beaten and kicked into unconsciousness by a group of men in broad daylight in the middle of a street as a crowd of bystanders were gawking at the victim and videotaping the assault, shouting homophobic slurs until several women intervened and carried the victim's limp body to safety.[13]

While Osama bin Laden was willing to tolerate moderate Muslims and condemned inter-Muslim violence, al-Zarqawi viewed moderate Muslims as "enemies of the faith."[14] When moderate Muslims in Europe formed a group called Democratic Muslims, extremist Islamists vilified and assailed them to such an extent that the group's leader, a secular Muslim lawmaker, Naser Khader, needed bodyguards. Naser says that the Islamists consider secular Muslims like himself as their principal enemies or traitors, and more dangerous than Christians and Jews.[15] In 2014, ISIS/Daesh in Syria crucified eight rebel fighters whom they deemed to be too moderate, although all of them were the same Sunnis fighting against the Assad regime.[16]

Designated terrorist groups are not the only ones that shun and condemn moderates and the independent-minded for "lacking loyalty." Iranian government officials are unduly suspicious of dual nationals (e.g., Iranians with American, Canadian, or British citizenship). Officials often harass them, accuse them of spying, and jail them with unsubstantiated, bogus charges.[17] Fourteen parliamentarians were forced to resign or ruled ineligible when Australia, in 2017, renewed its scrutiny on a constitutional clause banning dual nationals from becoming lawmakers.[18] In extremely partisan American politics, party loyalists consider moderate and independent party members who occasionally vote across party lines as "traitors" and "sell-outs" who lack loyalty to the party. Hardline Democrats shun such moderates calling them "Blue Dog" Democrats; loyalist Republicans occasionally "hunt down" the "spineless RINOs" (Republicans in Name Only) and punish them by cutting off campaign funding.[19] Pope Benedict XVI denounced so-called "do-it-yourself" or "cafeteria Catholics" who pick and choose parts of Catholic dictums they want to adhere to instead of following everything the Catholic Church preaches *en masse*, and suggested a "purity-test" for Catholics[20] for the same reason—aversion toward lukewarm moderates and independent-minded Catholics. In 2019, Pope Francis, during a mass in St. Peter's Basilica, exhorted the faithful to refrain from becoming "lukewarm Christians living by half measures."[21]

Hatred Toward People Who Cooperate with or Aid Outsiders

People with strongly ingrained "us vs. them" mindsets berate those who cooperate with, assist, or marry out-group members as "sell-outs" who "betray" the group. According to Tuskegee Institute's report, there were 4,743 recorded deaths by lynching in the U.S. between 1882 and 1968; 1,297 of the victims were whites, who were lynched by white mobs for "helping blacks" or being anti-lynching.[22] Among the 800,000 victims of the Rwandan genocide, which Hutu rebels committed against the Tutsis in 1994, there were countless *moderate* Hutus killed by Hutu rebels because they were sympathetic to the Tutsis.[23] In the aftermath of the U.S.-led Iraq invasion, the killing spree by Sunni insurgents targeted not only the Shiites but also Sunnis whom they suspected to be cooperating with the America-supported government.[24] In Pakistan, Islamic militants killed health workers distributing polio vaccines and parents who vaccinated their children against polio, because they consider them "collaborators of the West."[25] In Syria and Bahrain, government forces have killed or imprisoned medical doctors and nurses for treating injured rebel group members.[26] Over 850 Syrian health care providers have been killed by the Syrian regime during the civil war that began in 2011, both from the regime's bombing of hospitals or from targeted killings of those who treated injured rebel forces.[27]

Need for "Projection"

When people perceive the world to be an "us vs. them" dichotomy with associated implications of good versus evil, it becomes imperative for them to "project" themselves to be on the *right* side—e.g., as "good," not "evil," and "insider," not "outsider." Those who fail to do so can be accused of or be mistaken to be "on the wrong side" and be rejected, shunned, or even killed. Especially when people judge and sanction each other by neighborhood and peer gossip and vigilante mob attacks (extrajudicial punishments), they must be extremely mindful of how they present themselves to others regarding "to which side they belong." Anyone suspected or accused of aiding or sympathizing with outsiders or enemies can be killed without due process, along with their family members. Two days after Israeli strikes killed three Hamas leaders in 2014, Hamas executed eighteen *suspected* informants in broad daylight on a busy street, after accusing them of collaborating with Israel as informants without proof or investigation.[28] Within a few weeks following the 2016 failed coup, the Turkish government, under President Erdogan's push, arrested, detained, and jailed tens of thousands of public servants, soldiers, and educators who they *suspected* to be associated with the coup, and suspended 100,000 more from their occupation.[29]

In such precarious surroundings and situations, people must constantly demonstrate their loyalty to the group, even in exaggeration, to ensure that they are not mistaken to be on the "wrong side" or construed to be sympathetic to outsiders or "bad guys." The hyperbolic displays of hostility toward and rejection of outsiders signify their effort to demonstrate loyalty in order to guarantee acceptance by their "good guy" peers and evade suspicion of disloyalty. Probably for this reason, extremists frequently exhibit histrionic revulsion toward out-groups (e.g., "death to America" marches in Pakistan and Iran, "stoning deaths" of adulterers, homophobia, xenophobia, and Islamophobia) to "project" themselves to be on the "good" or "right" side, and shirk being mistaken to be on the "evil/wrong" side.

Shared Sense of Moral Superiority

When a group of people sustain an "us vs. them" dichotomy associated with implications of "good vs. evil," it is usually based on their collective belief in the group's moral superiority, righteousness, and pride and honor that validate their "superior" status and "goodness." With collectively shared belief in moral superiority, they can easily convince themselves that their group is always on the "right/good/superior" side and others are "wrong/evil/inferior."[30] When a group of people assures themselves that they are "morally superior and righteous," others subsequently become "inferior" heathens, heretics, sinners, savages, "evil-doers," and "morally decrepit" people who do not deserve the same respect and worth as they do.

For instance, extreme Christian fundamentalists and evangelicals may believe that Christianity is superior to other religions, as Islamists believe Islam is superior to other religions. Driven by their sense of superiority, they are urged to proselytize non–Christians, whereas extreme Islamists are compelled to attack infidels who threaten or humiliate them. According to a 2017 Baylor University poll, about half of conservative evangelicals in the U.S. believe that atheists have "inferior" values, and 44 percent of them believe Muslims have "inferior" values, compared to 30 percent and 21 percent respectively among the mainline churchgoers.[31] According to Gervais and Najle's[32] study of more than 3,000 people across 13 countries on five continents, the majority of people consider atheists to be more "morally depraved and dangerous" than believers, even in many secularized countries. The anti-atheist bias was strongest in nations with high numbers of believers, like the United Arab Emirates, U.S., and India. Similarly, some people may believe that the "chosen" people are superior to "un-chosen" people or civilized nations to "uncivilized barbarians." Male chauvinists believe men are superior to women, white supremacists believe whites are superior to non-whites, and homophobes consider heterosexuals as superior to homosexuals. Social conservatives call themselves the "value voters" because they believe that their values are more "righteous" than that of the "amoral, Godless liberals," and a host of far-right, white-supremacist, anti-immigrant, and anti-government hate/militia group members claim that they are the "true patriots," and accuse their critics of being "unpatriotic."[33]

When Americans believe in "American exceptionalism" and "American greatness," other nations become "not so great" or "inferior" and "secondary" in comparison, and other nations deserve less respect and their interests and rights become "less worthy" compared to that of America's.[34] Sachs[35] argued that the strongly-held American belief in "American exceptionalism"—conviction that America is a nation unlike any other, destined for greatness and bound to lead, and a nation that can do no wrong—has led America to be involved in endless, unnecessary, and unjust conflicts and wars of choice, covert and overt, from Guatemala and Iran in the 1950s to Iraq and Afghanistan in more recent years. The implication and expectation of such "exceptionalism" is that global peace can be achieved through American leadership with exceptional military prowess, economic power, and cultural hegemony, although such beliefs have been promoted for economic interests and proven to be an illusion repeatedly through history.

A cogent sense of moral superiority impels people to judge others based on their "superior" moral standard; look down upon and mistreat others they deem to be "inferior"; impose their "superior" values and moral standards upon others; and punish or root out those who do not accept their superiority, violate their "superior" moral codes, or contest it. Such collectively embraced senses of moral superiority and group righteousness are indispensable for extremist groups and movements, because they help leaders to effectively mobilize and convince followers to sacrifice personal interests and lives to defend their group's moral superiority, and justify their acts of atrocities inflicted upon "evil inferiors" without guilt or contrition.

Importance of Defending Group Moral Superiority

When a group of people tries to uphold their "superior" status based on their *claim* of moral superiority and righteousness, they must defend their presumed "superiority" with all their might, because failure to do so can mean losing their superior status and power. When a group of people fear losing their superior status, they become easily offended and outraged by even the slightest rebukes, challenges, and insults against their group. When such incursions occur, they retaliate and try to eradicate all sources of the insults and challenges to restore their group's *asserted* superiority and honor, using violence if necessary. As Bandura[36] confers, throughout history, countless ordinary and decent people have perpetrated reprehensible and destructive conduct in the name of *defending* their group's superior religious principles, righteous ideologies, and nationalistic imperatives. In the process of defending their superior moral values, they feel morally justified to carry out horrendous acts against those who subvert, violate, or challenge their superior standing. Innumerable people have suffered at the hands of such "group-righteous crusaders" bent on stamping out whatever they consider "evil," "barbaric," "heretic," or whoever questions their superiority.

Throughout history, men have ruthlessly defended their superior social status over women using traditions, religious beliefs, sexist ideologies, and legal systems, and viciously punished women who challenged their dominance. Similar acts of aggressively defending group-based moral superiority existed with white supremacists against non-white races, heterosexuals against homosexuals, slave-holders against slaves, aristocrats and noblemen against the commoners, the civilized against the uncivilized, capitalists against laborers, occupiers against the occupied, and among various religious and sectarian groups and nation-states.

Many Americans felt that the 9/11 terrorist attacks in 2001 were a humiliating blow to America's pride and honor of being the solely remaining superpower. They supported the invasion of Iraq, clamoring to restore America's superiority by showcasing America's military might and invincibility to the world (e.g., "shock and awe" statement by then–Secretary of Defense, Donald Rumsfeld).[37] Perhaps this is the reason why foreign terror groups' attacks infuriate Americans more profoundly than other serious crimes, or man-made disasters that engender greater loss of human life, such as criminally negligent industrial accidents and malfeasance, gun violence, drug abuse, mass shootings, auto accidents, pool accidents,[38] and killings by domestic terror groups, such as white supremacists.[39] Terrorist attacks by foreign groups are not just a "life-or-death" matter—it offends national pride and honor. It is an insult to and assault on *all* Americans and what America stands for—its immutable superpower status in the world. The ultimate goal of America's "war on terror" is not simply defending national security or protecting American lives. More importantly, it is to uphold America's image, status, honor, and respect on the international stage as the sole, remaining, immutable hegemon.[40]

Collectively upheld beliefs in moral superiority are usually the byproduct of meticulously orchestrated strategies of ideological indoctrination by extremist group leaders. I discuss the strategic sides of formulating and instilling a sense of moral superiority in Chapter 3.

Significance of Group Identity and Homophilic Affinity

Maintaining "us vs. them" and "insider vs. outsider" boundaries and distinctions cannot be sustained unless people share a clear sense of group identity among the likeminded, like-thinking, like-believing, like-originated, like-aggrieving, like-appearing, or like-behaving, whether the identities are determined biologically, culturally, geographically, nationally, religiously, politically, or ideologically. When there are no visibly discernable identity differences, people use arbitrary colors, signs, insignias, clothing, or tattoos as symbolic markers of their group identity to separate "us" from "them." In such cases, the designated symbolic objects and signs acquire "sacred" value because they represent the group[41]—e.g., Muslim headscarves, Sheik turbans, Jewish yarmulkes, Christian cross necklaces—and wearing or carrying them becomes a proof of membership and a display of loyalty ("membership ID").

Not every group with a strong sense of group identity becomes extremist. However, most extremist group members share such a robust sense of group identity, and group-based extremism is more likely to occur and prosper when group identities acquire preeminence to such an extent that they define and determine one's existence, identity, status, and raison d'être. Groups become more than just a collection of individuals, as they morph into a form of "sui generis"—a reified *moral* entity with a life of its own, with autonomous power to affect people's lives.[42] One's group becomes a "psychological anchor," "bedrock," and "frame of reference," upon which one's whole existence is shaped, judged, and appraised.[43] People become duty-bound devotees to uphold the group's honor, defend group-centric ideologies, and sacrifice their personal interests for the glory of the group.

Desire to Preserve Group Identity

An assortment of extremist groups and acts have born out of people's desire to maintain group identity and associated cultural traditions. Paul Tillich discussed that Nazi rhetoric resonated powerfully to Germans living in small towns and villages and members of the working class who yearned to preserve traditional German identity. They considered Nazism a "reactionary repudiation" of liberals and socialists who thought in "universalist" terms without respecting their particular communities and identities (which he calls "myths of origin"), whether they were ethnic, cultural, religious, nationalistic, regional, or a mixture of these.[44]

The mounting sentiments of anti–EU (European Union), anti-globalization, and xenophobic white nationalism in Europe since the 2008 economic recession have baffled many EU leaders. Since the 1970s, the EU has shifted wealth across borders under programs called "cohesion funding." Between 2000 and 2020, the EU was on track to spend around 858 billion Euros ($992 billion) to unify the continent by modernizing infrastructures, raising living standards, easing poverty, and opening new markets in the most needy regions or countries of Europe, chosen because their economic output per person is below 90 percent of the EU average. Yet, the countries and regions that are the largest recipients of this EU funding are the most notable hotbeds of xenophobic, anti–EU nationalism, brimming with voters resenting the cultural and political changes that accompanied European integration, threatening the bloc's cohesion. What they demand, more than money and economic prosperity, is their national and regional sovereignty, cultural identity, and respect. The discontent stretches from small towns in Europe's richest nations, including Britain and France, to struggling regions in fast growing post–Communist economies such as Poland and Hungary. Many locals repudiate the EU's obligation to accept migrants that followed the EU's economic funding. "The money, we got our share, but it's more important to save Wales" (from foreigners) said Ken Sullivan, a retired coal miner.[45]

Homophilic Affinity

When group identities define people's existence and worth, people tend to connect, bond with, and trust those with kindred identities and disavow others with dissimilar identities, a tendency called "homophily."[46] In order to assure that they are accepted and recognized as bona fide members of the group, they associate with in-group members only, shunning out-group members; offer help to and protect only their in-group members, not out-group members; and marry within, renouncing those who marry out. Homophilic tendencies can exist in any group where people wish to create a "safe zone" among the likeminded in which they do not have to defend their beliefs or lifestyles against outsiders and detractors. Studies have corroborated people's general tendency to categorize everyone into groups based on similarities[47] and select their "network structure" based on those similarities, rather than dissimilarities.[48] Scholars have observed homophilic preferences and affinity among people who share similar political views[49] and racial and ethnic identities,[50] and among those with similar religious views, especially among evangelicals and fundamentalists.[51] Similar preferences exist among graduates of "elite" schools, and people who share the same "regionality," and propinquity, also.[52] Not every group with homophilic tendencies becomes an extremist group. However, most extremist group members exhibit a strong sense of group identity and homophilic tendency, and rely on members who can ardently uphold and defend their shared identities and group-centric ideologies, and fight against all critics, deviants, and detractors.

In most extremist groups, the salience of group identity and "us vs. them" mindsets are often the products of deliberate and strategic indoctrination efforts by the extremist leaders who can sow group-centric ideologies, stoke fears, and foment revulsion toward out-groups in order to mobilize followers and garner political support for the group. The specific strategies of pivoting group identities are elaborated on in Chapter 3.

Seeking In-Group Solidarity and Unity Through Uniformity and Conformity

When group identities gain preeminence, people value and take pride in group unity and solidarity that are built on the fact that they share the same identity and like-mindedness. Conversely, they become uncomfortable, insecure, even intimidated when exposed to differences, deviances, and diversities. In extreme cases, they become intolerant of and hostile toward outsiders. They also become resentful of the in-group members who do not conform to the same beliefs, values, and lifestyles because they fear diversities may divide their group and subvert the unity and solidarity of their group. In order to maintain the group's unity and solidarity, therefore, they vehemently defend and protect the group's shared beliefs, values, and identities against all diverging influences and trends, whether they are from internal or external sources.

Such "groupish" people tend to value deference to authority, blind loyalty, and conformity as fundamental "moral foundations" of the group that they believe are necessary for building unity and solidarity of the group.[53] They prod and pressure each other to conform, not deviate; fit in, not stand out; and go along with the flow and crowd, not against it, thus, fostering a culture that is lacking innovation and prone to problems of "groupthink."[54] They shun, rebuke, and punish anyone whom they presume to be deviants, "disobedients," misfits, heretics, dissenters, critics, detractors, challengers,

1. Extremist Cultural Mindsets on a Group Level 41

provocateurs, agitators, and traitors without misgivings, while praising acts of blind submission, conformity, and obedience to all established authorities and traditions. Even minor differences and trifling deviations can become a source of significant contention in such cultures. In Amish communities that value uniformity, minute and subtle variations, such as in clothing and hats, can become a salient source of internal schisms with spiteful disputations and contentious bouts, because those slight disparities represent "serious symbolic boundaries of profound importance."[55] Minute and trifling differences have been a source of serious contention between Shiite and Sunni Muslims for centuries, such as the sitting positions and placing of hands during prayer, and the number of times Muslims should pray per day[56] probably for the same reason—i.e., the desire to defend symbolic boundaries that define the group's identity.

The "groupish" yearning for homogeneity and solidarity can exist in all groups to a varying degree. However, they are more pronounced and pervasive in extremist groups whose survival, mobilization, and potency hinge upon maintaining group solidarity and ideological purity among its members. In order to enforce unity through uniformity, extremist group members, leaders and followers alike, use repressive sanctions against their own group members, both formal and informal, aimed at deterring deviances and differentiations. The extremist strategies of enforcing unity through uniformity by means of repressive sanctions will be elaborated in Chapter 3.

Respect for and Duty to Uphold Group Traditions

When a group of people tries to maintain unity through uniformity and conformity, they inevitably become highly parochial and bound by group-prescribed traditions—i.e., they conform to traditional ways of life and the status quo, resisting changes. As Calhoun[57] discussed, in such cases, defending tradition can become "a critical source of radicalization." Particularly in most reactionary extremist groups, such as in socially-conservative and religiously-fundamentalist groups, people zealously guard their parochial beliefs and lifestyles, deeply entrenched in age-old traditions, rebuffing all modernizing, liberalizing or secularizing trends. Some even yearn to go back to what it was like in the past before changes took place—the "good old days." They cherish the simpler life of following age-old traditions they are familiar with, and they value continuity in culture embedded in "the past"—e.g., the solid and immutable "ground" and "bedrock" upon which they were raised. Changes are unsettling to these people, because they are unpredictable and unknowable, compared to the past that is already known and familiar. They feel more comfortable and secure in the habituated and routinized ways of life, absent-minded conformity, and simplified life of obedience and conformity, instead of exploring things that are atypical, foreign, and outside of their inherited frame of thoughts. They feel offended when their esteemed tradition is challenged, which they consider a "threat to their existence," and they become duty-bound to defend their tradition and fend off any subversive forces to their tradition, whether they are from internal or external sources. For them, maintaining their group's cultural distinction embedded in tradition is a form of "boundary maintenance" that is necessary for the group's continued existence ("fear of extinction"). Without the boundary, they fear, their group's identity may disappear and their existence may be threatened. Tradition becomes the symbol of their group identity: By upholding tradition, they believe they can preserve their group's identity and existence.

In African societies, people try to "stay the same" and seek to "fit in," not only for security and comfort, but also to *honor* the group's tradition ("the past"), which represents their group's identity.[58] Breaking-away from the past represents "dishonoring" their past, thus, their whole identity. Transmitting the inherited tradition to their children and then to grandchildren becomes their lifelong duty for the honor of their group. Not doing so can be a source of "shame" because it dishonors the group and tradition. They become proud bearers and dutiful custodians of group's tradition, and consider any reform-oriented trends or movements as a serious threat to the identity, existence, and honor of their group.

Throughout history, people have tolerated or participated in extremely unjust and violent acts without questioning their virtue or merit, simply because they have been the traditional ways of life for generations. Examples include patriarchy, polygyny, monarchy, slavery, caste systems, child labor, child brides, female genital mutilation, pedophile sexual abuse (e.g., "bacha bazi" in Afghanistan, practice of "chocoshi" in parts of Africa), and family honor killings. In rural parts of Nepal, people continue to sequester menstruating women and girls in "menstruation huts" or cow sheds despite the fact that many die from cold, smoke inhalation, attacks by animals, and snake bites, simply because it is a tradition that has been going on for centuries.[59] Atrocious acts of hazing lower-ranking soldiers are widely tolerated and ignored in the Russian military as scores of young conscripts are killed or severely injured at the hands of higher level officers, calling them "dedovshchina," which means "rule of the grandfathers." In 2005 alone, 17 conscripts died from hazing and many more were permanently injured, out of about 3,000 *reported* cases of hazing-related abuses.[60]

Yearning for "Tribalistic" Lifestyle

Scholars have noted that some people are attracted to extremist groups for the simple, traditional and "tribalistic" lifestyle they offer. People with nostalgic yearning for the "good old days" of tribal lifestyle find extremist groups enticing and gratifying (e.g., "re-tribalization" of Barber[61]; "prime shelter nostalgia" of Bauman[62]). They find psychological comfort and security in a "tribalistic" sense of belonging, in-group trust, camaraderie, and loyalty. One of the main reasons why jihadism resonates powerfully with young, alienated Muslims, according to Barber (1996), is because jihad delivers a promise of "tribalistic" group identity, unity, security, and sense of community among like-minded people, and a narrowly defined and conceived parochialism that is grounded in renunciation and exclusion of "others" and modernity. They embrace the traditional deference to leaders and intolerance toward outsiders and "enemies within" that were the hallmarks of tribalism. Riaz (2011) also discussed that the core essence all extremist Islamist groups in Afghanistan and Pakistan exhibit commonly is the "ardent and fearless resistance to modernity," which they believe is threatening their traditional ways of life and Islamic values.

Maintaining Power by Upholding Tradition

Reactionary extremist groups are not the only groups that try to uphold tradition. Some dominant extremist groups also try to preserve tradition because it is the source of their power—i.e., the tradition endorses and justifies their dominant status and power. Men have fought fiercely to preserve patriarchal tradition that justified their dominance and mistreatment of women for centuries repelling demands for sexual equality. Monarchs have defended monarchism ruthlessly for centuries as a part of immutable tradition. Caste systems, despite apparent injustices and cruelty, have persisted for centuries because they had become a part of the tradition enshrined in Hinduism. Christian nationalists in the U.S. are nostalgic for the "good old days" of the past when no one challenged Christianity as the dominant tradition and foundation of the nation impacting every aspect of American life. White nationalists are nostalgic for the "good old days" of the past when Eurocentric culture and tradition dominated America and minorities were "not so loud, so demanding, so numerous—a time when minorities were more grateful."[63]

Shared Belief That the Group Is More Important and Valuable Than the Individual

Extremist group members commonly believe that their *group* is more important and valuable than individual members are. Therefore, individuals' lives, interests, and rights can be easily sacrificed if it is for the honor and glory of the group or advancing the group's interests. Such a belief allows people to accept and justify violent acts of cruelty and human sacrifice for the group—such as the use of human shields, collaterals, hostages, suicide bombers, kamikaze attackers, child soldiers, and slave laborers— and make unjust demands from individual members of the group, such as extortion of exorbitant contributions for the group. Individual sacrifice for the group is revered and glorified to such an extent that people willingly die for the group's honor (e.g., suicide bombers), or kill their own family members who "dishonored" their family ("family honor killing"). By the same reasoning, group members do not hesitate to commit extreme acts of violence against individuals of out-groups, such as torture, terrorist attacks, mass killings, genocides, massacres, and ethnic cleansing, for the benefit of their own group. Such acts of cruelty can even become "honorable" and "morally imperative" duties when committed for the honor of their group. Followers of Charles Manson, a murderous cult leader, testified during their trials that they believed it was their "duty" to kill random victims to incite a race war following Manson's orders.[64] Some cult followers killed their own children and killed themselves for the honor of their group following the orders of their leaders (e.g., Heaven's Gate, Jim Jones' People's Temple, and Order of the Solar Temple).

Sacrificing Individuals for the Honor of the Group

Such group-bound cultural frames that debase individual lives and interests for the benefit of the group have existed throughout history, and they continue to persist in sundry traditional societies around the world. In some rural Arab/Muslim communities in Africa, the Middle East, and Southeast Asia, when a daughter or sister "dishonors" her family by losing her virginity, even by rape, parents and brothers are obligated, or at least pressured to kill their daughter or sister to restore the family's honor (called "family honor killing"). In Pakistan alone, at least 1,000 women, mostly teenage girls, die from "family honor killing" annually.[65] In Iraq, family members turn in their gay sons to be killed by vigilante police and mobs, in order to restore their family's honor that was besmirched by having a gay son.[66] For them, restoring the family's honor and reputation is more important than the life of their son or brother. In the U.S., some parents refuse modern medical

1. Extremist Cultural Mindsets on a Group Level

treatment and rely solely on "faith-healing" causing their children to die from diseases with known medical treatments (e.g., diabetes, kidney infection, intestinal blockage, and appendicitis), often in extremely excruciating pain. They willingly sacrifice their children's lives and health in honor of their religious beliefs that disavow modern medicine (e.g., fundamentalists in Christian Science and Jehovah's Witnesses). They can sidestep criminal prosecution because most states allow religious exemptions from child abuse charges for "prayer-healing" parents. At least 303 children died between 1975 and 2012 because parents withheld medical treatment on religious grounds.[67] A tight-knit community of Orthodox Jews in Brooklyn follows an implicit "code of silence" that prohibits Jews from reporting fellow Jews to external authorities. They try to take care of problems internally rather than taking them to outside authorities in order to protect their community's reputation and to dodge collective shame. Some even consider it permissible to kill a Jew who reports fellow Jews to the authorities. A school counselor in the Brooklyn Orthodox community, Avrohom Mondrovitz, sexually molested numerous young boys for years, yet victims and witnesses did not dare to report to authorities for years under death threats.[68] All of these cases illustrate situations where people willingly sacrifice or violate individuals' rights and lives in order to protect their group's honor and reputation.

SACRIFICING INDIVIDUAL RIGHTS IN U.S. LAW ENFORCEMENT AGENCIES

Similar acts of safeguarding group reputation and honor at the expense of individual rights occur in selected modern institutions and organizations, also. For the extremists in law enforcement agencies, advancing the interests of their organization supersedes their duty to protect the rights of innocent individuals. Some cops and prosecutors arrest and convict as many suspects as possible to inflate the crime-fighting records of their organization, and to accrue revenue from exorbitant fees, fines, and civil-asset forfeitures (e.g., "revenue generating" schemes). They do so for the benefit of their organization, even though such acts are prone to wrongful arrests and convictions of the innocent and hurt lower-income people who face jail time because they cannot pay fines and fees.[69] The goal of police interrogation is not necessarily to ascertain the truth, but it is structured to promote incrimination of the accused in order to "perk up their records."[70] Investigators, cops, and prosecutors use various tactics to entice defendants to make false confessions ("compliant or internalized"),[71] coerce plea bargain deals, lie in court to convince the judges and juries of their guilt (known as "testilying"), or prohibit defendants from post-conviction remedies to advance their "institutional goals."[72] Particularly when they face public outrage and pressure to solve high-profile crime cases, some overzealous cops and prosecutors knowingly arrest, prosecute, and convict innocent suspects to embellish their organization's image and reputation by "quickly wrapping up high-profile cases" by forging and hiding evidence and forcing confessions. Example cases include the "Central Park Five,"[73] "Beatrice Six,"[74] "Groveland Four,"[75] and Davontae Sanford cases.[76] According to the National Registry of Exonerations' report in 2018, at least 2,100 people were exonerated from their criminal convictions since DNA testing was introduced in 1989. In more than half of the exoneration cases, the wrongful convictions resulted from official misconduct, such as officers threatening witnesses, withholding evidence that would have cleared the defendant, and pressuring analysts to falsify test results.[77]

ORGANIZATIONAL COVER-UPS

Various modern institutions and organizations have tried to shield their reputation, ignoring potential risks to individual rights and lives. The Catholic Church has sheltered its pedophile priests and covered-up their sexual abuse of children for centuries in order to protect the Church's reputation, permitting more children to be abused.[78] In 2017, Australia's Royal Commission into Institutional Responses to Child Sexual Abuse reported that seven percent of priests in the Australian Catholic Church have been accused of sexually abusing children between 1950 and 2010, yet, the majority of accusations were ignored by the Church. Even worse, when accusations were made, victims were routinely punished, not the perpetrators.[79] Thomas O'Brien, who was a bishop of the Diocese of Phoenix, admitted to sheltering at least 50 priests accused of sexual abuse of children, often shuffling them around to parishes across the state, allowing more children to be abused.[80]

Most colleges and universities have their own law enforcement units, which enables them to hide criminal misconducts committed by students and officials, and dismiss charges to safeguard the institution's reputation, which can affect enrollment and alumni contributions. Such practices have placed many students at peril and denied justice to victims of criminal wrongdoing. When college athletes are accused of criminal misconduct, including rape, institutions are even more likely to dismiss accusations, and coerce victims to drop the charges for the benefit of the institution.[81] Military also maintain internal law enforcement units and investigative authority, which empowers them to dismiss wrongful conduct and sexual assault accusations to protect their institution's reputation.[82] Plentiful studies have reported how law enforcement officers abide by an implicit rule of "cop code" ("blue code of silence") that forbids reporting their colleagues' wrongdoings, and instead they cover-up each other's wrongdoings. They do so to shield the reputation of the organization as well as to shelter each other from criminal prosecution.[83]

Similar attempts at safeguarding institutional reputations take place in America's correctional institutions, also. According to a congressional report released in 2019, serious misconduct by senior federal prison officials, including sexual assault and abuse, are "largely tolerated or ignored altogether"; whereas, those who speak out about the misconduct and victims who file complaints against offenders are routinely subjected to punishment and retaliation.[84] A list of hospitals, even some of the most reputable ones, such as Cleveland Clinic, routinely shielded their staffs' criminally negligent mistakes and wrongdoings, including rape of patients, to protect the reputation of the institution, according to a *USA Today* investigation.[85] U.S.A. Gymnastics shielded pedophile sports doctors accused of sexual assault of young gymnasts for decades, because they valued the reputation of the organization and winning medals over protecting the children under their care. Larry Nassar, the team doctor, was convicted in 2018 of molesting over 250 children over a 20-year period, despite numerous charges and complaints made by the children and their parents.[86] Authorities of various agencies within the United Nations have repeatedly dismissed sexual assault and abuse accusations against the people they cared for and female coworkers, and refused to investigate them in order to protect the reputation of their agencies.[87] Plentiful corporations conceal misconduct allegations against high-ranking officials to protect the reputation of their organization, especially when the offenders are essential to the operation and profit of the corporation. When sexual misconduct complaints or retaliation scandals appear, even the most reputable corporations routinely pay hush money to the victims to protect the reputation of their organization, instead of reporting them to the police.[88] Such flagrant violations of individual rights occur because group members and leaders believe that shielding the group's reputation, profits, and interests are more important than safeguarding individual rights and public welfare.

NATIONAL HONOR OVER INDIVIDUAL RIGHTS/WELFARE

Some nation-states do not hesitate to jeopardize the lives of their citizens in order to preserve national pride and reputation. In 1976, when China had a massive earthquake that killed about a quarter of million people and left millions homeless, the Chinese government tried to cover-up the death toll and damage, and refused to accept foreign aid, fearing that it might tarnish the image of China and bring shame to China. In 2008, when a cyclone killed over 100,000 people and displaced millions of people, the government of Myanmar refused to accept foreign aid for the same reason—fear that it might bring shame to the nation and decrease people's loyalty to the government.[89] After Hurricane Gustav hit Cuba harshly in 2008, Fidel Castro, refused U.S. aid, because Cuba had "too much dignity" to accept U.S. handouts.[90] In 2016, Doctors Without Borders accused Haitian officials of grossly underreporting casualties from a cholera epidemic, risking the lives of its citizens and tourists, mainly to protect its national reputation and tourism industries.[91] For the leaders of these nations, national pride and honor are more important than aiding their suffering citizens.

Loyalty, Duty and Sacrifice for the Group

Extremist groups and their leaders rely heavily on loyal devotees who dutifully follow orders and sacrifice personal interests for the group. For the success of their causes, therefore, they try hard to instill values of loyalty, duty, and sacrifice for the group among their followers. Loyalty is valued over truth, justice, fairness, merit, and honesty. For instance, they applaud acts of loyalty over competence and integrity, and ignore foibles and malfeasance of the loyalists, while reviling earnest disagreements and whistleblowing by truth-seeking individuals. Out of loyalty, tribesmen, gang members, soldiers, cops, priests, and fraternity brothers conceal each other's criminal wrongdoings, and citizens ignore and justify the malfeasance of their political leaders, government, and military (e.g., "our nation, right or wrong"). Out of loyalty, people become obedient, conforming, submissive, and bravely sacrifice their personal interest for the benefit of the group.

While extremist groups rely immensely on loyal and dutiful members for their collective defense and resource mobilization, group members become loyal to their group to secure their own survival and protection. Members' loyalty to their group, therefore, deepens in proportion to how desperately members need the group for their survival and security. The more insecure people feel, the more they fear isolation from and rejection by the group, thus the more loyal they become to the group. In such a symbiotic coexistence, loyalty becomes a price people pay, as a form of insurance premium, to secure group-provided protection and support. Public display of loyalty becomes a form of "identity verification process" that is widely expected and demanded.[92] According to Horowitz's[93] study of gangs, in order to retain gang membership, members must continually demonstrate and bolster loyalty through acts of mutual sacrifice, which, in turn, solidify their partnership, brotherhood, camaraderie, and mutual support.

Intolerance of Disloyalty

When loyalty is highly esteemed, people become intolerant of disloyalty. Throughout history, people have considered wide-ranging acts to be disloyal, including even the most trifling forms of disobedience, dissenting, questioning, criticizing, defecting, and challenging of authorities. The price of disloyalty has been high, also. Innumerable groups in the past have imposed the death penalty for blasphemy, apostasy, defection, treason, espionage, desertion, snitching, whistleblowing, and disobedience. Parents and family elders viciously punished their children who disobeyed them, even killing them disguised as "family honor killings." In fear of being accused of disloyalty, people were reluctant to challenge or criticize their group leaders and in-group members ("one-of-their-own") no matter what they did, and reviled those who did as "traitors" and "sell-outs."

Extremist groups are especially ruthless when it comes to punishing what they consider to be "acts of disloyalty" committed by their own members. They routinely torture and execute their internal critics, dissenters, traitors, snitches, defectors, deserters, and whistle-blowers, accusing them of traitorous betrayal. Gangs and rebel groups are notoriously cruel when it comes to punishing their snitches, traitors, and deserters. One of the chief missions of extremist jihadi leaders, such as al-Zarqawi and al-Zawahiri, was killing those of the same sectarian faith, the Sunnis, who disapproved of the jihadi goals, who refused to subscribe to their extremist goals, or who tried to join peaceful political processes.[94]

In more traditional societies and communities, condemnation of disloyal acts continues to pervade with grave consequences. Apostasy is still a capital crime in numerous Islamic nations, such as Afghanistan, Sudan, Iran, and Saudi Arabia. In some places like Iran, Muslims tolerate Christians but repudiate Muslims' conversion to Christianity with capital punishment because they consider conversion a "traitorous" act.[95] According to Cottee,[96] Muslims living in Britain and Canada face serious obstacles when they renounce or attempt to leave the Muslim faith. Apostates are ostracized from their own family, and apostates' family members are shamed and stigmatized by the Muslim community. Jehovah's Witnesses prohibit members from communicating with those who leave the group, even their family members. Mothers go for years, even decades, without talking to their children; siblings write off siblings, and friends shun friends who desert the group. This practice of "shunning" can push the already vulnerable defectors over the edge toward severe depression and suicide.[97] During the U.S. occupation of Iraq (between 2003 and 2008), at least 250 Iraqi men who worked as interpreters or informants for American troops were killed, even by their own family members. Many more left Iraq after the war under threat from their neighbors who considered them "disloyal traitors" who dishonored their community and shamed their families by cooperating with Americans.[98]

Some soldiers in the U.S. military consider accusing fellow soldiers of committing a crime, including rape, as a "traitorous act" of "betrayal" and "snitching." Instead of the perpetrators, they vilify and punish the accusers, such as rape victims.[99] In 2015, Human Rights Watch reported that nearly two thirds of U.S. military personnel who reported sexual assaults faced reprisals, including bullying, isolation and career setbacks; yet, the Pentagon has failed to address the problem.[100] Sundry leaders of private sector corporations and governmental organizations rebuked whistleblowers as "traitors" and retaliated against them for disclosing organizational wrongdoings, despite legal protections applied to whistleblowers.[101]

Double-Standards, In-Group Protectionism and Patronage

Double-Standards

People with a robust sense of in-group loyalty tend to apply double-standards when judging or evaluating insiders and outsiders—i.e., they apply one set of standards and rules to in-group members, and a different set to out-group members. For instance, they are quick to exaggerate and revile even the most frivolous misdeeds of out-group members, yet, they grant generous benefit of doubt to and tolerate even the most serious wrongful acts of in-group members. They cannot be objectively critical of "one-of-their-own" yet are hypercritical of out-group members who commit the same acts.[102]

Deployment of double-standards can lead to extremely unfair acts of profiling, unwarranted suspicion, discrimination, and mistreatment of out-group members. Prejudicial white people with double-standards, for instance, may suspect black people of committing a crime even when they are acting normal, while dismissing apparently criminal acts committed by other whites. Extremely nationalistic Americans would rush to excoriate human rights violations and injustices committed by "rogue" adversarial nations, while ignoring, condoning, or justifying the same acts committed by the American government and military and its allies.

Such double-standard mindsets enable extremist group members to commit and condone atrocities against out-group members without guilt or contrition. They can commit terrorist acts because they believe out-group members' lives are not as valuable as in-group members' lives, and in-group members' rights and welfare must take precedence over that of out-group members. During a war, troops can kill enemies and commit atrocities against them without much compunction, because they do not consider enemies as fellow humans with equal rights and human worth. Enemies are routinely "dehumanized" and "demonized" to such an extent that they become simple "targets," "packages," "rats," "pigs," or "terrorists" who deserve to be slaughtered.[103]

Double-standard mindsets are pervasive in America's partisan politics. During the 2016 presidential campaign, the majority (63 percent) of Republicans did not believe sexual misconduct allegations by 13 women against Republican candidate Donald Trump, whereas, the majority of Democrats (64 percent) believed the allegations to be true. According to a 2018 CNN/SSRS poll, about 54 percent of Republicans believed the investigation into Russian interference in the 2016 election to elect Trump was a "witch hunt," compared to only 12 percent of Democrats.[104] In 2017, the majority of Republicans believed that Democratic Senator Al Franken should resign because of one sexual misconduct allegation, yet the majority believed that the Republican senatorial candidate from Alabama, Roy Moore, should not drop out of the race despite numerous accusations of sexual misconduct and assault against teenage girls.[105] The so-called "budget-hawk" Republican lawmakers advocate "fiscal responsibility," castigate "tax-and-spend" Democrats, and block spending bills only when their party is in minority, yet they eagerly cut taxes and raise federal spending in support of their partisan agendas, bloating the budget deficit when their party is the majority.[106]

In-Group Protectionism

People with a compelling sense of in-group loyalty are urged to protect their in-group peers irrespective of what they do, a tendency called "in-group protectionism."[107] Out of loyalty, family members, friends, tribesmen, frat brothers, church members, police officers, and military soldiers try to cover-up each other's and in-group members' wrongdoings and mistakes. Even among strangers, people of the same group identities, whether racial, ethnic, religious, or national, protect each other and hide each other's mistakes. This explains why African Americans have a tendency to shield high-profile African Americans accused of wrongdoing. During the O.J. Simpson murder trial in 1995, most African Americans assumed Simpson, a prominent African American football player accused of killing his ex-wife and her male friend, to be innocent, whereas most whites presumed him guilty of the murders. During the George Zimmerman murder trial in 2013 (Florida neighborhood watch volunteer who shot and killed a 17-year-old black teenager), most whites and Hispanics weighed George Zimmerman's killing of a black teen as "self-defense," whereas the majority of blacks regarded it as murder.[108]

In 2018, several Hindu men were arrested for kidnapping an eight-year-old Muslim girl and holding her in a Hindu temple in the northern state of Jammu, Kashmir, where she was drugged and gang-raped for three days before being murdered. Instead of denouncing the act, Hindu villagers protested to defend the suspected men, and blamed the "Muslim separatists" for infiltrating their neighborhood. According to the investigators' report, two Hindu police officers destroyed evidence when the girl's body was discovered, and Hindu lawyers physically blocked police officers from filing charges at a court. Prime Minister Narendra Modi was censured for being too slow to respond to the attacks, and two of his government ministers participated in a rally in support of the accused.[109]

In-group protectionism is one of the factors that motivates Islamists/jihadists to join extremist groups and commit extremist acts—they are inspired by their overarching desire to defend and protect "people-of-their-own-kind" or to avenge those who harm them, although they may be total strangers. When the Assad regime of Syria (mostly Alawites, an offshoot of Shiite) mercilessly persecuted Sunnis during the civil war that started in 2011, a salvo of Sunnis around the world vicariously aggrieved, and traveled afar to join Sunni rebel groups and ISIS/Daesh to defend Sunnis in Syria.[110] According to a U.S. state department official report, between 2014 and 2015, ISIS/Daesh attracted about 22,000 foreign fighters from approximately one hundred different countries; that figure is twice as large as those who went to battle against the Soviet Union in Afghanistan over a 10-year period back in the 1980s.[111] When ISIS/Daesh lost its ground in Iraq and Syria in 2017, seized documents revealed that more than 40,000 foreign fighters from 110 countries had joined ISIS/Daesh to fight on behalf of the Sunni "brotherhood."[112] A number of Muslim Americans have committed terrorist acts out of overwhelming outrage over America's foreign policy and military actions that they believe were responsible for killing scores of their fellow Muslims (or Sunnis) around the world. Example cases include the Tsarnaev brothers of the Boston Marathon bombing in 2013[113]; Army Major Nidal Malik Hasan who killed 13 at Fort Hood, Texas, in 2009[114]; 2016 Ohio State University knife attacker Abdul Razak Ali Artan[115]; and mass shooter Omar Mateen who killed 49 in an Orlando, Florida, nightclub in 2018.[116] Scores of other Muslim Americans have been arrested and convicted of financially supporting or trying to join ISIS and other jihadi groups, because they have been radicalized for the same reason—America's involvement or support for mistreatment of Muslims (or Sunnis) around the world.[117] Similarly, countless, enraged African Americans have reacted with violent riots and protests after police killed or ruthlessly injured "one-of-their-own" without justification and accountability (e.g., "Black Lives Matter" movement; 2014 riot in Ferguson, Missouri; Cincinnati riot of 2001; 1992 Los Angeles riot; Watts riot in 1965).

"Anti-Snitch" Culture

The so-called "anti-snitch culture" pervasive in gang subcultures evolved from group members' profound desire to protect their in-group members from the outside world and criminal justice system they distrust. It also exists in some underprivileged minority neighborhoods where community members distrust the criminal justice system to such an extent that they feel compelled to protect members of their community from (what they considered to be) an inherently unfair, unjust, and corrupt criminal justice system. People refuse to report crimes, testify in court against "one-of-their-own," and cooperate with the police, making criminal investigation virtually impossible.[118]

Such "anti-snitch" mindsets of protecting "one-of-their-own" are not limited to minority communities or gang subcultures. They exist in a variety of other legitimate groups and organizations in modern societies, also. Despite the fact that they swear an oath to serve and protect the public without bias, many cops follow an implicit "code of ethics" of their own, called "cop code" (or "blue wall of silence," "blue code," and "blue shield/curtain"). They hide information, cover-up each other's wrongdoings, and lie in court to protect their fellow cops in trouble.[119] "In-group protectionism" and "anti-snitch culture" exist in the military as well (e.g., Marines' "blue falconry"). Soldiers consider accusing fellow soldiers of wrongdoing, especially of rape, as "traitorous acts" of "betrayal" or "snitching," and the accusers (e.g., rape victims) are frequently punished and shamed instead of the perpetrators.[120] According to a 2007 Pentagon survey of U.S. troops fighting in Iraq, less than half of Marines and a little more than half of Army soldiers surveyed said they would report a member of their unit for illegitimately killing or wounding innocent civilians.[121] Catholic Church priests, for centuries, have considered sheltering and protecting their pedophile colleagues as a "sacred duty."[122] The desire to protect "one-of-their-own" is shared by lay people as well. When *National Catholic Reporter* initiated to expose priests' sexual abuse of children and the Church's cover-up for the first time in history in 1985, it lost droves of subscribers and a board member, and suffered intense castigation from civil and church authorities.[123] All of these example cases manifest how easily people can succumb to committing and supporting extremist acts out of well-intended desire to protect "people-of-their-own-kind."

Collective Shame, Blame and Rejection

Collective Shame and Blame

Group-bound extremists see individuals primarily as "members of a group" rather than persons with unique identity and autonomy, and consider each individual to represent and embody the group to which he belongs. When one of the out-group members transgresses, therefore, they shame and blame the whole group to which the offender belongs, and it becomes a "group thing." When one of their in-group members is offended or humiliated by one of the out-group members, all of the in-group members are obligated to avenge the whole out-group or anyone who belongs to the out-group to restore the group's honor. For instance, when a girl is raped, it brings shame to her whole family, and the family tries to avenge the rapist's whole family to restore family's honor.[124] When a Muslim converts to Christianity, it offends and brings shame to the whole Muslim community, and therefore, the convert must be executed and his family shunned.[125] When a few "rogue" cops mistreat and kill a crime suspect, all cops are presumed to be "guilty by association" and become targets of random assassinations. When a few immigrants commit crimes, they blame *all* immigrants, and seek to ban immigration. When a few Muslim Americans commit mass murder (e.g., in San Bernardino, California, in 2015 and Orlando gay club shooting in 2016), all Muslims become "guilty by association" and subjected to abhorrence and random attacks. Some extremist political leaders have indeed tried to ban *all* Muslims from entering America, as Donald Trump proposed during his presidential campaign in 2016 and attempted as president. Terrorist acts against civilians can be easily justified and condoned with a mindset of collective shame and blame. When the American government or an American corporation commits malfeasance and harms one or some of their group members, *all* Americans, including civilians who have nothing to do with the wrongful acts, become legitimate targets of aversion and violent revenge assaults. Osama bin Laden and his followers in al-Qaeda implored terrorist attacks against all Americans to "avenge" the American government's "meddling in Muslim nations."[126]

With collective shame and blame mindsets, even minor or localized confrontations and frictions can easily spiral into broader and bloodier conflicts with grievous consequences. After the 9/11 terrorist attacks by al-Qaeda in 2001, some Americans felt that the attacks brought shame on all Americans or all Christians, and presumed that *all* Muslims were to be blamed for the attacks and should be targeted for revenge attacks.[127] Meanwhile, some Muslims/Islamists regarded the U.S.-led invasion of Iraq as a shameful and humiliating assault on *all* Muslims around the world, and believed *all* the Christians around the world should be blamed and hated for the invasion. Sunnis around the world considered the fall of Iraq's Saddam Hussein in 2003 as a humiliating blow to all the Sunnis around the world, and blamed all the Shiites, along with Christians, for bringing the disgrace. After the U.S.-led invasion of Iraq in 2003, groups of Sunnis assailed Iraqi Christians who had lived in Iraq for centuries, simply because they were Christians, somehow associated with America. Eventually, more than half of the 1.4 million Iraqi Christians fled Iraq in fear, according to a U.S. State Department report.[128] When Sunni vs. Shiite feuding intensified after the U.S.-led invasion in Iraq, many inter-sectarian marriages broke apart. Especially in Baghdad, divorce rates almost quadrupled, and sectarianism accounted for more than half of them. Some inter-sectarian couples were forced to divorce under death threats from their neighbors and in-laws.[129] Sunnis blamed all the Shiites and Shiites blamed all the Sunnis for the chaos and devastation they faced.

Collective Rejection

A robust sense of in-group loyalty spurs feelings of suspicion and hostility toward out-groups, prompting "collective rejection" of everything and everyone which/who is associated with, represents, or reminds them of the out-group they hate, regardless of merit or justification. Scholars have discussed that Islamist/jihadist radicalism is a form of "collective rejection"—i.e., they reject every aspect of Western influence *en masse* because they hate Western governments' hegemonic power, political interference, and economic domination.[130] Simply because they hate *a few* aspects of Western culture and policies, they repudiate everything related to or representing the West regardless of merit, such as Western-style education, health care (e.g., vaccinations, midwifery schools), music, movies, shopping malls, hotels, hospitals, airports, humanitarian NGOs, and Western aid workers (although some of them use Western-made weapons to fight and internet to recruit followers).

Boko Haram's (in northern Africa) motto is that "Western education is sin," and they have forayed and burned schools and kidnapped children from schools. In 2014, denouncing the education of girls, they kidnapped 276 school-girls to be sold off as brides,[131] and 110 more in 2018.[132] Afghanistan's Taliban also attack schools, especially girls' schools, and kill students and teachers. The number of school attacks increased to 192 in 2018 from 68 in 2015, and as a result, 431 schools closed for security reasons in 2018, and millions of children can no longer attend school.[133] Al-Shabaab of the Somali region raided Western-style shopping malls (e.g., Westgate Mall of Kenya)[134] and hotels, effecting heavy casualties.[135] In 2017, al-Shabaab's effort to bomb a Somali airport failed, and instead killed 512 Somalis when the bomb detonated in a crowded street.[136] In 2018, Taliban militants attacked the Kabul International hotel killing scores, including many Westerners[137], and bombed a mosque because it was being used as a voting registration place.[138] In 2018, Islamic State militants attacked a Save the Children office in Afghanistan killing and injuring numerous aid workers.[139] In 2020, ISIS-inspired Islamist militants stormed a maternity hospital ran by Doctors Without Borders and shot 24, mostly mothers and infants, to death, and injured many more in Kabul, Afghanistan.[140] Between 2011 and 2016, 1,083 humanitarian aid workers were attacked, kidnapped, gang raped, and killed, about 70 percent of them by al-Shabab in Somalia and Taliban and Haqqani networks in Afghanistan and Pakistan.[141]

Even in-group members become targets of violent attacks when they collaborate with the hated out-groups. In Pakistan, Islamist militants have killed scores of Pakistani health workers for vaccinating children against polio.[142] In 2016, eight Islamist militants killed seven Pakistani police officers who were guarding Western health workers administering polio vaccination in Karachi, Pakistan.[143] In 2018, an Islamist group in Afghanistan waged a seven-hour assault on a midwifery school where 67 young Afghan female students were learning midwifery, killing two and wounding 11 others.[144]

Similar acts of "collective rejection" occur in the Western world as well. The upsurge of anti–Muslim hysteria and "Islamophobia" in Western societies after terrorist attacks is also a form of "collective rejection." People denounce and reject the *whole* group of Muslims and their religion altogether because a few Muslims committed terrorist acts against them.[145] After the fall of the Islamic State in 2017, a number of Western nations, including France, Germany, Denmark, Holland, the U.S., and Canada, refused to take back over 2,000 of their citizens—mostly women and children who followed their husband to the Islamic State or joined voluntarily, inspired by ISIS propaganda and married ISIS fighters—fearing they might spread radical Islamic ideology in their country. They remain "stateless" in dingy camps in northern Syria under the care of humanitarian organizations.[146] Legewie[147] documented how a few terrorist incidents had spawned profound effects of "collective rejection" and persecution of immigrants throughout history all around the world including in Western nations. The "Japanese Internment" during the Second World War was also a form of "collective rejection"—the U.S. government rounded up and detained Japanese Americans who had nothing to do with the war.

"Cultural Inversion"

"Cultural inversion"[148] is a consequence of a profound case of "collective rejection." When a group of people experiences a severely impeded

1. Extremist Cultural Mindsets on a Group Level 57

social mobility and opportunity for advancement for a long time owing to systemic discrimination and maltreatment by another group, they develop an "oppositional culture/identity" shaped by collective and indiscriminant rejection of *everything* that is associated with or indicative of the dominant group. The aforementioned "anti-snitch" culture among some minority residents in underprivileged neighborhoods is an example of "cultural inversion." They distrust the criminal justice system *en masse*, and reject the whole system including anyone who collaborates with it (e.g., "snitches"), a phenomenon called "legal cynicism." Studies have substantiated that persistent biases and unjust treatment of minorities in the criminal justice system have eroded minorities' trust in the system. They become cynical of the whole system, and refuse to comply with the law or accept legal decisions.[149] Criminal justice systems in Europe face similar dilemmas with their terror suspects in trial. Defendants accused of terrorist attacks (e.g., Salah Abdeslam, Sofian Ayeri, Ayoub el Khazzani) refuse to participate in or cooperate with the criminal justice system because they believe it is "fundamentally and unfairly stacked against Muslims." They try to delegitimize the system through "self-recusal" of silence or absentia as political acts of protest and rejection.[150]

Obstructionism in Partisan Politics

Extreme partisan politics often spur political obstructionism—i.e., lawmakers reject and renounce everything the opposition party is proposing regardless of merit and virtue—effecting congressional paralysis. Used primarily by the minority party, its goal is to obstruct every bill, or as many as possible, proposed by the party in power, which will then make the party in power appear dysfunctional and incompetent to such an extent that voters will turn their backs on the party in power. The practice occurs frequently in the U.S. Congress even though lawmakers know that it is counterproductive, risky, and costly, even to the obstructing party.[151] Not a single Republican cast their vote in favor when President Obama's Affordable Care Act was passed in 2009, although the bill was virtually identical to the Republican-proposed health care bill during President Clinton's attempt to pass a health care bill in 1993. After the passage, the Republican Party tried to repeal the act over 50 times in five years.[152] The Republican-dominated Congress refused to confirm more than half of the federal nominees during the seven years of the Obama presidency using 79 filibusters, far more than during any previous administration, causing operational dysfunction in multiple federal agencies and effecting much harm and inconvenience to the public.[153] Expanding border walls on the Mexican border was a bipartisan idea both Democratic and Republican lawmakers supported during the Obama administration. However, in

2019, the Democrat-dominated House refused to grant $5.7 billion to fund President Trump's border wall, mainly because they did not want to give Trump a chance to successfully accomplish one of his signature campaign promises.[154]

Even after winning elections, some political leaders try to reverse and repeal what their predecessors of the opposition party have achieved, instead of moving forward with their own agendas. Political analysts asserted that the Trump administration's primary agenda after taking power in January of 2017 was to repeal and reverse as many policies and achievements of President Obama as possible, thereby erasing and obliterating Obama's legacy, regardless of merit, value, or popularity. President Trump reversed a number of Obama-era regulations on the environment, finance industries, labor, and immigration; removed Obama-instituted national monuments; voided DACA (Deferred Action for Childhood Arrival) that protected immigrant children from deportation; and retreated from Obama-era deals, such as the Paris Climate Accord (global initiative to curtail global warming), Trans-Pacific Partnership (TPP) trade agreement, and the Iran nuclear deal, despite opposition from his own advisors and lawmakers of his own party.[155] Trump reversed Obama's vehicle emission regulation even when auto industries opposed the reversal.[156] After Congress failed to repeal and replace Obamacare, he singlehandedly initiated an effort to chip away and dismantle Obamacare with a series of executive orders and lawsuits, despite the majority opinion favoring Obamacare.[157] The partisan sentiments of "collective rejection" have spilled over to the public. Some analysts argued that most Trump supporters passionately opposed Obamacare, including those who benefit from it (e.g., low-wage working class and self-employed) simply because it was the work of President Obama, whom they loathed.[158]

REVOLUTIONS AND POLITICAL PURGING

Goals and ideologies of most revolutionary and rebel groups are extreme—i.e., they strive for a sweeping overhaul of the system and leadership, rather than making incremental modifications and adjustments to fix the problems of the existing systems and improve them. When they successfully overthrow the existing system, they reject everything that is associated with or reminds them of the system they abhor, and seek to eradicate *all* elements and personnel associated with the previous systems. Therefore, once revolutionary leaders appropriate power, they often turn into brutal dictators reigning in terror trying to erase and purge every vestige of the old regime and systems they replace. Communist revolutionary movements aimed at a total and complete overthrow of the capitalistic economic system, instead of making incremental adjustments to fix the problems of

1. Extremist Cultural Mindsets on a Group Level   59

capitalism and enhance the system. The goal of "cultural Revolutions" in China, Soviet Union, Cambodia, North Korea, and Cuba was to purge *all* potentially counterrevolutionary sources and intellectuals, and to remove every trace of what they perceived to be associated with intellectualism.[159] Dictatorial regimes often engage in such wide-ranging, "broad net," political purging and eradication efforts, which is a form of "collective rejection." Most recently, after the 2016 failed coup in Turkey, President Erdogan jailed anyone who, they suspected, might be remotely associated with the coup or the alleged leader of the coup, Fethullah Gülen, including hundreds of thousands of educators and public servants.[160]

❖❖ 2 ❖❖

Extremist Cultural Mindsets on a Personal Level

Seeking Belonging and Acceptance for Security

Extremist groups are alluring to people with an intense desire to belong, bond with, and be accepted by peers for security and comfort. People whose self-identity is fragile, as frequently is the case with young people, seek to bolster their identity through constant contact with others who can validate and enable them through mutual acceptance and recognition. Their ontological security comes from *belonging*, whether it is to a group, shared identity, ideology, common cause, common antipathy, or simply sharing feelings of "like-mindedness," "like-appearing," and camaraderie. They feel secure and protected when they are accepted and recognized as "one of them." Immersed in "solidarity-in-kind," group life makes their life "meaningful," and renders them a sense of comfort and security.

Scholars have discussed that people who are exceedingly fearful of and hypersensitive to existential threats (i.e., people who hold the schematic perception of the world as an inherently dangerous and threatening place as opposed to a safe and secure place) have a heightened desire to belong and be accepted by peers, and seek group-rendered security and protection.[1] Groups become their "protection mechanism" that can ease their fear, vulnerabilities, and insecurities.[2]

To secure acceptance, people endeavor to conform to group-prescribed norms and "go along with the flow."[3] To dodge rejection, isolation, or shame by their peers (e.g., "losing face"), they become hypersensitive to how they appear to others and how they will be judged by their peers. To gain acceptance, they demonstrate loyalty through exaggerated disgust toward out-groups, evince camaraderie through sacrifice, and try hard to impress their peers with bravery and audacity. Siegel et al.[4] documented how adolescents engage in extreme, risk-taking behaviors for the sake of gaining acceptance and popularity among peers, often without considering the consequences of their behavior. Gang members commit crimes and battlefield soldiers fight in bravery for the same reason—to be accepted and respected by their peers.[5] In extreme cases, their desire to belong is so intense that they willingly commit violent acts under peer pressure or following the orders of their leaders. Some have committed mass suicides (Heaven's Gate and Jim Jones' People's Temple members in Guyana)[6], and others participated in war crimes, mass killings, and random killings (e.g., Japan's terrorist cult Aum Shinrikyo, the murderous cult led by Charles Manson).[7] Fraternity pledges voluntarily submit themselves to brutal, humiliating, and painful hazing rituals; cult followers endure slavery-type labor and sexual abuses[8]; tribal members undergo brutally painful "rites of passage"[9]; and gang members participate in dreadful initiation ceremonies, branding rituals, and commit crimes for the same reason—i.e., to be accepted by the group.[10]

Seeking "Prime Shelter Refuge"

Studies have substantiated that disaffected youths are drawn to gangs because gang life offers them the "prime shelter refuge" with a tribal sense of identity, belonging, and protection that they cannot obtain from their family, school, or community.[11] After returning from the Iraq and Afghan Wars, some veterans become seriously depressed and suicidal, not necessarily because of the traumas they suffered during the war (e.g., PTSD, TBI), but due to a sudden loss of the "tribalistic" bond and camaraderie they relied upon during the war among soldiers.[12] The majority of outlaw motorcycle gang members are former veterans who strive to find the same camaraderie and group bonding they experienced during the war from the gang life. They are drawn to the group-based lifestyle bound by camaraderie, loyalty, and mutual-support the biker gang offers, according to Steve Cook, who heads the Midwest Outlaw Motorcycle Gang Investigators Association.[13]

Some gang members in Central America (e.g., Guatemala, El Salvador, and Honduras), when they are ready to leave the gang, join Pentecostal evangelical churches through dramatic conversion experiences, in an attempt to find another group that can embrace them and offer them an equivalent sense of belonging, acceptance, solidarity, and protection (e.g., against gang reprisal threats). They see conversion to evangelical Protestantism as a "legitimate," even only way to exit the gang and find a replacement refuge, because evangelical churches accept them, protect them, and offer them an opportunity for personal redemption and transformation with God's forgiveness.[14] Flores[15] reported similar "gang recovery" efforts in inner-city areas of Los Angeles. Through religious outreach programs like

Pentecostal Victory Outreach and Homeboy Industries, and their use of ritualized reintegration and spiritual practices, former "debauched nihilistic" gang members transform into "family men" and devout "men of God." They drift from one group to another hoping to satisfy their compelling need for belonging, acceptance, and communality. Lim and Putnam[16] also suggested that many religious people, regardless of denomination and doctrine, join church congregations seeking to satisfy their "craving for communal fulfillment"—e.g., belonging, acceptance, communality—rather than for the religious beliefs and doctrinal teachings.

Some second-generation immigrants who feel marginalized by the majority natives or have impediments assimilating to the host society and culture experience an "identity crisis"—i.e., feeling that they belong to neither their parents' native culture nor their host country[17]—or a state of "existential denial"—i.e., not being fully accepted by any group.[18] Feeling "loathed as outcasts," "misfits," and "aliens" in their own homeland,[19] craving belonging and searching for an alternative identity, they often form or join ethnic gangs (e.g., MS-13, Trinitario, Latin Kings, Korean and Chinese gangs) and try to protect each other against outsiders and rival gangs. Gangs become their "family," replacing the mainstream institutions that they feel rejected them.[20]

Some of the disaffected second-generation Muslim immigrants in Europe join transnational terrorist groups (e.g., ISIS/Daesh, al-Qaeda) for the same reason—seeking alternative identity, belonging, acceptance, and protection. ISIS/Daesh and al-Qaeda use loosely and often misleadingly redefined (or tweaked) versions of "Islamism/jihadism" as their identity, recruiting tool, and ideological cover to lure those vulnerable youths seeking identity and belonging.[21] Jihadist groups become their "family" substitute, the only group with which they can identify and feel they truly belong. They join the group to assure their "own survival in that hostile milieu," and in that sense, the goal is primarily about "belonging to a *group*," not necessarily about the religious beliefs or ideologies, says Didier Leroy of the Royal Higher Institute for Defense in Brussels.[22] The core constituents of the Nazi movement in Germany were mostly Protestants from the countryside or small towns who did not belong to the Catholic electorate of the Center Party, and resented the working class that supported Socialist and Communist parties. The Nazis became an attractive alternative identity and source of belonging for them.[23]

Ideological Belonging for Individual Extremists

Most of the individual terrorists (so-called "lone-wolf terrorists," such as Brenton Tarrant, Anders Behring Breivik, Omar Mateen, Dylann Roof, and Eric Rudolph) are also strongly attached to extremist groups or inspired by extremist groups' ideologies through the internet and have a robust sense of belonging and bonding, although the bond may not be physical.[24] They become connected, attached, and sympathetic to extremist groups' ideologies through the internet, where they operate as "virtual packs" seeking "virtual belonging" activated by online propaganda messages from extremist leaders.[25] The Tsarnaev brothers of the Boston Marathon bombing in 2013, Army Major Nidal Malik Hasan, who killed 13 at Fort Hood, Texas, in 2009, and San Bernardino shooter Rizwan Farook in 2015 were reportedly inspired by online jihadist messages of Anwar al-Awlaki.[26] Salman Abedi, Britain's suicide bomber at the Ariana Grande concert in Manchester in 2017, and the attackers of the London Bridge at Borough Market (Khuram Shazad and Rachid Redoune) in 2017 were also inspired by ISIS/Daesh propaganda messages online.[27] Dylann Roof, a self-avowed white supremacist who killed nine African-American parishioners during a Bible study at Charleston's Emanuel African Methodist Episcopal Church in 2015, subscribed to and was self-radicalized by white supremacist groups' propaganda messages online, as well.[28] Alek Minassian, who ran over and killed ten and injured 14, mostly women, with his van in Toronto, Canada, was a frequent poster to an online misogynist group called Incel ("Involuntarily Celibate") where frustrated young men with a history of rejections by women or unfulfilled sexual relationships share their grievances with other men with similar experiences.[29]

Importance of Defending Honor and Avoiding Shame

Most pre-modern societies of the past lacked a firmly instituted rule of law. Instead, people relied upon informal social exchange systems based on honor and shame, which operated as a powerful social control mechanism that regulated people's behaviors.[30] Appiah[31] defines "having honor" as "being entitled to respect." When one is shamed and "loses face" in the community, whether from misdeeds or public humiliation, he becomes "dishonored" and "disrespected," and becomes subjected to mistreatment by the community—e.g., he and his family face social disapproval, shunning, ridicule, and rejection. In order to elude such mistreatments, one must maintain his honor by vigilantly fending off acts of transgression and humiliation, even the slightest insults or non-deferential treatments in public. If one fails to do so, he is judged to be "weak" and "dishonored" with a sullied reputation. To restore one's honor, he is obligated to go out and avenge the source of the dishonor. In extreme cases, one would rather die valiantly upholding his honor (e.g., "dueling") than to live pusillanimously in shame and dishonor, stigmatized as a "coward" who could not defend his honor.[32]

According to Anderson,[33] inner-city "street kids" place prime importance on gaining respect because that is the only way they can deflect and deter transgression and mistreatment by others (e.g., being "dissed"). They crave respect to such a degree that they risk their own life to attain and maintain it, simply to send a message to others that they are not someone to be "messed with." Horowitz[34] detected an analogous mindset among Chicago gang members. One's honor revolves around a person's ability to gain respect and command deference in interpersonal relations. When a person is publicly humiliated, people regard him as "weak and dishonored." In order to restore his honor, he must physically take back his claim to dominance and regain respect. Heller et al.[35] ascertained that most youth murders in Chicago occur without premeditation and without utilitarian goals of obtaining something material. Instead, they happen when someone says something "stupid" to someone else that offends the other person's honor, and the offended person tries to defend and restore his honor through reprisal attacks. If the person happens to have a gun, it can result in murder.

In some rural areas around the world, such as in Pakistan, India and Iran, people consider it justifiable for men to throw acid at and disfigure the face of the women who refuse their marriage proposal, in order to restore their honor disgraced by rejection (called "acid attacks").[36] People also regard the killing of a wife as "legitimate defense of honor" when the wife commits adultery or is raped.[37] In 2015, a man was arrested in Dubai after he fought off lifeguards trying to save his drowning daughter, who was screaming for help. He told the guard that he would rather his daughter die in honor than be "dishonored" by having unknown men touch her.[38]

In the U.S., police officers at times overreact with excessive force when suspects do not show respect to them. There have been numerous incidences in the U.S. where police officers arrested, abused, even shot and killed citizens for petty acts of "disrespect," such as "flipping a finger," refusing to extinguish a cigarette, jaywalking in police presence, "running away" from police, and even for "making eye contact." In some of these cases, the suspects ended up being killed or found dead in suspicious circumstances while in police custody.[39] What police officers resent is (what they perceived to be) a "lack of respect" on the part of the suspects, and they overreact with vindictive violence to penalize the "disrespectful" behaviors, even when those acts do not pose any physical threat to the officers.[40] In 2017, Desiree Fairooz was arrested and convicted of disorderly conduct for laughing out loud during Attorney General Jeff Sessions' confirmation hearing; the case was later dismissed by a Superior Court judge in a retrial.[41]

Even some political leaders overreact when people show disrespect to them. When Putin became Russia's president in 1999, Russia's NTV mocked him in a political satire, as it did to President Boris Yeltsin before Putin. Unlike Yeltsin, however, Putin immediately jailed NTV's CEO and seized control over the network.[42] In 2016, North Korea's leader Kim Jong-un ordered the execution of two senior officials with an anti-aircraft weapon because one fell asleep during his speech and the other suggested his own ideas in a meeting. Both were charged with disloyalty and disrespect for Chairman Kim.[43] In 2018, two Venezuelan firemen who created a satirical video depicting President Nicolas Maduro as a donkey faced criminal prosecution with a sentence of 20 years in prison.[44] Honor-bound extremist leaders cannot tolerate even the most insignificant acts of affront or disrespect, because they believe such acts, albeit trifling, offend their *honor*, which they must defend forcefully to gain and maintain respect.

Defending the Group's Honor

In group-bound cultures, defending the *group's* honor is just as imperative as defending personal honor. Like the individual's honor, the group's honor is firmly affiliated with members' ability to defend the group's reputation against transgression, humiliation, and shame. Every group, like every individual, develops a reputation—i.e., people judge a group in terms of such attributes as power, dominance, respect, and ability to defend itself. The group's reputation determines the way the group is treated by both members and nonmembers.[45] When transgressions against the group occur, whether they are criticisms, mockery, insults, or threats, group members feel duty-bound to avenge the source of the transgression in order to restore the group's honor sullied by the transgression. The second rule in the membership handbook of the Dominican gang Trinitarios is "Anyone who disrespects the Trinitarios gang must be swiftly and severely punished." The punishment typically follows a pattern—a crowd of Trinitarios, armed with machetes and knives, hunt down and swarm their victims, stabbing and slashing them multiple times. Scores of teens have been killed at their hands for simply "quarreling with" Trinitarios, or rejecting the group's invitation to join, including those with mistaken identities.[46] In 2019, six MS-13 members hacked a man, whom they believed had defaced MS-13 graffiti, to death with a machete, dismembered his body, and carved out his heart before throwing the body parts into a canyon of Angeles National Forest.[47] Some extreme Islamists in Europe have murdered, assaulted, and threatened European cartoonists and satirical magazine publishers for publishing cartoons that they believe "mocked" their prophets, such as in the *Charlie Hebdo* incident and the ax attack on Kurt Westergaard.

The goal of so-called "family honor killing" is to defend the honor of the family. When one of the family members disgraces their family, the other family members must punish the transgressor to restore the family's honor. For instance, when a daughter or sister loses her virginity, even by rape, people consider it a grave dishonor to the whole family, and the family loses respect in the community as a result. In order to restore the family's honor and regain respect, brothers/fathers are obligated to kill their sister/daughter.[48] For them, acts of guarding family honor and "saving face" in the community are more important than protecting individual lives and the rights of their family members.

Historically, most religions and religious states of the past maintained anti-blasphemy laws that imposed the death penalty for whatever acts they believed to be insulting attacks on their religion. Even in modern times, hundreds of people in a given year languish in Pakistani jails under the anti-blasphemy laws that include a mandatory death sentence for acts such as "insulting" the Prophet Muhammad.[49] Asia Bibi, a Christian mother of five in Pakistan, received the death penalty for blasphemy after an argument with a coworker. In 2018, after spending eight years in prison, a judge commuted her sentence. However, she could not leave the prison for fear of death threats by mobs, and her lawyer Sariful Malook fled the country under death threats.[50] In 2015, several Pakistani secular bloggers were hacked to death by vigilante mobs in broad daylight for posting comments that "insulted" Islam.[51] A Pakistani police officer became a "hero" for killing cabinet minister Shahbaz Bhatti, who sought to reform anti-blasphemy law to be less prone to abuses. When the officer was executed for murdering Bhatti in 2016, violent riots erupted and people demanded mandatory death penalty for blasphemy and no punishment for anyone who kills a blasphemer.[52] People's passion for defending the honor of their religion and prophets is so overwhelming that as an anti-blasphemy political party has been formed and is gaining support in Pakistan, it has sparked violence, assassinations, and mass demonstrations. In 2018, the party garnered more than two million votes and finished third in Pakistan's most populous province of Punjab, and won two seats in the city of Karachi.[53]

Honor plays a central role in many resistant extremist groups whose goal is to rebel against their oppressors. The subjugated group members band together and revolt against the dominant group striving, to restore the honor and dignity of their group violated by the mistreatments. Scholars have argued that what inspires and radicalizes followers of Islamist/jihadist extremist groups are not necessarily the cultural values or beliefs they hold, whether religious or ideological, nor are they merely a part of identity politics. They are resisting and rebelling against the hegemonic power of the Western world and their history-long dominance, interference, and mistreatment, whether political, economic, military, or cultural, which they believe to have trampled their group's honor and pride.[54]

Even nations have behaved in extremist ways in defending national honor and pride. In 2018, a Cairo court sentenced Lebanese tourist Mona el-Mazbouh to eight years in prison for "insulting Egypt," because she posted a video on Facebook complaining about sexual harassment, poor restaurant services, and street thefts in Egypt.[55] In Thailand, numerous reporters and bloggers were jailed for insulting or criticizing royal family members, even their dogs, under the Lèse majesté law.[56] Samantha Power,[57] as U.S. ambassador to the United Nations, suggested that Russia's Putin invaded Georgia in 2008 "out of honor, or, put another way, out of perceived humiliation"—especially from the collapse of the Soviet Union in 1990, which gave way to a world in which the "sole superpower" (the U.S.) boasted about how it had "won" the Cold War. Diplomats and intelligence professionals should acknowledge that honor and humiliation weigh as heavily in the minds of statesmen and citizens as do economic and security interests, she warned. President Trump is widely regarded as having fixated on status and respect.[58] He sought to "regain" America's respect through "being strong" and "tough," and tried to achieve this goal through belligerent bravado, threats, and intimidation, vaunting military prowess and flaunting a superpower's upper hand in diplomacy and trading. He considered "being taken advantage of" by other nations as an intolerable shame. He mentioned numerous times how a plethora of other nations were "ripping off America," "raping us," and "laughing at us" because they could easily "take advantage" of America, and boasted how other nations began "to respect America once again" after he became the president.[59] One of the key profiles of extremists' mindsets, leaders and followers alike, is this profound aspiration for defending the group's honor and earning respect, which they believe comes from brute strength, toughness, bravery, military or physical prowess, and ability to dominate others.

Vindictiveness and the Duty to Avenge

When people feel urged to defend a group's honor, they are quick to overreact to transgressions against them, even the most insignificant ones, with a vindictive hankering for retaliation. Revenge-taking has been an essential part of the human political process, especially in the pre-modern era when societies generally lacked a firmly instituted rule of law. People customarily believed that only the appropriate revenge could restore the honor of the offended group and bring justice ("revenge justice"). Without revenge, the offended group loses its honor, and becomes vulnerable to further assaults and humiliations. In honor-bound cultures with a strong emphasis on vindictive justice, therefore, quarrelsome disputes and perceived perils from external sources, even trivial acts of boasting, blustering, and demeaning, can easily escalate into serious and violent collisions.

Throughout history, countless wars and violent conflicts have emanated from people's vindictive desire to avenge prior transgressions. Walker and Bailey[60] documented that the principal motive for the never-ending skirmishes among American Indian tribes was revenge for prior killings and capture of women and children, and less often for theft of material goods. Chagnon's[61] study of Yanomamo Indians in Venezuela also revealed that the primary aim of the incessant tribal skirmishes is revenge—e.g., to recover or avenge the previous abduction of their women. In much of Africa plagued with ethnic and tribal violence, political leaders face insurmountable obstacles in making reconciliations because people demand retaliation. Especially the survivors of violent assaults stipulate nothing short of equally violent revenge because any attempt at reconciliations "ignores their pains," "keeps the wound in their heart alive," and forces them to "re-live the pains all over again."[62] In Somalia, inter-clan and inter-family revenge-killings are not limited to the offenders and victims. They expand to include the innocent family members of the offenders and victims, and their tit-for-tat killings continue for multiple generations with devastating consequences to both sides of the conflict. Out of desperation, the Somali government in 2018 passed a law mandating the death penalty and hefty fines for inter-clan revenge-killings, but most people do not believe it will change anything.[63]

Extremists' vindictive desire to avenge often cascades down to following generations. A range of groups and nation-states that suffered a history-long trajectory of oppression, humiliation, and traumas (e.g., slavery, genocides, war crimes, occupations, annexations) have endeavored to transmit their "honorable" duty of avenging their traumas to their descendants. They try to make sure the "collective wounds" they or their ancestors suffered never heal by continuously reviving the memories of the past traumas and reminding their descendants of their duty to avenge. The revenge they or their ancestors could not accomplish becomes a generational duty to carry out for the descendants.[64]

Gangs' Retaliation Murders

Revenge is behind countless violent acts gangs and organized criminal group members commit. They avenge offenders who insult their group or assault anyone of the group to which offenders belong in order to restore their group's honor and reputation sullied by the affront and to deter future assaults. Although the intended goal may be "deterrence," instead of deterring, such tit-for-tat revenge-attacks frequently escalate into a vicious cycle of "retaliation murders," where each retaliatory murder plants seeds for another. After hurricane Katrina in 2005, gangs surfaced out of chaotic disorder in affected areas of New Orleans, spawning a surge of gang-related reprisal murders. Residents say, "It's like, you shoot my friend today; I'm gonna shoot your friend tomorrow: you shoot my brother; I'm gonna shoot your mama. It's a cycle that just doesn't stop."[65] The murders in Chicago have a clear pattern, police say—about 90 percent are gang-related, and the majority of those are in retaliation for previous murders. In 2012, when Chicago's murder rate shot up, Police Superintendent Garry McCarthy said, "They go back and forth like a tennis ball. You shoot us, we shoot you; you kill one of us, we kill one of you."[66] They do not forgive or forget; they must always avenge. The motorcycle gang Outlaw's patch "G-F-O-D" signifies "God Forgives, Outlaws Don't," says Neil MacBride, the U.S. attorney in the Eastern District of Virginia.[67] At times, police can become targets (or participants) of revenge attacks. In 2006, in Sao Paolo, Brazil, revenge attacks between one of the fiercest criminal gangs, First Command of the Capital (PCC), and police turned violent, lasting for five days, with ensuing deaths of 115 from both sides.[68] The tit-for-tat cycle of revenge attacks between the police and black communities in the streets of Rio de Janeiro, Brazil, escalated and reached a death toll of 30 police officers and 124 civilians in 2017 alone.[69]

Desire to Avenge Among Terrorist Groups

Revenge has been one of the prime motives behind numerous terrorist acts, also. Numerous extremist groups have committed terrorist acts in order to avenge their aggressors, especially when the aggressor group's military or political power is superior to theirs. In 1998, Osama bin Laden declared, "killing Americans and their allies—civilians and military—is an individual *duty* for every Muslim to avenge Western nations' meddling in Muslim nations."[70] After the ISIS/Daesh-backed terrorist attacks at six locations in Paris in September of 2015 that killed 130 people and wounded 494, many ISIS/Daesh sympathizers commented on Islamist websites with such statements as: "Do they think, after killing us and mocking our prophet, we will just stand and watch?"[71] In 2017, an ISIS/Daesh-inspired militant group in Egypt attacked a Sufi Muslim mosque and killed over 300 worshipping Sufi Muslims with suicide bombings and executions, because the Sufis allegedly handed over several people accused of having ties with ISIS/

Daesh to Egyptian police. It was a payback for the town's cooperation with the Egyptian government and a bloody warning of the consequences of further cooperation.[72] In 2014, Taliban militants in Pakistan raided the Army Public School and Degree College and killed 132 students and 10 staff in retaliation for the killing of their tribesmen during army operations in their provinces.[73] Nigeria's militant Islamist group Boko Haram began its brutal campaign of terror after the death of its leader Mohammad Yusuf while in police custody in 2009. During its ten-year rampage of terror attacks, over 30,000 people, mostly innocent civilians, were killed, and more than two million were displaced.[74] In 2019, Thowfeek Jamaath, a local Islamist group in Sri Lanka, coordinated multiple suicide bombings on three Christian churches and three high-end hotels and killed over 300 and injured over 500, in retaliation for the attacks at two mosques in New Zealand that killed 50 Muslims a month prior to the bombings.[75]

Escalation of Violence Through Retaliation Attacks

Even the most trifling disputes and affronts can spiral into large-scale conflicts when extremist political leaders exaggerate the threat and stir up people's emotions to avenge with forces greater than the original transgression. According to the declassified "top-secret" memo, the Johnson administration's decision to send U.S. ground troops to Vietnam in 1965 was primarily (70 percent) to "avoid humiliation" by retaliating against North Vietnam's successful surprise attacks on U.S. air bases and battle ships, followed by "containing China" (20 percent) and "aiding South Vietnam" (10 percent).[76] Vladimir Putin considered the fall of Soviet Union a humiliating defeat, and resented the West's belittling of Russia, ruminating for revenge. The goal of destabilizing the West by annexing Crimea and meddling in Western elections were part of his "strategic retaliation against the West."[77]

SECTARIAN VIOLENCE IN IRAQ

Cycles of revenge-taking have fueled the history-long sectarian violence between the Sunnis and Shiites in Iraq. After the U.S.-led invasion of Iraq in 2003 and subsequent fall of Saddam Hussein, Iraqi Shiites took revenge against the Sunnis who dominated Iraq for over twenty years under Saddam's brutally repressive regime. In the land where the concept of "an eye for an eye, a tooth for a tooth" was born nearly 4,000 years ago under the code of Babylonian King Hammurabi, revenge killings of Baathists (Saddam Hussein's party) became rampant, and the U.S.-led coalition forces and Iraqi police routinely dismissed their brutal "assassinations and counter-assassinations."[78] Instead of forming an inclusive Iraq, the Shiite-dominated Maliki government that took over power in 2006 systematically antagonized and marginalized Sunnis from politics. Such retaliatory discriminatory policies contributed to the rise of al-Qaeda–linked insurgency groups, and the development and infiltration of ISIS/Daesh in Iraq and Syria, the Sunni Islamist group in 2014, with the backings of a sizable Iraqi Sunnis marginalized under Shiites' dominance.[79]

Israel and Palestine

The large-scale conflicts between Palestinians and Israelis evolved from individual scuffles, which spiraled into all-out wars through a succession of revenge strikes. The Israel-Hezbollah War in 2006 started when two Israeli soldiers were kidnapped and five more were killed by Hezbollah in Lebanon.[80] The Israeli-Hamas conflict in 2014 came out of the kidnapping and murder of three Israeli teens by a (suspected) Hamas group.[81]

War Crimes by Soldiers

When troops commit atrocities during wars and torture prisoners of war, their acts are often goaded by their thirst for avenging prior assaults and losses. The My Lai massacre (the killing of over 500 Vietnamese civilians, mostly women and children, by U.S. troops in 1968) was an "expression of their anger and desire for revenge" after heavy casualties and the death of a popular sergeant.[82] The Haditha massacre, where a team of U.S. Marines led by Staff Sgt. Frank Wuterich killed 24 Iraqi men, women and children in the town of Haditha in 2005, was also attributed to the fury and urge for revenge after an unexpected bomb killed a popular marine.[83]

Retaliation Against Whistleblowers and Accusers

Vindictive desire for revenge persists in modern corporate cultures, also. Despite laws protecting corporate whistleblowers, an assortment of corporations and government agencies have retaliated against their own employees who exposed corruption, misconduct, and mismanagement.[84] More than two-thirds of workers who filed sexual harassment and misconduct charges with the EEOC (Equal Employment Opportunity Commission) say they suffered from all sorts of retaliation, ranging from job transfers and shift changes to getting fired, according to an analysis of more than 45,000 harassment complaints filed with the EEOC between 2012 and 2016.[85] Of those, nearly all were ultimately fired or left their jobs because they felt their work environment became intolerable.[86] After numerous scandals involving corporate fraud, such as Enron and WorldCom in the 1990s, Congress in 2002 passed the Sarbane-Oxley law to protect corporate whistleblowers from being retaliated against. Since then, the Department of Labor ruled in favor of only 17 cases out of 1,273 complaints of retaliation and 841 cases have been dismissed. Senators Patrick Leahy and Charles Grassley accused the Department of Labor of violating the "spirit and goals" of a federal law aimed at protecting employees who report corporate wrongdoing.[87] Victims of military rape in the U.S. are reluctant to bring rape charges, fearing retaliation by peers and their superiors. Even when they do, the military's rape prosecution rate is much lower than the civilian rate.[88] Even when they are prosecuted, less than 3 percent of the cases result in conviction.[89] Instead, in the majority of cases, the victims, not the alleged offenders, faced retaliation including wrongful discharges from the military with dubious charges of mental and personality disorders.[90]

Tendency to Justify Use of Violence

Violence has been "a fundamental means of relating and regulating social relationships" in human history. Sundry groups, past and present, used violence to dominate others, earn respect, achieve solidarity, protect honor, and eschew shame.[91] Extremist group members in particular regard violence as an acceptable, legitimate, even necessary means of achieving their group-centric objectives, whether it is to empower themselves, defend the honor of their group, or to punish and avenge perpetrators, enemies, and traitors.

Especially in redemptive extremist groups, therefore, violence has a personal meaning for the individual. It is a path to individual salvation and redemption, a means of "transcending reality," regardless of the political outcome for the collectivity in the real world.[92] Acts of cruelty and savagery become not only admissible, but also "morally justifiable" and "honorable" when they are committed by the "good people" for "good causes" against the "bad and evil" people and the "oppressors."[93] Terrorists become heroic "freedom fighters"; suicide bombers are revered as martyrs; killings are rewarded with awards and recognitions; and rape is touted as "winners' trophy."

Throughout history, countless extremist groups, including both dominant and resistant, have used violence to vent their grievances, take revenge, defend their dominant status, or promote their agendas and political goals. Dominant extremist groups typically kill men and boys, gang-rape women and girls, burn down villages, and throw babies into the fire, as happened during Arab Sudanese military attacks against non–Arab Darfuris in Darfur, Sudan, between 2003 and 2010; Buddhist Burmese military and government against Muslim Rohingya minorities in 2017; Rwandan genocide in 1994; and the Srebrenica genocide in 1995. On the other hand, resistant extremist groups, as military underdogs, often use insurgency guerrilla and surprise terror attacks and suicide bombings when they attack dominant groups with superior military power. Terrorism, as a "strategy of surprise," is necessary for small or underdog groups that must compensate for their weakness in membership and power and destructive capability.[94] Mulloy[95] documented how a litany of militia groups in the U.S. have been radicalized and justified use of violence to promote their anti-government ideologies, and Durham[96] and Michael[97] detailed how some of the right-wing, racist, and other hate groups turned violent in carrying out their "righteous" causes of advocating white supremacy. Clarke[98] and Kaplan[99] demonstrated how assorted religious fundamentalist groups (of Christianity, Islam, and Hinduism) became extreme and justified use of violence in defending their beliefs, and Haleem[100] documented how radicalized Islamist groups justify violence to achieve their jihadist goals.

Support for Violence Among the Public

Support for use of violence is not a mindset isolated to groups designated to be terrorist or extremist. Support for violence, as sympathizers or well-wishers, is also substantial among the general public. According to the Pew Research Global Attitudes Project in 2006, 29 percent of Jordanians, 17 percent of Turks, 14 percent of Pakistanis, and 28 percent of Egyptians say suicide bombings against civilian targets can be justified if it is "to defend Islam."[101] In 2017, an Iraqi photojournalist smuggled out and released a secret video to the Western media that captured six different incidences of apparent torture and murder of numerous Iraqi civilians accused of cooperating with ISIS/Daesh by the Iraqi troops after they reclaimed the territory ISIS/Daesh had occupied. The majority of Iraqis hailed and praised the special operations unit officers for their "heroic acts," and condemned and even threatened to kill the Iraqi journalist who released the video to the West.[102] Even a decade after the 9/11 terrorist attacks in 2001, the majority (59 percent) of Americans think that the CIA's "harsh interrogation" tactics used on terror suspects after 9/11 were justified.[103] In 2013, a Gallup poll found that 65 percent of Americans supported drone airstrikes against civilians suspected of terrorism abroad, although such attacks often cause deaths of innocent civilians.[104]

Support for Mob Killings

In India, people applaud lynch mobs who violently attack and kill suspected criminals and Muslims. In 2018 alone, dozens of people were beaten to death, often in cold blood, by crowds of young men who alternated between booting someone in the head and taking "selfies" with their victims. The eight Hindu lynch mobs, who were convicted of beating an unarmed Muslim man to death for herding cows in 2018, also shot pictures of themselves hitting their victim. When they were granted bail during an appeal, Jayant Sinha, a Harvard-educated Indian who was a partner at McKinsey & Co. before becoming a member of the Indian Parliament and then a minister in Modi's government in 2016, invited the mobs to his house and celebrated with sweets and wreaths of marigolds. He also financed their legal defense, including lawyers' fees.[105] In Ukraine, nationalist mobs stepped up their violent attacks on Roma people, emboldened by their government that ignores such actions. When one of the groups known as C14 filmed their violent attacks and posted them on the internet, the government, seeking populist support, instead of prosecuting them, gave the group a state grant in the form of free rent for auditoriums and "patriotic education." After several members of a nationalist group, Sober and Angry Youth, killed a Roma man and posted their killing online in 2018, only one of the suspects was convicted with two months of house arrest.[106]

Political Violence

Violence among political factions is endemic and routinely tolerated as a "fact of life" in various parts around the world. In Latin America, people generally accept the endemic political violence as a "necessary means of sustaining democracy." They consider violence not a failure of democracy but a form of "violent pluralism," as sparring political camps tussle for power and control in an environment where corruption, oppression, and coercive means prevail.[107] At least 136 politicians and political operatives were assassinated in Mexico during a several months campaign period leading up to the July 2018 election. More than a third were candidates or potential candidates, and others included elected officials, party members, and campaign workers.[108] Between August of 2016 and December of 2017, 40 members of South Africa's ruling party (African National Congress) were assassinated in factional in-fights as the party prepared to elect a new leader and members scuffled over power and lucrative party posts. Political violence is so common and widely accepted that there has not been a single conviction for the killings.[109]

Male Domination of Women Through Violent Acts

Throughout history, men have used violence to dominate and subjugate women, and people generally accepted it as a "fact of life" (e.g., wife beating, domestic violence, marital rape, and family honor killings). Even in the modern era, women face peril at home at the hands of their own family members and intimate partners. Of the approximately 87,000 women who were victims of intentional homicide in 2017 around the world, about 34 percent were murdered by an intimate male partner and 24 percent by his family member or relative, according to a 2018 report by the United Nations Office on Drugs and Crime. The rate of women killed by a partner or relative was highest in countries in Africa, followed by the Americas, where the culture is rooted in societal norms that espouse men's authority to exert control over and dominate women. The lowest rate was in Europe.[110] Numerous startup tech companies in Silicon Valley sustain a fraternity-style "bro culture" where sexual aggression and mistreatment of women by peers are routinely ignored, even collectively prodded and applauded as offenders boast of their offenses.[111]

Fraternity Hazing Rituals

Fraternity members justify violent hazing rituals, both afflicting and enduring, as "meaningful," "bonding experiences" that are necessary for building group camaraderie, trust, and "life-long brotherhood ties," according to the confessions of former and current fraternity members.[112] Some even consider enduring violent hazing attacks as an "honorable" act, instead of dodging it in cowardice. Florida A&M University drum major Robert Champion, who was beaten to death during a hazing ritual, reportedly wanted to be hazed to become a lead drum major, and considered the cruel ritual an "honor."[113]

Institutional Violence

Multiple governmental agencies and military forces of high-income nations have used violent means to infiltrate, control, and dominate the political and economic systems of less-developed nations, causing immense pain and suffering to the masses of indigenous population, through foreign invasion, colonization, economic imperialism, supporting military dictators favorable to their economic interests and supplying for their brutal crackdown of their own citizen protesters. A host of American multinational corporations and their paramilitary "death squads" cooperated with brutal, right-wing, military juntas that ruled Latin America in the 1970s and 1980s. Union leaders and democracy protesters were among the tens of thousands of people who disappeared or were sent to clandestine detention centers where they were arbitrarily detained, tortured, and killed. In 2018, a court in Argentina convicted two former Ford Motor executives for helping the country's military dictators kidnap and torture 24 of their own workers during the 1970s. The two convicted, Pedro Muller, 87 and Hector Francisco Sibilla, 92, "allowed a detention center to be set up inside the premises of Ford factory" in Argentina where such brutal acts were committed. The convictions were the first in which representatives of a multinational firm were found culpable in a human rights trial in Argentina.[114]

Violence as a Source of Power

Violence, especially terrorizing acts of cruelty, can be immensely empowering. Even a minor display or threat of violence by extremists can generate immense symbolic power by jolting the masses into awareness of their potency.[115] For this reason, extremists regard violence as a form of power—i.e., an effective means of achieving, exercising, and displaying power. They feel empowered, superior, and dominant when they are collectively engaged in cruel acts of violence against others. Torturing prisoners of war or captured rival gang members is usually a collective performance for the same reason—the goal is not necessarily to gather intelligence information or to seek justice, but to physically dominate and overpower the helpless groups of individuals in captivity.[116] Some gang members consider raping a woman as a show of power and domination by dishonoring her husband or boyfriend. The only way her husband or boyfriend can regain his honor is to kill the rapist.[117] Neo-Nazis in Germany routinely attack disabled people who cannot defend themselves,[118] and some teenagers in the U.S. randomly attack and kill homeless people in what law enforcement agents call "sports killings,"[119] probably for the same reason—enjoyment of exercising power through violent acts committed against the most vulnerable and defenseless groups of people.

Enjoyment of Violence

When people consider violence as a form of power, some might even enjoy committing acts of violence, as sadists enjoy overpowering the weak through humiliation and cruelty (e.g., bullying, sexual assaults and harassments, hazing, and physical abuse of children, the disabled, and the mentally challenged). Some battlefield soldiers reported "thrills of fighting"[120]; gang members express their pleasure when they demonstrate personal dominance over rival gangs through violence.[121] Bullying is another example of using violence for entertainment, as well as to establish or legitimize status hierarchy. Scholars have noted that teens' bullying, like gang violence, is almost always a group phenomenon—i.e., it occurs within the "peer context," often urged by a group of cheering bystanders and spectators.[122] Their acts indicate teens' desire to demonstrate "social prowess" that can elevate their social status, individually or group- or clique-based.[123] They target "easy prey" (e.g., minorities, homosexuals, small and weak kids, and the disabled), and taunt, harass, and bully them for the pleasure of feeling powerful and superior. By demeaning and humiliating weaker groups of people, they believe they earn respect and move up in the social hierarchy of statuses.[124]

Violence as a Source of Respect

In a social milieu where violence is associated with power, violence can become a source of respect—i.e., people respect the ability to commit atrocities as a "demonstration of bravery," and "status symbol."[125] According to Anderson,[126] honor-bound "street kids" try to earn respect and climb the status hierarchy through "violating" and "shaming" others, often with brute force. They gain respect by boasting of their manliness, toughness, ruthlessness, and fearlessness through committing violent acts—e.g., throwing the first punch; pulling the first trigger; raping and stealing the girlfriend or sister of others; and robbing valuable items from others and flaunting them as "trophies." They consider such acts of brutality as the embodiment of their status as "winners" who deserve respect among those who generally fear "the fearless." In such cultures where people admire violence, bravery, and audacity, people are more likely to join terrorist organizations, especially ones that are already established and known for violent character, because they seek to earn the respect and admiration of their peers, family, and community. This is especially the case among the nationalist and separatist groups that can appeal to a large number of popular constituencies.[127] When violence is respected, people openly swagger and exaggerate their violent acts to gain respect.

Respect for Political Leaders with Violent Swaggers

Some extremist politicians openly brag about their daring acts of violence to gain respect, and people with extremist mindsets admire such leaders with crudity, vulgarity, viciousness, and flaunting of their brute forces as a "strong man who is not afraid of anything." President Duterte of the Philippines boasted of killing someone and sexually assaulting a maid as a teenager during his presidential campaign and as president; nevertheless, the majority of Filipinos elected him and continued to support him during his presidency.[128] In 2017, as president, Duterte told a group of soldiers who were fighting rebel groups on the southern island of Mindanao that each of them was allowed to rape up to three women. He ordered his troops to shoot female rebels "in the vagina," because women are "useless without their vaginas." In 2016, when an Australian missionary was raped and murdered, he said that he should have been "the first in line" to rape her because she was so beautiful.[129] Italy's Prime Minister Silvio Berlusconi had bragged of his sexual prowess and conquests of underage girls (in so-called "bunga bunga parties") in public, yet continued to maintain popularity for decades[130] Despite the swaggering of his sexual aggression and assault against women in a leaked audio tape (the "*Access Hollywood*" tape) during the 2016 presidential campaign, and accusations of sexual assault and misconduct by 19 women, Americans elected Donald Trump to be president. His brash, bullying, daring, and bold bravado, vulgarity, and swagger, and propensity of provoking and condoning violence, may have helped him earn respect from his base followers with extremist streaks (e.g., white nationalists and supremacists, Christian nationalists, alt-right, anti-immigrant, anti-globalism economic nationalists and populists).[131] In 2017, Greg Gianforte, a Trump supporter, won Montana's U.S. House seat, despite being charged with assault after grabbing a reporter by the neck and throwing him to the floor during a campaign event.[132] President Trump, during the 2018 campaign in Montana, hailed his body-slamming, as crowds exulted.[133] The majority of Russians admire President Putin for his daring moves and use of brute force in defending Russia's interests overseas, including military interference in Ukraine and annexation of Crimea, despite his increasingly authoritarian power-grab, rampant corruption among his oligarchs, and targeted killings and jailing of journalists and political opponents who were critical of him.[134]

Exaggerating Violent Acts Among Prison Inmates

In prisons, inmates perceive violence as a broadly accepted, informal cultural norm that governs their social hierarchy and status—i.e., violence exerted over other inmates is a means of building social hierarchy and statuses among prisoners. Therefore, they rarely report acts of violence, such as gang fights, interpersonal assaults, and rapes. The degree of violence inmates committed prior to entering prison can also determine their social hierarchy in the prison. For instance, inmates who committed murder to defend their honor (e.g., killing of police officers, traitors, or snitches) usually earn higher status for their bravery and courage, compared to pedophile molesters or white-collar criminals.[135] Male inmates, thus, have a tendency to exaggerate their criminal past to ascend in the prison social hierarchy, augment their ability to dominate others, and deter acts of transgression against them.[136]

Violence Becomes a "Performance"

In a culture where people admire bravery and audacity, committing violent acts can become a "performance," designed and executed to impress peers and gain respect—e.g., "staged violence."[137] Depending on the situation, people flaunt their violent acts to maximize the "impression effects," hoping to gain respect and admiration. Some teenagers share videos of their own incriminating acts of violence (e.g., gang rapes, physical abuse of mentally disabled) on social media platforms, or share the recorded videos of their violent criminal acts with their peers.[138] Some terrorists and mass shooters also showcase their acts of violence for the same reason. Ian David Long, who gunned down a dozen people in a California bar in 2018, paused during his shooting spree to post his own rampage on Instagram.[139] Brenton Tarrant, the 2019 mass shooter of mosques in Christchurch, New Zealand, who killed 50 praying Muslims and wounded scores more, video-streamed his killing spree live for 17 minutes on social media sites including Facebook, YouTube, and Reddit.[140] The 2019 gunman who killed two while trying to enter a Jewish synagogue as members were celebrating Yom Kippur in Halle, Germany, also used a head-camera to live-stream his terrorizing acts.[141] Saudi students at Pensacola Naval Air Station recorded part of the deadly attacks against U.S. military officials committed by one of their peers, Mohammed Alshamrani, a Saudi national, in 2019.[142] In 2017, a Hindu man in Ahmedabad, India, attacked and killed a Muslim man with an iron pickax and burned his body. He asked his nephew to film the entire episode and proudly posted it on social media, bragging that he had killed the man to protect his Hindu community from Muslim jihadists.[143]

Bystanders and witnesses to violent criminal acts, on the other hand, become spectators cheering and prodding the acts as if they are watching a staged "performance," instead of intervening to stop the act or calling the police.[144] Most recently, in 2019, several teenagers in Long Beach, New York, assaulted and stabbed 16-year-old Khaseen Morris to death during a "pre-arranged" fight over a girl, as 50 to 70 teenagers looked on, recording and sharing the act on social media.[145]

Conviction-Driven Absolutism and Blind Certitude

Extremists tend to be absolutists who consider upholding and acting upon absolute and unwavering convictions as signs of strength and courage, thus a source of admiration. Absolutists, like dogmatists and fundamentalists, refuse to acknowledge the "context-bound" and relative nature of human knowledge and perspectives—i.e., how our views and beliefs are shaped by the fortuitousness of our surroundings and continually evolve as circumstances evolve.[146] Instead, they value and admire rigidity in views and resolute defense of one's beliefs, and regard self-doubt, self-questioning, introspection, and willingness to adapt and modify as signs of weakness and flaws in character. They seek out simple and immutable certainty, because uncertainties, ambiguities, complexities, and relativities make them feel uneasy and insecure. They would rather be certain and convinced of (what may be) "wrong" beliefs, rather than to be cautiously doubtful of their beliefs.[147] Sibley and Duckitt[148] demonstrated that one of the key incentives for pursuing group-based dominance and superiority is the underlying personality dimension that values "tough-mindedness" *over* "tender-mindedness." People high on the "tough-mindedness" scale seek power from absolute convictions and refuse to negotiate compromises or reconcile differences, because they believe those are the qualities necessary for pursuing dominance and intergroup superiority (e.g., "social dominance orientation"). Extremists tend to be such "tough-minded" absolutists who consider unwavering and unyielding absolutism as a source of power as well a show of power. They believe that upholding and acting upon absolute convictions not only make them *feel* powerful, but also *appear* powerful to others.

Seeking Group Empowerment Through Absolutism

Power-seeking and power-hungry individuals often gravitate toward extremist groups where members strive to empower themselves with absolutist beliefs and attitudes, particularly regarding the group's moral superiority and righteousness. With steadfast and unshakable convictions, group members can believe in whatever they *want* to believe, regardless of facts and truthfulness. Facts and truths become irrelevant, or they can be tweaked and cherry-picked to corroborate their convictions (e.g., "confirmation bias," "deductive reasoning" or "self-censorship"). Realities can be manufactured, self-defined, re-defined, and re-constructed to fit their ideological convictions (e.g., "make-believe realities," "definition of situation," "historical revisionism"). Gradually, they develop a "tunnel-vision" of the world, trapped in "willful blindness," impervious to contrary views and factual evidence, and in so doing, make themselves prone to problems of "groupthink" and "certainty traps." As they seek power and refuge in deeply-entrenched and ideologically-biased convictions, snubbing all doubts and contrary views, extremists become oblivious to other people's and group's perspectives, as well as evidence-based scientific facts, and become unable to make impartial or balanced judgments.

For this reason, conviction-driven "groupthink" can occur in extremely partisan, identity politics. For instance, what influenced the decision to invade Iraq in 2003 was the resolute conviction of the majority of leading figures within the Bush administration that Saddam Hussein possessed weapons of mass destruction, or their production was imminent, which later turned out to be untrue.[149] President Bush in 2002 told the nation: "Facing clear evidence of peril, we cannot wait for the final proof, the smoking gun that could come in the form of a mushroom cloud." Consumed by their own "messianic" convictions, he and his administration ignored contrary evidence, warnings, and divergent views from intelligence sources, advisors, and experts, and decided to invade Iraq.[150] Nevertheless, the majority of Americans, facing the Iraq invasion, admired President Bush as a "man of strong conviction," as he repeated "there is no doubt in my mind," and trusted his decision to invade Iraq.[151]

At least in the U.S., as political leaders become ideologically polarized by openly discrediting scientific evidence, especially among the pro-business economic conservatives who seek to promote corporate interests at any cost, the general public's views about science seem to be changing, also. Studies have confirmed that trust in the sciences and scientific evidence has attenuated considerably during the past few decades among Americans who identify themselves as "strongly conservative," "traditional" or "religious" (e.g., attend church frequently); whereas, among others it remained steady.[152] There is evidence that conservative political leaders have endeavored to delegitimize science and scientific institutions altogether in an attempt to promote their conviction-driven, absolutist beliefs and ideologically conservative political and economic agendas.[153]

Refusal to Negotiate, Compromise and Reconcile

When people are convinced of their moral superiority and group righteousness with absolute and blind certitude, it becomes virtually impossible for them to engage in negotiations, make compromises, or reconcile differences with out-groups in confrontational situations. Their sanctimonious ideologies can never be compromised, criticized, or contested; their way is always the "higher- and nobler-way," and "their views and beliefs" should always prevail over those of others. As righteous "good-doers," they become eager to crush or eradicate the "inferiors," "infidels" and "evil-doers," instead of negotiating compromises. The only way to resolve confrontational situations is by winning a decisive victory with total destruction, eradication, and capitulation of the enemies.

Extremists regard negotiating a compromise as a sign of weakness, a form of "surrender," a source of humiliation, and a show of vulnerability, and therefore, they must avoid it at all costs to defend the group's honor and to stave off future assaults and incursions. They would rather die valiantly or suffer in honor, rather than be humiliated in disgrace by giving in to others' demands, or even meeting them half way. In 2017, the Pakistani government struck a deal with leaders of a militant fundamentalist Islamist group, and agreed to dismiss its law minister, whom the militants accused of blasphemy, in return for ending violent riots. Masses of enraged Pakistanis hit the street and protested the deal, because they considered such negotiation and compromise as "nothing but a humiliating capitulation." The militant group indeed celebrated the compromise deal as a sign of "capitulation" on the part of the Pakistani government.[154] For extremists, even "meeting with enemies" is considered a disgrace. In the U.S., some hardline, conservative Republican lawmakers openly castigated President Obama's willingness to meet with leaders of renegade nations, such as Cuba, North Korea, and Iran, because it would demean the superior status of the U.S.[155]

Hypersensitivity to Fear

Fear is probably one of the most potent human emotions that can spark and fuel extremist acts and movements. When people become fearful, like most other animals, the so-called "pack mentality" or "herd mentality" sets in—i.e., they try to "gang up together" against the presumed source of their fear to defend themselves using violent means. A group of people who face threats from another group fear losing the group's existence, identity, culture, honor, and ideology; they will do anything to preserve their group's distinctive cultural tradition, doctrinal autonomy, political sovereignty, and purity in identity. Throughout history, most violent situations were shaped by emotions of fear[156], and fear was behind many group-based acts of violence—e.g., by fascist groups of all kinds,[157] ethno-nationalisms and ethnic wars,[158] populisms of the left and right,[159] militia groups,[160] and a multitude of hate groups.[161]

Psychologists have noted that some people are more "fear-sensitive" and "hyper-sensitive to threats" than others—i.e., they are more likely to believe that the world is an inherently dangerous and threatening place, as opposed to people who believe it to be a safe and secure place—and, they tend to be more fear-prone.[162] Fear-prone people tend to be "groupish"[163]—e.g., they join groups to protect themselves against the presumed sources of the threat and use aggressive measures to defend themselves. This fear-prone personality dimension impels individuals to identify with the existing social order for stability shunning changes, and emphasize social cohesion for collective security (e.g., RWA—"right-wing authoritarianism").[164] Some political pundits have asserted that the conservative Republican base, the "right-wing" extremists who supported Trump, is comprised of people with a heightened sense of existential fear, and as a result, they have a stronger than normal desire to seek protection from manifold sources. Some believe guns and robust military power will protect them (e.g., defense hawks and gun-rights advocates); others believe God will protect them (e.g., religious conservatives and fundamentalists), and others believe their money and wealth will protect them (e.g., high-income economic conservatives; pro-business, anti-tax, free-market fundamentalists). Some believe border walls will protect them from "invading" and "intruding" outsiders (nativists and white nationalists); others are inspired by Trump's slogan of "Make America Great Again," hoping to return to the "good-old-days" when whites monopolized power and dominated over minority groups.[165]

Human emotions of fear are often artificially induced and intensified by extremist leaders who use "fear-mongering" strategies to stir up fear for mobilization purposes. Such strategies of inducing fear will be discussed in the following Chapter 4.

The "End-Justifies-the-Means" Mindset

A group becomes extremist when members try to achieve group-centric goals and maximize group-centric interests using extreme measures, disregarding or trampling the rights and interests of others. Their end goal of securing group-centric interests supersedes even the most basic existential needs and human rights of other group members, as they justify use of *any* means to achieve their goals, notwithstanding the rules, laws, ethics, fairness, morality, or justice. On the individual level, people with such "end-justifies-the-means" mindsets may become sociopathic egoists and criminals who try to satisfy their selfish interests using extreme measures that violate others' rights, interests, even lives. Students cheat to get good grades; athletes default to illegal doping to win in sports games; robbers rob to make easy money; business owners knowingly produce and sell products that are harmful to consumers or the environment to make more profits; and politicians lie, take bribes and kickbacks, rig votes, and rely on illegal campaign contributions to win in elections. They do not hesitate to violate rules and ignore ethics and morality in the process of procuring their *personal* goals, whether it is survival needs, winning in competition, or furthering self-interests.

Extremist group members apply the same mindsets and justification to securing their *group's* honor, glory, and interests. If it is for the sake of achieving group-centric goals and interests, facts do not matter; truths can be tweaked; rules can be violated; people can be harmed or used as means; and acts of atrocities can be readily justified. Throughout history, sundry groups of people and nation states have committed extremist acts of cruelty to promote their group's interests, such as torture, political purging, terrorism, genocide, ethnic cleansing, mass murders, war crimes, slavery, and a host of discriminatory and abusive acts. Numerous visionary leaders, convinced of and infatuated with their own grandiose vision of achieving a group-centric vision of utopia, caliphate, "God's kingdom," "classless society," "pure race," or any other forms of "new world order," have committed and justified inhumane acts of savagery and injustice. Countless corporations have engaged in unethical business tactics for the end goal of making greater profits, placing people in harm's way—e.g., exploiting workers, injuring consumers, crushing competitors, damaging environments, bribing lawmakers, and prodding others to go to war. Hawkish, militant political leaders, in the name of achieving "national security," protecting "national sovereignty," or "spreading democracy and freedom around the world," have initiated illegal wars, invaded foreign nations, ruined people's lives, and justified cruelty and human sacrifice.

Extremists have no scruples about exploiting human lives to achieve their political goals, including lives of civilians, women, and children. An assortment of militant extremist/terrorist groups have committed terrorist acts against civilians and exploited their own group members, including children (e.g., child soldiers, sex slaves, and suicide bombers) to achieve their group-centric political agendas. In Uganda, the Lord's Resistance Army (LRA) abducted and exploited about 20,000 boys and girls, and used them as soldiers and sex slaves in their effort to establish the "Lord's Kingdom" ruled by the Ten Commandments.[166] The warring tribal groups in South Sudan recruited more than 19,000 children as soldiers, about 10 percent under the age of 13. In 2018, the United Nations successfully negotiated the release of almost 2,000 of them.[167] Sundry extremist groups, such as ISIS/Daesh, al-Qaeda, and Boko Haram, also used teenage boys and girls to carry out suicide bombings on their behalf.[168]

State-Sponsored Extremist Acts

Officially designated extremist/terrorist groups are not the only ones that exploit innocent humans as instruments to achieve their political goals. Led by Crown Prince Mohammed bin Salman, the Saudi military recruited tens of thousands of desperately poor Sudanese children in the Darfur region of Sudan to fight in Yemen against a hostile faction backed by Iran (Houthis). Of about 14,000 Sudanese militiamen Saudis recruited, about 20 to 40 percent were estimated to be under the age of 17.[169] North Korean and Iranian regimes, on numerous occasions, tried to obtain diplomatic advantage by taking human collaterals and foreign hostages to blackmail or extort concessions from their host nations.[170] The former Bosnian Serb leader Radovan Karadzic denied all the war crimes charges against him during his tribunal at the International Criminal Court in The Hague in 2010, arguing that those actions were "necessary for Serbian survival." His crimes included genocide, mass murders, extermination, persecution, forced deportation, and the seizing of 200 United Nations workers as hostages.[171] Numerous advanced nations do not hesitate to supply lethal weapons to warring parties around the world for economic gains in their weapons industries ("war profiteering"), most recently in Yemen. In 2019, a United Nations panel reported that the U.S., U.K., France, and Iran are "complicit in war crimes in Yemen" by supplying weapons to a plurality of parties involved in the civil war. Their supply of weapons "perpetuated the conflict and prolonged the suffering of the Yemeni people" causing an "immense and wide-ranging humanitarian crisis."[172]

Plenty of Americans harbored the "end-justifies-the-means" mindset after the 9/11 terrorist attacks in 2001, and approved of and justified the extreme acts of their government and military that violated international agreements for the end goal of achieving national security, despite criticisms and warnings from international organizations—e.g., foreign invasion, use of torture, indefinite detention of terror suspects without due process, and substantial violation of civil liberties of U.S. citizens. Military leaders routinely justified civilian casualties as "necessary" and "unavoidable" "collateral damages." Secretary of Defense Donald Rumsfeld, in a Pentagon news conference about the high casualties in Iraq, inadvertently blurted that "people are fungible," indicating that troops can be easily replaced.[173] The American troops who tortured and abused Iraqi prisoners in Abu Ghraib, according to the whistleblower Joseph Darby, were led to believe that they were "doing something good" for America by "breaking them (prison inmates)" to solicit intelligence information.[174]

Toward the end of the Second World War, the American government and military justified the use of atomic bombs against civilians in Japan with the familiar rationale of "saving more (American) lives by ending the war." The U.S. military sprayed toxic chemical defoliant Agent Orange, a herbicide mixed with dioxin, across about one-third of Vietnam, knowing its long-term hazards to human health, including that of American troops,[175] based on the same rationale—winning the war justifies sacrificing human lives and wellbeing, including that of American troops and allies. The Vietnam government is still struggling to clean up the long-term environmental effects from Agent Orange 40 years after the war, and innumerable Vietnamese continue to suffer from the long-term effects of dioxin-contaminated soils, that cause debilitating health problems like cancer and birth defects.[176]

The American government's involvement in human rights violations and mass murders in Latin America has been well documented (e.g., "Dirty War" and "Operation Condor"). They were carried out in pursuit of a single-minded goal of "crushing" leftist and democracy movements in Latin America, for the economic benefit of American multinational corporations and their collaborators in Latin America.[177] Thirty years later, in Afghanistan, the CIA-recruited, trained, and equipped Afghan paramilitary "strike forces" are engaged in brutal acts of atrocities against scores of Afghan civilians in their effort to search for militants, including night raids, torture, and killings of family members of the suspects, including women and children, and burning their houses with virtual impunity.[178]

End-Justifies-the-Means Mindsets in Corporate Culture

The "end-justifies-the-means" mindset prevails in business sectors, also. Business owners and management routinely believe that the bottom line of running business enterprises is always maximizing profit at any cost. Making profit justifies rule violations (e.g., tax evasion, violation of labor laws, anti-trust laws, environmental regulations, consumer safety rules), deceiving consumers (e.g., false advertisements), and destroying competitors. They lobby and bribe lawmakers to lower taxes, deregulate their business activities, and change laws so that they can maximize profit and get away with wrongdoing. A litany of corporations have cheated and engaged in fraudulent and illegal activities to make more profits at the expense of unwitting consumers and the public (e.g., financial frauds by Enron, Worldcom, Cendant, Wells Fargo, Bernard L. Madoff Investment Securities; the Volkswagen emission cheating scandal, and other criminal negligence that caused industrial disasters). Weapons industries and defense contractors (e.g., Boeing, Lockheed Martin, General Dynamics, Northrop Grumman, BAE Systems, DynCorp International, Raytheon, General Electric) and other privatized military and defense support industries (e.g., Blackwater, Halliburton, KBR) have tried to maximize profit from violent wars and conflicts (called "war profiteering")[179] that has wrecked the lives of many civilians and children, by bribing lawmakers. The so-called "too-big-to-fail" banks and finance industries deliberately targeted less-educated, lower-income people with abusive and unethical financial schemes (e.g., "sub-prime loans") that caused a massive housing market collapse in 2008 hurting scores of lower-income homeowners, all the while "securitizing" their own risk with taxpayers' bailout.[180]

Drug companies continue to produce deadly addictive painkillers, even in increasingly higher dosages, and market them aggressively, bribing lawmakers, doctors, and distributors as over 60,000 Americans die every year from prescription drug overdose[181], and firearm industries produce ever-more lethal weapons, and lobby intensely to impede any gun control legislations, as about 40,000 Americans die every year from firearm-related incidences, through homicide, accidents, mass shootings, and suicides.[182] Tobacco industries have surreptitiously raised the nicotine content in their products and aggressively targeted young teenagers, knowing that their products are highly addictive and harmful to health, and got away with their wrongdoings for decades by bribing lawmakers.[183] Teen vaping of e-cigarettes has become an epidemic that affects 3.6 million underage teenagers, outpacing cigarettes, alcohol, marijuana, and other substances, baffling doctors as to how to treat them. To lure younger smokers, industries offer easy-to-conceal devices like the Juul, which vaporizes a high-nicotine solution sold in flavors such as cream, mango, and cucumber.[184] As of September 2019, there were over 500 vaping-related illnesses and nine deaths, mostly among teenagers, in 38 states of the U.S.[185]

Some business enterprises are established specifically to exploit the most vulnerable and unfortunate groups of people, such as sex tourism industries, especially for pedophiles (for example, in Thailand, Cambodia, and Indonesia). Government officials and tourism industries routinely turn a blind eye to such illegal business activities because they are good for the nations' economy and businesses by luring international tourists.[186] Even in the U.S., there are businesses that profit from human trafficking and use of "bonded laborers" (also called "indentured servitude" or "modern slavery"), child labor, and prostitution. In July of 2013, the FBI arrested over 150 people and recovered 105 children, ages between 13 and 17, involved in child prostitution rings in 76 cities across the country.[187] These example cases illustrate that the "end-justifies-the-means" mindsets are not confined to the officially designated extremist/terrorist groups; they are pervasive in sundry groups and organizations of modern societies that try to maximize profit by using the most vulnerable people, ruining their lives, and infringing upon their basic human rights.

Zero-Sum View of the World

The "end-justifies-the-means" mindset is prevalent among people with a zero-sum view of the world. On the individual level, people with a zero-sum view believe that one can survive or advance only by destroying competitors, and other people's success devalues one's standing in the social hierarchy, even signifies his failure, because the sum of all resources are always zero. On the group level, they believe that a group can advance only when other groups regress, and can promote its interests only at the expense of another group's interest, because the sum of all resources is always "fixed"—i.e., does not increase or decrease. For instance, Americans with a zero-sum view are inclined to believe that the Soviet Union's collapse was America's triumph, and China's rise is America's loss, even a threat to America's status in the world.[188] In the 1980s, the target of fear-mongering hysteria was against Japan, as the Japanese economy expanded rapidly and accumulated a large trade surplus with the U.S. Zero-sum minded Americans were gravely concerned that the rise of Japan was threatening America's economic supremacy and world standing.[189] For men with a zero-sum view, women's advances in gaining equal rights mean abatement of men's status. For white people with a zero-sum view, minority groups gaining equal opportunity for success indicates loss of power for whites. Similarly, some believe that allowing gay marriage poses a menace to the sanctity of heterosexual marriage; having too many Muslim immigrants erodes the Christian foundation of America; and money spent on helping the poor in foreign nations (e.g., foreign aid, humanitarian assistance) hurts America's poor. Some may even believe that people become righteous "do-gooders" by disparaging and punishing the sinners and "bad guys" as severely as possible, and a group can become morally "righteous" and "superior" by condemning and demonizing other groups.

People with a zero-sum view of the world are, therefore, obsessed with "winning." For them, everything in life is a competition, and people (or groups) either win or lose. With such a zero-sum battlefield mentality, every confrontational situation becomes a "win or lose" and "kill or die" situation, desperate and exigent. The only way one group can survive or advance is by winning a decisive victory by crushing others at all costs and by any means possible (e.g., demeaning, demonizing, destructing, and unfairly taking advantage of other groups), not by negotiating compromises, sharing power for peaceful coexistence, or pursuing mutually-benefitting collaborative progress—e.g., "making the whole pot bigger."

Pundits have discussed how the zero-sum worldview guides foreign policy agendas of Russia's President Putin. He tries to make Russia strong by upending the West, specifically NATO and the United States. To achieve this goal, Putin instigated an "all-against-all" type of campaign aimed at exploiting internal divisions and creating chaos within the Western world by meddling in elections, spreading disinformation and propaganda online, crafting disruption and internal division, and sowing distrust in the political system. He hopes that will weaken the legitimacy, stability, and people's trust in the government, and eventually upend the West's "liberal world order," which, he believes, will strengthen Russia.[190]

During times of economic duress and internal stress with shrinking resources, nested subgroups tend to splinter, spurring combative identity politics and intergroup conflicts (e.g., nationalism, racism, anti-immigrant nativism, and partisan politics). As people feel insecure about their survival needs, and feel "attacked" by some "other groups" and "enemies within," they succumb to a zero-sum competition mentality, pitting themselves against other groups, and begin to hate them.[191] Under

2. Extremist Cultural Mindsets on a Personal Level

precarious and insecure situations, people who are hypersensitive to fears and threats accede to a zero-sum survival mindset. With constant and paranoid fear that other people are about to harm or take advantage of them, they lose trust in outsiders and whoever appears to be "different." They see the reality as a "dog-eat-dog" type of anarchy, where every group must be on its own in a "survival of the fittest" competition until the strongest group survives and dominates others. In constant fear of "losing" in the battle, they do not hesitate to apply extreme measures to defend and enhance their survival chances by unfairly taking advantage of other groups and trampling on their rights.

This zero-sum worldview explains why the dominant, majority, and privileged groups become extremists when their dominant status is threatened or challenged. They fear the "rise of the rest," because they believe it means losing the monopoly of power and privileges they enjoy. To shirk loss of power, they use extremist measures to defend their dominant status against any challenges and threats to their power,[192] including brutal repression of the powerless groups of people who try to gain equal access to power and resources. In their zero-sum mindset, powerless and minority groups' advances in gaining equal rights and resources (e.g., employment, education) signify "loss" of their power and privilege. Political analysts discussed that the white, working-class populist base who supported President Trump in 2016 were people with a zero-sum view of the world who felt threatened by the rise of China and other "emerging economies" and growing size and electoral power of minority groups in the U.S. (e.g., blacks, Hispanics, Asian Americans, Muslims). They felt insecure that the rise of China means that America is "falling behind," and minority groups' advances indicate whites are "losing ground."[193] They supported President Trump because he promised to "make America great again" by restoring the hegemonic power America had before, and by "building the wall" to protect white Americans from an invasion of immigrants.

In areas where a "winner-takes-all" principle governs, such as in wars, politics, competing businesses, and sports, people are more inclined to embrace a zero-sum view of the world that fosters an "end-justifies-the-means" mindset. In politics, for instance, the end goal of winning elections dictates everything, as the winner usually takes all the power. When winning becomes the only goal, people try to win by crushing their opponents at all costs and with whatever means available, effecting viciously negative "smear campaigns," partisan bickering, and obstructionist gridlock. Opposition parties become "enemies" to be demonized and annihilated and party members refuse to cooperate with the opposition. Instead, they debase each other with wrongful accusations and "smear tactics." Political parties become a form of extremist group engaged in all-out wars with a single-minded end goal of winning and promoting their ideological agendas to the fullest extent by obliterating opponents, instead of attaining cooperative and negotiated compromises for the benefit of everyone and every group in the society.

Authoritarianism

In authoritarian cultures, people tend to be hypersensitive to and obsessed with power and hierarchy of statuses, whether they are of individuals or groups. They rank and assign individuals and groups in a hierarchical order of statuses, formally or informally, explicitly or implicitly. They become hypersensitive to status hierarchies and behave in accordance to hierarchy of statuses—e.g., they are subservient to their superiors, yet bullying to their inferiors ("kiss up, kick down" attitude). They eagerly submit themselves to and heedlessly admire persons of authority, power, wealth, and fame regardless of merit; yet, they demean, despise, and oppress people and groups with lower status or less power than them. They are exceedingly intolerant and critical of even the most trifling infractions committed by people of lower-statuses, such as women, minorities, lower-castes, the poor, prostitutes, crime suspects, ex-cons, homosexuals, and gypsies (e.g., "social-dominance orientation [SDO]"), yet, unreservedly tolerant and forgiving of even the most egregious and damaging rule-violations committed by the high-status persons with power and wealth.

Studies have documented that white working-class Americans have a tendency to admire the wealthy and despise the poor who they assume rely on public assistance,[194] and have "romanticized reverence" for the police and support their hardline, racist tactics against crime.[195] Studies also corroborated that right-wing authoritarianism is a strong predictor of prejudice against minority groups of all categories.[196] Some people with an authoritarian predilection find pleasure in acts of exercising power and dominance over the less powerful and vulnerable, as exhibited in such behaviors as bullying, sexual harassment, hazing, vigilante mob attacks, police abuse of power, prisoner abuse, misogyny, and racial hatred.[197]

For these reasons, extremism and authoritarianism tend to feed each other in a cycle—i.e., extremism thrives in authoritarian cultures, and the threats posed by extremist acts activate people's predisposition toward authoritarian preferences and behaviors.[198] Taagepera[199] has ascertained that people who spend a considerable amount of time in authoritarian group cultures tend to view extremism more favorably than those who do not. Probably for this reason, most gangs and criminal cartels maintain a strict authoritarian command structure, where higher-ranking members discipline and punish ruthlessly lower-ranking or wayward members of their own group.[200]

Attachment to "Strongmen" Authoritarian Leaders

People with authoritarian mindsets tend to idealize, romanticize, and even idolize strong, authoritarian leaders who dictate to them what to do, what is right and wrong, and what to believe in, and offer clear-cut, black-and-white, and grossly simplified answers to all the complicated and controversial issues and events affecting their lives. Lacking an "internal locus of control" (the ability to ascertain one's own choice of action and destiny), they eagerly place their fate in the hands of their authoritarian leaders in blind trust and faith. They feel secure and protected under a leader who *appears* to be strong, decisive, commanding, and overbearing, even if it requires forsaking their personal liberty and autonomy.[201] On the other hand, they regard political leaders who are more measured, introspective, civil, and nuanced, who seek balanced compromises to avert violent conflicts as "weak" and "spineless" leaders ill-suited to protect them. They search and long for a father- or prophet-like "strongman" leader who, they believe, can protect them from enemies, restore law and order they perceive to be in turmoil, and miraculously "save" them from perils and misery ("messianic savior").

Once they accept a leader as their "savior," they follow and devote to him unconditionally; become emotionally attached to him; refuse to acknowledge any flaws, missteps, or other undesirable traits of the leader; and become hostile toward others who disapprove of or criticize their enshrined leader (e.g., "authoritarian submission").[202] Infatuated with their own longing for and idealization of strong leaders, they become vulnerable to emotional manipulations, ideological propagandas, divisive demagoguery, and a utopian or revolutionary world vision their leaders present.

During her five-hour testimony, Leslie Van Houten, one of Charles Manson's followers who killed the LaBianca family upon Manson's order, described Manson as a "Christ-like man who had all the answers."[203] Donald Trump, as a presidential candidate in 2016, boasted of his unwavering popularity by saying: "I could stand in the middle of 5th Avenue and shoot somebody and I wouldn't lose any voters."[204] His followers may have been such desperate seekers of a "messianic savior," who flocked to Trump infatuated by their own yearnings for a strong, authoritarian leader who could institute the dramatic reforms they longed for. In such situations, the actual quality and ability of the leaders becomes inconsequential. Instead, leaders become *symbolic* figures representing the group's identity, interests, or aspirations.

When leaderships become symbolic and leaders embody the group and its aspirations—e.g., "who they are" and "what they yearn for"—people cannot tolerate critics who assail their leader or media accusing their leader of malfeasance. They become indignant and duty-bound to go out of their way to defend their embattled leader, accusing the accusers and attacking the attackers, heedless of the wrongdoings their leaders commit. A number of Trump supporters have attacked or were arrested for plotting to attack critics of Trump (e.g., CNN, Bill and Hillary Clinton, Joe Biden, Barack Obama, members of Congress, and the actor Robert De Niro).[205] In Italy, news about pedophile clergy sexual abuse is rarely reported in the media because most Italians are indifferent to it or refuse to pay attention to it.[206] In 2010, when the media reported that Pope Benedict, as a Cardinal (Joseph Ratzinger), was involved in covering up child sexual abuses committed by numerous priests, about 4,000 Catholics from around the world, gathered in Rome for a convention, rallied in defense of the Pope in St. Peter's Square, and accused the journalists of being "sowers of mistrust."[207]

Probably for the same reason, despite the sexual assault accusations from 19 women, Donald Trump won the presidential election in 2016. When eight women accused Alabama's 2017 Republican senatorial candidate Roy Moore, a Christian evangelical "moral crusader," of sexual misconduct and assault against multiple teenage victims, scores of white evangelical women came out in droves to defend Moore, and accused the media of propagating "fake news" and "persecuting" Moore for his faith. They insisted that he is a "strong leader" who "does not bend or change," a person more like a "biblical prophet speaking out for God than a politician."[208] When Andy Savage, a popular pastor at an evangelical mega-church in Memphis, Tennessee, admitted that he committed sexual assault against a teenager (after the incident was exposed through the #MeToo movement), and asked for forgiveness during a sermon, over 2,000 worshipers gave him a 25-second standing ovation, some weeping.[209] In 2017, when India's spiritual leader Gurmeet Ram Rahim Sing was convicted of rape, the verdict elicited violent protests from the guru's followers in two states, Haryana and Punjab, resulting in a military curfew. When another 77-year-old "self-styled godman" Asaram Bapu was convicted of raping a 16-year-old girl in 2018, masses of devotees protested and said, "even if Brahma [creator God in Hinduism] says he's a rapist, we won't believe it."[210]

Illiberal Democracies

The fervent longing for a messianic leader probably explains why people in numerous less-developed societies *democratically* elect and passionately support authoritarian, even autocratic dictators who rule with extremist, undemocratic manners and policies (by Western standards)—a phenomenon called "illiberal democracy"[211] and "authoritarian voters."[212] Levitsky and Ziblatt[213] discussed how "democracies die democratically"

2. Extremist Cultural Mindsets on a Personal Level 93

because of such people who prefer authoritarian dictatorship over democratic leaders. Despite the economic chaos, political oppression, and deaths of millions during the Cultural Revolution, many Chinese people continue to revere Mao as a heroic leader who stood up against the West, and celebrate his achievement and legacy with giant statutes of him all over China.[214] The power of and support for Cambodia's brutal Pol Pot regime that was responsible for the genocide of over 1.5 million people was the outcome of years of war, corruption, and chaos which devastated Southeast Asia during the Vietnam War. In a state of deeply rooted insecurity and vulnerability, Cambodians tolerated dictators hoping that such a strong leader could bring stability, order, and security back to their country.[215] When the Soviet Union left Afghanistan after ten years of war, Afghanistan descended into chaos without firm leadership. In the power vacuum, multiple warring factions sparred against one another, jockeying for power and effecting widespread chaos and desolation. The Islamist Taliban rose to power despite its brutal oppression of Afghan people, because people hankered for a strong, authoritarian leadership, which, they believed, could restore order, stability, and security.[216]

When Russia sank into economic chaos and political turmoil after the fall of the Soviet Union, Russians yearned for a strong leader who could restore order and stability. They reelected President Putin after he demonstrated decisive leadership during the brutal crackdown of the Chechen rebels, which the majority of Russians esteemed to be the quality they longed for—a strong, decisive, and authoritarian leader who could put up a fight against the rebels and the West, and restore national pride and stability. To the amazement of Westerners, Mr. Putin enjoyed over 80 percent approval rating for decades, despite the fact that, during his first term as president, he took over all six independent national television stations that existed before his election in 2000, and purged and killed scores of political opponents and journalists who criticized him.[217] Even during economic downturns from diminishing oil prices and economic sanctions by the West, Putin continued to enjoy high popularity in Russia.[218] In 2018, Russians reelected Putin for a fourth term for the same reason—e.g., they consider Putin a "strong man" who can "protect them," "maintain stability," and "make them proud" by "standing up to the West."[219]

After three years of chaotic revolution and riots to remove military dictator Hosni Mubarak, followed by economic turmoil and political mayhem under President Morsi of the Muslim Brotherhood, Egyptians in 2014 democratically elected another repressive military dictator, General el-Sisi.[220] Yearning for stability and order, Egyptians preferred a strong dictator with a commanding governmental control and firm grip on its people, renouncing democracy and freedom.[221] Despite the reign of terror and extra-judicial killings of thousands of suspected drug dealers and users, and outlandish public displays of crude vulgarity and flagrant incivility, three-quarters of Filipinos support President Duterte and regard him as a "strong" leader who can push for reforms, control rampant drug abuses, and corruption, and stand up against foreign leaders.[222]

Myanmar's military officials consider a "campaign of atrocity" against ethnic minority Rohingya Muslims as their "path to power and riches." Myanmar's hardline general Min Aung Hlaing's popularity soared after his brutal crackdown of Rohingya people in 2009. He has further cemented his power and status with galvanizing popularity in 2017 after a ruthless "ethnic cleansing" of the Rohingya people. Despite the systematic murder, rape, and arson of Rohingya villages, which forced over 700,000 Rohingya refugees to flee to Bangladesh, the majority of the public in Myanmar supported and admired him as a "strong and heroic leader."[223]

After the 9/11 terrorist attacks in 2001, President Bush's approval rate rose to an all-time high of 92 percent, although he was elected with 49 percent of the popular vote in 2000.[224] The majority of Americans, in fear and fury, endorsed Bush's hardline tactics to fight against terrorism, believing that he was "a man of strong conviction" who could protect America against terrorists.[225] On the other side of the world, threatened by the U.S.-led invasion of Iraq, Iranians elected their hardline, Islamist, authoritarian leader, Mahmoud Ahmadinejad, hoping that his forceful position on defense against the U.S. might unite the nation in self-defense.[226] Turkish voters, reeling from a debilitating economic crisis in 2001, and fed up with series of unstable coalition governments, rampant corruption, and economic mismanagement, merged to support the strong authoritarian leadership of President Recep Tayyip Erdoğan for over 16 years. As a pious person with strong belief in political Islam, Erdoğan instilled an "us vs. them" mindset and image of himself as the "strong man" who could stand up against the non–Islamic West and crack down on dissenters, successfully creating an enduring supporter base.[227] These examples lend increased credence to scholars' assertions that extremist mindsets emerge and authoritarian leaders gain popular support when people face heightened senses of collective fear, anxiety, instability, and insecurity.[228]

In Chapter 4, I discuss how authoritarian leaders strategically seize on people's aspiration for "strongmen leadership" when faced with fear and insecurity, and expand their power base.

Emotional Attraction to Group Power

Extremist groups are alluring to people who are emotionally excitable and obsessive, who seek to obtain psychological gratification from experiencing group power and euphoric elation from collective rituals and fanatical zeal. Extremist groups can offer them opportunities to experience group power through various theatrical rituals and collective acts. As Durkheim[229] understood, group rituals and gatherings can conjure up "collective effervescence"—i.e., an "awe-inspiring" feelings of "we-ness," a passion-filled energy, collective power, and a state of ecstasy. People attain emotional exultation and spiritual feelings of solidarity, and experience group power from participating in collective rituals and mass gatherings, such as religious pilgrimages, mega churches, political rallies and ceremonies, military parades, mass marches, protests, and riots. The vigor and potency of all collective movements emanate from such emotional energy, obsession, excitement, and passion of the participants.

Extremist groups, whether they are racist, Marxist, communist, Islamist/jihadist, Nazis, revolutionary, religious fundamentalist, far-right, far-left, or street gangs, offer an ideal and effectual conduit for people to satisfy their *emotional* need for obsessive fixation and longing for attachment, excitement, and empowerment, which can, at times, turn into a form of enjoyment. Researchers observed that many ISIS/Daesh members, leaders and followers alike, are such emotionally volatile and excitable people who mix violence with music, poetry, and art, to satisfy their varying emotional needs of the time. For instance, they would "kill in the morning" in rampages, and "weep in the evening" in an emotional trance during prayers and religious rituals.[230] Similarly, a sufficient number of Nazi officers in the concentration camps were "sensitive music lovers" who enjoyed classical music played by Jewish inmates as "musical slaves" in "camp orchestras and ensembles" (called Lagerkapellen) to "relax" after executions and "selections" (picking who should die).[231] Extremists seem to attain psychological gratification from emotionally arousing collective acts of violence, power, and obsessively single-minded passion, in a similar way as some people passionately enjoy music, art, poetry, and sports events.

Soufan[232] maintains that ISIS/Daesh offers "a cradle" for young Muslims who yearn for group-rendered "excitement, enjoyment, comradeship, and collective power" while entrapped in "mediocrity, isolation, and tedium" in Europe. According to Kotkin[233] and Sebestyen,[234] Russian Bolshevik revolutionaries under Lenin and Stalin were driven largely by the "emotions of personal obsession," not necessarily the communist ideologies. What incites and excites extremists may be the "shared passion": Without the emotions of fanatical passion, ideologies do not transform into action, they concluded. Gaylin[235] contends that all heinous, group-based extremist acts (e.g., genocides, massacres, terrorist acts, gang rapes, and mass murders) evolve out of fixated emotions of hatred, which gain traction through ritualized performances. Through ritualized acts of violence, people experience collective power, thrills, excitement, synergy, camaraderie, and group spirit, which can eclipse any personal feelings of doubt, guilt, or compunction. Depending on their political goals, collective acts of violence may even become a catharsis or "purification ritual" through which participants can "cleanse" their group by eradicating "undesirable" and "impure" elements. The Khmer Rouge's genocide of over 1.5 million people happened because of the Pol Pot regime and his followers' fanatical obsession and revolutionary zeal to establish a unified socialist utopia by brutally removing all dissenters and critics. They even documented the killings and recorded the victims meticulously because they did not believe what they were doing was wrong, blinded by their passion and obsession.[236]

Searching for Spiritual Sense of "Higher/Nobler" Meanings of Life

Some people's obsessive passion for group-bound causes extends beyond enjoyment of group power and excitement. It satisfies their compulsive search for a *spiritual* sense of "higher/nobler" meanings of and purposes in life, in preference to a mundane, self-absorbed, materialistic life. Extremist groups are palatable to such people because they offer "higher/nobler" causes and meanings in life, packaged in group-centric ideologies and presented as "spiritual" accomplishments. Participants can become passionately absorbed into something that is greater than they are and worthy of their sacrifice. They find personal redemption in pursuing the group's glory and honor, which, in return, can fulfill their spiritual aspirations for elevation, achievement, and atonement. Spiritually aroused and consumed by their own passion, they become "true believers"[237] and "righteous believers"[238] obsessed with their "noble" and "worthy" causes without reservations or doubts, who can act upon uncanny bravery without fear and commit atrocities without guilt or contrition in their single-minded pursuit of obsessive goals. Similar types of emotional obsession also explain behaviors of so-called "single-issue fanatics" and "single-issue-voters" who are fanatically obsessed with only one issue—e.g., anti-abortion, pro–gun rights, pro–animal rights, environmental preservation— ignoring everything else in the society. They seek "higher meaning" in life and redemption in pursuing what they consider to be a "noble" and indispensably compelling issue worthy of fight and sacrifice of personal interest.

A life devoted to group-centric, "lofty" causes satisfies these people's craving for spiritual fulfillment, emotional gratification, and self-elevation. They become "righteous" crusaders with unwavering moral conviction, blissfully reveling in emotional trances they experience in the process. For this reason, Tololyan[239] argued that terrorism is not simply the product of a collective sense of alienation or grievances, but "the manifestation of a desire to give one's individual life an iconic centrality in the eyes of the community" that values defending honor of the group and sacrifice for the group. Similarly, Elisha[240] described how Christian evangelical activists are driven by a similar desire to move beyond materialistic needs and individualistic pleasure from consumption, and seek spiritual satisfaction from their devotion to the "lofty" evangelical mission of "saving lost souls."

Recognizing the emotional vulnerabilities of humans, extremist leaders use a variety of strategies to appeal to human emotions and invoke emotional exuberance and passion to be used for mobilization purposes. The extremist strategies of manipulating human emotions will be detailed in Chapter 4.

♦♦ 3 ♦♦

Extremist Strategies of Pivoting Group Identities

As it was with extremist mindsets, typical strategies extremists use also display considerable similarities across all extremist groups, regardless of culture, religion, race, ethnicity, nationality, and civilization. In Chapters 3 and 4, I elaborate on some of the common strategies they use to attain their extremist goals, both as leaders and followers—strategies of pivoting group identities in Chapter 3, followed by strategies of enhancing group power in Chapter 4. As it was with extremist mindsets, not every extremist group uses all of these strategies, and not every group that applies a few of these strategies would be considered an extremist group. Groups that rely on more of these strategies in higher frequency and intensity, however, are more likely to be regarded as extremist groups.

Cultivating Group Identities

As Tilly[1] and Tilly and Tarrow[2] examined, one of the essential tasks of all contentious group leaders is constructing and maintaining group identities and boundaries. All group-centric movements are founded upon a collectively embraced group identity, and thrive when members passionately and proudly identify themselves with and rally around the identities. When a group of people take on the same identity, experience the same adversity or fate, and observe parallel emotions and collateral behaviors, a sense of common destiny and empathetic connection arises, which is called "empathetic solidarity"—i.e., "a reciprocated sense of merged consciousness and alliance, with faith in others' commitments to shared purposes."[3] It is the group leaders' task to invoke this "empathetic solidarity" by pivoting group identities to energize desired movements.[4] For these reasons, the process of constructing group identities lies at the heart of all contentious politics

3. Extremist Strategies of Pivoting Group Identities 99

and is central to all power relations.[5] Multiple researchers have discussed how the notion of collective identity works and plays a pivotal role in imbuing a group with a coherent message and the collective energy necessary to mobilize its constituents into collective action.[6] Polletta and Jasper[7] substantiated how group identity construction and branding processes are deeply ingrained in all aspects of group-centric social movements, including movement emergence, recruitment and participation, movement strategy, and interpretation of outcomes.

Using Identities for Political Goals

Effective formulation and delineation of identities are crucial not simply because they determine what it means to be a part of a group at an ontological level and distinguish one's group from other groups, but, often more importantly, because they define and accentuate social hierarchies of group-based "status distinction." For this reason, the process of constructing group identities usually involves imposing inferior identities upon others, a vital process of defining who can be included or excluded, allies or enemies, and which group deserves higher status and respect than others in a broader context of the society.[8] Rohlinger et al.[9] argued that the implicit goal of constructing group identities is to build "borders" and "boundaries" between "us vs. them" and to claim superiority or distinctiveness, which can be used to justify unequal treatment of "others." By claiming "authenticity," "superiority," "chosen people" status, or "pure breed," for instance, one group can claim greater resources and remove the "unwanted and undesirables" from sharing limited resources.

Throughout history, therefore, group identity construction process has always been an essential *political* process: group leaders purposefully created, erased, revived, reformulated, and rejuvenated group identities in accordance with evolving political goals and needs.[10] In every society, the dominant groups use identity politics to determine which groups should be included or excluded in resource distribution, whether they are racial, ethnic, religious, regional, or sexual[11], and subordinate groups frame political protests by formulating or reviving identity politics of resistance.[12]

Underneath the cloak of identities leaders put forth, therefore, there are always more fundamental political motives of securing the group's interests (e.g., security, domination, subjugation, exploitation, or resistance) or economic benefits (e.g., control over limited resources, monopolization, or market expansion) group members try to procure collectively. Klandermans[13] and Klandermans and de Weerd[14] detailed this political process by documenting how Dutch farmers collaborated to craft their own identity in their movement of opposing European Union and national regulations to protect their own economic interests. Thomson[15] and Hunter[16] argue that the so-called "culture war" in America is also an example of such an "identity construction process" orchestrated by religious leaders and social conservatives, and inflated and exploited by opportunistic political leaders. They used popular, attention-grabbing, and culturally sensitive wedge issues such as abortion, LGBTQ rights, gun rights, religious freedom, school prayers, and evolutionism to define, redefine, reformulate and redesign their group identities and allegiances (e.g., "value voters," "Moral Majority," "pro-lifers," "people of faith") for political goals of winning in elections. Capitalizing on the "culture war," American politics have become aggressively partisan "identity politics," and political campaigns have become an "identity construction" process as political leaders aggressively pivot partisan identity by demonizing the opposition party and claiming moral superiority.

Privileged groups have always formed distinctive identities to artificially elevate their social status and subsequent privileges, and expand their power-base. As Weber[17] discusses, privileged groups of people assemble "status groups" to protect and augment their political and economic power by supporting each other's interests. Historically, privileged class member—e.g., royal families, aristocrats, and upper-class people—have used their time, effort, and resources to form "status groups" through networking, formally and informally, and generated a sense of shared "consciousness of kind" to further their collective interests. They try to *differentiate* themselves through cultural means to justify their superior status, political power, and economic privileges. Royal family members and aristocrats have devoted themselves to acquiring distinctive manners, etiquette, nurturing aesthetics and taste in art, music, poetry, and playing high-class sports (e.g., polo, yachting). As Collins[18] discusses, *cultural* distinctiveness can help cloak the economic interests and prestige underneath, and thus can be used to *justify* their privileges. By *appearing* distinctive and distinguished from the lower-class members, it becomes easier for the privileged class to *justify* their superior status, power, and privileges. Underprivileged "outsiders" can be easily identified and excluded from competition, and thus can limit privileges only to those who *seem* like "the right kind."

Constructing Group Identities

Typically, group leaders construct and pivot group identities by accentuating the distinctiveness and superiority of their group compared to competing out-groups.[19] As Eriksen[20] argued, this process is carried out by the political and cultural elites who can pick and choose whatever aspects of a culture can serve their political purpose by convincing the masses.

3. Extremist Strategies of Pivoting Group Identities

Group leaders forge identities out of manifold sources—e.g., biological distinctions, locations, commonly-shared economic and political interests, group-centric ideologies, divisive issues, and collectively-shared traumatic events or experiences[21] (e.g., slavery, genocide, persecution, terrorist attacks). For instance, when there are extremely unfair economic inequalities or injustices unfairly inflicted upon a group of people, victimized groups of people form identities to protest against the mistreatment and injustices perpetrated by the perceived "oppressors" and "perpetrators" (e.g., persecuted and discriminated minority groups, labor unions, communist and Marxist revolutionary and rebel groups such as FARC and ELN in Colombia). At times, people form groups and forge identities out of an urgent need for social reform or addressing key issues—e.g., issue- or agenda-related activisms and movements (e.g., civil rights, gay rights, women's rights, abortion rights, gay rights, animal rights, anti-war, environmental concerns).

Even the most seemingly-ascribed group identities, such as race and ethnicity, are not always "fixed" or biologically determined, but subject to processes of identity formulating, reformulating, redefining, and reclassifying (both self-identification and classification by others) depending on situations and political motives.[22] Through elaborate processes of "racial formation,"[23] "ethnic project," and "ethnic 'marketing' campaigns,"[24] people have contrived or reinforced racial identities, hierarchies, etiquettes, myths and stereotypes for political gains, and determined how each racial group should behave (e.g., racial etiquettes), and to which category each person should belong (e.g., the "one-drop rule," "hypo-descent rule").[25] For this reason, people in different regions have conceived race and ethnicity in variant ways, and the definition of race and ethnicity have transmuted throughout history depending on historical backgrounds and political needs of the situation.[26]

The concept of the nation-state is also a modern construction, and subject to changes depending on geopolitical circumstances.[27] Ethno-nationalism is a modern ideology which appeared only in the 20th century when political leaders convinced peasants to adopt national identities on the basis of shared language, religion, and historical mythology.[28] The promulgation and constitution of a nation state was a deliberate process carried out by leaders, either for political (e.g., going to war) or financial purposes (e.g., collecting taxes). The process typically entailed construction of commemorative artifacts, such as monuments, flags, and anthems, and creation of myths, legends, and special occasions designed to honor national identity, history, and heroic leaders (e.g., national holidays, memorializing ceremonies of war heroes). In so doing, the sacred dimension and concept of "chosenness" of the collectivity were promulgated with "romanticized" primordial themes. In the process, the notion of "us" and "them/others" are demarcated, and the designated "others" are marginalized.[29] Large and pluralistic, modern states must constantly endeavor to uphold their national identity by constructing and appealing to what Peter Loewenberg calls a "synthetic nationhood." Nations with a highly diverse population in culture and ethnicity, like the U.S., Brazil, and Indonesia, must somehow forge an alternative concept of unity in identity that resonates with people's "shared-fates" and national pride.[30] This supports Barth's[31] suggestion that group identities depend not so much on the content of culture or "primordiality" but the *purpose* for which the group is created.

Symbolic Nature of Group Identities

Within the "constructionist" framework, therefore, once successfully created, group identities and identity differences become mere *symbols*—i.e., "a product of human imagination"—leaders invoke to use as mobilization tools.[32] They are nothing more than "tribal marks" or "color-coded gang symbols" people use to differentiate "us" from "them" and "friends" from "foes" in political or economic power scuffles. In fact, many of the European youths who joined Islamist extremist group ISIS/Daesh were not even religious or well-versed with Islam.[33] Most of the "lone-wolf" terrorists who committed terrorist acts inspired by ISIS/Daesh and al-Qaeda (e.g., Omar Mateen, Ahmad Rahami) had not been particularly religious.[34] Islam, as they interpreted, become a symbolic identity leaders use to mobilize resources for their movement.

As Barth[35] suggests, the question of who is and is not a member of a group depends not upon the contents of the culture or beliefs, but upon the *purpose* for which the community acts together.[36] Cultural disparities are not the central causes of animosity as group leaders try to make them appear to be (e.g., Islamism, jihadism, "clash of civilizations," and Islamophobia). They are *symbolic* tools or markers leaders use to appeal to and mobilize people and to demark allies from enemies, and therefore, cannot be blamed for the acts of aggression people commit.

Independent Role of the Identities

Although cultural differences and symbolic identities may not constitute direct causes of group contentions, once meaningfully constructed and effectively cultivated, cultural and identity variances *can* make group conflicts harder to resolve, because they "expand the potential misunderstandings and misperceptions of other groups."[37] In all extremist groups and movements, therefore, the "reified" concepts of symbolic identities play a pivotal role—i.e., it is this "sense of identity" that can invoke people's

3. Extremist Strategies of Pivoting Group Identities 103

passion for the movements, not necessarily the actual differences in identities.[38] When people are viscerally compelled to join and fight for a cause, therefore, we need to detect where that passion comes from, not just *how* they are mobilized into actions. The passions derive from people's *perception* of "who they are" as collectivities and as individuals, which takes shape within relational settings and interactions.[39] This is why McAdam et al.[40] argue that actors take actions in contentious politics "in the name of identities," and scholars have placed prominent emphasis on the identity *construction* process as a crucial "mechanism" for all social movements.[41] Probably for the same reason, in all extremist groups, group identities are critically important and group leaders place great emphasis on identity distinctions, boundaries, and maintenance.

MARKING OF GROUP IDENTITIES

Once group identities are constructed, leaders and members try to define and distinguish "us" from "them" by using some form of "markers." When ascribed, natural, or biological characteristics cannot separate "us" from "them," they use arbitrary symbols that can epitomize identities to separate "us" from "them." When gangs and criminal cartels are organized based on regional boundaries and turfs, instead of easily identifiable racial or ethnic differences, they use colors, hand-signs, tattoos, and other insignias as symbols of their identity and to differentiate themselves from rival gangs.[42] Indigenous tribes in Africa and Australia used facial tattoos for identification of a person's tribal lineage; sundry religions use wearable symbols to identify which religion people belong to (e.g., Christian cross, Jewish yarmulke, Muslim headscarves and body covers).

At times "inferior" groups of people were forced to wear their group symbols to be identified as "inferior" groups by the majority group. Nazis in Europe forced Jews to wear identifying badges or garments symbolizing Jews (e.g., Star of David), and executed those who refused to wear them.[43] Rohingya Muslim men in Myanmar are forced to wear only their traditional clothing of sarons or longyis, and prohibited from wearing pants. To the dominant majority Buddhists, they became unofficial uniforms that identified minority Muslims as "inferior people" to be discriminated against. Rohingya Muslim refugees in Bangladesh who fled Myanmar in 2017 after ethnic massacres in Myanmar reveled at being able to wear pants.[44]

Invoking Group Identities

For a group movement to gain a momentum, leaders must successfully invoke a shared sense of group identity and consciousness by accentuating group boundaries that distinguish "us" from "them" and "insiders" from "outsiders."[45] Throughout history, leaders have used an assortment of myths, legends, fairy tales, and dramatized stories of past heroes and prophets to glorify their group and arouse pride in groups. Some leaders appealed to blood ties and ethnic/racial purity. Bismarck exhorted "Germans, think with your blood!"; Adolf Hitler urged ethnic purity of the German nationals ("Volk"); Italy's Benito Mussolini stressed consanguinity of "pure Italian blood," and Mao Zedong equated the Communist Party as "part of the Great nation, flesh of its flesh and blood of its blood."[46] Some groups use family-type epithets such as brotherhood, motherland, brothers and sisters, as in the Catholic Church, fraternities and sororities, gangs, military, and some African American communities, since those familial terms can invoke a "familistic" sense of belonging and loyalty, eternal and unconditional. Such appeal to consanguinity, blood-ties, and kinship-ties, inevitably bifurcate humanity into "us" and "them" and "insiders" and "outsiders," and this propensity toward bifurcating humanity into groups of "us" vs. "them" has been the major sources of ethnic conflicts, divisions, and animosity toward out-group members.

Nurturing Group Identities

When identities are successfully manufactured, they should be constantly invoked, inculcated, and reminded of through a multiplicity of means and strategies. For instance, "Birthright Israel" is an educational program funded by the Israeli government and non-profit organizations that pay young Jews around the world to go to Israel to connect with their Jewish roots and reinforce Jewish identity and ties with Israel.[47] In just one decade since it was launched in 2000, more than 250,000 Jews from all over the world went on Birthright tours. A study demonstrated that alumni of the program were much more likely to feel connected to the Jewish state, defend Israeli political causes, and marry a Jew.[48] China is in the process of reinventing and rejuvenating parochial nationalism among its citizens, fighting against Western influences. On the eve of 90th anniversary of the ascent of China's Communist Party, the Chinese government produced and released a $124 million movie of Mao, *Beginning of the Great Revival*. The movie dramatically glorified the ascension of China's Communist Party and its heroic leader, Mao Zedong, despite the fact that his movement caused the death of tens of millions people in China through executions and starvation.[49] It was the Chinese government's deliberately orchestrated effort to raise people's attachment and loyalty to the Communist Party and strengthen national pride in identity by invoking, romanticizing and idealizing their "heroic" leaders of the past.[50]

Especially when new identities are constructed, group leaders try to replace the pre-existing identities and loyalties of the members and recruits with the new identities they constructed. Communist states have tried to erase people's pre-existing traditional identities and loyalties, whether they were familial, tribal, religious, or social status-related, and forcibly rebrand them with communist party identity demanding undivided loyalties only to the party.[51] Like most gangs, one of the initial tasks of Nxivm, a self-empowerment group for women, is breaking down recruits' preexisting identities and replacing them with a Nxivm identity through intensive initiation ceremonies that include physical "branding."[52]

Appealing to and Enforcing Group Unity, Solidarity and Uniformity

As Collins[53] states, groups gain power when "selfish individuals develop moral feelings of solidarity that binds them to groups they belong to." Rational individuals, without the moral feelings of group solidarity, will pursue calculated, short-term, self-interests without caring about the group they belong to. Social scientists have discussed the power of moral consensus and its "binding effects" on human collectivity. In contentious groups, therefore, group unity, consensus, and uniformity become powerful "moral foundations" of the group, especially when they face external enemy groups.[54] Group leaders have vested interests in appealing to in-group unity, solidarity, consensus, and conformity, and such efforts tend to be more forceful in extremist groups.

Social Cohesion as a Source of Group Power

Group cohesion can be an effective source of group power. Social cohesion is good for a group's morale, and good morale is what keeps men fighting in wars and improves their odds of survival in prison camps, because when a group of people achieves solidarity of camaraderie, they feel empowered, energized, and protected.[55] Cohesively unified groups can exert power that is greater than the sum of its parts, and members' experience collective power that can empower each member to act in an uncannily courageous manner. Extremist group leaders are particularly adept at evoking group unity and solidarity because they rely heavily on the courage and sacrifice of their members in carrying out extremist acts. Throughout history, extremist groups have tried to build group unity and solidarity by enforcing unity through uniformity, and discouraging deviation and dissent. Deviants and "people of differences" have been demonized, persecuted, and killed for no reasons other than the desire to enforce "unity through uniformity"—e.g., heretics, apostates, traitors, dissenters, critics, criminals, homosexuals, and even those with birth defects, deformity, or mental illness. Their effort to preserve territorial boundaries with a pure and uniform population, ethnically, culturally, religiously, or ideologically, has often been a murderous one, as they tried to enforce uniformity and homogeneity through repulsive means—e.g., population transfers, expulsions, ethnic cleansing, and genocide.[56] Most nationalistic sentiments have also been centered on the idea of seeking uniformity and consensus, such as having uniform language, religion, race, ethnicity, and tradition. Under these schemes, anyone who deviates, disputes, questions, or dissents are labeled as "unpatriotic," "disloyal," even "traitorous." The manifestation of patriotic loyalty instigated by well-meaning nations has frequently generated perpetual vigilance against the "fifth column," "undesirables," and "the enemies within," all aimed at achieving "purity" and "uniformity" of the population, whether they are national, religious, or ethnic identities.[57]

Enforcing Uniformity ("Homogenizing Pressure")

Once group identity is constructed, membership is defined by the commitment to the group's culture[58] and the recognition of boundaries.[59] To pivot group identities, therefore, leaders impose and enforce uniformity in beliefs and values and conformity to norms and traditions with repressive forces and threat of severe punishment. Members are pressured to accept whatever is defined to be conventional or traditional by the leadership, maintain purity in their identity and ideology, and obey leaders without questioning or challenging them. For the sake of the group's unity, dissenters should acquiesce and submit to the dominant views and opinions, and minority groups should forego their heritage and assimilate to the majority or dominant culture for the sake of the group's unity.

FORCED ASSIMILATIONS

Some extremist groups try to force their "unlike," "dissimilar" or "un-pure" members to assimilate into the dominant culture. The French Third Republic prohibited use of local dialects in favor of standard French, and penalized violators in a wide-ranging campaign orchestrated to stamp out local customs, dialects, and calendars, consigning local histories to oblivion.[60] The U.S., Canada, and Australia forced their native populations (e.g., Native Indians, aborigines) to assimilate. Their children were forcibly removed from their parents and sent off to be raised by white foster parents. In Canada, for over a century, more than 150,000 indigenous children, about 70 percent of the total indigenous children population, were forced to attend Catholic boarding schools, where they suffered mentally and some even died under physical and sexual abuses. The goal was to obliterate indigenous cultures and languages and force them to assimilate to Western, Catholic theology, and culture.[61]

In modern times, the Chinese government is deliberately trying to "erase" the Muslim culture of the minority group of Uighurs, an act critics call "cultural genocide." They detained hundreds of thousands of Uighur adults in "Adult Education Camps," and separated children from their families and housed them in "Children's Education Camps" where they are taught only Han Chinese language and culture. It was estimated that there were at least hundreds of thousands of Uighurs who had been incarcerated and subjected to "indoctrination programs" in 2018.[62] They also systematically demolished traditional Uighur neighborhoods, mosques, Uighur-language books, and other cultural artifacts, and imprisoned Muslim religious and Uighur cultural leaders. Their goal is to forcibly assimilate the Uighurs into the China's dominant Han culture.[63]

Some Europeans resent their immigrant populations for "refusing to assimilate" to European culture,[64] and support policies designed to force assimilation. In 2018, the Danish government issued a rule that, beginning at the age of 1, so-called "ghetto children" (children of 25 low-income and predominantly Muslim enclaves) must be separated from their families for at least 25 hours a week, not including nap time, for mandatory instruction in "Danish values," including the traditions of Christmas and Easter, and the Danish language. Noncompliance could result in a stoppage of welfare payment.[65]

Use of Repressive Sanctions to Enforce Uniformity

In order to achieve and uphold unity through uniformity, extremist leaders use repressive sanctions and threats of punishment against their own deviants, dissenters, critics and other "non-conformists." In 2014, the self-proclaimed Islamic State (ISIS/Daesh) offered Christians in Mosul an ultimatum—"leave, pay a fine, and convert; or, be killed," and the group issued laws legalizing enslavement of non–Muslim women and children in Mosul, which were posted on the walls of mosques throughout the city.[66] Amish communities sustain unity and uniformity through strict, repressive sanctions, both formal and informal—e.g., humiliating rituals of punishment, overbearing informal social control by the watchful eyes of the prying neighbors, and constant fear and threat of being rejected, banished, and shunned from the community.[67]

Boundary Maintenance and Expansion

The central core of all group- and identity-based movements is, therefore, "constructing cultural, symbolic, social, organizational or institutional boundaries" of collectivities, which becomes the basis of trust, deservedness, and solidarity.[68] Constructing and maintaining boundaries—whether physical, social, or "conceptual space"—are of supreme concern because boundaries remark and legitimize social criteria that account for groups' structural (or hierarchical) positions; facilitate negotiations of intergroup and intragroup exchanges; and reinforce group consciousness.[69] In extremist group movements, delineating and accentuating group boundaries and differences in contrasting forms and patterns (e.g., "oppositional consciousness"),[70] are of particular importance because they signify the "power differential" and define resource "deservedness" between "insiders" and "outsiders"—i.e., boundaries dictate the "range of moral obligation" of defining who "deserves" consideration, compassion, and resources. People in "our" group are entitled to attention and concern, especially when resources are scarce, opposed to people "outside" the group.[71] The concept of citizenship, for instance, is not just a formally addressed legal status; it is a matter of belonging, which requires recognition by other members of the community as "deserving" the same civil, political, and social rights as the rest.[72]

Once boundaries are erected and the definition of "insiders/outsiders" is established, groups face the business of *maintaining* the boundaries[73]—e.g., what to do with people who cross the boundary; how a stranger becomes an insider; and when a member becomes an outsider.[74] Extremist groups in particular employ boundary maintenance strategies extensively because they rely heavily on identity-based "oppositional consciousness"[75]—e.g., "us vs. them" and "allies vs. enemies." They try to suppress "diverging" tendencies within the group; trap or force members to stay within; and prohibit unwanted "outsiders" from infiltrating (except in "expansionary" groups). In extreme cases, they try to remove the "undesired outsiders" via mass killings (e.g., genocide, ethnic cleansing), or "drive them out" by dismantling their access to life-sustaining resources, such as land, food, and water, leading to a "genocidal elimination" of group life,[76] as happened most recently in the Darfur region of Sudan and to the Rohingya people in Myanmar. When the boundaries become blurred, they fear that the distinctiveness of their group's identity may efface, along with their unity, solidarity, and privilege. In 2016, as a presidential candidate, Donald Trump, from the first day of his campaign, announced his plan to build a wall along the Mexican border, and his supporters chanted "build that wall" during his rallies and even sports events throughout the campaign season.[77]

Calling illegal immigrants "rapists," "drug dealers," and "criminals," Trump appealed to the group-bound extremists who feel secure and safe when borders are tightly enforced and intruders are scrupulously fended off (e.g., "border psychology").

Punishing Boundary-Crossers

Extremist groups try to uphold group boundaries using strict rules against boundary-crossing and punish violators with repressive sanctions. Religious leaders in the past have brutally punished acts of apostasy, heresy and blasphemy with executions following atrocious tortures. Apostates were considered traitors who were worse than enemies, because their acts signified crimes of *betraying* their own people and identity—an act of crossing the group boundary. Political leaders have punished subversive, traitorous and treasonous acts; the military punished defectors and deserters, as gangs punish snitches and defectors, and corporations retaliate against whistle-blowers, all for the same goal—i.e., maintaining group boundaries by punishing the disloyal acts of boundary-crossers.

Even in some present-day states, people consider apostasy and defection as serious crimes that warrant severe punishment. In 2006, the Afghan government sentenced an Afghan man who converted to Christianity, Abdul Rahman, 41, to death under Islamic law.[78] In 2011, an Iranian pastor, Youcef Nadarkhani, who converted to Christianity and refused to renounce his Christian faith, received the death penalty, and the sentence was upheld by a higher court in Iran.[79] In 2014 in Sudan, a 27-year-old pregnant woman, Meriam Yehya Ibrahim, was convicted on charges of apostasy with the death penalty. She was brought up as a Christian by her mother, but because her father was Muslim, she was considered an apostate.[80] According to a 2012 survey, the majority of Egyptians (84 percent), especially among the older generation, support the death penalty for those who renounce the Muslim faith.[81] Adam Gadahn, a grandson of a Jewish doctor who grew up in California, converted to Islam and joined al-Qaeda in Pakistan. In 2010, he received the first treason charge the U.S. government had imposed since World War II, which carries the death penalty. In 2015, he was killed in U.S. drone strikes.[82]

Al-Qaeda's leader Al-Zarqawi frequently announced to his followers that there are only two ways to leave the organization—either be killed in battle, or be killed by al-Qaeda.[83] In 2014, the Britain-based Syrian Observatory for Human Rights (SOHR) reported that ISIS/Daesh had executed about 200 of its own fighters from foreign nations who had sought to return home.[84] Some hard-core gangs and criminal cartels enforce the so-called "blood in, blood out" code to forbid defections—i.e., once you join the group, you cannot leave the group without risking your life. In 2019, five MS-13 members were arrested for the stabbing death of a 16-year-old fellow gangbanger. They stabbed him over 100 times and torched his body because he wanted out of his crew.[85] During the war against rebel groups in Colombia, paramilitary groups routinely killed their own members when they tried to leave the group.[86]

Revulsion toward homosexuals and transgender people may also reveal people's resentment against those who cross boundaries of sexual orientation and gender stereotypes. Even in some modern states, such as the U.S., homophobia is still pervasive, and assorted legal barriers continue to hamper homosexuals' access to equal rights and treatments. At least 29 transgender people were beaten to death for being transgender in the U.S. in 2017 alone, according to Human Rights Campaign, followed by 26 in 2018. The majority of the victims were women from minority backgrounds who transitioned to become men.[87]

Typical victims of lynching assaults against blacks after slavery in the U.S. were those who were successful or "dared" to demand racial equality, which whites considered acts of "crossing boundaries" of racial norms and statuses. The goal of their violent assaults against blacks was to "put them down" and "place them back" to where blacks should belong—the "lower status." Emmett Till, a 14-year-old black teen, was lynched to death in Mississippi in 1955 after being accused of "whistling" at a white woman.[88] White lynch mobs considered that Emmet Till "crossed" the racial boundaries by "courting" white women.

Violence Against Women Who Cross Gender Boundaries

Sexual harassment of and violence against women are also motivated by men's desire to protect the social hierarchy of patriarchy and male dominance. Men who fear and resent women "crossing" the traditional boundaries of gender roles try to "punish" women to keep them in a subservient "women's place." Especially when women "encroach into" traditionally male-dominated occupations, men react with sexual harassments, assaults and discrimination. In the U.S., while men in traditionally female occupations (e.g., nursing) reap the rewards of a "glass escalator" to leadership positions[89]; women, when they enter traditionally male-dominated occupations (e.g., the military, firefighters, police force, construction, and sports commentators) face bullying, harassment, and sexual assaults.[90] Women supervisors who hold authority over male co-workers and women who are considered "too assertive," threatening the gender hierarchy are more likely to be targeted for sexual harassment by men[91] and discrimination.[92]

Probably for the same reason, campaigns of violence against women

3. Extremist Strategies of Pivoting Group Identities 111

in traditional societies have targeted professional women, female university students, and girls who seek education, as happened in Iraq after the fall of Saddam Hussein, in Afghanistan, and in areas occupied by ISIS/Daesh.[93] Men regard such women as "boundary-crossers" who must be punished and tamed to be back in their "right" place. The Taliban in Afghanistan outlawed educating girls as soon as they took power in 1996. When girls' education was reintroduced under U.S. control, they kidnapped and killed teachers; mutilated their faces; burned down girls' schools; and threatened parents of girls who sent their kids to school.[94] Most victims of domestic violence are also women who challenge or disobey male authority in the family. Of the approximately 87,000 women who were victims of intentional homicide in 2017 around the world, about 34 percent were murdered by their intimate partner, and 24 percent by their family member or relative, according to a 2018 report by the United Nations Office on Drugs and Crime. The rate of women killed by a partner or relative was highest in countries in Africa, followed by the Americas, where culture is rooted in societal norms that espouse men's authority to exert control over and dominate women. The lowest rate was in Europe.[95]

Trapping Through Dependency Relationship

Some extremist groups use strategies of "trapping" that makes it virtually impossible for members to leave the group. Establishing a paternalistic dependency relationship is an example of such a strategy. When a group maintains a "paternalistic system" or "patronage system" based on membership identity, members' social and economic livelihoods and survival depend completely upon others in the group. In such situations, one cannot leave the group without forsaking his social livelihood, economic sustainability, and possibly his survival chances. Marriage and slavery systems of the past resembled such "paternalistic" dependency relationships. Through marriage, the husband and in-law families become "providers and caretakers" of the bride and women: the women's lives become completely dependent upon their husbands' and his family's support and mercy, and they thus become unable to leave their husband and his family. In such systems, women are more prone to abuse by their in-laws, who take advantage of the fact that women must remain dependent on their in-laws for survival. Under slavery, a slave's whole life was at the mercy of their masters and owners, and, therefore, they could not leave their masters without risking their lives. Being enslaved and trapped without options of leaving the group, they frequently became victims of abuse and mistreatment.

Some religious groups (e.g., Mormons, Jehovah's Witnesses, the Amish, and some cults, and monasteries) and communes (e.g., Israeli Kibbutzim, religious and polygamous cults) maintain similar types of paternalistic dependency relationships. When members' survival and livelihoods depend on the communal support system and commune-based economic cooperation, it becomes extremely difficult for the members to leave the group. They become permanently trapped within, although they may be "free" to leave. For instance, some Jehovah's Witnesses groups maintain a very tightknit, group-sufficient support system, and forewarn deviants and dissenters with threats of excommunication, banishment, ostracization, and shunning. Members become trapped inside and unable to leave the group, fearing loss of their entire support system as well as friends, family, and business network. This "shunning" policy can push the already vulnerable defectors over the edge toward severe depression from isolation even from their own family members. As a result, the suicide rate is much higher among those who are ostracized after leaving the group than the U.S. population's average suicide rate.[96] The ultimate goal of "trapping" is to maximize the power and control group leaders can exert over their members and followers. When members are trapped within and fear rejection, it becomes easier for the leaders to control members' behaviors as they wish and demand compliance.

Isolation and Segregation

Some extremist group leaders try to sustain group boundaries by keeping their members isolated and segregated from the outside world, and forbidding contacts with the outside world. An assortment of religious cults, polygamous groups, Amish communities, and Native Indian reservations continue to use this strategy, as well as a few contemporary rogue nations and tribes, such as North Korea, the Taliban, Druze, and Kurds to some extent.[97] They demonize the outside world as "evil" or "dangerous," and pressure their children to stay within and marry within. Isolating the group from the outside world also makes it easier for them to control the inflow of information from the outside. In isolation, indoctrination of group-centric ideologies becomes easier and more effective, as does shielding inside affairs away from outsiders.

As soon as ISIS/Daesh occupied the city of Mosul in Iraq, they cut all internet services in the city, and declared that anyone caught trying to connect to the web would be lashed. The group also imposed severe travel restrictions outside the city.[98] According to Roy Jeffs, son of polygamous group FLDS leader Warren Jeffs, who was expelled from the group by his father, FLDS members "were told that everybody outside the church was terrible, and the whole world wants to kill us, that people wanted to destroy us and our moral values."[99] Amish groups have employed various techniques of isolation, aiming to preserve a separate and autonomous culture and enforcement of norms, including prohibition of accessing modern media (e.g., internet, radio, television) for information ("psychic insularity"). Once baptized, they are forbidden from leaving the group. Parents and the community may abandon those who leave the group possibly "for eternity."[100] Sexual abuse of young girls by family members, neighbors, and church leaders was allowed to fester for generations within Amish communities, because isolation without outside scrutiny made it easier for them to cover up such acts.[101]

Conservative Hasidic Jewish communities in New York and New Jersey maintain their enclave and remain within their communities for generations, socialize among themselves and shun the outside world, and educate their children in their parochial schools that serve to preserve their tradition and identity. They pressure politicians to protect their housing and education subsidies and make sure the state doesn't interfere with the educational approaches of yeshivas, despite laws requiring all students to receive an education equivalent to that of public schools.[102] Despite a high poverty rate and welfare dependency, most polygamous groups prohibit sending children to public school; Jehovah's Witnesses and Hasidic Jewish communities discourage sending children to college.[103]

Demanding Purity in Identity and Ideology

In typical extremist groups, particularly in reactionary groups, leaders try to retain group boundaries by enforcing purity in identity, culture, and ideology. They prohibit mixing, mingling, and fusing of identities (e.g., intergroup or inter-faith marriages and socializing), and repudiate ambiguities in identities or "in-between" statuses. A litany of extremist leaders had advocated racial, ethnic, and ideological "purity" to preserve their group boundaries—e.g., Adolf Hitler of Germany, Italy's Benito Mussolini, Mao Zedong of China, Ho Chi Minh of Vietnam, and Kim Il-Sung of North Korea[104]—because they believe intergroup breeding producing mixed-group offspring poses a threat to sustaining group boundaries. Intergroup marriages, such as inter-caste, inter-race/ethnicity, inter-faith, and the marriage of royal family members to outside commoners, was banned in manifold parts of the world in the past. The U.S. retained the "one-drop rule" or "hypo-descent rule" to prohibit interracial marriages for centuries; some states had anti-miscegenation laws until 1967 when the Supreme Court ruled it unconstitutional. In some parts of the world, mixed-race people are discriminated against with a social status lower than both parents' races, such as in Vietnam, Korea, Uganda, and the Basque region of Spain.[105] In small villages of northern India, men and women are murdered by family members or vigilante mobs for daring to date or marry outside of their caste boundaries.[106]

Religious fundamentalist group leaders stipulate rigid orthodoxy in perspective and adherence to the original scriptures, condemning any efforts of modification, reinterpretation, revision or alteration, in their effort to uphold the group's doctrinal "purity." Al-Qaeda leaders often say that if the Muslim world wants to restore its strength, it needs to go back to the "pure days of Islam" when it was a monoculture unsullied by foreign cultures, although the Muslim world was already a poly-culture during the "Golden Age" between the 8th and 13th centuries.[107] Pope Benedict frequently warned followers against becoming "Cafeteria Catholics" or "do-it-yourself" Catholics who pick and choose whichever doctrine they want to adhere to.[108] If one is to be a Catholic, he should accept and follow *all* Catholic teachings as a package, instead of selecting whatever he wants particularly regarding such issues as divorce, contraception, abortion, and gay marriage.

Bashing of the Moderates

In their effort to maintain group boundaries and purity in identity, extremists tend to bash, punish, or condemn "lukewarm" believers, half-hearted followers, and independent-minded moderates. For them, loyalty means total submission to and blind acceptance of the group's doctrines *en masse*, without the option of selecting one's own beliefs and course of action. Al-Qaeda's Osama bin-Laden made a statement: "There is no middle-ground in the struggle between God and Satan. All Muslims, therefore, must take up arms in this fight. Any Muslim who renounces this idea is just one more nonbeliever worthy of destruction."[109] Al-Zarqawi viewed moderate Muslims as "enemies of the faith,"[110] and sent his suicide bombers to kill fellow Sunnis who tried to join peaceful political negotiations.[111] In U.S. partisan politics, extremist partisan lawmakers stipulate ideological purity from their party's rank-and-file members. They call moderates and swing-voters "Blue Dogs" (Democrats who occasionally vote across party lines) and "RINOs (Republicans In Name Only)" (Republicans who occasionally vote across party lines), accuse them of lacking loyalty, and punish them by cutting off campaign funding.[112]

Dealing with "Outsiders Within"

For the extremists who are gripped with maintaining group boundaries and preserving purity in group identity and ideology, "outsiders within," whether they are immigrants, migrants, minority groups, dissenters, or criminals, pose threats to their existence and security, and, therefore, ought to be purged or "cleansed."

ANTI-IMMIGRANT NATIVISM

Throughout history, people have resented immigrants and migrants, and perceived them as outsiders "invading their territory," "corrupting" their culture, and eroding their group's unity and solidarity. White majority Americans' desire to preserve "cultural and racial purity" turned into belligerent aversion toward immigrants throughout America's immigration history. During the 19th and 20th centuries, some WASP Americans loathed Catholics, Jews, Japanese and Chinese Americans; in more recent years, the targets have shifted towards Hispanic and Muslim immigrants. Their resentment stems from the "patriotic" (from their perspective) fear that the newcomers may not share *their* values, do not believe in democracy and Christianity, and, subsequently, American culture and heritage may disappear. Such fears were often stoked and fueled by politicians engaged in political demagoguery for their own political gains.[113] Europeans' resentment toward Muslim immigrants manifest parallel sentiments—fear of losing European identity and "cultural purity." Especially during Europe's prolonged and chronic economic malaise in the aftermath of the Great Recession that started in 2008, resentment over immigrants surged, giving political ascent to the anti-immigrant, anti-globalization, anti–EU, right-wing extremist political parties.[114]

PURGING OF "OUTSIDERS WITHIN"

At times, extremists feel it is necessary to remove by force or "root out" those who are not deemed legitimate or "deserving" members or "insiders." Throughout history, countless groups have tried to eliminate "outsiders-within" and "un-pure misfits" through genocide, ethnic cleansing, and forced expulsion and segregation. Even in the contemporary era, numerous "purging" or "eradication" campaigns continue to persist in various places—e.g., against Tamil Tigers in Sri Lanka; Rohingyas in Myanmar; Christians in some Arab nations; Kurds in Turkey; Roma people in Europe; and illegal immigrants, migrants, and refugees in advanced nations.

Boundary Expansion (Group Expansionism)

Some groups try to expand their group boundaries by recruiting outsiders and expanding their territories (e.g., Max Weber's "open groups"). Their goal is to enlarge their power base and manpower resources as much as possible.[115] The Cold War was a showdown between the Soviet Union–led communist expansionism for global dominance and U.S.-led capitalistic market expansion, which escalated as both sides tried to expand their territory and alliances transcending differences in race, ethnicity, culture, and religion, using military powers and initiating wars. Multiple religious groups have endeavored to expand their boundaries through aggressive proselytizing and transnational missionary outreach across racial, ethnic, national, and geographic boundaries.[116] Since the Middle Ages, Christian missionaries—revered by some, reviled by others—have been history's most flourishing cross-cultural "pollinators." A host of America's mainline Christian churches, mobilized and funded by local congregations, continue to engage in missionary work around the world, although not as imposingly as they once did in the past.[117] In more recent decades, Islam, Hinduism, Catholicism, and Pentecostalism are competitively spreading rapidly in Africa more than mainline Christianity.[118]

According to Pipes,[119] Islamism is an effort to expand the territories ruled by Muslims by taking over territories ruled by non-Muslims (called "infidels"). The purpose of jihad is not simply to spread the Islamic faith but to extend sovereign Muslim power, with the eventual goal of achieving Muslim dominion over the entire world. According to *The 9/11 Commission Report*, in the 1980s, awash in sudden oil wealth, Saudi Arabia launched a propaganda blitz designed to spread its Sunni fundamentalist interpretation of Islam called Wahhabism throughout the world, funded by Zakat, a mandatory contribution all Muslims must pay, to build mosques and religious schools that could recruit more adherents and expand their power, territory, and global clout.[120] To entice potential recruits to join their group, most militant Islamist/jihadist groups, such as Hamas, Hezbollah, al-Qaeda, and the Muslim Brotherhood, offer social services to the destitute (e.g., food, shelter, education) and entice their conversion and loyalty, as many Christian missionaries did in the past. They enter impoverished areas and build houses and provide education their government cannot offer, often infused with religious and ideological indoctrination.[121]

Any attempt to re-define or broaden group boundaries and establish more inclusive identities (e.g., pan–Islamism, Muslim Brotherhood, jihadism, Marxism, the European Union, corporate globalism) always manifest hegemonic implications, whether for political, religious, or economic motives. When it happens, it becomes a form of "identity politics"—i.e., an effort to coalesce groups of dissimilar identities and interests to form *higher-order* groups of more inclusive identities and greater power, a form of group expansionism.[122] The implicit connotation behind broadly inclusive mottos, such as "clash of civilization" and "global war against terror," carry analogous insinuation—i.e., the Western, civilized nations must unite together to defend themselves against the "non–Western" civilizations represented by Islamist/jihadist terror groups. Although those terms may not have been introduced for that specific goal initially,[123] the media and politicians have used (or misused) the terms with such implications, and have resonated forcefully with people in the western world who felt the urgency to band together to fight against escalating anti–West terrorist threats. In that sense, it appears that the implications of "clash of civilizations" (from the way it is used and quoted) is akin to that of "jihadism"—i.e., both imply the political aspiration of constructing wider circles of group identities and boundaries that can transcend and encompass a multitude of nested-groups for the purpose of expanding groups' boundaries and subsequent power base.

Cultivating a Sense of Moral Superiority

For any group-centric extremist movement to be fruitful, members must believe in the "morally righteous and superior" status of their group juxtaposed to the "evil and inferior" others. It is the leader's task to instill this sense of moral superiority and righteousness that can inspire members to defend their group sacrificing their lives.[124] By claiming moral superiority, extremist movements become a "moral and spiritual cause" with a heightened sense of urgency and calling worthy of individual sacrifice. Convinced of their moral superiority, followers become partial to the values of their group and the interests of their in-group members and hostile toward "inferior" outsiders, and they willingly sacrifice their lives and self-interests to defend the group against all detractors and challengers.

People have used and devised an assortment of concepts and ideas to formulate a sense of moral superiority and group-centric pride, such as beliefs in superiority of men over women (sexism), whites over other races (racism), certain ethnicities (ethnocentrism), nations (e.g., "American exceptionalism"), the group ("royal blood," "value voters"), and religion over others (e.g., claiming of "authenticity," "orthodoxy," "Christendom," "Islamic exceptionalism").[125] A plethora of racist hate groups and anti-government militia groups infuse their ideology with religion to justify superiority of their group's status over others. Paul Mullet, priest at a Christian Identity church in Bainbridge, Ohio, near Cincinnati, preaches: "Only a select group of white people is chosen by God—not the Jewish, not blacks, not mongrels, not half-breeds, yellows, Chinese, Koreans, homosexuals, or bisexuals."[126] When a group is deemed to be "chosen by God," it implies that they are bestowed with a special mission to lead the world, and therefore, deserve special privilege and nobler status.[127]

Similarly, Kaufman[128] holds that chauvinistic nationalism is based on, and prompted by the belief that one's own nation is superior to others (e.g., "American exceptionalism"), and therefore, has the right to dominate or displace others. McDougall[129] argues that Americans' belief in the nation's "special purpose and blessing from God," implanted as a sort of "civil religion," has led to series of foreign policy follies around the world as an aggressor and "nation-builder." In the name of "divine-right inspired" foreign policy, when in fact the goal was achieving "grasp for world power" and extortion of resources, leaders were keen to use military might on the side of the moralistic ideals of "spreading peace and freedom around the world" by removing "unholy" enemies.

Moral Superiority as a Source of Group Power

When a group of people claims and believes in moral superiority, they experience a sense of power and elevation. By imposing their moral values on others, and judging others based on their own moral standards, they "feel" powerful, confident, righteous, and virtuous with "God on their side," fighting against the "less worthy" and "immoral" infidels and heathens. When a group of people believes in their group's superiority, they become unwilling to tolerate or cooperate with "inferior others." Instead, they feel compelled to defend their superiority and impose their superior beliefs on others, which they believe to be a "noble" mission that deserves their devotion and sacrifice. Wars become "holy crusades": violence and atrocities become necessary and justifiable acts.

Moral Superiority as a Hierarchical Positioning Tool

Claiming moral superiority is a form of "hierarchical positioning tool."[130] By elevating one group above others, other groups become "inferior" and less deserving of power, resources, privilege and respect. People need inferior groups to feel superior, righteous and powerful. When there is no external group to be degraded, they try to find or create "inferior groups within" to "feel superior," whether they are criminals, gypsies, undesirable minorities, foreigners, political dissidents, or homosexuals (e.g., McCarthyism, racism, sexism, homophobia, Islamophobia). It is extremists' strategy to manufacture a sense of moral superiority to position themselves above "inferior" others, and to justify their privilege and esteem over the "inferior" others. As Moon[131] discusses, the processes of constructing and reconfiguring group identities and claiming superior status upon themselves, therefore, signify the politics of defining which group deserves higher status and respect than others in a broader context of the society. In so doing, they are imposing "inferior" status upon others.

3. Extremist Strategies of Pivoting Group Identities

According to Stark,[132] most cults and sects are not new religions, but are splinter groups that branched out from mainline denominations and institutions by claiming authenticity, doctrinal purity, and superiority. Marty and Appleby[133] call this a "tendency to separate from fellow believers and to redefine the sacred community in opposition to 'lukewarm believers.'" In so doing, they can place their group above other competing groups. If everyone is Christian, for instance, they claim to be "born-again" or "professing" Christians, implying that they are exclusive and more authentic than "regular" or "lukewarm" Christians. Being Jewish is not enough for orthodox Jews; they distinguish themselves as "orthodox" Jews, even "ultra-orthodox." The social and religious conservatives who turned out in droves to vote for President Bush in the 2000 and 2004 elections labeled themselves as "value voters." Implicit in their label is that their values are "morally superior" over that of the opposite side—the "liberal elites" who they believe to be secular, Godless, immoral, and have no respect for family values and tradition (for supporting abortion rights and gay rights). Sundry militia and racist hate group members, anti-immigrant activists, anti-tax Tea Partyers, and gun rights activists call themselves "true patriots," indicating that others who do not share the same views as they do are less righteous "unpatriots." The white supremacist group Ku Klux Klan regards itself as an "organization of patriotic Americans" that advocates patriotism, community, and commitment to a "moral order," while unabashedly engaging in violent acts against racial and ethnic minorities.[134]

People with strong sense of moral superiority are more likely to become "moral crusaders" who exhibit histrionic indignation over other people's trivial violation of morality, to show off or reaffirm their *own* superior stance on moral righteousness. Such a dramatic display of "moral panic or outrage" is a strategy aimed at elevating their group to a "morally superior" status by viciously denouncing "deviants" as "sinners" and "evil/bad-doers," especially when such acts are committed by disliked "out-group" members.[135]

Moral Superiority Used to Justify Violence and Injustice

When a group of people feel morally superior and righteous, it becomes easier for them to justify maltreatment of "inferior" groups, including violent acts against them (e.g., domination, subjugation, persecution, genocide, ethnic cleansing, terrorism, foreign invasion, and slavery). In such cases, their violent acts become "righteous violence," committed for their "noble causes." Individual acts of violence and atrocities may be symptoms of mental or psychological disorders as criminologists and psychologists explain. On the other hand, collective acts of violence are usually propelled by this moral sense of group superiority and righteousness.

Use of Group-Centric Ideologies

Contentious group leaders try to formulate and deliver motivational narratives and ideologies that justify the group-centric interests and goals they pursue.[136] Ideologies are a set of beliefs used to promote and justify one group's interests at the expense of another—e.g., to justify unfair inequalities, injustices, discrimination, persecution, subjugation, and domination. Use of group-centric ideologies is a vital aspect of most extremist groups. Throughout history, countless extremist group leaders have formulated and propagated an array of ideologies to promote their group-centric causes and interests and justify mistreatment of others, and instituted laws and implemented policies in support of such ideologies. For instance, people used beliefs in racism and white supremacy to justify slavery and discrimination against non-whites, and men justified domination of women by monopolizing power to define morality, tradition, beliefs, values, and interpretation of religious scriptures in their favor ("ideology construction"). Politicians promulgated nationalistic narratives disguised as "patriotism" (e.g., national pride and honor, "American exceptionalism," "shining city on the hill") and "national security" imperatives to justify wars, war crimes, foreign invasions, and expansion of military budgets. Pro-business, economic elites used "economic efficiency and progress" to justify aggressive de-regulation of businesses and tax cuts for the wealthy, ignoring the safety of consumers and workers, environmental protection, and fairness in economic redistribution in the society.

Power of Ideologies

Historically, ideas and emotions have been much more effective in cultivating loyalty, solidarity, and sacrifice to a common cause than knowledge, reason, physical force, or military might can. Ideologies are more than just ideas. When they are successfully inculcated, they become a potent emotional fixation that can conjure up a sense of "moral cause," because ideologies, unlike other beliefs, tap into people's emotions, instead of reason. Arousing emotions can have the power to animate movements, goad people into action, for "good or evil," and justify human cruelties and systemic injustices without reservations.[137] Ideologies can steer people to overcome the sense of logic and facts, triumph over scientific evidence, and

3. Extremist Strategies of Pivoting Group Identities   121

enable people to believe in what they *want* to believe in, not what are factual, truthful, or just. In so doing, ideologies can make "good" people commit "evil" acts and transform injustices into justices, unfairness into fairness, and undeserved wealth and poverty into deserved wealth and poverty, without reservations or misgivings.

With successfully inculcated and legitimated ideologies, slavery can become a "paternalistic system" in which the "magnanimous" slave-owners safeguard the helpless and naïve slaves; colonialism becomes "white men's burden of civilizing the uncivilized"; and terrorist acts against civilians become a "holy war" against infidels. With group-centric ideologies, acts of war and atrocities can turn into "moral crusades" waged for "noble" causes of eradicating "evil-doers." Even genocides and ethnic cleansing can become a "patriotic duty" necessary for "cleansing" the nation. Terrorists become "freedom fighters"; suicide bombers are admired as "martyrs"; racist white nationalists become "true patriots"; homophobes become "defenders of religious freedom"; violent street gangs become "protectors" of the vulnerable; and the wealthy becomes benevolent "job creators" to be protected and respected.

IDEOLOGY AS EMOTIONAL OBSESSION

To the extremists, the effects of ideology can reach far beyond passion and enthusiasm. It becomes an emotional obsession that consumes one's entire life, controls thought patterns and courses of action, and delivers people with a divine, spiritual, and lofty mission and vision.[138] For instance, as Volkan[139] describes, an SS officer in Nazi Germany would not have thought of stealing a watch from a fellow officer, but participated in the extermination of Jews, as was expected under Nazi ideology. Ideology can blind people, and make them lose objectivity, rationality, critical thinking, and deliberative reflection, and it turns normal people into fanatics, extremists, and terrorists. With an ideological definition of the situation and goals, a group's activity becomes a missionary movement with evangelical zeal to spread, recruit people, and expand their territory, influence, and power. When a group's ideology becomes "sacred," infallible, and held beyond question or error, threats to group identity, real or perceived, are frequently met with "righteous violence." Understanding this power of ideologies, extremist group leaders strive to contrive, indoctrinate, and propagate group-centric ideologies when they launch extremist movements.

Using Religion as Ideology

Typically, extremist group leaders use God and religion as a part of ideological narratives to bolster their own or their group's power and supremacy, and to justify bigotry, injustice, discrimination, and atrocities. When the concept of God is invoked on their behalf, their ideologies become "unchallengeable," regardless of how unfair and unjust they may be. Monarchs and noblemen claimed to have "divine" or "God-given" rights to justify their unlimited and unchallenged power and privilege; people revered kings and emperors as "God-sent" leaders who were "anointed by God," an image which was carefully stage-crafted through elaborate "anointment ceremonies" and use of "Seal of the Heaven's Mandate." During the Middle Ages in Europe, religion was basically a collective ritual that worked to solidify and perpetuate the status hierarchy of the communities. The clergies' implicit role was to furnish means for noble persons of privilege and power to demonstrate their virtue, honor, and magnanimity.[140]

Using Religion to Justify Violent Acts

People have justified wars, atrocities, and cruelty against those of different faiths as a "divine mission" that is required to defend their faith, "commanded" by God.[141] When religion is used to justify violent and terrorist acts, they become "holy and sacred" terror committed "in God's name" with His blessing. By "sacralizing" violent acts, atrocities are given an aura of legitimacy. By elevating a temporal struggle to the level of the cosmic, people can bypass the usual moral restrictions on killing. Because their actions are "morally sanctioned" by religion, they feel empowered to commit atrocities without feeling guilt or compunction.[142] Religious extremist groups used the "lofty" goals of achieving dominion, whether it is Islamism (e.g., a global Islamic State), a caliphate, or Christendom, to justify their brutal acts of violence, atrocities, and human sacrifices (e.g., "religious crusades," Lord's Resistance Army). Islamist/jihadist groups (e.g., Muslim Brotherhood, al-Qaeda, ISIS/Daesh) use the concept of "Islamic exceptionalism" sanctioned by Allah, to mobilize and energize their followers and to justify their unjust acts of violence.[143] A number of Islamist terrorists have shouted "Allahu akbar!" ("God is great") while committing mass killings and suicide bombings.[144] Abortion clinic bombers regularly cite Bible scriptures, and there have been several scripture-based messianic terrorist groups, such as the "Covenant," "the Sword," the "Arm of the Lord," and "The Order."[145]

Even the raping of preteen girls becomes "virtuous" if performed in a ritualized, "spiritual" manner—e.g., pray before and after the rape—and if the victims are non–Muslims, as practiced by ISIS/Daesh fighters against young Yazidi girls.[146] In 2014, the Nigerian rebel group Boko Haram kidnapped over 200 schoolgirls, and sold the girls as brides in forced marriages. Shekau, the leader of the group said, "In Islam, it is allowed to take infidel women as slaves."[147] Some Muslims justify taking a child-bride, as young as nine years old, because the "Prophet Mohamed had a nine-year-old child bride."[148] In Iraq, some Islamic clerics groom vulnerable teen girls as young as nine years of age to be used as sex slaves for dowries as part of a controversial religious practice known as a "pleasure marriage" or "temporary marriage" ("mutaa marriage"). A man can marry a girl for as short as half an hour, sometimes in a hotel room, with a brief ceremony officiated by clerics, even over the phone without the presence of the bride. One cleric, Sayyed Raad, said it is acceptable because the practice "descends from the Prophet Muhammad." Although it is difficult to estimate how many young girls have been subjected to these "temporary marriages," eight out of ten clerics the BBC interviewed admitted to officiating such marriages. The practice is spreading in recent years because of two wars (the Iraq War and war against ISIS/Daesh) that produced over a million widowed mothers of young girls struggling to survive and needing the support of the clerics.[149] According to Lynch,[150] the Catholic Church, for centuries, considered covering up pedophile sexual abuse by priests as a "*sacred* duty"; Polygamous commune FLDS leaders call their multiple marriages with pre-teen brides "spiritual" or "celestial" marriages "blessed by God."[151]

USING RELIGION TO JUSTIFY UNJUST SYSTEMS

Numerous extremist leaders used religion to justify unjust and unfair *systems* from which their group (or their benefactors) benefited. Hinduism was used to justify a caste system for centuries, and later used to symbolize Indian nationalism, justifying mistreatment of Muslim minorities.[152] Shintoism was constructed to assign religious justification or surrogate for Japanese nationalism and military aggression overseas.[153] Confucianism defended the power and authority of the elders in the family and leaders of the community, and quotes from the Bible were used to justify slavery and sexual inequality. Saudi Arabia's ruling royal family prohibits public protests because it is considered "un–Islamic"[154]; Saudi princes justify their enormous wealth as "God's blessing," as the majority of the population struggles to survive.[155] Christian Identity Group is a religious movement that unites a plethora of white supremacists groups throughout the U.S. with a belief that the white race, specifically the Anglo-Saxon, Celtic, Scandinavian, and Germanic peoples, are the racial descendants of the tribes of Israel and God's true "chosen people." They use religion to justify their racist and anti–Semitic ideologies and systemic discriminations against non-whites.[156]

Class-Based Ideologies

After the end of the Second World War in 1945, communism became a potent ideology used in the globalized class war, justifying violent revolutions, human sacrifices, and political repression, in hopes of achieving classless societies. In most cases, they turned into an extremist movement as leaders sought to empower themselves and monopolize power and privilege using violence and threat to control masses of people. The Marxian ideals of egalitarian society turned into tyrannical dictatorships ruled by *political* elites "representing" the working class.[157] Economic elites in the capitalistic societies, on the other hand, used the ideologies of free-market, free competition, meritocracy, and "survival of the fittest" to *justify* extreme inequality, poverty, and their own economic wealth and interests. They used distorted versions of supply-side economic theories and "trickle-down wealth effect" arguments (the wealthy must become wealthier first for their wealth to trickle-down to the lower-class) to justify tax cuts for the wealthy and deregulation of industries, which enlarged wealth of the already privileged class exponentially without "trickling down" to the majority at the bottom, magnifying economic inequality and impairing the overall economy by depressing consumption by the masses.[158]

Likewise, the use of ideology is not a strategy limited to the terrorist or rebel groups. Throughout history, the wealthy, privileged, and powerful have devised a host of class-based ideologies to justify their wealth, power, and economic interests. The eventual goal of all class-based ideologies of the privileged economic elites is to persuade (or fool) the underprivileged masses to believe in ideologies that support the interests of the wealthy (e.g., Marx's "false consciousness") instead of their own group's interests ("class consciousness"). They constructed a benevolent "job creator" image of the wealthy, which is used to justify why everyone except the wealthy should sacrifice during economic hard times (although jobs cannot be created without consumption by the middle- and lower-class). They misuse belief in the "American dream" to justify the "deserving" statuses of the wealthy—the "wealthy should be *admired* for achieving the American Dream." They advocate ideology of "personal responsibility" to justify curtailing or eliminating social welfare programs funded by taxation, and in extreme cases, they rationalize unbridled capitalism using ideology of "self-interest"—i.e., "greed is good," "virtues of selfishness,"[159] and "self-interest of each will produce the best interest of all."[160] The privileged economic elites have become so successfully self-inoculated into such pro-business, pro-wealthy, neoliberal economic ideologies that justify the ruthless pursuit of money-making and profiteering that they no longer feel uncomfortable or care about social responsibility to the rest of the society.[161]

Using Tradition as Ideologies

Groups of people who benefit from the existing systems, such as men, the dominant, wealthy and powerful, monarchs, aristocrats, higher-caste people, and political and religious leaders, have an interest in maintaining the status quo, using tradition as justification for resisting reforms. They are more likely to believe in following, respecting, and honoring a group's traditions without questioning or challenging them, and punish those who do, establishing a form of dominant extremism. When successfully indoctrinated, people, in the name of tradition, readily put up with extremely intolerable situations and unjust systems. Throughout history, people have endured and participated in preserving extremely unjust and unfair systems without questioning their virtue or merit, out of respect for the traditional ways of life for generations. Examples include patriarchy, polygyny, monarchy, slavery, caste systems, child brides, female genital mutilation, pedophilia (e.g., "bacha bazi" in Afghanistan, practice of "chocoshi" in parts of Africa), and family honor killings. In such cases, tradition becomes an ideology that is used by the dominant and privileged groups to justify the systems from which they benefit, denying the same interests and rights to underprivileged groups.

Using "Freedom" as Ideology

Even the concept of "freedom" can become an ideology when misused by ideologues. Racists and white nationalists use the constitutional right to "free speech" to justify their racially incendiary and offensive hate speeches and rallies, and wealthy corporate executives use "freedom of speech" to push for virtually unlimited corporate donations to sway politics, tilting the playing field in favor of corporations and the super-wealthy, away from the public. Religious fundamentalists use "freedom of religion" to justify their prejudice and discrimination against religious minorities and homosexuals; hardline, neo-conservative politicians use the slogan of "spreading democracy and freedom" to justify foreign invasion, military intervention, and capitalistic expansionism in foreign countries for the benefit of their donor multinational corporations.

Ideological Indoctrination and Dissemination

Throughout history, extremist group leaders have strived to indoctrinate their followers with group-centric ideologies to mobilize them. Religious cults are well-known for their effectiveness in ideological indoctrination. According to the former members of FLDS, Warren Jeffs' polygamous commune, the leader Warren Jeffs is "in charge of devising church history." "So for a lot of us children who were born into this, our days would be forever listening to these tapes of Warren's voice playing over and over of him teaching us church history. It became the backdrop of our childhood."[162] When the Taliban took power in Afghanistan in 1996, they removed English, history and physical education classes and all aspects of Western influence from school curricula, and replaced them with Islamic subjects, consisted mainly of memorizing the Quran.[163] When Pakistani kids graduate from Islamic schools for teens, known as madrassas, they have memorized the Quran and finer points of Islamic law, yet learned little else. "They need little else," argues Muhammad Saleem Asif, a religious scholar and the principal of the madrassa, the Roza Tul Quran Al Kareem School. "These students, repeating the words of God, will raise the spirits and morals of their community," he asserts.[164] These madrassas flourish in impoverished and disadvantaged areas in Pakistan where parents are too poor to send their kids to public schools. These schools are funded by Zakat contributions from foreign nations, such as Saudi Arabia, which tries to fulfill its mission of propagating the Saudi's extreme version of Islam, Wahhabism.[165]

Some modern nation states endeavor to shape their people's beliefs through ideological indoctrination designed to boost nationalism and patriotism. For decades, the Chinese Communist Party has pushed a stiff regiment of ideological education on students, requiring lessons on Marx and Mao, and canned lectures on the virtues of patriotism and loyalty. In 2017, amid fears that the party was losing its grip on young minds, President Xi Jinping re-invoked and reshaped Mao's "Red Army Schools," a political education and indoctrination policy across China's more than 238,000 primary and secondary schools that are designed to promote "Chinese traditional and socialist culture"—a mix of party loyalty and patriotic pride in China's past.[166] The Chinese government also sends observers to nearly 2,600 universities to monitor mandatory ideology classes, which include staples like "Mao Zedong thought," Marxism-Leninism, and Communist Party history and Party-building.[167] In 2018, after President Xi secured his lifetime presidency, dozens of state universities founded centers devoted to studying the political doctrine known as Xi Jinping Thought, similar to what the Communist Party under Mao did with Mao Zedong's Thought. Under this program, all students will be required to take lessons in Xi's philosophy.[168]

Use of Enemies: "Enemization and Demonization"

In group-bound extremist cultures, as Salman Rushdie describes, one's identity is defined through hatred—i.e., "who you *hate* defines which group you belong to."[169] The existence of enemies delineates and accentuates group identity and heightens people's sense of unity and solidarity

3. Extremist Strategies of Pivoting Group Identities

by raising their fear and anxiety, which, in turn, inspires loyalty and willingness to sacrifice for the group. Extremist groups, therefore, *need* external enemies to retain internal solidarity and unity. As Hoffer[170] describes, "without a devil to hate, mass movements often falter." Without enemies to hate, leaders cannot conjure up the emotional energies that are necessary for their mobilization effort.

The goal of the leaders is to capitalize on the group psychology that the greater the threat group members perceive from outsiders, the more ardently members coalesce around their central leader.[171] When confronted with external enemies, people, feeling insecure, flock to authoritarian leaders who *appear* to be strong, decisive, and audacious—someone they believe can protect them from the enemy and restore security.[172] The greater their perceived threat, the more intensely members rally around their authoritarian leader. For this reason, extremist leaders try to exaggerate or create external threats using incendiary narratives and hate-filled invectives, and present themselves as commanding "saviors" who can deliver their flock out of fear and restore security. North Korean leaders refer to America as the "evil imperialist regime"; Iranian supreme leaders call America the "Great Satan" and Israel, the "Little Satan" which should be "wiped off the map."[173] President Reagan's "evil empire" was the former Soviet Union; President Bush's "axis of evil" referred to Iran, Iraq and North Korea.[174] Such warlike slogans and belligerent diatribes are designed to instill fear and loathing among their *own* followers, hoping that they will rally around their leader seeking protection.

According to Soufan,[175] most people join Islamist/jihadi terror groups such as al-Qaeda and ISIS not necessarily to wage war against the West; rather, they do so for a variety of other reasons, such as economic trouble, ethnic or sectarian rivalry, or to "protect" fellow Muslims. However, once they join the group, the group leaders place them in a non-stop "ideological echo chamber" indoctrinating them with hate-filled, anti–West ideologies and narratives. Al-Qaeda successfully peddled the view that the West is engaged in a "war against Islam" to destroy them. The invasion of Iraq, subsequent mistreatment of Muslims (e.g., humiliating treatment of prisoners in Guantanamo Bay and Abu Ghraib), and the failure to curtail civilian casualties from drone attacks have all contributed to the fulfillment of this propaganda message offered by their leaders.

The most common enemies of sundry right-wing and militia extremist groups in the Western world have been ethnic/racial minorities, immigrants, homosexuals, Jews, and communists whom they consider inferior, alien, and corrupt. However, in recent decades, they redirected their enmity toward the government and governmental authorities and establishments, whom they see as "traitors" for letting foreigners "invade" and "occupy" the country and giving them equal rights and "preferential treatments."[176]

Russia's President Putin tries to maintain his power by invoking external enemies. He presents the Western world, especially the U.S., as enemies that pose a threat to Russia's existence and convinces Russians that only he can put up a fight against the Western world and secure Russia from their threats. Many Russians, scarred by the unrelenting economic, social, and security hardships of the 1990s, welcomed the rise of the security state and the authoritarian leadership of Putin. They continue to support him, despite a suffering economy and crippling civic institutions under Putin's reign.[177] Thanks to Putin's relentless "demonization" efforts, 68 percent of Russians considered the U.S. their "enemy" in 2018, up from 22 percent in 1999.[178]

Creating Enemies

When there is no discernable enemy group to hate, extremist leaders try to find or create one. The ulterior goal of the European witch craze (15th through 17th centuries) for the Church was to *create* an enemy group (mostly poor single women) they could blame for all the social ills of the time, and, in so doing, dodge the blame themselves.[179] Nazi Germany's effort to *create* enemy groups to blame and hate resulted in extermination of six million Jews. Both communist and anti-communist movements turned into hysteric "witch-hunts" that led to persecution and execution of millions of innocent political dissidents, critics, and intellectuals as "enemies of the state"—e.g., Mao's "Cultural Revolution," Stalin's the "Great Purge" and "Great Terror," McCarthyism in America, and 30 years of violent political turmoil in Latin America. According to John Erlichman, President Richard Nixon's policy advisor, the Nixon administration during the 1968 campaign had two enemies—black people and the anti-war liberal left. Using the slogan of "war on drugs," they successfully associated heroin with black people and marijuana with the "anti-war hippies" and demonized both groups night after night on the evening news.[180] During his presidential campaign in 2016, Donald Trump invoked many enemies—e.g., China was "raping America" with trade surpluses and unfair trades; Mexico was sending "rapists and drug dealers" to the U.S.; the "fake media" was the "enemy of the people," and the "Dems" were spreading false rumors about him.[181]

Jihadism, especially the al-Qaeda brand under the leadership of Osama bin Laden, sought to achieve pan–Islamic unity by creating and identifying a commonly-perceived external enemy, the West. As Islamic societies modernize and develop economically, they become more diverse, and face *internal* disputes and divisions among competing sects, as well as between traditionalists and reformists who challenge the traditional orthodox Islamic authority and control. Fearing the internal division and loss of dictatorial authority, leaders try to restore unity and maintain their unchallenged power by identifying the West as their common enemy to be detested and targeted with terrorist attacks.[182]

Sowing Hatred by Dehumanizing and Vilifying Enemies

Once an enemy group is identified, extremist leaders try to sow hatred to energize their followers. They magnify the "evilness" of their enemies in order to justify their hatred and acts of violence and mistreatment against them as "self-defense," even a "holy" mission. When the targeted enemy group becomes the repository of all the bad and evil, devalued, and dangerous elements in the group's psyche, it becomes virtually impossible for anyone to develop a fragment of empathy either for the enemy group's positions or for any losses it has suffered.[183] Brustein[184] conferred that the main cause of the Holocaust was the anti–Semitic hatred that was successfully planted and spread especially among the Germans in rural areas by the Nazis with the help of Hitler's charisma, more importantly than other competing theories of explanations—e.g., modernization theory, strong state theory, political culture theory, and rational economic theory.

Extremist leaders use dehumanization tactics to demote enemy groups into objects with sub-human qualities, lowest to the level that deserves to be mistreated, even annihilated. When people portray enemies as "targets," "dogs," "pigs," "rats," "Nazis," or "terrorists," they can no longer regard their enemies as their "fellow humans": their enemies no longer belong to the legitimate community of "the people."[185] Nazis characterized Jews as "the louse, carrier of typhus," "a filthy, parasitic, blood-sucking disease vector that had penetrated the German nation."[186] Leaders of the Khmer Rouge in Cambodia called their genocide victims (about 1.5 million) to be "worth less than garbage."[187] Germany's anti-migrant far-right-wingers are unafraid to show their hostility toward Muslim immigrants, openly calling them "scumbags," "animals," and "trash."[188] In North Korea, where systematic indoctrination of anti–Americanism starts as early as in kindergarten, U.S. soldiers are depicted as "cruel, ghoulish barbarians" with big noses and fiendish eyes, trained to kill North Koreans.[189] In 2019, China's state-owned media sources called Hong Kong's democracy protesters "cockroaches."[190]

Fomenting "Victimhood Mentality" ("Persecution Complex")

Some extremist group leaders, even of dominant groups, try to contrive or exaggerate an image that their group is being persecuted, attacked, and victimized by other groups, because the group-felt sense of persecution can conjure up or intensify urgency and saliency of their group-centric causes. Their goal is to incite senses of urgency, indignation, and fear that are effective for group mobilization. Some religious fundamentalist group leaders exaggerate foreign intrusion into their self-established "lonely omnipotence," in an effort to create a perception that their beliefs are continually under assault by non-believers, scientists, or even by rival fundamentalist groups.[191] Al-Qaeda and its offshoot jihadist groups try to mold an image that infidels—the West, especially America—are trying to *destroy* Islam, by exaggerating all the injustice and malfeasance the West had inflicted upon them in the past, and clamoring for revenge.[192]

When dominant group members try to portray themselves as *victims* of attack, their goal is to turn their dominant status to appear as vulnerable victims who must defend themselves and to justify use of violence against powerless groups of people. One of the Nazi leaders, Joseph Goebbels, had some of the Nazi storm troopers attack their own group while disguised as communists and socialists, and claimed that Nazis were the victims of communist violence. By effectively blaming the Jews, communists, and socialists, Germans became the "victims" and their violent onslaught against Jews, communists, and socialists become legitimate "defensive" attacks necessary for Nazi survival.[193] In 2016, when people protested and the media berated police for their brutality against and killings of unarmed minority suspects, law enforcement responded with a claim that there was an endemic "war on cops" in the U.S.[194] President Trump constantly portrayed America as the "victim" of mistreatment by other nations. He stated in numerous speeches how other nations were "taking advantage of America," "raping" and "laughing at us." In so doing, he was sowing a "victimhood mentality"—i.e., America is the "victim" of foreign assault and mistreatment, not the aggressor, and we must be united to defend ourselves against aggressions from foreign nations.[195]

"War on Whites"

When governments implement policies and laws to extend equal rights and opportunities to disadvantaged and discriminated-against racial or ethnic minority groups, white supremacists declare such efforts as a government-orchestrated "war on whites," which implies that whites are being attacked with "reverse discrimination," and they must unite

3. Extremist Strategies of Pivoting Group Identities 131

and defend themselves against unjust governmental intrusion[196]—a strategy that effectively turns their movement into a "defensive movement."[197] They portray themselves as "victims," whose rights are being trampled by the influx of immigrants and liberal policies designed to help discriminated minorities. White-supremacist groups' websites frequently mention the notion of "white genocide" and discuss how the whites in the U.S. will suffer as whites in Zimbabwe and Rhodesia did, when minorities "take over" the U.S., unless whites band together and defend themselves forcefully.[198] Dylann Roof, who shot and killed nine black Bible class members at the Emanuel African Methodist Episcopal Church in South Carolina in 2015, said that "blacks are taking over the world" and "someone needs to do something about it for the white race."[199] A Republican Congressman, Jason Lewis of Minnesota, said that "blacks are waging racial wars against whites" and that "the real victims of most racial violence are not members of the minorities in America—they are white people."[200] Similarly, white nationalists in Europe often use such terms as "reverse-colonization" and "genocide by substitution," referring to the "invasion" of non-white immigrants and migrants to Europe, especially those coming from Africa and Middle East.[201]

War on "People of Faith"

Some Christian evangelical and fundamentalist group leaders in the U.S. use the same strategy. Whenever people disagree with their position on controversial issues, such as abortion, gay marriage, teaching of evolution, euthanasia and stem-cell research, they claim that "liberal elites" or "people against faith" are attacking "people of faith,"[202] and that they are "under siege" and being "silenced" and "persecuted."[203] In 2005, when Senate Democrats threatened to filibuster Bush nominees to the Supreme Court, Republicans used the slogan: "Stop the filibuster against 'people of faith.'"[204] In 2019, Vice President Mike Pence told Liberty University graduates to prepare to be "shunned and ridiculed for being a Christian."[205]

The Politics of Fear ("Fear-Mongering")

Social scientists have observed that some political leaders wittingly exaggerate and even fabricate threats to the existence and well-being of their group, because they understand how perceived threats engender a sense of cohesiveness among the threatened group members.[206] When people's fear and insecurity levels are high (e.g. "group hysteria" and "collective panic"), they lose rational reasoning abilities, and become more willing to sacrifice their individual rights and freedom hoping to secure safety and stability,[207] making it easier for leaders to recruit and mobilize their flock. At times, they use exaggerated "shock" and "fear" (e.g., fear of terrorism, crime, foreign invasion, and influx of immigrants) as a pretext for dramatic policy modifications that are designed to serve their own political interests—e.g., getting reelected, procuring campaign contributions, solidifying power base, muzzling opponents and critics. Examples of such policy changes included waging "wars of choice" and foreign invasions, limiting civil liberties and rights, punishing dissenters and protesters using legal means, expanding police and military expenditures, and increasing defense contracts as a payback to large donor corporations.[208] Throughout history, extremist political leaders have orchestrated and stoked group hysteria and paranoia with devastating consequences to humanity, while delivering favors to their donor groups.

North Korea's Kim dynasty has been firmly ensconced in power for three generations (Kim Il-sung, Kim Jong-il, and Kim Jong-un) by effectively using this "fear-mongering strategy"—invoking hysterical paranoia over "imminent" U.S.-led invasion. They purposefully induce fear and insecurity among people to bolster their dictatorial power and justify brutal persecution of dissenters.[209] Leaders of racist hate groups and right-wing extremists also spread paranoia, panic-inducing conspiracy theories, and predictions of calamities for the same reasons of boosting group solidarity and resource mobilization efforts,[210] as well as various doomsday cult leaders and apocalyptic "endtimers" that preyed upon people's fear of "judgment day."[211] NRA (National Rifle Association) leaders deliberately create a sense of fear among its members and supporters by constantly reminding them that their gun rights are under attack by the "coastal, socialist, media elites who hate guns," and that they are "at the mercy of evil," especially after tragic incidences of mass murders and school shootings.[212]

America's History of Fear

The history of hysteric fear of immigrants that swept through America for centuries was against all immigrants, including Irish, Italians, Jews, Chinese, and Japanese, stoked by political demagogues who preyed upon people's fears. The Know Nothing movement spread hysteric fear of Catholics, the so-called "Catholic menace," and anti–Semitic screeds regularly warned that Jews were plotting to destroy the U.S. in one way or another. During World War I, Nazis were depicted as the "worst evil in the Axis," and rumors, even propagated by U.S. government agencies, spread that German-Americans were poisoning food.[213] During the Cold War era, America's politicians constantly instilled a fear of communism and nuclear onslaught from the Soviet Union in order to garner unbound support for their power and agendas of boosting military spending. White supremacist groups exaggerated fear of black men attacking white women to justify their racial hatred, and anti-feminist groups hyped the danger of rape and sexual assault when women went into the public arena to discourage women from seeking gainful employment.[214]

After the 9/11 terrorist attacks in 2001, America underwent another wave of fear-driven hysteria, which led to the Afghan and Iraq Wars and support for massive military spending increases. President Bush's "mushroom cloud" speech in 2002 effectively persuaded Americans to endorse the Iraq invasion.[215] Vice President Dick Cheney, during the 2004 re-election campaign of Bush, said: "It is absolutely essential that on November 2, we make the right choice, because if we make the wrong choice, the danger is that we will get hit again, and we will be hit in a way that will be devastating from the standpoint of the U.S."[216] Tom Ridge, the first secretary of Homeland Security created after 9/11, stated in his memoir that top advisors in the Bush administration pressured him to raise the national security threat to the highest level of "orange" just before the 2004 election, which he suspected was an effort to sway voters by raising people's fear level.[217]

Invoking Fear to Attain Loyalty and Dependency

At times, some extremist leaders commit random acts of violence against innocent civilians and create chaos and instability in the community deliberately, for no other reason except to invoke fear and distrust among people. One of the main goals of Islamist/jihadist extremist groups like al-Qaeda, ISIS/Daesh, al-Shabaab, and Boko Haram is to create zones within the Muslim world that are so lawless and chaotic that the authority of the state will collapse, and people will lose trust in their government. When that happens, they will move in to fill the vacuum left by governmental failure, and earn people's trust and loyalty by providing much-needed security, order, and services like education, water, and electricity.[218] They are exploiting the psychological vulnerability of people—i.e., fear-driven people tend to flock to "strongmen" leadership with authoritarian control.

Taliban insurgents attack and kill random Afghan civilians in Kabul for the same reason. People may wonder why they kill innocent Afghan bystanders through senseless acts of terror in civilian locales, such as hotels, hospitals, mosques, and election sites.[219] The United Nations reported that at least 10,453 Afghan civilians were either killed or wounded by Taliban terrorist onslaughts in 2017 alone,[220] and the number of civilian deaths and injuries doubled since 2009, while that of Afghan security and military personnel have decreased during the same time,[221] marking 2018 as the "deadliest year" for Afghan civilians in a decade.[222] Their goal is to instill fear by creating instability with random terror attacks, which will destabilize the U.S.-backed Afghan government and decrease people's trust in the government. That will give the Taliban an opportunity to retake power and control in Afghanistan and earn people's trust. With enough chaos and fear, they believe, people will turn to the Taliban, "the stronger and mightier," away from the hopelessly dysfunctional government.[223]

Presenting Leadership as "Savior" Amid Fear and Chaos

Having created enough fear that terrorizes their followers, extremist leaders present themselves as the only potential "savior" who can deliver people out of fear and insecurity, protect them from the presumed enemies, and "stand up" against the external sources of threat. Sundry political and religious leaders have used this strategy—i.e., stoking intergroup divisions and fears with "doom and gloom" predictions and conspiracy theories to incite fear, only to present themselves as "saviors" who can heroically deliver security and stability for the people. Donald Trump, as a 2016 presidential candidate, repeatedly depicted the world as a "terrible and dangerous place" where "every nation is trying to take advantage of America; radical Islamic terrorists are gathering strength; Christians are being executed *en masse* in the Middle East; illegal immigrants infiltrate and lurk in the shadows, and gangs operate with impunity in our cities." "The murder rate is the highest it's been in 47 years [although all violent crimes including murder have continued to abate since the peak in 1990]; drugs are 'pouring' across the border, and bad people are flooding through our airports." He declared that the world is "a horrible mess" and America is "heading toward hell." And then, he repeated "I alone can fix it," and "make America great again."[224] His strategy was to brand his image as the only "savior" who could "save America from hell," "protect America," and "stand up" against external enemies. Philippine President Duterte used the same strategy to be elected—i.e., he grossly exaggerated threats from drugs and corruption, and presented himself as a "strongman" who could fix all the problems.[225] During the COVID-19 pandemic in 2020, assorted authoritarian leaders around the world capitalized on the hysteric fear to expand their power and authority beyond legal limits, such as by proclaiming national emergencies, changing laws, enhancing public surveillance, and muzzling the media. Example cases include President Putin of Russia who changed the law to expand his presidency; Hungary's Orban who declared an indefinite

3. Extremist Strategies of Pivoting Group Identities 135

"order-by-decree"; Israel's Netanyahu who delayed the criminal indictment against him using emergency decrees; and others who implemented similar measures, such as the Philippines' Duterte, Chile's Piñera, Turkey's Erdoğan, Thailand's Prayuth, Cambodia's Hun Sen, and Myanmar's Tatmadaw.[226]

Stoking Fear to Justify Violence

Fear often turns into hatred and anger against the source of the fear, which make it easier for people to justify their acts of violence, cruelty, and atrocities. The greater the fear, anger, and hatred, thus, the more cruel and violent people become toward their enemy groups. Behind all tragic mass murders and atrocities, there were human emotions of fear, anger, and hatred stoked by political and religious leaders working as demagogues—e.g., the Catholic Church's execution of heretics during the Inquisition; Puritans' of witches; Nazis' of Jews; Mao's persecution of intellectuals during the Cultural Revolution; persecution of communists and their sympathizers in Latin America and during the McCarthyism era in the U.S. By inflating the size, power, and diabolic images of their enemy groups, leaders were able to make far-reaching appeals to popular sentiments of hatred that justified atrocities of extraordinary scale.[227] Hermann Göring, who was second in command to Hitler, said, during his trial in Nuremberg, that the Nazis were able to get the German people to go along with such absurd and ruinous policies of war and onslaught by scaring them. He said: "Of course, the people don't want war. Why would some poor slob on a farm want to risk his life in a war? But, after all, it is the leaders of the country who determine the policy. The people can always be brought to the bidding of the leaders. All you have to do is tell them they're being attacked and denounce the pacifists for lacking patriotism. It works the same way in every country."[228]

Stoking Fear for Financial Gains

Some extremist group leaders use the same fear-mongering strategy to obtain financial gains for their causes. For instance, Taliban insurgents in Afghanistan create an environment of fear by raiding and harassing businesses, and then, demand "protection money" if they do not want to be raided. In 2009, the media reported that about 20 percent of U.S. taxpayers' money for rebuilding Afghanistan went to the Taliban, the terrorist group the U.S. is trying to eradicate, as "protection money." When the U.S. military pays foreign contractors to rebuild roads, buildings, and bridges that are mangled by war, the contractors must pay Taliban "protection money." If they don't, Taliban insurgents will blow up the buildings and bridges. Taliban insurgents then arm themselves with the extortion money funded by U.S. taxpayers, and strike U.S. troops.[229]

One of the strategies gangs and criminal cartels use is to deliberately incite fear through violence on the street, and collect "protection money" from residents and businesses, promising them "protection" from violence—a strategy called "protection racketeering."[230] Gangs in Juarez, Mexico, stoke fear by killing people randomly (more than 3,000 in 2010) and harassing people with a barrage of criminal acts, such as extortions, carjackings, and kidnappings. After stirring up enough fear, they demand "protection money" from the terrorized people and businesses—i.e., if they pay, they will be spared from violent attacks. The local newspaper *El Norte* reported that 90 percent of small businesses in Juarez are forced to pay local gangs for "protection." Those who do not pay must risk being killed or having their businesses torched.[231] In 2015, one of the San Salvadoran gangs ordered banning of 40 bus routes when a bus company refused to pay the demanded "protection money" or "rackets." When the drivers continued to drive the buses, they killed eight bus drivers while they were driving.[232] It is estimated that El Salvadoran gangs earn about $20 million a year from extortion. MS-13 alone earns as much as $600,000 a month in extortion payments from bus companies, retailers, and other businesses, with little pressure from authorities in 248 of the country's 262 municipalities. MS-13 and its rival Barrio 18 are El Salvador's largest employers with as many as 60,000 people as lookouts, collectors, and assassins. In San Salvador, the nation's capital, gangs control the local distribution of consumer products, such as diapers and Coca-Cola, and extort commuters, call-center employees, restaurants, and store owners. In the rural east, gangs threaten to burn sugar plantations unless farmers pay up.[233]

The apocalyptic predictions embedded in "doomsday" cults are designed to invoke fear (e.g., of not going to heaven) and a sense of insecurity (e.g., from not knowing their status of salvation) among believers by presenting the ultimate "test of faith"—a means of separating the "wheat from the tares"[234]—or a chance of "reaffirmation of faith" before the final judgment.[235] The leaders try to take advantage of the fact that people become more submissive to their leaders when they are fearful, helpless, and desperate. The threat of an imminent "end of the world" and "judgment day" can induce a heightened state of anxiety among believers. In fear, they contribute more money, sometimes their lifetime savings, to the church leaders, hoping to assure their salvation,[236] as happened most recently with California's radio minister Harold Camping ("Family Radio"), who predicted the end-of-the-world "Rapture" on May 21, 2011.[237]

Labeling, Stereotyping, Blaming, Scapegoating

Labeling

Labeling is a strategy groups of people use commonly to accentuate differences between "us" and "them," and to elevate their group's status by degrading out-groups.

LABELING AS "HIERARCHICAL POSITIONING" PROCESS

Acts of labeling indicate intergroup power dynamics and struggles—i.e., a group of people uses labels to empower themselves and degrade others. They apply positive labels to themselves to elevate their own status compared to other groups (e.g., "chosen people," "royal blood," "race realists," "true patriots," "white patriots," "born-again Christians," "value voters," "job creators," "crusaders"). For instance, white nationalist, racist, and anti-government militia groups call themselves "true patriots" and their movement "patriot movement."[238] By calling themselves "true patriots," they are implying that those who do not support their cause are "less patriotic" or "unpatriotic." On the other hand, they apply negative and derogatory labels to out-groups—e.g., pejorative terms and disparaging descriptions, such as racial, sexual, and religious slurs and epithets—to humiliate, demonize, belittle, or mock other groups to elevate their own status above the "labeled," or legitimize their superior status over the "labeled." There are plenty of religion-related labels, such as infidels, heathens, heretics, pagans, gentiles, "godless liberals," "religious nuts," and "Jesus freaks," and there are others applied to racial/ethnic minority groups, such as the N-word, gooks, chinks, and japs. There are labels for rural residents, such as rednecks, hillbillies, and hicks; for criminals, ex-cons, ex-felons, sex offenders, druggies, and terrorists; for sexual deviants, such as sluts, fags, faggots, whores, and for the poor, such as "welfare queens," "bag ladies," and "bums." Negative labeling is an act of verbal branding and bullying with the purpose of "putting down" people of out-groups, and therefore, always implies intergroup power struggles and hierarchical status-construction processes.

Labeling can occur within racial/ethnic groups when there are intragroup contentions and struggles for power and resource domination. Members contrive labels to differentiate themselves or to elevate themselves over others within the same group. Shirley[239] demonstrated that in predominantly-white rural communities in Mississippi, people draw intra-racial distinctions between "rednecks" and "non-rednecks" to separate themselves. "Non-rednecks" describe "rednecks" with negative characterizations, marginalize them, and discriminate against them.

Labeling in U.S. Politics

Some political leaders of modern times also use derogatory labels to assail, demean, and disparage their opponents, and elevate the status of their own political party. Conservative nationalistic politicians label humanistic liberals who challenge unethical foreign policies of the U.S. government as "unpatriotic" and "anti–American" "traitors," and economic conservatives bemoan their critics by calling them "socialists" and "communists." Those who oppose war or disapprove of hardline counterterrorist measures are labeled as "terrorist sympathizers" who like to "cozy up with terrorists." Some liberal Democrats call economically and politically conservative Republican lawmakers the "country club Republicans" and "right-wing zealots," and foreign policy hardliners the "war-mongering" "defense-hawks." Even within the same party, the hardliners label "moderate" independent voters who at times vote across the party lines "RINOs (Republicans In Name Only")" and "Blue Dogs" (Democrat lawmakers who at times vote with the Republican Party). The Nixon administration labeled anti-war protesters "communists," "hippies," "radical incendiaries," and "liberal bastards" to delegitimize their causes until thousands of Vietnam veterans started to protest against the Vietnam War (VVAW).[240] President Trump successfully labeled mainstream media that reported stories unfavorable to him as "fake news" and "enemy of the people," and berated his own government organizations (e.g., CIA, FBI, Justice Department) and their employees who did not comply with his demands as the "deep state" elements that conspired to subvert him.

Using Negative Labeling to Justify Mistreatments

When a group of people labels others as infidels, heretics, communists, witches, gypsies, ex-cons, illegals, druggies, traitors, felons, and terrorists, it becomes easier for them to justify their mistreatment, discrimination, and persecution of the labeled. For instance, by labeling a group of people as "enemies," "terrorists," "agitators," "commies" (meaning communists) and "fascists," it becomes legitimate to use deadly force and violence against them, deny them due process, and mistreat them, because the labels degrade the people to a level lower than their labelers' status. During the 30 years of "dirty war," Latin America's military dictators labeled democracy protesters and labor union leaders as "internal enemies of the state" and justified their brutal executions and "disappearances" with the help of paramilitary death squads.[241] In 2017, embattled Venezuelan President Nicolas Maduro's administration labeled protesters against Maduro "terrorists," and ordered brutal crackdowns against them, although they were protesting over economic chaos, inflation, chronic shortages of basic goods, high

3. Extremist Strategies of Pivoting Group Identities   139

levels of urban violence, and the constitutional crisis the Maduro administration engendered to maintain its power.[242]

LABELING PERSECUTED MINORITIES AS "TERRORISTS"

Labeling persecuted minority groups protesting to gain equal status as "terrorist groups" has been a convenient and popular strategy for dominant groups throughout history, because it made it easier for them to justify violent raids aimed at "elimination" and "extermination" of the group. For this reason, the powerless minorities and underdog groups have been much more likely to be labeled as "extremist" and "terrorist" groups than the majority and powerful groups when they commit equally extremist acts.[243]

The Buddhist-dominated government and people of Myanmar have systematically discriminated against the Muslim minority group called Rohingya (about 1.3 million, which is about 3 percent of the population) since 1948. They are persecuted, deprived of citizenship rights for generations, driven out of their land, and sporadically subjected to ethnic cleansing, despite the fact that they have lived there for centuries. In 2012, when the government confiscated their land, confined them in segregated camps, and prohibited them from working or moving to other areas, they protested with violence. The Myanmar government promptly labeled them as a "terrorist group," killed scores of protesters, and detained over 146,000 Rohingya people.[244] In Sri Lanka, the government and military seized the land owned by Tamil Tigers (ethnic minority group) and removed them from their land where they had lived forever. When Tamil Tigers revolted in protest, the Sri Lankan government declared them as "terrorists," and justified brutal assaults and persecution to a level of virtual extinction of the group in 2015.[245]

Uighers (Muslims who speak Turk) are ethnic minorities in Urumqi, China, who are discriminated against by the majority ethnic Han Chinese. When the dominant Han Chinese moved into their area, took their jobs, and forced them to speak Mandarin, Uighers protested, some of them violently. The Chinese government quickly labeled all Uighers as a "terrorist group," and beginning in 2017, started a "mass detention" program—i.e., they arrested hundreds of thousands of Uighurs for having "extremist thoughts," and detained them in "reeducation camps" for months and years. Their children were forcibly separated from their parents, and kept in children's camps where they were forced to learn Han tradition and language.[246]

In 2018, Israel responded to rock-throwing Palestinian teens protesting against the move of Israel's capital to Jerusalem with live ammunition, killing 189 Palestinians and injuring over 9,000, including many children who posed no threat to the Israeli troops. Yet, Hamas, the Palestinian resistance group Israel labeled a "terrorist organization," is accused of instigating the violence, not the Israeli government. After investigating the incident, the United Nations reported that Israeli troops committed crimes against humanity, and recommended a resolution measure, which the U.S. vetoed arguing that it was "one-sided" and "unfair" to Israel.[247] In 2015, the Nigerian army invaded the compound of a minority sect Shia group called Islamic Movement of Nigeria (IMN), killed about 350 members, and arrested the leader Zakzaky. Despite its aggression, in 2019, the Nigerian court granted the government permission to label the group as a "terrorist organization," a move that allows authorities to clamp down harder on the group, because its members demanded release of their leader Ibrahim el-Zakzaky who has been detained since 2015 despite a court order to release him.[248]

USING "TERRORISM" CHARGES TO PERSECUTE DISSENTERS AND CRITICS

Authoritarian states use terrorism charges to purge and persecute political dissenters and critics. Saudi Arabia routinely executes dissenters and critics accusing them of terrorism or having extremist ideologies. In 2016, it executed 47, mostly minority sect Shia members, including a prominent Shia leader Nimr al-Nimr under terrorism-related charges. In 2019, it executed 37 men, mostly political prisoners convicted of terror-related crimes, the kingdom's official news agency reported.[249] In Turkey, anyone who openly criticizes the government faces imprisonment with "terrorism" charges. During the COVID-19 pandemic in 2020, Turkey's parliament decided to release over 90,000 prisoners to address the immediate threat of the pandemic in overcrowded prisons, except tens of thousands who were rounded up and charged with "terrorism" during the purging spree following the 2016 failed military coup against Erdogan. They were mostly civil servants, judiciary officials, military personnel, journalists, and politicians[250]

Stereotyping

Group-bound people tend to see individuals as a representation of their group, and therefore, they are more prone to stereotyping—i.e., they believe in grossly over-generalized and misrepresented images of a group of people ignoring individual variations, underlying circumstances, and factual truths about the group. Stereotypes can be positive or negative—e.g., people apply positive stereotypes to in-group, allies, or "favored" group members, and negative ones to disliked out-groups (e.g., Muslims are terrorists; Mexican Americans are illegal immigrants; illegal immigrants are criminals; blacks are criminals and lazy; Jews are miserly).

To a certain extent, stereotyping exists probably in every society where group dynamics are at play. In extremist groups, because they are strongly bound by "us vs. them" mindsets and group-centric ideologies, stereotyping is more common and pronounced, defining and justifying their worldviews, causes, beliefs, and goals. Extremist group *leaders* may use negative stereotypes for the purpose of group mobilization, to justify mistreatment of out-groups, or to place their group above others in a hierarchy of social statuses (used as a "positioning tool"). Group *followers*, meanwhile, may believe in stereotypes of outsiders because of limited exposure to out-group members, or as a result of unfavorable and unpleasant experiences with outsiders (e.g., being robbed or conned), as well as as a result of indoctrination by their leaders. For instance (in hypothetical situations), extremists are more likely to assume that all black teens are criminals after being mugged by a black teen, than non-extremists. When they see a white cop abusing a black criminal suspect, they are more likely to assume that *all* white cops are abusive and racist. In both cases, race may have nothing to do with the events, yet they tend to interpret them as a "racial" issue. When a Democratic lawmaker is accused of bribery, extremist Republicans are quick to assume that all Democrat lawmakers are corrupt. Extremists use a few cases of illegal immigrants arrested for committing crimes as proof that *all* over 11 million illegal immigrants are criminals.[251] After the 9/11 terrorist attacks, some Americans refused to fly with Arab- or Muslim-appearing passengers, publicly demonstrated to oppose building of mosques in their neighborhoods, and demonized Islam, as if all (over one billion around the world) Muslims were "terrorists."

EFFECTS OF STEREOTYPING

Irrespective of what the genesis is, negative stereotypes, once widely accepted, can have a pervasive impact on the lives of the groups of people who are negatively stereotyped. They are more likely to be suspected, arrested, and convicted of crimes, even wrongfully, simply based on stereotypes ("profiling"), and they become less likely to be hired or accepted in social circles and business trades. They cannot live in certain neighborhoods or send their children to schools of their choice, and their voices are ignored and credibility diminished, all because of stereotypes.[252] The basic causes and goals of stereotyping are generally similar to that of labeling as discussed above—to accentuate the differences between "us and them," degrade out-groups and to elevate in-group status, and justify mistreatment of the negatively stereotyped groups of people.

Blaming and Scapegoating

Extremists, when their group is under a threat or in a crisis (e.g., due to natural disasters, spread of pandemic, external threats, internal chaos due to economic hardship, political turmoil and divisions), yet they cannot face the *real* source of the threat, try to blame and scapegoat powerless minority groups of people for their troubles. In so doing, leaders can dodge the blame and divert attention away from themselves, and followers can vent and release their anger and frustration on the scapegoated groups of people, instead of their leaders who are responsible for resolving the problems.

WITCH CRAZE

During the 16th and 17th centuries in Europe, hysteric fear of witches swept through Europe, which prompted rampant occurrences of witchcraft trials and executions of (accused) witches. This occurred as European societies were going through a major transformation with massive turmoil, politically, socially and culturally, and the Church attributed all the undesirable phenomena of lawlessness, crime, disorganization, and misery to the witches. By blaming the witches and executing over 500,000 mostly unmarried women (e.g., singles and widows), whether deliberate or not, they were able to dodge the blame for the chaos and instability.[253]

COMMUNIST MOVEMENTS

When the Marxist and Maoist experimental "collectivization" plan failed miserably with disastrous consequences (e.g., food shortage, economic chaos, and millions of deaths from famine) in the Soviet Union, China, and Cambodia (under Khmer Rouge), leaders blamed "internal enemies" of critics and dissenters for the failure, and responded with brutal purges, coordinated torture, mass executions, and incarcerations in prison camps.[254]

JIHADIST MOVEMENTS

Anti-West Islamist/jihadist groups blame Western powers for the problems their societies face, overlooking the internal shortcomings of the Muslim world. They argue that all of the political problems and social ills are the result of the Western world's imperialistic power, political interference, and economic dominance, which trampled their nations' sovereign power, honor, and pride.[255] According to a global survey by Pew Research Center in 2006, the majority of Muslims around the world, including those in Europe, blamed the Western world for their problems.[256]

BLAMING THE POWERLESS GROUPS

Throughout history, a litany of dominant group leaders have blamed powerless minorities to dodge responsibility and divert attention when they faced calamities they could not handle. In America, every time the economy turned sour, right-wing, anti-immigrant nativists blamed immigrants for the social ills of their time, such as high crime rates, economic woes, unemployment, the spread of diseases, rising costs of health care, social service resource drain, the epidemic of drug abuse, and illegal voting, usually inflamed by political leaders and demagogues.[257] Nazis in Germany blamed Jews for their economic trouble, and persecuted and executed over 6 million Jews during the Second World War. Germans scapegoated Turkish immigrants during the economic trouble in the 1990s, shortly after the reunification of East and West ("Turkey-bashing"), and repatriated many back to Turkey. After the U.S.-led invasion of Iraq in 2003, Iraqi Sunnis blamed Iraqi Christians for the invasion, and persecuted them. The U.S. State Department reported that more than half of 1.4 million Iraqi Christians fled Iraq fearing onslaughts.[258]

Similarly, powerful groups of people have often blamed the powerless to escape culpability on their part. In 2012, 41,200 South African platinum mine union workers walked out in protest, during which 34 striking workers were shot to death *by* the police. The South African government charged 270 miners with manslaughter for "causing deaths" of their 34 fellow miners who were killed by the police.[259] In 2013, an Egyptian court sentenced 21 soccer fans to death for their role in a riot during which 74 fans were killed *by* police.[260] When 96 Liverpool football fans were crushed to death in 1989, British police and the government quickly blamed the fans for the disaster to dodge the responsibility. Twenty-seven years later, under the unrelenting pressure from the victims' families, a newly-formed Hillsborough Independent Investigative Panel accused the police of misconduct and cover-up.[261] In 1970, when the Ohio National Guard opened fire, killing four and injuring nine Kent State University students protesting against the Vietnam War on the university campus, the state of Ohio indicted 24 student activists and a professor with the deaths and injuries of the students, not the National Guard who fired the shots.[262]

Blaming the Victims

Extremists try to divert the blame they deserve by blaming the victims (of their own wrongdoings), attacking the attackers, accusing the accusers, and discrediting the detractors. Throughout history, men who abuse their wives often blame their wives for their abuse, even accusing their wives of infidelity to justify their abusive behaviors.[263] Men have blamed rape victims for "causing" or "seducing" them to rape. Even in modern times, in rural and traditional parts of less-developed societies, rape victims are punished, even stoned to death, not the rapists; victims are accused of "provoking" rape, or going outside without proper cover or male escort.[264] More than 99 percent of sexual assaults in India are never reported. Victims do not report because authorities and people shame and blame the victims, not the perpetrators. Even when an 11-year-old girl was repeatedly gang-raped by an elevator attendant, security guards, plumbers, and electricians of an apartment complex for months in 2018, people blamed the girl's mother and dismissed the rape allegations by saying that the girl was "deaf and dumb."[265] In 2016, an Indian woman who was gang-raped by five men was gang-raped again by the same men out on bail as a punishment for reporting the rape instead of committing suicide for "shaming" herself.[266] In 2019, a 23-year-old Indian woman who was heading to testify against a man who allegedly raped her was attacked by a group of men, including her rapist, and fatally set on fire.[267] By blaming the weaker and vulnerable women, men can get away with rape and sexual harassment, and sustain their dominance over women.

A similar "blaming the victims" attitude persists in the Western world, also. When rape victims report the crime in the U.S. military, they are often "wrongfully discharged" from the military with bogus charges of mental or personality disorder.[268] In 2016, Baylor University removed its president, Kenneth Starr, for systematically ignoring rape charges against athletes, and instead, punishing and retaliating against the rape victims for reporting.[269] According to internal studies, hundreds of nuns who were raped by priests did not report, because they were taught to believe "they're the guilty ones for having seduced that holy man into committing sin." Raped nuns who become pregnant are "outcasted" from their orders, but not the priests who impregnate them. Victims are forced to leave their order and live alone, raising their children with no help, according to the report.[270] Amish girls who are sexually abused by family members, neighbors, and church leaders do not report, because, in their "victim shaming and blaming culture," victims who report are bullied, mocked, spit on, and called "sluts" and "whores," and the whole community, including their mothers, overwhelmingly support the abusers, not the victims.[271]

♦♦ 4 ♦♦

Extremist Strategies Designed to Enhance Group Power

Producing Loyal Followers Willing to Sacrifice for the Group

The success of all extremist group movements depends on leaders' abilities to produce loyal followers who are willing to sacrifice their lives or personal interests for the group without expecting material reward. Therefore, leaders have a stake in generating and assembling as many loyal, devoted, and obedient followers who are submissive yet valorous, "happy-to-die warriors," as possible.

Valuing Loyalty to Induce Sacrifice

With loyal followers willing to sacrifice, leaders do not have to deploy physical force or material compensation for their sacrifice—they will voluntarily sacrifice their personal interests for the "higher" and "nobler" causes of defending the group's pride and honor. In order to induce sacrifice for the group, leaders glorify martyrdom as an ultimate display of loyalty and sacrifice. While condemning egoistic suicides, most religions, including various branches of Christianity and Islam, have encouraged martyrdom as an act of "cleansing one's sins" or a form of "atonement"—i.e., an effort to "cleanse and redeem oneself from earthly, mortal evil" and "earning peace in heaven."[1] In Islamist extremist groups, suicide bombers earn the highest respect and honor, and their families gain higher status in the community for their acts of martyrdom.[2] Political leaders acclaim sacrificing one's life for nationalistic causes, also. Former Iranian President Ahmadinejad stated: "Is there an art that is more beautiful, more divine, and more eternal than the art of the martyr's death?"[3] Turkey's President Recep Tayyip Erdoğan, in front of a raucous rally, said to a 6-year-old girl weeping in fear holding the Turkish flag, that "if she becomes a martyr, she will be wrapped in Turkey's flag."[4]

Cultivating Loyalty

Loyalty, unlike conformity, cannot be physically coerced; it must be shrewdly and strategically cultivated using the power of ideas and manipulation of human emotions.

Soliciting Loyalty with Social Services

Like in most human relationships, symbiotic relationships between group leaders and followers are embedded in reciprocal, give-and-take, trade-offs of loyalty and protection.[5] Leaders proffer (or promise) security and protection in return for loyalty from their followers. For this reason, religious organizations, especially in the past, performed charity functions—e.g., provided some form of subsistence level aid and social services to the needy and destitute. In return, people offered their loyalty to the church. Some contemporary religious cults and communes continue to provide basic existential security in a communal setting—e.g., food, shelter, education for children, and health care. Religious missionary efforts, whether they were Christian, Muslim, or Hindi, incorporated charity functions and provision of social services into their proselytizing and outreach efforts around the globe for this reason.[6] Especially in areas where the state fails to deliver the basic services and protection, religious groups can easily step in to fill the void and gain people's loyalty.[7] Most well-known "extremist/terrorist" groups, such as al-Qaeda, Hamas, Hezbollah, al-Shabaab, Boko Haram, and the Muslim Brotherhood, operate as charity organizations providing food, shelter, and education to the poor, funded by Islam's obligatory alms-giving called Zakat, in their effort to recruit members and solicit loyalty. They enter impoverished areas, build houses, and provide education their government cannot provide, often infused with ideological and religious indoctrination to gain people's loyalty.[8]

Gangs' Effort to Procure Loyalty

In areas where the central state cannot maintain rule of law, tribal warlords, rebel groups, and gangs take over, and jockey for power and obtain people's loyalty by providing social services and security the state cannot offer. In areas in El Salvador where the government is unable to maintain law and order, people form and join gangs to protect each other. Gangs control street-level drug sales, charge local residents for "protection," and battle to keep their rivals out. In such neighborhoods and environments, people regard these gangs as "social organizations that protect the civilians," because they deliver necessary services to the people the government is unable to—e.g., they help get water lines connected or refurbish the community hall.[9] In Honduras, many economically-struggling parents leave their children behind to work in the U.S., and the children become vulnerable prey for violence without parental protection and guidance. For these children without protection from parents and the government, gangs become the only available source of protection. They become loyal to the gang seeking protection and security.[10] During the economic lockdowns due to the COVID-19 pandemic, sundry gangs and rebel groups turned the government's failure to control the virus into their own propaganda opportunity. In areas where the government is not able to help the people in need, they take over the governmental role and try to appear to be the "responsible, accountable actor." Mexico's drug gangs distributed aid packages with food and masks to people struggling in fear; MS-13 in El Salvador instituted and enforced its own curfew and distributed masks. In Afghanistan, Taliban militants dispatched health teams with impressive medical gear and offered health care services to the fear-stricken people[11]; in South Africa, instead of fighting, rival gangs started to distribute much needed food and water to people in their territory.[12] In southern Italy, Mafia clans took advantage of the pandemic lockdown by providing everyday necessities to residents of poor neighborhoods and offering credit to businesses that were near bankruptcy.[13]

Strategies of Invoking Loyalty in Modern Organizations

Using loyalty to mobilize manpower and procure resources is not a strategy exclusive to traditional groups of the past or terrorist groups and street gangs. Some modern institutions and organizations continue to use similar strategies of invoking loyalty from their members and employees for organizational benefit. Having loyal members and followers makes it easier for organizations to hide their wrongdoings and deter whistle-blowing, hence, they can protect their reputation and promote organizational interests.

Colleges and Universities: Colleges and universities try to induce a "familial" sense of loyalty among their students and alums. They offer legacy admission privileges to children of the alums to enhance loyalty to the institution across generations, because their loyalty and intergenerational allegiance can bring in higher alumni contributions.[14] The Penn State Alumni Association, with more than 165,000 members, is the largest dues-paying alumni group in the world. "Even when you leave State

College," says Professor Scott Kretchmar, "it's attached to you like an umbilical cord." That is why these alums, out of loyalty, coalesced to embrace the beleaguered football head coach Joe Paterno when he was accused of covering up the child sexual abuse case of his assistant coach for many years.[15] At Harvard, the legacy admission rate was more than five times higher (33.6 percent) than non-legacy applicants (5.9 percent) in 2017[16]; at Princeton, legacies are admitted at four times the general admission rate, and at the University of Notre Dame, University of Virginia, and Georgetown University, the rate is about twice higher.[17]

Corporations: Like the military, large corporations of the past offered an assortment of corporate-sponsored benefits (e.g., healthcare, retirement pension, housing accommodations, and continuing education) to their employees, called "corporate paternalism." Whether intentional or unintentional, such policies can render similar effects of inducing loyalty for the corporation. When corporations become the primary "protector," "caretaker," and "provider" of employees' (and their families') whole life and livelihood, employees tend to be more loyal to the corporation, more devoted and productive, and less likely to blow whistles against the corporation. According to Fukuyama,[18] Japanese corporations have long maintained such a paternalistic system that guarantees their workers' lifetime job security, training, and extensive welfare benefits for life, in return for loyalty and hard work. Employees *want* to do their best for the company because it looks after their family's whole life and lifetime welfare. The sense of employee loyalty is not formal or legal; it is entirely internalized—the result of a subtle process of corporate-centered socialization.[19] Without loyalty, corporations have to rely solely on financial rewards as compensation and incentive, which can be costlier for the corporation.

Political Parties: Communist parties tried to instill loyalty and moral obligation to the state and party through provision of life-encompassing benefits, such as state-guaranteed employment, rationed food, housing, education, healthcare, and childcare. They sought to monopolize people's loyalty by making people's whole life dependent upon the state, bypassing other institutions.[20] Political leaders frequently promise to offer sundry social services and benefits to their constituents to obtain their loyalty and vote. Saddam Hussein's Baath Party had pushed for women's rights—e.g., right to vote, be educated, and other legal rights—to gain their loyalty and votes.[21] Nazis in Germany advocated for higher old-age pensions, greater educational opportunities for the poor, an end to child labor, and improving maternal health care for the same reason.[22] They tried to earn political loyalty by offering social services to the most vulnerable segments of the population who needed help.

Monopolizing Loyalty

Once successfully cultivated, loyalty must be vigilantly safeguarded against competing sources of loyalty. As societies enlarge and diversify, multiple subgroups compete to monopolize people's loyalty, allegiance, and trust. Extremist group leaders try to convince their followers that only *they* can be trusted, no one else, and *they* are the only ones who are looking after the interest of their loyal followers. Islamist leaders in Europe preach how Muslims in Europe should be "Muslims first," before being Europeans[23], and American nationalists call for people to be "Americans first, before being a part of humanity." In their effort to monopolize people's loyalty, communist states (e.g., former Soviet Union, North Korea, China) eradicated religion, and tried to minimize people's loyalty to their family and kinship. The state carried out constant political vigilance and spying over everyone, and coerced the same from everyone against everyone else, even children against their parents, and brothers against each other. Children were required to be raised and educated by the state from a young age, and in some cases, they were prohibited to call their parents "mom and dad."[24]

Most religions in the past condemned heresy and idolatry—i.e., believing in or worshipping anything other than their own designated god and doctrines. ISIS/Daesh, when occupying the city of Palmyra in Syria in 2014, demolished Roman-era ancient tower tombs built in approximately 103 AD, because they "promote idolatry."[25] They also took over university buildings and burned all the books in the libraries, because those artifacts offered views contrary to their religious beliefs.[26] Some political leaders of developing nations try to limit or ban NGOs (Non-governmental organizations) and international charity groups, fearing that their people may become loyal to the NGOs instead of their state leaders. Leaders of Russia, China, and India had tried to limit NGO activities; Egyptian leaders have put foreign NGO workers on trial[27], and in Kenya, leaders have labeled NGOs as "terrorist" organizations.[28] In 2010, militants in Pakistan attacked and killed six World Vision workers.[29]

Appealing to Human Emotions

François-René de Chateaubriand said about 200 years ago, "Men don't allow themselves to be killed for their interests; they allow themselves to be killed for their passions."[30] Psychologists have discerned that when people choose to act politically, they often do so prodded by their emotions rather than reason. Emotions commit one to act more fervently than does the cost-benefit calculation of intellective cognition. Studies have shown that emotional judgments and motivations are more spontaneous and stronger than cognitive ones, and people have more affective responses to emotionally keyed information than purely cognitive information, sometimes even without reckoning the full details of the information.[31] Throughout human history, it has been passion-filled emotion that turned people into fanatical extremists, not reason or intellectual cognition.[32] Emotionally aroused, they easily succumb to hysteric fears, conspiracy theories, irrational exuberance, and exaggerated fears extremist leaders foment and cultivate, embrace group-centric ideologies, and execute group-prescribed extremist acts without reservations.

Emotions Suppress Rational Reasoning Process

Emotions are far more effective in generating collective sentiments and mobilizing actions, because emotions quell rational reasoning ability that can suppress emotional urges. When people become emotionally aroused, they lose rational and critical thinking ability, act more impulsively and thoughtlessly, and become more vulnerable to ideological propagandas and indoctrinations. For instance, when people go to war or leaders initiate a war, the decision is usually based on emotions, such as fear, hatred, outrage, and desire to seek revenge and protect group honor. Consumed by their emotions, they do not think or calculate the potential costs of the war—e.g., loss of human life and financial liabilities. Had Americans been given the information about potential costs of war prior to waging a war, not too many Americans would have supported the wars. The last U.S. World War I veteran died in 2011. Yet, 4,038 widows, sons and daughters continue to get monthly VA pension and other benefit payments, which totaled $16.5 million in 2011 alone. Spouses, parents and children of deceased veterans from World War II, Korea, Vietnam, Kuwait, Iraq and Afghanistan received about $6.7 billion in 2013. These payments do not include the costs of fighting or caring for the actual veterans—i.e., they include payments to care for their dependents. A Harvard University study in 2013 projected the final bill for the Iraq and Afghanistan wars to be $4 trillion to $6 trillion in the coming decades.[33] Blinded by the drumbeat of passion-filled rhetoric and spirit-raising slogans and propaganda designed to stir up emotions of passion and fervor, people eagerly support wars, go to war, and fight for the group risking their lives, without considering the cost of the wars.

Goals of Appealing to Emotions

To Invoke Collective Sentiments of Solidarity

Appealing to human emotions has been an effective mobilization technique in all combative groups, because emotions can generate collective sentiments of loyalty and group allegiances. Only human emotion, not reason, can inspire such passionate and spiritual feelings of group solidarity, camaraderie, loyalty, and pride that can bind a group of people together. For this reason, all political movements gain momentum when leaders effectively instill a collective sense of group solidarity and belonging by appealing to human emotions.[34] To arouse passion-filled feelings of solidarity, leaders appeal to group unity and exaggerate fears of disunity.[35]

To Encourage Sacrifice

Extremist groups in particular rely heavily on members' willingness to sacrifice their personal interests and lives for the group, because extremist acts tend to be high-risk with perilous consequences. If people can think and calculate costs and benefits rationally, most people will shun extremist groups and extremist acts, because any person with a rational inclination to calculate will realize that the costs and risks of committing extremist acts usually outweigh the benefits from them. In the case of suicide bombings, for instance, one must sacrifice his life for the sake of the group's causes, so that other members of the group can benefit from his act. No rational human being would volunteer to be a suicide bomber if he can rationally calculate the costs and benefits of this action. When people willingly sacrifice their lives and interests for the sake of the group, leaders reap the benefits from their sacrifice without having to spend material compensation for their services. For this reason, throughout human history, scores of religious and political leaders have exhorted and glorified sacrifice for the group by appealing to human emotions.

To Inspire Courage and Bravery

When people are passionately incited, whether with fear, hatred, anger, or pride, they exert a high degree of emotional energy, become overly confident about their abilities, and act in heroically courageous and audacious ways in response to danger and challenges, without thinking about the potential dangers and harmful consequences to themselves or to others. At times, they can be equally audacious in committing extraordinary acts against targeted enemies, including atrocities, brutalities, and wanton destruction without compunction. Behind all the brutal atrocities committed by extremist groups throughout human history, there have been strong, visionary, conviction-driven, and authoritarian leaders and demagogues who successfully invoked emotional zeal and passion in their followers and convinced them to fight bravely, risk their lives, commit atrocities, and believe that their sacrifice and carnage are for "noble" and worthy causes.

Strategies of Appealing to Emotions

Kaufman[36] argues that most political decisions people make are emotional expressions, and therefore, politics is largely about manipulating people's emotions using symbols as tools, which he calls "symbolic politics"—i.e., political activity focused on arousing emotions rather than addressing interests. The majority of extremist strategies I discuss in this chapter are geared toward appealing to and arousing people's emotions that are necessary for energizing and mobilizing a collectivity—e.g., inculcating a sense of moral superiority, group righteousness, and group pride; strategically exaggerating external threats and demonize enemies as subhuman species; using collective rituals to conjure up mystical and spiritual experiences of group spirit and solidarity and to stage-craft "superhuman" images of the leaders with uncanny abilities. Their goal is to generate a primordial or Gemeinschaft-like spiritual community with a moral sense of solidarity by emphasizing and exaggerating the fate-sharing elements of the members to an extent that individuals lose their individuality and exist only for the sake and interest of the group.[37]

Even in modern times, extremist leaders use emotionally-charged rhetorical ploys, slogans, propaganda, symbols, and rituals that can exude group-centric emotions (e.g., patriotism, ethno-nationalism, racism, Nazism) to rally up emotional energy for the group's causes and passionate feelings of solidarity. Nazis in Germany paraded with such emotion-arousing slogans as "Germany, Awake!" "The Jews are our Misfortune!" and "Today Germany, Tomorrow the World!"[38]; communist parties held mass parades with people holding placards with slogans like "Workers of the World Unite" and "Land to the Peasants," and white supremacist and nationalist groups continue to engage in large rallies filled with such catchphrases and slogans as "White Pride World Wide (WPWW)," "Our Race is Our Nation (ORION)" and "stop white genocide." North Korea's Kim regime frequently performs elaborately choreographed mass rallies and military parades to conjure up emotional feelings of patriotism and loyalty to the regime leaders. Donald Trump, during the 2016 presidential campaign, held massive campaign rallies suffused with emotion-arousing slogans, such as "lock her (Hillary Clinton) up," "build that wall" (Mexican border), "make America great again," and "drain the swamp" (ending Washington corruption). At every rally, thousands of his supporters zealously chanted these slogans, creating a drumbeat of "echo chamber" akin to those used by Nazis and Islamist/jihadist groups. Even after winning the election, President Trump continued to hold and revel in campaign-style, emotion-arousing rallies with thousands of frantically cheering followers, boasting his achievements and demonizing the media.[39]

Use of Collective Rituals

One of the common strategies contentious groups use is performing collective rituals to invoke group unity and solidarity and to display group size and power (e.g., how "large" and "mighty" the group is).[40] Rituals have always been a salient part of human collectivities, whether they are political, religious, social, or familial—e.g., coronation and anointment ceremonies of kings and queens, inauguration ceremonies of presidents, political conventions and rallies, military parades and ceremonies, religious worships, baptism, canonization, beatification, pilgrimages, weddings, funerals, rites of passage, public executions, and gangs' initiation ceremonies—because of their emotional appeals and power to bind people together.[41] Group marches, parades, festivals, and even public protests and demonstrations can generate analogous "ritualistic" effects on human emotions (e.g., Civil Rights marches, Forth-of-July parades, Labor Day and Veterans' Day parades, "Million Men March," and "March for Life"). Motorcycle gangs engage in mass "ride outs" (e.g., "Rolling Thunder"), and some hate groups (e.g., KKK) periodically stage large marches, rallies, and parades to gain attention and to raise a sense of group pride and camaraderie.

According to Alexander's[42] social performance theory, collective rituals are core components of groups' social performance, where actors act in accordance to scripts with dramatized stage effects. Efficacious use of theatrical performances imbued with emotion-arousing narratives, symbols, slogans, and coordinated gestures can connect "defused" realities together, give meaning to public settings, and bring the collectivities together. Ritualized performances bring human emotions out, connect them to the concept of the "sacred," and make participants "*feel* the sacred" (as opposed to knowing the "sacred").[43] The emotions generated from collective rituals are instrumental in all social movements because they can corral people's grievances and anger and channel them toward collective actions.[44] When people's emotions are aroused and encapsulated through collective rituals, they exert forceful energy, which can make people perform uncanny acts of bravery, gallantry, and heroism, as well as commit atrocities and brutalities in a ritualistic fashion.

As Fine[45] observed, ideologies are not just "held together" by a group, but they must be dramatically *enacted* through rituals and performances in order for members to continue to identify themselves with the group and pledge to contribute resources to the group. For this reason, religious, military, and political leaders throughout history, even in modern times, rely heavily on collective rituals to bolster their group's identity, ideology, pride, and members' emotional attachment to groups.[46] Religious services are always filled with ritualized and coordinated movements and chants, often boasting their size and number of participants (e.g., mega-churches, pilgrimages); politics is also filled with ritualized and stage-crafted dramas that include skillfully choreographed ceremonies, parades, and rallies, and the military routinely performs mass rituals adorned with colorful uniforms, parading soldiers, and display of medals and weapons.

Rituals Enhance Group Solidarity and Collective Power

Group rituals are symbolic acts that are carefully choreographed and orchestrated to produce emotional bonding experiences and invoke spiritual and moral feelings and an aura of group cohesion and power. Through rituals, members are reminded of their group identity and belonging, their sense of solidarity and allegiance is reinforced, and they renew their vows of loyalty and duty. While chanting, bowing, praying, singing, and dancing together, group members experience the *spiritual* feelings of "one-ness," expressed and reverberated through "one-voice" and "one-action" in a ritualized and synchronized coordination. Through collective rituals, people experience spiritual power and energy they cannot feel alone, and group solidarity and unity is reinforced as members repeatedly avow, renew, and pledge their loyalty and allegiance.[47]

Durkheim[48] argued that the key aspect of all religions, therefore, is not necessarily its beliefs but the social rituals its members perform together. When a large number of people who share the same identity or beliefs congregate together ("physical co-presence"), focus on the same objects that represent the group (e.g., flags, cross, image of God), and coordinate their activities in unison (e.g., gestures, prayers, singing, dancing), they *feel* the existence of "greatness" and "forcefulness"—something that overpowers individuals. They become mesmerized and "awe-struck" by "something greater than the sum of each individual." Such emotional and spiritual experiences of exaltation and empowerment spread quickly among participants ("contagion effect"), and they extol together in "group power," which renders them a sense of security and protection. Studies have substantiated this Durkheimian theory of ritual elaborated by Collins,[49] with an assortment of religious groups—i.e., collective rituals indeed raise people's emotional feelings of group solidarity, affinity, effervescence, and the spiritual experience of a superpower's (e.g., God's) presence and manifestation.[50]

People who attend the Million Man March, March for Life, "megachurches," and even sports events also experience a similar "spiritual awakening" of being a part of "group power." They *enjoy* the experience of "group power," and depending on the circumstances, some may even become addicted to it, seeking to experience it repeatedly. When rituals are designed to produce such feelings of "greatness" and "collective power," the *size* of the group matters—i.e., the greater the size, the more power the group exerts.[51] People are drawn to mega-churches, mega-marches, huge rallies, parades, protests, and massive pilgrimages, because the bigger the crowd, the more powerful they feel.

Using Rituals to Stagecraft Powerful Image of Leaders

Extremist group leaders use collective rituals to conjure up impressively commanding, "bigger-than-life" images of themselves. They try to contrive and aggrandize a cultic persona of themselves through dramatized, theatrical, and stage-managed collective rituals centered on them. Through meticulously stage-managed rituals, and with the help of fancy and elaborate costumes, props, gears, and supporting casts, ordinary humans can transform into "divine," "sacred," and authoritative "super-humans" with uncanny abilities to lead a group. Only the carefully-crafted rituals, such as lavish coronation and anointment ceremonies of kings and queens, politicians' and Pope's elaborate and expansive inauguration ceremonies, canonization and beatification rituals, can bestow such a "sacred" image and symbolic aura upon ordinary individuals. To make themselves appear powerful, in modern political campaigning, some candidates use "fake crowds" who are paid to gather and show enthusiastic support for the candidates, called "astro-turfing." There are businesses (e.g., Crowds-on-Demand) which supply such attention-grabbing crowds for politicians at press conferences and campaign rallies for pay as a part of a "media stunt."[52] Their goal is to forge a popular, commanding, and cardinal image of a person through theatrical stage-managing and acting by "made-to-believe" supporting casts.

Use of Symbols

Jenkins[53] discusses that symbols are necessary in all group-based movements because group identities are products of human imagination, purposefully conjured up by leaders. They need symbols that can bring people together under the *imaginary* identities. Durkheim[54] noticed the instrumental function of cultural symbols in religions. When symbolic objects are imbued with special meaning and "sacredness," they become central for defining people's identities and their relationships. With symbols, the relationship between community members and their common values are defined, and the group as a whole gains a "sacred" purpose of forming and reinforcing the core existence of the communities. Effectively deployed and "sacralized" symbols can bring community members together, raise their sense of solidarity and cohesion, and mobilize people for group-centric causes.

For this reason, creating and "sacralizing" symbols using various tools, such as myths, legends, and collective rituals, has been a crucial role of group leaders in all group-based movements. When certain objects, artifacts, and acts are designated or branded to be "sacred" and "holy," whatever they represent or symbolize becomes unchallengeable, uncontestable, and unassailable. Group leaders are acutely aware of this "symbolic" significance of symbols and effectively use them to represent the group, demark boundaries, and inspire a sense of group unity and solidarity. Symbols can be anything—e.g., objects or emblems, real or imagined, such as flags, totems, shrines, "holy" scriptures, crosses, swastikas, hammer and sickle, iron/Celtic crosses, yarmulkes, headscarves, tattoos, insignias, color-coded attires, and signs and gestures—that is bestowed with sacrosanct meaning and epitomizes the group, and is then revered as the "group in reification." Once effectually reified, they can inspire and energize people the same way the venerated group leaders can.

Connor[55] argues that the core of all ethno-nationalism rests in symbols that represent the nation and arouse emotional feelings of solidarity and belonging (e.g., flags, national anthems, swastika, concepts of rising sun and Britannia). Kaufman[56] discusses how people join political groups in response to symbols that represent their group ("symbolic politics" or "symbolic choice theory"). One of the core assumptions of "symbolic politics" (or "symbolic choice") theory is that people choose political courses of action responding to the most emotionally potent symbol evoked. Effectively applying emotionally-laden symbols, therefore, leaders can inspire people to participate in ethnic movements. Successfully "sacralized" symbols can simplify a complex reality, short-circuit the convoluted problem of making tradeoff decisions, and urge people to put group-centric issues ahead of personal concerns. For this reason, the essential "how" of all ethnic wars in the past has been "symbolic politics"—i.e., leaders manipulating symbols that tap into nationalist myths to mobilize people for wars.[57]

Symbols as Group Identification Marks

As Collins[58] states, when two people both respect the same sacred emblems and the same holy names, they know that they belong to the same ritual community. Those who share common symbols feel a moral tie among themselves and a righteous anger against outsiders who violate the respect for the symbols they revere. To be a part of a group, therefore, members must embrace, display, and respect collectively-shared symbols as a part of the "identity verification process."[59]

Symbols are particularly important in extremist groups whose existence indomitably depends on group identities and distinctions of "insiders" from "outsiders." Symbols become crucial tools of "group identification" where people's desire to "differentiate" is closely tied to their imperative need to maintain psycho-spatial distance between groups.[60] The flagrant display of symbols is regarded as proof of membership identity and loyalty, and a cultural expectation in such groups.[61] Tribes in the past used tattoos as tribal marks to identify which tribe people belonged to; gangs use symbolic emblems and color-coded outfits to identify each other. Religious groups have historically relied on a litany of symbolic objects, images, required attires and hairstyles that distinguish in-group members from outsiders. Nations use flags and anthems to symbolize their country; military units use color-coded uniforms, insignias and badges to identify each other, and colleges and universities use mascots and colors to differentiate them from others.

The outlaw biker group Mongols are unified under their trademark logo—a drawing of a brawny Genghis Khan–like figure sporting a queue and sunglasses riding a chopper while brandishing a sword. This symbol is emblazoned on their jackets, shirts, caps, and motorcycles of all members. For Mongols, the "patch," as they call it, is key to "belonging" and the optics of appearing tough, and members can spend months or even years proving their "worthiness" before they can earn the right to wear it. "The patch is like the American flag to these guys and speaks to the identity of the club, the individual, and the culture," says gang expert William Dulaney.[62]

Importance of Defending Symbols

When symbols are considered representative of a group, people become compelled to defend the symbols with the same passion and vehemence as defending their group. They become indignant when their symbolic objects (e.g., national flags, cross, Quran, Bible) are desecrated or insulted, as much as when their group is threatened, and they retaliate violently to restore their group's honor smeared by the disrespectful acts against their "sacred" symbolic objects. In 2011, masses of Afghans rioted for days to protest against the (alleged) burning of a Quran in Florida, resulting in the death of nine people and more than 80 injured in Kandahar alone. In Mazar-i-Sharif, eleven people died in related riots including seven foreign U.N. workers who were attacked by the mob.[63] Mobs in India lynch Muslims suspected of transporting cows or eating beef and boast about their killings by posting videos of their executions; yet, authorities refuse to investigate or prosecute perpetrators. At least 44 Muslims have been lynched to death in three years, yet no one has been prosecuted. Instead, injured victims of lynch assaults are often jailed as perpetrators.[64] In 2015, a Hindu mob stormed into a Muslim neighbor's residence and killed family members over a rumor that the Muslim neighbors were eating beef, which Hindus consider sacred.[65] They were willing to kill their neighbors in order to defend their sacred symbol that represents their group.

Symbolic Leadership

In group-bound cultures unified by symbols, leaders can acquire symbolic status and a spiritual persona that represent the group by orchestrating judiciously choreographed collective rituals, legendary narratives, and a drumbeat of self-aggrandizing slogans. Once leadership is successfully "symbolicized" to represent the group, people revere and worship their leaders as "symbols" of their group (e.g., monarchs, prophets, the Pope). Once a leader attains a "spiritual" persona representing the group, their actual leadership qualities and abilities become inconsequential: their principal role turns into one of rallying up group members' spirits and upholding the group's unity and solidarity. Disrespecting or criticizing leaders, therefore, becomes tantamount to dishonoring the whole group, a treasonous act. Hereditary transmission of leadership becomes easily justifiable, natural, and unchallenged, because the descendants of the symbolic leaders are considered to be born with the same aura of symbolic legitimacy as their forefathers. European and Japanese people's adulation for and attachment to their loyal family members and Catholics' adoration of and veneration for Popes resemble such blind attachment and loyalty to symbolic leaders. For supporters of Donald Trump during the 2016 presidential campaign, facts did not matter and what Trump said and did were immaterial. The only thing that mattered was what Trump "represented" and "symbolized," whether that was the "change" they longed for, white nationalism, or going back to the 1970s when America dominated the world's manufacturing industries. They took *him* seriously as a *symbolic* leader representing their yearnings and aspirations, not necessarily for his policy agendas, messages, or personal qualities.[66]

In North Korea, one cannot escape statues and murals of three generational leaders of the Kim dynasty—Kim Il-sung, Kim Jong-il, and Kim Jong-un. North Korean leaders have long relied on myths and legends to legitimize the three-generation autocracy that started with the first president, President Kim Il-sung, after the liberation of Korea from Japanese occupation in 1945. The sudden death of Kim Jong-il (the second heir) in 2011 led to an accelerated "myth-making" process to legitimize ascension of his youngest son, Kim Jong-un (reportedly at 28 years of age at the time).⁶⁷ Once leaders are entrusted with symbolic status, people defend the honor of their leaders with the same solemnness and zealotry as they defend the honor of their group. When some cartoonists and authors in Europe (e.g., *Charlie Hebdo*, Salman Rushdie, and Kurt Westergaard) mocked or insulted Islamic prophets, Muslims all over the world reacted with violent riots, and Islamic fatwas were declared against the cartoonists and authors.⁶⁸

Memorializing Past Legendary Heroes and Leaders as Symbols of the Group

In group-bound extremist cultures, people's need for and adulation of "symbolic leadership" is pervasive, because such groups rely heavily on leadership that can invoke *spiritual* feelings of group solidarity, irrespective of the actual deeds and qualities of the leader. Capitalizing on such needs, leaders try to turn images of heroic, legendary leaders of the past into symbols that embody the group. They construct statues and monuments to memorialize such heroes in perpetuity, because by remembering and worshipping their heroic leaders, group members solidify their union, identity, and belonging.

Every nation and religion has its fair share of heroic and legendary leaders with images artfully crafted and preserved through various myths, legends, embellished biographies, and impressive statutes and murals, even hundreds of years after their death. Even the leaders who led millions of their own people to tragic deaths in wars, man-made famines and disasters, and brutal political purging, such as Stalin of Russia and Mao of China, are revived, re-envisioned, and re-embellished to conjure up nationalistic feelings of pride and glory. Over 40 years after the death of Mao, China is building giant statues of him all over the country, even a pure golden statue, to re-create his *symbolic* image as a heroic leader of China.⁶⁹ In 2018, China passed legislation that requires "all of society" to "honor, study, and defend" Communist party-approved heroes and martyrs. Criminal penalties will apply to anyone who defames members of that "select group" of leaders of the past.⁷⁰ In 2017 the Russian government begun to erect new monuments of Josef Stalin—the Soviet Union's leader once disgraced for orchestrating mass murders and causing the death of millions by starvation after failed economic experiments. Its goal is to revive and restore Stalin's image as a national hero who defeated the Nazis in World War II, not as a brutal mass murderer reviled by historians.⁷¹ Historians have documented that at least 800,000 people were executed during the 16 months of Stalin's "Great Terror" and "Purge,"⁷² and about 3.9 million Ukrainians (13 percent of Ukraine's population) died because of Stalin's failed experimental collectivization between 1932 and 1934 (called "hunger extermination").[73] Thanks to the Russian government's orchestrated revisionist effort, in 2018 the number of Russians who viewed Stalin in positive ways reached the highest level since the fall of the Soviet Union in 1990.[74] Even when all mass gatherings were banned during the COVID-19 lockdown in 2020, Moscow allowed people to gather at Lenin's Tomb to celebrate the 150th anniversary of the birth of Vladimir Lenin, another Soviet leader.[75]

Over 150 years after the end of the Civil War, America is still quarreling—in state capitols and courtrooms, college campuses, and around town squares—over how, or whether, to commemorate Confederate soldiers and their legacies. White nationalist and white supremacy groups strive to preserve the statues of Confederate leaders, soldiers, and flags, and even build new statues of Confederate leaders, because they symbolize their group's pride and honor and the segregationist ideologies they espouse. As more state authorities decide to remove Confederate and Civil War monuments in public places, new monuments are rising on private properties. In recent years, about 75 Confederate memorials (e.g., statutes, monuments, place names, symbols) have been renamed or removed from public places across the U.S., especially on college campuses, according to Southern Poverty Law Center. However, 350 new Confederate memorials have been added to the list since 2016, raising its total to 1,740.[76]

Offering Simplified Worldviews and Explanations ("Simplism")

Extremism is particularly alluring to people who favor a simplified and totalistic vision of the world, and believe in and seek simplistic explanations and solutions for all the world's problems, ignoring the intricacies, ambiguities, and arbitrariness of complex modern realities.

Attraction to "Simplism"

Simplified worldviews and solutions to problems make people's lives easier, thus, they feel more comfortable, secure, and confident, in contrast to feeling bewildered, lost, and confounded by complexities they do not quite comprehend. As Bauman[77] describes, living among a multitude of competing values, norms and lifestyles, without a firm and reliable guarantee of being on the right side, is a high psychological price to pay in the modern world. Instead, these people try to take refuge and comfort in a simple, emotionally-charged, ideological world vision that furnishes them with a sense of moral rectitude, power, certainty, comfort, and confidence. Even more, accepting the simplified and justified vision of the world renders them a sense of empowerment, instead of feeling "ignorant," confused, insecure, and powerless.

Extremist leaders intuitively understand that they can appeal to and capture the attention of such vulnerable people by offering them a clear, easy-to-understand, and grossly simplified utopian vision of the world (e.g., the "Promised Land" strategy) and options for solutions to all the intricate issues and problems of the world. They use simple, emotionally charged, and attention-grabbing slogans and catchphrases that can quickly appeal to and stir up human emotions, ignoring concrete, data-based factual information and rational explanations. Adolf Hitler once explained: "I will tell you what has carried me to the position I have reached. Our political problems appear complicated. The German people could make nothing of them…. I, on the other hand, reduced them to the simplest terms. The masses understood this and followed me."[78]

Some people are attracted to cults, rebel and revolutionary groups, gangs, and fundamentalist groups because these groups offer them a clearly delineated and simplified view of the world, with simply defined goals and meanings of life, that makes easy sense to them.[79] For instance, Marxian/communist revolutionary leaders campaigned with a simple message that capitalism was the source of all problems, and socialism would solve all the world's problems and bring about a utopian world of "classless society." Despite the brutalities and atrocities leaders committed, scores of youths gravitated toward Taliban and ISIS/Daesh, even from the western world, because these group leaders effectively imparted a simplified utopian vision of caliphate.[80] Hassan Abu Hanieh, a Jordanian authority on jihadist groups, said, "Their (ISIS's) judiciary system is brutal but simple, swift and effective—the killer is killed; the adulterer is stoned; and the thief's hands are cut."[81]

Effects of "Simplism"

Yearning for and attraction to a simplified world vision and answers to complex and controversial issues continue to exist among plenty of people in modern societies, affecting various policy decisions. For instance, some Americans believe that terrorism can be eliminated simply by killing (or "rooting out") all the terrorists, as crimes can be eradicated by locking up all the criminals, and all the world's geopolitical problems can be resolved by removing regimes unfavorable to U.S. from power by force. For instance, neo-conservatives had long believed that spreading American-style capitalism and democracy around the world, even by force, would establish peace and prosperity for everyone all over the world.[82] The Iraq invasion was based on such a naively simplistic belief that America could introduce democracy in Iraq and solve all the complex political problems in the Middle East by removing Saddam Hussein from power and building a huge embassy in Baghdad from which America could control the Middle East. The U.S. Embassy complex in Iraq, completed in 2009, is the largest and most expensive embassy in the world, nearly as large as Vatican City. It occupies 104 acres (42 hectares), and cost $750 million to build, and was maintained with a staff of 15,000 employees and contractors in 2012, until its size and activity were significantly curtailed to a minimum after U.S. troops left Iraq in 2011.[83]

Donald Trump, as a presidential candidate in 2016, was able to appeal to masses of working-class whites by offering a grossly simplified worldview and solutions to all of America's problems. He explained all the complex world problems with a few simplified "blames" (e.g., illegal immigrants, China, and Democrats), and deflated all the complicated policy agendas into a few simple slogans, catchphrases, and jingles. For instance, he blamed illegal immigrants for the crimes and drug problems America faces; blamed China and globalized treaties previous administrations instituted for all the job losses in America; derided all the "establishment" politicians and Democrats as "stupid"; and promised that he would deliver tax cuts and deregulation that would solve all the economic problems and raise wages.[84] Regarding ISIS/Daesh, he said he would "bomb the hell out of ISIS,"[85] and to secure America, ban all Muslims from "entering" the U.S.[86] He ignored all the complexities related to the issue of immigration, and offered the one simple solution embodied by the "build that wall" chant, and presented his anti-corruption message summed up as "lock her (Hillary Clinton) up" and "drain the swamp," mantras which he repeated at every rally. Trump's use of Twitter was particularly effective in reaching out to a base audience seeking simplified answers. All the complex policy issues and arguments were pared down into 140 characters, grossly simplified and streamlined, without having to explain the details and complexities of the true reality.

Authoritarian Leadership

Extremist group leaders tend to be aggressively authoritarian—e.g., seek unchallenged power, and command absolute obedience, submission, and undivided loyalty from their followers. To maintain unassailable power, they suppress all sources of challenges to their power using bellicose threats and excessive force. They try to control their followers' minds and behaviors using ideological indoctrination and framing, oppressive means of social control, and rule by fear, aimed at turning individuals into mindless instruments that can be used for their group-centric causes.

Oppressive Means of Social Control

Repressive regime leaders throughout history have mercilessly persecuted their critics, detractors, opponents, dissidents, protesters, and "disobedients," accusing them of being "subversive," "seditious," or "treasonous." Saddam Hussein of Iraq demanded and expected unwavering loyalty from his followers, and ruthlessly punished whomever he suspected of being disloyal. Once in a while, he would call out a list of names of *presumed* "traitors" who lacked loyalty, and they were removed from the assembly one by one to be executed by their colleagues.[87] North Korea's three generations of the Kim regime are notorious for executing anyone suspected of being disloyal or disobedient. Kim Jong-un reportedly had his own uncle executed and his half-brother assassinated in Malaysia in 2017.[88]

In extremely traditional and fundamentalist groups under authoritarian control, even the most trivial infractions (by modern standards), such as disobedience, wearing improper attire, showing hair, losing virginity, adultery, and blasphemy, can incur severe punishments, including death. Fearing repressive sanctions and social rejection, people have no choice but to conform, obey, fit in, go along, and blend in with the peers and the status quo, and accept whatever is conventional, routine, traditional, or imposed upon them, without impugning the authority sources, whether they are political and religious leaders or elders in the family.

In the polygamous commune FLDS, according to defectors, disobeying the orders of its leader Warren Jeffs meant "eternal damnation," causing members to live in a constant fear of being expelled and "damned."[89] In 2019, *Politico* reported a "culture of fear" at the largest Christian college in the world, Liberty University in Lynchburg, Virginia, founded by Jerry Falwell, Sr., based on anonymous interviews with more than two dozen current and former Liberty University officials. Employees are prohibited from talking to media without approval or openly discussing what goes on inside the institution; those who speak risk being fired. "It's a dictatorship," one current high-level employee of the school said. "Everybody is scared for their life. Everybody walks around in fear," said a current university employee who agreed to speak only after purchasing a burner phone, fearing that Falwell was monitoring their communications. The fear is not limited to Liberty's campus. Several people who lack any tie to Liberty but live in the school's hometown of Lynchburg, Virginia, refused to go on the record for this reporting, fearing Falwell would take revenge upon them and their families.[90]

Anti-Media, Anti-Science and Anti-Intellectual Policies

In order to consolidate their power and control, extremist leaders denounce, discredit, or obstruct any alternative, contrary, or competing sources of authority and knowledge that challenge or undermine their own power and authority, such as critics, dissenters, opponents, and competitors as well as traitors, skeptics, and half-hearted moderates. In modern societies, authoritarian leaders feel particularly threatened by the media reports and scientific knowledge that contradict their claims and corrode their credibility and authority. In order to silence media and academia, they strive to either take control of the media and academia, or discredit factual information and scientific findings that are contrary to their views and ideologies by calling them politically-motivated "fake news" and "disinformation campaigns." Numerous contemporary political leaders and autocrats around the world have blamed and attacked the media for spreading "fake news" to discredit media scrutiny and purged their critics, such as Putin of Russia, Syria's al-Assad, Maduro of Venezuela, Myanmar's military regime, Turkey's Erdogan, as well as President Trump.[91] Hungary's Prime Minister Viktor Orban, following Putin's path, after being elected, took over state media groups and expelled the internationally renowned Central European University out of Hungary in 2018.[92]

Some Christian fundamentalist groups oppose the teaching of evolution theories fearing that people may no longer believe in the creationist view presented in the Bible. Others prohibit their followers from seeking medical treatment, which they see as "threatening" their religious authority and tenets, and instead, instruct them to rely only on faith-healing (e.g., some Christian Scientists and Jehovah's Witnesses groups). Jehovah's Witnesses groups consider higher education, especially in the sciences, to be "spiritually dangerous," and discourage members and their children from going to college.[93]

Persecution of Journalists

Extremist leaders detest the media that report stories that are unfavorable to them, and persecute journalists who expose their wrongdoings. In Russia, 42 liberal journalists and news editors were murdered in contract-style killings between 1997 and 2007; of those, 21 were killed under President Putin (2000–2007).[94] The majority of those killed had reported stories critical of Russian political leaders, and many more are in jail for reporting corruption in the government and pro–Putin business oligarchs.[95] In 2018, 15 Saudi agents brutally murdered and mutilated the body of *Washington Post* journalist Jamal Khashoggi, a Saudi national, who was a frequent critic of Saudi royal families, inside the building of the Saudi consulate in Istanbul, Turkey.[96]

In 2015, the Taliban in Afghanistan declared that journalists could be "military targets" to be hit, after journalists reported on atrocities and rapes that occurred after they took over the city of Kunduz.[97] Since then, Afghanistan has become one of the most dangerous countries in the world for journalists—more than one hundred journalists have been killed, including ten in one suicide bombing in 2018.[98] In Mexico, at least 88 journalists were killed between 1995 and 2005 and 22 between 2006 and 2010, and scores more are threatened into silence by drug cartels and corporate-sponsored paramilitaries for reporting their criminal activities and collusion with corrupt politicians and police.[99] Multiple newspapers had to shut down their businesses because they cannot secure the lives of their journalists without protection from the government and police.[100]

Anti-Science and Anti-Media Sentiments Among U.S. Political Leaders

Some conservative American leaders have openly displayed their aversion toward the "liberal" and "biased" media and academia. President Richard Nixon, talking to National Security Advisor Henry Kissinger in 1972 in a declassified taped Oval Office conversation, said, "Never forget: the press is the enemy; the establishment is the enemy; the professors are the enemy."[101] President Trump repeatedly branded mainstream media sources (e.g., CNN, *Washington Post, New York Times*) that reported news stories critical of or unfavorable to him as "crooked" and "dishonest" "enemy of the state (or people)" that spread "fake news," and "garbage journalism."[102] Economically-conservative, pro-business politicians (who receive campaign funding from large corporations and industries) also have a penchant for denouncing media and science, because scientific research (e.g., about global warming, endangered species, and environmental destruction) often threatens their donor corporations' business interests, and media sources often expose corporate malfeasance. Studies have reported that, thanks to their concerted efforts to delegitimize science and secular institutions,[103] trust in science among Americans who identify themselves as "conservatives" and "religious" (who attend church frequently) in the U.S. has waned significantly between the 1970s and 2010s, while, among others it remained steady.[104]

A deluge of scientists and research institutions (e.g., Commerce Department and NASA) complained and accused the Bush and Trump administrations of censoring and suppressing federal research on global warming.[105] In 2006, 8,000 concerned scientists (The Union of Concerned Scientists), including 49 Nobel laureates, 63 National Medal of Science recipients and 171 members of the National Academies, submitted a letter to the Bush administration, accusing them of an unprecedented level of political intrusion into their research and academic activities.[106]

Purging of Intellectuals

Throughout history, plenty of dogmatic and ideological leaders, especially in religious and political realms, have persecuted independently-minded scientists and intellectuals—e.g., Spanish Inquisition, Nazi Germany, China under Mao's rule ("Cultural Revolution"), Soviet Union under Stalin (the "Great Purge/Terror"), Cambodia under Pol Pot, and North Korea under the Kim dynasty. Tens of millions of scholars and intellectuals were executed without due process, and millions more languished and perished in concentration and labor camps under their rules of terror. Communist revolutions set off as "class-based" populism; yet, after winning power, they turned into a "cultural" populism, "rooting out" intellectuals who criticized the communist rule and posed threats to their power.[107] After the Iranian Revolution of 1979, Ayatollah Ruhollah Khomeini fired thousands of university professors and expelled many more students. In 2006, Iran's hardline President Ahmadinejad urged purging of liberal and secular university professors from the country's universities, complaining that reforms in the country's universities were difficult to accomplish when the educational system was affected by secularism.[108] After the failed coup attempt in Turkey in 2015, Turkish president Recep Tayyip Erdoğan blamed liberal academia, and detained nearly 150,000, more than half of them educators.[109]

Hardline Approaches to Conflict Resolution

Group-bound extremists tend to take hardline approaches to confrontational situations, either to defend the honor of the group or to avoid "appearing weak." Groups, like individuals, must *appear* mighty and formidable to defend their honor and to scare-off potential enemy groups. They fear that other groups will try to take advantage of them and mistreat them if they appear "weak." They fight "fire with fire" and "guns with guns"; they respond to violence with violence, and threat with threat, preferably with greater vehemence than their enemies have inflicted upon them. Anything less means an affront to their group's honor and pride, and will be taken as a sign of weakness by the enemies that can invite more incursions.

Refusing to Negotiate, Compromise and Apologize

In conflict resolution situations, extremists seek to maximize gains without giving up anything—i.e., they pursue "win-win" deals, not "give-and-take." They use whatever leverage they can exploit to maximize their group-centric benefits. For instance, they take human hostages and use them as bargaining chips in political or economic negotiations. They make hyperbolic threats and demand "take-it-or-leave-it" ultimatums, instead of negotiating compromises with mutually-sacrificing concessions.[110] They refuse to compromise because they have a dire existential need to be "winners and victors," not "losers and failures." Every deal or sparring confrontation is a dire "win or die" situation in their hostile "zero-sum" world view. They must always "win" in every confrontational situation, whether their end goal is to survive, protect group honor and pride, or to maximize group-centric interests. For this reason, people who are most easily mobilized in extremist campaigns and movements tend to be the most willing to fight and least willing to make concessions for negotiated peace.[111] Without willingness to negotiate compromises and reconcile differences, all intergroup contentions and disputes escalate, not de-escalate, and result in violent conflicts.

Such hardline extremism subsists in American politics, also. "Freedom Caucus" is a small group of (around 30) tightly-knit, ultra-conservative, "my-way-or-no-way," "hell-no," hardline extremists within the Republican Party that is known to take "no compromise" positions on all issues they oppose or are proposed by opposition party members. Republican Representative Rob Poe, who left the group in 2017, said that the Freedom Caucus "would vote no against the Ten Commandments if it is up for a vote."[112] The National Rifle Association (NRA) refuses to make any concessions or compromises in gun-control legislation discussions because they fear such concessions may open doors to a flood of anti-gun legislation, eventually leading to a total ban on guns (fear of a "slippery-slope" effect).[113]

Hardline, no-compromise stances in wars often lead to tragic consequences of massive destruction, loss of life, and human suffering. After the U.S.-led invasion of Iraq in 2003, the Bush administration, instead of negotiating peace with Saddam's supporters and forming an inclusive Iraq, sought to "root out" all Saddam's Baath Party officials and disband the Iraqi military, against U.S. military generals' advice. Such totally exclusive extremist measures alienated millions of former Iraqi civil servants, teachers and soldiers, mostly Sunnis, who joined al-Qaeda–linked insurgency groups that eventually thwarted U.S. efforts to rebuild Iraq, resulting in violent conflicts for several years with heavy U.S. casualties.[114] Within a few months after the U.S. invaded Afghanistan in 2001, the Taliban, facing defeat, proposed a peace deal with surrender. Afghan officials considered accepting the surrender deal from Taliban leaders, but Defense Secretary Donald Rumsfeld quickly knocked that down, and sought complete destruction of the Taliban with swift justice for Taliban leaders like Mullah Omar. In the meantime, the Taliban regained power and launched serious raids while the U.S. was busy fighting in Iraq. In 2019, after 18 years of fighting with over 2,300 American deaths and over 20,000 injured, U.S.-led efforts to rebuild Afghanistan failed; any progress made in Afghanistan was all but lost, and a U.S.-initiated peace deal was rejected by the Taliban that is regaining power in Afghanistan.[115]

Never Apologize for Mistakes and Wrongdoings

Extremists value "being tough" and "appearing strong," which includes acts of not "backing down" from their initial positions, never giving in or giving up their causes, and never admitting wrongdoings or apologizing for their mistakes. Mitt Romney, 2012 Republican presidential candidate, and Marco Rubio, 2016 candidate, excoriated President Obama for "apologizing" to other nations for what America did in the past (e.g., prisoner abuse and other mistakes during Iraq War). Romney wrote a book titled *No Apology: The Case for American Greatness* (2010), in which he argues that the case for America's greatness rests on "never apologizing." President Trump in 2018, in his speech to graduating Naval Academy cadets, also criticized President Obama and said, "We are not going to apologize for America. We are going to stand up for America. No more apologies."[116]

Militaristic Jingoism and Attachment to Weapons

Extremists value military might, and take refuge in military prowess and stockpiles of deadly weapons. They believe that a group's security can be achieved primarily through military might, which signifies the group's pride and strength, and gives them sense of ontological security. In confrontational situations, extremists are quick to fall back on military forces and weapons, instead of diplomacy and negotiations, because they believe in "achieving peace through dominance"—i.e., by "crushing, eliminating, and annihilating" enemies, not coexisting in harmony.

Military prowess with deadly weapons has always been an obsession with extremist leaders seeking autocratic personal power and hegemonic group power. Most militia groups, such as the Christian Identity Group, stockpile weapons and ammunition in their communal compounds. Some mandate that their followers own and be ready to use the most advanced weapons available, such as M-16 assault rifles, to arm themselves against

4. Extremist Strategies Designed to Enhance Group Power 169

governmental invasion.[117] Way and Peeks' study[118] corroborated that political leaders of highly centralized and "personalistic" dictatorships are substantially more likely to pursue the building of military power, especially nuclear weapons, than democratic types. In 2014, India's Prime Minister Narendra Modi announced that he would augment multinational defense industries operating in India by 100 percent, although India is already one of the world's largest importers of weapons (over $30 billion in 2013).[119] His decision was met with heavy criticism because about half of Indians still do not have electricity, running water, and access to toilets. Every day, women have to risk their safety and life (through the risk of being raped or killed) while performing the simplest bodily functions. Open defecation also contaminates food and water, and transmits diarrhea-related diseases that kill 200,000 Indian children every year.[120] The U.S. has the most aircraft carriers (13 as of 2015), while Russia has only two and China has one, a used one they bought from Russia and refurbished in 2011.[121] Yet, President Trump, a month after taking office, authorized a national defense authorization bill of $716 billion, the largest in history, a 10 percent increase from the previous year, mostly for upgrading weapons, especially the F-35 fighter jets, compared to President Obama who slashed it by 11 percent.[122] At the same time, Trump drastically cut funding for foreign aid and non-military domestic programs, especially for the EPA, labor, arts, public broadcasting, education, and health- and science-related research.[123] Both President Trump and President Putin of Russia precipitated weapons production and air defense systems violating and threatening to withdraw from the Nuclear Arms Treaty agreed upon after the Cold War to curtail weapons production.[124]

Importance of Out-Frightening Enemies

Extremists try to intimidate potential enemies with incendiary bravado and stockpiles of deadly weapons to send a message—"don't mess with us." They amass arsenals of weapons and show them off to scare potential enemies and hopefully fend them off. The 2012 Republican Party presidential candidate Mitt Romney's position on defense and military was, "America must preserve a military that is so strong that no nation would ever dare to test it."[125] Donald Trump, as a presidential candidate, said, "We're going to make our military so big, so strong, so great, and so powerful that we're never going to have to use it" because no one will "mess with us."[126] On the eve of the U.S.-led invasion of Iraq, Secretary of Defense Donald Rumsfeld said that the campaign was intended to instill "shock and awe" among Iraqis, bombing hundreds of targets in Iraq at once.[127] Extremists' constant struggle to out-fear, out-bully, and out-power their enemies often leads to ever-escalating stockpiles of weaponry and hostilities on both sides. In the 1960s, during the peak of the Cold War, with mounting fear and suspicion of each other, the U.S. and U.S.S.R. stockpiled nuclear weapons in competition. At its peak, U.S. had over 30,000 nuclear warheads that could destroy the whole world several times, and the Soviet Union had even more.[128]

Purposeful Use of Brutality to Out-Frighten Enemies

Some extremists go beyond "show of force," and try to boast of their fearlessness by being excessively brutal, atrocious, and destructive. In their effort to out-frighten their enemies, they commit "atrocities in competition," amplifying fear and terror. Rebel groups in northeastern Congo, according to a 2003 U.N. report, use systematic lootings, killings, massive gang rapes of women and girls, and cannibalism as "premeditated tools of war" used to *terrorize* the population.[129] ISIS/Daesh split from al-Qaeda because al-Qaeda was not "brutal enough," and its members captured and decapitated members of more moderate al-Qaeda-linked groups, such as al-Nusra Front and Army of Islam in Syria.[130] To maximize the "fear effect," they publicize their ostentatiously brazen acts of brutality in social media platforms for the whole world to see. In 2015, ISIS/Daesh released their videos of atrocities online which displayed their militants murdering people by drowning them in a cage, decapitating them, stoning them to death, throwing them from buildings, and burning a captured Jordanian pilot alive. Videos of the killings, even by young boys, are their propaganda tool used to "shock and terrify" their enemies.[131] In 2013, Abu Sakkar, Syria's rebel leader, cannibalized a Syrian soldier's heart and posted his act on their propaganda video. During an interview, he said, "I did not want to do it, but I had to do it to terrify enemies." In the video, Abu Sakkar picks up a bloody handful of something and declares, "We will eat your hearts and livers of you—soldiers of Bashar the dog."[132] In Honduras, street gangs commit cruelty and brutality to out-frighten rival gangs in competition to such an extent that it reached a point of skinning women alive.[133]

Preemptive Attacks

Hardliners believe that the best defense is always offense—e.g., they must strike enemies *before* enemies can assail their group. By scaring the enemies preemptively, they believe they can circumvent costly confrontations and humiliating assaults. The Israeli government attacks Palestinians based on this rationale—they must go into Gaza and destroy their weapons and tunnels *before* they can strike Israel. Saddam Hussein of Iraq, in 1980, invaded Iran preemptively because he believed Iran's revolutionary leader

Ayatollah Khomeini was a threat to his regime, and might attack Iraq.[134] President Bush's decision to invade Iraq derived from the same doctrine of "preemptive strike"—i.e., the U.S. must strike Iraq *before* Iraq can attack the U.S. with weapons of mass destruction. His policy of massive detention of terror suspects after the 9/11 attacks was also to fend off possible future bouts against America.[135]

Collective Punishments

In group-bound extremist cultures, when "one-of-us" is wronged by "one-of-them," "all-of-us" become responsible for revenge attacks on "all-of-them," because they become guilty by association. When a fellow troop is killed by an enemy soldier, for instance, it justifies killings of anyone *associated with* the enemy group, including civilians, women, and children. When the U.S. kills Pakistanis by drone strikes, Pakistanis turn around and kill anyone who is Western in return, including international charity and United Nations aid workers and health care providers.[136] During the Israeli-Hamas conflict in 2014, anti–Semitic violence committed by Muslims spiked in France and Germany. They assaulted Jews and attacked Jewish synagogues, especially, although Jews in Europe had nothing to do with Israeli aggression.[137] In 1988, Saddam Hussein of Iraq ordered mustard gas attacks on the Kurdish town of Halabja that instantly killed over 5,000 mainly women and children, and massacred over 12,000 survivors, mostly civilians. It was a revenge attack against the whole Kurdish population in Iraq for a few violent insurgency attacks committed by a few Kurdish militia groups.[138] When a few Muslim Americans committed mass murders (e.g., in San Bernardino, California, in 2015), some people supported banning of all Muslims from entering America, as President Trump tried with his executive order in 2017.

Terrorist attacks are a form of collective punishment extremists justify based on the this rationale—i.e., when a nation's policy violates or offends another group's members, the whole nation, or anyone who belongs to the nation, including innocent civilians and children, becomes legitimate targets for revenge strikes because they all become "guilty by association." In 1998, Osama bin Laden declared that "killing Americans and their allies, civilians and military, is an individual duty for every Muslim."[139] America's rationale for waging wars in Iraq and Afghanistan in response to the 9/11 terrorist attacks was also based on collective punishment. When a few Islamist groups commit terrorist attacks against Americans, all Islamist groups become "guilty by association," and become targets of retaliatory attacks, including nations that harbor terrorist groups.

The goal of collective punishment is to maximize terrorizing effects, hoping to deter future occurrences of assaults. After winning a war, extremist leaders try to "root-out" every vestige of their enemies, and everyone who may be remotely "associated with" the enemy, rather than trying to reconcile and reintegrate them. The Bush administration spearheaded policies of "de-Baathification" and disbanding of the 400,000-men Iraqi military after the U.S.-led invasion of Iraq in 2003, despite opposition from U.S. military leaders. The goal was to remove and punish *everyone* who was "associated" with Saddam Hussein and his Baath Party, which included most public officials, career soldiers, police, and school teachers. These policies produced a large number of disaffected, marginalized, and disgruntled Sunnis who joined al-Qaeda insurgent groups in Iraq, which later became ISIS/Daesh.[140]

Punishing Family Members of the Offenders

Punishing family members of offenders, which used to be commonplace in traditional societies of the past, is also a form of collective punishment extremist groups continue to employ. In some traditional societies of the past, it was customary to kill "three generations" or "nine-family-relatives" of traitors, defectors, and enemies to eliminate even the most remote possibility of revenge attacks by their descendants and relatives (called "nine-kinship extermination" policy in China; "three-generation extermination" in Korea). Even in the contemporary world, vestiges of collective punishment linger, especially in extremist groups. According to Pakistan's Frontier Crimes Regulation (FCR) policy (called FATA laws): "When a member of a tribe commits a crime, the whole tribe members are responsible for the acts committed by the person: their houses are demolished, they are arrested and fines are imposed on the whole tribe."[141] In 2014, in a small village in Jharkhand state's Bokaro district in India, a man raped his neighbor's wife, and the victim's family was permitted to gang-rape the offender's 14-year-old sister in retaliation.[142] In various parts of Africa, when a person commits a crime, mobs go after his family members to avenge the victim.[143] Israel maintains a long-standing policy of demolishing the homes of Palestinians when terrorists assault Israeli citizens, despite international condemnation.[144] In 2018, Saudi Arabian officials arrested family members and friends of a political refugee in Canada who fled to Canada and made videos denouncing Saudi Arabia.[145] Donald Trump, as a presidential candidate, said that he would "kill the families of terrorists" in order to win the fight against terrorist groups.[146]

Typically, extremist groups, like the Taliban, try to maximize the killing effect by targeting weddings and funerals, when all the family members are gathered.[147] In July of 2019, at least 65 people were killed following an attack by Boko Haram on a funeral gathering in northeastern Nigeria, according to local officials, and many more were injured.[148] In August of 2019, ISIS/Daesh claimed responsibility for a suicide bombing at a crowded wedding party in the Afghan capital of Kabul that killed 63 and injured 182, including women and children.[149]

State-Sponsored Collective Punishments

Collective punishment was a common, state-sponsored policy in the pre-modern era. Even in modern times, states occasionally carry out collective punishment explicitly or covertly under extraordinary circumstances. For instance, after the Pearl Harbor onslaughts by the Japanese, Franklin D. Roosevelt ordered the internment of all Japanese-American citizens, with the approval of Congress and the Supreme Court, even though the majority of them were U.S. citizens, born in the U.S., and had nothing to do with the Pearl Harbor attacks.[150] America's atomic bomb attacks on Japan's Hiroshima and Nagasaki in 1945 were also a form of collective punishment—they killed over 200,000 Japanese, mostly civilians, on the first day of bombing alone.[151] We can also reason that initiating the Afghan war and invasion of Iraq in response to the 9/11 terrorist attacks were a form of collective punishment—i.e., punishing the Taliban for harboring al-Qaeda and Iraq for attempting to develop weapons of mass destruction, although they were not directly associated with the 9/11 attacks.

After ISIS/Daesh was driven out of Iraq in 2017, the Iraqi military executed anyone suspected of collaborating with ISIS/Daesh, many of whom were foreigners, relatives, bystanders, and functionaries (e.g., cooks, medical doctors), as well as the wives of the fighters, without any investigation or due process. It is estimated between 13,000 and 20,000 civilians have been detained on suspicion of ties to ISIS/Daesh since 2017, and 2,900 trials performed with a 98 percent conviction rate, with the death penalty. In April of 2018, they convicted and sentenced 14 women to death within two days, after military trials that lasted only about ten minutes for each woman.[152] In 2017, when about 40 Rohingya insurgents attacked and killed 12 Myanmar police, the Buddhist Myanmar military responded with a policy that amounted to "ethnic cleansing" in a reprisal for the Rohingya militants' attack on police. The massacres, rapes, and the wholesale burning and destruction of villages by the Myanmar military in Rakhine state forced nearly 700,000 Rohingya Muslims to flee to Bangladesh.[153]

Economic Sanctions and Embargoes

Economic sanctions and embargoes Western nations frequently impose against "rogue nations" (e.g., Iraq, Syria, North Korea, Iran,

Cuba, and Venezuela) and Israel against Palestine are a form of collective punishment. Most economic sanctions, embargos and blockades, although they are intended to punish unruly dictators and their regimes, end up hurting civilians more than the dictators.[154] For instance, because of the economic embargo imposed against Iraq for invading Kuwait in 1991, nearly everything in Iraq's infrastructure—electricity, roads, telephones, water treatment—has been affected by the shortage of equipment needed to maintain it, and much of the supplies needed for survival, such as food and medicine, have been on shortage, creating a deplorable humanitarian disaster for the civilians. According to a UNICEF official report, 25 percent of Iraqi children suffered from chronic malnutrition and diseases that were mostly eradicated in Iraq beforehand (e.g., cholera and typhoid), and child mortality rates more than doubled in consequence.[155] According to Global Policy Forum's report,[156] the sanctions caused the deaths of about 450,000 Iraqi children, many of diarrhea, because one of the prohibited items held under the "dual purpose mission" (items that can be used for military purpose as well as civilian) was chlorine that is used to treat water.

◆◆ 5 ◆◆

Typical Goals of Extremist Groups

There are as many goals extremist groups pursue as there are various types of extremist groups. Nonetheless, there seem to be a few generalizable and overlapping commonalities in goals that spur groups of people to act in extremist ways, irrespective of culture, nationality, religion, civilization, race, ethnicity, and ideology. Not every extremist group is driven by all of the goals included in this chapter. However, every extremist group seems to be motivated by at least one of the goals discussed in this chapter.

Most extremist groups grow out of or transmute from ordinary groups, movements and activism. Some of the goals of extremist groups are, therefore, analogous to those of the ordinary group movements. What distinguishes extremist groups from ordinary groups is their adaptation of extremist ideologies and strategies that manifests members' extremist mindsets, in their relentless pursuit of achieving group-centric goals, impinging upon the welfare and interests of other group members. In this chapter, I discuss some of the archetypical goals extremist groups pursue using extremist strategies.

Group Empowerment for Dominance or Resistance

The ultimate goal of all extremist groups is seeking group empowerment, whether the goal is to dominate others and limited resources, to resist domination by other groups, to promote change, to resist change, or to advance their social and political agendas. Throughout history, an array of tribes, gangs, militias, rebel and revolutionary groups, ethnic and racial groups, religious groups, political parties, interest groups, nation-states, and other ideological groups have collided and combated in pursuance of greater power and dominance using extremist means. The dominant group members try to secure or expand their superior power, status, privilege, and access to resources, and the oppressed and powerless group members strive to empower themselves to resist domination and achieve equal status and power in the society. Powerful groups, whether they are nations or corporations, bully the powerless ones (e.g., chauvinistic nationalism and "corporate bullying") for the same reasons and goals as a group of teenagers bully and gangs fight—i.e., for greater power, dominance, financial gains, and ascendency in statuses. For the powerless groups, on the other hand, the only way they can demand equal status and rights is to fight against the dominant groups that do not want to give up their superior status and share power and resources (e.g., rebel groups, resistance movements, independence movements, feminist, civil rights, and gay rights movements).

Dominant Extremist Groups

Dominant groups become extremists prodded by their desire to preserve the status quo from which they benefit, or to expand their power and privilege by taking advantage of other groups. Dominant groups react with extremist measures when their privileged status is challenged and threatened by resistance groups requesting equality. In order to preserve their dominant status, they band together and systematically obstruct subordinate groups from rising up or challenging their superior status. Throughout history, men strived to preserve patriarchal systems and systematically subjugated women using extremist strategies. They created sexist ideologies to justify domination of women, which they incorporated into traditions and religions, and denied women's access to equal rights by using sundry legal schemes, backed up by traditions, norms, and beliefs. Powerful nations colonized powerless nations and exploited indigenous populations and natural resources, violently suppressing their independence movements with superior military power. After the Second World War when these former colonies gained independence, these nations used their economic might to force global compliance to enjoy the economic "benefits of empire" without claiming populated territories ("domination without annexation").[1]

A plethora of dominant racial and ethnic groups around the world have systematically subjugated and discriminated against powerless minority groups using extremist ideologies and strategies, treating them as second-class citizens, if not virtual slaves. Monarchs and aristocrats fought hard to quell democratizing demands for centuries to maintain their dominant status and privileges, as did upper-caste members who ruled over lower-caste members. Countless right-wing, anti-immigrant, nativist groups have tried to protect their "superiority in identity" by limiting non-native people's access to equal rights and benefits. Dominant extremism also includes abusive acts committed by people of authority against those without, such as the police's use of excessive force over criminal suspects and protesters; similar acts by prison guards over inmates and detainees; employers exploiting employees; and acts of bullying and hazing by upperclassmen over underclassmen.

Maximizing Group-Centric Interests

One of the most common goals of dominant extremisms is *maximizing* one group's collective interests by taking advantage of other groups of people—e.g., patriarchy, slavery, aristocracy, colonialism, exploitation of laborers, corporate monopoly—instead of sharing benefits. Historically, the wealthy and the privileged have always banded together to protect and expand their wealth and power by forming "status group ties" (M. Weber's term) or "profit-sharing" alliances—e.g., "pay-for-play" and "quid-pro-quo" exchange of favors between politicians and corporate elites, called "crony capitalism." Industry-friendly business elites and interest groups, united by collectively-shared economic interests, develop a sense of "consciousness of kind," and try to advance policies and agendas they benefit from by collectively peddling influence in Congress (e.g., ALEC, American Crossroads, and Progressive States Network).[2] Burris[3] and Mizruchi[4] exposed how the powerful and tight-knit social networks among corporate elites, working as "interlocking directorates" (those who serve numerous boards of large corporations), facilitated political cohesion within the business community and peddled influence in politics toward their collective economic interests. In a modern globalizing economy, economic and corporate elites' effort to expand their power and wealth is globalizing also. Multinational business elites form an "interlocking networks of TCC" (transnational capitalist class) of plutocrats, and collaboratively wield their power globally, bound only by their business interest and corporate profits, ignoring national loyalties or humanity's concerns.[5]

Corporate Extremisms

Countless corporations engage in ruthless competition to get ahead of others and dominate the market by crushing competitors. Some corporations engage in illicit or illegal acts to maximize profit, such as bribery, corruption, market manipulation, illegal campaign contributions, illegal dumping of toxic wastes, and misrepresentation of financial statements ("cooking the books"). Others abuse their employees using various tactics, such as underpaying, unequal pay, denying benefits, forced overtime work, unsafe working environments, unjustified termination, anti-competition clauses, prohibiting formation of labor unions, abuse of non-disclosure agreements, illegally retaliating against whistle-blowers, and covering up their wrongdoings. They use "mandatory arbitration" clauses to circumvent legal liabilities and lawsuits from employees and get away with their mistreatment of employees. Globalized giant oil industries (e.g., Shell, BP, Exxon, Chevron) and mining industries (e.g., Vale, BHP) have wrecked natural environments and animal habitats and caused an assortment of man-made disasters (chemical and oil spills, explosions, dam failures, air and water pollution, etc.) in less developed nations endangering indigenous people's lives, and gotten away with their wrongdoings by bribing corrupt political leaders of those nations.[6]

Drug Companies: While lawmakers turned a blind eye to corporate wrongdoing as a payback for campaign contributions, drug companies used an array of scams to scare patients into taking drugs with marginal benefits and conjured up new ailments and treatments, which they claimed required pricey drugs to "cure." They funded scientific research or did their own research to claim effectiveness of the drugs they developed, and paid bribes to bury negative studies. They used manifold gimmicks to bypass patent laws (e.g., "evergreening") and forestalled generic drug productions for as long as possible, raising the cost of drugs for consumers without any governmental oversight.[7] The HIV prevention pill Truvada (or PrEP), for instance, is sold for $1,780 per month in the U.S., whereas in the rest of the world, it is sold for $5 per month. Gilead Sciences, which is the only company that sells Truvada, patented the drug, although the research to produce the drug was funded by taxpayers, and also stymied the production of generic versions of it that could significantly lower the price.[8] Drug companies continued to produce opioid-based painkillers that were more addictive and powerful than existing drugs, and aggressively marketed them by paying off lawmakers, doctors, and distributors, as more than 60,000 Americans a year died from overdose, a 266 percent increase between 1999 and 2016. As a result of their unscrupulous activities, Americans consume a staggering 80 percent of all opioids the world produces, although just 4.4 percent of the world's population is American.[9] All of these activities occurred not only with the blessing of, but also in collaboration with lawmakers who received generous contributions from drug companies, only to pass laws that made it virtually impossible to curb illegal distribution of opioid-related painkillers, such as the Marino Bill. In 2017 alone, drug companies gave $60 million to lawmakers.[10] As a result of the widespread malfeasance by the drug companies collaborating with lawmakers, Americans spend 2 to 3 times more on average for the same drugs compared to most other industrialized nations.[11] The total cost of prescription drugs Americans consume rose to $330 billion, 10 percent of total health care cost in 2016, from just $12 billion that is 5 percent of total health care cost in 1980, according to a report by the Peterson Center on Healthcare.[12]

5. Typical Goals of Extremist Groups 179

Tobacco Industries: It took over 40 years to convince Americans to believe in the harmful and addictive effects of tobacco smoking, because tobacco industries evaded the regulatory powers of the FDA by aggressively lobbying lawmakers. Even in recent decades, they were able to surreptitiously raise the nicotine content of their products without FDA scrutiny, making their products more addictive. As a result, millions more people became addicted to nicotine, and about 400,000 people a year died in the U.S. for several decades as a consequence, according to the Centers for Disease Control and Prevention.[13] In recent years, as tobacco sales dwindled in the U.S., industries started to produce e-cigarettes for vaping, arguing without proof that it was a "safer" alternative to smoking, and aggressively marketed them to teenagers, knowing that their products were highly addictive and harmful to people's health, especially when people started using them at an earlier age.[14] Teen vaping of e-cigarettes has become an epidemic that affects 3.6 million underage teenagers, outpacing cigarettes, alcohol, marijuana, and other substances, baffling doctors as to how to treat them. Since debuting in the U.S. in 2007, e-cigarettes and other vaping devices have grown into a $6.6 billion business.[15]

Environmental Destruction: When the government fails to oversee and regulate industries, all of humanity can suffer immensely from environmental pollution, as can animals from destruction of wildlife habitats, because the primary goal of profit-motivated businesses is maximizing short-term profits, even if it involves harming the public.[16] Fossil fuel industries have been successful in delegitimizing scientific data supporting global warming for decades, bribing lawmakers to continue to support their industry-friendly agendas, and thwarting development of renewable energy sources that are necessary to slow global warming.[17] Agricultural pest control industries continue to produce toxic chemicals as a pervasive part of the agricultural landscape, ignoring harm-reduction technologies, distorting and refuting scientific databases and research, and vigorously fighting against environmental concerns by bribing lawmakers.[18]

War Profiteering: Weapons industries profit from violent conflicts. The 9/11 terrorist attacks have been particularly profitable for the weapons and defense industries. The U.S. alone has spent over $2.8 trillion on the fight against terrorism since the 9/11 attacks in 2001 (until 2018), according to a study by the Stimson Center think tank, including spending on the wars in Afghanistan, Iraq, and Syria,[19] largely for the benefit of U.S. weapons industries (e.g., Boeing, Lockheed Martin, General Dynamics, Northrop Grumman, BAE Systems, DynCorp International, Raytheon, General Electric) and other privatized military and defense support industries (e.g., Blackwater, Halliburton, KBR), which are generous donors to policy makers and lawmakers.[20] Even after the war, advanced nations continue to supply high-tech weapons to conflict-prone areas around the world for the benefit of their weapons industries, knowing that they are being used to kill civilians in civil wars. Most recently in Yemen, the Saudi-UAE coalition forces launched over 19,000 airstrikes between 2015 and 2018, and one third of these have struck non-military targets—homes, hospitals, schools, markets, and mosques—and killed more than 50,000 Yemeni civilians, according to the United Nations' estimates. In 2019, a panel of UN experts pointed the blame not only at Saudi Arabia and the UAE, but also at the parties supplying the coalition with weapons—the U.S., U.K., and French and German companies. It said, they are "complicit in war crimes in Yemen" by supplying weapons to multiple parties involved in the civil war. Their supply of weapons "perpetuated the conflict and prolonged the suffering of the Yemeni people" causing an "immense and wide-ranging humanitarian crisis."[21]

These are just a few examples of dominant extremisms perpetrated by corporate entities that try to maximize their special interests by causing immense harm, pain, and suffering to innocent people around the world. If such corporate malfeasance continues to fester for a long period of time, people lose trust in their economic system, and try to protest against economic injustice (e.g., communist, anti-war, environmental protection, labor union, and other economic justice movements, such as the "Occupy Wall Street" movement in the U.S. and "Yellow Jacket" movement in France). Of course, not all protesters and resistance movements are extremists. However, they can always turn into violent resistant extremist movements if the extremely unfair and unjust social, economic, and political acts persist with impunity, augmenting the wealth and privileges of a few already wealthy and privileged exclusive groups of people who continue to control and manipulate the system to advance their self-interests through corporate special interests at the expense of the rest of the society and humanity.

Resistant Extremist Groups

Moon[22] argued that collective identities ("collective selfhood") often emanate or strengthen out of "systematic stigmatization and structural disadvantage" a group of people experience together, as a way of making sense of their situation, or in an effort to change the social conditions of stigmatization and disadvantage. Although not all subordinate or oppressed groups of people seeking equal rights and access to power resort to extremist means, they are more likely to do so when their access to legitimate means of achieving desired outcomes is systematically blocked or nonexistent.

Most resistance movements are activated by a shared sense of grievances and indignation, either by the victims of oppression or by their sympathizers—e.g., over history of mistreatment, humiliation, persecution, prejudice, discrimination, alienation, rejection, exclusion, exploitation, and injustice. Radicalized revolutionary movements, independence movements by occupied natives, leftist insurgency and rebel groups, labor unions, anti-establishment populist movements (of left and right), and equal rights movements by discriminated minority groups are some of the examples that had been violent in the past (e.g., feminist, women's suffrage, Black Power, Black Panther, Civil Rights movements, anti-Apartheid movements, Irish Republican Army, Palestinian revolts against Israeli occupation). When the state becomes ineffective in enforcing the rule of law, or becomes a collaborator colluding with the oppressors and wrongdoers, victimized private citizens target the offenders directly in lieu of the state authorities by forming social movements, activisms, and protests, which can turn violent at times.[23]

Hierarchical Positioning

Hechter[24] argues that all group-based struggles for dominance and resistance are a part of the "hierarchical positioning" effort—i.e., a group of people trying to position themselves above other groups by degrading other groups in the social hierarchy structure (comparable to "status competition theory"). It is a deliberate and collaborative effort to establish or solidify a group-based "pecking order" of social positions using arbitrarily constructed identities, such as in caste systems, monarchism, slavery, patriarchy, and assertions of racial and ethnic superiority. Such "hierarchical positioning" efforts often involve extremist measures of coercion and violence when subjugated groups resist subordination.[25] In such cases, contentious groups become a *mechanism* through which categories and identities provide grounds for generating and structuring inequality of positions and rewards.[26]

At times, the "positioning" strategy can be explicit and legal (e.g., caste system, slavery, apartheid), and in other situations, it is implicit—e.g., using elaborate cultural norms and etiquettes that can establish and justify "inferior" statuses imposed upon the powerless groups by the dominant groups. For instance, Blumer[27] argued that racial/ethnic prejudice is a concerted effort to establish hierarchical social standing among diverse racial/ethnic groups. By defining and constructing racial/ethnic identities, images, stereotypes, and social norms and etiquettes that govern intergroup relations, people can assign superior status to one group and inferior status to other groups. Prejudice, therefore, does not necessarily connote individual feelings or personality defects, but a collective and collaborative *process* of establishing group-based hierarchical social standings for political purposes and economic gains.[28]

Numerous groups of people have tried to forge a "superior status" by claiming their "specialness," "authenticity," "purity," "orthodoxy," "exceptionality," "royal blood," and "chosen people" concepts. Monarchism, caste system, slavery, white supremacy, colonialism, sexism, and Nazism embody such efforts that are carefully engineered and efficaciously legitimated and justified by self-serving ideologies, and reinforced by negative stereotypes. By claiming to be "born-again Christians," some Christians try to elevate their status above "regular" or "ordinary Christians" whom they judge to be "lukewarm" or "half-hearted" believers. Scores of religious and sectarian groups have split from mainline groups by claiming that their beliefs are "purer," "more orthodox," or "more authentic" than others, and their interpretation of scripture to be superior or the "only truth," which makes others to be "inferior," "untrue," "impure" or "inauthentic." By calling themselves the "value voters" (by taking an anti-abortion and anti-gay standing), social and religious conservatives during the 2004 presidential election implied that their moral values were "superior" to and more "righteous" than others who did not share the same position on abortion and homosexuality.

Most gang fights, both internal and external, are carried out for the same goal—jockeying and jostling for power and dominance in an effort to move up in the implicit hierarchy of social standing. Papachristos[29] documented that Chicago gang murders occur through an "epidemic-like process of social contagion" as competing gangs vie for positions of dominance—i.e., "who kills whom" determines hierarchical order and status within the institutionalized social networks of gang conflicts. The 2015 "bikers' brawl" in Waco, Texas, which left nine people dead and 18 others injured, exemplifies the group-based power struggle among competing biker gangs. The incident highlighted the ongoing dispute between the Bandidos, the most commanding biker gang in Texas, and the Cossacks, a club that recently had begun vying for greater power in competition. "It's all about power, status, and honor," says James Quinn, a biker gang expert.[30] Teenage bullying, like gang fights, mirrors the same "hierarchical positioning" process in their own "status achievement struggle." They try to elevate their standing in the social hierarchy (e.g., popularity, respect) through displays of "social prowess" and physical aggression.[31] For this reason, teens' bullying behaviors, like gang violence, are mostly a group phenomenon that occurs within the peer context,[32] urged and cheered by a group of bystanders.[33]

Redemption

Redemptive extremist groups can evolve out of assorted motives, such as religious, ideological, political, or issue-oriented. Members commit extremist acts driven by "moralistic" aspirations of "saving the world" from whatever source they perceive to be evil or unjust, even when they are not directly affected by the "evilness" and injustice. The sources of the evil can be diverse, such as abortion, homosexuality, war, nuclear weapons, animal abuse, environmental damage, the West, "evil empires," capitalism, communism, fascism, police, "big banks," the government, and corrupt corporations. In such groups, participants commit extremist acts to "transcend reality" as much as to transform it, with a "moralistic" sense of mission and the duty of "saving the world."[34] Such groups can transition to extremism when members begin to justify their extremist/terrorist acts as a necessary means of "saving the world," which they perceive to be a sacred and moral duty, and perceive committing violent acts to achieve redemption as a path to individual salvation. Achieving their "moralistic causes" outstrips their personal security, comfort, even life, and their goal of redemption justifies their extremist acts, irrespective of law, justice, and human rights.

Members of Aum Shinrikyo, Japan's doomsday terrorist cult, motivated by their urgent mission of "controlling Japan in the name of salvation," committed sarin nerve gas attacks in the subway, killing 13 and injuring thousands.[35] Some of the right-wing extremist movements also share redemptive aspirations as they define them—e.g., "saving America" from a basket of "undesirable" segments of the society, such as ethnic minorities, immigrants, homosexuals, and communists.[36]

Seeking Redemption on Behalf of Victims

Not everyone who seeks redemption through extremism is the actual victim of injustice or "evilness." Many are driven by the desire to "save" others who are being persecuted unjustly. The majority of the radical leftist movement members in the 1960s and 1970s had been children of the upper middle-class with above-average education, who did not suffer from poverty, injustice, or the "evils of capitalism." Yet, they joined groups (e.g., the Weathermen) with a visionary mission of "making the world a better place" free of capitalist expropriators. Many terrorists have claimed that they commit violent acts to "make the world a better place," as they define it, although over time terrorism becomes a career as much as an idealistic passion.[37] Countless young Muslims joined jihadist groups and committed violent acts urged by their "moralistic" desire to "save" "people-of-their-own" who were being persecuted, or to avenge those who persecuted them on behalf of the victims of persecution. When Syria's Assad regime (mostly Alawites, an offshoot of Shiite Islam) brutally persecuted Sunnis during the civil war that started in 2011, Sunnis around the world were vicariously aggrieved, and some of them traveled afar to join Sunni rebel groups and ISIS/Daesh to defend Sunnis in Syria.[38] A number of Muslim Europeans and Americans committed terrorist acts out of their overwhelming outrage over (what they perceived to be) "unjust" Western foreign policies and military actions responsible for killing many of their fellow Muslims or Sunnis around the world. Europe endured multiple terrorist attacks committed by "homegrown" jihadi terrorists protesting against Western aggression targeting their "fellow" Muslims around the world—e.g., 2005 London bombings, 2015 "Paris Massacre," 2016 Brussels bombings, 2016 Bastille Day attack in Nice, France, 2016 Christmas Market attack in Berlin, and the 2017 Manchester Arena bombing in UK. There were similar jihadist attacks in the U.S., such as the San Bernardino attack in 2015, Orlando nightclub mass shooting in 2016, 2017 Lower Manhattan attack, 2013 Boston Marathon bombing, 2009 Fort Hood mass killings, and 2016 New York and New Jersey bombings. Many whites joined "Black Lives Matter" protests after the police killing of George Floyd in 2020, because they were vicariously indignant over the racial injustice in America's criminal justice system, although they were not directly affected by it.

Collective Defense

Most human collectivities are formed at least in part to achieve collective defense. Throughout history, people have formed a plethora of groups, from families to nation states, to defend themselves collectively against external sources of threat. The greater the perceived threats to people's existential security, the greater the probability that such groups will adopt extremist measures to protect themselves. Their desire to defend themselves supersedes all other moral and legal accountabilities, including respect for other people's rights, welfare, and lives. Gangs proliferate in areas with a high degree of social disorganization and disorder where people live on the margins of society with severely limited economic means and structural protection, or under constant threats to existential security,[39] such as in prisons, areas of high crime and corruption, and in places where rule of law is absent or unenforced (e.g., "failed states" or anarchic or lawless environments where law enforcement is ineffective or seriously biased).[40] In such situations, people join whichever group they believe can protect them, or band together under a contrived identity to protect each other and survive.

5. Typical Goals of Extremist Groups

Prison gangs are formed for the purpose of collective defense. The Aryan Brotherhood is a white supremacist gang that was formed inside California's San Quentin State Prison. Whites, as numeric minorities, needed to band together to protect each other from being assaulted by non-white inmates.[41] Various "Latino protection gangs" (e.g., Latin King, Trinitarios, MS-13) were formed in U.S. cities among Hispanic immigrants who tried to defend themselves and their territory against black gangs in their disorganized neighborhoods populated by disadvantaged minority groups without adequate police protection.[42] Although they are formed to defend themselves, the incessant brawls between rival gangs often exacerbate the hostile and volatile environment with escalating tension and violence that can erupt in deadly fights. Most recently, in 2019, a five-hour gang fight inside Brazil's prison between two rival gangs resulted in the death of at least 52. Many were decapitated or burned to death.[43] At times, when they face an enemy too powerful to fight against alone, gangs, even the competing ones, merge and cooperate to form a collective defense force. In 2009, Los Angeles police reported that, after nearly two decades of vicious fighting, members of the Bloods and the Crips, two rival nemeses, met amicably in restaurants, shook hands, and collaborated to fight against the mounting pressure from police. "They really are united against what they perceive to be a common enemy—the law enforcement," said Jorja Leap, a gang expert.[44]

The rise of unified pan–Arabic hostility toward the West and Israel surfaced after the creation of Israel in 1948. According to Hays,[45] Arabs had been historically a tribal people, dominated by tribal leaders, that adhered to separatist traditions and identities. The driving force toward pan–Arabic, unified ethno-nationalism in the postwar Arab world and battle against the West was not a religious one, as it had been in earlier ages, but grew out of a desperate need for collective defense under the Zionist threat. The creation of Israel and growing number of Jews in "Arab land" impelled them to unite under the pan–Arabic, ethno-nationalistic goals to defend themselves collectively.[46] When U.S.-led coalition forces invaded Iraq in 2003, tens of thousands of Sunni sympathizers from all over the Middle East (Saudi Arabia, Jordan, Yemen, and Syria) slipped into Iraq, eager to fight "Americans in Muslim country," although they had no affection for Saddam and his loyalists.[47] One of the fighters, Abu Abdullah said, "Nobody pays us to fight; we fight because America has come to kill *our* people."[48] Although not every group mobilized for collective defense becomes an extremist group, many extremist groups' primary goal has been forming a group-based collective defense force among the like-minded, like-identified, and like-believing groups of people who seek to protect their collective identity and their pride and honor. The greater their perceived threat of extinction or humiliation, therefore, the more likely they will radicalize and turn to extremist means to fight.

Reactionary Extremist Groups

Multiple traditional, socially conservative, right-wing, and religiously fundamentalist groups and movements have turned extremist in their efforts to *defend* their group's identity, tradition, distinction, and existence by resisting or fighting against changes that threaten their group's identity, whether they are modernizing, liberalizing, or secularizing trends in the society. In most reactionary extremist groups, as Calhoun[49] noted, tradition becomes an essential source and resource for radicalization. They fiercely defend their tradition-bound status-quo, whether they are religious, racial, ethnic, national, or regional in origin, because their traditions symbolize their group's identity. They fear that losing tradition will obliterate their group's distinctive identity and existence.

Most Amish, Mennonites, Native Indian communities, and religious fundamentalist groups around the world have been fierce defenders of their age-old traditions, resisting changes and fearing that their community and identity may disappear. Although not all reactionary groups are extremists, when their "fear of extinction" becomes heightened, they adopt extremist measures to defend their group's identity and tradition. This "fear of extinction" has heightened in traditional communities around the world because of the rising tide of globalization, immigration, migration, and penetration of techno-media that threatens their traditional cultures. Scholars have regarded the ascent of anti–West and anti-globalization extremisms in the Arab/Muslim world as a "reactionary backlash" against the Western hegemonic power, technology, culture, and modernization,[50] combined with aspirations of "de-secularization."[51] Their resistance movements mirror their desire for "indigenization" and "re–Islamization" of the Middle East, aggressively rejecting Western and modern influences ("undoing of modernity"), fearing "extinction" of their cultural identity.[52] Anti-West extremist group leaders capitalize on such fears and resentment to recruit fighters (e.g., Boko Haram, al-Qaeda, al-Shabaab, ISIS/Daesh, Taliban, and Muslim Brotherhood). Under the sway of such anti–West and re–Islamization movements spreading in the Arab world, some prominent political leaders have gained authoritarian power by exploiting people's fear of and resentment against the West, including Ruhollah Khomeini and Mahmoud Ahmadinejad of Iran, Mohamed Morsi of Egypt, and Turkey's Recep Tayyip Erdoğan. For instance, Turkey's Erdoğan, who is an extremely conservative political Islamist who rejects Western influence, chipped away at Turkey's democratic institutions; modified the constitution in his favor for longer term limits; revamped Turkey's court systems by removing judges and civil servants he disliked; brought the media under his control; and left Turkey in a constant state of emergency and economic chaos. Yet, the majority of Turkish people supported him for decades because they believed he can stand up against the West and defend Turkey.[53]

Pooling Resources for Collective Support and Patronage Systems

Groups build solidarity and cohesion through generalized exchange systems of reciprocity—i.e., individuals give up certain portion of their resources to obtain greater benefits from the group.[54] Groups use pooled resources to build a "collective support system" by managing and spreading individual adversities.[55] The group's ability to pool resources is directly associated with the group's power and control over its members. The more resources they can pool, the more power and control they can exert and secure members' lives. For this reason, throughout history, groups have earned people's trust by furnishing people's safety net, security blanket, and means of survival against uncontrollable, unpredictable misfortunes and crises in people's lives. By relinquishing some of their resources, people can render themselves with jointly produced goods—e.g., cooperative production of food, insurance from natural disasters, and greater access to information and mates—that they cannot obtain through individual efforts alone.[56]

Pooling resources for redistribution has been a common practice for many groups, past and present. Religious organizations collect obligatory contributions, such as tithe and zakat, and states impose taxes. With the revenue, they provide protection for the members' lifetime hardships, such as old age and illness, and social services to the unfortunate and destitute. Members will not be motivated to contribute their resources unless they believe they will gain something better or more from the group in return, whether it is security, protection, survival needs, or psychological comfort of belonging. In India, people regularly evade paying taxes because most Indians rely on their family for security and protection, not the government.[57] The Nazis, even during the war, advocated for more generous old-age pensions, greater educational opportunities for the poor, an end to child labor, and improved maternal health care to garner loyalty from the most vulnerable segments of the population.[58]

Extremist groups operate in a similar way—they need resources to maintain their operation and to keep members content and loyal to the group by providing security, safety, food and basic welfare. Except, for extremist groups, the need for pooling resources is more urgent and means are more coercive, compared to more conventional groups and organizations where resource pooling has been largely institutionalized and legitimated either by tradition or legal measures. To obtain loyalty, extremist groups operate as "charity groups"—e.g., they pool resources and redistribute them to spread risks among their members. The Islamic extremist/terrorist groups, such as al-Qaeda, Hamas, Hezbollah, and Muslim Brotherhood, offer social services to the poor, funded by Islam's obligatory alms-giving called zakat. They enter impoverished areas, build houses, and offer education the government cannot provide, often infused with ideological and religious indoctrination, and gain people's loyalty.[59] ISIS/Daesh, as soon as it occupied territories in Iraq and Syria, collected exorbitant taxes from everyone and every activity people engaged in, especially from the farmers, to fund the war and to deliver services and food rations to people. They generated much more revenue from taxation and extortion schemes than they earned from illegal selling of oil and kidnapping of Westerners.[60] If groups cannot pool resources legitimately, they extort them as "protection money" and "rackets" for "safeguarding" local residents and businesses from other rival groups, as do gangs and criminal cartels (called "protection racketeering").[61] In such cases, pooling resources becomes the group's primary goal, and they do not hesitate to use extreme measures to achieve this goal, infringing upon people's rights and security.

In-Group Patronage System

Groups thrive by successfully pooling resources, and using the resources to build a broader internal patronage system where jobs, opportunities, and favors are bestowed and exchanged within the group boundary, irrespective of merit or ability. In pre-modern traditional societies, families and tribes operated as a powerful and effective patronage system in which leaders doled out favors to their favorites and cronies within the group in return for their loyalty. Such patronage systems and politics prevailed throughout much of the world before the 19th century, at which time wealthy Western nations implemented protracted civil-service reforms that reflected merit, replacing the loyalty-based patronage systems.[62]

When members trade, exchange, and cooperate only with in-group members, it can have wide-ranging repercussions to multiple aspects of people's lives, such as opportunities for education, employment, promotion, business connections and contracts, housing, and marriages. What most Americans call the "culture of corruption" in Iraq and Afghanistan is actually a traditional patronage system, in which rulers mete out favors

5. Typical Goals of Extremist Groups

to their favorites and cronies in return for their loyalty. Whatever "foreign aid" the U.S. gave them was also distributed as rulers' "favors," which, in effect, undermined Western efforts to build democracy in those nations.[63] When U.S. troops invaded Iraq, their effort to "introduce democracy" was hampered by Iraqis' firm loyalty to their family. Iraqis describe nepotism not as a civic problem but as a "moral duty" and "virtue." "In this country, whoever is in power will bring his relatives in from the village and give them important positions," says Sheik Yousif, one of the patriarchs in charge of a powerful clan in Baghdad. "That is what Saddam did, and now those relatives are fulfilling their obligation to protect him from Americans."[64] With such patronage systems, groups gain inordinate power over individuals, commanding undivided loyalty and allegiance, because of the group's ability to dole out favors and privileges and control the livelihood of members and their families.

Even in the modern world, there are families that operate as nepotistic "tribal patronage systems" especially in Asia and the Middle East.[65] Businesses in Asia are still predominantly a family affair. From family shops and restaurants of Hong Kong and Taiwan to huge, clannish conglomerates of South Korea called "chaebol" (e.g., Samsung, Hyundai, SK, LG, Lotte), the majority of Asia's businesses and even most of the publicly-traded companies continue to be family-owned and controlled, and have been passed down for generations, shunning professional managers from outside. Family businesses commonly operate like secret cartels or "ancient tribes" influencing political power for the family, independent from outside oversight, and rife with bribery, kickbacks, racketeering, corruption, stock manipulation, illegal campaign contributions, tax evasion, and fraud.[66] Saudi Arabia's autocratic royal family is essentially a family-incorporated business empire that intermingles commercial business ventures with government affairs. Family members own and control most of not only the oil businesses, but also most of the key industries in Saudi Arabia.[67]

Politics in Africa are notoriously violent because which tribe-based party wins in elections has far-reaching consequences beyond politics, as elected officials distribute key governmental positions and resources to their own tribal members, ignoring others ("tribal patronage system").[68] Africans who live a marginal economic existence must rely on those nearest to them—the first is family, and second is tribe. African politicians know this psychology very well, and exploit it ruthlessly. "Vote for me," they say, "because I'm from your tribe and you can trust me."[69] In 2008, in Kenya, after a highly disputed election that brought about re-election of President Mwai Kibaki, a member of the Kikuyu tribe, violence erupted targeting his tribal members by the opposition party leader's tribal members, resulting in the deaths of over 1,000.[70]

Building a Self-Contained, Autonomous Entity

Some extremist groups strive to build a self-contained and self-sustained patronage system in order to achieve an autonomous political entity that is self-sufficient and self-reliant with as little outside pressure or interference as possible. With complete self-sufficiency, they believe they can strive toward achieving their group-centric goals, without having to negotiate, cooperate, or give in to others' demands for group survival. Sundry extremist groups and autocratic regimes, even in the contemporary modern world (e.g., North Korea and Cuba to a certain extent), have strived to achieve an autonomous, self-contained system with complete autonomy and independence. Militia groups also seek autonomy, rebuffing a host of societal rules that they consider to be "governmental overreach" (e.g., gun control measures, public land use restriction, governmental regulations, protection of minority rights).

Tribalism

For much of human history, before modern nation-states developed, tribal communities dominated people's lives,[71] and they still do in rural parts of Africa, Asia, and the Middle East. Tribalism remains robust in areas where the government is unable to protect and provide for the people. In such areas, tribes operate as self-contained and autonomous groups fully equipped with their own military forces determined to secure their territory, power, and group-centric interests, ignoring the laws and regulations the state imposes. In some areas, endemic revenge-killings among rival tribes are spreading thanks to easy access to and availability of high-tech weapons through illicit arms-trade and smuggling. For instance, in Yemen, about 2,000 people are killed every year as a result of tribal conflicts and the warrior culture that condones killings, abetted by the spread of modern weapons.[72] Even the nations with a burgeoning democracy like the Congo face great difficulty controlling traditional tribal chiefs and their militias with autonomous power, because people pledge their loyalty to their tribal leaders instead of the state.[73]

Religious and Ethnic Communes

Most religious cults and polygamous communes endeavor to maintain autonomy, fighting against society's rules and oversight that interfere with their beliefs and activities (e.g., laws against multiple marriages, marriage with preteen girls, illegal drug use, labor law violations, and refusing education and medical treatment of children). Even some established religious

5. Typical Goals of Extremist Groups 191

groups and isolated ethnic communes and enclaves try to maintain a self-contained economic unit built on collaborative in-group business ties and social networks within, shunning outsiders and institutions (e.g., education, employment, even legal systems in some cases),[74] and enforce intragroup marriages.[75] In so doing, groups can boost their resource pooling ability and effectively trap members within the group. When members trade, exchange, socialize, and cooperate only with in-group members, members' survival and livelihoods depend exclusively on the communal support system and commune-based economic cooperation. They become permanently trapped within the group, although they may be "free" to leave. For instance, within the tightknit, group-sufficient economic and support system Jehovah's Witnesses maintain, members become trapped inside and unable to leave the group fearing loss of their entire support system as well as friends, family, and business network.[76] Being trapped without an option of leaving the group, they have no other choice but to be loyal to the group and stay within.

Amish communities have maintained autonomy, outside of federal or state legal systems and jurisdictions. This practice allowed Amish communities to cover up rampant sexual abuses of young girls by family members, neighbors, and church leaders, which have become an "open secret spanning generations." Members are conditioned not to seek outside help, and victims of sexual assault are threatened with excommunication if they report crimes.[77] The Catholic Church has tried to maintain autonomy from state rules as much as possible. By claiming that they follow "God's rule," not man-made rules, they were able to shelter their pedophile priests from criminal prosecution for centuries.[78] During the COVID-19 pandemic in 2020, many fundamentalist churches all over the world and Jewish orthodox communities in New York and Israel disobeyed the "social distancing" orders enacted to curb spread of the virus, and continued in-person worship services, arguing that "faith will protect the congregation." Some Catholic Churches continued their "holy drink" practices by sharing spoons and drinking cups.[79]

Expansion of Territory, Membership and Influence ("Expansionism")

Most extremist groups are "expansionistic"—i.e., they aspire to recruit more members for the purpose of expanding group manpower, territory, and resources. Especially for groups whose success and power depends on the *size* of the group, their mobilization of resources and bargaining power directly correlates with their group size—i.e., "more is always better." Weber[80] calls these "open groups," because they benefit from being more open and inclusive to enlarge their membership, such as in religious organizations, political parties, labor unions, gangs, rebel groups, militia, hate-groups, and activist groups. To expand their power base, gangs, criminal cartels, hate groups, and militias actively recruit members. Most gangs start out locally, yet once they gain popularity, they try to expand membership globally, using internet and social-media networks. The motorcycle gang Bandidos that started in Texas has about 93 chapters throughout the U.S. and in 13 other countries[81]; the Mongols gang of California has more than 60 chapters globally, including branches in Sweden and Germany.[82] Nation states also engage in expansionistic mission. The Cold War was a showdown between Soviet Union–led communist expansionism for global dominance and U.S.–led capitalistic expansion of market-based hegemonic economic power, which escalated into a globalized conflict as both sides tried to expand their territory and alliances transcending differences in race, ethnicity, culture, religion, and national boundaries, using military powers and committing atrocities.

The purpose of jihad is not simply to spread the Islamic faith but to expand sovereign Muslim power, with the eventual goal of achieving Muslim dominion over the world. According to *The 9/11 Commission Report*, in the 1980s, awash in sudden oil wealth, Saudi Arabia started to spread its Sunni fundamentalist interpretation of Islam called Wahhabism throughout the world, using money collected from Islamic mandatory donations called zakat, and built mosques and religious schools. Such efforts have been effective in recruiting global adherents and expanding their power, territory, and influence around the world.[83] Their effort has contributed to the rise and empowerment of Sunni Muslims, including their extremist subgroups, transcending racial, ethnic, geographical, and national boundaries, bound only by the common sectarian identities. Christian expansionistic zeal, both Protestant and Catholic, has also been fruitful in reaching out to non–Christians around the world, transcending tribal, racial, ethnic, national, and class boundaries, through aggressive proselytizing and global missionary outreach efforts.[84]

Such expansionistic groups, whether for political or religious reasons, are prone to extremism because their expansionistic "mission" reflects their group-centric ideologies that are designed to achieve "hegemonic dominance," such as Islamism, "Christian Dominion," "Proletarian Internationalism," and "capitalistic imperialism." In the process of achieving these hegemonic goals, they readily rely on multiple extremist strategies, such as ideological indoctrination, religious proselytization, and occupation of foreign land of unassuming people, infringing upon their rights to autonomy and sovereignty.

Monopolization of Power, Resources and Rewards

As Olzak's[85] competition theory stipulates, when competition over scarce resources intensify, whether they are natural resources, financial rewards, or employment and educational opportunities, intergroup relations strain and identity-based feuds heat up, making use of extremist means more likely. Groups that seek *monopolization* of resources and power are by definition extremist groups, because pursuing monopoly means refusing to share the resources and power with others who also have rightful claims to equal shares of the resources and power. They try to maximize group-centric interests by denying or violating other people's rights and interests, even if their actions do not involve *physical* violence. Such groups become more extreme as resources become scarcer and competition becomes fiercer.

Dominant groups use extremist strategies to *maintain* their monopoly over resources, fending off any attempts and demands by the subordinate groups to share the resources. Groups with comparable power and status can also turn extremist when they seek to monopolize power, resources, and rewards through competition. Innumerable competing groups have sparred for dominance throughout history, such as families, tribes, street gangs, criminal cartels, and nation states, as well as various religious and sectarian groups (e.g., Christians vs. Muslims; Catholics vs. Protestants; Sunnis vs. Shiites; Buddhists vs. Muslims; Hindis vs. Muslims).

Many corporations and businesses compete for market monopolization, at times using extremist strategies, infringing upon the rights of their competitors and wellbeing of their consumers. In South Africa, two minibus taxi companies have been in violent competition for over a decade, a battle over taxi routes and turfs that has claimed hundreds of lives. In July of 2018, gunmen with automatic weapons killed 11 drivers and critically injured four of the rival company's as they were returning from a murdered colleague's funeral. "Large parts of the industry have begun to look very much like the Mafia, where you must defend and expand your business turf through the use of violence," says Mark Shaw, an expert on organized crime.[86] At times, competition among companies and industries can involve collision between nation states. The U.S. has engaged in a stealthy, occasionally threatening, global campaign to impede China's Huawei and other Chinese firms from participating in the most dramatic remaking of the internet plumbing that controls internet services since it sputtered into being—5G technology. Whoever controls 5G technology globally can acquire an enormous economic, intelligence, and military edge for the future. Fearing the loss of the technological hegemony it enjoyed for decades with 4G technology, the United States is trying to obstruct Huawei's infiltration in Europe and other places, applying diplomatic pressure and intimidation tactics to EU allies.[87]

Monopolization of Resources by "Closed Groups"

In contrast to "open" groups, some groups are "closed"—their goal is to elevate members' social status by monopolizing resources, and enhance group power by restricting membership and eliminating competition.[88] They try to monopolize resources and rewards by limiting others from joining their group, and obstructing outsiders from sharing the same benefits, opportunities, and privileges they relish. Various dominant groups, such as monarchs, royal families, aristocrats, high-caste members, dominant racial/ethnic groups, and autocratic regimes operate with group-centric goals of maximizing and monopolizing power, resources, and rewards within their own circles of "legitimate" members, excluding others.

Although they may not be considered extremist groups by most people, professional guilds, federations, and "status groups"[89] operate with the same goal—monopolizing resources and rewards by limiting others' access to them. Modern professional and occupational organizations, such as AMA (American Medical Association), ABA (American Bar Association), American Realtors, Plumbers, and Auto-dealers Associations, for instance, try to limit competition by instituting assorted types of credentials, such as diplomas, certificates, licenses, mandatory training and testing processes, and membership dues, to curb their membership from growing. By restricting others' access to the same occupations, they can secure higher wages and greater privileges for themselves, a strategy called "credentialism" by Collins[90] and "occupational closure" by Bol and Weeden.[91] Such "closed" groups pressure lawmakers to establish *legal* orders to limit competition to make their monopoly *legal and formal*. In such cases, the groups become "legally privileged groups," which can determine who can become "insiders" and discriminate against "outsiders" legally. In some parts of California, even pet groomers, tattoo artists, tree trimmers, and shampooers must go through extensive training, pass exams, and pay fees to get licenses, making their access to employment costlier and more arduous than functionally necessary for the jobs.[92]

Fiel[93] argued that sundry policies and informal efforts people used to sustain school segregation in the U.S. are also a "mode of monopolistic closure strategy" amid status competition, where racial and ethnic groups compete for school-based statuses and resources. A parallel argument can be made for the history-long, race-based housing segregation. Such exclusionary actions violate the rights and welfare of the people who are being excluded from their rightful access to the societal resources and rewards they deserve equally as a result of the arbitrarily crafted exclusionary "closure" schemes.

Creating Alternative Opportunities for Empowerment, Advancement and Belonging

Some extremist groups are formed to create alternative opportunities for pursuing power, success, autonomy, and achievement by those who cannot accomplish these goals through conventionally-approved or legitimate ways. When gainful employment becomes unobtainable or unsustainable, for instance, some people commit crimes to make a living. When societal systems (e.g., educational, economic, political, legal, justice) do not offer equal justice or adequate opportunities for sustainability and advancement, marginalized people with frustrated aspirations form groups of their own or join groups that can offer them *alternative* opportunities to achieve the same goals of power, success, and acceptance, such as gangs, cartels, criminal syndicates, rebel and revolutionary groups, and cults.[94] Within the group, they find alternate means of earning income and a chance to move up in the organizational hierarchy, as well as gain acceptance, a sense of belonging, camaraderie, and life meaning they could not find in conventional or legitimate groups and social milieu.

"Social Misfits"

Such "alternative" groups are particularly appealing to alienated "social misfits" who search for alternative ways of survival, acceptance, and life meaning.[95] Gangs develop in structurally deprived or disadvantaged neighborhoods without adequate access to legitimate opportunities for making a living and earning respect, as an alternative means of survival and achievement. Gangs serve as a way of fulfilling members' status-attainment goals and peer-group needs (e.g., identity, belonging, attachment) that they could not satisfy in the conventional world that is "hostile" to them.[96] Living in a marginalized neighborhood, feeling systematically obstructed from attaining legitimate opportunities and status, teens find alternative means of empowerment opportunity within the gang, although most gang members eventually recognize the internal contradictions and subsequently leave the gang as they age.[97]

Some teens join gangs because gangs can offer them protection and support their families cannot provide. Street gang Trinitarios members testified in court, "When you become a member of the Trinitarios, if you have any outstanding debts, they are paid for." "If you have any problems with any individuals or any type of conflicts, they are resolved, whether it is diplomatically or with violence." "These are the people that look out for you, and take care of you when you go to prison," they said.[98] Gangs become a source of protection, support, and attachment that their families and community cannot offer them.

Elijah Anderson's[99] study of inner-city street culture also deliberated that the prevailing "code of the street" among gangs and "street kids" is actually a "cultural adaptation mechanism" that surfaces where there is a "profound lack of faith in the police and the judicial system," called "legal cynicism."[100] A lack of accountability in police and judicial systems in disorganized neighborhoods has abetted youths to create an alternative "status system" where "tough" people who can "take care of themselves" through displaying manhood, toughness, ruthlessness, and fearlessness are accorded with deference and respect, and establish an alternative "justice system" where they can punish "violators" of their honor promptly on their own. In such an alternative social milieu with alternative norms, people respect the ability to commit violence as a "demonstration of bravery," and "status symbol."[101] Hagan et al.[102] also documented a similar scenario that unfolded in Iraq in the chaotic aftermath of the U.S.-led invasion in 2003—how "legal cynicism" played a key role in fostering Sunni insurgency and violence against U.S. forces and Shiite militias.

Some second-generation immigrants who feel rejected by the mainstream culture, or have difficulty assimilating to it, experience a form of "identity crisis"—i.e., they cannot fit into their parents' native country, nor can they assimilate to the host countries.[103] As a reactionary measure, they band together and form a group of their own, an alternative identity and culture, which can take on a form of "oppositional culture" with radicalized agendas of a rebellious nature (e.g., ethnic gangs, "homegrown terrorists"), violently rejecting and attacking their host culture and people. In their pursuit of and yearning for "belonging" and "identity," they become easy prey for transnational terrorist groups (e.g., ISIS, al-Qaeda), which use a loosely and misleadingly-redefined (or tweaked) version of "Islamism/jihadism" as an ideological cover.[104] Islamist/jihadist messages and narratives resonate forcefully with these "power-hungry powerless" youths, particularly the college educated youths without decent jobs or prospects for advancement, as well as the unfairly marginalized, discriminated, and alienated groups of people.[105] For them, "terrorist groups offer a route for advancement, an opportunity for glamour and excitement, a chance at world renown, a way of demonstrating one's courage, as well as a way of earning income."[106] For marginalized and disaffected Muslim youths in Europe, ISIS's/Daesh's message of building a caliphate or "Islamic State" was exceptionally alluring—a legitimate state where they could pursue a career and seek advancement, surrounded by the like-minded and like-believing, without being subjected to racism, discrimination, suspicion, and hatred.[107]

In the early 1900s, in small American towns with limited career opportunities for the young, belonging to the KKK (Ku Klux Klan) offered opportunities for career advancement and access to powerful political networks. The KKK was well-organized, well-structured, and expansive, from its code words to its machine-like control over City Councils and state legislatures. It was never a political party, but it wielded substantial clout in politics. Klan members or Klan-endorsed politicians held governors' offices in Oregon, Texas, and Colorado; it controlled many mayors' offices from Portland, Maine, to Portland, Oregon. It also sponsored baseball teams, county fairs, college fraternities, and beauty pageants, offering a social sense of belonging as well as opportunities for advancement.[108]

Pursuance of Autonomy

Some people form or join unconventional or alternative groups because they are dissatisfied or disagree with the existing institutions and frames of established norms. Scores of extremist groups are "off-shoot" or "splinter groups" separated from more conventional groups, formed by people who seek autonomy, "purity" in identity or ideology, and independence from the established groups, which they believe rejected them or they find to be corrupt or unorthodox. In such groups, leaders create alternate sets of norms, rejecting the conventional norms, and enjoy becoming "kings in their own world of creation," while the rank-and-file members enjoy the empowering experience of freedom and opportunities to shine and gain attention in newly-created movements and causes. Most rebel groups and revolutionary movements develop out of discontent toward the existing and established norms, systems, and institutions, and most far-right and far-left extremist and populist groups challenge established norms and systems. Such groups often turn into extremist groups, or acquire an "extremist" label because of their rebellious nature and the "unconventional" positions they take on issues.

The Freedom Caucus and Tea Party movements are such "anti-establishment" rebel groups that arose within the Republican Party in the 1990s and gained political power. They are made of around 30 ultra-conservative, pro-business, and libertarian Republican lawmakers who are vexed with the "established" or moderate Republicans who make compromises with Democrats in the legislative process. They take "hell-no," "my-way-or-no-way" type of hardline positions on all issues, obstructing the legislative process in Congress.[109]

According to Stark and Bainbridge,[110] most cults and sects are not entirely new religions, but are splinter groups that branch out from the mainline denominations and institutions, seeking autonomy and alternative ways of achieving power and recognition independent from the conventional leadership that rejected them. Marty and Appleby[111] also consider "cult formation" a "tendency to separate from fellow believers and to redefine the sacred community independent from the established mainline denominations." Their ultimate goal is gaining legitimacy as an autonomous group independent from the established religious institutions and authorities. Most Islamist extremist groups in South Asia are anti-government rebel or separatist groups seeking *regional autonomy* ruled by their own norms (e.g., Abu Sayyaf in the Philippines, Jemaah Islamiyah in Indonesia, Islamic Defenders Front in Malaysia and Indonesia, Taliban in Afghanistan, Haqqani network in Pakistan and Afghanistan) fighting against religious discrimination or secularizing policies imposed by the government.

Organizational Survival

Once a group is organized, its primary goal becomes group survival—i.e., maintaining continuation of operation by averting extinction of the group. Group survival becomes critical because, with time, the group becomes a lifeline, means of survival, and source of power for its members, especially for the leaders. The older the organization, therefore, the more imperative their survival goal becomes.[112] The survival goal becomes more imperative in extremist/terrorist groups, as they become "professional" over time with sophisticated organizational maneuvering. The initial cause of a "moral crusade" turns into an existential necessity for maintaining and perpetuating their cadres that is critical for group survival.[113] Group survival is particularly critical in groups that are labeled as "extremist" or "terrorist," because members are stigmatized as "criminals," and unable to return to conventional life. Without alternative options to fall back upon, the group becomes the only means toward career, survival, and status. Terrorism becomes a person's profession, not just a passion, whether the goal is money, political power, status, or attention.[114]

For this reason, extremist groups strive to secure their organizational survival, often resorting to extremist measures, whether they are dictatorial regimes, revolutionary and rebel groups, cults, gangs, or criminal cartels. Most autocratic regimes' ultimate goal is also organizational survival. To secure their survival, they commit atrocities, violence, and cruelty against their opponents, dissidents, and critics. Some established religious institutions of the past, such as the Catholic Church, also committed grave

5. Typical Goals of Extremist Groups

atrocities against scientists, pagan intellectuals, and priests who did not follow their doctrinal beliefs (e.g., Spanish Inquisition) for its organizational survival and maintenance of unchallenged authority.[115]

When group survival is threatened by the "exit" of their own members, leaders try to trap members within with threats of severe punishments. Some religious groups punished acts of apostasy with death; political leaders reproached traitorous and treasonous acts with the death penalty, and the military reprimanded defectors and deserters, all for the same goal of forestalling group "exits." Some hard-core gangs and criminal cartels enforce a "blood in, blood out" code to forbid defections—i.e., once you join the group, you cannot leave the group without risking your life. Al-Qaeda leader Al-Zarqawi frequently announced to his followers that there were only two ways to leave the organization—either being killed in battle, or be killed by al-Qaeda.[116]

For this reason, terrorist groups tend to persist even in the face of evident failure of achieving political goals.[117] To secure group survival, some groups "morph" themselves into different versions of the same or a related species that will permit continuity of the organization,[118] or find a new cause once their first one is achieved.[119] Other groups broaden their goals in order to attract a wider variety of recruits; merge with groups of different ideologies, forcing both sides to adapt; or transform themselves into profit-driven organized criminal groups.[120]

Reactionary Extremist Groups

Most reactionary extremist groups' primary goal is their survival. They try to preserve their distinctive or authentic identity by keeping their group's beliefs and traditions intact, warding off all adulterating outside influences (e.g., Amish, Mennonites, Orthodox and Hasidic Jews, polygamous communes, religious fundamentalist groups). Conservative Hasidic Jewish families in New York and New Jersey, for instance, maintain their enclave and remain within for generations. They socialize among themselves only, shunning the outside world, and educate their children in their parochial schools only. They pressure politicians to protect their segregated housing and parochial education subsidies to make sure the state does not interfere with their educational approach within yeshivas, despite laws requiring all parochial school students to receive an education equivalent to that of public schools.[121] In spite of high poverty rates and welfare dependency, polygamous groups prohibit sending children to public schools, and Jehovah's Witnesses discourage sending children to college.[122] Members of these groups try to insulate themselves from the outside world to secure their group's survival for generations to come.

◆◆ 6 ◆◆

Factors That Facilitate the Rise of Extremist Groups

People form or join groups for sundry reasons, and groups become extremists for multiple causes, depending on circumstances and objectives. Yet, there are certain situations and conditions that seem to contribute to the radicalization of people, exhorting them toward extremist actions. Those facilitating factors are summarized in this chapter. Not every group of people facing these factors turns to extremism. However, the majority of extremist groups seem to sprout out of at least one of these causes and conditions. In this chapter, I discuss some of the causes and conditions that prompt regular movements to adopt extremist means and strategies.

Threats to Existential Security

Under perilous situations that threaten people's existential security, causing them to feel insecure or indignant, people band together and try to protect each other and defend their group's collective interests, using any available means. In order to secure their survival, they try to create a "safe space" among the most trusted groups of people, often the like-minded, like-believing, like-appearing, and those who share the same identities, shunning outsiders and whomever they deem to be "different" and "untrustworthy." Group identities become more salient; members become more hostile toward out-groups; in-group loyalty and camaraderie strengthen; and leaders become more authoritarian, demanding loyalty, submission, and sacrifice. The "us vs. them" mindset proliferates, infused with "good vs. evil" distinction, and people try to identify and define allies and enemies with a heightened sense of group distinctions and boundaries. Behind all exclusive, homophilic extremist movements, such as anti-immigrant activists, racists, nationalists, white nationalists, Christian nationalists, and religious fundamentalists, Brexiteers (seeking Brexit from European Union), and homophilic sentiments, such as xenophobia, homophobia, Islamophobia, anti–West hysteria, and prejudice against any "different" groups of people, there lies a fundamental, psychological desire to "feel safe" among the like-minded, without being threatened by the "differences" and "outsiders."

In such cases, groups become a "collective coping arrangement" or "defense mechanism" that is necessary for people to advance their survival chances collectively against the perceived levels of uncertainty that threatens existential security.[1] Feeling insecure and threatened, people become loyal to the group which they believe can protect them and provide for them, physically, financially, or psychologically, and pledge their loyalty to the group as an "insurance premium" they pay to be protected and provided for by the group. To assure their security, they freely submit themselves to groups and their authorities, forgo their own freedom and civil rights, and violate other people's rights and welfare on behalf of their group.

Not every group under existential threat falls back on extremist responses. However, when they do, it is often as a reaction to some form of threat from external sources, whether the group's existence is threatened, collective interests are at stake, status challenged, dignity trampled, or honor smeared. Threatened groups become more prone to extremism when the collective fear comes from a leader who deliberately exaggerates threats for the purpose of mobilizing resources (e.g., "fear-mongering").

Factors That Threaten Existential Security

Multitudes of sources can threaten people's existential security, such as threats from external groups, wars, lawlessness, chaos from disasters, whether manmade or natural, and absence of justice. In most resistance groups, the sources of the threat are usually systemic persecution and mistreatment by the dominant groups. Persecuted, oppressed, stigmatized, and marginalized groups, however, are not the only groups that experience threats to existential security. Dominant group members (e.g., men in a patriarchy system, whites in racist societies, aristocrats, monarchs, upper caste members, capitalists, and the wealthy and powerful) can also feel threatened when their superior status and privileges are challenged, either through populist revolts or legislative amendments.

External Factors

In large groups, threats to existential security can be twofold—from external (out-groups) or internal sources (e.g., economic and political chaos, civil wars, and other forms of internal feuds and divisions). When people feel that their existential security is under threat by *external* sources, nested subgroups merge together to defend the whole group they belong to, forming a "collective defense mechanism."[2] In such cases, in-group identification heightens and the "out-group liking" index falls, along with willingness to cooperate with out-groups.[3] Rise of chauvinistic aggression from one group poses a security threat to the targeted group, which also turns to chauvinism to defend itself. Each side becomes a threat to the other, generating a vicious cycle of escalating fear, suspicion, and enmity, resulting in "securities dilemma."[4]

Canetti-Nisim et al.[5] ascertained that exposure to terrorist attacks raises people's support for right-wing extremism and hostility toward *all* out-groups, including minority groups within. Shortly after the 9/11 terrorist attacks in 2001, many Americans reverted to extremist mindsets propelled by the fear of terrorism and exigent desire to protect themselves (e.g., support for nationalistic, defensive, aggressive authoritarianism). They endorsed hardline, militaristic counterterrorist policies and authoritarian leadership (e.g., supporting Iraq and Afghan wars, torture, and limitation of civil liberties; anti–Muslim sentiments).[6] Anti-Muslim and anti-immigrant sentiments soared with random attacks on Mosques, Muslim Americans, and their gathering places, along with support for politicians who advocated restrictions on all immigration (e.g., President Trump). By the same logic, we should be able to understand how Muslims' view of America altered following the U.S.-led invasion of Iraq and a handful of ill-fated foibles and mishaps that followed the invasion. Muslims around the world, particularly the Sunnis, perceived the invasion and removal of Saddam as painfully threatening and humiliating assaults on their group's honor and dignity, and coagulated their support for the Islamist/jihadist extremist groups fighting against the West.[7]

Internal Factors

On the other hand, when people face *internal* stress threatening their existential security (e.g., economic recession, extreme inequality, systemic injustice, and chaos from systemic failures and corruption), nested groups tend to splinter and "parochialize" (or "tribalize") as people "hunker down" to the core, most immediate identity circles whom they can trust the most ("bunker mentality"). Williams[8] corroborated how people, when insecure, tend to "stay put," "stay rooted," and "stay local." "Staying local" is a form of self-protection—i.e., staying near family and friends they can rely on as their "safety net." Such behaviors of "parochializing" and "burrowing" are a form of "group regression" that can fragment large groups, as nested subgroups seek autonomy, self-determination, self-containment,

6. Factors That Facilitate the Rise of Extremist Groups 203

and self-support, antagonizing what they perceive to be the "out-groups (or enemies) within."[9] Multiple scholars corroborated this tendency of large group fragmentation under duress.[10]

During economic hard times and internal stress, resources diminish (e.g., high unemployment, shrinking wages, falling share prices), and every group feels attacked and pitted against other groups, not just for jobs and spoils but for the right to define their group's identity—a condition that devolves into "zero-sum" group competition, a pure form of "political tribalism."[11] The dominant or the majority groups try to secure their economic benefits despite shrinking resources for the whole group, instead of sacrificing for or sharing with others, and the subordinate or powerless and moneyless groups rebel against the dwindling shares of their economic benefits that threaten their livelihood and survival. When "there isn't enough to go around," foreigners and immigrants in particular appear as "dangerous outsiders" who try to take away shares of resources (e.g., jobs, health care, education opportunities, and access to social services).[12] Prejudice and discrimination against racial/ethnic minorities and immigrants build up, and nations turn to isolationism, protectionism, nationalism, and xenophobia, spurning globalization, transnational alliances, and international cooperation.

The rise of far-right, nationalist, anti-immigrant, racist, anti-globalization, anti-establishment, and anti–EU extremisms and populisms that swept throughout Western societies in the aftermath of the Great Recession that began in 2008 would be an apt example of the rise of political tribalism. Masses of jobless, working-class, white voters with bleak economic prospects fueled the anti-establishment, anti-immigrant, extreme-right populism and "strongmen" autocracy.[13] Native populations' support for redistributive social service and welfare policies waned in Europe and the U.S.,[14] because more native-born people saw immigrants and foreigners as "undeserving" of public assistance they funded by paying taxes.[15]

Even among the same racial and ethnic groups, economic hard times can fragment large groups spurring regional, separatist movements. Catalans tried to secede from Spain in 2012 and 2017; Scotland tried to gain independence from the United Kingdom in 2014, and two Italian regions (Lombardy and Veneto) sought to gain greater autonomy from Rome through referendum in 2017.[16] In 2014, Indians elected anti–Muslim Hindu nationalist Prime Minister Narendra Modi, who endorsed and implemented policies and rules that threatened India's long maintained status as a democratic, secular republic. Under his rule, Hindu nationalist mobs brazenly attacked Muslims and burned Muslim mosques, businesses, and houses; authorities ignored most of such violent behaviors with the support of the majority Hindis.[17] Turkey turned to political Islamism under President Erdoğan and Israelis rallied around right-wing, Jewish nationalist Prime Minister Benjamin Netanyahu, despite multiple bribery investigations and his hardline and racist positions against Palestinians.

Effects of Improving Existential Security

By the same reasoning, we can surmise that when structural conditions for existential security improve (e.g., with rule of law, economic affluence, public safety nets, and abated threats of war), extremist cultural mindsets will dissipate. Scholars have discussed such dialectic and reciprocal interaction between the culture and structure—e.g., how political and economic events and structural conditions shape people's cultural mindsets, and how those cultural mindsets contour political and social activities and events,[18] including the ebb and flow of extremisms. It seems to elucidate why people in unstable and deprived societies and situations with lower existential security are more prone to extremism compared to people in stable and affluent societies and situations with higher existential security, irrespective of race, ethnicity, religion, nationality, and civilization.

During the pre-modern era, people's lives were generally precarious and insecure, and reliance on a support group was necessary for survival. Most people did not have enough resources or reserves to care for their families in times of adversity, such as in the aftermath of natural disasters or unfortunate accidents and illnesses. Without a well-established and fairly enforced rule of law, people could not rely on authorities when they were wronged by others or falsely accused of wrongdoing. Violent tribal or ethnic skirmishes were common, making people's lives highly unpredictable and perilous. In fear, people tried to survive by becoming loyal to whichever group they believed could protect them and provide for them. When people must rely on group support systems, they become more conforming to group-prescribed norms, submit themselves to their leaders, and become loyal to the group in order to secure acceptance by the group and eschew rejections. When groups gain unchallenged power over individuals, group interests, honor, and glory supersede individual rights, happiness, and even life. This allows leaders to exploit individuals for the benefit of groups, ignoring their rights, dignity, and life.

As societies evolved and advanced with technological innovation and economic development, surpluses and reserves needed for survival accrued.[19] Increasing surpluses enabled more individuals to accumulate wealth and join pooled resource protection programs (e.g., various insurances programs against unforeseen perils in life), and societies to offer public assistances to vulnerable people without means of survival, improving people's general sense of existential security. According to Mann's[20] study, the number of people dying per decade due to famine in the world has steadily attenuated since 1860, down to 3 per 100,000 in 2010. Effectively instituted and enforced rule of law and fairer political and economic systems (e.g., liberal and inclusive democracies, economic redistributions) have abated much of the group-felt grievances and need for extremist melees between the privileged and underprivileged, as well as between the dominant and subordinate groups. With the expansion of scientific explanations, natural events became more controllable and manageable; with medical technology and institutionalized rule of law, people's lives became much more predictable and secure.[21]

Such structural transformations in life and improved existential security allowed more people to liberate themselves from the group-prescribed constraints and loyalties that controlled people's mindsets in the past, permitting more individualistic cultural mindsets to proliferate (e.g., "post-materialist values").[22] As deprivation-compensation theories suggest,[23] the improved existential security people enjoy in most affluent, post-industrial societies has attenuated people's psychological vulnerability to mortal events (e.g., famines, floods, wars, poverty, and diseases).[24] With rising existential security, extremist cultural mindsets and people's desire to form extremist groups and employ extremist measures to secure survival have considerably withered.

"Securities Dilemma"

The "securities dilemma" created by the escalating hostilities between two groups with a series of "feedback loops" of revenge attacks spawn what Collins[25] calls the "C-escalation" of crisis as involved groups seek allies for support, drive out neutrals, and mobilize material resources. Each side becomes a threat to the other, generating a vicious cycle of accelerating fear, suspicion and animosity.[26] Groups ensnared in such "securities dilemmas" are more likely to adopt extremist measures trying to out-fear each other, boosting volume and scope of their threats and deepening people's fear and aversion toward each other. Gang violence intensifies with existence of rival gangs. Each gang faces threats to its existence, and overreacts to protect itself with a series of retaliatory strikes and acts of brutality and mayhem designed to out-fear rival gangs.[27] During the Cold War era, both the U.S. and Soviet Union were ensnared in such a "securities dilemma" with a mounting nuclear arms race, as fears and suspicion spiraled out of control. Between 1940 and 1996, the U.S. spent at least $8.75 trillion (adjusted for 1996 terms) on production of over 70,000 nuclear warheads, which was more than enough to obliterate the whole world several times. The Soviet

Union produced over 55,000 warheads,[28] as both countries were enmeshed in a hysterical level of fear and suspicion of each other.

Throughout history, especially during the pre-modern era, humans have endured devastating conflicts and large-scale wars resulting from escalating "securities dilemmas." Even in the modern era, some nations test the limits of their boundaries and power, and threaten their neighboring nations, generating "securities dilemmas." The growing economic power and nationalistic expansionism of China engendered an equally virulent upsurge of nationalism in neighboring nations under threat, such as in Japan, Vietnam, and the Philippines. In May of 2014, rampaging anti–Chinese rioters in Vietnam left at least two dead, scores of people, mostly non–Chinese foreigners injured and their businesses ruined, in response to a tense standoff over an oil rig China placed in a disputed part of the South China Sea.[29] Responding to Chinese aggression and territorial reclamation projects in the South China Sea (e.g., building of artificial islands, presence of warships and fishing boats in other nations' territory) in 2015, Japanese parliament amended its constitution to allow Japanese troops to fight in foreign territory even when Japan itself is not attacked, gradually moving away from its post–World War II pacifism. The nationalistic expansionism of Russia in 2014 (annexation of Crimea and military invasion in Ukraine) led to anti–Russian responses by Europe and America that led to economic sanctions and buildup of anti-missile defenses in NATO nations.[30]

Anarchy and "Legitimation Crisis"

When a society operates by a system of just and impartial rule of law, people tend to trust the system, and have diminished need to rely on extremist groups to protect themselves against injustices and corruptions. Conversely, when people perceive that their government is too corrupt and incompetent to enforce rule of law, they will find alternative sources that they believe will deliver law and order and protect them. In the absence of an effective state that can enforce rule of law, whether due to incompetency, corruption, economic crisis, natural disasters, or war, society turns into a state of anarchy and lawlessness.[31] Seeking an alternative source of protection, people turn to localized groups which, they believe, can protect and provide for them, such as family, kinship, tribal, militia, church, gang, rebel, and extremist groups. A study of international data corroborated that people who had been more intensely affected by the violence of war were more likely to join or participate in religious groups and their rituals. The more profound the impact of war on an individual—such as the death, injury or abduction of a household member—the greater the likelihood that the person would turn to religion.[32]

"Failed States"

According to the *Arab Human Development Report,*[33] one of the main reasons why extremisms spread in Arab societies is because of the endemic "crisis in legitimacy" in the Arab world. There is a collective failure in many Arab states to address and resolve crucial issues and problems people face, due to economic chaos, political upheavals, endemic corruption, systemic injustice, and lack of advancement in human development. In such "failed states" without a functioning or effective central government—e.g., Somalia, Afghanistan, and much of central Africa—tribal warlords, militias, rebel groups, and gangs proliferate, jockeying and jostling for power and territory using brute force, amplifying people's fear and insecurity. Scores of people in Somalia follow al-Shabaab because their government cannot deliver security and uphold rule of law. As taxi driver Mahmood Abdullahi says: "If the government can disarm the militias and get rid of the checkpoints where they steal money from us, then we would support the government."[34] When the U.S.-led coalition and newly formed Iraqi government could not secure safety and economic viability for the majority of the Iraqi population after the fall of Saddam Hussein, a deluge of Iraqis turned to local militia and tribal warlords for protection, turning away from the central government, making it virtually impossible for the coalition forces to build a functioning democracy.[35]

Extremist groups and extremist leaders gain popular support in areas where the government cannot maintain law and order, security, and public services for its citizens. In such places and situations, extremist groups try to gain people's support and trust working as "charity groups" (providing education, health care, shelter, and food) and "security providers" (maintaining law and order in their own haphazard way) (e.g., Muslim Brotherhood, Hamas, Hezbollah, al-Qaeda, Taliban, and some gangs in some urban areas of Latin America). In El Salvador, because the government is unable to control the infiltration of Mexican drug cartels and protect its people from them, people are joining gangs and cartels instead to be protected from rampant violence and lawlessness. The gangs control street-level drug sales, charge local residents for "protection," and battle to keep their rivals out. In such neighborhoods, people generally regard these gangs as "social organizations that protect the civilians," because the gangs deliver necessary services to the people (e.g., they help get water lines connected; refurbish the community hall), which the government is unable to do.[36] In Honduras, competing gangs take over the poor neighborhoods, and threaten youth to join them using violence. Scores of economically struggling parents leave their children behind to work in the U.S., and the children become vulnerable prey for gang violence without parental protection. For these children without protection from parents and the government, gangs become the only available source of protection.[37] People seek gangs' protection because cops are outnumbered and out-powered by drug cartels, if not "bought out" by the cartels to turn a blind eye.[38]

During economic lockdowns due to the COVID-19 pandemic, in areas where government could not control the spread of the virus, gangs and rebel groups took advantage of the government's failure as their own propaganda opportunity—they took over the governmental role and tried to appear to be the "responsible and accountable actors." Mexico's drug gangs distributed aid packages with food and masks to people struggling in fear; MS-13 in El Salvador instituted and enforced its own curfew and distributed masks. In Afghanistan, Taliban militants dispatched "health teams" with impressive medical gear and offered health care services to the fear-stricken people[39]; in South Africa, instead of fighting, rival gangs started to distribute much needed food and water to people in their territory.[40] In southern Italy, Mafia clans took advantage of the pandemic lockdown and delivered everyday necessities to residents of poor neighborhoods and offered credits to businesses that were near bankruptcy.[41]

Chaos and Economic Meltdown

Merolla et al.[42] ascertained that societal-level threats and uncertainties ("collective crisis") tend to activate people's predisposition toward extremist preferences and behaviors and authoritarian leadership. Europe's fascist regimes rose to power after the First World War during the time of economic, social, and political disarray. Fascist Germany of the Weimar Republic resulted from the Great Inflation and the Great Depression, which spurred both left- and right-wing extremists and uprisings. In Italy, high inflation and pervasive unemployment led to violent strikes and lockouts that paralyzed its economy for almost two years while left- and right-wing gangs battled violently in the streets. In such dreadful conditions, people yearn for extremist "strongmen" leaders who rule by fear and total control, even if they disrespect people's civil rights and due process. Russia's Putin rose to power in the midst of economic and political chaos after the collapse of the Soviet Union; Venezuela's Chavez rose to power fueled by deteriorating social and economic conditions rife with corruption and extreme inequality, and Hungary's Viktor Orban amassed authoritarian power as Europe was experiencing the painful fallout from the financial crisis of 2008 and upsurge of migrants from the war-torn Middle East and Africa.[43]

When fears of crime and lawlessness mount, more people tolerate or even embrace police brutality, hoping that they will restore law and order for them. Police brutality and killings are rampant in Brazil, reaching the highest level in 2018 when 51,000 people were killed by police. They shoot people from helicopters, armored personnel carriers, or at close range in the streets. Yet, the majority of people continue to support the police and politicians who promise to be "tough on crime" (e.g., President Jair Bolsonaro), hoping that "fighting violence with violence" will end violence.[44] In the 1960s and 1970s, when the city of Philadelphia was beleaguered by high crime, racial conflicts, and economic stagnation, working-class whites abandoned the liberal agendas of labor unions, and became "law and order" conservatives supporting hardline, racist law enforcement tactics with "romanticized reverence" for police officers, hoping that they would restore law and order.[45] Amidst lawless chaos with high crime rates, people voluntarily forgo liberty, justice, fairness, and civil rights for security, stability, and protection.

INCITING CHAOS TO SOLICIT SUPPORT

Understanding this group psychology, in order to garner support for themselves, some extremist groups deliberately stir up chaos with violence, hoping that will undermine people's trust in the state. One of the main goals of Islamist extremist groups like al-Qaeda, ISIS/Daesh, al-Shabaab, and Boko Haram was to create zones within the Muslim world that are so lawless and chaotic that the authority of the state would collapse, and people would lose trust in their government. They would then move in to fill the vacuum left by government's "failure," and earn people's trust and loyalty by providing much-needed security, order, and services like education, water, and electricity.[46] Taliban insurgents attack and kill random Afghan civilians in Kabul for the same reason—they create chaos with violent attacks against large numbers of civilians hoping that will undermine people's trust in the U.S.-backed Afghan government. In just one week of January 2018, they rocked Afghanistan with a hotel siege that killed 22 and a car bomb that killed 95.[47] In 2018, a suicide bomber targeted a group of Islamic clerics gathered to discuss how to reduce violence, killing at least 12 and wounding many more.[48] According to a United Nations report, at least 10,453 Afghan civilians were either killed or wounded by Taliban attacks in 2017 alone[49]; the number of civilian deaths and injuries doubled since 2009, while that of Afghan security personnel have decreased during the same time,[50] marking 2018 as the "deadliest year" for Afghan civilians in a decade.[51]

Vigilante Violence

When the government and police cannot enforce rule of law, or they apply laws unfairly and unjustly, people turn to vigilante justice or extrajudicial revenge attacks with mob violence. In parts of Mexico infested with drug cartels, a form of "citizen self-defense groups" are arising to fight against drug cartels that are ravaging their communities and overpowering or conspiring with police and political leaders. These paramilitary vigilantes patrol their neighborhoods, catch smugglers who are employed by the drug cartels, and punish them on their own.[52] In South Africa's poor neighborhood of Diepsloot Township near Johannesburg, rape is rampant and the government is unable to prosecute perpetrators. In frustration, vigilante gangs formed and started to capture and kill accused rapists.[53] In parts of India where the government is unable or unwilling to prosecute sexual offenders, vigilante mobs started to kill those who were suspected of rape, including those who were falsely accused, prompting the Supreme Court to urge the government to pass an anti-lynching law in 2018.[54]

In certain areas of Latin America where people do not have much faith in their law enforcement and criminal justice system to bring criminals to justice, mobs routinely attack and kill suspected criminals with impunity and public support. Lynch mobs are made up of ordinary citizens, from students to old ladies. They kill the accused with the same grisly cruelty as gangs do—e.g., mutilating victims' sex organs, gouging their eyes, and burning them alive in broad daylight. Even police officers give tacit approval to lynching, making little effort to intervene or collect evidence to bring assailants to trial—fewer than one in ten vigilante murder cases are resolved by arrest. Without fear of prosecution, murder rates peaked and reached the highest level in unstable nations in Latin America, such as El Salvador (40.29 per 100,000 in 2016), Venezuela (34.77), Guatemala (26.81), and Honduras (20.56), compared to 0.56 in Europe and 3.85 in the U.S.[55]

Mob lynching is rarely a response to a single crime, researchers say. Rather, the crimes are simply the last straw for a community living in fear of endemic violence and lawlessness. In such situations, lynching becomes a cathartic act that gives offenders a sense of redemption through "re-imposing order," says Gema Santamaria, an expert in extralegal justice and adviser to the United Nations.[56]

Collective Fear

Fear is probably one of the most potent human emotions that can spark and fuel extremist acts and movements. When people become fearful, like other animals, the so-called "pack mentality" or "herd mentality" sets in—i.e., they try to "gang up together" against the source of their fear to defend themselves, often using extreme measures. An elevated sense of

6. Factors That Facilitate the Rise of Extremist Groups 211

fear collectively shared by a group of people foments rage and abhorrence against the presumed source of the fear, whether they are "out-groups" or "enemies," triggering violent acts and destructive conflicts.[57] Emotions of tension and fear prompt people to commit violent acts[58]; fear is behind an array of group-based acts of violence—by fascist groups of all kinds,[59] ethno-nationalisms and ethnic wars,[60] populism on the left and right,[61] militia groups,[62] and assorted hate groups.[63]

Sources of Fear

Depending on the circumstances, people can become fearful for an assortment of reasons, as discussed below.

Fear of Rejection

When individuals must depend on their group for protection and survival, rejection by the group can mean losing group protection and means of survival. To survive, people must try hard to ward off rejection—whether it's being shunned, mocked, isolated, shamed ("losing face"), ostracized, or excommunicated. To guarantee acceptance, people demonstrate their loyalty to the group through conformity, sacrifice, and submission. Some people commit atrocities against their enemies, out-group members, and "traitors" as manifestation of their in-group loyalty. According to Ruble,[64] people in Native Indian communities have considered banishment as the ultimate punishment they fear the most. Banishment meant casting offenders out of the community, forcing them to fend for themselves alone in the forest or on the plains. It meant stripping them of their tribal membership, which is equivalent to losing their social identity, safety net, and protection. For this reason, tribal members fear banishment more than death or imprisonment.

Fear of rejection is greater in groups with a paternalistic dependency relationship where members' whole lives and livelihoods depend on the communal support system or commune-based economic cooperation (e.g., Mormons, Amish, Jehovah's Witnesses, Israeli Kibbutzim, polygamous communes, and an assortment of cults). In such situations, social rejection can mean the loss of one's entire livelihood, means of survival, and support system as well as friendship, family ties, and business networks.[65] In some religious communities, the fear of rejection can extend to people's life after death. One of the ex–FLDS (a polygamous commune) members, Tonia Tewell, described how FLDS members live in constant fear and threat of "not going to heaven," because their leaders told them since childhood that anyone who is disloyal to the group and disobeys their leaders will be damned and not go to heaven.[66]

Fear of Group Extinction

Some groups become extremists when members fear that their group's identity, culture, and existence is on the verge of disappearing because of various reasons, such as immigrants, globalization, scientific explanations, technological innovations, cultural changes, modernization, or foreign invasion. They consider maintaining the group's cultural distinction and purity in identity as a form of "boundary maintenance" that is necessary for the group's continued existence. Without the boundary, they fear, their group's identity may disappear along with its existence. Particularly in reactionary extremist groups, tradition becomes the symbol of group identity; by upholding tradition, members believe they can preserve the group's identity and existence. Ethnic/racial "purity" can also become a sign of group identity; by deterring racial/ethnic mixing, they believe they can preserve the group's identity and status.

Some groups deploy extremist strategies to preserve their distinctive identity and tradition, such as religious fundamentalist groups, white supremacists, anti-immigrant nativist groups, indigenous groups, and a host of communal groups—e.g., Amish, Mennonite, and polygamous groups. Fear of extinction prompted a litany of violent ethno-national conflicts throughout history all around the world. According to Kaufman,[67] Armenians' mythology placed fear of a repetition of the 1915 genocide at the center of their concerns, while Azerbaijanis feared the destruction of their state, on which their identity depended. In some cases, these fears of extinction were exaggerated or fanciful; yet, once people believed in it, they became one of the primary causes of destructive ethnic wars.

Fear of Change

If not extinction, people fear changes, whether they are from modernization, secularization, diversity, pluralism, or whatever they perceive to be disruptive to the status quo. Most reactionary extremist groups emanate from fears of change, including fundamentalist and radically conservative reactionary groups, whether socially or religiously. For instance, Christian fundamentalists are aggressively evangelical and defensive of their beliefs, fearing the spread of secularism and religious pluralism, which they believe will chip away at the Christian hegemony in the U.S.[68] Their desire to resist change often shapes their positions on public policy issues toward anti-liberalism, anti-intellectualism, anti-modernism, anti-multiculturalism, anti-secularization, anti-internationalism, anti-gay, and anti-feminism, even when they benefit from the changes (e.g., anti-feminist women). They romanticize the past and yearn for a fanciful image of the "good-old-days" of "tribalistic" and tradition-based simpler lifestyles, dictated by the elderly and authorities. They become proud defenders of age-old traditions, with hate-filled condemnation of those who violate the tradition or try to reform the status quo.

The globalizing and "heterogenizing" trends of the modern world have been an unsettling experience for the identity-bound traditionalists around the world. As more people migrate, mix, mingle, and switch identities, it is becoming increasingly harder for them to define and maintain their traditional identities and culture.[69] For instance, instead of accepting changes, some Muslims strive for "indigenization," "re-tribalization," and "re–Islamization" of the Middle East.[70] Scholars have discussed that most Islamist/jihadist terror groups are driven by the fear of "westernization"—i.e., fear that Western culture is encroaching and corrupting their culture.[71] Boko Haram of Nigeria and the Taliban of Afghanistan are well-known for their militant opposition to Western influence, and violently reject modern education, healthcare, missionaries and NGOs, as well as Western political interference. On the other hand, the so-called "Islamophobia" among the right-wing, anti-immigrant, nationalistic parties and groups in Europe also stems from the fear that European culture and identity may alter because of what they see as "Islamic invasion" and "Islamization of Europe."[72] Similar sentiments exist among American counterparts who fear "Latin-Americanization" of America with an influx of Hispanic immigration. These groups of people try to uphold the status quo, resisting changes, if not wishing to return to the past, fearing that external influence will tarnish their group's distinctive identity and tradition, whether they are religious, cultural, political, national, or regional.

The dominant and privileged groups who benefit from the status quo (e.g., men, aristocrats, monarchs, racial/ethnic majority, the wealthy, and the powerful) also fear changes that might undercut their privileged status, and try arduously to sustain the existing systems and status quo, advocating tradition and stability as their ideological cover. Most white supremacist group members share nostalgia for the past when "minorities were not so loud, so demanding, so numerous—a time when minorities were more grateful."[73] The goal of most violent acts against blacks throughout American history has been to "put them down" and "put them back in their place," to where they used to or should belong—at a lower status. It was probably for this reason that typical victims of lynching in American history were blacks who were successful, who dared to demand equality (e.g., equal pay, access, opportunities), and black men who were accused of "courting" white women, as Dray[74] documented. The KKK has always envisioned the future based upon a mythological vision of the past—an America without immigrants, an America ruled by Anglo-Saxon whites, and an America that prayed in unison to an evangelical Christian God.[75]

FEAR OF LOSING POWER AND SUPERIORITY

The privileged groups can become extremists when members fear losing their monopoly of power and the dominance they enjoy.[76] In such cases, they use extremist measures to defend their dominant status against all challenges to their power, including brutal repression of powerless groups that try to gain equal access to power and resources. In some cases, they exaggerate their superiority and over-exercise their power to compensate for their fear of losing superiority.[77]

Throughout history, men have feared losing their patriarchal system and their power and dominance over women. In order to maintain their privileged status, they practiced aggressively authoritarian and discriminatory measures to control women, and used extremist strategies to denigrate and marginalize women and prohibited women from obtaining education and equal rights (to vote, to work, drive, or own property). The history-long and widespread practices of abuses and violence against women, systematic denial of equal rights, sexual discrimination and harassment, buttressed with sexist ideologies and misogynous beliefs, are testaments to and examples of male subjugation of women, motivated by their fear of losing male superiority and dominance over women. This is probably the reason why campaigns of violence against women in traditional societies usually target professional women, female university students, and girls who seek education, as happened in Iraq after the fall of Saddam Hussein, Afghanistan, and in areas occupied by ISIS/Daesh.[78] In the U.S., it took over 70 years of struggle for women to obtain the right to vote,[79] and the ERA (Equal Rights Amendment)—a proposed constitutional amendment to protect women's equal rights—has still not been ratified, over 45 years after it was proposed.[80] Almost 60 years after President John F. Kennedy signed the Equal Pay Act in an effort to abolish wage discrimination based on gender, in 2017, the Census Bureau reported that, full-time, year-round working American women earned an average of 80 percent of what their male counterparts earned doing the same work in various occupations.[81] Only six countries in the world (Belgium, Denmark, France, Latvia, Luxembourg, and Sweden) give women and men legally protected equal rights as of 2019, the World Bank reported.[82]

At times, the sheer growth in "size" of the minority groups can cause the majority group to feel threatened, although they continue to enjoy dominance and privilege. White supremacist and racist groups are agitated by the fear of (potentially) losing their numeric superiority, which, they fear, might threaten their dominant status, power, and privilege.[83] Increase in minority population has irked the majority group to react with daring hostilities against minorities consumed by the fear of being outnumbered by the minorities. Most mass shooters of recent years against racial/ethnic minority groups (e.g., Brenton Tarrant, who killed 57 Muslims in Christchurch, New Zealand in 2019; the synagogue shooters in Pittsburgh, Pennsylvania, and Poway, California, and Patrick Crusius, who killed 22 mostly Mexican American shoppers at Walmart in El Paso, Texas) reportedly believed in a so-called "Great Replacement" theory spreading on racist websites, claiming that white people are being "replaced" by people of color through mass immigration.[84] Political analysts have discussed that the white working-class populist base who supported President Trump were the people who felt threatened by the growing size of the racial and ethnic minority population in the U.S., the result of immigration and high birth rates.[85] They supported Trump because he promised to "make America great again" (presumably back to when whites dominated America) and "build a wall" to protect whites from the "invasion" of immigrants.

Group-Felt Grievances

Not every oppressed group adopts extremist measures, and not every oppression spawns a resistance movement, as Devenport et al.[86] observed. However, most resistance or reform-seeking extremisms, when they do occur, arise out of seething grievances and rage that arise from oppression, abuse, or violation of human dignity afflicted upon a group of people. Scholars and pundits have long suspected the group-felt grievances to be one of the main causes of resistance movements, especially among people who have been systematically mistreated, deprived, exploited, or abused at the hands of another group for an extended time period and those who are sympathetic to such victims of mistreatment.

Sources of Grievances

Sources of grievance can be diverse, such as extremely unfair and unequal systems of reward and distribution of resources; unequal access to power and opportunities (e.g., due to corruption, discrimination, cronyism, nepotism, inherited wealth and statuses, and rigged economic, legal, and political systems); and civil and human rights violations from abuses of powers (e.g., unfair treatments of the powerless in the social and justice systems). When a group of people's future prospects become bleak, unpredictable, or uncontrollable, because of systemic failures and biases, not because of one's own misdeed, the like-afflicted people aggrieve together and try to improve the situation. When their demands for reform are systematically blocked or dismissed, they turn to extremist means to achieve equal rights and human dignity. Under Apartheid, black South Africans revolted; under Israeli occupation, Palestinians continue to rebel, often violently; and under Turkish repression, Kurds resist violently at times. Numerous leftist and communist rebel groups, such as FARC and ELN, revolutionary guerrilla movements, independence movements by occupied people, labor unions, Civil Rights, feminist, women's suffrage, and Black Power movements are some examples of such reform-seeking resistant movements born out of collectively experienced or perceived grievances.

GRIEVANCES AGAINST THE WEST: ISLAMIST/JIHADIST GROUPS

Crotty[87] argues that the root cause of anti–West grievances around the world stems not only from the past experiences of colonialism, but also from how colonialism transformed into *economic* domination and political manipulation in modern times (called "economic colonialism") since most former colonized nations gained independence in 1945 after the Second World War. Without occupying the nations, the wealthy countries continue to extract resources, exploit cheap labor, and dispose of consumer goods they produce, turning the nations into impoverished and extremely unequal societies ruled by a few corrupt oligarchs and dictatorial puppet regimes. Such regimes tend to Western powers instead of their citizens, in exchange for protection of their regime. This is the reason why multitudes of Muslims regarded Osama bin Laden as a "Robin Hood" and supported Saddam Hussein as a pan–Arabic leader who stood up against the Western powers, even as they launched terrorist attacks on Western nations and their people and institutions around the world.

The 9/11 Commission Report to Congress[88] concluded that Osama Bin Laden and his followers brooded over a long-festering history of grievances against the West, which were used as their justification for the 9/11 attacks. Their stated grievances included the U.S. military presence in Saudi Arabia, the home of Islam's holiest sites, and suffering of the Iraqi people because of sanctions imposed after the Gulf War. Particularly offensive to them was the Western endorsement of their repressive dictators and oppressive police states, both military and financial, motivated by oil interests, which produced a new class of rich and spoiled economic elites and royal families protected by the American military. Also included in their list of grievances was America's unconditional sponsorship for Israel and willful blindness toward its inhumane treatment of over one million Arabs in Palestine.[89]

SECTARIAN VIOLENCE IN IRAQ

Group-felt grievances were the driving force behind the century-old sectarian violence between the Sunnis and Shiites in Iraq. Under Hussein's rule, until the U.S.-led invasion in 2003, the oppressed group of Shiites grieved collectively. After the fall of Saddam, the Sunnis grieved over Shiite oppression and their revenge attacks. "Their sect is nothing more than a uniform, a convenient way to tell friends from enemy," says Ghanim Hashem Kudhir, who teaches modern Islamic history at Baghdad's Mustansiriya University. "What binds them is not religion but a common history of grievances: Shiites saw themselves as the oppressed, and they saw Sunnis as the oppressors."[90]

Frustrated Aspirations: "Incel"

As McGregor et al.[91] documented, an ordinary group of people can be driven to commit extremist acts when they feel frustrated because their aspirations for achieving important life goals and desires are flustered. "Incel" (meaning "involuntary celibacy") refers to an online community of misogynous men who are frustrated by their inability to form sexual relationships with women. Instead of blaming themselves, they vent their anger on social media platforms where they share their thoughts of virulent misogyny with other men like them. Lamenting "involuntary celibacy," they share broader resentments against women, whom they believe to be the source of their frustration. They spread their hate-filled messages online, calling for violent attacks against women. Elliot Rodger, a self-identified "incel" who randomly killed six women and wounded more than a dozen others near the University of California–Santa Barbara in 2014, was reportedly motivated by his desire for retaliation against women who rejected him, as manifested in the videotaped monologue on YouTube he left behind. After killing himself, Rodger became a hero to other "incels" who lauded Rodger's action in online discussion platforms, which were shared with over 40,000 participants and sympathizers.[92] Alek Minassian posted a message hostile to women on this platform moments before his deadly rampage in Toronto in 2018 that killed ten people, mostly women. In the message, he praised "incels" and blamed women for denying them their right to sexual intercourse.[93] Their collectively shared feelings of frustration and anger became a bonding cause for these men, goading them to act out with violence.

Controversy Over Role of Grievances in Collective Actions

Until the 1970s, most well-known perspectives on collective actions and social movements highlighted such grievances and economic deprivation as principal causes of violence and extremism. Since the 1970s, however, researchers had downplayed the role of economic deprivation and grievances in explaining collective contentions (e.g., "deprivation theory of collective actions"), as empirical evidence did not corroborate the connection.[94] For instance, a sizable portion of the arrested rioters, protesters, and rebel group members, especially among the leadership positions, were not the most deprived, oppressed, unemployed, or underprivileged.[95] In response, instead of "deprivation theories," scholars introduced resource mobilization and political process theories that placed greater emphasis on the roles of the group leadership and their mobilization efforts.[96] In recent years, however, attention to grievances is reemerging as one of the notable determinants of collective actions.[97] The focus, however, has shifted toward "*relative* deprivation" (e.g., poverty amidst the wealth; deprivation amid the plentiful),[98] which tends to cultivate a sense of injustice and unfairness, not necessarily a level of *absolute* poverty and deprivation.[99]

"Sympathetic Indignation"

Others introduced such concepts as "vicarious indignation" or "sympathetic grievances" that occur among people who become indignant over how their "fellow humans" or "some of their own" people are being persecuted and mistreated, although they may not be directly afflicted by the mistreatment.[100] Studies have ascertained that most riots and violent protests in recent history were triggered by events where police and authorities acted unjustly against powerless minority groups. Such events incited participants who were not directly affected or victimized by the authorities (e.g., non-minorities), yet felt indignant over how "some of their fellow humans" were mistreated and abused by the authorities.[101] This seems to suggest that the participants of collective actions, whether spontaneous or organized, can be *sympathizers* of the victims of injustice or "vicarious participants,"[102] not necessarily the victims of injustice. In such cases, these sympathetic extremists would be considered redemptive extremists who try to "right the wrong," as well as resistant extremists.

A sizable portion of the Civil Rights Movement activists in the 1960s were well-educated whites who were not subjected to racial bias and discrimination. Yet, they were enraged by how their fellow citizens and humans were being mistreated simply because of the color of their skin, and risked their lives to help them to gain equal rights. Multitudes of gay rights activists were heterosexuals who were indignant over how homosexuals' basic rights were violated unjustly. The majority of the leftist movement participants and terrorists in the 1960s and 1970s in the U.S. and Europe were also well-educated, and came from middle- and upper-middle-class backgrounds, yet began to sympathize with the working-class struggles.[103] Participants in the 2011 London Riots (protesting against discrimination

6. Factors That Facilitate the Rise of Extremist Groups 219

and maltreatment of racial minorities) were from highly diverse backgrounds—racially, ethnically, culturally, and socio-economically—including many who were not subjected to discrimination and mistreatment.[104]

"Home-Grown" Terrorists

Most of Europe's so-called "home-grown" terrorists are not necessarily economically-deprived or uneducated—they have a middle-class background with a relatively high level of education.[105] What lures them to "betray" their European host nations and join Islamist/jihadist groups is their indignation over injustices inflicted not necessarily upon themselves, but upon their *own* group of people, not only in their own nation but also around the world.[106] They are radicalized over how their fellow Muslims—whether they are Palestinians, Sunnis, or Arabs—are mistreated and persecuted by Western leaders and their allies. The fact that their fellow, "identity-sharing" strangers are being persecuted angers them enough for them to risk their lives to fight for justice, even though they may not be directly affected by the persecution and mistreatments. Those who joined ISIS were also motivated by stories of the persecution of Palestinians, Syrians, and other Muslims around the world.[107] The majority of the nine suicide bombers of three churches and three high-end hotels in Sri Lanka that killed over 250 and injured over 500 in 2019 were well-educated men and women from middle- and upper-class families.[108] They were members of a local Islamist group, Thowfeek Jamaath, who committed the attacks with the help of ISIS/Daesh in retaliation for the mass shootings at two mosques in New Zealand that killed 50 Muslims a month prior to the bombings.[109]

Group-Felt Humiliation ("Shame Complex")

What infuriates a group of people and drives them toward extremist responses are not always deprivation and economic hardships per se; rather, it is a sense of collectively-felt humiliation—e.g., the feeling that they are being shamed, affronted, and slighted without due respect and dignity. A person, who feels he has endured an unbearable indignity and anguish, after a period of brooding, may run amok and lash out his aggression by attacking or killing others, as happens with most mass killers.[110] A *group* of people who collectively suffers unbearable shame and degradation at the hands of another group does the same—commits terrorist/extremist acts against the group they perceive to be the oppressors and perpetrators. Even without systematic persecution, group-felt humiliation can charge members with forceful emotions of rage. If extremist leaders can capture and channel those emotions, and effectively mobilize the people for action, it becomes a potent resistant movement.

Nation-States' Response to Humiliation

Group-felt humiliation has ignited a plethora of extremist aggressions and "group regressions" throughout history.[111] Scholars have argued that China's territorial and economic aggression and nationalistic fervor stem from the century of humiliation China suffered under the Western states' "preeminence and global supremacy with superior technological and economic prowess."[112] The humiliating defeat and concession it was forced to make to the British Empire after the First Opium War (1839–43), and the bitter experience of foreign incursions and exploitations during the two World Wars, in particular, led to the ascent of the Chinese Communist Party and its oppressive, isolationist ideologies and policies for over 40 years.[113]

After the First World War, Western allies, as "victors," punished and humiliated Germany and left it out of the new international world alliances. Such maltreatment and isolation left Germans wounded and angry, pinning for revenge, and eventually led to the Second World War.[114] Historians argue that the humiliating experience of the fall of the Soviet Union and subsequent belittlement and alienation of Russia by the West, whether real or perceived, may have contributed to the upsurge of Russian nationalism and aggression (e.g., the annexation of Crimea, involvement in Ukraine and Syria) under President Putin. Despite his authoritarian rule and allegations of corruption, President Putin maintains soaring popularity among Russians who regard Putin as a strong leader who can stand up against the West, making Russians feel "proud" again.[115]

Role of Humiliation Among Islamist/Jihadist Groups

What inspires people to gravitate toward radicalized Islamist/jihadist groups is also their overwhelming sense of humiliation. Osama bin Laden's speech after the 9/11 terrorist attacks in 2001 described the long history of humiliation Muslims had endured (as they perceive) as: "What America is tasting now is something insignificant compared to what we have tasted for scores of years. Our nations (the Islamic world) have been tasting this humiliation and this degradation for more than 80 years. Its sons are killed, its blood is shed, its sanctuaries are attacked, and no one hears and no one heeds."[116] Osama bin Laden's deputy, Ayman al-Zawahiri, described globalization and the new world order as "deeply humiliating to Muslims," and prescribed "youth of Islam to carry arms and defend their religion with pride and dignity," rather than submit to the humiliation of globalization. They felt that "Muslims have been overpowered and trampled by the West," and that "their ego hurts."[117]

Role of Humiliation in Working-Class Populism

According to Guillur,[118] the far-right, anti-immigrant populism that has swept much of the Western world since the 2008 economic recession was the "working-class's rebellion against years of economic gouging and belittlement by the economic elites." Instead of empathizing with the deteriorating economic conditions of the working class as a result of automation technologies, outsourcing of manufacturing jobs, and an influx of migrant workers, elites continue to disparage the working-class populism as "stupid, racist, and fascist." For instance, British businessman and political advisor, Alain Minc, lamented that "Brexit [Britain's departure from European Union] was the victory of the uneducated people over educated people"; and French intellectual and philosopher Bernard-Henri Levy described Brexit as "victory of ... stupidity over the mind." In the U.S., Hillary Clinton, as the U.S. Democratic presidential nominee, described Trump supporters as a "basket of deplorables" who were "racist, sexist, homophobic, xenophobic, and Islamophobic."[119] What drove and energized the rural "gun culture" and support for the powerful gun lobby group the NRA (National Rifle Association) in the U.S. was the "liberal media's demonization and belittling of the gun-rights activists." The media's perceived condescension and vilification of them were what drove many more people to join and donate to the NRA, and support its causes, according to members of the association.[120]

White People's Sense of Humiliation

Indignation over humiliation is not an experience limited only to the oppressed or marginalized groups. After the election of first African American president Barack Obama in 2008, according to the Southern Poverty Law Center, a plethora of white supremacist, anti-government militia, and (self-proclaimed) "patriot" groups have sprouted, revived, or expanded their membership ranks, and have become more active and violent. They perceived election of an African American president as a humiliating blow and insult to the honor and pride of the white race, enough to take extremist actions.[121] The KKK also became more active playing on white people's sense of "fear, humiliation, and victimization," by spreading misinformation about their enemies—e.g., minorities, immigrants, the government—and planted fake stories about Jews and Catholic priests plotting conspiracies against whites.[122]

Extreme Inequalities and Injustices Created by Dominant Extremisms

Extreme inequalities and injustices result when societal systems are rigged by the dominant groups that try to expand their power by monopolizing benefits and resources, at the expense of or by taking advantage of the powerless groups of people. They manipulate the systems in such a way that the unequal arrangements they benefit from become systemic, legitimate, traditional, "natural," "God-given," and therefore, unchallengeable. Once their superior status and power are legitimated, they control the systemic procedures and outcomes in their favor using political, legal, and ideological maneuvering. When inequalities and injustices become extreme and intolerable, it foments grievances among the disadvantaged groups of people, and their rage against the dominant group spawns resistant extremisms. Throughout history, sundry groups had dominated other groups and violently quelled reform efforts, such as in cases of patriarchy, slavery, caste systems, aristocracy, monarchy, imperialism, colonialism, exploitive capitalism, and discrimination based on racial, ethnic, and religious classifications. Oppressed groups, on the other hand, reacted with violent resistance movements, such as riots, protests, uprisings, rebel movements, and revolutions. Human history has been awash with clashes and conflicts between the dominant and resistant groups, especially as more people become educated and embrace modern values of fairness, equal rights, and justice.

Resistant Extremisms Against Dominant Extremisms in Modern World

Most modern societies, through vicissitudes of turmoil, have achieved higher degrees of equality, justice, and rule of law, compared to the traditional societies of the pre-modern era, despite intermittent relapses. Nevertheless, even in modern societies and times, violent protests, uprisings, and terrorist attacks occur sporadically. Most of the terror attacks against the Western world have been committed by resistant extremist groups fighting against the injustices perpetrated by the Western dominant extremisms, including Islamic/jihadist terror attacks. Most of the domestic extremist/terror acts have been resistant in nature, protesting against dominant extremisms committed by the wealthy and powerful. The "Arab Spring"

6. Factors That Facilitate the Rise of Extremist Groups 223

of 2011 was a middle-class uprising against the repressive dictators in Middle East nations, as was the unsuccessful "Green Movement" of Iran in 2009. Almost one-third of Hong Kong citizens participated in months-long protests demanding democracy independent from Beijing's authoritarian pressure and encroachment into their political activities. Tens of thousands of Iraqis demonstrated in central Baghdad and across mostly Shiite southern Iraq in 2019, fueled by anger at endemic corruption, high unemployment and poor public services. Over 300 protesters were shot and killed by security forces who used live ammunition against the protesters, and nearly 15,000 were wounded one month into the anti-government protests that started in October 2019, the Iraqi High Commission for Human Rights (IHCHR) reported.[123]

The Western world is not free of violent protests against injustices and inequalities. In 2018, over 300,000 angry "Yellow Vest" protesters swept through Paris streets every weekend for several months, and some of their actions were violent. The ordinary middle- and working-class Frenchmen vented their seething resentment against the nation's privileged "economic elite" class, to which President Macron belongs, who continue to further their own political and economic interests at the expense of the majority of the French working-class.[124] After the killing of Michael Brown in Ferguson, Missouri, in 2014, when police continued to kill black men and teenagers without cause and consequences to themselves, blacks around the U.S., along with sympathizers, organized nation-wide protests called the "Black Lives Matter" movement. Although the vast majority of the protests were peaceful, the movement has prompted a few rogue assailants from different groups to ambush and assassinate random police officers. After the housing market collapse of 2008 that brought the global economy into the Great Recession owing to the abusively speculative practices of the "too-big-to-fail" Wall Street banks, "Occupy Wall Street" movements and protests spread in large cities across America, some violently.

What mobilized the far-right nationalist movements that swept throughout Europe in the aftermath of the 2008 Great Recession were angry and frustrated working-class Europeans protesting against the globalist economic elites and "invasion" of immigrants and migrants. The rise of extreme-right populism in the U.S. that culminated in the election of Donald Trump was also a form of working-class revolt against the globalizing elites who benefited from free trade and immigration at their disadvantage. Although they may not have committed large-scale terrorist acts, their pugnaciously anti-immigrant stance, hate-filled xenophobic statements, and mass shooting incidences against immigrants were frightening to immigrants and minority groups of people.

Dominant Extremisms in the Corporate World

Studies abound when it comes to the detrimental effects of the most ostensibly unjust forms of dominance extremisms, such as persecution and discrimination against sexual, racial, ethnic and religious minorities, as well as, colonialism, imperialism and dictatorial regimes. On the other hand, how brazenly abusive business practices orchestrated by rapaciously profit-seeking economic elites (e.g., "plutocrats" and "transnational capitalist class") and their multinational corporations collaborating with corrupt politicians, can also ferment large scale grievances and resentments prodding resistant extremisms has not been widely explored as much, and implores critical attention. When multinational corporations unjustly harm indigenous people in foreign nations, disrupt their economy, deplete resources, and desolate their natural environment, and get away with their devastating malfeasance by bribing their corrupt leaders and with the blessing of their "parent" nations, the rage among the afflicted people and their sympathizers can extend not only to the multinational corporations, but also to the nations to which the multinational corporations belong, including their innocent civilians ("collective punishment").

Fueling Anti-West Sentiments

Most radicalized anti–West jihadist/Islamist groups harbor the same sense of grievances—e.g., a long history of oppression, mistreatment, manipulation, and humiliation they believe the Western world has inflicted upon them.[125] Their entrenched grievances emanate from the unfair and unjust political policies and economic exploitations carried out by Western corporations in collaboration with their corrupt politicians and policy makers—meddling into their politics, staging military coups, propping up and defending unscrupulous dictators, economic manipulation, unfair trade deals, exploitation of their resources and labor forces, and, at times, regime change through foreign invasions. Especially since the Second World War, large multinational corporations have become progressively more powerful and influential in shaping foreign policy issues involving investment in developing nations in their favor, disregarding even the most basic welfare of the indigenous population, geopolitical stability, and environmental concerns.[126] The U.S., for instance, for the benefit of its powerful multinational corporations, collaborated with, even sponsored, rigid, ethnocratic dictators who were not only corrupt, but also brutal in cracking down on their own people, especially against political dissidents and protesters.[127] America's unrestrained endorsement and protection of oppressive dictators, the "thugs and tyrants," and their repressive police states have produced "a new class of rich, spoiled elites and royal families" much reviled by the citizens in developing nations.[128] Scholars concur that the boiling resentments and grievances among oppressed populations in parts of the non–Western world have become the main sources of their radicalization against the West, spawning terrorist attacks.[129]

Effects of Multinational Corporations

The unregulated and unrestrained trends of globalization have created not only political instability, but also high and increasing economic inequality in most developing nations.[130] Studies have corroborated the suspected outcomes of MNCs (multinational corporations) and FDI (foreign direct investment) in developing nations, such as escalating income inequality and weakened domestic autonomy,[131] and reduction of economic growth, particularly in the post-socialist nations,[132] except in a few nations with solidly established democratic institutions that can mitigate the strains from FDI by granting workers freedom of association rights and facilitating institutional grievance resolutions.[133] Nevertheless, without globalized regulatory entities, multinational corporations have virtually no legal restrictions or liabilities against the fallouts from their ravenous pursuit of profit-seeking. They can ignore the interests and welfare of the people in host nations, and generate ravaging effects to the indigenous population, such as extreme inequality, exploitation of labor, corruption, political oppression and instability, and environmental destruction, with virtual impunity. Such injustices are bound to instigate resistance extremisms, some with terrorist tactics targeting vulnerable citizens of the Western nations as well as their own corrupt political leaders who collaborate with the West.[134]

Wherever the Western multinational corporations operate, trails of grievances seem to spread, spurring extremist groups to arise, whether they are in the Middle East, Africa, Asia, or Latin America. For instance, globalized giant oil industries (e.g., Shell, BP, Exxon, Chevron) and mining industries (e.g., Vale, BHP) damaged much of the natural environment and human and animal habitats around the world, and caused numerous manmade disasters with massive human casualties (e.g., chemical spills and explosions, oil spills, mine collapses and explosions, dam failures, mud slides) in less developed nations, and repeatedly got away with their malfeasance and liabilities by bribing the corrupt political leaders of those nations.[135] Thanks to the irresponsible practices of oil companies, for instance, Nigeria had over 7,000 oil spills between 1970 and 2000, which contaminated much of its water, soil, and air (from gas flares burning), ravaging fishing and farming industries, and causing serious health problems in the population.[136] The Movement for the Emancipation of the Niger Delta (MEND) arose to fight against the abusive practices of Western oil companies that were responsible for the air and water pollution, contaminated beaches and soil, destruction of fishing industries, and effecting political corruption and instability. Yet, instead of heeding their demands, the Western world quickly condemned the group as "terrorists" and helped the Nigerian military to eradicate it.[137] In 2019, Archbishop of York John Sentamu, speaking on behalf of a commission investigating oil spills in the Niger Delta, said that "a slow environmental genocide is taking place in Nigeria's Bayelsa State" as a result of decades of oil spills, and that oil companies must "end the culture of double standards in Nigeria."[138]

Between 2009 and 2011, Somali pirates terrorized the Horn of Africa region, assailing vessels transporting oil and kidnapping sailors for ransom. The Somalis were protesting against and trying to fend off illegal dumping of toxic wastes (including chemical and nuclear wastes) by the oil-transporting vessels traveling near their shallow seashores, wrecking their fishing activities. Without a functioning government and military, they had no other way but to turn to terrorist tactics to protect their territory and economic needs on their own, going against the foreign shipping industries of the powerful nations polluting their seashores. Without addressing the root causes of their "terrorist" acts, the Western nations captured, prosecuted, and imprisoned those responsible for the attacks against oil tankers, ending the hostage dramas.[139]

Similar scenarios of destruction of environment, political meddling, staging of military coups, and brutal crackdown on protesters rampaged all over Latin America for several decades. The American government's role has been to protect the interests of U.S. multinational corporations operating in Latin America, despite their abusive acts of exploiting cheap labor, devastating the natural environment without legal liability, and producing extreme inequality and subsequent political instability.[140] Leftist groups, such as FARC and ELN, arose owing to the endemic, unfair, and exploitative business practices of U.S. multinational corporations in collaboration with Latin American business oligarchs. The U.S. military and CIA ferociously backed and even instituted military dictators who can brutally crush leftist rebel groups, democracy movement leaders, student protesters, and religious leaders with complete impunity, labeling them as "internal enemies of the state." Most Latin American nations suffered for over 30 years from brutal dictators and their regimes that committed rampant violence, mass murders, and disappearances of tens of thousands of young democracy protesters and union leaders in the 1970s and 1980s. These acts were perpetrated by U.S.-backed and trained military and corporate-sponsored paramilitary "death squads" with the blessing of their corrupt, pro–American dictators. When people democratically elected political leaders who were not pro–America, America staged military coups to replace them with pro–American leaders. The American government's involvement in human rights violations in those nations has been well documented (e.g., "Dirty War" and "Operation Condor"), as they were driven by a single-minded goal of "crushing" leftist movements, for the economic benefits of American multinational corporations operating in Latin America.[141]

The same imputation goes to most high-income nations and their multinational corporations, which profit tremendously from Africa, Asia, and the Middle East, exploiting their natural resources and cheap labor. They also get away with unfair trade deals and unscrupulous practices by bribing and empowering corrupt and brutal dictators (e.g., the Shah of Iran, Saudi royal families, Mubarak of Egypt, Marcos of the Philippines, Suharto of Indonesia, Teodoro Obiang Nguema Mbasogo of Equatorial Guinea, Goodluck Jonathan of Nigeria, and Saddam Hussein of Iraq before his invasion of Kuwait), even removing (e.g., staging of military coups and through political assassinations) democratically-elected, anti–West or "uncooperative" leaders. Emboldened by the superpowers' political and military backings, these corrupt dictators, reigning for decades and generations, have been unafraid to plunder nations' revenue from selling resources, and commit war crimes and human rights violations against their own people.

Policies of "Regime Change"

The history of U.S. involvement in removing foreign leaders who are "not so friendly" to U.S. interests has been long and ruthless. For instance, in 1953, the CIA instigated a coup d'état in Tehran and removed democratically-elected Iranian Prime Minister Mohammed Mosaddeg and his government. The U.S.-backed Mohammad Reza Pahlavi, the Shah of Iran, ruled for 26 years in tyrannical repression, working on behalf of U.S. oil companies and under the protection of the U.S. government. In 1979, Iranians, fed up with the corrupt and brutal Shah's regime, overthrew the regime and embraced the equally repressive theocratic leadership of Ayatollah Khomeini. During the revolution, crowds invaded the U.S. embassy in Tehran, and took 52 American hostages for 444 days.[142] In Iraq, in the 1960s, the CIA recruited a group of street thugs, including Saddam Hussein, to oust democratically elected leader Karim Kassem, who was seen as a threat to U.S. oil interests. After taking power, the U.S.-backed Saddam Hussein became a horrendous dictator who terrorized his own people and executed political opponents. The U.S. continued to support Hussein despite his and his family members' atrocities until he betrayed the U.S., nationalized Iraqi oil, and invaded Kuwait in 1990.[143] Three years after the U.S.-led invasion of Iraq, Saddam was executed, in 2006.

More recently, in 2009, democratically elected Honduran president

Manuel Zelaya was ousted in a military coup when he raised the minimum wage by 60 percent, which was unfavorable to U.S. multinational corporations (particularly the garment industries) and collaborating Honduran corporate elites. Although the U.S. initially denied any involvement in the coup, later a number of U.S. officials—most notably then–Secretary of State Hillary Clinton—were reported to have played an important role, at least in thwarting Zelaya from returning to office, if not directly involved in plotting the coup itself, despite massive citizen protests against the coup.[144] Former President of Haiti Jean-Bertrand Aristide was also overthrown in 2004, after he angered business owners collaborating with U.S. multinational corporations by approving an increase of the minimum wage.[145]

Emerging Economies Following in Western Footsteps

U.S. and Western multinational corporations no longer monopolize the use of abusive tactics of exploitation and violence in less developed nations. More recently, Asian multinationals have begun to infiltrate resource-rich regions in less-developed nations. For instance, as Western multinationals pulled out of oil production in South Sudan because of high risks from political turmoil, oil companies from Asia (including the Chinese National Petroleum Co., Petronas of Malaysia, and the Indian Oil and Natural Gas Corporation) moved in to compete over the lucrative "top prize" oil fields using the same violent and unethical tactics the advanced nations had used in the past. In 2019, a United Nations War Crimes Panel's report accused these oil companies, along with Sudan's Nilepet, of "contributing to the ongoing violence and war crimes" in South Sudan by funding South Sudan's security forces that committed atrocities against their own people on behalf of the oil companies, including such brutal acts as burning elderly people alive in their huts, sexually mutilating children, slamming babies against trees, and raping women and girls as young as seven years old. The report concluded that the role of foreign oil industries was "a major driver for the continuing violence in South Sudan, [and the] ensuing inconceivable level of human suffering," aimed at securing control of areas close to oil fields by removing and driving out the civilian population.[146]

These are just a few examples of the abusive acts multinational corporations have been engaged in throughout the world with the blessing of and protection by governments. Although not every multinational corporation is engaged in abusive and exploitive practices, when some of them do, people in the affected areas assume that *all* multinationals operate likewise, and blame their hosting nations and their citizens for their acts ("collective punishment").

Militarized Dominant Extremisms

Iraq War

The Iraq invasion in 2003 was not so much (or genuinely) about spreading democracy and freedom as President Bush touted, but to secure America's oil interests by removing Saddam Hussein.[147] One of the architects of the Iraq War, Richard Perle, as Defense Department advisor to President Bush, frankly admitted during an interview: "The idea that we went to Iraq to impose democracy is nonsense: Democracy would be icing on the cake."[148] After the successful removal of Saddam Hussein in 2007, the Bush administration drafted a law and pressured Iraq's newly elected Prime Minister Nouri al-Maliki to pass the law that would give Western oil companies, especially BP, Shell and Exxon/Mobil, 30-year, no-bid contracts to extract Iraq's crude oil with up to 75 percent of the profits, from 70 out of 80 existing oil fields and all of the future developments, under Executive Order 13303. This oil law pressed by the U.S. permitted the first large-scale operation by foreign oil companies in Iraq since Saddam nationalized the industry in 1972, with complete legal immunity.[149]

It is not just the oil companies that benefited from the Iraq War. The major beneficiaries of the war included U.S. firms with lucrative weapons and reconstruction contracts, mostly without bidding, who were major donors to President Bush's political campaigns, according to the CPI (Center for Public Integrity) report that disclosed 70 companies and individuals who won reconstruction contracts in Afghanistan and Iraq worth over $8 billion.[150] According to Chellie Pingree, president of the citizens' activist group Common Cause, Halliburton (the company of which Dick Cheney was CEO before becoming vice president under Bush) *alone* procured about $1.7 billion for contracts, ranging from hot meals to hunting for weapons of mass destruction, which the company obtained with exclusive, no-bid contracts. Bechtel's contract to rebuild Iraqi infrastructure also exceeded $1 billion.[151]

As Cox[152] argued, corporate interests, especially that of the military-industrial complex, were powerfully at play in structuring the *military* response to the 9/11 terrorist attacks in 2001. Even after the Iraq War, in 2012, taxpayer-funded, defense-related contracts constituted 76 percent of Lockheed Martin's revenue; 95 percent of BAE Systems; 92 percent of Raytheon; 66 percent of General Dynamics; and 77 percent of Northrop Grumman. The constellation of economic interests comprising the military-industrial complex has helped to determine, shape, and refine the definition of "national security interests" with a single-minded goal of maximizing their corporate profits and protecting their access to resources in foreign nations by shoring up policies of "military expansionism," using the 9/11 terrorist attacks as a convenient excuse.[153] By invading Iraq, the country that had "nothing to do with 9/11" (as the 9/11 Investigation Commission concluded and as President Bush admitted),[154] American corporations, especially the military-industrial and oil-related companies, reaped enormous profit, at the expense of American taxpayers' money and lives of thousands of American troops and tens of thousands of Iraqi citizens.

MILITARY-INDUSTRIAL COMPLEX

Ever since President Eisenhower warned Americans of the dangers of the military-industrial complex in 1961, the power and political clout of it have accelerated. The military- and defense-related corporations have guided and pushed much of the foreign policy agendas, even before the Iraq and Afghan Wars.[155] For instance, during the eight-year war between Iraq and Iran (1980–1988), which the U.S. prodded Iraq to initiate largely in retaliation for Iran's humiliating treatment of U.S. diplomats during the Iranian Revolution in 1978 and 1979, an estimated 680,000 Iraqis and Iranians were killed, including over 100,000 civilians. During the war 9,000 tanks and armored vehicles, 950 warplanes, 30 naval ships and 72 commercial vessels were destroyed, totaling about $1.1 trillion. The major suppliers of those mangled weapons to *both* warring nations were the weapons industries of the U.S., Israel, and Soviet Union.[156] In 2015, the U.S. sold $40 billion in weapons mostly to conflict-prone developing nations, which was about half of all weapons sales in the world, far ahead of France, the number two weapons dealer with $15 billion in sales, followed by Russia with $11 billion,[157] knowing that these weapons were used in civil wars, massacres, and against civilian protesters by dictators and autocrats who want to crush their people's aspirations for democracy. Despite international criticism and condemnation, America's weapons industries continue to sell high-tech weapons to Saudi Arabia, knowing that they are used against Houthi rebels in Yemen, killing scores of civilians indiscriminately, including women and school children, and displacing millions of civilians who now face starvation.[158] During Yemen's civil war, America's arms deliveries to Saudis increased dramatically, to $5.5 billion in 2017 from $1.7 billion in 2009. In 2017, in Trump's first trip abroad as president, his first stop was Saudi Arabia, where he announced $100 billion in immediate sales of U.S. weapons, with $350 billion additional deals over the next 10 years. Even after the gruesome murder of Jamal Khashoggi, a well-known *Washington Post* journalist and critic of the Saudi government, President Trump rejected bipartisan support for sanctions against Saudi Arabia by saying "weapons export to Saudi creates jobs in the U.S."[159] In 2019, when Congress passed a bill to end military support for Saudi Arabia because it is committing acts that amount to war crimes and creating a huge humanitarian crisis in Yemen, President Trump vetoed the bill arguing that Saudi Arabia is a key ally and vital importer of U.S.-made weapons.[160] In 2019, the United Nations reported that there were at least 7,000 confirmed civilians deaths in Yemen, and 65 percent of the deaths were directly attributed to air strikes by the Saudi-led coalition forces.[161]

The U.S.'s military intervention in foreign countries to protect U.S. corporate interests, and the unrestrained supply of weapons in conflict-prone regions around the world can be seen as the pinnacle of state-sponsored dominant extremisms in modern times. American corporations, including weapons and oil industries, colluding with and bribing corrupt politicians, both foreign and domestic, promote their own economic interests at the expense of masses of people around the world—impairing their lives, infrastructure, and the environment, and destabilizing their nations' political autonomy and economic systems, in violation of their national sovereignty. Their unscrupulous extremist acts are bolstering anti–West sentiments and causes in afflicted areas of the world, fueling resistant extremist groups plotting terrorist threats against the West.

Fate-Sharing Experiences

Enduring dramatic, fate-sharing events or experiences together, whether positive or negative, shame or glory, *can* be a powerful bonding experience that can generate a shared sense of identity, camaraderie, and "collective conscience."[162] Martin Buber said a group is not necessarily defined by common ethnic origin, but instead by a common *fate*. For instance, he argues, nationalism is a reaction of a nation to a crisis, an insufficiency, or a wound from which it suffers, whether caused by external forces that limit political or economic autonomy, or by internal forces, such as rootlessness and social chaos.[163] Grand'Maison also stated that nations are not a given, determined by their ethnic origin: nations are cultural constructions made under the pressure of historical circumstances that arise from shared *fates*.[164] If a nation's fate-sharing experience is a positive one, citizens exalt and celebrate together in honor and glory; for a negative or humiliating one, they commiserate together, share a sense of anger and grievances, and seek atonement and revenge collectively. The 9/11 terrorist attacks in 2001 were catastrophic "fate-sharing" events that bonded Americans together with a profound sense of collective anger, shame, and hatred. They believed that, as a Christian nation, all Americans should unite together to fight against Islamic terrorists for retribution and justice, with unusually robust and militant patriotic fervor and nationalistic zeal in modern history.[165] The attacks aroused an unusual sense of group solidarity in recent history—e.g., the feeling that "we are all in this together; we are all part of a larger national project, and we all need to make some shared sacrifices and look beyond our narrow self-interest."[166]

Fate-sharing events and experiences can invoke "collective consciousness" and "consciousness of kind" among the afflicted, whether they are from violent acts of crime, humiliating trauma, or disasters, natural or man-made, the same way collective victimization by oppression, abuse, and persecution can.[167] The sense of sharing the same fate, enduring an ordeal and trauma together can be a powerful bonding agent that can strengthen existing group identities or bring about a new identity bound by the shared feeling that "only those who went through the same experience can understand." Their in-group ties and loyalties grow strong, and their antipathy toward out-groups upsurges, at times transcending their primordial differences in race, ethnicity, nationality, and religion. As Long[168] and Fine[169] discussed, a form of "social capital" emerges from fate-sharing experiences, shaping people's collective aspirations of fulfilling collectivity's common goals.

Examples of Shared Fates

The sources of trauma and shared fate a group of people experience can be diverse. The following illustrates some examples.

WAR TIME TRAUMAS

Wars and traumas pull battlefield soldiers closer together with an acute sense of bond, camaraderie, and brotherhood, because they share the same life-threatening experiences together during which they have to rely on each other for survival and protection.[170] Marines serving in the Iraq War reported that they do not fight for politics, ideologies, national honor, or duty to the country. They fight for their "brothers," meaning fellow Marines—i.e., they fight to protect each other and look after each other under life-threatening hostile situations.[171] Probably for this reason, acts of war crimes occur usually in response to collectively experienced traumatic events, such as after heavy losses of their fellow "brothers."[172]

TRAUMAS FROM CORPORATE WRONGDOINGS

In a similar way, when a group of workers experience an unusually harsh and unsafe working environment or mistreatment at the hands of management, they are more likely to unite and fight against management to demand better treatments (e.g., labor unions, strikes, walkouts), with an unusually robust feeling of group solidarity, camaraderie, and loyalty to each other. When a large number of consumers are injured by corporate

6. Factors That Facilitate the Rise of Extremist Groups

wrongdoings (e.g., defective or harmful products, toxic material dumping), the unjustly afflicted can band together and seek redress collectively with unusually high feelings of collective bonding (e.g., public protests, class-action lawsuits). Their "collective consciousness" stems from the feeling that no one else can understand what they experienced except their peers who lived through the same experiences of being afflicted or victimized by corporate wrongdoings.

Imprisonment Experiences

Some extremist groups have sprouted out of some form of life-altering, fate-sharing experiences, whether real or perceived. According to Chulov,[173] ISIS/Daesh has grown out of Camp Bucca, a U.S. detention center in Iraq, which became a breeding ground for Sunni insurgents while they served time with other "like-minds with shared grievances," plotting about what they would do when they were eventually released. It was in this facility where they met and connected, impelled by the same "fate" they experienced and endured, and they networked and plotted an insurgency movement. Ten years later, the group developed into ISIS/Daesh. Of the 25 members of the ISIS's military council, 17 were prisoners held for months or years at Camp Bucca.[174] French officials also reported that a handful of Muslim petty criminals with no history of prior radicalization are becoming radicalized in prisons. About 50–60 percent of roughly 67,000 prison inmates in France are Muslims (who represent 7.5 percent of French population)[175]; in Paris region prisons, where a lot of preaching and proselytizing go on, up to 70 percent of inmates are identified as Muslim.[176] Convicted terrorists claim the highest "social pecking order"; with the respect they earn, they recruit and indoctrinate fellow inmates.[177] British officials also reported that locking up masses of young Muslim petty criminals in prisons created an unintended consequence of "convergence effect"—i.e., the like-minded and like-experienced Muslims grieve and seethe together, radicalize each other, and join jihadist groups after release.[178] In Britain, Muslims make up roughly 5 percent of the population, but between 14 to 40 percent of the prison population are Muslims, depending on the prison.[179] By sharing the same humiliating fate of imprisonment, mistreatment, and stigmatization with disproportionately higher frequency, they become more motivated to connect, bond, and empathize than before they entered prison, reinforcing their collective senses of grievances, resentments, and anger.

Committing Collective Acts of Violence

At times, committing acts of violence together can become a form of "fate-sharing" experience that bonds people together with a staunch sense of group solidarity and loyalty. Gang members' initiation activities often involve criminal or violent acts committed together. Perhaps they intuitively understand the "bonding effects" of committing violence as a collectivity. By committing criminal acts together, they become permanently "bound by" the same fate, whether stigma or honor, and secrecy of their criminal acts. They are forced to deter any member from leaving the group because departure of a member and the possible revelation of their secret criminal acts can pose a serious threat to the remaining members of the group.[180]

Blockage of Legitimate Means of Achieving Changes

Most resistant extremist groups and movements occur when oppressed groups of people do not have legitimate means or ability to transform the system in their favor through non-violent ways, because they are legally prohibited, politically repressed, or systematically obstructed.[181] In truly democratic societies, therefore, people will have diminished need to resort to extremist means to demand changes, because the system offers a variety of opportunities and means for oppressed and disgruntled groups to voice their grievances and request reforms legitimately, and participate in political actions legally and legislatively to bring about reforms. Any group of people, even the most powerless and moneyless, has the right to assemble freely for collective actions, organize and fight for their rights and interests, legally and legitimately. When the system, whether due to authoritarian leadership or non-democratic systems, does not allow people to organize themselves to pursue changes legitimately, resistant groups have no other recourse except to turn to illegitimate means, often labeled as "extreme" measures, to demand changes.

In authoritarian "police" states (e.g., Saudi Arabia, Iran, Egypt, North Korea), free speech and assembly rights are limited, and public protests are prohibited. Anyone who dissents, challenges or protests against authorities can be labeled as "terrorists" with "subversive" motives, and detained or executed without due process. Most recently, in 2019, Iraqi security forces killed 149 civilians and injured over 4,000 who were protesting over high unemployment, poor public services, and corruption. More than 70 percent of the deaths were caused by shots to the head or chest.[182] In 2018, an Egyptian court sentenced 75 people to death, including top figures of the outlawed Muslim Brotherhood group, for their involvement in a 2013 sit-in protest.[183] During the seven years of Syrian civil war, tens of thousands of public protesters have disappeared into government jails where torture and mistreatments, and mass disappearances were rife, human rights groups reported. In 2018, the Syrian government revealed names of over 300 arrested for protesting against the government who died in jail, in just one year—2013.[184] In 2018, when hundreds of thousands of people marched on Nicaragua's Mother's Day to honor the mothers of students killed at previous rallies, the Nicaraguan military opened fire, killing at least 15 people.[185] Even in presumably "democratic" societies where protests are permitted, they require authorization, and masses of protesters have been arrested for dubious charges, such as "resisting authority," "covering face," or "creating public nuisance."[186] In 2015, the Spanish government ended freedom of assembly rights under the revised Citizens' Security Law. Under the new provision, police have discretionary ability to arrest and hand out fines up to $650,000 to unauthorized demonstrators. They will be allowed to issue fines of up to $30,000 for such acts as taking pictures of police during protests, failing to show police an ID, or just gathering in an unauthorized way near government buildings.[187] If people cannot express their grievances and protest against injustice, maltreatment, and corruption, oppressed groups of people see no other way to reform the system except violent resistance and uprising, especially when the dominant groups refuse to change the system or share powers, and, instead, violently suppress their effort to change, or keep the pace of change too slow.[188]

Military Underdogs' Terrorist Attacks Against Dominant Groups

Military underdogs are more likely to adopt insurgency and terrorist attacks against civilian targets ("soft targets"), because they cannot fight against the more powerful and dominant groups with superior military power *legitimately*—i.e., conventional military confrontations. Their aim is to send a *political* message to the dominant groups by terrorizing a large audience of people, hoping to compel the government or a third party such as an international organization to intervene and attend to their grievances.[189] Without a third-party intervention, such as an independent and neutral international organization, extremist/terrorist attacks appear to be the only option for the military underdogs with overarching grievances against the superpowers that refuse to share power and resources and violate their rights, wellbeing, and sovereignty.

Geographic and Cultural Isolation

Segregation by all group boundaries, whether they are geographical, cultural, social, associational, or physical, whether based on race, ethnicity, income level, religion, nationality, tribal identity, or region, tends to reinforce and accentuate group identities and solidarities, and cultivate extremism-prone mindsets by restricting chances for "intersectionality," "multiple group affiliations,"[190] and "intersecting group affiliations."[191] People who live an encapsulated life in a parochial surrounding most of their lifetime, without much contact with outsiders or exposure to diverse experiences, tend to place high emphasis on conformity to the traditional, particularistic views, and are more likely to offer their loyalty to their localized groups rebuffing differences and diversities.[192] Even in urban, metropolitan areas, when people live most of their lives in localized enclaves (what Herbert Gans referred to as "little peasant villages") where the social structure creates a kind of "cocoon around the individuals,"[193] they develop group-centric mindsets with dutiful desire to defend their group, which is predisposed to extremism.

Without intergroup exposures and cross-pollination of ideas and cultures, people become more firmly rooted in their group-prescribed cultures, and develop group-centric mindsets. Isolation produces a form of cultural and mental "insularity," in which people acquire and solidify a parochial view of the world, which tends to be dogmatic, inwardly-defined, and unidimensional in perspective—i.e., events are explained from their vantagepoints only. They become suspicious of and hostile toward outsiders; resolutely defensive of their own beliefs and views, and consequently, they try to stave off all outside influences and viciously denounce "one-of-their-own" deviating from their group's tradition. A study by Sperling et al.[194] corroborated that people in isolated rural areas in America hold more fundamentalist religious beliefs and are less open to or accepting of racial/ethnic minorities and immigrants, and less supportive of professional women and gay rights than urban and metro residents.

In gang-infested urban "cocoons," gang subcultures dictate every aspect of their lives, becoming the "most dominant culture" of the situation. In order to alleviate deadly gang violence problems in Chicago, former gang members suggested a "mentoring program" for the gang members, which they believe will expose them to the outside world and views. For the gangs, they say, "all they know is their block."[195] This is probably the reason why extremist group leaders and autocratic regimes try hard to shelter their members from outside influences by banning education, internet, and traveling, as discussed in earlier chapters. They fear losing members and their loyalty when members are exposed to diverse worldviews and information that contradicts what they indoctrinate.

Extremist Leaders with Organizational Skills

None of the above-mentioned factors and conditions alone would be enough to elicit extremist groups and movements without an organizational leadership. Some extremist *acts* can be situational and spontaneously-occurring without a leader, such as mob violence, riots, and vigilante attacks, and some spur-of-the-moment protests and demonstrations can crop up without instrumental leadership and organizational structures. For a collectivity to develop into an organized extremist group, however, effective leadership is indispensable. Most organized extremist groups have a captivating leader who can evoke extremist mindsets out of ordinary people and channel their passion-filled emotions toward a group-centric movement using extremist strategies. Without such a leadership, people's extremist mindsets and grievances are likely to stay dormant and inactive.

When violent civil war was going on in Iraq between the Shiites and Sunnis following the U.S.-led invasion in 2003, among the Iraqi refugees congregated in Syria and Jordan, there was only one, unified Iraqi community where all the Iraqi refugees, regardless of sectarian differences, lived together without conflicts, sharing the same theater, cafes, and restaurants.[196] It seems to allude that the sectarian animosity is not an inherent or inevitable cause of their clash as their leaders assert it to be. Without the political and religious leaders, Iraqi refugees *can* be united as one ethnic group in peace. After the controversial election in 2008, Kenya plunged into intertribal violence, causing the deaths of thousands of civilians and the displacement of millions. The unrest, however, did not start until a few angry and power-hungry politicians, dissatisfied with the election result, began to exploit the situation by pivoting tribal identities and protesting the election result.[197]

Leaders as Instrumental Medium

When group movements emerge, leaders become instrumental mediums connecting people's traumas and grievances with collective actions. They formulate and invoke a sense of group identity and cause by defining collective aspirations and goals, and propagate the need for their movements.[198] They contrive group-centric ideologies that can justify their movement, and convince potential recruits with incentives and reasons why they should join and sacrifice for their causes.[199] When that happens, leaders can effectually procure and pool resources and build the organizational infrastructure needed for the movement—e.g., creating communication channels, and building social infrastructure and social networks that can facilitate collective actions.[200]

Scholars have discussed how contentious groups and collectivities gain momentum when leaders effectively stir up people's fear, anger, and grievances, and corral those emotions toward group-centric causes and actions.[201] By capitalizing on people's emotional vulnerabilities, such leaders can mobilize people and their resources to initiate contentious movements and activisms.[202] People with passion-filled emotions become easy prey for their collective mobilization efforts, because emotionally aroused people become readily inspired and mobilized by the leader's pleas, and vulnerable to ideological propagandas and rhetorical narratives and slogans leaders present. For this reason, extremist group leaders try to hype fear and transform it into anger and aversion toward out-groups—the presumed source of the threat and fear. By exaggerating threats, stoking fear, and inciting anger, they can transform ordinary people into fanatic extremists willing to commit violent acts on behalf of the group without reservations. The more fearful and angry people become, the more passionate, energized, even vicious they become, with a single-minded obsession of achieving their group-centric, "holy" goals and agendas, disregarding notions of justice, fairness, and the human rights of their victims.

Charismatic leadership and ideological propaganda have always played a pivotal role in shaping and invoking violently extremist groups and movements of the past and present. Brustein[203] discussed that the main cause of the Holocaust was the anti–Semitic hatred that was successfully manufactured, propagated, and implanted among Germans in rural areas by Hitler, more importantly than any other competing theories (e.g., modernization theory, strong-state theory, political culture theory, rational economic theory). According to Soufan,[204] most people join Islamist/jihadi terror groups, such as al-Qaeda and ISIS/Daesh, not necessarily to stage a war against the West; rather, they do so for other reasons, such as economic trouble, ethnic or familial motives, sectarianism, ethnic chauvinism, or tribal rivalries. However, once they join the group, the group leaders place them under a non-stop "ideological echo chamber" in which they are indoctrinated with hate-filled, anti–West ideologies and narratives. Al-Qaeda leaders, particularly Osama bin Laden, had successfully peddled the view that the West is engaged in a "war against Islam" to vanquish Islam. The invasion of Iraq, subsequent mistreatment of Muslims (e.g., humiliating treatment of prisoners in Guantanamo Bay and Abu Ghraib), and the failure to curtail civilian casualties from drone attacks afterwards have all contributed to "fulfilling" their propaganda messages.[205]

In violence-prone extremist groups, leaders' mobilization strategies to facilitate collective actions expand beyond convincing potential recruits or building organizational infrastructures. They rely heavily on members' willingness and eagerness to sacrifice their lives and personal interest for

6. Factors That Facilitate the Rise of Extremist Groups 239

the group, and to commit unjust and cruel acts against out-groups, enemies, and "traitors" on behalf of the group. In order to achieve this goal, leaders transform the group into a "spiritual and moral" entity that is "greater and holier than the sum of all individuals," by instilling a sense of moral superiority and group righteousness. When this effort succeeds, acts of self-sacrifice for the group become a "moral" duty, and fighting for the group, even committing atrocities against "enemies" becomes a "holy crusade." The success of such groups depends on the leader's ability to produce as many "righteous" soldiers as possible who would gladly participate in "righteous violence" committing atrocities without feeling guilt or contrition, for the "noble" and "holy" causes of defending their group.

♦♦ 7 ♦♦

Deterring Extremist Group Aggressions

In examining extremist aggressions, it becomes apparent that they have multiple causes, and countering them calls for comprehensive, multi-pronged approaches. I discuss some of those approaches with three objectives in mind—improving existential security for all groups of people; restraining extreme and unfair inequalities and injustices in all aspects of the society and the globe; and stamping out dominant extremisms that incite resistant extremisms to foment.

Balancing of Clashing Groups' Interests

Most group-based extremisms arise because different groups' collective interests collide, whether they are between dominant and subordinate groups, majority and minority groups, or between groups with equal power or size. When one group tries to monopolize power and resources and maximize its group-centric interests at the expense of another, whether through subjugation, abuse, exploitation, or discrimination, the wronged group of people is likely to rebel, some with extreme measures. To achieve stability, peace and progress devoid of extremisms in a given society or a community, therefore, all competing groups' interests must be fairly balanced, and at the same time, personal and special interests must be balanced with collective and public interests. Each nested group's interests should be balanced with national interests, and national interests should be balanced with international and humanity's interests for safe and balanced growth and prosperity of humanity devoid of extremist aggressions.

For instance, individuals and corporations must pursue personal interests and corporate profits within the moral and ethical boundaries of protecting collective interests—e.g., assuming social responsibility, causing no harm to others, and protecting shared environments. Each nation's economic prosperity must be achieved within the limitations of promoting social justice and responsibilities to the public good and global communities. All benefits from economic development and progress must be shared fairly and equitably among all groups involved. When individual sacrifices are required for the collective interests, or national sacrifices are needed for the good of humanity, the sacrifices should be equally shared by every party involved, along with the benefits, to minimize resentments and grievances among the disaffected and marginalized groups of people who must bear greater burden of sacrifice without rightful share of the benefits.

Intergroup power struggles, ranging from inter-family to inter-nation collisions, are as old as human history. Most of the Western world endured a tumultuous era of violence for centuries over labor vs. management disputes, which culminated in Communist revolutions and counter-communist aggressions. Many continue to struggle with sparring political ideologies (e.g., right vs. left, pro-business vs. pro-labor, elitism vs. populism) and various wedge issues that pit traditionalists against the progressives—e.g., gender roles, abortion, gun rights, gay rights, religious freedom, human rights, and environmental protection. However, in the broader historical spectrum, historians concur that most modern societies have made enormous progress in achieving more egalitarian systems, politically, economically and socially, albeit with periodic relapses. Religious freedom, liberal democracies, and equal rights and opportunities for everyone regardless of backgrounds and group identities exist much more broadly in modern, advanced nations, compared to the repressive authoritarian and hierarchical states of the past with hereditary transmission of statuses and wealth, bound by tradition and religion (e.g., caste systems, aristocracy, theocracy, patriarchy). Modern societies achieved societal progress largely through successfully balancing competing interests and demands among an array of groups, a process that contributed to reduction of extremist aggressions.

Integration of Marginalized Groups

Human history is awash with violent intergroup feuds between the native and immigrant population, as well as various majority and minority groups, whether in size or power. As more people travel, immigrate, and migrate across national boundaries, the type and scope of intergroup interactions and contentions are bound to surge, reshaping the general ethos of modern, globalizing, cosmopolitan societies. In pluralistic modern societies with a large immigrant and transient population, some people experience distress from "loss of identity" competing loyalties, and "identity crisis"—i.e., feeling that they don't belong to any group,[1] especially when they are marginalized and mistreated by other groups of people, threatening their sense of existential security. Such an "alienating" experience can be more pronounced among immigrant minority groups. When people dis-embed from their native groups and re-embed into another group, they commonly find themselves in situations where their identities are questioned, loyalties clash, and their allegiance is suspected. In general, immigrants' loyalty and allegiance to the hosting nation vary subject to how well they are *accepted and treated* by the natives. If they are well received and treated, they are more likely to identify themselves as one of the hosting nation's member, and quickly assimilate to the dominant culture. If not, they are more inclined to retain or repatriate their allegiance to their birth place and parents' national identity, resisting assimilation.[2]

Muslim immigrants in Europe, even some of the second generation Muslims, face such dilemmas—e.g., loss of "belonging," clashing loyalties, allegiances, "identity crisis." In fact, a number of terrorist acts in Europe had been committed by so-called "home-grown terrorists"—Muslims who were born and raised in Europe, yet radicalized by Islamist/jihadist ideologies. They are more common among those who are marginalized, disaffected, and aggrieved by prejudice and maltreatment, or outraged by the way their fellow Muslims (whether they are Sunnis or Palestinians) are mistreated, either real or perceived. Their Muslim identity is rejuvenated and reinvigorated; they resist assimilation; they rebuff European identity all together in rebellion[3], and find sense of identity and belonging in anti–West Islamist/jihadist groups, such as ISIS/Daesh.[4] Radicalized Islamist groups lure these youths searching for belonging with easy-to-grasp answers and twisted versions of "authentic Muslim."[5] For a society to minimize extremist rebellions, social, political, and economic integration of all marginalized groups is essential.

Balancing Group's and Humanity's Interests

At times, one group's interests (e.g., national, industries', or corporate interests) can clash with humanity's interests, and instigate international instability, geopolitical disturbance, or environmental destruction for the detriment of the humanity.

Curtailing Nationalism in the Globalizing World

Global stability and peace are hard to achieve because nationalistic concerns tend to prevail when they clash with humanistic values. For the majority of people, nationalistic mandates for self-determination and security tend to be much more socially pervasive than those relate to international or humanity's concerns.[6] Political leaders are elected for the job of defending national interests and security, not sponsoring global or humanity's interests, unless there is international pressure to help or they expect some posterior benefits from aiding other nations. Even with the international pressure, nationalistic leaders often resist international cooperation blinded by short-term national interests, or for the interest of their donor corporations. For instance, in 2001, President Bush snubbed the Kyoto protocol on tackling climate change (which would have committed the U.S. to cutting greenhouse gas emissions) for the benefit of the U.S. economy, especially that of the fossil-fuel industries.[7] In 2003, the first permanent international tribunal, International Criminal Court (ICC) was founded after decades of international collaborative endeavor, and embarked on an ambitious project of enforcing the international rule of law and punishing those responsible for war crimes and genocides. The Bush administration, fearing that it might exercise its jurisdiction to investigate and prosecute U.S. military and political officials over the Iraq invasion, decided not to join it.[8] President Trump in 2017 pulled out of the Paris Agreement that was designed to curb global warming for the same reason—refusal to sacrifice short-term national economic interests, particularly that of the U.S. fossil-fuel industries. Trump also withdrew from the INF Treaty—the nuclear arsenal reduction agreement with Russia—to build more lethal nuclear weapons, which he believed were necessary for America's military dominance and for the benefit of U.S. weapons industries who contributed to his election.[9]

Modern states cannot achieve long-term global peace and stability free of extremist violence unless they balance national and humanity's interests, even if it involves sacrificing a certain degree of short-term national interests. If developed nations continue to maximize their national interests, or their corporate interests, at the expense of, or trampling less-developed nations' sovereignty and their citizens' rights and welfare, the imperiled groups of people will resort to extremist acts, such as terrorist attacks seeking revenge or reform.

AMERICA'S SUPPORT FOR AUTHORITARIAN REGIMES FOR ECONOMIC INTERESTS

In the process of maximizing America's economic interests, the American government has maintained a long-standing policy of supporting and empowering regimes that were committing atrocities against their own people, at times even replacing democratically elected heads with corrupt, pro–American dictators. Such political interferences for the benefit of multinational corporations' economic interests have been one of the primary root causes of people's grievances and resentments against the West in many developing nations of Latin America, The Middle East , and Africa, prodding rise of resistant extremist groups. Western support for repressive dictators and oppressive police states in the Arab world has produced a new class of rich, spoiled elites and royal families protected by the American military, stifled their efforts to build democracy, and contributed to the rise of anti–West sentiments and Islamic radicalism in the Arab world.[10]

The American government's involvement in human rights violations in Latin America for the benefit of U.S. multinational corporations' interest has been well documented. They were motivated by the single-minded goal of "crushing" leftist movements in Latin America for the economic benefit of American corporations and their collaborating oligarchs in Latin America.[11] According to Howard,[12] this has become a "habit" in U.S. foreign policy, driven by its desire to secure its corporate interests overseas. Such an extremist pursuit of global economic hegemony for the benefit of U.S. multinational corporations using U.S. military might must be tamed and replaced with more balanced approaches of promoting fair trades, mutually-benefitting cooperation, and democracy, in conjunction with respectfully power-sharing diplomacy. Instead of maximizing America's corporate interest at the expense of wellbeing of other nations and their people, both sides must adhere to achieving mutually-benefitting collective interests that are fairly balanced with shared benefits and sacrifices.

Balancing Globalizing and "Parochializing" Forces

As with all social transformations, the common reactions to globalization have been twofold. Some groups of people see globalization as a positive trend leading toward cultural amalgamation and economic cooperation removing boundaries and de-emphasizing particularities (e.g., "cosmopolitanism," the idea of "global village"), and try to take advantage of the new opportunities it offers. Others see globalization as a threat to their cultural identity, political sovereignty, and economic independence, and resent it—e.g., fear of "westernization" in non–Western world; fear of "Islamization of Europe"; desire to preserve America as a "white Christian nation"; anti-immigration and anti-multiculturalism. Some people feel "free and liberated" from the repressive, "tribalistic," group-bound constraints and parochial loyalties, and are happy to join the "humanity of mankind" with cosmopolitan vision of the world; others fear globalization and "parochialize" or "burrow" deeper into localized groups and identities, and become stauncher fundamentalists and defenders of their group's traditions, ideologies, dogmas, and autonomy, responding aggressively against all external "threats" to their group (so-called "hunker-down effect" and "bunker mentality").

Whether to be "inclusive or exclusive" toward people of differences—e.g., race, ethnicity, religions, and nationalities—has become a controversial issue as modern states globalize and transform into a "mosaic of diversity with profound cultural and social consequences."[13] Nations grapple with whether to "open or close" doors for immigrants and migrants; adopt protectionist or free-trade economic policies; take unilateral isolationist or multilateral approaches to geopolitical issues; and whether to embrace multiculturalism and pluralism or stipulate one-sided assimilation from their "not-so-pure" members and immigrants. Modern societies observe the necessity of globalizing for economic benefits (e.g., greater resources, trade partners, and market potential; flow of labor and capital, and cross-stimulation of ideas for innovation) and political power that stems from broader trade partnership and alliances. Yet, at the same time, there is palpable unease among the traditionalists over "openness" and diversity that follow globalization—i.e., fear of change and loss of group identity, heritage, "purity," and "safe zone."[14] For instance, British rural farmers are torn between their dire need to rely on immigrant workers *and* nationalistic desires to retain British culture unadulterated by immigrants.[15] Residents in some East German towns with seriously shrinking populations are dithering between the economic benefits from migrant workers and fear of losing their cultural heritage.[16]

For a safer and more secure world order, societies must respect and balance both sides' needs and desires, even if it means slower economic growth and lower profits for the multinational corporations. Policies can become more flexible in "opening" and "closing" depending on changing economic circumstances, and offer temporary compensation or alternative means of survival to groups of people who are negatively affected by "opening."

Reactionary Trends of "Parochializing"

Some people in developing societies resent globalization because they construe globalization as "cultural imperialism" or "ideological colonialism" imposed by Western nations[17] that does not respect their local values and traditions, particularly concerning their traditional notions regarding gender roles, sexual orientation, gender identity, sexual equality, marriage, and religion. In their yearning to preserve their group's identity, tradition, sovereignty, autonomy, and cultural distinction, they turn to chauvinistic and xenophobic nationalism, political isolationism, and economic protectionism.[18] Scholars regarded the proliferation of anti–West, anti-globalization extremist groups in the Arab/Muslim world (e.g., Islamist/jihadist radicalism and fundamentalism) as a "*reactionary* backlash" against the West's hegemonic power facilitated by Western interests in oil and the modernization it symbolizes.[19] Berger[20] considered the radicalized "revival of fundamentalist Islamism" as a form of "de-secularization movement"; Barber[21] called it a "retribalization" effort that indicates desire for "indigenization." Huntington's[22] "re-Islamization" and Modood's[23] "re-empowerment of Islamic identity" also point toward the same phenomenon—Muslims asserting their autonomy and self-empowerment against Western domination. All of these efforts and movements are a type of "parochializing" trend in the form of reactionary extremism. The world has become a more unsettling place with globalization, because it incited reactionary "parochializing"[24] among those who seek to ward off Western powers[25] and violently reject all modern, cosmopolitan values and lifestyles.[26]

"Parochializing" can occur among some subgroups of people of the most advanced nations, also, especially when they face threat to their existential security (e.g., terrorist attacks, economic recession, political chaos, high crime). During the economic crisis of the 1930s, many European nations turned to isolationism, protectionism and nationalism, which aggravated economic troubles steering toward the Great Depression, and eventually the Second World War. One of the reasons behind creation of the EU (European Union) was to avert such intra-Europe wars and economic competition, which devastated the continent for almost a century.[27] However, in the aftermath of the Great Recession of 2008 and slow recovery that followed, Europeans' endorsement of the EU has waned: a plethora of far-right, anti–EU, anti-immigrant, anti-multiculturalism, nationalistic political parties have gained political backing.[28] Scholars consider the renewal of nationalism and anti-immigrant (mixed with racist) "populist movements" as repudiation of economic globalization and cultural cosmopolitanism among the traditionalists.[29] The Brits who voted for "Brexit" (leaving the EU) in the 2016 referendum reflected similar "parochializing" sentiments. They consisted of far-right and far-left from *both* the conservative/Tory and liberal/Labor parties who sought to reclaim Britain's political sovereignty and economic autonomy independent from the EU, and reclaim British identity and cultural heritage.[30] In economic hard times, people desire to return to or preserve their localized, national, racial, ethnic, or religious identities and political autonomy rebuffing globalizing or transnational trends, even at the expense of economic prosperity, and search for "ontological security" in a localized context of "tribalistic" affinities rejecting outsiders and globalization.[31]

Americans who rallied for Donald Trump in the 2016 presidential election shared the same emotions and desires. Frustrated with economic insecurity as a result of globalization (e.g., outsourcing of working-class manufacturing jobs; influx of immigrant and migrant workers) and fear of terrorism from Islamist groups, they wanted to restore nationalistic or identity-based parochialism (e.g., white nationalism and Christian nationalism),[32] and economic autonomy through isolationism and protectionism. They included "America first" nationalists, anti-immigrant and anti–Muslim nativists and racists, and anti-globalization and anti–free trade protectionists and isolationists, diverging from the typically pro-business, economically-conservative, "establishment" Republicans who espoused economic globalization (e.g., global free-trade treaties, outsourcing, and supporting interest of the multinational corporations) for decades.

As a result, globalizing post-industrial Western societies face extremisms on both ends of the political spectrum—the extreme globalists seeking to maximize corporate profits as much and fast as they can at the expense of lives of the working class people, on one side, and the anti-globalists, the working class populists who reject globalism *en masse* and wish to go back to the "good-old-days" of a manufacturing economy and white- and Christian-dominated traditional culture without immigrants. Modern societies must balance both sides' needs and interests, heeding to the fears and grievances of the people who have been negatively afflicted by globalization, even if it means decelerating the globalization process.

Resolving Problems of Globalization

Globalization, if managed properly and effectively, can produce enormous economic benefits to every group and nation involved. Problems occur when globalization processes are not properly regulated and benefits from globalization are not fairly and evenly distributed, effecting systemic injustice and widening the income gap. For the most part, the current form of globalization has been pushed too far too fast, largely for the benefit of the multinational corporations, ignoring its harsh impacts on the working class population who are negatively affected by the process—e.g., loss of jobs from outsourcing and lower wages from increased immigrants. To make the matters worse, the "winners" from globalization—e.g., economic elites of the multinational corporations and their shareholders, along with collaborating politicians—reaped most of the benefits from globalization, and refused to share them with the "losers" from globalization who suffer greatly *as a result* of globalization and outsourcing of jobs, particularly the working-class population in the manufacturing industries.[33] Instead of redistributing income and wealth, the U.S. introduced an assortment of pro-business policies that exacerbated the plight of the working class—most notably, corporate and high-income earners' taxes were cut substantially (e.g., President Bush's and Trump's tax cuts in 2001 and 2017 respectively) despite their massive increase in income; whereas, minimum wage and middle-class wages have been stagnant for decades and their tax burden has increased proportionately (e.g., regressive payroll taxes and rise of excise and state income taxes that are mostly "flat"). For instance, despite a slight increase in minimum wage over several years ending in 2009, in the 2010s about one third of economic gains in the U.S. went to the richest 1 percent, which is much more than during the 1980s and 1990s, according to the Federal Reserve's report.[34]

To turn globalization into a "win-win" process for all, the societies involved in globalizing economies must carefully balance the competing interests between the "winners" and "losers" from the globalization. For instance, the government can redistribute income and rewards through more progressive taxation and compensation; create jobs in the non-manufacturing sectors for the working-class; raise minimum wage for low-skill service sector jobs; introduce re-education and job training programs for the workers displaced as a result of corporate outsourcing; and curb illegal immigration to protect domestic workers. Multinational corporations can be forced to defray the cost of reeducation programs and incentives for the workers, or offer them temporary financial relief to ease the pains of economic transition (from manufacturing to service-oriented economies). Instead, America has been expediting outsourcing with tax incentives for the multinational corporations, and kept the minimum wage low for decades for the benefit of employers and businesses, exacerbating the economic situation of the working class negatively affected by globalization. If societies are unable or unwilling to redistribute the gains from globalization equitably, at least they can slow down the globalization process to ease the pains of transition for the working class (e.g., applying tax penalties for outsourcing corporations and imposing import tariffs), giving them more time to adapt and adjust to the changes.

Whenever an implementation of a policy creates winners and losers, efforts must be made to balance and redistribute gains and losses between the winners and losers, even if it entails slower economic growth. If not, the system becomes unfair to the losers, and they will try to apply extremist measures if their demands are not met promptly and properly, disrupting the whole society.

Balancing Corporate and Public Interests

As Kay[35] discusses, every government is confronted with "rent-seeking" lobbyists, who push for policies that do not always coincide with the interests of the public. The direct consequences of their actions affect various economic policies, such as price controls, tariffs, subsidies, tax breaks, and environmental protections that benefit the "rent-seeking" special-interest groups, yet are damaging to the general public. A number of studies have demonstrated how special interest groups have persuaded lawmakers to make policy decisions for their own interests, and *against* the interests of the general public, both in Europe and the U.S.,[36] with heavy pro-business, especially large corporations' biases[37], and in so doing, established quid-pro-quo "profit sharing" schemes between the corporations and lawmakers at the expense of the public's interests, even harming the public.[38]

As examples, some coal and mining companies have operated and made profits by risking the lives of their workers and damaging the environment (e.g., mountain top removal mining, mismanagement of wastes, fatal mine explosions) for decades; globalized giant oil companies have ruined the natural environment and animal habitats and caused numerous man-made disasters as a result of criminal negligence (e.g., chemical and oil spills, explosions, fires) especially in less developed nations, and gotten away with their wrongdoings by bribing corrupt leaders and lawmakers.[39] Drug companies have used sundry scams to manipulate the drug approval process; bypassed patent laws and government oversight; raised drug prices; and evaded negotiations for discounts.[40] Weapons industries and supporting private equity groups have profited handsomely by donating to politicians and pressuring lawmakers to wage unjustified wars, to get more taxpayers' money (via defense contracts), and to export more weapons to conflict-prone areas knowing that they are used in killing civilians in civil wars.[41]

Politicians Colluding with Industries

Too often, the nefarious business activities of the corporations continue with impunity, and even flourish with the help of corrupt politicians who ignore such activities as a payback to their political contributors, be they from campaign contributions, consulting and speaking fees, gifts, and other quid-pro-quo "profit-sharing schemes."[42] Despite the "drain the swamp" campaign slogan Trump promised, industry lobbying in Washington more than doubled when the Trump administration took power in Washington in 2017. The most notable cases include oil and gas industries pressing to roll back federal regulation on drilling implemented under the Obama administration; telecommunication industries seeking to reverse net neutrality rules passed during the Obama administration; Boeing and Lockheed Martin and other defense contractors seeking to restore cuts in the Pentagon's budget made during the Obama administration; and finance industries trying to rescind a range of Frank-Dodd finance reform bills passed after the financial crisis of 2008 to avert another financial crisis.[43] In 2019, the Trump administration vastly expanded the amount of federal lands potentially open to industrial use, including parts of national parks, and rolled back several major regulations meant to safeguard offshore drilling rigs, ending a bevy of safety measures put in place after the 2010 *Deepwater Horizon* oil spill, which spewed 4.9 million barrels of oil into the Gulf of Mexico with long-term, devastating consequences.[44] As large corporations' power and sway over lawmakers builds up, it is becoming increasingly arduous for governments, even in the most advanced democracies, to contain corporate special interests on behalf of the public, effecting wide-ranging pro-business policy implementations for both domestic and foreign policy issues. When corporations continue to harm the public in collaboration with the government, the public has no recourse to protect itself and the environment other than public protests and demonstrations that can turn extreme and violent.

Taming Corporate Interests on the Global Level

With economic globalization, the need for systemic justice expands to international communities. This is becoming an acutely pressing issue because whenever Western corporations and governments commit malfeasance in non–Western worlds, the people victimized by their wrongdoings blame the *whole* West, not the few individuals and corporations responsible for the act, the same way masses of Americans blamed the whole Muslim world for the 9/11 terrorist acts in 2001 ("collective rejection"). Unless the politicians and government officials of the advanced economies resume their oversight duties *over* the corporations, instead of collaborating with and prodding their nefarious activities overseas, corporations' insatiable greed to maximize profit and raise share prices will continue, plundering the world's resources, exploiting workers, infringing upon their human rights, and destroying the natural environment with virtual impunity. Such abusive activities by the multinational corporations exacerbate extreme inequalities and political instability in the developing nations, and cultivate resistance extremisms with radicalized ideologies and terrorist threats to the West.[45]

During his speech to the United Nations in 2015 Pope Francis implored against "a selfish and boundless thirst for power and material prosperity" that "leads both to the misuse of available natural resources and to the exclusion of the weak and disadvantaged."[46] During his visit to the Nairobi slums, where half the city's residents live, Pope Francis decried their destitute living conditions, and said that those communities are the "victims of new forms of colonialism" by the rich countries. "These are the wounds inflicted by minorities who cling to power and wealth, who selfishly squander while a growing majority is forced to flee to abandoned, filthy and rundown peripheries," he said.[47] Nigeria is not an isolated case. Similar problems exist throughout the developing world plagued with poverty, inequality, injustice, and corruption, and these are the places where extremist groups pose grave threats to political stability, economic progress, and social wellbeing of the people. Some of the extremist groups are "globalizing," also, merging together and recruiting members from all over the world, to fight against the hegemonic power of the Western world.

For the sake of humanity and future generations, multinational corporations must be persuaded and regulated to pursue profit in more ethical manners, becoming more responsible for humanity's wellbeing and global stability. Political leaders and lawmakers must also heed long-term global and humanitarian interests instead of the short-term corporate profits of their campaign donors. The citizens of the high-income nations also bear a moral duty to stand up against the abuses committed by their nation's multinational corporations and government to protect humanity and ward off violent conflicts in the future, instead of reveling over rising corporate stock prices and the lower price of consumer goods. Without their actions, our future descendants will have to pay a hefty price for the "sins of inaction" committed by the current generation, with growing terrorist threats, possibly armed with weapons of mass destruction.

By all means, we cannot blame the advanced nations and their multinational corporations for *all* the world's problems and extremist/terrorist threats. Not every conflict or problem the world faces is the result of the misdeeds multinational corporations commit, or the superpower nations that support them. In fact, countless people around the world benefit from the activities of the multinational corporations, including those in the developing nations who collaborate with the multinational corporations. To promote politically stable globalization, the developing nations must also implement their fair share of reforms to improve existential security of their people—e.g., instituting democratic rule of law, improving systemic justice, stamping out corruption, and investing in education and infrastructure for long-term economic growth and prosperity. Scores of people in developing nations suffer from the endemic problems of corruption (so-called "culture of impunity"), which is rampant because their governments are unable to enforce the rule of law.[48] Advanced nations can assist developing nations to strengthen the rule of law and build democratic systems, instead of aggravating their "culture of corruption" by bribing their unscrupulous leaders and oligarchs and manipulating their politics for the benefit of their multinational corporations. In fact, studies have shown that Western efforts to assist democratization in developing nations through various "democracy assistance programs" have effectively curtailed corruption, violent conflicts, and civil wars in those nations, strengthened their key political institutions, such as the legislature and judiciary, and empowered non-state actors, such as civil society organizations.[49]

Structural Changes to Improve Existential Security and Fairness in Systems

As discussed in previous chapters, threats to people's existential security, for individuals and groups alike, can cultivate extremist mindsets for ordinary people. To deter extremism, therefore, it is essential that societies strive to secure everybody's and every group's equal rights, welfare and survival needs. Threats to existential security can derive not only from material deprivation or attacks from external forces, but also from precariousness of life circumstances as a result of anarchy, lawlessness, and uncontrollable life crises (e.g., weakened rule of law, failed states, wars, pandemics, and natural disasters). In addition to improving existential security, instituting robust governing systems that can enforce rule of law, regulatory oversight, and maintenance of order is essential to deter extremist aggressions from arising.

Enforcing Democratic Rule of Law

Democratic rule of law, when it is firmly instituted and fairly enforced, depresses corruption, favoritism, injustice, and the cruel effects of the "survival of the fittest" type of anarchy that pits everyone and every group against everyone else, allowing the strongest and the cleverest to thrive by taking unfair advantage of the weak, vulnerable, less fortunate, and underprivileged. Well instituted and enforced rule of law, therefore, obviates the need for extremist outbursts among the insecure and disaffected groups of people in a given society.

RULE OF LAW MAKES PEOPLE'S LIVES MORE PREDICTABLE AND SECURE

Institutionalized and well-enforced rule of law, provided that it is fair and just, makes people's lives and interactions more predictable, accountable, and secure. In the absence of well-established and enforced rule of law, people's life events become unpredictable and precarious. For instance, people cannot rely on authorities when they are wronged by others or falsely accused of wrongdoing. They can be wrongfully punished by informal, arbitrary, extrajudicial executions by vigilante mobs, yet, there is no means to prove their innocence or protest against the injustice. People become reluctant to form interpersonal trades, transactions, and exchanges, because there is no recourse if the other party violates the terms of the contract. Instead, people tend to "hunker down" to the most trusted, localized circle of groups (e.g., family, tribes), distrusting and shunning the outside world. In most modern states, effectively instituted and enforced rule of law and fairer political and justice systems have attenuated much of people's fears, uncertainties, and grievances that fomented extremist feuds between groups, including those between the privileged and underprivileged and the dominant and subordinate groups, making people's lives much more predictable, accountable, and secure.

Rule of Law Reduces Corruption

Well-established and enforced rule of law is essential in paring down the corruption and injustice that foster extremism. Without the rule of law, corruption spreads wildly with high reward, determining people's life chances and quality of life. Masses of people in less-developed societies feel hopeless because of rampant corruption and a culture of impunity in large scales. In such societies, what controls one's survival and well-being is tied to connections to the powerful and the ability to bribe, not personal merit, hard work, and ability. The "unconnected" and marginalized become discontent and hanker for rebellion, while the powerful, wealthy, and well-connected dominate the society reaping all the benefits from the toils of the powerless, poor, and "unconnected," turning the society into an extremely unfair, unjust, and corrupt system ripe for extremist resistance and rebellions.

Rule of Law Protects Powerless Minority Groups

Democratic rule of law is particularly crucial for the oppressed, disadvantaged, and discriminated against minority groups, whether by size or power. Effectively enforced rule of law can moderate abuses of power, corruption, discrimination, and exploitation of the powerless and vulnerable by the powerful, privileged, and well-connected groups of people. Without the democratic rule of law, the powerful, majority groups can abuse, exploit, and dominate powerless minorities without fear of punishment, and the discriminated against and violated minority groups hanker for protest against the injustice, at times forming or joining armed rebel groups.

Rule of Law Instills Trust in the System

When a society operates by fair and impartial rules of law and the government enforces the rule of law effectively and honestly, people trust the systems and the government that runs the systems. When people generally trust the systems, they are more likely to cooperate with the government—e.g., pay taxes, vote in elections, and abide by the law. On the other hand, when the government cannot enforce the rule of law or enforces laws unfairly, people lose trust in the system and refuse to cooperate with the government, and even rebel against it. People's trust in the system can have far-reaching consequences in every corner of the society. Without trust, people's interactions with others and economic activities become precarious, unpredictable, and arbitrary, making everyone's lives insecure and defenseless.

SEARCHING FOR ALTERNATIVE SOURCES OF LAW AND ORDER

When people lose trust in the state because the state cannot enforce rule of law and maintain order and stability, they turn to alternative groups which they believe can protect them and maintain law and order for them.[50] In areas where the rule of law is absent or weakened (e.g., "failed states" or lawless areas where law enforcement is ineffective or seriously biased), people join whichever localized group they believe can protect them, or they band together under a contrived identity to protect each other and implement "quick and effective" vigilante justice. Armed groups with "strongman" leadership and brutal means of violence emerge and gain popular support, whether they are rebel groups, gangs, criminal cartels, tribes, anti-government militia and rebel groups, hate groups, or riot mobs, and they rule with violence and intimidation in a brutal "war of all against all," trying to survive by out-fearing each other with exaggerated acts of bravery, cruelty, audacity, and violence.[51] For this reason, Pinker[52] argued that the government's enforcement of the rule of law has "pacifying effects," which contribute to the abating rates of interpersonal and intergroup violence and killings in a given society.

Pakistani youths join militant Islamist groups because they are fed up with political corruption. If the government cannot provide rule of law and justice, they would rather follow the "rule of God" the Taliban's justice offers, albeit cruel and primitive, they say.[53] ISIS/Daesh performed and publicized notoriously "cruel and inhumane" forms of public executions, even of their own members who tried to leave or did not obey leaders, including beheadings, crucifixions, stoning to death, and other monstrous forms of torturous deaths. Yet, tens of thousands of people from all over the world flocked to join the ISIS Caliphate and fought for its cause, risking their lives. In their minds, crude and brutal means of enforcing law and order is better than a corrupt and dysfunctional system without law and order.[54]

Reducing Extreme and Unfair Inequalities

Throughout history, extreme inequalities in power and wealth have spawned scores of violent revolutions and uprisings by the poor and powerless and their sympathizers, spurring resistant extremisms. Such movements were frequently suppressed with even more violent and brutal extremist responses by the wealthy and powerful who were determined to preserve their power and privileges instead of sharing them with the less powerful—e.g., dominant extremisms. Moderating inequalities through

7. Deterring Extremist Group Aggressions

more inclusive economic development and fairer and equitable distribution of rewards and resources, thus, will deter both dominant and resistant extremisms.

In every society and on global geopolitics, the degree of inequalities must be reasonable, reflect merit, and be balanced with equal opportunities and fairness in the system to deter extremist rebellions by the marginalized and disaffected. The main problem regarding inequalities is not necessarily "how much inequality" there should be (the degree of inequality), but *how* inequalities develop and intensify—i.e., how the unfair policies, rigged systems, and corrupt business practices and political favors perpetuate and expand inequalities disproportionately and generate extreme, unfair, and unjustifiable inequalities.[55] For instance, inequalities that arise from corruption, exploitation, unchecked inheritance, rigged systems, crony capitalism, and "quid-pro-quo" and "pay-to-play" schemes are not only unfair and unjust, but also detrimental to free competition, eroding the spirit of hard work and innovation.

Systemic Inequalities Disable Personal Responsibilities

Political and economic conservatives emphasize the virtues of *personal* responsibility—that is, that everyone should be responsible for his or her own life, instead of relying on government handouts or blaming others and systemic shortcomings for their own unmet needs. Of course, individuals must be responsible for their own actions and lives; yet, at the same time, society must maintain fair and just economic systems that can *enable* people to become self-sufficient and personally responsible. If the system is rigged or tilted in favor of certain groups of already privileged people against others, and opportunities for advancement are not meted out equally, the disadvantaged groups will not be able to achieve "self-sufficiency" no matter how hard they try.

No society can expect or demand everyone to become self-sufficient unless the *means and opportunities* to achieve self-sufficiency are available and provided equally to everyone. When the system is inherently unjust and unfair, the underprivileged and marginalized people, living on the fringe of the margins, will be deprived of equal access to means and opportunities regardless of how hard they work, and face greater difficulty to achieve the same level of self-sufficiency, if at all. In such cases, the society, and everyone in the society, becomes responsible for their welfare at least to the subsistence level with public assistance to those who cannot become self-sufficient for systemic reasons that are beyond individual control. For instance, when the average family's health insurance premium is $19,000 per year[56]; average childcare cost is over $10,000 per year per child[57]; and average college cost (tuition and fees, excluding room and board) for one year is $34,740 for private colleges, and $9,970 for public colleges (in-state tuition),[58] while federal minimum wage jobs pay less than $20,000 per year, and the median family's pre-tax income is $61,372 per year in 2018,[59] there are grave *systemic* limitations for the majority of American families and individuals to become self-sufficient in caring for themselves and educating their children. This is why the majority of the most advanced European societies turned into "welfare states," offering public assistance to the underprivileged from a collective pool of taxes. Under this system, the elites, wealthy, lucky, fortunate, and healthy assume a greater share of the collective responsibilities for the subsistence of the non-elites, poor, unfortunate, and sick who cannot become self-sufficient for *systemic* reasons that are beyond their control. If a society is unwilling to financially compensate for systemic injustices, and drives a large number of its citizens to the margins of the society, it becomes a systemically unstable society ripe for extremist revolts.

Liberal and Inclusive Democracies

On the political side, to deter extremist aggressions from arising, societies must implement and exercise more inclusive and democratic political systems that respect all groups of people equally and guarantee their equal rights and access to political power. Such democratic political systems can deter extremist aggressions for the following reasons.

Democracy Allows Peaceful Transfer of Powers

Modern liberal democracies allow peaceful and periodic transfer of power, averting the ascent of autocratic dictators and extremist regimes that rule for decades and generations, without going through tumultuous and violent revolutions and uprisings. Through constant debates with dissenting forces and changes of leadership, whether they are between the left and right, conservative and liberal, traditional and progressive, societies move forward with moderate and incremental changes of adaptation and adjustments, sidestepping extremist takeovers and sweeping overhauls of the systems.

Democracy Respects Equal Rights of Every Group

Most resistant extremist groups surface when the dominant groups refuse to share powers with the subordinate groups, and instead, they use repressive means to oppress the subordinate groups from challenging the system that protects their powers (dominant extremism). Democracy is predicated upon a belief that there is no group defined to be above others by its belief, creed, race, ethnicity, nationality, occupation, and birth right, regardless of its size, wealth, or power, and a belief that every group deserves equal respect and to be treated with equal rights. It incorporates various measures to protect rights of the minority and powerless groups, thus, can deter the rise of dominant extremisms and the "tyranny of the majority" which, in turn, incite resistant extremisms. By instituting checks and balances on the powers of the established and privileged groups, and allowing legitimate means for the powerless and moneyless to voice their opinion, democracy includes everyone and every group into the political decision making process.[60]

DEMOCRACY ENCOURAGES INCLUSIVENESS

Democracies have an inherent propensity to be inclusive, drawing diverse groups of people together as politicians try to win as many electoral votes as possible. In democratic electoral systems, therefore, ideological doctrinaires and extremist politicians have difficulty winning the majority votes. Even the most prejudiced demagogues, in order to win in elections, must appeal to as many diverse segments of the population as possible, including the powerless and disadvantaged minority groups. Even the most economically conservative, pro-business politicians are forced to appease the poor by offering more generous social benefits and services to court their votes. Even the most racist and ethnocentric leaders are constrained to support racially and ethnically inclusive policies if they were to win votes of the racial and ethnic minorities.

Seeking presidential election in 2014, candidates in Afghanistan actively courted minority ethnic groups that were persecuted or discriminated against for centuries, such as the Hazara minorities. Some even selected minority ethnic group members to be their vice presidential candidates.[61] Shortly after America's Civil War, the Republican Party in the South pushed for the 14th and 15th Amendments to give equal citizenry and voting rights to black men in order to win in elections in the South.[62] In 2013, fearing loss of young voters, Republican National Committee chairman Reince Priebus pleaded to religious conservatives to be more inclusive and tolerant of immigrants and gays. "If we are not," he implored, "we will limit our ability to attract young people and many others, including many women, who agree with us on some but not all issues."[63]

DEMOCRACY ALLOWS LEGITIMATE OUTLETS FOR EXPRESSING GRIEVANCES

In non-democratic, oppressive and authoritarian political systems, underprivileged groups face substantial restrictions on their ability to organize for collective actions, and their likelihood of achieving success from collective action is severely restricted, if not impossible. On the other hand, democratic systems offer a variety of opportunities for the oppressed and dissident groups to voice their grievances legitimately with the help of free and independent media sources, and participate in political actions legally and peacefully, thereby abating the need for violent collective actions.[64] The freedoms of speech, expression and assembly built into the democratic system facilitate groups with grievances to assemble and organize activisms, protests, and movements to demand reforms legitimately and peacefully without extremist means. They can also contact political leaders, make campaign contributions, volunteer in campaigns, and even run for political offices. Without the guarantee of such rights, balance of power in the society will be inevitably tilted in favor of the powerful, dominant, connected, and privileged, solidifying their dominant positions, and in so doing, sow grievances and fester resentment among the marginalized, rooting for change with violent means.

DEMOCRACY PROMOTES PEACEFUL RESOLUTION OF CONFLICTS

One of the greatest achievements of democratic systems has been instituting means of making collective decisions on contentious issues without resorting to violence. In that sense, democracy is a system that provides non-violent and civilized means of conflict resolution by moderating competing interests among multitudes of groups. Functioning democracy will continue to have conflicts but they are more likely to be resolved peacefully, diplomatically, and fairly, without fostering extremist violence. The peaceful resolution of conflicts requires diplomacy of compromises and concessions from all parties involved, through which all involved parties share benefits and burdens equally—i.e., no group emerges as a "winner," or is forced to sacrifices more for the benefit of other groups. When one group demands greater sacrifice from another group as a resolution option, the resolution becomes an expression of group-centric, extremist ideology, not democracy. When one group's interests are seriously threatened and unfairly curtailed for the benefit of another group, fighting the threat becomes an all-important and all-consuming end that justifies all means for its members, including violence,[65] which spur extremist rebellions.

Institutional Assistance

Promoting and maintaining systems that are fairly balanced and equitable to all require not only effective government but also oversight by various non-governmental institutions, such as the media, academia, and international organizations that can assume informal regulatory functions on behalf of the people, *provided that* they operate in a value-neutral and objective manner independent from any group-centric special interests.

Role of the State

When the government cannot safeguard the safety, rights, and interests of everyone and every group, the persecuted minorities and those who are wronged by the powerful will rise up and protest. It is the government's role to institute and enforce rule of law to restrain abuse of power and malfeasance committed by the dominant groups, which can deter violent revolts by the persecuted groups. Among the myriad roles the state assumes (e.g., providing security, protecting liberty and individual rights, and provision of public services, law enforcement, and basic welfare of the citizens), I focus on a few key roles that can tame extremist aggressions.

INSTITUTING AND ENFORCING RULE OF LAW FAIRLY AND JUSTLY

As discussed above, the rule of law represses corruption; instills trust in the systems; makes people's lives more predictable and secure; protects powerless groups' rights; and promotes economic development. For these reasons, people's demands for the state to enforce rule of law have grown steadily in the Western world since the 1870s, and the demand and expectation are strongest in the economically advanced Western nations where the sentiment of individual freedom is strongest.[66] Concerning economic activities in particular, history has manifested that not everyone voluntarily behaves in a moral and ethical manner, and not every business willingly pays taxes and assumes social responsibility. Some cheat and bend the rules to maximize profit and beat competitors often harming the public in the process. Without the government vigilantly enforcing the rule of law, more will defraud and manipulate the system to be winners of the free-market competition, leaving behind masses of the aggrieved and discontented, brooding for changes, eroding the collective good of the society.

PROTECTION OF EQUAL RIGHTS FOR EVERY GROUP AND INDIVIDUAL

One of the main roles of the modern governments is to protect individual rights, especially that of the most vulnerable, disadvantaged, persecuted minorities and oppressed groups, and to ensure equal justice and opportunity for all citizens, regardless of background and group identity. Without the state's protection of equal rights and opportunities, a state of anarchy takes place where the rights and welfare of the underprivileged and discriminated groups of people can be trampled without due recourse to "right the wrong," and the systems become rigged in favor of the dominant and privileged groups, fueling resistance extremisms to foment.

BALANCING OF CLASHING INTERESTS AND VALUES

Another key role of the government is to be a neutral mediator and to balance clashing interests and intergroup conflicts that arise in pluralistic modern societies, whether they are racial, ethnic, religious, sexual, class conflicts, or "culture wars." Contention can also be between labor vs. management, industry vs. public consumers, and individual rights vs. national interests. It is government's role to make sure that no single group ascends as the dominant group, hoarding resources or rewards, abusing its power over others.

The duty of keeping corporate power in check falls largely upon the governmental agencies and their policies. Only the government can institute rules and regulations over corporations to protect the public, environment and natural resources, maintain fairness in the systems, and deter the economic havoc of panics and depressions that are characteristic of unregulated capitalism.[67] In most modern societies, government also assumes the responsibility of redistributing resources equitably. As scholars noted (e.g., Josiah Warren, Karl Polanyi), in a society entirely built on the free-market exchange of services, the accumulation of property and economic power of a few can enslave the majority, generating "class conflicts" that can become violent and costly. Without government's redistribution effort, the whole capitalistic system can collapse, either from violent uprisings or economic imbalance between supply and demand by weakening consumption power of the impoverished mass.[68]

GOVERNMENTAL REGULATIONS PROTECT FREE AND FAIR ECONOMIC COMPETITION

The free-market works properly only when everyone follows the rules that are designed to deter cheating and rigging of the free competition.[69] Only the government has the legal power to institute and enforce those systemic and operative rules and regulatory policies to preclude manipulation of the system by profit-motivated businesses and individuals to the detriment of everyone else in the society.

Problems of Laissez-Faire: Almost every noteworthy American political thought in the 19th century had centered on the radical concept of laissez-faire as the "natural order" of society. Demanding the "sovereignty of the individual," advocates of laissez-faire econimics argued that "the best government is that which governs least."[70] However, after undergoing the vicissitudes of economic chaos, political turbulence, and social injustice,

7. Deterring Extremist Group Aggressions 261

social thinkers from as early as in the 1890s (e.g., Saint-Simmon) started to rebuke the laissez-faire doctrine as "a thin disguise for exploitation of the working masses by the owners of property."[71]

Laissez-faire liberalism of the 20th century produced many more losers than winners in the economic sphere. The right to compete on an equal basis with one's fellows for advancement, an idea that was based on the work of the "invisible hand" in the marketplace, inexorably produced insecurity, uncertainty, and anxiety among the masses, and extreme economic inequality. The discontent among wage laborers and subsistence farmers soon spread to the middle-class wage-earners who lived on the margins of the society working for the privileged few.[72] For the original laissez-faire doctrine to work, insisted Orestes A. Brownson, "equality of conditions and powers of all the members of society" must preexist, and the state must assume the role of enforcing that equality in conditions. To maintain truly fair and just "laissez-faire" economic systems, therefore, states need not less but more effective and broader governmental regulations.[73]

Regulation Is Necessary to Protect the Public: When the government fails to regulate abusive acts of profit-seeking by industries, whether by willful misconduct or criminal negligence, people's lives can be threatened—e.g., through chemical spills, hazardous waste mismanagement, environmental destruction, unsafe working environment, exploitation and abuses of workers, and production of defective products. When the government fails to regulate economic activities, people do not trust the economic system, assuming it to be inherently inept, unfair and corrupt. Instead of abiding by the rules of the state, they will find other means to get ahead of others, such as corruption, bribery, fraud, and abuses, producing a sweeping culture of corruption and impunity, eventually degenerating into a lawless anarchy, where the strongest survive by taking advantage of the weaker. Without governmental regulation, thus, society becomes a fertile ground for both dominant and resistant extremisms to fester and collide violently, causing even greater chaos and destruction to the wider range of population.

Regulation Is Necessary to Protect the Free-Market System: The goal of governmental regulations is to protect and promote free and fair competition, *not* to limit them. The "free enterprise system" cannot be "free" without the state's enforcement of rule of law that safeguards "fair competition" by regulating and punishing cheaters and riggers. If not, the "free enterprise system" turns into "rigged enterprise system" that rewards only the selfish cheaters, riggers, and sociopathic fraudsters at the expense of honest businesses trying hard to earn a living playing by the rules. For societies to maintain a truly competitive free-market system, there must be effective and efficient government that can regulate economic activities to make sure people who "do the right thing" can survive and thrive, while weeding out those who cheat to win. Only when the cheaters and riggers are caught and punished does the system become fair, allowing the ethical businesses to survive in free competition, for the benefit of everyone.

For instance, the 2008 financial crisis and market collapse occurred largely because government agencies (e.g., SEC, FTC) failed to regulate finance industries, allowing the "big banks" to devise exotic schemes of dubious and unethical nature, taking advantage of the loopholes in the system—sub-prime loans, mortgage backed securities, derivative trading, credit default swaps, collateralized debt obligations, synthetic credit derivatives, and structured asset-based securities—which eventually devastated the global financial market and world economy[74] to such an extent that taxpayers had to bail them out to deflect further destabilizing effects from the panic and ripple effects from the crisis.[75] As a result, the world economy suffered major setbacks for many years as a consequence of what became known as the "Great Recession"; scores of the world's businesses collapsed, and masses of people lost their jobs, housing, and lifetime savings.[76] In the aftermath of the Great Recession and economic chaos, the world has witnessed the rise of "Occupy Wall Street" protests, far-right extremisms and populisms, and support for "strongmen," authoritarian leaders.

Media and Academia

Independent and unbiased media and academia play a crucial role in providing factual information and research-based analyses people need to make informed judgments on controversial issues and policies. Their job is to report factual events, present data-based analyses, and explain the causes and consequence of social and natural phenomena without ideological and group-centric biases and prejudices, for the benefit of *everyone* in the world. Their input is vital in curbing extremism because such information can debunk myths, misinformation, stereotypes, propagandas, conspiracy theories, and misguided ideologies concocted by the extremist leaders, and expose falsehood, corruption and malfeasance committed by the powerful and privileged. Without the trusted media and academia, people lose access to valid and truthful sources of information, and they can easily succumb to false rumors, conspiracy theories, fake news, and ideological indoctrination.[77] Realities can be easily distorted and truths can be crafted by extremist leaders who try to spread group-centric or self-serving ideologies they benefit from, whether they are for political, religious, or economic interests. They can keep the public in the dark, and manipulate people's beliefs and lives with fabricated truths they manufacture.

To impede such distortions of realities and truths, societies need to institute, support, and empower autonomous, independent, and objective media and academia, and guard them from becoming "tribalistic," representing group-centric interests and ideologies, whichever group they may be. "Tribalized" and extremely partisan media not only reinforce extreme positions of the already extremism-prone citizens, but also inspire some of the moderate audiences to become extremists, also.[78]

Media's Oversight Role Over Established Powers

With its investigative capacity, the media plays an informal oversight role over the established power-sources, such as the government, corporations, industries, institutions, interest groups, and a plethora of for-profit and group-centric organizations. Media is one of the very few sources in every society that can expose malfeasance of the society committed by the powerful, such as corruption, injustice, misconduct, and abuse of power. Especially when politicians, instead of safeguarding the public, receive money from industries and the wealthy and turn a blind eye to their wrongdoings, even changing laws and policies in their favor harming the public, there is no other notable countervailing power against them other than the media. Without the fear of media's "exposure," power of the privileged groups becomes limitless, and can continue to rig the system and abuse power to maximize their self-serving interests, turning into a form of dominant extremism. Corruptions, abuses, and wrongdoings will continue with impunity as power gets concentrated in a few hands, and the majority of the public will remain voiceless, powerless, abused, neglected and marginalized, seething for revolt.

Modern media had exposed numerous incidences of human rights violations, war crimes, corporate misconduct, political corruption, abuse of power by police officers and criminal justice systems, and priest sexual abuse of children. Without the media's disclosure, the American public would not have known about the quagmires of the Vietnam War and war crimes committed by American troops in Vietnam, Abu Ghraib prisoner abuses, and police shootings of crime suspects. Precisely because of this informal oversight role of the media—i.e., exposing wrongdoings by the powerful—the media has been vilified and persecuted by the world's dictators, ideologues, and right-wing extremists throughout history. Many rulers and corporations have tried to control, even take over the media to silence critics, some successfully (most recent examples include Putin of Russia, al-Sisi of Egypt, and Maduro of Venezuela); or, tried to muzzle journalists with threats of lawsuits, bribery, and intimidation, if not imprisonment and assassination.

Public Shaming by the Media

Governmental regulation is frequently inadequate and insufficient because the government does not have enough resources, manpower, and information about the private sector businesses sufficient enough to regulate them ("asymmetric information" problem). The "self-regulation," frequently clamored for by industry, does not work well because corporations have no incentive to voluntarily implement profit-reducing regulations.[79] One possible way to raise incentives for "self-regulation" is public shaming campaigns through media sources, which can force private-sector corporations to be more heedful about "self-regulating," for the sake of maintaining their reputation and image. Public shaming is an "informal social control mechanism" that can complement legal measures that are often insufficient, costly, and ineffective. Without the public shaming through media, societies lose the balance of power, and become unable to curb wrongdoing by the powerful groups.[80]

Public shaming has been quite effective in changing the behaviors of corporations, such as in cases of anti–Apartheid movements in the 1980s and anti-sweatshop movement in the 1990s, and is becoming even more effective on the global level with the use of the internet. Countries and corporations are becoming more concerned about protesters' and activists' "moral coercions" that can spread rapidly through social media platforms, to eschew damaging effects on their public image and reputation that are directly tied to their profit and interests.[81]

Role of Academia and the Sciences

Academia has always tried to encourage people to engage in critical dialogues and analytic reasoning, and understand the paradigmatic, path-dependent, and relativistic nature of knowledge, as opposed to the absolutistic, doctrinal, and ideological sources of knowledge as frequently found in extremist groups. Scientific education, in particular, cultivates independent, objective and critical mindsets that can cultivate autonomous and independent thinking abilities among people, rebuking ideological manipulation and authoritarian control. In the process, it enables people to become more creative and open-minded about exploring different views while formulating factual, knowledge-based decisions and choices of action.

Scientific pursuit of knowledge is non-dogmatic—i.e., it does not claim absolute and everlasting truth; instead, scientific endeavor is an ongoing, evolutionary "process," involving dialectical discourses and disputes, and subject to falsification. Scientific knowledge and community are universal—i.e., they transcend above all group-centric interests, loyalties, and boundaries. Scientists' ethical codes of conduct require all scientists to share their research endeavors and findings with the global community of scientists. For these reasons, the spread of scientific mindsets and education in a given society can mitigate extremist and group-centric mindsets and activities.

International Governing Bodies

Most economically advanced nations have learned, through a long and tumultuous history of violent and destructive labor movements, protests, riots, and revolutions, that a free-market economy requires governmental interference and regulation to maintain free, fair, safe, balanced, and equitable economic growth. However, in the global arena, there is no such governmental apparatus that can effectively regulate globalizing economies and their political ramifications to ensure fairness in the system. As Haass[82] addresses, "the world isn't self-organizing or self-regulating: there is no 'invisible hand' to bring peace and order in geopolitics." Consequently, the world's capitalistic economy operates as the "war of all against all" type of anarchy where powerful nations and corporations exploit the powerless with impunity, becoming wealthier and more powerful, similar to the system that wrecked the free-market capitalism in Europe a century ago giving rise to communist revolutions.

In order to achieve balanced and equitable economic growth and more stable geopolitical order, the world needs a robust international body that can regulate the globalizing economy to become fairer, safer, and more accountable. We must restructure the globalization process in such a way that everyone, every group, and every nation involved can benefit equally from the globalization through effective management, oversight, and regulation. This can be achieved only with the help of autonomous international organizations that are impartial and independent from the political clout of the powerful nations.

Growing Power of Multinational Corporations

With unregulated economic globalization, the power of large multinational corporations and globalized business elites are becoming ever more formidable, shaping foreign and domestic policies in their favor, and dismissing negative consequences that affect geopolitical events. Problems of unfair trade, economic exploitation, and political manipulation have been exacerbated as economic globalization intensified with rising powers of multinational corporations and borderless trade of goods and labor without adequate oversights and regulations.[83]

When matters like balancing the global economy, protecting the environment, and the regulation of derivatives trading are left entirely to market forces, outcomes tend to serve the most powerful, because markets neither have a conscience nor do they ensure equal opportunities.[84] Yet, there is no international governing body that is powerful enough to counter their powers and regulate their activities to safeguard the rest of the people who are negatively affected by their abusive acts. In fact, for multinational corporations, "the ideal world is one of *no states*, or at least of smaller rather than larger states," as Eric Hobsbawm observed, because "the smaller the state, the weaker it is, the less money it takes to *buy* the government"—i.e., it becomes easier and cheaper for multinational corporations to control, manipulate, and exploit the country, without legal obligation to heed to their regulatory measures or welfare of their people.[85] When their economic power alone is not enough to control and dominate smaller nations, they rely on the strong military protection and political backing of their parent nations—the powerful, mostly Western nations with formidable military prowess. Such situations are extremely vulnerable to corruptions, abuses, and exploitations of the indigenous population of the developing world, generating extreme economic inequality and political instability, which often contribute to the rise of anti–West extremist groups.[86]

REGULATING MULTINATIONAL CORPORATIONS

Most extremist, radicalized groups that pose terrorist threats to the West are motivated by the economic injustice and political interference they suffered in the hands of powerful Western nations and their multinational corporations. Their grievances includes such acts as plundering of natural resources, exploitation of labor, environmental destruction, political manipulation, and military intervention to protect their corporate interests. Most of all, they resent how the Western nations prop up corrupt and brutal "pro–Western" dictators, and ignore their abusive acts against their own people, driven by the single-minded goal of maximizing profits of their multinational corporations. Islamists'/jihadists' deep-seated resentment over what they perceive to be unjust and unfair arrangements between the powerful and powerless nations have been expressed in their manifestos, as in that of al-Qaeda's leader Osama bin Laden.[87]

What instigates nations and groups to become "rogue" or radicalized is not necessarily the absolute level of poverty and deprivation, but more often, their sense of *injustice*—e.g., feeling that they are unfairly exploited or humiliated by external forces. The sense of "global injustice," whether economic, political, military, or cultural, whether real or perceived, is also what drives masses of young Muslims to join Islamist/jihadist extremist groups, and aspire to be "freedom fighters" and "holy warriors" engaged in "holy war" and "crusade" against the "evil empires" of the West who have no other interest except exploiting their natural resources and cheap labor.

With geopolitical stability at stake, the world must institute and rely on robust, autonomous, and effective international organizations that can enforce international rule of law and regulate globalizing economic activities to safeguard interests of the less-developed and less-powerful nations and their people. Only the international governing body that is truly independent, value-neutral, and authoritative can effectively mediate the competing interests of powerful and powerless nations fairly and justly, and remedy the grievances of the mistreated groups of people around the world. A globalized free-market economy requires globalized regulation to function properly, fairly, freely, and safely. "Capitalism without borders" needs "regulation without borders," for the same reasons as the "capitalism within borders" requires "regulation within borders" to maintain free and fair competition and to protect the powerless groups of people, such as laborers, consumers, and indigenous people affected by environmental destruction, whose rights can be easily trampled by the powerful and corrupt businesses and corporations operating without oversights and accountabilities. Without the globalized regulatory mechanisms and agencies, and without the fear of legal accountabilities for the victims of corporate wrongdoings they can impose, the powerful nations will continue to pillage the powerless nations and exploit their people with impunity, fomenting fertile ground for extremist aggressions to arise using terrorist tactics.[88]

Mediating Conflicts and Disputes Among Nations

International organizations can also take on a more active role in mediating international contentions and disputes around the world, such as in cases of civil wars, territorial disputes, foreign invasions, annexations, ethnic and religious feuds, trade wars, and threats from transnational terror groups, *before* they turn into violent and destructive large-scale conflicts. When conflicts and wars do occur, they can intervene and ensure that the warring parties follow the international "rules of engagement" agreements, and punish violators to deter disastrous consequences, such as torture, war crimes, mass murders, and human rights violations. International organizations should be the "go-to" place for all nations, groups, and parties with political and economic grievances when their sovereign rights and fair-trade rules are violated.

Especially when dealing with anti–West, transnational extremist groups, the world must rely on international organizations to investigate the causes of their grievances and mediate peaceful resolutions to deter violent conflicts from widening and escalating. When superpowers respond with military powers and try to "root out" or "exterminate" terrorist groups militarily, it will only validate their anti–West causes, and reinforce their movements by eliciting more sympathizers to join the groups, as we have already witnessed after the Soviet Union's invasion of Afghanistan in 1979 and the U.S.-led invasion of Iraq in 2003. In response to the U.S.-led invasion of Iraq, Sunni Muslims from all over the world joined al-Qaeda, went to Iraq as insurgent fighters, and later contributed to the formation of ISIS/Daesh.[89] Instead of a few superpowers, which are already perceived to be the primary culprits for the world's injustices and grievances by these extremists, the world needs to rely on independent international organizations that are trusted by all to resolve geopolitical conflicts working as *neutral* agents.

Promoting Global Democracy

Most conflicts in the international arena stem from the same causes as conflicts in the domestic realm—i.e., powerful nations do not want to share power with others or make concessions and compromises, and instead, try to maximize their national interests by taking advantage of less powerful and vulnerable nations, trampling their rights and sovereignty. To regulate and mitigate nationalistic fervor, therefore, the same principles of democracy most modern nations adopted for domestic affairs must be extended to the international world. Especially with the rapid expansion of a globalizing world economy, there is an exigent need for a powerful international governing apparatus which can enforce global democracy and the rule of law regulating geopolitical events and activities. The world needs to institute global democracy by empowering international organizations that can uphold order and the international rule of law to protect the powerless nations and groups around the world, just as modern state governments do in domestic politics to protect powerless and minority groups of people. To achieve geopolitical stability, all nations should be more mindful of the principles of global democracy and the international rule of law, forming democratic partnership at home and abroad based on core liberal values of mutual respect and equality.[90]

Empowering International Organizations

For global governing bodies to enforce global democracy and the rule of law, they must gain authority and trust from all nations and people around the world by instituting democracy and enforcing the rule of law fairly, objectively, and impartially. If they are perceived to be merely a proxy power or "puppets" operating on behalf of the powerful nations, regardless of the truth, they will lose support from the rest of the world, eroding their authority and effectiveness. Global organizations should be empowered to enforce the rule of law and punish violators accordingly, yet, at the same time, must also be subjected to vigorous oversight and regulation, both internally (within the organization) and externally (by the international community). Their officials must maintain political neutrality, pledging their loyalty only to humanity, transcending national or regional identities, allegiances, and loyalties.

To institute such democratic institutions, the powerful nations must share power and cooperate with the powerless; respect sovereign rights of every nation, regardless of differential power, wealth, and size; and recognize the long-term, "shared-fate" aspects of the globalizing world. As Cottam and Cottam[91] pressed, one of the pivotal integration strategies needed in a multi-group, pluralistic modern world is the "devolution of power"—i.e., the dominant groups must strategically cede their preeminent power and share the power with other groups, by respecting their autonomy and including them in decision making processes for the greater benefits for all groups involved. For long-term geopolitical stability and global prosperity, it is imperative that the international organizations, not a few powerful nations, try to settle disputes and resolve conflicts fairly and justly, averting military confrontations with tragic consequences. The era of achieving "peace through force (or strength)"—such as "Pax Romana, Britannica, and Americana,"[92] has practically effaced. The modern globalizing world needs a modern globalized governing body that can ensure fair and respectful trade and diplomacy to achieve the mutually-benefitting peaceful coexistence of all nations through democratic cooperation with equal rights and mutual respect.

Held[93] suggests that global democracy ("cosmopolitan democracy") can be achieved by democratizing and empowering existing international bodies, holding referenda where the constituencies are defined by particular transnational issues that cut across nations and states, and creating world-regional parliaments equally represented by the nations of groups involved.[94] Others have suggested that transnational democracy may be better served by creating new institutions that are functionally redefined and non-territorial political communities or associations, rather than territorially delimited ones, because many vital issues, such as environmental, trade unionism, trade and labor disputes, and other social movements, are becoming increasingly global.[95] At the present time, the powerful nations are the only ones which have the ability and resources to form and fund international organizations designed to promote global democracy. Unfortunately, however, most of them do not want democratic institutions because they fear losing dominant power and leadership roles, and they are the ones who are responsible for the most acute forms of human suffering in the developing world.[96] Instead, Falk[97] argues that the world needs "globalization from below," to counter the dominant forms of "globalization from above," by incorporating a variety of democratizing measures to the present world order. He suggests transnational social movements animated by a vision of humane governance can offer better hopes of extending the domain of global democracy by challenging globalized monopolies by the powerful nations and their multinational corporations.

Limitations of Existing International Organizations

The existing international organizations, most notably the United Nations and its subsidiary organizations, such as the World Bank, IMF, WTO, WHO, UNESCO, and UNICEF, have contributed a great deal to improving quality of life for the myriads around the world. Studies reported that international organizations have been effective in promoting human rights and children's health,[98] democracy,[99] environmental protection,[100] and equal rights of women and homosexuals.[101] However, the existing international organizations have been far from perfect. Lacking trust, funding, and resources, their powers are severely limited and they struggle with internal problems of bureaucracy and ineptitude. They are frequently accused of being unfair in favor of powerful nations, as well as of corruption, mismanagement, and waste.[102]

Scholars have also doubted whether existing international organizations operate in a truly fair and democratic manner. Some discovered that powerful member states largely determine the policies of international organizations and coerce endorsement of the weaker members to mold the bargaining outcomes to their advantage, at times using intimidation tactics.[103] Many agree that existing organizations are not seriously heeding to the acute issues of unfair economic activities and global inequality, mainly because they are funded and controlled by the powerful nations that try to advance their own economic interests by securing their market base and coercing market-liberalizing reforms in the developing world.[104] Babb[105] and Stiglitz[106] documented that there is a great deal of secrecy and hidden agendas in decision making in favor of the high-income donor nations that fund the IMF and World Bank (developed economies, including the U.S.) sidestepping transparency and accountability and endangering economies of the developing societies which must rely on these globalized financial institutions.

Busby[107] and Alpert[108] reported that there have been rigorous efforts by the U.S. government, particularly the Treasury Department, to mold the behavior of these international banks to promote long-term economic interests of the U.S. (e.g., pushing for market liberalization in the developing nations), and that they periodically threatened to withdraw or cut off funding when U.S. interests were not met by the organizations. The U.S. has repeatedly declined to endorse international initiatives for moral action, often assuming the role of "gatekeeper" and "veto player," refusing to cooperate with other nations in the international arena, to maximize its own economic and political interests—e.g., Kyoto Treaty, International Criminal Court, United Nations Arms Trade Treaty of 2013, and Paris Climate

Agreement. In 2019, the Trump administration refused to renew or confirm judges of the WTO's highest court of "appellate body," reducing the number of judges to one from seven, arguing that "America is better off without it." America's inaction has virtually crippled the WTO's ability to settle international trade disputes in a fair manner, making it impossible for disgruntled nations to seek justice regarding unfair trade deals. The Trump administration resented the fact that the court had ruled against U.S. interests in about half of the cases in which ruled.[109] In 2020, during the peak of the global COVID-19 pandemic, President Trump pulled the U.S.'s funding for the World Health Organization, arguing without presenting evidence that the WHO was biased toward China and covered up China's misdeeds in dealing with the spread of COVID-19.[110]

The dilemma international organizations face is that they must be funded by the powerful nations; yet, at the same time, they must operate with democratic principles, holding every nation accountable, working for the collective, global interests, on behalf of every nation involved. Unfortunately, this principle is not welcomed by the superpower nations who contribute considerably more to maintain the organizations' operational budget than other nations, and for that reason, prefer to have control over the organizations. On the other hand, if the organizations heed to the demands of the major donor nations, the superpowers, the powerless nations, which are the numeric majorities, will lose trust in the organizations, and withdraw their support, obviating the democratic principle and the very purpose of founding international organizations. For future geopolitical stability and economic progress, the powerful nations must cede some of their powers and embrace international organizations, and cooperate with the rest of the world through power-sharing democracy and mutually benefitting economic policies. In the long run, the powerful nations, including their multinational corporations, will benefit *more* from a peaceful and stable world order and economy, instead of a conflict-prone, unstable, and violent world with constant threats from terrorist groups.

Cultural Changes That Cultivate Moderate Centrism and Fair-Mindedness

Modifying people's cultural mindsets and attitudes is usually more challenging and time-consuming than making systemic and structural reforms by implementing new policies and laws. Unfortunately, however, systemic changes cannot gain wide-ranging support or be sustained for a long time unless people's cultural mindsets alter enough to understand why such reforms are needed. In order to make systemic changes that can deter extremist aggressions, therefore, people's cultural ethos must be modified. Among multitudes of cultural mindsets that can mollify extremisms, I discuss three—i.e., pragmatic centrism, humanistic individualism, and communitarian spirits.

Pragmatic Centrism

In a given society, extremist aggressions can be mollified if more people embrace moderated and negotiated centrist positions on quarrelsome issues as a preferred and valued cultural ethos, for practical purposes of resolving conflicts without violent confrontations. People with pragmatic centrist mindsets can forestall extremist rivalries because they are more likely to negotiate compromises with fairer tradeoffs for all sides involved, through respectful dialogues and diplomacy, and to regard mixture of diverse voices as a desirable outcomes. In order to achieve balanced growth and progress devoid of extremisms of all types, thus, societies need more pragmatic centrists, not obsessive, group-righteous, and conviction-driven ideologues, and more people who can make decisions based on rational reasoning and factual data, not passion-filled emotions, blind convictions, and utopian visions. They seek out union-building coalitions not divisive confrontations; recognize the wisdom in the middle-grounds, not extreme ends; and believe in the mixture of diverse voices, not in the power of ideological and doctrinal "purity," "authenticity," and proclaimed "righteousness." They are more willing to give up and give in, enough to achieve negotiated compromises to obviate conflicts for the greater good of *all* groups and individuals involved.

FLEXIBILITY, OPEN-MINDEDNESS

Negotiated compromises are possible only when people have flexible mindsets, not when people rigidly uphold their group-centric views of righteousness, which is typically associated with fundamentalisms and extremisms (e.g., "our way or no way" and "our beliefs are the only true beliefs"). People with flexible mindsets are more likely to be open-minded about differing, contrasting, even dissenting views, and more willing to adjust and adapt to changing circumstances and situations. Open-minded centrists are more likely to value and appreciate the dissenting, opposing and contrarian views, compared to ideological loggerheads, and deliberate before they make decisions, considering all sides' positions, deflecting problems of "groupthink." As Robert Holmes stated in *On War and Morality*, it is always necessary to approach disagreements not in the spirit of conviction that you are right and your opponent wrong but rather with an openness to the possibility that each side may hold a part of the truth, and that only by taking every side seriously progress toward a completer truth becomes possible.[111]

Seeking Gradual Changes Through Adaptations and Adjustments

Pragmatic centrism does not necessarily mean that societies must always stay in the middle to maintain balance without changes. Throughout history, people have adapted and adjusted through evolutionary changes, not necessarily because of some ideological shifts or changes in values, but simply to improve their survival chances by adapting to changing circumstances. People have learned, through evolutionary processes, that flexible adaptations and adjustments raise their chances of survival better than rigidity and obstinacy of resisting them.[112] Pragmatic centrists pursue piecemeal and incremental changes through a series of adaptations, adjustments, and problem-solving, constantly recalibrating, reformulating, and fixing problems as they arise, instead of pursuing radical, sweeping overhaul of the total system, such as in violent revolutions and upheavals inspired by a grandiose vision of "new world order" extremist leaders.

Evolutionary Reforms, Not Revolutionary Overhauls: We have learned from history that the perils of radical and revolutionary upheavals led by charismatic, ideological leaders with grandiose visions of "saving the world" often end up in catastrophic systemic failures with tragic consequences of human suffering in epic proportion and long-term devolution of societies (e.g., "Black Famine" of 1933 which killed 5 to 8 million under Stalin's failed "Forced Collectivization"; Mao's failed experiment of "Great Leap Forward" which resulted in 30 to 40 million deaths by starvation).[113] Researchers have documented that revolutions often do not contribute to the promotion of liberty and equality; instead, they generate a new ruling class of oligarchy, stronger armed forces, and more war-prone regimes.[114] Throughout history, people have witnessed how revolutionary leaders, once they achieve power through violent revolutions, frequently turn into brutal dictators, more repressive than the previous ones, with paranoiac fear of losing power to counterrevolutionary forces, and engage in merciless persecution and purging of critics and dissenters—e.g., the "Reign of Terror" after the French Revolution, Mao's Cultural Revolution, Stalin's "Great Purges," and the Cambodian genocide.

In large and complex modern societies, political and economic systems are so profoundly complex and intricately interconnected and interdependent that any attempts at abrupt, large-scale, systemic transformation are not only impossible, but also destined to fail, presaging equally large-scale oppositional resistance or reactionary forces auguring violent conflicts. Most extreme, sweeping changes implemented by extremist leaders have invited equally extreme counter-extremist forces, destabilizing the whole equilibrium, and forcing the society to leap from one extreme to another in cycles, with much destruction, chaos, and economic regression.

Humanistic Individualism

Notable social thinkers have deliberated that the rise of individualistic cultural ethos in modern societies contributed to the spread of humanistic values based on the idea of "rules of reciprocity." As people desire to be treated with respect, they realize that they must treat others with respect, also. As they clamor for their individual rights and freedom, they are forced to admit the same rights and freedom of others, as well. They must value other people's lives if they want their own life to be valued by others, an idea that is analogous to Rotenberg's "reciprocal individualism."[115] Thus, individualism fosters humanistic values—e.g., respect for equal rights and dignity of every individual and concern for the welfare of humanity as a whole.[116] Most types of "individualism of *equality*"—e.g., "moral/ethical individualism"; "affective individualism" of John Locke; "inverted individualism" by Walter Davis[117]—originated from the moral philosophy of Immanuel Kant—i.e., "treat each man as a moral agent, as an end in himself"—with an equal claim to autonomy and respect as everyone else, and never should he be treated as a means to others' ends.[118] This view of humanity has become the underpinning principle of humanistic individualism, highlighting respect for each and every person's human rights and dignity, which led to the advancement of social justice and equal rights for all humanity.

Respect for Human Dignity

Humanistic individualism is predicated upon the principal belief that everyone must respect the dignity and worth of each and every person equally, regardless of his or her group identity, belonging, status, or background. When people regard individuals as having intrinsic value with sovereign right over their own body and mind, they are forced to place the highest value on each human life, as an ultimate value, and thus, no one can be treated solely as a means to the interest of another person.[119] Humanistic individualists, therefore, become indignant whenever human dignity is trampled upon and human rights are violated, irrespective of who the culprits or the victims are—e.g., allies or enemies, and insiders or outsiders. As Émile Durkheim conferred, humanistic individualism embodies "glorification not of the self, but of the individual in general—the humanity," and under this view, the humanity becomes "sacred and worthy of respect," not groups or collectivities.[120] The underlying principle behind humanistic individualism is not egocentric self-glorification but "sympathy for all that is human," a wider pity for all human sufferings and miseries, with more ardent desire to combat and alleviate them, and greater thirst for social justice.[121] Individuals become free from any group, god, religion, tradition, or any other forms of established authorities and group-prescribed constraints, and instead, they are encouraged to respect the rights of others and worth of fellow humans, with a profound concern for social justice and fighting against injustices.[122]

For the humanistic individualists, respect for humanity extends to society's "least respected and accepted" groups of people, such as the deviants, criminals, criminal suspects, prison inmates, and ex-felons, who should be treated fairly and respectfully under the law, as well as the most disadvantaged, underprivileged, deprived, discriminated, and unfortunate (e.g., the poor, disabled, mentally-ill, sick, persecuted) who cannot take care of themselves for reasons that are beyond their control. Their rights and human dignity should be equally respected and protected by the rule of law applied to everyone as basic *human* rights.

Fairness

The concept of equality is intrinsically interconnected with that of fairness, because some types and degrees of inequalities can be considered justifiable if they arise from *fair* competition under *just* distributive systems that reflect merit. Therefore, humanistic individualists generally highlight *fairness* as the core determinant of equality.

Fairness as Rules of Reciprocity: One simple aspect of fairness originates from the "rule of reciprocity." If one wants to be treated with respect, he is obligated to treat others with respect, also. If one were to demand or relish her individual rights and freedom, she is forced to grant the same rights and freedom of others, as well. One can pursue self-interests, happiness, and self-fulfillment only within the limitation that he does not violate others' same interests and opportunities while pursuing his own interests.

Fairness in Distribution of Resources: Another aspect of fairness refers to how resources and rewards are distributed. Many financially well-off economic conservatives argue that resources should be distributed solely based on merit (e.g., ability, intelligence, talent, skills, hard work, entrepreneurial and managerial skills) and individuals' contribution to the society and economy (called "fairness based on proportionality").[123] For instance, those who create jobs for others have a more important role in the society and contribute more to the society than those who work for them, and those who pay more taxes in absolute amount should have greater voice and sway in the society than those who do not pay as much taxes. The problem with this perspective is that this type of resource distribution becomes fair *only when* the *systems and procedures* of meting out resources and opportunities are fair and just ("systemic fairness" and "competitive fairness"). In other words, the "*rules* of the game" must be fair and rigorously enforced—i.e., the system provides everyone the same chance of winning in the competition. When the system is rigged or tilted in favor of one group against another, and, as a result, rules become unfair or are not enforced fairly and justly, the *system* becomes unfair, and the distribution of resources does not reflect merit, because not everyone has the same opportunities to become wealthy and successful on an equal footing. In such cases, either the system must be amended to be fairer, or the distribution system should be adjusted to compensate for the unfairness in the system through "redistributive justice"—e.g., regressive taxes, provision of social services and public assistance to the disadvantaged and marginalized. For instance, unless jobs are available and wages are high enough for everyone to make a decent, subsistence living, some form of redistribution through progressive taxation becomes necessary to compensate for unfairness in the systems.

Systemic and Procedural Fairness: The "systemic" and "procedural" fairness refers to whether institutional procedures are carried out fairly without discriminatory effects.[124] If the system is unfair or the institutional procedures are carried out unfairly (e.g., discrimination, exclusion, and profiling), the outcome of reward, notwithstanding merit, becomes unfair. For instance, when the criminal justice system goes after petty thefts and non-violent drug offenders who commit crimes mainly to survive in an unfair economic system, and incarcerates them for years, while ignoring, even rewarding the "big guys" in the "big banks" who already have much more than enough to survive, yet, rig the system with fraudulent schemes to make more money, fooling and taking advantage of the most vulnerable population of the society (e.g., sub-prime loans schemes applied to poor, less-educated, and minorities), it is not a "fair" system. Even worse, when these "big guys" bribe politicians with campaign contributions and consulting and speaking fees to make or alter the laws so that they can get away with such fraudulent schemes or legal liabilities, it is not a "fair" system; it becomes a "rigged" system, tilted for the benefit of the already wealthy and privileged at the expense of the underprivileged. When the super-wealthy managers of hedge fund and private equity firms and corporate CEOs and CFOs pay proportionately lower rates of taxes (e.g., by taking advantage of "carried-interest tax loopholes"; paying lower taxes by abusing business tax deduction privileges: pay virtually zero payroll taxes due to extremely low level of "maximum caps" on earned income and by claiming capital gains income instead of earned income, and hiding money in foreign "tax-haven" shelters to avoid paying taxes) than the majority of the middle-class and minimum-wage earners (whose regressive payroll taxes, state tax, and sales tax burdens that are proportionately much greater than the higher-income people), it becomes an "unfair" system. It burdens the poor and middle-class population with heavier tax burdens, for the benefit of affluent property-owners, capital gains income earners, and business-owners.[125]

Universalistic Views and Concerns

Humanistic values include hopes of bringing people away from concerns only about their own lives or interests of the groups they belong to, and push toward a sense of much broader, greater social responsibility applied to humanity in general.[126] For humanistic individualists, therefore, their "core identity" becomes the humanity of mankind. As Simmel[127] described, "Even the national solidarity should recede behind the idea of 'mankind.'" "The particularistic rights of status groups and circles should be replaced by the rights of the individual, the 'human rights,'" the rights that "derive from belonging to the widest conceivable circle."[128] Saint-Simon also stated that the final stage of human progress is the integration of all men into one humanity[129]—the vision of a "global village" where everyone becomes a "citizen of the world." John Lennon famously envisioned such a world devoid of heaven or hell, religion or nation-states in his song "Imagine."[130] The distinction between "us vs. them" and "in-group vs. out-groups" that dominated the traditional, group-bound extremists' mindsets fades, and people begin to understand and humanize out-groups, even their adversaries, instead of fearing and demonizing them. Every group cooperates with others to achieve long-term peace and balanced prosperity with fairness and justice, for the benefit of *all* humanity, not just of one particular group or a few powerful who seek to maximize their self-interests at the expense of others, because concerns for global interests, in the long run, will eventually override all other egocentric or group-centric interests.

Social Justice on the Global Level

Numerous social thinkers have discussed the close association between individualism and social justice.[131] They equate or define "societal progress" as "rise in social justice"—a foundation that establishes and uplifts well-being *for all*, especially improving the lives of the most vulnerable with basic social support of security, stability, health, and resources.[132] Even the most competitive economic order, John S. Mill argued, should be based on the ethical values of a responsible society made of true justice, not just freedom in economic competition. In that sense, Mill's attitude toward the equitable distribution of wealth was deeply tinged with his humanistic philosophy of social justice. For this reason, he advocated for state regulation of monopolistic tendencies, public works, and social legislation, and insisted on limitation of property rights in land and its fair distribution among actual farmers.[133]

All of these aspects of humanistic individualism are intrinsically antithetical to group-bound extremisms that seek to maximize group-centric and self-interested (on the part of the extremist leaders) goals and interests by denying other people's rights, interests, and wellbeing. Spread of humanistic individualism in a given society, therefore, will erode extremist mindsets and deter rise of extremist groups.

Communitarian Spirit

ENHANCING SELF-INTERESTS THROUGH COLLECTIVE INTERESTS

A utilitarian view of social justice—"providing the most good for the most people"—orients the regulatory state toward cost-benefit analysis and risk assessment. A libertarian approach to justice is associated with maximizing individual liberty and private property, where "free" market becomes protector of liberty, and regulation is seen as culprit. Within libertarian views, therefore, the collectivity progresses when each individual tries to maximize his self-interests in free competition uninhibited by external regulation. Communitarians, on the other hand, believe that specified groups and communities share common interests and desires, and thus social justice should be identified in an egalitarian manner.[134] For the communitarians, the concept of pursuing collective interests, including affirmation for social responsibility and justice for humanity, is not merely out of humanitarian empathy or altruistic concern for humanity. It arises out of recognition that "individuals' interests are best served by serving the collective good" as Tocqueville addressed, because "everybody does better when everybody does better."[135] Individuals' ability to pursue self-interests can be "shored up" by promoting the public good, because people cannot promote personal interests unless they collectively protect the public interests that safeguard everyone's right to pursue personal good.[136] Even the most egoistic person, for instance, cannot achieve individual success and wealth accumulation, unless the collectivity protects the system that enables individual's right to pursue personal achievement by upholding rule of law and guaranteeing fair competition—e.g., curbing corruption and rigging of the system by selfish individuals. Without the collectivity's effort to defend the fair systems and rule of law, the individuals' pursuit of self-interests and personal fulfillment becomes unattainable, at least not by legal means.

Instead of being antithetical, therefore, private and public interests are

7. Deterring Extremist Group Aggressions 279

inexorably intermingled and interdependent—i.e., they enable and facilitate each other. This idea is akin to what Waterman calls "ethical individualism," and "ethical pursuit of self-interests" that can simultaneously enhance social *and* individual interests in a reciprocal and balanced manner.[137] This is the reason why, although individualism is a prevailing creed in the U.S., the causes for *limiting* individualism is also a pervasive idea, deeply ingrained in Americans' commitment to communitarian involvement and belief in measured, compromised, and more balanced individualism.[138] This is also the reason why the majority of the world's most advanced, high-income, and democratic nations with the strongest individualistic values are also the most "regularized" societies where the governments actively regulate their corporate activities to preserve collective interests, *not* the most "laissez-faire" type of capitalism, which is more common in developing nations with fledgling economies.[139]

Recognizing Interdependency and "Shared Fates" of Collectivities

In order to nurture communitarian spirit, society's leaders must emphasize and inspire people to recognize the "shared fate" aspect of the community and humanity—i.e., the idea that everyone's and every group's interests and fates are ultimately interdependent and mutually-reinforcing, not autonomously independent and unilaterally evolving. Everyone in the community, every group in the humanity, therefore, "rise together and fall together," because everyone is "in the same boat together." Even the most unashamedly profit-motivated businesses and corporations reckon that they cannot maximize profit *at the expense* of their employees and communities they serve. For instance, they cannot evade paying their fair share of taxes, pay below living-wages to their workers, harm consumers, and pollute the environment to maximize profit, because their businesses rely on the welfare and consumption power of their community. Their businesses will eventually suffer if their workforce is not properly educated or too sick to work; if there is no dependable infrastructure necessary for their businesses (e.g., transportation system, utilities, internet, water, sewage); if the political and natural environments are unsafe or damaged; and most of all, if their employees, as consumers, are not paid enough to consume the products and services they produce. Every sector of the community must cooperate to sustain the interdependent and symbiotic relationship and balance of interests in support of each other, for the benefit of everyone in the community including the business owners. To secure a cleaner environment for future generations to come, everyone should sacrifice a bit of luxury in life—e.g., reduce carbon emissions, energy conservation, recycling, and higher mileages in cars. To build collective "herd immunity" from which all children benefit, people must take the slight inconvenience and risk that may come with vaccinating their children. Overall, it is about accepting and respecting the implicit societal rules of reciprocity—everyone must "give a little, to take a little"—and taking responsibility for humanity's interdependent destinies for generations to come.

SHARED-SACRIFICES AND SHARED-BENEFITS

When situations turn dire or resources diminish, contentions arise over who should sacrifice more than others. When situations improve, people debate over who should benefit more and faster than others. When there is a budget deficit, for instance, who should bear the burden of paying higher taxes—lower- and middle-income families or upper-income families? During economic recession, who should sacrifice more—the executives of the corporations or their employees? When there is war, who should go to war, and who should pay for it? When burdens and benefits are not equally shared and distributed, people who sacrifice more and benefit less become discontent sensing unfairness, and such grievances, when discerned acutely and shared broadly, can incite resistant extremisms. In cases of sacrificing, some go further than equal sharing, and argue that those who can *afford* to sacrifice more—e.g., the wealthy with greater reserves not the poor, higher-income nations not the lower, larger corporations over small businesses, and corporate executives over employees—should sacrifice more than those who cannot afford to sacrifice because of limited margins of reserve needed for survival. Robert Reich[140] argued that if the U.S. were to wage another war, unlike what happened during the Afghanistan and Iraq Wars, the burden of fighting the war must be widely shared among all Americans. If the wealthy and privileged do not want to sacrifice their children in the "volunteer army," at least, they should shoulder a greater burden of paying higher taxes to finance the war.

Supporters of "supply-side," "pro-(big)-business" economic doctrine which became popular after the fall of the Soviet Union in 1989, often argue that the benefits from expanding economy from recession should go to the business owners and corporate executives, instead of the working-class and the public, because they are the ones who can reinvest their profits to create jobs for others, triggering the wealth to "trickle down" to lower classes. What they refuse to admit is the fact that if masses of population do not gain from the recovery with higher wages and benefits, they cannot *consume* the goods and services the business-class produces with their "reinvested" profits, hampering the economic recovery. In mature capitalist "consumption economies" like in the U.S., both demand and supply sides of the economy must be adequately balanced to achieve prolonged economic progress. After the 2008 Great Recession, large corporations and

7. Deterring Extremist Group Aggressions   281

the stock market rebounded within a few years, but the wealth they recovered did not "trickle-down" to the general population, dragging the recession on for years, which contributed to the rise of populism among the economically marginalized working-class with deep-seated grievances and resentment toward economic elites.[141] It was their bitterness and ire that galvanized political support for the presidential candidates of Donald Trump and Bernie Sanders in the 2016 presidential election who ran as "anti-establishment" populists on both right and left extremes. When benefits and sacrifices are not fairly shared in a given society, the system becomes unfair and unjust, nurturing resistance extremisms to surface.

INTERDEPENDENCY IN GLOBALIZING WORLD ORDER

The same communitarian principle applies to the globalizing world order with economic interdependence as well. Especially with globalization, every nation's economic and political interests are intricately interconnected and interdependent, and as a result, every nation must cooperate and try to balance their national interest with international and humanity's long-term objectives. Even the most nationalistic states must consider the long-term consequences of maximizing nationalistic interests at the expense of other nations—e.g., risk of violent resistance movements and stirring up geopolitical instability. In the long run, every group benefits from peaceful world order by respecting international rule of law and promoting "fair play" to protect effective functioning of the global economy and maintain geopolitical stability.

As recent examples, we observed how the Great Recession that started in 2008 in the U.S. destabilized the world order not only economically but also politically, with large numbers of migrants crossing borders to find work, which prompted a rise of anti-immigrant populism.[142] In the globalized economy, Europe's economic trouble hurts the U.S. economy, and China's economic downturn, as happened in 2015 and 2016, threatens economies of the developing nations around the world, as well as the U.S., because their economies rely on trade with China. The environmental pollution in China affects Japan and Korea, as well as contributes to global warming; spread of infectious diseases in one nation can quickly kick off health crises in the global population (e.g., AIDS, Ebola, SARS, MERS, N1H1, and COVID-19), as people travel and migrate at an unprecedented rate and speed. COVID-19, a respiratory disease first reported in China, became a global pandemic within three months in 2020, infecting over 4.8 million and killing more than 318,000 as of May 2020, and continues to pose grave threats to humanity.[143] In March of 2020, United Nations Secretary-General António Guterres warned the world that COVID-19 will be "a threat to all humanity," and pleaded to the world's rich nations to cooperate and help the vulnerable countries. He stated that if the richer countries do not help out the poor nations to cope with the COVID-19 pandemic, the virus will "circle back around the globe" and haunt the rich countries again.[144]

In such an interdependent globalized world and economy, all nations must cooperate to achieve *humanity's* "collective interests" with fair, balanced, and shared burdens and benefits. The era of nationalistic competition over territorial aggrandizement, military prowess, and imperialistic "pax" is no longer feasible or ideal in a modern world, as Giddens[145] noticed decades ago. The "America first" type of nationalistic foreign policy or "our country, right or wrong" type of chauvinistic nationalism will further disrupt geopolitical stability by allowing the strongest nations to advance by taking advantage of the weak. In the long run, such nationalistic policies will pose a greater threat to strong nations' national security by inspiring rebellious extremist groups with terroristic means threatening the activities of the Western multinational corporations. Ironically, nationalistic foreign and economic policies designed to maximize economic interests and national security can very well threaten economic interests and national security instead of safeguarding them.

Strategic Changes in Dealing with Extremist Groups

Extremists and extremist groups exist in every society. Even the most developed and modernized societies have a fair share of extremists, and their extent and virulence fluctuate contingent upon political and economic situations—e.g., higher during economic hard times and under existential threat, and lower in more prosperous and stable times. In general, however, modern, advanced societies have fewer extremists and more humanistic individualists who rebuff hardline extremists and counter-extremist responses to extremist aggressions, compared to more traditional and less developed societies. Political leaders, therefore, must care a great deal about how to morally justify violent counterterrorism measures to punish terrorists without violating societies' own democratic principles and standards of civilized conduct. The use of violent counter-extremist measures that involve sacrificing innocent lives is usually justified on utilitarian grounds—e.g., for the long-term aftereffects of saving *more* lives. However, others have queried such arguments because "fighting terror with terror," like "fighting fire with fire," often escalates the conflicts and retaliatory violence, causing greater human suffering than the original attacks.[146] We must appraise the counterproductive effects of such hardline approaches in fighting extremisms, and come up with more humane, civilized, and effective strategies that are more amenable to modern democratic aspirations and values of the modernites.

De-escalating Extremist Aggressions

Counter-extremism/terrorism studies suggest that modern societies should focus on strategies of deescalating intergroup contentions, restraining extremist urges to counterattack violent assaults, because hardline, militaristic, retaliatory counter-extremist measures tend to strengthen solidarity and loyalty among members of extremist/terrorist groups, instead of weakening them.[147] As discussed in previous chapters, most extremist aggressions are impelled by momentary fear, anger, and animosity that arise due to threats to people's existential security, whether they are physical, financial, political, or cultural, or humiliating assaults on the pride and honor of the group inflicted by another group. With extremist counter-extremist measures, extremist hostilities on one side tend to raise security threats on the other side, generating a vicious cycle of "securities dilemma" as both sides sharpen their extremist hostilities with vindictive retaliatory urges.

For instance, the hardline counter-terrorist measures the U.S.-led Western world initiated after the 9/11 terrorist attacks in 2001, such as military invasion of Iraq and Afghanistan, solidified the existing terror groups, such as the Taliban, al-Qaeda, and propelled the rise of even more radicalized jihadist/Islamist terror groups, such as ISIS/Daesh and its satellite groups, drawing more recruits and sympathizers from all around the world. Indiscriminate killings of terrorism suspects and civilian bystanders with drone attacks in Somalia, Sudan, Pakistan, and Afghanistan are generating a second generation of extremists with a graver sense of revenge against the Western world for killing their progenitors, dragging on the so-called "war on terror" for decades without any vision of success in sight.[148]

Using military forces to "crush" extremist/terrorist groups tends to aggravate their sense of indignation and grievances, validate their causes, and precipitate their radicalization instead of mollifying them. Studies have shown that heavy-handed police tactics of responding to riots with armored tanks, military assault weapons, bayonets, and protection gear (so-called "militarized policing") *intensified* rioters' fury and rage and provoked violent reactions, drawing larger number of sympathizers into the crowd, instead of deescalating the tension.[149] The Kent State shooting of college students by the Ohio National Guard in 1970 inflamed the anti–Vietnam War movement nationwide, instead of abating it. In 2019, Hong Kong's months-long pro-democracy protests had been peaceful until riot police began to use aggressive means of control (e.g., tear gas, rubber bullets, and live ammunition), injuring and killing some of the protesters.[150] In 2019, when Iranian securitiy guards responded to demonstrators protesting against economic hardships and corruption with live bullets, killing at least 250, many more Iranians joined the protest and demanded regime change.[151]

Especially in a modern, civilized world order, a group can no longer gain power and respect by showcasing its military prowess or by decimating and humiliating weaker groups of people. The assaulted group will eventually regroup and retaliate with graver vengeance and vehemence. More importantly, whichever group engages in violent attacks against innocent civilians, whether extremist or counter-extremist, will *lose* respect and support from the growing number of humanistic modernities worldwide. When terrorist attacks occur, instead of waging an all-out counterterrorist war on the whole group deem to be associated with the terrorist groups, we can turn to a *criminal justice* approach that involves criminal investigation, and prosecution of only those who are directly responsible for the terrorist acts. That was what America did with Oklahoma City bombers in 1995, Britain with its London subway bombers in 2005, and France with its Paris concert hall bombers in 2015. The U.S. did not go after all militia groups, and Britain and France did not launch revenge attacks against Islamist/jihadist groups that were responsible for the attacks.

Rectifying the Root Causes of Grievances

The most crucial measures the world must take to assuage resistance extremisms are investigating the *root causes* of their grievances and frustrated aspirations, and trying to rectify the political, economic, structural, and systemic sources of the problems that galvanize their radicalization. As criminologists often state, violence is always a symptom of more fundamental root causes of the society. Gangs are not the main *sources* of a community's crime problems; rather, gang violence is a *symptom* of underlying societal ills—e.g., highly insecure, unjust, neglected, and deprived living conditions because of mistreatment, segregation, neglect, isolation, and lack of reliable and trustworthy law enforcement and systemic protections of the affected people.[152] Likewise, the rise of resistant extremist/terrorist groups is also a symptom of more fundamental geopolitical problems that cause segments of the world's vulnerable population to aggrieve and suffer whether in deprivation or humiliation. Modern, civilized societies cannot "kill" their way out of extremist/terrorist threats without resolving the underlying problems that cultivate them in the first place, for the same reason as why we cannot "arrest" our way out of high rates of crime and drug abuses, as criminologists often caution. Unless the *root causes* of their radicalization are properly addressed and resolved, killing and threatening them are not going to eradicate their extremist causes and redemptive aspirations.

Most radicalized Islamist/jihadist group members, for instance, harbor deep-seated grievances against the West for the long history of occupation, oppression, mistreatment, exploitation, manipulation, and humiliation they believe the Western world has inflicted upon them.[153] Their deeply-ingrained grievances emanate not only from the past history of colonialism, but also from the unfair and unjust political and economic policies the Western nations commandeered for the benefit of their multinational corporations—e. g., meddling into their politics, staging military coups, propping up and defending unscrupulously corrupt and brutal dictators, economic manipulation, and exploitation of their resources and labor forces. Large multinational corporations, protected by their "parent" nations, have become progressively more powerful and influential in shaping domestic policies of the developing nations in their favor, disregarding even the most basic rights and welfare of the indigenous population, geopolitical stability, or environmental concerns.[154] Unless the Western world recognizes and rectifies these root causes, the grievances and anger that fuel anti–West aggression will not subside.

Restraining Dominant Extremisms

As discussed in previous chapters, most resistance extremisms arise as a revolt against dominance extremisms that engender systemic unfairness, injustice, and extreme inequalities. Slaves fought against the system of slavery to be liberated; colonized against the colonizers; exploited workers against the capitalists; women against male domination; and persecuted and discriminated minority groups, whether religious, racial, ethnic, or sexual orientation, against the dominant majority groups.

Latin America's leftist rebel groups arose owing to the endemic, unfair, and exploitive business practices of the U.S. multinational corporations colluding with Latin American business oligarchs. In order to quell the leftist rebel groups, they formed and funded paramilitary "death squads," trained by the American military and CIA, which were responsible for the killing and disappearance of countless democracy movement leaders, student protesters, and religious leaders who disapproved of their exploitive practices. They escape prosecution or liability by propping up murderous puppet regimes through "regime change" and military coups. The same imputation goes to other high-income nations and their multinational corporations, which have profited momentously from Africa, Asia, and the Middle East for centuries. They have exploited natural resources and indigenous labor forces, and gotten away with malfeasance and unfair deals and practices by bribing and instituting ruthlessly brutal, pro–Western dictators, obviating people's democratic aspirations (e.g., the shah of Iran, Saudi royal family, Mubarak of Egypt, Saddam of Iraq before his invasion of Kuwait, Marcos of the Philippines, Suharto of Indonesia, PRI of Mexico, and multitudes of military juntas in Latin America and Africa). In numerous incidences, they forcibly replaced democratically-elected, anti–West or uncooperative leaders with pro–West rulers by staging of military coups, political assassinations, or military invasions (so-called "regime change"). Emboldened by the superpowers' political and military backing, these corrupt dictators became unafraid to commit atrocities, war crimes, and human rights violations against their own people, reigning for decades and generations with impunity.[155]

With such unrestrained Western endorsement of oppressive dictators, the "thugs and tyrants" and their brutally repressive police states have produced "a new class of rich, spoiled elites and 'royal' families," who are much reviled by the public,[156] fomenting anger and aversion toward the Western world. The Western world must acknowledge these problems and become more proactive in regulating corruption, abuse, environmental destruction, and injustices committed by multinational corporations, instead of protecting and prodding their exploitive activities and empowering corrupt, abusive, pro–Western dictators on their behalf.[157]

Dominant extremisms with hegemonic motives foster resistant extremisms with anti-hegemonic aspirations. Unless such hegemonic interests of the dominant groups—the powerful nations and their multinational corporations—can be tamed and regulated, anti–West extremist groups with terroristic tactics will not fade away.

Negotiating Compromises with Respectful Diplomacy

As societies evolve and people become better educated and informed, their expectations of the societies and leadership change, also. What people want, regardless of culture, religion, race, ethnicity, geography, nationality, and ideology, is not simply food, shelter, and tools for survival, but also human dignity—i.e., people desire to be treated with respect and live under fair and just social systems. When they are repeatedly mistreated and humiliated, they find dignity in resisting and protesting, even when their basic needs are not threatened.[158] For instance, according to the Pew Research Center's global survey in 2006, nearly 90 percent of Muslims in Jordan, Egypt, Indonesia and Turkey blamed the "Muslim furor" on the "Western world's disrespect" for Islam and Muslims.[159] Insulting, threatening and humiliating them with greater force, whether military, political, or economic, will only aggravate their furor, not pacify them. The traditional, hardline measures of quelling extremist belligerence with force, especially using militarized threats and oppression (e.g., "scare the hell out of them") become not only ineffective in resolving conflicts but also counterproductive—i.e., they fortify a sense of humiliation and exasperation, fueling radicalization instead of subduing it.

Instead, in order to pacify extremist aggressions, leaders of modern societies must adopt more civilized and mutually-respectful diplomacy and negotiations with fair deals and equally-benefiting and sacrificing compromises, combined with legal and strategic incentives for cooperation. The ultimate goal should always be averting emotionally charged acceleration of animosity that can spiral into more serious conflicts with graver consequences for everyone involved.

Peaceful Conflict Resolution Through Negotiated Compromises

With respectful diplomacy, conflicts can be resolved peacefully with negotiated compromises, trade-off deals, and collaborative problem-solving efforts. The preference for a negotiated centrist approach is not necessarily for civilized mannerisms or humanistic idealism; but, more importantly, it is for the pragmatic and practical goals of problem-solving and a quest for risk-averse means of conflict-resolution. Violent conflicts and confrontations are always costlier, deadlier, and more destructive than peaceful negotiations, and often exacerbate problems instead of resolving them.

There are ample examples of successful negotiations of peace deals that ended or averted violent conflicts. Most recently, in 2016, following President Juan Manuel Santos' leadership, Colombia ended 50 years of bloody conflict that claimed over 230,000 human lives, by reaching a full cease-fire and disarmament agreement with leftist rebel groups FARC and ELN.[160] After three decades of violent and brutal border conflicts, during which over 100,000 people died and millions were displaced, in 2018, Ethiopia and Eritrea reached a peace deal that opened transportation and communication links for separated families and communities to reestablish contact. Most rebel groups involved in the conflicts agreed to end their armed struggle and registered as political parties.[161] In 2015, Tunisia's National Dialogue Quartet, a coalition of labor union leaders, businesspeople, lawyers and human rights activists with conflicting agendas and interests, received the Nobel Peace Prize "for its decisive contribution to the building of a pluralistic democracy in Tunisia in the wake of the Jasmine Revolution of 2011," averting a civil war. All other countries that went through the "Arab Spring" uprising in 2011 failed to achieve democracy except Tunisia, thanks to their contribution.[162] In 2009, Bosnia's two armies who fought against each other in the 1990s—one representing the Serbs, and the other, the Muslim-Croat Federation—took steps toward merging and reconciling, leaving behind their past atrocities committed against each other during the war, including the genocide of over 8,000 Bosnian Muslims.[163]

Use of Third Party Mediation: When the situation does not offer legitimate means of reconciling conflicts between two parties, mediation by a third party can be effective in resolving clashes. Numerous conflicts and civil wars have been averted or curtailed and bloodshed diffused or mitigated with mediation by a neutral party of governments or international body of intermediaries that negotiated compromises, inclusive engagements and power-sharing agreements and treaties. For instance, under the leadership of CARE International, three different ethnic groups in Kosovo—Serbs, Roma, Albanians—who killed, raped, and drove each other out of their houses and neighborhoods during the ethnic conflicts in the 1990s, reached a peace agreement and rebuilt their community together again.[164] Peace agreements in El Salvador in 1992 with rebel group FMLN and the Brussels Agreement in 2013 between Serbia and Kosovo are also example cases that achieved peace deals with the help of third party intermediaries.

RECONCILIATION, NOT REVENGE AND RETALIATION

As discussed in Chapter 1, in extremist cultures, people consider avenging perpetrators as a duty that is necessary to restore a group's honor when it has been maligned by transgression. Even when one of the in-group members is offended by one of the out-group members, the entire in-group feels obliged to avenge any one (or ones) belonging to the out-group, because they all become "guilty by association." In such an environment, violence and hostility fester through cycles of retaliatory attacks. The only way groups can diffuse such escalation of violence is by initiating diplomatic reconciliations, overcoming extremist desires to avenge. With respectful diplomacy, sparring groups can reconcile differences and mend past grievances peacefully, deescalating tension and violence.

Nelson Mandela, who was jailed for almost three decades for fighting against the brutal Apartheid policy carried out by the white-dominated regime in South Africa, forgave his captors, warded off retaliatory violence against whites, maintained his presidency with respectful cooperation with the white captors, and willingly walked away from the presidency after a single term despite huge popularity.[165] Japanese Emperor Akihito, after inheriting the throne in 1989, visited all the nations Japanese military had occupied or devastated during the Second World War, and apologized for the atrocities its military committed under his father's rule (Emperor Hirohito), instead of rooting for another revenge war to restore the honor of the country suffering from humiliating defeat.[166] After the Second World War, the allied forces did not retaliate against Germany and Japan, and instead, embraced them as allies and helped them with reconstruction efforts (e.g., the Marshall Plan), contributing to the peaceful world order for generations to come.

Inclusion of Extremist Groups Into the Society

POLITICAL INCLUSION

Most extremist/terrorist groups, when they are included in the democratic political system with legitimate electoral power, tend to become less extreme to gain legitimacy and people's votes. Koopmans's[167] study demonstrated that between 1986 and 1994, right-wing extremist political parties in Germany, Norway, and Denmark ceased to engage in extremist violence after winning seats in the Parliament. Zimmermann[168] also documented how far-right extremist groups in Europe, such as NPD (National Democratic Party, a neo-fascist German party), ended their radical activities when they scored electoral success. Hezbollah, a terrorist group designated by the West, ceased to commit violent acts after Israel pulled out of their territory in 2000, and instead, astutely endeavored to harvest admiration inside southern Lebanon by launching itself into mainstream politics.[169] Other example cases of democratic political inclusion of extremist/terrorist groups include South Africa's peace deal with ANC (African National Congress), which became a legitimate political party in 1990; embracing of KLA (Kosovo Liberation Army) as a legitimate political group under NATO guidance in 1998; recognition of PLO (Palestinian Liberation Army) by international organizations in 1994; Britain's peace agreement with IRA (Irish Republican Army) in 1998[170]; Colombia's peace deal with rebel group FARC in 2018; and the Mali government's agreement with the Plateforme in 2015. In 2007, the Ecuadoran government legalized some of its notorious gangs, such as the "Latin Kings," as "cultural and social organizations," and integrated them into university life with job training programs. Ten years later, most of them separated their ties from gangs and criminal life, and murder rates among gangs plummeted dramatically.[171]

"RE-EMBEDDING" OPPORTUNITIES

According to Crenshaw,[172] when making peace negotiations with extremist/terrorist groups, offering members constructive opportunities for "exit" from terrorist groups is essential. Exit opportunities can be employment-related or community-oriented living arrangements, where ex-members can be accepted and re-embedded back into the community. Without the guarantee of safe "exits" and opportunities for "re-entering," members of extremist/terrorist groups, stigmatized by their violent past, will not leave the group or participate in negotiations fearing rejection and retaliation. Offers of amnesty, employment opportunities, and financial rewards, for instance, can make it easier for members to exit from the groups. Colombia's peace deal with the violent leftist rebel groups FARC and ELN in 2012 and 2014 respectively, despite much opposition from the hardliners, included amnesty to most rebel group members, estimated to be about 29,000, except a few offenders of serious crimes. Some were even consolidated into political parties and the Colombian army, to the surprise of former rebel members.[173]

What most extremist/terrorist group members seek is attention, recognition, legitimacy, acceptance, and respect. When they cannot obtain them legitimately, they try to obtain them through illegitimate ways that are often extremist and violent. When they gain legitimacy, recognition, and acceptance, they have no reason to be extreme and violent any more. Even when extremist/terrorist groups appear to die out, it is often because they just got "burned out" or imploded as a result of internal disputes, and not necessarily because of successful counter-extremist/terrorist efforts.[174]

It seems that the hardline campaigns of "exterminating" and "rooting out" extremist groups with equally extremist measures are not the most effective means of combatting extremisms, as scholars have repeatedly discoursed.[175] Instead, abating extremisms can be achieved, possibly more effectively, by including them in the democratic process through respectful negotiations, acceptance, and gaining their trust.

Fostering and Empowering the Moderates and Technocrats

One of the most crucial and effective ways of fighting against the threats from extremist/terrorist groups is to expand and empower the moderates and independent thinkers of the society, who are normally reserved about voicing their opinions on controversial issues and reluctant to participate in activisms. Moderates and independents can play a mediating role in subduing and placating the polarizing extremists, and become a buffer between the polemic extremes of the ideological spectrums when they collide, whether they are between left and right, conservatives and liberals, pro-business and pro-labor, rich and poor, Republicans and Democrats, traditional and modernists, or fundamentalists and progressives. They can help to balance the opposing extremes in the society by endorsing political leaders who are pragmatic centrists and technocratic problem-solvers, rebuffing dogmatic ideologues and extremists.

In most modern societies, moderates probably outnumber extremists;

yet, they do not *appear* to be a sizable group, because they tend to remain reticent and restrained, unlike the extremists who frequently capture the media's attention by "crying out loud" or engaging in "attention-grabbing" extremist acts (e.g., committing violent and terrorizing acts and atrocities; violent protests and movements; spreading outrageous rumors and conspiracy theories). In fighting against extremisms, societies, especially the media, can pay more attention to moderates, and give them greater opportunities to voice their opinions, instead of so often spotlighting the sensational and attention-grabbing speeches and acts of the extremists. Without moderates' input, extremists will dominate the public attention and social dialogues in media and politics (e.g., "shock talk hosts," angry demagogues, propagandists, and conspiracy theorists) distorting the reality and misleading the public with fabricated definitions of the reality, spawning an unnecessarily divisive, combative, and volatile atmosphere.

EMPOWERING THE MODERATES

To encourage and empower the moderates, leaders of the society can make a deliberate effort to nurture and expand the size of moderates and independent thinkers, who tend to be better-educated, well-informed, and middle-class members of the society. The middle class had expanded immensely in the Western nations from the 1940s through the 1970s, maintaining a barrier between the sparring interests of the upper- vs. lower-classes and labor vs. management, and steering the society toward more balanced progress.[176] Since the 1980s, however, as higher-income, mostly Western nations entered the service-oriented and knowledge-based post-industrial economy shedding manufacturing jobs, the size of the middle-class has been steadily shrinking and their economic conditions have worsened, producing large and growing income disparity and a discontent working class coveting populist revolt.[177]

Modern societies must reinvest their resources in nurturing middle-class moderates with higher wages especially for less-skilled service-sector jobs, more progressive taxation and income redistribution, and increased funding for public education and academia which play vital roles in nurturing moderates. Especially in the developing societies, generous funding for public education, increased economic opportunities for educated youths, and support for independent media can expand the size of middle-class moderates and tame extremisms across the spectrum, including dominant and resistant.

When dealing with Islamist/jihadist extremisms, empowering moderate Muslims may be the only peaceful option the West has if it wants to deescalate tension with the Islamist/jihadist groups without turning to military options.[178] The Western nations must keep moderate Muslims *on their side*, because they can moderate their own extremists with a show of disapproval, and they can aid the Western intelligence communities with information needed to foil potential terrorist attacks before they happen. Without their help, the West's counterterrorist efforts will face a daunting challenge collecting intelligence information that is necessary in foiling terrorist plots. If the Western nations respond to terrorist attacks with an overpowering military might with mass civilian casualties and destruction, they will lose the support from moderate Muslims by prodding the moderates to become more sympathetic to the extremists' causes, as happened after the U.S.-led invasion of Iraq in 2003.

Conclusion

In 2003, U.N. Secretary-General Kofi Annan warned world leaders that the war against terrorism must go beyond simply fighting extremists but also hold out the promise of a "better and fairer world. Terrorism will only be defeated if we act to solve the political disputes and long-standing conflicts which generate support for it. If we don't, we shall find ourselves acting as a recruiting sergeant for the very terrorist groups we seek to suppress. Paradoxically, terrorist groups may actually be sustained when, in responding to their outrages, governments cross the line and commit outrages themselves—whether it is indiscriminate bombardment of cities, torture of prisoners, targeted assassinations or accepting the death of innocent civilians as 'collateral damage,'" Annan stated. "These acts are not only illegal and unjustifiable, they may also be exploited by terrorists to gain new followers and to generate cycles of violence in which they thrive," he added.[1]

To fight against anti–West extremisms and extremist groups, the Western world must admit and remedy the root causes of the grievances inflicted upon them by the Western world for decades. Needless to say, the West and its multinational corporations are not responsible for *all* of the problems developing nations face. Developing nations must also perform their fair share of problem-solving—e.g., by instituting the rule of law, which can curtail corruption and injustice; buttressing democratic systems; investing in public education and economic development; as well as debunking extremist ideologies and disempowering extremist groups. At the same time, the Western world and its multinational corporations can *help* the developing nations to achieve these goals more expeditiously, instead of hampering the process by interfering and meddling in their politics and "crushing" people's democratizing and egalitarian aspirations and endeavors by empowering corrupt dictators who terrorize their own people, all for the benefit of Western multinational corporations and a few collaborating oligarchs.

Keeping the world safe from terrorist attacks is an exigent matter for the survival and progress of humanity for generations to come, which should not be compromised for the benefit of a few powerful nations and their multinational corporations. For a safer and more stable future world and humanity's progress, we must understand the mutually causative nature of dominant and resistant extremisms—i.e., how they provoke and inflame each other—and try to reconcile their competing interests and demands in mutually beneficial and respectful ways before they turn into violent clashes. Unless the world can tame and restrain *both* dominant and resistant extremisms concurrently, with the help of regulatory and interventionist measures implemented by governments and international organizations, extremist aggressions and threats of terrorism, possibly armed with weapons of mass destruction, will continue to pose grave threats to humanity, with escalating cycles of fear, hatred, and violence spiraling out of control.

Chapter Notes

Introduction

1. For the latest studies regarding this trend, see Steven Pinker, *The Better Angels of Our Nature: Why Violence Has Declined* (New York: Viking, 2011); Steven Pinker, *Enlightenment Now: The Case for Reason, Science, Humanism, and Progress* (New York: Viking, 2018); Michael Shermer, *The Moral Arc: How Science and Reason Lead Humanity Toward Truth, Justice and Freedom* (New York: Henry Holt, 2015); Angus Deaton, *The Great Escape: Health, Wealth, and the Origins of Inequality* (Princeton, NJ: Princeton University Press, 2013); Johan Norberg, *Progress: Ten Reasons to Look Forward to the Future* (London: OneWorld Publications, 2016); Peter Wagner, *Modernity as Experience and Interpretation: A New Sociology of Modernity* (Cambridge, UK: Polity, 2008); Gregg Easterbrook, *It's Better than It Looks: Reasons for Optimism in an Age of Fear* (New York: Public Affairs, 2018); Matt Ridley, *The Rational Optimists: How Prosperity Evolves* (New York: HarperCollins, 2010).
2. Feliz Solomon, "Myanmar Stands Accused of Ethnic Cleansing. Here's Why," Time.com, September 12, 2017; Foster Klug, "Myanmar Limiting Food to Reduce the Rohingya," Associated Press, February 11, 2018.
3. BBC World Service Newshour, February 22, 2018.
4. BBC World Service Newshour, July 22 and 23, 2018.
5. Elaine Weiss, *The Woman's Hour: The Great Fight to Win the Vote* (New York: Viking, 2018).
6. Steven M. Gillon, *Separate and Unequal: The Kerner Commission and the Unraveling of American Liberalism* (New York: Basic Books, 2018).
7. PBS Documentary, *The Vietnam War* (Aired in September, 2017).
8. Kim R. Holmes, *The Closing of the Liberal Mind: How Groupthink and Intolerance Define the Left* (New York: Encounter Books, 2016); Oliver Roy, "The Closing of the Right's Mind," *New York Times* (Op-Ed), June 4, 2014.
9. Kimiko de Freytas-Tamura, "Extremist Messaged British Suspect," *New York Times*, January 24, 2018, A7; Katrin Bennhold, "Political Murder and Far Right Shock Germany," *New York Times*, July 8, 2019, A1 & A9; BBC, "Decoding Far-right Online Hate after Christchurch," March 23, 2019.
10. Matthew W. Hughey, *White Bound: Nationalist, Antiracists, and the Shared Meaning of Race* (Stanford, CA: Stanford University Press, 2012); Ian Lovett, et al., "Antifa Violence Splits the Left," *Wall Street Journal*, September 20, 2017, A1 & A12.
11. Colin J. Beck and Emily Miner, "Who Gets Designated a Terrorist and Why?" *Social Forces* 91, no.3 (2013), 837–872; Austin T. Turk, "Sociology of Terrorism," *Annual Review of Sociology* 30, no. 1 (2004), 271–286; David Boyns and James D. Ballard, "Developing a Sociological Theory for the Empirical Understanding of Terrorism," *The American Sociologist* 35, no. 2 (2004), 5–25.
12. John W. Patty, "Signaling through Obstruction," *American Journal of Political Science* 60, no. 1 (2016), 175–189.
13. Shanto Iyengar and Sean J. Westwood, "Fear and Loathing Across Party Lines: New Evidence on Group Polarization," *American Journal of Political Science* 59, no. 3 (2015), 690–707; Shanto Iyengar et al., "Affect, Not Ideology: A Social Identity Perspective on Polarization," *Public Opinion Quarterly* 76, no.3 (2012), 405–31.

14. See Martha Crenshaw, "Theories of Terrorism: Instrumental and Organizational Approaches," in *Inside Terrorist Organizations*, ed. David C. Rapoport (Portland, OR: Frank Cass, 2001), 13-31.

15. See Charles Kurzman, *The Missing Martyrs: Why There are So Few Muslim Terrorists* (New York: Oxford University Press, 2011); John L. Esposito and Dalia Mogahed, *Who Speaks for Islam? What a Billion Muslims Really Think* (New York: Gallup Press, 2008); Steven Fish, *Are Muslims Distinctive: A Look at the Evidence* (New York: Oxford University Press, 2011); Carl Ernst and Richard Martin, *Rethinking Islamic Studies: From Orientalism to Cosmopolitanism* (Columbia, SC: University of South Carolina Press, 2010).

16. See Peter Berger, *The Desecularization of the World: Resurgent Religion and World Politics* (Washington, D.C.: Ethics and Public Policy Center, 1999); Rodney Stark and Roger Finke, *Acts of Faith: Explaining the Human Side of Religion* (Berkeley, CA: University of California Press, 2000); David Martin, *A General Theory of Secularization* (New York: Harper & Row, 1993); Steve Bruce, *God Is Dead: Secularization in the West* (Oxford: Blackwell, 2002).

17. See Samuel P. Huntington, *The Clash of Civilization and the Remaking of World Order* (New York: Simon & Schuster, 2011); Kurzman, *The Missing Martyrs*; Benjamin Barber, *Jihad vs. McWorld: Terrorism's Challenge to Democracy* (New York: Ballantine Books, 1996).

18. Craig J. Calhoun, *The Roots of Radicalism: Tradition, the Public Sphere, and Early Nineteenth Century Social Movements* (Chicago, IL: University of Chicago Press, 2012), 18.

19. Akbar Ahmed, *Journey into Europe: Islam, Immigration, and Identity* (Washington, D.C.: Brookings Institution Press, 2018), 249-304.

20. See Jonathan Fox, "Paradigm Lost: Huntington's Unfulfilled Clash of Civilizations Prediction into the 21st Century," *International Politics* 42, no. 4 (2005), 428-457; Paul Berman, *Terror and Liberalism* (New York: W. W. Norton, 2003); A. Mungiu-Pippidi and D. Mindruta, "Was Huntington Right? Testing Cultural Legacies and the Civilization Border," *International Politics* 39, no. 2 (2002), 193-213; E. A. Henderson and R. Tucker, "Clear and Present Strangers: The Clash of Civilizations and International Conflict," *International Studies Quarterly* 45, no. 2 (2001), 317-338; Ali Soufan, *Anatomy of Terror: From the Death of bin Laden to the Rise of the Islamic State* (New York: W. W. Norton, 2017); Irm Haleem, *The Essence of Islamist Extremism: Recognition Through Violence, Freedom Through Death* (New York: Routledge, 2014).

21. Mehran Kamrava, "Repression, Fundamentalism, and Terrorism in the Middle East," in *Democratic Development & Political Terrorism: The Global Perspective*, ed. William Crotty (Boston, MA: Northeastern University Press, 2005), 167-193.

22. Thomas Omestad, "Culture Clash in Denmark: The Close-knit Danes Find Their Liberal Ideals Tested by a Growing, Alienated Muslim Population," *U.S. News & World Report*, January 8, 2007, 40-45; Douglas Waller, "An American Imam," *Time*, November 21, 2005, 60-62; Fareed Zakaria, "Why Do They Hate Us?" *Newsweek*, October 15, 2001; Fareed Zakaria, "Why Do They Hate Us?" Global GPS, CNN, July 3, 2016.

23. Christopher A. Bail, *Terrified: How Anti-Muslim Fringe Organizations Became Mainstream* (Princeton, NJ: Princeton University Press, 2014); CBS, "The Holy Warrior," *60 Minutes*, September 15, 2004; Michael Kinsley, "The Religious Superiority Complex," *Time*, November 3, 2003, 106.

24. Dick Meyer, "Rush: MPs Just 'Blowing off Steam,'" CBS, May 6, 2004; Susan Sontag, "Regarding the Torture of Others," *New York Times*, May 23, 2004.

25. For similar discussions, see Stuart J. Kaufman, *Modern Hatreds: The Symbolic Politics of Ethnic War* (Ithaca, NY: Cornell University Press, 2001), 38; Ted R. Gurr, "Terrorism in Democracies: Its Social and Political Bases," in *Origins of Terrorism: Psychologies, Ideologies, Theologies, States of Mind*, ed. Walter Reich (Washington D.C.: Woodrow Wilson Center Press, 1998), 86-102.

26. See James D. Hunter, *Culture Wars: The Struggle to Define America* (New York: Basic Books, 1991); Martin Marty and Scott Appleby, *Fundamentalisms Observed: The Fundamentalism Project, Book 1* (Chicago, IL: University of Chicago Press, 1994).

27. Deirdre Shesgreen, "Republicans Face a Fresh Fight Over Obamacare," *USA Today*, January 3, 2018, 3A.

28. Yascha Mounk, *The People vs. Democracy: Why Our Freedom Is in Danger and How to Save It* (Cambridge, MA: Harvard University Press, 2016), 1-22.

29. See W. G. Stephan et al., "Intergroup Threat Theory," in *Handbook of Prejudice, Stereotyping, and Discrimination*, ed. T. D. Nelson (New York: Psychology Press, 2009), 43–59.

30. Stanley Feldman, "Enforcing Social Conformity: A Theory of Authoritarianism," *Political Psychology* 24, no 1 (2003), 41–74.

31. See Marc J. Hetherington and Elizabeth Suhay, "Authoritarianism, Threat, and Americans' Support for the War on Terror," *American Journal of Political Science* 55, no.3 (2011), 546–560; Feldman, "Enforcing Social Conformity," 41–74; Karen Stenner, *The Authoritarian Dynamic* (New York: Cambridge University Press, 2005); Marc J. Hetherington and Jonathan D. Weiler, *Authoritarianism and Polarization in American Politics* (New York: Cambridge University Press, 2009), 109–130; Reza Aslan, *Beyond Fundamentalism: Confronting Religious Extremism in the Age of Globalization* (New York: Random House, 2010).

32. Hope Yen (Associated Press), "9/11 Panel Disputes Iraq Link to Attacks," Yahoo News, June 16, 2004; Suzanne Goldenberg, "Bush: Saddam Was Not Responsible for 9/11," *The Guardian*, September 11, 2006; Jean E. Smith, *Bush* (New York: Simon & Schuster, 2016), 326–356.

33. Smith, *Bush*, 472–498.

34. See Clem Brooks and Jeff Manza, *Whose Rights? Counterterrorism and the Dark Side of American Public Opinion* (New York: Russell Sage Foundation, 2013); Lori Peek, *Behind the Backlash: Muslim Americans After 9/11* (Philadelphia: Temple University Press, 2011); James Vicini (Reuters), "FBI Abused Power to Get Private Records: Report," Yahoo News, March 9, 2007; Michael J. Sniffen, "Terror Prosecution Fall to Pre-9/11 Level," Associated Press, September 4, 2006; Jeff Stein, "A CIA Man Speaks His Mind on Secret Abductions," *Congressional Quarterly*, April 20, 2007; Tom Lasseter, "America's Prison for Terrorists Often Held the Wrong Men," *McClatchy Newspapers*, June 15, 2008; David G. Savage, "Judge Orders 17 Chinese Muslims Released from Guantanamo Bay," *Los Angeles Times*, October 7, 2008; Chitra Ragavan, "A Fine Legal Mess in Motown," *U.S. News & World Report*, September 13, 2004, 39–40.

35. Linda Herrera and Asef Bayat, "Introduction: Being Young and Muslim in Neoliberal Times," in *Being Young and Muslim: New Cultural Politics in the Global South and North*, eds. Linda Herrera and Asef Bayat (New York: Oxford University Press, 2010), 3–26.

36. Seumas Milne, "After Iraq, It's Not Just North Korea That Wants a Bomb," *The Guardian*, May 27, 2017.

37. "Securities Dilemma" of Robert Jervis, from Kaufman, *Modern Hatred*, 34; "C-escalation" of Randall Collins, "C-Escalation and D-Escalation: A Theory of the Time-Dynamics of Conflict," *American Sociological Review* 77, no 1 (2012), 1–20; Stephan et al., "Intergroup Threat Theory," 43–59.

38. Gary A. Fine, "Group Culture and the Interaction Order: Local Sociology on the Meso-level," *Annual Review of Sociology* 38, no. 1 (2012), 159–179; Kathleen Carley, "A Theory of Group Stability," *American Sociological Review* 56, no. 3 (1991), 331–54.

39. Gary Fine, *Tiny Publics: A Theory of Group Action and Culture* (New York: Russell Sage Foundation, 2012a), 36.

40. Oleg Kharkhordin, *The Collective and the Individual in Russia: A Study of Practices* (Berkeley, CA: University of California Press, 1999); Michael Walzer, *The Revolution of the Saints: A Study in the Origins of Radical Politics* (Cambridge, MA: Harvard University Press, 1965); David Apter, "Political Religion in the New Nations," in *Old Societies and New States*, ed. C. Geertz (New York: Free Press, 1964), 57–104; Emilio Gentile, "The Sacralisation of Politics: Definitions, Interpretations and Reflections on the Question of Secular Religion and Totalitarianism," *Totalitarian Movements and Political Religions* 1, no. 1 (2000), 18–55.

41. Will Carless, "White Supremacists Are Killing in the Name of an Ancient Nordic Religion," *PRI's The World*, NPR.org, May 25, 2017; BBC, "Decoding Far-right Online Hate."

42. C. Mitchell, "The Religious Content of Ethnic Identities," *Sociology* 40, no. 6 (2006), 1135–1152; Mălina Voicu, "Effect of Nationalism on Religiosity in 30 European Countries," *European Sociological Review* 28, no. 3 (2012), 333–343.

43. Wade C. Rowatt et al., "Associations among Religiousness, Social Attitudes, and Prejudice in a National Random Sample of American Adults," *Psychology of Religion and Spirituality* 1, no. 1 (2009), 14–24.

44. Kurt Eichenwald, "Right-wing Extremists Are a Bigger Threat to American Than ISIS," *Newsweek*, February 4, 2016; Michael Barkun, *Religion and the Racist Right: The Origins of the Christian Identity Movement* (Chapel Hill, NC: University of North Carolina Press, 1997); Jeffrey Kaplan, "Right-wing Violence in North America," in *Terror from the Extreme Right*, ed. Tore Bjørgo (London, England: Frank Cass, 1995), 44–95.

45. Bob Schenck, *Costly Grace: An Evangelical Minister's Rediscovery of Faith, Hope, and Love* (New York: Harper, 2018); Jeremy W. Peters and Katie Benner, "N.R.A.'s Web Voices Warn 'We're at the Mercy of Evil,'" *New York Times*, February 22, 2018, A17.

46. Tore Bjørgo, "Introduction," in *Terror From the Extreme Right*, ed. Tore Bjørgo (London, England: Frank Cass, 1995), 1–16.

47. Bjørgo, "Introduction," 3; Kaplan, "Right-wing Violence," 44–95.

48. Zeke Turner, "Culture Clash in Arts Capital," *Wall Street Journal*, April 21, 2016, A9; Tom Beyerlein and Valerie Lough, "Growing Culture: Militia Mentality," *Dayton Daily News*, April 4, 2010, A8; Joshua R. Miller, "Michigan Militia Group Preparing for Antichrist, Web Site Says," FOX News, March 29, 2010; Peters and Benner, "N.R.A.'s Web Voices Warn," A17.

49. Eugene Scott, "Most White Evangelicals Say Non-white Majority Bad," *New York Times*, July 22, 2018, A24.

50. BBC, "Non-Jewish Holocaust Victims: The 5,000,000 Others," January 20, 2005.

51. PBS, "Three Murder Suspects Linked to Atomwaffen: Where Their Cases Stand," *Frontline*, aired on June 19, 2019.

52. Marina Pitofsky, "Far-right Women State a Claim," *USA Today*, August 10–12, 2018, 1A & 8A.

53. Gabrielle Steinhauser and Kjetil M. Hovland, "EU Bickering Pauses for Nobel," *Wall Street Journal*, December 11, 2012, A12; John-Thor Dahlburg, "After Anti-EU Parties Surge, What's Ahead?" Yahoo News, May 26, 2014; Esme Nicholson, "Germany's Right-wing AfD is Accused of Exploiting Jewish Members," NPR News, October 5, 2018.

54. Anthony Oberschall, *Social Conflict and Social Movements* (Englewood Cliffs, NJ: Prentice-Hall, 1973), 125; David Meyer and Nancy Whittier, "Social Movement Spillover," *Social Problems* 41, no. 2 (1994), 277–298; Larry Isaac et al., "Taking It from the Streets: How the Sixties Mass Movement Revitalized Unionization," *American Journal of Sociology* 112, no. 1 (2006), 46–98; Doug McAdam, "'Initiator' and 'Spin-off' Movements: Diffusion Processes in Protest Cycles," in *Repertoires and Cycles of Collective Action*, ed. M. Traugott (Durham, NC: Duke University Press, 1995), 217–239.

55. Doug McAdam, "Micromobilization Contexts and Recruitments to Activism," *International Social Movement Research* 1 (1988), 125–154; Ann Mische, "Cross-talk in Movements: Reconceiving the Culture-Network Link," in *Social Movements and Networks*, Vol. 1, eds. M. Diani and D. McAdam (Oxford, UK: Oxford University Press, 2003), 258–281.

56. Xiaohong Xu, "Belonging Before Believing: Group Ethos and Block Recruitment in the Making of Chinese Communism," *American Sociological Review* 78, no. 5 (2013), 773–796.

57. Scott Helfstein, *Edges of Radicalization: Individuals, Networks and Ideas in Violent Extremism* (Combating Terrorism Center, U.S. Military Academy, CreateSpace Independent Publishing Platform, 2014).

58. For discussion of "cultural frames," see Ann Swidler, "Culture in Action: Symbols and Strategies," *American Sociological Review* 51, no. 2 (1986), 273–286; Ulf Hannerz, *Soulside: Inquiries into Ghetto Culture and Community* (New York: Columbia University Press, 1969); Michele Lamont and Mario L. Small, "How Culture Matters for the Understanding of Poverty: Enriching Our Understanding," in *The Colors of Poverty: Why Racial and Ethnic Disparities Persist*, eds. Ann C. Lin and David Harris (New York: Russell Sage, 2008), 76–102; Erving Goffman, *Frame Analysis: An Essay on the Organization of Experience* (Cambridge, MA: Harvard University Press, 1974).

59. Khachig Tololyan, "Cultural Narrative and the Motivation of the Terrorist," in *Inside Terrorist Organizations*, ed. David C. Rapoport (Portland, OR: Frank Cass, 2001), 217–233.

60. Ibid., 220–224.

61. See Mustifa Emirbayer and Chad A. Goldberg, "Pragmatism, Bourdieu, and Collective Emotions in Contentious Politics," *Theory and Society* 34 (2005), 469–518; Inmaculada Adarves-Yorno et al., "What Are We Fighting For?: The Effects of Framing on

Ingroup Identification and Allegiance," *The Journal of Social Psychology* 153, no. 1 (2013), 25–37.

62. See Randall Collins, "The Contentious Social Interactionism of Charles Tilly," *Social Psychology Quarterly* 73, no. 1 (2010b), 5–10; Verta Taylor and Nella Van Dyke, "'Get Up. Stand Up': Tactical Repertoires of Social Movements," in *The Blackwell Companion to Social Movements*, eds. David A. Snow et al. (Malden, MA: Blackwell, 2004), 262–293; Francesca Polletta and James M. Jasper, "Collective Identity and Social Movements," *Annual Review of Sociology* 27, no. 1 (2001), 283–305; Dawne Moon, "Who Am I and Who Are We. Conflicting Narratives of Collective Selfhood in Stigmatized Groups," *American Journal of Sociology* 117, no. 5 (2012), 1336–1379.

63. Kate Nash, "The Cultural Turn in Sociology: Toward a Theory of Cultural Politics," *Sociology* 35, no. 1 (2001), 77–92; Collins, "The Contentious Social Interactionism," 8.

64. Moon, "Who Am I and Who Are We," 1342.

65. Andrew McKinnon, "Elective Affinities of the Protestant Ethic: Weber and the Chemistry of Capitalism," *Sociological Theory* 28, no. 1 (2010), 108–126.

66. Jonathan Haidt, *The Righteous Mind: Why Good People Are Divided by Politics and Religion* (New York, NY: Vintage, 2012); J. Duckitt, "A Dual-process Cognitive-motivational Theory of Ideology and Prejudice," in *Advances in Experimental Social Psychology*, Vol. 33, ed. M. P. Zanna (New York: Academic Press, 2001), 41–133.

67. Similar to "prospect theory"; see Jeffrey D. Berejikian, "Model Building with Prospect Theory: A Cognitive Approach to International Relations," *Political Psychology* 23, no. 4 (2002), 759–786; "large group regression," Vamik Volkan, *Blind Trust: Large Groups and Their Leaders in Times of Crisis and Terror* (Charlottesville, VA: Pitchstone Publishing, 2004); For related discussion, see also Feldman, "Enforcing Social Conformity," 41–74; Stenner, *The Authoritarian Dynamic*; Michael J. Gilligan et al., "Civil War and Social Cohesion: Lab-in-the-Field Evidence from Nepal," *American Journal of Political Science* 58, no. 3 (2014), 604–619; Renee F. Lyons et al., "Coping as a Communal Process," *Journal of Social and Personal Relationships* 15, no. 5 (1998), 579–605; James W. Pennebaker and Kent D. Harber, "A Social Stage Model of Collective Coping: The Loma Prieta Earthquake and the Persian Gulf War," *Journal of Social Issues* 49, no. 4 (1993), 125–145; James D. Fearon et al., "Can Development Aid Contribute to Social Cohesion After Civil War? Evidence from a Field Experiment in Post-Conflict Liberia," *American Economic Review* 99, no. 2 (2009), 287–291; Sam Whitt and Rick K. Wilson, "The Dictator Game: Fairness and Equity in Postwar Bosnia," *American Journal of Political Science* 51, no. 3 (2007), 655–668.

68. John D. McCarthy and Mayer N. Zald, "Resource Mobilization and Social Movements: A Partial Theory," *American Journal of Sociology* 82, no. 6 (1977), 1212–1241.

69. Craig N. Murphy, "The Emergence of Global Governance," in *International Organization and Global Governance*, eds. Thomas G. Weiss and Rorden Wilkinson (New York: Routledge, 2018), 25–36.

70. See Pinker, *The Better Angels* and *Enlightenment Now*; Shermer, *The Moral Arc*; Deaton, *The Great Escape*; Norberg, *Progress*; Wagner, *Modernity as Experience and Interpretation*; Easterbrook, *It's Better than It Looks*; Ridley, *The Rational Optimists*; Charles C. Mann, *The Wizard and the Prophet: Two Remarkable Scientists and Their Dueling Visions to Shape Tomorrow's World* (New York: Alfred A. Knopf, 2018).

Chapter 1

1. For related discussions, see Michele Lamont and Virag Molnar, "The Study of Boundaries in the Social Sciences," *Annual Review of Sociology* 28, no. 1 (2002), 167–195.

2. Salman Rushdie, from "Fareed Zakaria GPS," CNN, September 23, 2012.

3. Aparisim Ghosh, "The Apostle of Hate," *Time*, June 19, 2006, 36–37.

4. Scott Atran, "Can We Construct a Counter-Narrative to ISIS's End Goal?" NPR News, November 22, 2015.

5. Penny Edgell et al., "Atheists as 'Other': Moral Boundaries and Cultural Membership in American Society," *American Sociological Review* 71, no. 2 (2006), 211–234.

6. Reza Aslan, *Beyond Fundamentalism: Confronting Religious Extremism in the Age of Globalization* (New York: Random House, 2010).

7. PBS, "The Spirituality of George W. Bush," *Frontline*, aired on April 29, 2004.
8. Somini Sengupta, "Nikki Haley Puts U.N. on Notice: U.S. Is 'Taking Names,'" *New York Times*, January 27, 2017.
9. Shanto Iyengar and Sean J. Westwood, "Fear and Loathing Across Party Lines: New Evidence on Group Polarization," *American Journal of Political Science* 59, no. 3 (2015), 690–707; Shanto Iyengar et al., "Affect, Not Ideology: A Social Identity Perspective on Polarization," *Public Opinion Quarterly* 76, no. 3 (2012), 405–431.
10. James F. Davis, *Who Is Black?: One Nation's Definition* (State College, PA: Penn State University Press, 1991).
11. CBS News, "Gay Sex Now Officially Punishable by Death by Stoning in Brunei," April 3, 2019.
12. Associated Press, "Black Trans Woman Killed in S. Carolina Is the 12th in 2019," July 25, 2019.
13. CBS News, "Arrest in Brutal Beating of Dallas Transgender Women in Broad Daylight in Front of Crowd," April 15, 2019.
14. Romesh Ratnesar, "Face of Terror," *Time*, December 27–January 3, 2004–2005, 96–100.
15. Thomas Omestad, "Culture Clash in Denmark: The Close-knit Danes Find Their Liberal Ideals Tested by a Growing, Alienated Muslim Population," *U.S. News & World Report*, January 8, 2007, 40–45.
16. Reuters, "ISIL Crucifies Eight Rival Fighters, Says Monitoring Group," June 29, 2014.
17. Human Rights Watch, "Iran: Arrest Shows Peril for Dual Nationals," February 15, 2016, available at https://www.hrw.org/news/2016/02/15/iran-arrest-shows-peril-dual-nationals; BBC, "Iran Accuses Dual National of Spying for British Intelligence," August 16, 2016.
18. Paul Karp, "Australia Citizenship Crisis Reignites as Senator and Four MPs Quit," *The Guardian*, May 9, 2018.
19. John Nichols, "Hunting for RINOs," *The Nation*, August 26, 2005; Paul Bedard, "Angry Tea Party Leaders Go 'RINO' Hunting for Would-be Republicans," *Washington Examiner*, November 4, 2013; Scott Shepard, "Political Moderation Could Get Test in Ohio," *Dayton Daily News*, May 31, 2005, A1.
20. Carol Glatz, "Ignorance of Faith Risks Creating Cafeteria Catholics, Pope Says," *Catholic News Service*, October 17, 2012.
21. Associated Press, "Pope Warns Against 'Lukewarm' Christians at Vatican Mass," ABC News, June 29, 2019.
22. NAACP, "History of Lynching," Accessed 2017, Available at http://www.naacp.org/history-of-lynchings.
23. BBC, "Rwanda: How the Genocide Happened," May 17, 2011.
24. Ben Gilbert, "An Eye for an Eye," *U.S. News & World Report*, February 20, 2006, 27–28.
25. Jason Beaubien, "Taliban in Pakistan Derail World Polio Eradication," NPR News, July 29, 2014; Associated Press, "Gunmen Kill 2 Polio Workers in Pakistan, Mother and Daughter," ABC News, January 18, 2018.
26. BBC World Service Newshour, December 8, 2015; Associated Press, "Bahrain: Protesters Are Sentenced," *Wall Street Journal*, June 15, 2012, A10.
27. CBS News, "When Hospitals Become Targets in Syria's Civil War," *60 Minutes*, August 5, 2018.
28. Asa Fitch and Joshua Mitnick, "Hamas Kills Alleged Israel Collaborators," *Wall Street Journal*, August 23–24, 2014, A6.
29. Josh Keller et al., "The Scale of Turkey's Purge Is Nearly Unprecedented," *New York Times*, August 2, 2016; Tim Arango et al., "Turks See Purge as Witch Hunt of 'Medieval' Darkness," *New York Times*, September 16, 2016.
30. Akin to "in-group projection theory" and "social-dominance orientation [SDO]"; see Felicia Pratto et al., "Social Dominance Orientation: A Personality Variable Predicting Social and Political Attitudes," *Journal of Personality and Social Psychology*, 67, no. 4 (1994), 741–763.
31. Julie Zauzmer and Michelle Boorstein, "Evangelicals Fear Muslims; Atheists Fear Christians: How Americans Mistrust One Another," *Washington Post*, September 7, 2017.
32. Will M. Gervais and Maxine B. Najle, "How Many Atheists Are There?" *PsyArXiv*, March 3, 2017.
33. Wade Goodwyn, "Alt-Right, White Nationalist, Free Speech: The Far Right's Language Explained," NPR News, June 4, 2017.
34. For related discussions, see Amy Chua, *Political Tribes: Group Instinct and the Fate of Nations* (New York: Penguin Press, 2018), 15–36.
35. Jeffrey D. Sachs, *A New Foreign Policy: Beyond American Exceptionalism* (New York: Columbia University Press, 2018).

36. Albert Bandura, "Mechanisms of Moral Engagement," in *Origins of Terrorism: Psychologies, Ideologies, Theologies, States of Mind*, ed. Walter Reich (Washington D.C.: Woodrow Wilson Center Press, 1998), 161-191.

37. Matt Duss, "Iraq: Because Rumsfeld Needed Better Targets," Thinkprogress.com, July 28, 2009.

38. For similar discussions, see Jacob N. Shapiro and David A. Siegel, "Understanding in Terrorist Organizations," *International Studies Quarterly* 51, no. 2 (2007), 405-429; Navin A. Bapat and Sean Zeigler, "Terrorism, Dynamic Commitment Problems, and Military Conflict," *American Journal of Political Science* 60, no. 2 (2016), 337-351; Ronald Bailey, "Don't be Terrorized." *Reason*, August 11, 2006.

39. Alex Sundby, "White Supremacists Committed Most Extremist Killings in U.S. in 2017, Group Says," CBS News, January 19, 2018.

40. Bapat and Zeigler, "Terrorism," 337-351.

41. Emile Durkheim, *The Division of Labor in Society*, Translation by George Simpson (New York: Macmillan, 1964 [1933]).

42. Durkheim, *The Division of Labor*.

43. Donald M. Taylor, *The Quest for Identity* (Westport, CT: Praeger, 2002), 44.

44. Gregory Baum, *Nationalism, Religion, and Ethics* (Quebec City, Canada: McGill-Queen's University Press, 2001), 119-122.

45. Laurence Norman and Drew Hinshaw, "EU Finds $1 Trillion Doesn't Buy Love," *Wall Street Journal*, August 9, 2018, A1 & A8.

46. See Marilynn B. Brewer, "The Psychology of Prejudice: Ingroup Love or Outgroup Hate?" *Journal of Social Issues* 55, no. 3 (1999), 429-444; M. Hewstone et al., "Intergroup Bias," *Annual Review of Psychology* 53 (2002), 575-604; Christopher L. Aberson, Michael Healy, and Victoria Romero, "Ingroup Bias and Self-esteem: A Meta-analysis," *Personality and Social Psychology Review* 4, no. 2 (2000), 157-173; Chua, *Political Tribes*, 165-188.

47. Henry Tajfel and John C. Turner, "An Integrative Theory of Intergroup Conflict," in *The Social Psychology of Intergroup Relations*, eds. W. Austin and S. Worchel (Monterey, CA: Books/Cole, 1979), 33-47.

48. Miller McPherson et al., "Birds of a Feather: Homophily in Social Networks," *Annual Review of Sociology* 27 (2001), 415-444; Gueorgi Kossinets and Duncan J. Watts, "Origins of Homophily in an Evolving Social Network," *American Journal of Sociology* 115, no. 2 (2009), 405-450; Nicolas Gueguen et al., "Similarity and Social Interaction: When Similarity Fosters Implicit Behavior Toward a Stranger," *The Journal of Social Psychology* 151, no. 6 (2011), 671-673; Jerry M. Burger et al., "What a Coincidence! The Effects of Incidental Similarity on Compliance," *Personality and Social Psychology Bulletin* 30 (2004), 35-43.

49. Elisabeth R. Gerber et al., "Political Homophily and Collaboration in Regional Planning Networks," *American Journal of Political Science* 57, no. 3 (2013), 598-610.

50. David E. Broockman, "Black Politicians are More Intrinsically Motivated to Advance Blacks' Interests: A Field Experiment Manipulating Political Incentives," *American Journal of Political Science* 57, no. 3 (2013), 521-536; Dimitri Landa and Dominik Duell, "Social Identity and Electoral Accountability," *American Journal of Political Science* 59, no. 3 (2015), 671-689; Dingeman Wiertz, "Segregation in Civic Life: Ethnic Sorting and Mixing Across Voluntary Associations," *American Sociological Review* 81, no. 4 (2016), 800-827; Jeffrey A. Smith et al., "Social Distance in the U.S.: Sex, Race, Religion, Age, and Education Homophily Among Confidants, 1985-2004," *American Sociological Review* 79, no. 3 (2014), 432-465.

51. Kerem O. Kalkan et al., "Will Americans Vote for Muslims? The Impact of Religious and Ethnic Identifiers on Candidate Support," Presented at the annual meeting of the American Political Science Association, Boston, MA., 2008; Monika L. McDermott, "Religious Stereotyping and Voter Support for Evangelical Candidates," *Political Research Quarterly* 62, no. 2 (2009), 340-354; David E. Campbell et al., "The Party Faithful: Partisan Images, Candidate Religion, and the Electoral Impact of Party Identification," *American Journal of Political Science* 55, no. 1 (2011), 42-58; Smith et al. "Social Distance in the U.S."

52. Andreas Wimmer and Kevin Lewis, "Beyond and Below Racial Homophily: ERG Models of a Friendship Network Documented on Facebook," *American Journal of Sociology* 116, no. 2 (2010), 583-642.

53. Jonathan Haidt, *The Righteous Mind:*

Why Good People are Divided by Politics and Religion (New York: Vintage, 2012), 219–255.

54. Scott E. Page, *The Difference: How the Power of Diversity Creates Better Groups, Firms, Schools and Societies* (Princeton, NJ: Princeton University Press, 2007).

55. Charles E. Hurst and David L. McConnell, *An Amish Paradox: Diversity and Change in the World's Largest Amish Community* (Baltimore, MD: Johns Hopkins University Press, 2010).

56. Al-Islam.org, "The Major Difference Between the Shi'a and the Sunni," available at https://www.al-islam.org/shiite-encyclopedia/major-difference-between-shia-and-sunni, Accessed 2019.

57. Craig J. Calhoun, *The Roots of Radicalism: Tradition, the Public Sphere, and Early Nineteenth Century Social Movements* (Chicago, IL: University of Chicago Press, 2012), 82–120.

58. Daniel Etounga-Manguelle, "Does Africa Need a Cultural Adjustment Program?" in *Culture Matters: How Values Shape Human Progress*, eds. Laurence E. Harrison and Samuel P. Huntington (New York: Basic Books, 2001), 65–77.

59. Jeffrey Gettleman, "Nepal's Grim Superstition, Known to Lead to a Death by Shame," *New York Times*, June 20, 2018, A1 & A6.

60. Steven L. Myers, "Hazing Trial Bares Dark Side of Russia's Military," *New York Times*, August 13, 2006.

61. Benjamin Barber, *Jihad vs. McWorld: Terrorism's Challenge to Democracy* (New York: Ballantine Books, 1996).

62. Zygmunt Bauman, *Liquid Modernity* (Cambridge, UK: Polity, 2000).

63. Chua, *Political Tribes*, 137–164.

64. Ina Jaffe, "Manson Dies at 83: Lead Cult Members Who Committed 1969 Murders," NPR Morning Edition, November 20, 2017.

65. Terrence McCoy, "In Pakistan, 1,000 Women Die in 'Honor Killings' Annually. Why Is This Happening?" *Washington Post*, May 28, 2014; Julia Dahl, "Honor Killing Under Growing Scrutiny in the U.S.," CBS News, April 4, 2012.

66. BBC, "Anti-gay Attacks on Rise in Iraq," August 17, 2009.

67. Todd Richmond (Associated Press), "Court Upholds Parents' Convictions in Prayer Death," *U.S. News*, July 3, 2013.

68. Cynthia McFadden, Nightline, ABC News, October 3, 2006.

69. Peter Moskos, *Cop in the Hood: My Year Policing Baltimore's Eastern District* (Princeton, N.J.: Princeton University Press, 2008), 85–90; Matt Apuzzo, "Justice Dept. Condemns Profit-Minded Court Policies Targeting the Poor," *New York Times*, March 14, 2016; Ben, Kesling, "Lawsuit Alleges Ferguson, Mo., Legal System Violates Constitutional Protections," *Wall Street Journal*, February 9, 2015; Kate C. Greer, "Oklahoma Takes a Hard Look At What Police Seize—and How It's Spent," NPR News, July 26, 2015; Jeva Lange, "New York City Is Reportedly Ending Bail for Low-level Crimes," *The Week*, July 8, 2015; Norm Stamper, *To Protect and Serve: How to Fix America's Police* (New York: Nation Books, 2016); Marie Gottschalk, *The Problems and the Gallows: The Politics of Mass Incarceration in America* (New York: Cambridge University Press, 2006); John F. Pfaff, *Locked In: The True Causes of Mass Incarceration and How to Achieve Real Reform* (New York: Basic Books, 2017); Patrick Sharkey, *Uneasy Peace: The Great Crime Decline, the Renewal of City Life, and the Next War on Violence* (New York: W. W. Norton, 2018); Michael Wines, "Lawsuit Cites 45 Cases of Prosecutor Misconduct," *New York Times*, January 18, 2018, A18.

70. Richard A. Leo, *Police Interrogation and American Justice* (Cambridge, MA: Harvard University Press, 2009); Norm Stamper, *To Protect and Serve: How to Fix America's Police* (New York: Nation Books, 2016).

71. Brian L. Cutler, *Conviction of the Innocent: Lessons from Psychological Research* (Washington D.C.: American Psychological Association, 2011); Del Quentin Wilber, *A Good Month for Murder: The Inside Story of a Homicide Squad* (New York: Henry Holt, 2016).

72. Daniel S. Medwed, *Prosecution Complex: America's Race to Convict and its Impact on the Innocent* (New York: New York University Press, 2012); Joseph Goldstein, "Scrutiny of Decorated Detective Raises Specter of Lying as Routine," *New York Times*, October 11, 2017, A1 & A20; Joseph Goldstein, "'Testilying' by Police Persists as Cameras Capture Truth," *New York Times*, March 19, 2018, A1 & A16.

73. Natalie P. Byfield, *Savage Portrayals: Race, Media, and the Central Park Jogger Story* (Philadelphia, PA: Temple University Press, 2014); Associated Press, "Central Park Five Sets Record Straight," NPR News, November 27, 2012; PBS, "Central

Park Five," Aired on April 8, 2019 (released in 2012).

74. Associated Press, "Exonerated Inmates Awarded $28 Million," *Wall Street Journal*, July 7, A2, 2016.

75. Samantha J. Gross, "After Nearly 70 Years, Florida Clemency Board Pardons Groveland Four," *Miami Herald*, January 11, 2019.

76. Erik Ortiz, "Davontae Sanford, Wrongly Convicted of 4 Murders at Age 14, to Be Freed," NBC News, June 8, 2016.

77. Niraj Chokshi, "False Confessions, Mistaken Witnesses, Corrupt Officials: Putting the Innocent in Jail," *New York Times*, March 15, 2018, A22.

78. Marie Keenan, *Child Sexual Abuse and the Catholic Church: Gender, Power, and Organizational Culture* (New York: Oxford University Press, 2011); Rachel Zoll (Associated Press), "Study: 4,392 Priests Accused of Sex Abuse," *Washington Post*, February 26, 2004; Associated Press, "Vatican Defrocks 848 Priests in 10 years for Abuse," Fox News, May 7, 2014.

79. Alison Thoet, "7 Percent of Australia's Catholic Priests Accused of Sexually Abusing Children," PBS Newshour, February 6, 2017.

80. USA Today Network, "Parishes Across Nation Under Shadow of Abuse," *USA Today*, August 25–27, 2017, 1A & 6A.

81. Rajini Vaidyanathan, "Sexual Assault Survivors Challenge Universities," BBC World Service Newshour, February 20, 2014; Monika J. Hostler, "Making Campuses Safer for Women," *Wall Street Journal*, February 24, 2014; Joel Roberts, "College President Fired After Cover-Up," CBS News, July 16, 2007.

82. Ben Kesling, "Assault Reports Rise in Military," *Wall Street Journal*, December 29, 2017, A5; Rebecca Kheel, "Report: Sexual Assault Victims Wrongfully Discharged from Military," *The Hill*, May 19, 2016.

83. See Gennaro F. Vito et al., "Police Integrity: Rankings of Scenarios on the Klockars Scale by 'Management Cops,'" *Criminal Justice Review* 36, no. 2 (2011), 152–164; Vedat Kargin, *Peer Reporting of Unethical Police Behavior* (Philadelphia, PA: LFB Scholarly Publishing, 2010); Gabriel J. Chin and Scott Wells, "'The Blue Wall of Silence' as Evidence of Bias and Motive to Lie: A New Approach to Police Perjury," *University of Pittsburgh Law Review* 59 (1998), 233–299; Quint Thurman and Andrew Giacomazzi, *Controversies in Policing* (New York: Routledge, 2016); Peter Moskos, *Cop in the Hood: My Year Policing Baltimore's Eastern District* (Princeton, NJ: Princeton University Press, 2008); Eugene A. Paroline, "Taking Stock: Toward a Richer Understanding of Police Culture," *Journal of Criminal Justice* 31, no. 3 (2003), 199–214; Eugene A. Paroline and William Terrill, *Police Culture: Adapting to the Strains of the Job* (Durham, NC: Carolina Academic Press, 2013).

84. Kevin Johnson, "Congress: U.S. Prison Misconduct Regularly 'Covered up,'" *USA Today*, January 7, 2019, 3A.

85. Jayne O'Donnel, "Hospitals Shield Doctors in Sex Cases," *USA Today*, January 8, 2018, 1A & 5A.

86. Maggie Astor, "U.S. Gymnasts Worry That Program's Chaos Will Ruin Their Chances," *New York Times*, February 27, 2018.

87. Jina Moore, "U.N. Cases Read Like 'Manual in How Not to Investigate' Sex Assault," *New York Times*, June 29, 2018, A7.

88. For example cases, see Daisuke Wakabayashi and Katie Benner, "How Google Has Protected Its Elite Men," *New York Times*, October 26, 2018, A1 & A16; Rachel Abrams and John Koblin, "CBS Made Secret Deal with Actress Over Abuse," *New York Times*, December 13, 2018, B1 & B3; James B. Stewart, "'Disaster for CBS Shareholders': Damning Report on Moonves Reveals Total Failure at Top," *New York Times*, December 4, 2018; Emily Steel, "Fox Establishes Workplace Culture Panel After Harassment Scandal," *New York Times*, November 20, 2017.

89. Lijia Zhang, from Robin Young, Here and Now (podcast), WBUR, June 15, 2008.

90. Associated Press, "Fidel Castro Sees U.S. Aid Offer as Hypocritical," *USA Today*, September 17, 2008.

91. Rick Gladstone, "Cholera Deaths in Haiti Could Far Exceed Official Count," *New York Times*, March 18, 2016.

92. Jan E. Stets and Michael J. Carter, "A Theory of the Self for the Sociology of Morality," *American Sociological Review* 77, no. 1 (2012), 120–140.

93. Ruth Horowitz, "Honor and Reputation in the Chicano Gang," in *The Meaning of Sociology: A Reader*, 5th edition, ed. Joel M. Charon (Moorhead, MN: Moorhead State University Press, 1996), 59–66.

94. Ghosh, "The Apostle of Hate," 36–37.

95. Joshua R. Miller, "Iranian Pastor Faces Execution for Refusing to Recant

Christian Faith," Fox News, September 28, 2011.

96. Simon Cottee, *The Apostates: When Muslims Leave Islam* (London, UK: Hurst, 2015).

97. Tresa Baldas, "Ex-Jehovah's Witnesses Break Silence on Shunning," *USA Today*, March 28, 2018, 6A.

98. Walter Pincus, "Asylum Program Falls Short for Iraqis Aiding U.S. Forces," *Washington Post*, January 22, 2008; Anthony Shadid, "For an Iraqi Family, 'No Other Choice,'" *Washington Post*, August 1, 2003.

99. Bruce Smith (Associated Press), "Citadel Deals with Fallout from Sex Abuse Claims from Campers," *Washington Post*, December 11, 2011; Quil Lawrence, "New Report Says Pentagon Not Doing Enough For Sexual Assault Victims," NPR News, May 19, 2016; Susan Burke, "Prosecuting Military Sexual Assault Cases," Diane Rehm Show, NPR News, July 17, 2013; Kheel, "Report: Sexual Assault Victims"; Thomas Gibbons-Neff, "'It's Marine Corps Wide': Female Marines Detail Harassment in Wake of Nude Photos Scandal," *Washington Post*, March 7, 2017; PBS, RetroReport, October 16, 2019.

100. Felicia Schwartz, "Pentagon Faulted in Assault Cases," *Wall Street Journal*, May 18, 2015, A5.

101. For example cases, see Chris Arnold, "Reports on Wells Fargo Whistleblowers Spark Inquiry in Congress," NPR News, December 30, 2016; Joe Davidson, "Victims: Whistleblower Retaliation Is Growing," *Washington Post*, October 30, 2017.

102. Similar to "biased moral outrage"; see Shunsuke Uehara et al., "What Leads to Evocation of Moral Outrage? Exploring the Role of Personal Morality," *International Journal of Psychological Studies* 6, no. 1 (2015), 58–67; C. Daniel. Batson et al., "Pursuing Moral Outrage: Anger at Torture," *Journal of Experimental Social Psychology* 45, no. 1 (2009), 155–160; C. D. Batson et al., "Anger at Unfairness: Is it Moral Outrage?" *European Journal of Social Psychology* 37 (2007), 1272–1285; Erin M. O'Mara et al., "Will Moral Outrage Stand up? Distinguishing Among Emotional Reactions to a Moral Violation," *European Journal of Social Psychology* 41, no. 2 (2011), 173–179; Debra Liberman and Lance Linke, "The Effect of Social Category on Third Party Punishment," *Evolutionary Psychology* 5, no. 2 (2007), 289–305.

103. See Ehud Sprinzak, "The Psycho-political Formation of Extreme Left Terrorism in a Democracy: The Case of the Weathermen," in *Origins of Terrorism: Psychologies, Ideologies, Theologies, States of Mind*, ed. Walter Reich (Washington D.C.: Woodrow Wilson Center Press, 1998), 82; Vamik D. Volkan, *Blind Trust: Large Groups and Their Leaders in Times of Crisis and Terror* (Charlottesville, VA: Pitchstone Publishing, 2004), 107–108.

104. Charles M. Blow, "Trump, Treasonous Traitor," *New York Times* (Op-Ed), July 16, 2018, A19.

105. Steven Shepard, "Poll: Half Think Franken Should Resign." *Politico*, November 22, 2017.

106. Benjy Sarlin, "Economists Scratch Their Heads as Congress Ramps up Deficits," NBC News, February 9, 2018; Jennifer Steinhauer, "Deficit Soars but Republicans, Once the Fiscal Watchdog, Remain Quiet," *New York Times*, October 17, 2018, A17.

107. Katheryn Russel-Brown, *Protecting Our Own: Race, Crime, and African Americans* (Lanham, MD: Rowman & Littlefield, 2006).

108. Jon Cohen and Dan Balz, "Race Shapes Zimmerman Verdict Reaction," *Washington Post*, July 22, 2013.

109. Corrine Abrams and Krishna Pokharel, "India Is Shaken by Rape of Young Girl," *Wall Street Journal*, April 16, 2018, A6; Jeffrey Gettleman, "A Child Is Killed, and Empathy Goes Missing," *New York Times*, April 26, 2018, A8.

110. Craig Smith and Don Van Natta, Jr., "Officials Fear Iraq's Lure for Muslims in Europe," *New York Times*, October 23, 2004; Brian Bennett and Michael Ware, "Behind the Enemy Lines," *Time*, December 15, 2003, 28–35; Robert Siegel, "Foreign Policy Experts Weigh in on U.S. Strategy Against the Islamic State," NPR News, May 28, 2015.

111. Siegel, "Foreign Policy Experts."

112. BBC, "IS Foreign Fighters: 5,600 Have Returned Home—Report," October 24, 2017.

113. Masha Gessen, *Tsarnaev Brothers: The Road to a Modern Tragedy* (New York: Riverhead Books, 2015).

114. Philip Sherwell and Alex Spillius, "Fort Hood Shooting: Texas Army Killer Linked to September 11 Terrorists," *The Daily Telegraph*, November 7, 2009.

115. CBS Evening News, November 29, 2016.

116. Ashley Fantz et al., "Orlando Shooting: What Motivated a Killer?" CNN, June 14, 2019.
117. Alan Feuer, "Court Papers Detail a Drift Toward Jihad," *New York Times*, January 4, A17, 2018.
118. See Leonard Pitts, "Stop-snitching Culture Is Weak and Cowardly," *Dayton Daily News* (Op-Ed), February 6, 2009, A12; Nathan Thornburgh, "Looking for a Few Good Snitches," *Time*, February 27, 2006, 54–56.
119. See Joe Domanick, *Blue: The LAPD and the Battle to Redeem American Policing* (New York: Simon & Schuster, 2015); Vito et al., "Police Integrity"; Kargin, *Peer Reporting*; Chin and Wells, "The Blue Wall of Silence"; Thurman and Giacomazzi, *Controversies in Policing*; Moskos, "Cop in the Hood"; Carl B. Klockars et al., *Enhancing Police Integrity* (New York: Springer, 2006); Paroline, "Taking Stock"; Tom Barker and David Carter, "'Fluffing Up the Evidence and Covering Your Ass': Some Conceptual Notes on Police Lying," *Deviant Behavior* 11, no. 1 (1990), 61–73.
120. Schwartz, "Pentagon Faulted in Assault Cases"; Bruce, Smith (Associated Press), "Citadel Deals with Fallout from Sex Abuse Claims from Campers," *Washington Post*, December 11, 2011; Lawrence, "New Report Says"; Burke, "Prosecuting Military Sexual Assault Cases"; Kheel, "Report: Sexual Assault Victims."
121. Pauline Jelinek (Associated Press), "Lapses Found in Battlefield Ethics Study," *Houston Chronicle*, May 4, 2007.
122. Gordon Lynch, *The Sacred in the Modern World: A Cultural Sociological Approach* (Oxford, UK: Oxford University Press, 2014); Keenan, *Child Sexual Abuse*.
123. William F. Baker, "The Story Left Out of 'Spotlight,'" *USA Today* (Op-Ed), February 23, 2016, 7A.
124. For example cases, see Mujib Mashal and Zahra Nader, "In Lawless Afghan Province, 'No Value' and No Justice for Women," *New York Times*, July 9, 2017, A6; BBC, "Pakistan Village Council Orders 'Revenge Rape' of Girl," July 26, 2017.
125. Rachel Morarjee, "The Afghan Christian: A Problem for Karzai," *Time*, March 24, 2006.
126. Osama bin Laden, "Text of Fatwah Urging Jihad against Americans," *Al-Quds al-'Arabi*, February 23, 1998.
127. See Christopher A. Bail, *Terrified: How Anti-Muslim Fringe Organizations Became Mainstream* (Princeton, NJ: Princeton University Press, 2014); CBS News, "The Holy Warrior," *60 Minutes*, September 15, 2004; Michael Kinsley, "The Religious Superiority Complex," *Time*, November 3, 2003, 106.
128. Paul Schemm (Associated Press), "Iraqi Christians Giving Up" *Dayton Daily News*, May 15, 2009, A8.
129. Lourdes Garcia-Navarro, "From a War Outside to a War at Home," NPR News, July 7, 2008.
130. See Charles Kurzman, *The Missing Martyrs: Why There are So Few Muslim Terrorists* (New York: Oxford University Press, 2011); Carl Ernst and Richard Martin, *Rethinking Islamic Studies: From Orientalism to Cosmopolitanism* (Columbia: University of South Carolina Press, 2010); John L. Esposito and Dalia Mogahed, *Who Speaks for Islam? What a Billion Muslims Really Think* (New York: Gallup Press, 2008); Steven Fish, *Are Muslims Distinctive: A Look at the Evidence* (New York: Oxford University Press, 2011).
131. BBC World Service Newshour, April 14, 2016.
132. BBC World Service Newshour, February 28, 2018.
133. Thomas Gibbons-Neff, "Attacks by Extremist Groups on Afghan Schools Triple, UNICEF Reports," *New York Times*, May 28, 2019, A4.
134. Douglas K. Daniel (Associated Press), "39 People Killed in Kenya Mall Attack Claimed by Somali Militants; Hostages Still Held," *Washington Post*, September 21, 2013.
135. Abdirahman Hussein et al., "Al Shabaab Car Bomber Strikes Hotel in Somali Capital, at Least 15 Dead," Reuters, June 1, 2016; Abdi Guled, "Deadly Suicide Blast Hits Mogadishu Hotel," Associated Press, October 29, 2017.
136. Abdi Guled, "Final Death Toll Hits 512 in Truck Bomb Attack many Call Somalia's 9/11," Associated Press, December 3, 2017.
137. Ehsanullah Amiri and Craig Nelson, "Attacks Kill 19 at Afghan Hotel," *Wall Street Journal*, January 22, 2018, A7.
138. NBC Nightly News, May 1, 2018.
139. BBC World Service Newshour, January 25, 2018.
140. Saphora Smith et al. "'They Came to Kill the Mothers': Shock, Blame Swirl after Afghan Hospital Attack," NBC News, May 15, 2020.

141. Malaka Gharib, "In Their Own Words: Why Armed Fighters Attack Aid Workers," NPR News, September 14, 2017.
142. Associated Press, "Gunmen Kill 2 Polio Workers."
143. Qasim Nauman, "Gunmen Kill Police Guarding Polio Drive," *Wall Street Journal*, April 21, 2016, A14.
144. Zabihullah Ghazi and Rod Nordland, "Attack on Afghan Midwives School Kills 2," *New York Times*, July 29, 2018, A10.
145. Kurzman, *The Missing Martyrs*.
146. Ben Hubbard, "Scorned and Trapped: Wives and Children of ISIS," *New York Times*, July 5, 2018, A1 & A14.
147. Joscha Legewie, "Terrorist Events and Attitudes toward Immigrants: A Natural Experiment," *American Journal of Sociology* 118, no. 5 (2013), 1199–1245.
148. See John Ogbu, *Minority Education and Caste* (New York: Academic Press, 1978).
149. See David S. Kirk and Andrew V. Papachristos, "Cultural Mechanisms and the Persistence of Neighborhood Violence," *American Journal of Sociology* 116, no. 3 (2011), 1190–1233; Robert J. Sampson and Dawn J. Bartusch, "Legal Cynicism and (Subcultural?) Tolerance of Deviance: The Neighborhood Context of Racial Differences," *Law and Society Review* 32 (1998), 777–804; Robert J. Duran, *Gang Life in Two Cities: An Insider's Journey* (New York: Columbia University Press, 2013), 66–93; Raymond Paternoster et al., "Do Fair Procedures Matter? The Effect of Procedural Justice on Spouse Assault," *Law and Society Review* 31, no. 1 (1997), 163–204; Tom R. Tyler, "Enhancing Police Legitimacy," *Annals of the American Academy of Political and Social Science* 593 (2004), 84–99; Charis E. Kubrin and Ronald Weitzer, "Retaliatory Homicide: Concentrated Disadvantage and Neighborhood Culture," *Social Problems* 50, no. 2 (2003), 157–180; Elijah Anderson, *Code of the Street: Decency, Violence, and the Moral Life of the Inner City* (New York: W.W. Norton, 2000), 34; Rod K. Brunson, "Police Don't Like Black People: African American Young Men's Accumulated Police Experiences," *Criminology and Public Policy* 6 (2007), 71–101; Robert J. Kane, "Compromised Police Legitimacy as a Predictor of Violent Crime in Structurally Disadvantaged Communities," *Criminology* 43, no. 2 (2005), 469–498.
150. Alissa J. Rubin, "In Europe, Terrorism Trial, a Mostly Silent Protest," *New York Times*, February 11, 2018, A4.
151. John W. Patty, "Signaling Through Obstruction," *American Journal of Political Science* 60, no. 1 (2016), 175–189.
152. Ryan Tracy, "Candidates' Views on Banks," *Wall Street Journal*, November 12, 2015, C7.
153. Mike DeBonis, "Mitch McConnell's Senate Is Confirming Very, Very Few Presidential Nominees," *Washington Post*, May 5, 2016; Kristina Peterson and Corey Boles, "No Breakthrough on Filibuster," *Wall Street Journal*, July 16, 2003, A4.
154. T. Christian Miller, from Scott Simon, "Private Landowners Along Trump's Proposed Border Wall Risk Losing Property," NPR News, January 12, 2019.
155. Juliet Eilperin and Darla Cameron, "How Trump Is Rolling Back Obama's Legacy," *The Washington Post*, July 31, 2017; Scott Horsley, "Trump to Put Iran Nuclear Deal in Limbo by Refusing to Certify," NPR News, October 13, 2017.
156. Coral Davenport, "Trump's Environmental Rollbacks Find Opposition Within," *New York Times*, March 27, 2020.
157. Scott Horsley, "Trump Uses Executive Pen to Chip Away at Obamacare," NPR News, October 12, 2017; Max Greenwood, "Poll: ObamaCare More Popular Than House GOP Healthcare Bill," *The Hill*, June 22, 2017; Robert Pear and Reed Abelson, "President Plots His Own Course on Health Care," *New York Times*, October 13, 2017, A1 & A15.
158. Chris Cillizza, "The Real Reason Trump Is So Dead Set on Crushing Obamacare," CNN, October 13, 2017.
159. Lewis S. Feuer, *The Conflict of Generations: The Character and Significance of Student Movements* (New York: Basic Books, 1969), 139–142.
160. Keller et al., "The Scale of Turkey's Purge"; Arango et al., "Turks See Purge"; Thomas Grove, "Turkey President Reshapes Military after Coup," *Wall Street Journal*, February 24, 2017, A8.

Chapter 2

1. See Jonathan Haidt, *The Righteous Mind: Why Good People Are Divided by Politics and Religion* (New York: Vintage, 2012); John Duckitt, "A Dual-process Cognitive-motivational Theory of Ideology and Prejudice," in *Advances in Experimental Social Psychology, Vol. 33*, ed. M. P. Zanna,

41–113 (New York: Academic Press, 2001); "dangerous world belief holders" by Bob Altemeyer, *Enemies of Freedom: Understanding Right-wing Authoritarianism* (San Francisco, CA: Jossey-Bass, 1988); Chris G. Sibley et al., "Effects of Dangerous and Competitive Worldviews on Right-Wing Authoritarianism and Social Dominance Orientation Over a Five-month Period," *Political Psychology* 28, no. 3 (2007), 357–371; Justin H. Park and Edward Isherwood, "Effects of Concerns about Pathogens on Conservatism and Anti-fat Prejudice: Are they Mediated by Moral Intuitions?" *Journal of Social Psychology* 151, no. 4 (2011), 301–394; Mark Schaller, Justin H. Park, and Jason Faulkner, "Prehistoric Dangers and Contemporary Prejudices," *European Review of Social Psychology* 14 (2003), 105–137.

2. Alain Van Hiel and Barbara De Clercq, "Authoritarianism Is Good for You: Right-wing Authoritarianism as a Buffering Factor for Mental Distress," *European Journal of Personality* 23, no. 1 (2009), 33–50; Francesca Dallago et al., "Predicting Right-wing Authoritarianism via Personality and Dangerous World Beliefs: Direct, Indirect, and Interactive Effects," *The Journal of Social Psychology* 152, no. 1 (2012), 112–127; Schaller et al., "Prehistoric Dangers."

3. For similar discussion, see Paolo Riva et al., "Orders to Shoot (a Camera): Effects of Ostracism on Obedience." *The Journal of Social Psychology* 154, no. 3 (2014), 208–216.

4. Jason Siegel et al., "Dying to Be Popular: A Purposive Explanation of Adolescent Willingness to Endure Harm," in *Extremism and the Psychology of Uncertainty*, eds. Michael A. Hogg and Danielle L. Blaylock (West Sussex, UK: Wiley-Blackwell, 2011), Chapter 7.

5. Sebastian Junger, *Tribe: On Homecoming and Belonging* (New York: Twelve Publisher, 2016).

6. See John R. Hall, "Mass Suicide and the Branch Davidians," in *Cults, Religion and Violence* (London, UK: Cambridge University Press, 2002), 149–169; Robert W. Balch and David Taylor, "Making Sense of the Heaven's Gate Suicides," in *Cults, Religion and Violence* (London, UK: Cambridge University Press, 2002), 209–228.

7. Jeff Guinn, *Manson: The Life and Times of Charles Manson* (New York: Simon & Schuster, 2014).

8. James R. Noblitt and Pamela S. Perskin, *Cult and Ritual Abuse: Its History, Anthropology, and Recent Discovery in Contemporary America* (Westport, CT: Praeger, 2000).

9. Jina Moore, "In Kenya, Sparing Girls from a Painful Rite of Passage," *New York Times*, January 14, 2018, A9; Tenny Onyulo, "'I'm Still Feeling the Pain': Girls Forced to Undergo Mutilation," *USA Today*, January 23, 2018, 4A.

10. Barry Meier, "Branding Ritual Scarred Women in Secret Circle," *New York Times*, October 18, 2017, A1 & A26.

11. Donald M. Taylor, *The Quest for Identity* (Westport, CT: Praeger, 2002), 123; Richard Cloward and Lloyd Ohlin, *Delinquency and Opportunity: A Theory of Delinquent Gangs* (New York: The Free Press, 1966).

12. Junger, *Tribe: On Homecoming*.

13. From Krishnadev Calamur, "Uneasy Rider: The Origins of Motorcycle Gangs and How They Remain a Force." NPR News, May 22, 2015.

14. Robert Brenneman, *Homies and Hermanos: God and Gangs in Central America* (New York: Oxford University Press, 2011); Emily Green, "For Some Gang Members in El Salvador, the Evangelical Church Offers A Way Out," NPR News, July 2, 2018.

15. Edward O. Flores, *God's Gangs: Barrio Ministry, Masculinity, and Gang Recovery* (New York: New York University Press, 2014).

16. Chaeyoon Lim and Robert D. Putnam, "Religion, Social Networks, and Life Satisfaction," *American Sociological Review* 75, no. 6 (2010), 914–933.

17. Andreas Wimmer and Thomas Soehl, "Blocked Acculturation: Cultural Heterodoxy Among Europe's Immigrants," *American Journal of Sociology* 120, no. 1 (2014), 146–186; Fouad Ajami, "Within the Gates," *U.S. News & World Report*, July 25, 2005, 24.

18. Dawne Moon, "Who Am I and Who Are We. Conflicting Narratives of Collective Selfhood in Stigmatized Groups," *American Journal of Sociology* 117, no. 5 (2012), 1336–1379.

19. David D. Kirkpatrick, "They're Loathed as Outcasts, but This Is Home," *New York Times*, November 11, 2017, A1 & A6.

20. PBS, "The Gang Crackdown," *Frontline*, aired on February 16, 2018; Ellen Barry

and Christina Anderson, "Grenades and Gang Violence Rattle Sweden," *New York Times*, March 4, 2018, A8.

21. Andreas Wimmer and Thomas Soehl, "Blocked Acculturation: Cultural Heterodoxy Among Europe's Immigrants," *American Journal of Sociology* 120, no. 1 (2014), 146–186; Ajami, "Within the Gates," 24.

22. Alissa J. Rubin, "In Europe, Terrorism Trial, a Mostly Silent Protest," *New York Times*, February 11, 2018, A4.

23. Benjamin C. Hett, *The Death of Democracy: Hitler's Rise to Power and the Downfall of the Weimar Republic* (New York: Henry Holt, 2018).

24. Terry D. Turchie and Kathleen Puckett, *Hunting the American Terrorist: The FBI's War on Homegrown Terror* (Palisades, NY: History Publishing, 2007).

25. Alexander Meleagrou-Hitchens et al., *The Travelers: American Jihadists in Syria and Iraq* (Program on Extremism, George Washington University, 2018), 68–70.

26. Scott Shane, "YouTube Erases an Extremist Cleric," *New York Times*, November 13, 2017, A8.

27. Kimiko de Freytas-Tamura, "London Driver Held in Terrorism Inquiry after Car Crash," *New York Times*, August 14, 2018.

28. Scott Newman, "Sister of Charleston Shooter Dylann Roof Arrested after Menacing Social Media Post," NPR News, March 15, 2018.

29. Robyn Urback, "Terrorist? Misogynist? Labeling the Toronto Van Attacker a Pointless Exercise," CBC News, April 25, 2018.

30. Daniel Etounga-Manguelle, "Does Africa Need a Cultural Adjustment Program?" in *Culture Matters: How Values Shape Human Progress*, eds. Laurence E. Harrison and Samuel P. Huntington (New York: Basic Books, 2001), 65–77.

31. Kwame A. Appiah, *The Honor Code: How Moral Revolutions Happen* (New York: W. W. Norton, 2010).

32. See Virginia Andreescu et al., "The Violent South: Culture of Honor, Social Disorganization, and Murder in Appalachia," *Criminal Justice Review* 36, no. 1 (2011), 76–103; Richard E. Nisbett and Dov Cohen, *Culture of Honor: The Psychology of Violence in the South* (Boulder, CO: Westview Press, 1994); Elijah Anderson, *Code of the Street: Decency, Violence, and the Moral Life of the Inner City* (New York: W.W. Norton, 2000); Sara Heller et al., "Preventing Youth Violence and Dropout: A Randomized Field Experiment," Working Paper 19014, National Bureau of Economic Research, May 2013; Chris Walsh, *Cowardice: A Brief History* (Princeton, NJ: Princeton University Press, 2014); Randall Collins, *Violence: A Micro-Sociological Theory* (Princeton, NJ: Princeton University Press, 2008), 229–236.

33. Anderson, *Code of the Street*, 66–106.

34. Ruth Horowitz, "Honor and Reputation in the Chicano Gang," in *The Meaning of Sociology: A Reader*, 5th edition, ed. Joel M. Charon (Moorhead, MN: Moorhead State University Press, 1996), 59–66.

35. Heller et al., "Preventing Youth Violence."

36. Bonnie Allen, "Acid Attacks on the Rise in Uganda," PRI's The World, July 20, 2011; Steve Inskeep, "Documentary Follows Pakistan's Acid Attack Victims," NPR News, February 21, 2012.

37. Mala Htun, "Culture, Institution, and Gender Inequality in Latin America," in *Culture Matters: How Values Shape Human Progress*, eds. Laurence E. Harrison and Samuel P. Huntington (New York: Basic Books, 2001), 189–199.

38. Hugh Tomlinson, "Man Lets Daughter Drown to Save Honour," *The Times*, August 10, 2015.

39. For examples, see Holly Yan and Dana Ford, "Video of Sandra Bland's Arrest Ignites Firestorm of Reactions," CNN, July 22, 2015; Eyder Peralta, "University Of Cincinnati Police Officer Charged in Killing of Unarmed Black Man," NPR News, July 29, 2015; Larry Neumeister (Associated Press), "NY Court: Flipping Finger at Cops Not Worth Arrest," *San Francisco Chronicle*, January 3, 2013; Diane Rehm Show, "Update on Violence in Baltimore," NPR News, April 28, 2015; CNN, March 9, 2018; Fox News, November 20, 2017.

40. Hans Toch, *Cop Watch: Spectators, Social Media, and Police Reform* (Washington D.C.: American Psychological Association, 2012).

41. Maya Salam, "Case Is Dropped Against an Activist Who Laughed," *New York Times*, November 8, 2017, A17.

42. PBS, "Putin's Revenge, Part I," *Frontline*, aired on October 25, 2017.

43. Darren Boyle, "Kim Jong-un Uses

an Anti-aircraft Gun to Execute One High-ranking Official for Sleeping in a Meeting and Another for Coming Up with His Own Idea," *Daily Mail*, August 30, 2016.

44. Adam Forrest, "Venezuelans Who Made Video Showing President Maduro as a Donkey Face 20 Years in Prison," *Independent*, September 17, 2018.

45. See Nyla R. Branscombe et al., "The Context and Content of Social Identity Threat," in *Social Identity: Context, Commitment, Content*, eds. Naomi Ellemers et al. (Hoboken, NJ: Wiley-Blackwell, 1999), 35–58.

46. Jan Ransom and Al Baker, "Behind Teenager's Death: Machete-Wielding Gang in a Civil War," *New York Times*, July 19, 2018, A1 & A17.

47. Steve Almasy, "MS-13 Members Hacked Up One Victim and Cut Out His Heart, Federal Indictment Says," CNN, July 16, 2019.

48. Julia Dahl, "Honor Killing Under Growing Scrutiny in the U.S.," CBS News, April 4, 2012.

49. Saeed Shah, "Woman in Blasphemy Case Is Caught in Legal Limbo," *Wall Street Journal*, November 13, 2018, A6.

50. Sophia Saifi, "Asia Bibi Stuck in Pakistan Prison Over Death Fears," CNN, November 5, 2018.

51. BBC World Service Newshour, August 7, 2015.

52. Saeed Shah, "Pakistan Steps Up Blasphemy Fight," *Wall Street Journal*, December 4, 2017, A7.

53. Saeed Shah and Bill Spindle, "Anti-blasphemy Party Flexes Its Muscle in Pakistan," *Wall Street Journal*, August 2, 2018, A9.

54. See Charles Kurzman, *The Missing Martyrs: Why There are So Few Muslim Terrorists* (New York: Oxford University Press, 2011); Malcolm Fairbrother, "Economists, Capitalists, and the Making of Globalization: North American Free Trade in Comparative-Historical Perspective," *American Journal of Sociology* 119, no. 5 (2014), 1324–1379; Carl Ernst and Richard Martin, *Rethinking Islamic Studies: From Orientalism to Cosmopolitanism* (Columbia, SC: University of South Carolina Press, 2010); John L. Esposito and Dalia Mogahed, *Who Speaks for Islam? What a Billion Muslims Really Think* (New York: Gallup Press, 2008); Steven Fish, *Are Muslims Distinctive: A Look at the Evidence* (New York: Oxford University Press, 2011); Samuel P. Huntington, *The Clash of Civilization and the Remaking of World Order* (New York: Simon & Schuster, 2011 [1996]); Fareed Zakaria, "Why Do They Hate Us?" *Newsweek*, October 15, 2001; Andrew J. Bacevich, *America's War for the Greater Middle East: A Military History* (New York: Random House, 2016).

55. BBC World Service Newshour, July 8, 2018; Aljazeera, "Lebanese Woman Sentenced to Eight Years for 'Insulting' Egypt," July 8, 2018.

56. Oliver Holmes, "Thai Man Faces Jail for Insulting King's Dog with 'Sarcastic' Internet Post," *The Guardian*, December 15, 2015.

57. Samantha Power, "A Question of Honor," *Time* (Op-Ed), August 25, 2008, 22.

58. Michael Kranish and Marc Fisher, *Trump Revealed: An American Journey of Ambition, Ego, Money, and Power* (New York: Scribner, 2016), 290.

59. See Jacob M. Schlesinger, "Trump Forged Trade Ideas in 1980s—and Never Deviated," *Wall Street Journal*, November 16, 2018, A1 & A9; Reinhard Wolf, "'Make America Great Again': Donald Trump's Mission to Restore Respect for America," Researchgate, 2017, Available at https://www.researchgate.net/profile/Reinhard_Wolf/publication/314870929; Michael Barbaro, "What Drives Donald Trump?: Fear of Losing Status," *New York Times*, October 25, 2016; Edward Alden, "The Roots of Trump's Trade Rage," *Politico*, January 16, 2017; Greg Myre, "U.S. Woman and Family Freed After 5 Years In Captivity In Afghanistan," NPR News, October 12, 2017; ABC World News, October 12, 2017.

60. Robert S. Walker and Drew H. Bailey, "Marrying Kin in Small-scale Societies," *American Journal of Human Biology* 26, no. 3 (2014), 384–388.

61. Napoleon Chagnon, *Noble Savages: My Life Among Two Dangerous Tribes—the Yanomamo and the Anthropologists* (New York: Simon & Schuster, 2014).

62. Jina Moore, "Wounds Too Deep for a Handshake to Heal," *New York Times*, March 15, 2018, A4.

63. Will Ross, "Somalia Clans Secure Peace with Death Sentences and Hefty Fines," BBC, March 18, 2018.

64. Vamik D. Volkan, *Killing in the Name of Identity: A Study of Bloody Conflicts* (Charlottesville, VA: Pitchstone Publishing, 2006), 107–125.

65. Debbie Elliott, "New Orleans

Struggles with Murder Rates and Trust," NPR News, July 6, 2012.
66. Douglas Belkin, "Chicago Hunts for Answers to Gang Killings: Police Build Facebook-Like Database to Prevent Swift Cycles of Retaliation," *Wall Street Journal*, July 13, 2012, A3.
67. Carrie Johnson, "Feds Peel Back Chrome on Motorcycle Gangs." NPR News, July 29, 2010.
68. Associated Press, "Brazilian Gang Attacks the Police," *New York Times*, May 14, 2006; Paulo Prada, "5 Days of Violence by Gangs in Sao Paulo Leaves 115 Dead Before Subsiding," *New York Times*, May 17, 2006.
69. Samantha Pearson and Luciana Magalhaes, "Killing of Activist Jars a Divided Brazil," *Wall Street Journal*, March 26, 2018, A13.
70. Osama bin Laden, "Text of Fatwah Urging Jihad Against Americans," *Al-Quds al-'Arabi*, February 23, 1998.
71. Nour Malas and Dana Ballout, "In Arab World, Some Praise Amid Condemnations," *Wall Street Journal*, November 16, 2015, A11.
72. Nour Youssef, "Pondering Motives in Egypt's Deadliest Terrorist Attack," *New York Times*, December 2, 2017, A4.
73. Sophia Saifi and Greg Botelho, "In Pakistan School Attack, Taliban Terrorists Kill 145, Mostly Children," CNN, December 17, 2014.
74. Mayeni Jones, "Boko Haram: A Decade of Terror Explained," BBC, July 30, 2019.
75. Morgan Winsor and Dragana Jovanovic, "ISIS Claims Responsibility for Sri Lanka Easter Bombings That Killed Over 300," ABC News, April 23, 2019.
76. PBS, "The Vietnam War," *Frontline*, aired in September of 2017, Part 4.
77. PBS, "Putin's Revenge."
78. Bay Fang, "An Eye for an Eye," *U.S. News & World Report*, November 24, 2003, 24–26.
79. PBS, "The Rise of ISIS," *Frontline*, aired on October 28, 2014.
80. Greg Myre and Steven Erlanger, "Israelis Enter Lebanon After Attacks," *New York Times*, July 13, 2006.
81. Ian Deitch (Associated Press), "As Israel Buries Teens, Airstrikes Target Hamas," Yahoo News, July 1, 2014.
82. Robert J. Lifton, *Home from the War—Vietnam Veterans: Neither Victims nor Executioners* (New York: Simon & Schuster, 1973); PBS, "The Vietnam War."
83. Associated Press, "U.S. Military Mourns 'Tragic' Haditha Deaths," CNN, June 1, 2006.
84. For example cases, see Richard Wolf and Mary Orndroff, "Justices Say Public Workers Can Testify About Corruption," *USA Today*, June 19, 2014; Michael Corkery, "Lehman Whistle-blower's Fate: Fired," *Wall Street Journal*, March 16, 2010, C1; Howard Berkes, "Second Whistle-blower Complain for Massey Miner," NPR News, August 11, 2010.
85. By the Center for Employment Equity at the University of Massachusetts at Amherst.
86. Lauren Weber, "Harassment Claims Still Bring Retaliation," *Wall Street Journal*, December 13, 2018, B6.
87. Jennifer Levits, "Senators Write Chao over Whistleblowers," *Wall Street Journal*, September 10, 2008, A4.
88. Felicia Schwartz, "Pentagon Faulted in Assault Cases," *Wall Street Journal*, May 18, 2015, A5; Bruce Smith (Associated Press), "Citadel Deals with Fallout from Sex Abuse Claims from Campers," *Washington Post*, December 11, 2011; Quil Lawrence, "New Report Says Pentagon Not Doing Enough for Sexual Assault Victims," NPR News, May 19, 2016; Susan Burke, "Prosecuting Military Sexual Assault Cases," Diane Rehm Show, NPR News, July 17, 2013.
89. PBS, "The Invisible War," Independent Lens, May 13, 2013.
90. Ben Kesling, "Assault Reports Rise in Military," *Wall Street Journal*, December 29, 2017, A5; Rebecca Kheel, "Report: Sexual Assault Victims Wrongfully Discharged from Military," The Hill, May 19, 2016.
91. Alan P. Fiske and Tage Shakti Rai, *Virtuous Violence: Hurting and Killing to Create, Sustain, End and Honor Social Relationships* (Cambridge, UK: Cambridge University Press, 2015).
92. Martha Crenshaw, "Theories of Terrorism: Instrumental and Organizational Approaches," in *Inside Terrorist Organizations*, ed. David C. Rapoport (Portland, OR: Frank Cass, 2001), 20.
93. E.g., "moral consequentialism," see Irm Haleem, *The Essence of Islamist Extremism: Recognition Through Violence, Freedom Through Death* (New York: Routledge, 2014).
94. Crenshaw, "Theories of Terrorism," 14.

95. Darren Mulloy, *American Extremism: History, Politics and the Militia Movement* (New York: Routledge, 2005).

96. Martin Durham, *White Rage: The Extreme Right and American Politics* (New York: Routledge, 2007).

97. George Michael, *Confronting Right Wing Extremism and Terrorism in the U.S.* (New York: Routledge, 2012).

98. Sathianathan Clarke, *Competing Fundamentalisms: Violent Extremism in Christianity, Islam, and Hinduism* (New York: Routledge, 2017).

99. Jeffrey Kaplan, *Radical Religion and Violence: Theory and Case Studies* (New York: Routledge, 2015).

100. Haleem, *The Essence of Islamist Extremism*.

101. Pew Research Center, "The Great Divide: How Westerners and Muslims View Each Other," Pew Research Global Attitudes Project, June 22, 2006.

102. ABC World News, May 25, 2017.

103. Adam Goldman and Peyton Craighill, "New Poll Finds Majority of Americans Think Torture Was Justified After 9/11 Attacks," *Washington Post*, December 16, 2014.

104. Alyssa Brown and Frank Newport, "In U.S., 65% Support Drone Attacks on Terrorists Abroad," *Gallup News*, March 25, 2013.

105. Jeffrey Gettleman and Hari Kumar, "Far-right Politics in India's Year of the Lynch Mob," *New York Times*, July 21, 2018, A1 & A8.

106. Julia Mendel, "Attacks on Roma Camps Force Ukraine to Confront an Old Ethnic Enmity," *New York Times*, July 22, 2018, A8.

107. Enrique D. Arias and Daniel M. Goldstein, "Violent Pluralism," in *Violent Democracies in Latin America* (Durham, NC: Duke University Press, 2010), 1–34.

108. Paulina Villegas and Kirk Semple, "With Vote Near, Mexican Killers Go More Local," *New York Times*, July 1, 2018, A1 & A16.

109. Gabriele Steinhauser and Nthabiseng Gamede, "Killing Shake South Africa's ANC," *Wall Street Journal*, December 16–17, 2017, A7.

110. Karen Zraick, "Home Is Perilous to Women, U.N. Says," *New York Times*, November 28, 2018, A7.

111. David Gelles and Claire C. Miller, "Schools Teach MBAs Perils of 'Bro' Ethos," *New York Times*, December 26, 2017, A1 & A15.

112. 1A, "How to Stop Hazing," NPR.org, November 15, 2017.

113. Daily Mail, "Band Mates of Florida A&M University Drum Major Beaten to Death Say He 'Asked' to Be Hazed and Saw It as an 'Honor,'" *Daily Mail*, May 23, 2012.

114. Daniel Politi, "Ex-Ford Officials Guilty in '70 Argentina Abuses," *New York Times*, December 12, 2018, A9.

115. Mark Juergensmeyer, "The Logic of Religious Violence," in *Inside Terrorist Organizations*, ed. David C. Rapport (Portland, OR: Frank Cass, 2001), 182.

116. See Fiske and Rai, *Virtuous Violence*; Haleem, *The Essence of Islamist Extremism*; Horowitz, "Honor and Reputation"; Anderson, *Code of the Street*.

117. Horowitz, "Honor and Reputation."

118. BBC World Service Newshour, November 21, 2017.

119. Ashley Fantz, "Teen 'Sports Killings' of Homeless on the Rise." CNN, February 20, 2007.

120. E.g., "joy of combat," see Collins, *Violence*, 66–67.

121. Horowitz, "Honor and Reputation."

122. Debra Pepler et al., "Peer Processes in Bullying: Informing Prevention and Intervention Strategies," in *Handbook of Bullying in Schools: An International Perspective*, eds. S. R. Jimerson et al. (New York: Routledge, 2010), 469–479; Beth Doll et al., "Classroom Ecologies That Support or Discourage Bullying," in *Bullying in American Schools: A Social-ecological Perspective on Prevention and Intervention*, eds. D. L. Espelage and S. M. Swearer (Mahwah, NJ: Erlbaum, 2004), 161–183; Anthony D. Pellegrini and Jeffrey D. Long, "Part of the Solution and Part of the Problem: The Role of Peers in Bullying, Dominance, and Victimization During the Transition from Primary School Through Secondary School," in *Bullying in American Schools: A Social-ecological Perspective on Prevention and Intervention*, eds. D. L. Espelage and S. M. Swearer (Mahwah, NJ: Erlbaum, 2004), 107–117.

123. Nancy Guerra et al., "Understanding Bullying and Victimization during Childhood and Adolescence: A Mixed Methods Study," *Child Development* 82, no. 1 (2011), 295–310; Robert Faris and Diane Felmelee, "Status Struggles: Network Centrality and Gender Segregation in Same- and Cross-gender Aggression," *American*

Sociological Review 76, no. 1 (2011), 48–73; Philip C. Rodkin et al., "Social Goals, Social Behavior, and Social Status in Middle Childhood," *Developmental Psychology* 49, no. 6 (2013), 1139–1150; P. H. Hawley et al., "Sidestepping the Jingle Fallacy: Bullying, Aggression, and the Importance of Knowing the Difference," in *Bullying in North American Schools*, 2nd edition, eds. D. L. Espelage and S. Swearer (New York: Routledge, 2011), 101–115.

124. See Janna Juvonen, "Bullying among Young Adolescents: The Strong, the Weak and the Troubled," *Pediatrics* 112, no. 6 (2003), 1231–1237; Eryn Brown, "Bullying Tied to Social Status," *Los Angeles Times*, February 11, 2011.

125. For similar discussions, see Horowitz, "Honor and Reputation"; David S. Kirk, and Andrew V. Papachristos, "Cultural Mechanisms and the Persistence of Neighborhood Violence," *American Journal of Sociology* 116, no. 4 (2011), 1190–1233; Robert J. Sampson and Dawn J. Bartusch, "Legal Cynicism and (Subcultural?) Tolerance of Deviance: The Neighborhood Context of Racial Differences," *Law and Society Review* 32 (1998), 777–804.

126. Anderson, *Code of the Street*, 66–106.

127. Crenshaw, "Theories of Terrorism," 19.

128. Megan Specia, "President of Philippines Boasts of Killing Someone as a Teenager," *New York Times*, November 11, 2017, A7; Jason Gutierrez, "Philippine President Says He Sexually Abused a Maid," *New York Times*, January 1, 2019, A1 & A12.

129. Amanda Erickson, "Philippine President Rodrigo Duterte Kissed a Random Woman on the Mouth in Front of a Crowd," *Washington Post*, June 4, 2018.

130. ABC World News Tonight, September 18, 2011.

131. See Janell Ross, "Donald Trump's Baffling Explanation for Violence at his Campaign Rallies," *Washington Post*, March 11, 2016; Gerald F. Seib, "How a Trump Victory Could Happen." *Wall Street Journal*, June 21, 2016, A4.

132. Bobby C. Calvan and Nicholas Riccardi, "Gianforte Apologizes to Reporter after Winning U.S. House Race," Associated Press, May 26, 2017.

133. BBC, "Trump Hails Body Slamming Congressman Greg Gianforte in Montana," October 19, 2018.

134. Brian D. Taylor, *The Code of Putinism* (London: Oxford University Press, 2018).

135. Michael S. James, "Prison is 'Living Hell' for Pedophiles," ABC News, August 26, 2003; Christopher Hensley et al., "The Evolving Nature of Prison Argot and Sexual Hierarchies," *The Prison Journal* 83, no. 3 (2014), 289–300.

136. Rebecca Trammell, *Enforcing the Convict Code: Violence and Prison Culture* (Boulder, CO: Lynne Rienner Publishers, 2012).

137. Collins, *Violence*, 198–192, 223–229, 253–256.

138. For example cases, see Saeed Ahmed and Scottie Andrew, "A Man Killed His Girlfriend and Then Shared Photos of Her Dead Body on a Gaming Platform, Police Say," CNN, July 17, 2019; Richard A. Oppel, Jr., "Ohio Teenagers Guilty in Rape That Social Media Brought to Light," *New York Times*, March 18, 2013; Elisha Fieldstadt, "New Jersey Judge Spared Teen Rape Suspect Because He Came from 'Good Family,'" NBC News, July 3, 2019; David Heinzmann, "Teens Tape Selves Beating Homeless Men, Cops Say," *Chicago Tribune*, August 19, 2003.

139. Larry McShane, "Country Bar Shooter Ian Long Paused for Instagram Post in Middle of Rampage," *New York Daily News*, November 10, 2018.

140. Kevin Roose, "A Mass Murder of, and for, the Internet," *New York Times*, March 15, 2019.

141. BBC World Service Newshour, October 10, 2019.

142. Travis Fedschun, "NAS Pensacola Shooting Presumed to be 'Terrorism,' Saudi Student Recorded Attack on Video, Officials Say," Fox News, December 8, 2019.

143. Jeffrey Gettleman and Suhasini Raj, "Filmed Killing of Muslim Goes Viral, Rattling India," *New York Times*, December 10, 2017, A16.

144. For example cases, see John Keilman, "Hunt for Suspects in Facebook Live Sexual Assault Intensifies after 14-year-old Boy Charged," *Chicago Tribune*, April 3, 2017; Mark Berman and Derek Hawkins, "Hate Crime Charges Filed After 'Reprehensible' Video Shows Attack on Mentally-ill Man in Chicago," *Washington Post*, January 5, 2017; Oppel Jr., "Ohio Teenagers Guilty"; Michael B. Farrell, "Homecoming Rape: When Do Bystanders Become

Notes—Chapter 2

Accomplices?" *Christian Science Monitor*, October 29, 2009.

145. Jay Croft and Laura Ly, "Police Charge 7 More Teens in Fatal Stabbing That Crowd Watched," CNN, September 28, 2019.

146. Raymond A. Belliotti, *Seeking Identity: Individualism versus Community in an Ethnic Context* (Kansas City: University Press of Kansas, 1995), 180.

147. See Haidt, *The Righteous Mind*, 131–149.

148. Chris G. Sibley and John Duckitt, "The Personality Bases of Ideology: A One-year Longitudinal Study," *Journal of Social Psychology* 150, no. 5 (2010), 540–559.

149. Jean E. Smith, *Bush* (New York: Simon & Schuster, 2016), 300–325.

150. Kevin Whitelaw, "The Vanishing Case for War," *U.S. News & World Report*, October 18, 2004, 38–40; Smith, *Bush*; Evan Thomas, "The 12 Year Itch," *Newsweek*, March 30, 2003.

151. PBS, "The Spirituality of George W. Bush," *Frontline*, aired on April 29, 2004.

152. Gordon Gauchat, "Politicization of Science in the Public Sphere: A Study of Public Trust in the United States, 1974 to 2010," *American Sociological Review* 77, no. 2 (2012), 167–187; Chris Mooney, *The Republican War on Science* (New York: Basic Books, 2005); Timothy L. O'Brien and Shiri Noy, "Traditional, Modern, and Post-secular Perspectives on Science and Religion in the United States," *American Sociological Review* 80, no. 1 (2015), 92–115; Steven Yearley, "Understanding Science from the Perspective of the Sociology of Scientific Knowledge: An Overview," *Public Understanding of Science* 3 (1994), 245–258.

153. Gerald Holton, *Science and Anti-Science* (Cambridge, MA: Harvard University Press, 1993), 153.

154. Salman Masood, "Pakistan's Deal with Islamists to End Protests Is Seen as a Capitulation," *New York Times*, November 28, 2017, A4; Saeed Shah, "Pakistan's Capitulation Bolsters Islamists," *Wall Street Journal*, November 28, 2017, A6.

155. Tom Raum (Associated Press), "Obama Debate Comments Set Off Firestorm," *Washington Post*, July 24, 2007.

156. Collins, *Violence*, 19–20.

157. Madeleine Albright, *Fascism: A Warning* (New York: HarperCollins, 2018), 1–14.

158. Stuart J. Kaufman, *Modern Hatreds:*

The Symbolic Politics of Ethnic War (Ithaca, NY: Cornell University Press, 2001).

159. John Lukacs, *Democracy and Populism: Fear and Hatred* (New Haven, CT: Yale University Press, 2005).

160. Mulloy, *American Extremism*, Chapter 1.

161. Willard Gaylin, *The Psychological Descent into Violence* (New York: Public Affairs, 2003).

162. See Haidt, *The Religious Mind*; Duckitt, "A Dual-process"; Bob Altemeyer, "The Other 'Authoritarian Personality,'" in *Advances in Experimental Social Psychology* Vol. 30, ed. M. P. Zanna (New York, NY: Academic Press, 1998), 47–92; Sibley et al., "Effects of Dangerous and Competitive Worldviews"; Park and Isherwood, "Effects of Concerns"; Schaller et al., "Prehistoric Dangers."

163. Haidt, *The Righteous Mind*, 219–255.

164. Duckitt, "A Dual-process."

165. See Molly Ball, "Donald Trump and the Politics of Fear," *The Atlantic*, September 2, 2016; Sean McElwee and Jason McDaniel, "Fear of Diversity Made People More Likely to Vote Trump," *The Nation*, March 14, 2017; Candace Smith, "Some White Trump Supporters Fear Becoming Minority," ABC News, November 2, 2016; Paul Singer, "White Christians Decline in USA but Dominate GOP," *USA Today*, September 6, 2017, 5A.

166. John Pike, "Lord's Resistance Army: Uganda Civil War," Global Security Organization, July 28, 2002. Available at http://www.globalsecurity.org/military/world/para/Ira.htm; Keith Somerville, "Uganda's Rebels Keep the Faith," BBC, July 3, 2002; Martin Plaut, "Profile: Uganda's LRA Rebels," BBC, February 6, 2002.

167. Associated Press, "A Mass Release of Child Soldiers in South Sudan," *New York Times*, February 8, A8, 2018.

168. Brent Swails and David McKenzie, "Kidnapped to Kill: How Boko Haram is Turning Girls into Weapons," CNN, April 13, 2016; Dionne Searcey, "Boko Haram Strapped Suicide Bombs to Them: Somehow These Teenage Girls Survived," *New York Times*, October 26, 2017, A1 & A7; Craig Nelson, "Islamic State Claims Kabul Attack," *Wall Street Journal*, November 1, A6, 2017.

169. Kirkpatrick, "They're Loathed as Outcasts."

170. Andrew Jeong, "Ex-Envoy Says

Blackmail Is Part of Regime Playbook," *Wall Street Journal*, July 9, A6, 2018.

171. Mark Tran, "Karadzic Defends 'Just and Holy' Bosnian War," *Guardian*, March 1, 2010.

172. Sarah El Sirgany and Tamara Qiblawi, "U.S., UK, France, and Iran May Be Complicit in Yemen War Crimes, UN Says," CNN, September 3, 2019; Aljazeera, "Yemen: War Profiteers," August 2, 2019.

173. Clarence Page, "Rumsfeld Does It Again with His 'Fungible' Troop Remarks," *The Dispatch*, April 20, 2004.

174. Claudia Wallis, "Why Did They Do It" *Time*, May 17, 2004, 38–41.

175. PBS, "Agent Orange Puts a New Generation at Risk in Vietnam," Newshour, September 27, 2017.

176. BBC World Service Newshour, April 20, 2019.

177. For discussion of this issue see Ronald W. Cox, *Power and Profits: U.S. Policy in Central America* (Lexington: University of Kentucky Press, 1994); Ronald W. Cox and Daniel Skidmore-Hess, *U.S. Politics and the Global Economy: Corporate Power, Conservative Shift* (Boulder, CO: Lynne Rienner, 1999); Bruce Cumings et al., *Inventing the Axis of Evil* (New York: New Press, 2004); David Gibbs, *Political Economy of Third World Intervention* (Chicago: University of Chicago Press, 1991); David Gibbs, "Pretexts in U.S. Foreign Policy: The War on Terrorism in Historical Perspective," *New Political Science* 26, no. 3 (2004), 293–321; Jerry Harris, *The Dialectics of Globalization: Economic and Political Conflict in a Transnational World* (Tyne, UK: Cambridge Scholars Publishing, 2006); Alexandra Homolar, "Rebels Without a Conscience: The Evolution of the Rogue State Narrative in U.S. Security Policy," *European Journal of International Relations* 17, no. 4 (2010): 705–727; Chalmers Johnson, *Blowback: The Costs and Consequences of American Empire* (New York: Holt Paperbacks, 2004); Chalmers Johnson, *The Sorrows of Empire: Militarism, Secrecy and the End of the Republic* (New York: Metropolitan Books, 2004); Chalmers Johnson, *Nemesis: The Last Days of the American Republic* (New York: Metropolitan Books, 2007); Associated Press, "A Look at the Operation Condor Conspiracy in South America," *The New York Times*, May 27, 2016; BBC, "Operation Condor: Landmark Human Rights Trial Reaches Finale," May 27, 2016.

178. Mujib Mashal, "C.I.A.-led Afghan Forces Leave Grim Trail of Abuse" *New York Times*, December 31, 2018, A1 & A10.

179. See Jeffrey E. Stern, "Tracing a Tragedy in Yemen Back to an American Bomb Factory," *New York Times Magazine*, December 16, 2018, 40–47, 65; Burton F. Brinkley, "The U.S. Wants the Yemen War to End. Will It Stop Selling Arms to Saudi Arabia?" NBC News, November 5, 2018; Daniel Brown, "These Are the 20 Defense Companies Donating the Most Money to American Politicians," *Business Insider*, October 24, 2018.

180. Adam Tooze, *Crashed: How a Decade of Financial Crises Changed the World* (New York: Viking, 2018).

181. CBS Evening News, September 10, 2019; Barry Meier, *Pain Killer: An Empire of Deceit and the Origins of America's Opioid Epidemic*, 2nd Edition (New York: Random House, 2018); Barry Meier, "OxyContin Strategy Scrutinized," *New York Times*, February 1, 2019, B1 & B6.

182. Sarah Mervosh, "Nearly 40,000 Deaths from Firearms in 2017," *New York Times*, December 19, 2018, A19.

183. Jan Hoffman, "Teenagers Can't Stop Vaping Nicotine. Experts Can't Help Much," *New York Times*, December 19, 2018, A1 & A24.

184. Matthew Perrone, "Concern Rises for Teens Addicted to Nicotine." Associated Press, January 18, 2019.

185. NBC Nightly News, September 23, 2019.

186. See Neil Connor, "Sex Tourism Expanded into New Destinations Thanks to Cheap Flights, Says Landmark Report." *Telegraph*, May 13, 2016; ECPAT, "Sexual Exploitation of Children Is an Increasing Concern Across Southeast Asia: New Report," 2018, Available at http://www.ecpat.org/news/sexual-exploitation-children-increasing-concern-across-southeast-asia-new-report; BBC, "Asia's Child Sex Tourism Rising," August 22, 2000; *South China Morning Post*, "Global Child Sex Tourism 'Has Expanded' as Landmark UN-Backed Study Paints Grim Picture," May 12, 2016.

187. Kevin Johnson, "150 Arrested, 105 Children Rescued from Prostitution Ring," *USA Today*, July 29, 2013.

188. See Gideon Rachman, *Easternization: Asia's Rise and America's Decline* (New York: Other Press, 2017); Hall Moroz, *America at Sunset: The End of Pax Americana*

(South Carolina: CreateSpace Independent Publishing, 2015).

189. Peter Landers, "When the Feared Trade Rival Was Japan," *Wall Street Journal*, December 15–16, 2018, C1 & C2.

190. Molly K. McKew, "Putin's Real Long Game," *Politico*, January 6, 2017.

191. See Amy Chua, *Political Tribes: Group Instinct and the Fate of Nations* (New York: Penguin Press, 2018), 165–196.

192. Similar to power-devaluation theory, see Rory McVeigh, *The Rise of the Ku Klux Klan: Right-wing Movements and National Politics* (St. Paul, MN: University of Minnesota Press, 2009), 32–48.

193. David Brooks, PBS Newshour, May 10, 2018; Martha C. Nussbaum, *The Monarchy of Fear: A Philosopher Looks at Our Political Crisis* (New York: Simon & Schuster, 2018), 97–134.

194. Joan C. Williams, *White Working Class: Overcoming Class Cluelessness in America* (Boston, MA: Harvard Business Review Press, 2017), Chapters 3 & 4.

195. Timothy J. Lombardo, *Blue-collar Conservatism: Frank Rizzo's Philadelphia and Populist Politics* (Philadelphia, PA: University of Pennsylvania Press, 2018), 49–77.

196. E.g., Bob Altemeyer, *The Authoritarian Spector* (Cambridge, MA: Harvard University Press, 1996); Sibley et al., "Effects of Dangerous and Competitive"; Sibley and Duckitt, "The Personality Bases of Ideology"; Sam McFarland, *Prejudiced People: Individual Differences in Explicit Prejudice* (Bowling Green, KY: Western Kentucky University Press, 2001).

197. For similar discussions, see Altemeyer, *The Authoritarian Spector*; T. W. Adorno et al., *The Authoritarian Personality* (New York: Harper & Brothers, 1950); Stanley Feldman, "Enforcing Social Conformity: A Theory of Authoritarianism," *Political Psychology* 24, no. 1 (2003), 41–74; Karen Stenner, *The Authoritarian Dynamic* (New York: Cambridge University Press, 2005); Felicia Pratto et al., "Social Dominance Orientation: A Personality Variable Predicting Social and Political Attitudes," *Journal of Personality and Social Psychology*, 67 (1994), 741–763.

198. See Jennifer Merolla et al., "Authoritarianism, Need for Closure, and Conditions of Threat," in *Extremism and the Psychology of Uncertainty*, eds. Michael A. Hogg and Danielle L. Blaylock (West Sussex, UK: Wiley-Blackwell, 2011), Chapter 13; Rein Taagepera, "Prospects for Democracy in Islamic Countries," in *Democratic Development & Political Terrorism: The Global Perspective*, ed. William Crotty (Boston, MA: Northeastern University Press, 2005), 93–101; William Crotty, "Democratization and Political Terrorism," in *Democratic Development & Political Terrorism: The Global Perspective*, ed. William Crotty (Boston, MA: Northeastern University Press, 2005), 3–16.

199. Taagepera, "Prospects for Democracy," 93–101.

200. Ransom and Baker, "Behind Teenager's Death."

201. See Marc J. Hetherington and Elizabeth Suhay, "Authoritarianism, Threat, and Americans' Support for the War on Terror," *American Journal of Political Science* 55, no. 3 (2011), 546–560; Feldman, "Enforcing Social Conformity"; Stenner, *The Authoritarian Dynamic*; Marc J. Hetherington and Jonathan D. Weiler, *Authoritarianism and Polarization in American Politics* (Cambridge, UK: Cambridge University Press, 2009), 109–130.

202. See Adorno et al., *The Authoritarian Personality*; Zalmay Khalilzad, *The Envoy: From Kabul to the White House, My Journey through a Turbulent World* (New York: St. Martin's Press, 2016).

203. Clemence Michallon et al., "Charles Manson Condemns Parolee Leslie Van Houten, Sending Letters to Her in Prison Saying She Had Let Him Down," *Daily Mail*, November 24, 2017.

204. Jeremy Diamond, "Trump: I Could 'Shoot Somebody and I Wouldn't Lose Voters,'" CNN, January 24, 2016.

205. Associated Press, "Man Guilty of Sending Bombs to Trump Critics," March 24, 2009.

206. Elisabetta Povoledo, "As Other Nations Take a Hard Look at Clerical Abuse, Italy Mostly Ignores It," *New York Times*, February 23, 2019, A9.

207. Philip Pullella (Reuters), "Catholic Students Attack Media Over Abuse Charges," *Washington Post*, March 31, 2010.

208. Eric Levenson, "Why Roy Moore Supporters Are Standing by Him, in Their Own Words," CNN, November 13, 2017; Ian Lovett, "Moore's Faithful Firewall," *Wall Street Journal*, November 20, 2017, A3; Jay Reeves, "Many Christian Conservatives Are Backing Alabama's Roy Moore," *Washington Post*, November 19, 2017.

209. Kyle Swenson, "A Pastor Admitted a Past 'Sexual Incident' with a Teen. His

Congregation Gave Him a Standing Ovation," *Washington Post*, January 10, 2018.

210. Bill Chappell, "Influential Guru Asaram Bapu Given Life Sentence for Raping Teenage Girl," NPR News, *Business Standard*, April 25, 2018; "Asaram Verdict: Even if Brahma Says He's Rapist, Won't Believe Say Devotees," April 25, 2018.

211. Fareed Zakaria, *The Future of Freedom: Illiberal Democracy at Home and Abroad* (New York: W.W. Norton & Co, 2007).

212. Molly Worthen, "Is There Such a Thing as an Authoritarian Voter?" *New York Times, Sunday Review* (Op-Ed), December 16, 2018, 1 & 6.

213. Steven Levitsky and Daniel Ziblatt, *How Democracies Die* (New York: Crown Publishing, 2018).

214. BBC, "China's Cultural Revolution," September 10, 2013; AFP (Agent France Press), "Eight Stone Chairman Mao Statues Unveiled," December 13, 2013; Yang Su, *Collective Killings in Rural China During the Cultural Revolution* (New York: Cambridge University Press, 2011); Kerry Brown and Simone van Nieuwenhuizen, *China and the New Maoists* (London, UK: Zen Books, 2016).

215. BBC, "North Korea Leader Hails Political Purge," January 1, 2014.

216. Khalilzad, *The Envoy*.

217. Stephen Dalziel, "Russia's Love Affair with Strong Leaders," BBC, March 12, 2004; Arkady Ostrovsky, *The Invention of Russia: From Gorbachev's Freedom to Putin's War* (New York: Viking, 2016); Brian D. Taylor, *The Code of Putinism* (London, UK: Oxford University Press, 2018).

218. Nathan Hodge, "Prospect of New Sanctions Unsettles Russia's Elite," *Wall Street Journal*, January 23, 2018, R12.

219. NPR News, March 18, 2018; BBC News, March 18, 2018.

220. Leila Fadel, "As Egypt Votes on New Constitution, Space for Dissent Closes," NPR News, January 13, 2014; Leila Fadel, "Egyptian Media Encourages Voters to Get to Polls—Or Else," NPR News, May 27, 2014; David Greene, "After Mubarak, Egypt Appears Ready to Elect Another Military Man," NPR News, May 26, 2014.

221. Frank Gardner, "Bloodshed in Egypt: Security Forces Given 'Green Light' to Shoot," PRI's The World, August 16, 2013.

222. Trefor Moss, "Poll Shows Majority Support Duterte," *Wall Street Journal*, October 7, 2016.

223. Richard C. Paddock, "Ethnic Purge Elevates Myanmar's Other Leader," *New York Times*, November 27, 2017, A1 & A10; Richard C. Paddock, "For Myanmar Military, Ethnic Atrocity Is Path to Power and Riches," *New York Times*, January 28, 2018, A10.

224. Washington Post, "Washington Post/ABC News Poll," Available at http://media.washingtonpost.com/wp-srv/politics/ssi/polls/postpoll_072307.html, 2007; Roper Center, "President Approval" Available at http://www.ropercenter.uconn.edu/polls/presidential-approval/, accessed 2015.

225. Célia Belin, "Old Enmities or New Beginnings?" in *The Second Bush Presidency: Global Perspectives*, eds. Amit Gupta and Cherian Samuel (New York: Dorling Kindersley, Pearson Longman, 2006), 85.

226. BBC World Service Newshour, August 3, 2005.

227. Lisel Hintz, from Andrew Wilks, "What Keeps Recep Tayyip Drdogan in Power?" *Al Jazeera*. June 8, 2018.

228. Merolla et al., "Authoritarianism."

229. Emile Durkheim, *The Elementary Forms of Religious Life*, trans. Joseph W. Swain (New York: Pantianos Classics, 2016 [1912]), 12–30.

230. Thomas Hegghammer, *Jihadi Culture: The Art and Social Practices of Militant Islamists* (Cambridge, UK: Cambridge University Press, 2017).

231. Guido Fackler (trans. Peter Logan), "Music in Concentration Camps, 1933–1945," *Music & Politics* 1, no. 1 (2007), 1–25.

232. Ali Soufan, *Anatomy of Terror: From the Death of bin Laden to the Rise of the Islamic State* (New York: W. W. Norton, 2017), 297.

233. Stephen Kotkin, *Stalin: Waiting for Hitler, 1929–1941* (New York: Penguin Press, 2017).

234. Victor Sebestyen, *Lenin: The Man, the Dictator, and the Master of Terror* (New York: Pantheon, 2017).

235. Gaylin, *The Psychological Descent into Violence*.

236. Alexander L. Hinton, *Why Did They Kill? Cambodia in the Shadow of Genocide* (Berkeley, CA: University of California Press, 2005).

237. Eric Hoffer, *True Believer: Thoughts on the Nature of Mass Movements* (New York: Harper & Brothers, 1951).

238. Haidt, *The Righteous Mind*.

239. Khachig Tololyan, "Cultural Narrative and the Motivation of the Terrorist," in *Inside Terrorist Organizations*, ed. David C. Rapoport (Portland, OR: Frank Cass, 2001), 227.

240. Omri Elisha, *Moral Ambition: Mobilization and Social Outreach in Evangelical Megachurches* (Berkeley, CA: University of California Press, 2011), 123, 151.

Chapter 3

1. Charles Tilly, *Identities, Boundaries, and Social Change* (Boulder, CO: Paradigm Publishers, 2005); Charles Tilly, *Contentious Performances* (Cambridge, UK: Cambridge University Press, 2008).

2. Charles Tilly and Sidney Tarrow, *Contentious Politics* (Boulder, Co: Paradigm, 2007).

3. David R. Heise, "Conditions for Empathic Solidarity," in *The Problem of Solidarity: Theories and Models*, eds. Patrick Doreian and Thomas J. Fararo (London: Routledge, 1998), 197–212.

4. See Francisca Polletta and James M. Jasper, "Collective Identity and Social Movements," *Annual Review of Sociology* 27 (2001), 283–305.

5. Patricia H. Collins, "The New Politics of Community," *American Sociological Review* 75, no. 1 (2010), 10.

6. See Alberto Melucci, *Nomads of the Present: Social Movements and Individual Needs in Contemporary Society* (Philadelphia, PA: Temple University Press, 1989); E. Laraña et al., *New Social Movements: From Ideology to Identity* (Philadelphia, PA: Temple University Press, 1994), 101–132.

7. Polletta and Jasper, "Collective Identity," 283–305.

8. Dawne Moon, "Who Am I and Who Are We. Conflicting Narratives of Collective Selfhood in Stigmatized Groups," *American Journal of Sociology* 117, no. 5 (2012), 1371; Verta Taylor, and Nancy E. Whittier, "Collective Identity in Social Movement Communities: Lesbian Feminist Mobilization," in *Waves of Protest: Social Movements Since the Sixties*, ed. J. Freeman and V. Johnson (Oxford, UK: Oxford Univ. Press, 1999), 169–194.

9. Deana A. Rohlinger et al., "Constructing Boundaries: Collective Identity in the Tea Party Movement," in *Border Politics: Social Movements, Collective Identities, and Globalization*, eds. Nancy A. Naples and Jennifer B. Mendez (New York: New York University Press, 2014), 177–205.

10. See Joane Nagel, "Constructing Ethnicity," in *Majority and Minority: The Dynamics of Race and Ethnicity in American Life*, 6th Edition, ed. Norman R. Yetman (Boston, MA: Allyn & Bacon, 1999), 65–66; Shmuel N. Eisenstadt, "The Construction of Collective Identities and the Continual Reconstruction of Primordiality," in *Making Sense of Collectivity: Ethnicity, Nationalism and Globalisation*, ed. Malesevic, Sinisa and Mark Haugaard (London: Pluto Press, 2002), 45; Collins, "The New Politics," 10; Jack D. Eller, and Reed Coughlan, "The Poverty of Primordialism: The Demystification of Ethnic Attachments," *Ethnic and Racial Studies* 16, no. 2 (1993), 183–202.

11. Etienne Balibar, "Racism and Nationalism," in *Race, Nation, Class: Ambiguous Identities*, eds. E. Balibar and I. Wallerstein (New York: Verso, 1991), 37–67.

12. Boaventura S. Santos et al., "Introduction: Opening up the Canon of Knowledge and Recognition of Difference," in *Another Knowledge Is Possible: Beyond Northern Epistemologies*, ed. B. S. Santos (New York: Verso, 2007), vii–xix.

13. Bert Klandermans, *The Social Psychology of Protest* (Oxford, UK: Blackwell, 1997).

14. Bert Klandermans, and Marga M. De Weerd, "Group Identification and Political Protest," in *Self, Identity, and Social Movements*, eds. Sheldon Stryker et al. (Minneapolis, MN: University of Minnesota Press, 2000), 68–90.

15. Irene T. Thomson, *Culture Wars and Enduring American Dilemmas* (Ann Arbor, MI: University of Michigan Press, 2010).

16. James D. Hunter, *To Change the World: The Irony, Tragedy, and Possibility of Christianity in the late Modern World* (Oxford, UK: Oxford University Press, 2010), 101–132.

17. Max Weber, "Open and Closed Relationships," in *Inequality and Society*, eds. Jeff Manza and Michael Sauder (New York: W. W. Norton, 2009 [1920]), 94–98.

18. Randall Collins, *Four Sociological Traditions* (New York: Oxford University Press, 1994), 86–92.

19. Stuart J. Kaufman, *Modern Hatreds: The Symbolic Politics of Ethnic War* (Ithaca, NY: Cornell University Press, 2001), 23.

20. Thomas Eriksen, *Ethnicity and Nationalism: Anthropological Perspectives* (London, UK: Pluto Press, 1993).

21. E.g., "chosen traumas" by Vamik Volkan, *Blind Trust: Large Groups and Their Leaders in Times of Crisis and Terror* (Charlottesville, VA: Pitchstone Publishing, 2004).

22. See Aliya Saperstein and Andrew M. Penner, "Racial Fluidity and Inequality in the United States," *American Journal of Sociology* 118, no. 3 (2012), 676–727; Andreas Wimmer, *Ethnic Boundary Making: Institutions, Power, Networks* (New York: Oxford University Press, 2013); Michael L. Walker, "Race Making in a Penal Institution," *American Journal of Sociology* 121, no. 4 (2016), 1051–1078.

23. Michael Omi and Howard Winant, "Racial Formations," in *Rethinking the Color Line*, ed. Charles A. Gallagher (New York: McGraw Hill, 2007), 21–27.

24. Vilna B. Treitler, *The Ethnic Project: Transforming Racial Fiction into Ethnic Factions* (Stanford, CA: Stanford University Press, 2013).

25. Wimmer, *Ethnic Boundary Making*, 12–32; Mustafa Emirbayer and Matthew Desmond, *The Racial Order* (Chicago, IL: University of Chicago Press, 2015), 184–233.

26. See Kenneth Prewitt, *What Is Your Race? The Census and Our Flawed Efforts to Classify Americans* (Princeton, NJ: Princeton University Press, 2013); Julie A. Dowling, *Mexican Americans and the Question of Race* (Austin, TX: University of Texas Press, 2014); Ann Morning, *The Nature of Race: How Scientists Think and Teach about Human Differences* (Berkeley, CA: University of California Press, 2011); George Yancey, *Who Is White? Latinos, Asians, and the New Black/Nonblack Divide* (Boulder, CO: Lynn Rienner, 2003); Mara Loveman, *National Colors: Racial Classification and the State in Latin America* (New York: Oxford University Press, 2014); Edward Telles and Tianna Paschel, "Who Is Black, White, or Mixed Race? How Skin Color, Status, and Nation Shape Racial Classification in Latin America," *American Journal of Sociology* 120, no. 3 (2014), 864–907.

27. See Kaufman, *Modern Hatreds*, 15–48; Andreas Wimmer and Yuval Feinstein, "The Rise of the Nation-State Across the World, 1816 to 2001," *American Sociological Review* 75, no. 5 (2010), 764–790; Charles Tilly, "States and Nationalism in Europe, 1492–1992," *Theory and Society* 23, no. 1 (1994), 131–146.

28. Kaufman, *Modern Hatred*, 4–5.

29. See Eisenstadt, "The Construction of Collective Identities," 64; Angeliki Koukoutsaki-Monnier, "Understanding National Identity: Between Culture and Institutions," *American Journal of Cultural Sociology* 3, no. 1 (2015), 65–88.

30. From Volkan, *Blind Trust*, 27.

31. Fredrik Barth, "Introduction," in *Ethnic Groups and Boundaries: The Social Organization of Culture Difference*, ed. Fredrik Barth (Long Grove, IL: Waveland Press, 1998), 6–38.

32. Richard Jenkins, "Different Societies? Different Cultures? What Are Human Collectivities?" in *Making Sense of Collectivity: Ethnicity, Nationalism and Globalisation*, eds. Sinisa Malesevic and Mark Haugaard (London: Pluto Press, 2002), 21.

33. Lydia Wilson, "What I Discovered from Interviewing Imprisoned ISIS Fighters," *The Nation*, October 21, 2015; John Graham, "Who Joins ISIS and Why?" *Huffington Post*, December 29, 2015.

34. Evan Perez et al., "Omar Mateen Pledged Allegiance to ISIS, Official Says," CNN, June 12, 2016; Zolan Kanno-Youngs and Ted Mann, "Suspect Not Well Known at Mosque," *Wall Street Journal*, September 22, 2016, A2.

35. Barth, "Introduction," 6–38.

36. See also John Rex, "The Fundamentals of the Theory of Ethnicity," in *Making Sense of Collectivity: Ethnicity, Nationalism and Globalisation*, eds. Sinisa Malesevic and Mark Haugaard (London: Pluto Press, 2002), 95.

37. Tatsushi Arai, "When the Waters of Culture and Conflict Meet," in *Conflict across Cultures: A Unique Experience of Bridging Differences*, eds. Michelle Lebaron and Venashri Pillay (Boston, MA: Intercultural Press, 2006), 92.

38. Margaret Somers, "The Narrative Constitution of Identity: A Relational and Network Approach," *Theory and Society* 23, no. 5 (1994), 605–649.

39. Somers, "The Narrative Constitution of Identity," 624–625.

40. Doug McAdam et al., *Dynamics of Contention* (Cambridge, UK: Cambridge University Press, 2001), 137.

41. E.g., Tilly, *Contentious Performances*; McAdam et al., *Dynamics of Contention*.

42. Nicholas Casey and Laurence Iliff, "Drug War Grinds on After Cartel Arrest," *Wall Street Journal*, July 17, 2013.
43. Holocaust Memorial Center, "Jewish Stars and Other Jewish Badges," available at: https://www.holocaustcenter.org/visit/library-archive/holocaust-badges/.
44. Vidhi Doshi, "Rohingya Men in Bangladesh Revel in the Newfound Right to Wear Pants," *Washington Post*, June 18, 2018.
45. For similar discussions, See Tilly, *Identities, Boundaries, and Social Change*; Tilly, *Contentious Performances*, 116–145; Tilly and Tarrow, *Contentious Politics*, 119–144.
46. Walker Connor, *Ethnonationalism: The Quest for Understanding* (Princeton, NJ: Princeton University Press, 1994), 198–203.
47. Shaul Kelner, *Tours That Bind: Diaspora, Pilgrimage, and Israeli Birthright Tourism* (New York: New York University Press, 2010).
48. Lourdes Garcia-Navarro, "Should Israel Birthright Include Implication for Occupied Territories?" NPR News, January 10, 2010.
49. Yang Su, *Collective Killings in Rural China During the Cultural Revolution* (New York: Cambridge University Press, 2011).
50. Fareed Zakaria, "China's New Parochialism," *Time*, July 14, 2011; Andrew Browne, "Mao Now," *Wall Street Journal*, May 14–15, 2016, C1.
51. Lewis S. Feuer, "Science and the Ethic of Protestant Asceticism: A Reply to Professor Robert K. Merton," *Research in Sociology of Knowledge, Sciences, and Art* Vol. II (Stamford, CT: JAI Press, 1979), 1–23.
52. Vanessa Grigoriadis and Stefan Ruiz, "The Empowerment Cult," *New York Times Magazine*, June 3, 2018, 28–34.
53. Randall Collins, *Sociological Insight: An Introduction to Non-Obvious Sociology* (New York, NY: Oxford University Press, 1992), 3–29.
54. Jonathan Haidt, *The Righteous Mind: Why Good People Are Divided by Politics and Religion* (New York: Vintage, 2012).
55. Dora L. Costa and Matthew E. Kahn, *Heroes and Cowards: The Social Face of War* (Princeton, NJ: Princeton University Press, 2008).
56. Zygmunt Bauman, "Cultural Variety or Variety of Cultures," in *Making Sense of Collectivity: Ethnicity, Nationalism and Globalisation*, eds. Sinisa Malesevic and Mark Haugaard (London: Pluto Press, 2002), 184; Philip Spencer and Howard Wollman, "Blood and Sacrifice: Politics versus Culture in the Construction of Nationalism," in *Nationalism Old and New*, eds. Kevin J. Brehony and Naz Rassool (London: Macmillan Press, 1999), 114.
57. Bauman, "Cultural Variety," 174.
58. K. M. Carley, "A Theory of Group Stability," *American Sociological Review* 56, no. 3 (1991), 331–354.
59. Mark A. Cravalho, "Toast on Ice: the Ethnopsychology of the Winter-over Experience in Antarctica," *Ethos* 24 (1996), 628–656.
60. Bauman, "Cultural Variety," 167–180.
61. Ian Austen and Jason Horowitz, "A Pope Given to Apologies Has Nothing for Indigenous Canada," *New York Times*, April 24, 2018, A7.
62. Austin Ramzy, "Exiled Uighurs Take Fight with Beijing Online," *New York Times*, February 18, 2019, A4.
63. Josh Chin and Clement Burge, "China Razes Territory, Dismantling a Culture," *Wall Street Journal*, March 21, 2019, A1 & A10; Ramzy, "Exiled Uighurs"; John Sudworth, "China Muslims: Xinjiang Schools Used to Separate Children from Families," BBC, July 4, 2019.
64. Matthew Karnitschnig, "Merkel Enters Immigration Fray," *Wall Street Journal*, October 18, 2010, A15; Andreas Wimmer and Thomas Soehl, "Blocked Acculturation: Cultural Heterodoxy Among Europe's Immigrants," *American Journal of Sociology* 120, no. 1 (2014), 146–186.
65. Ellen Barry and Martin S. Sorensen, "For Help from Danish State, a Demand: Give Us Your Children," *New York Times*, July 2, 2018, A1 & A8.
66. Nour Malas, "Year of Islamic State Rule Transforms Mosul," *Wall Street Journal*, June 19, 2015, A8.
67. John A. Hostetler, "The Amish: A Small Society," in *Seeing Ourselves: Classic, Contemporary, and Cross-cultural Readings in Sociology*, 7th Edition, eds. John J. Macionis and Nijole V. Benokraitis (Upper Saddle River, NJ: Prentice Hall, 2007), 72–75; Charles E. Hurst and David L. McConnell, *An Amish Paradox: Diversity and Change in the World's largest Amish Community* (Baltimore, MD: Johns Hopkins University Press, 2010).

68. Eisenstadt, "The Construction of Collective Identities," 33.
69. See Jan N. Pieterse, "Ethnicities and Multiculturalism: Politics of Boundaries," in *Nationalism, Ethnicity and Minority Rights*, ed. S. May et al. (London: Cambridge University Press, 2004), 27–49; Taylor and Whittier, "Collective Identity," 179.
70. Similar to "oppositional consciousness" by Aldon D. Morris, "A Retrospective on the Civil Rights Movement: Political and Intellectual Landmarks," *Annual Review of Sociology* 25 (1999), 517–539.
71. Cara J. Wong, *Boundaries of Obligation in American Politics: Geographic, National, and Racial Communities* (New York: Cambridge University Press, 2010).
72. Evelyn N. Glenn, "Constructing Citizenship: Exclusion, Subordination, and Resistance," *American Sociological Review* 76, no 1 (2011), 3.
73. See Christena E. Nippert-Eng, "Boundary Work: Sculpting Work and Home," in *Cultural Sociology*, ed. Lynette Spillman (Oxford, UK: Oxford University Press, 2002), 79–86.
74. Eisenstadt, "The Construction of Collective Identities," 36.
75. Morris, "A Retrospective on the Civil Rights Movement," 517–539.
76. John Hagan and Joshua Kaiser, "The Displaced and Dispossessed of Darfur: Explaining the Sources of a Continuing State-led Genocide," *British Journal of Sociology* 62, no. 1 (2011), 1–25.
77. *New York Daily News*, April 11, 2016.
78. Rachel Morarjee, "The Afghan Christian: A Problem for Karzai," *Time*, March 24, 2006.
79. Joshua R. Miller, "Iranian Pastor Faces Execution for Refusing to Recant Christian Faith," Fox News, September 28, 2011.
80. Lucy Kinder, "Pregnant Doctor to Be Hanged for Not Being a Muslim," *Independent News*, May 16, 2014.
81. Shashank Joshi, "Film Protests: What Explains this Anger?" BBC, September 15, 2012.
82. Ralph Ellis, "Adam Gadahn, American Mouthpiece for al-Qaeda, Killed," CNN, April 23, 2015.
83. Romesh Ratnesar, "Face of Terror," *Time*, December 27-January 3, 2004–2005, 96–100.
84. Ben Tufft, "ISIS Executes Up to 200 Fighters for Trying to Flee Jihad and Return Home," *The Independent*, December 29, 2014.
85. Dean Balsamini, "MS-13 Members Allegedly Stabbed 16-year-old 100 Times for Wanting Out," *New York Post*, March 16, 2019.
86. Jason P. Howe, "In Bed with an Assassin," BBC Outlook, June 2, 2019.
87. Christina Caron, "Transgender Women Is Found Shot to Death in Alabama," *New York Times*, January 13, 2019, A19.
88. Philip Dray, *At the Hands of Persons Unknown: The Lynching of Black America* (New York: Modern Library, 2003).
89. Mia Hultin, "Some Take the Glass Escalator, Some Hit the Glass Ceiling?" *Work and Occupations* 30 (2003), 30–61; Christine Williams, "The Glass Escalator: Hidden Advantages for Men in the Female' Professions," *Social Problems* 39, no. 3 (1992), 253–267.
90. Jennifer L. Berdahl, "The Sexual Harassment of Uppity Women," *Journal of Applied Psychology* 92, no. 2 (2007), 425–437; Ellen Rosell et al., "Firefighting Women and Sexual Harassment," *Psychology of Women Quarterly* 32 (2008), 362–376; Kimberly A. Lonsway et al., "Sexual Harassment in Law Enforcement," *Police Quarterly* 16, no 2 (2013), 1177–1210; Christopher Uggen and Amy Blackstone, "Sexual Harassment as a Gendered Expression of Power," *American Sociological Review* 69, no. 1 (2004), 64–92; Carl A. Castro et al., "Sexual Assault in the Military," *Current Psychiatry Reports* 17, no. 7 (2015), 54–67; Julie Dicaro, "Threats, Vitriol. Hate. Ugly Truth About Women in Sports and Media," *Sports Illustrated*, September 27, 2015.
91. Aniruddha Das, "Sexual Harassment at Work in the United States," *Archives of Sexual Behavior* 38, no. 6 (2009), 909–921; Stacy de Coster et al., "Routine Activities and Sexual Harassment in the Workplace," *Work and Occupations* 26, no. 1 (1999), 21–49.
92. Kevin Stainback et al., "The Context of Workplace Sex Discrimination: Sex Composition, Workplace Culture, and Relative Power," *Social Forces* 89, no. 4 (2011), 1165–1188.
93. Mona Mahmoud and Mike Lanchin, "Basra Militants Targeting Women," BBC World Service Newshour, November 15, 2007; Soraya S. Nelson, "Taliban Wages War on Afghan Girls' Schools," NPR News, April 5, 2007; AFP (Agence France Presse),

"Islamic State Executing 'Educated Women' in New Wave of Horror: UN," from NDTV. com, January 21, 2015.

94. Nelson, "Taliban Wages War"; Ron Moreau and Sami Yousafzai, "A War on Schoolgirls," *Newsweek*, October 16, 2007.

95. Karen Zraick, "Home Is Perilous to Women, U.N. Says," *New York Times*, November 28, 2018, A7.

96. Tresa Baldas, "Ex-Jehovah's Witnesses Break Silence on Shunning," *USA Today*, March 28, 2018, 6A.

97. Anthony D. Smith, *Nationalism and Modernism: A Critical Survey of Recent Theories of Nations and Nationalism* (London: Routledge, 1999), 64; Hostetler, "The Amish," 72-75.

98. Malas, "Year of Islamic State Rule."

99. Krista Johnson, "'I genuinely believed I would be destroyed because my dad told me that constantly," *USA Today*, April 19, 2018, 1A & 4A.

100. John A. Hostetler, *Amish Society*, 3rd ed. (Baltimore: Johns Hopkins University, 1980); PBS, "The Amish," American Experience, February 24, 2012.

101. Sarah McClure, "The Amish Keep to Themselves. And They're Hiding a Horrifying Secret," *Cosmopolitan*, January 14, 2020.

102. Elizabeth Llorente, "Insular Hasidic Jews Struggle to Preserve Customs as Legal and Social Pressures Build," Fox News, June 11, 2018.

103. Baldas, "Ex-Jehovah's Witnesses"; Stephanie Nolasco, "Former Child Bride Who Helped Take Down Cult Leader Warren Jeffs Speaks Out in New Documentary," Fox News, February 19, 2018; Johnson, "I Genuinely Believed"; Llorente, "Insular Hasidic Jews."

104. Connor, *Ethnonationalism*, 198-202.

105. F. James Davis, *Who Is Black?: One Nation's Definition* (University Park: Penn State University Press, 1991); Robert P. Clark, "Patterns in the Lives of ETA members," *Terrorism* 6, no. 3 (1988), 423-454.

106. Simon Denyer, "Indian Village Proud After Double 'Honor Killing,'" Reuters, May 16, 2008.

107. Thomas Friedman, "Kansas and Al-Qaeda," *New York Times* (Op-Ed), August 10, 2013.

108. Carol Glatz, "Ignorance of Faith Risks Creating Cafeteria Catholics, Pope Says," Catholic News Service, October 17, 2012.

109. U.S. Government Printing Office, *The 9/11 Commission Report: Final Report of the National Commission on Terrorist Attacks upon the United States* (Washington, D.C., 2004).

110. Ratnesar, "Face of Terror," 96-100.

111. Aparism Ghosh, "The Apostle of Hate," *Time*, June 19, 2006, 36-37.

112. Mitch Frank, "Conservatives Go RINO Hunting," *Time*, November 19, 2004.

113. See Nicholas D. Kristof, "America's History of Fear," *New York Times* (Op-Ed), September 4, 2010; Tyler Anbinder, *City of Dreams: The 400-Year Epic History of Immigrant New York* (New York: Houghton Mifflin Harcourt, 2016).

114. Matthew Karnitschnig et al., "Europe's Anti-Immigrant Parties Stand to Gain Ground in Wake of Paris Attacks," *Wall Street Journal*, January 16, 2015, A1 & A6.

115. Mayer N. Zald and John D. McCarthy, *Social Movements in an Organizational Society* (New Brunswick, NJ: Transaction, 1987).

116. Scott Hibbard, "Religion and State in India: Ambiguity, Chauvinism, and Tolerance," in *Religion and Regimes: Support, Separation, and Opposition*, eds. Mehran Tamadonfar and Ted G. Jelen (Lanham, MD: Lexington Books, 2013), 251; Afe Adogame and Shobana Shankar, *Religion on the Move! New Dynamics of Religious Expansion in a Globalizing World* (Laiden: Brill Press, 2013); Afe Adogame and James V. Spickard, *Religion Crossing Boundaries: Transnational Religious and Social Dynamics in Africa and the New African Diaspora* (Leiden: Brill Press, 2010).

117. Robert Wuthnow, *Boundless Faith: The Global Outreach of American Churches* (Berkeley: University of California Press, 2009).

118. Adogame and Shankar, *Religion Crossing Boundaries*; Adogame and Spickard, *Religion on the Move*.

119. Daniel Pipes, "What Is Jihad," *New York Post*, December 31, 2002.

120. U.S. Government Printing Office, *The 9/11 Commission Report*.

121. Fareed Zakaria, "Why Do They Hate Us?" *Newsweek*, October 15, 2001; Fouad Ajami, "The Heartbreak of History," *U.S. News & World Report*, July 31, 2006, 41; Dan Murphy (Associated Press), "Hamas's Approach to Jihad: Start 'tm Young," Yahoo News, August 20, 2007; Mark Mazzetti, "Saudi Arabia Warns of Economic Fallout if Congress Passes 9/11 Bill," *New York Times*, April 15, 2016.

122. Moon, "Who Am I and Who Are We," 1336-1379; Taylor and Whittier, "Collective Identity," 169-194.
123. By Samuel P. Huntington, *The Clash of Civilization and the Remaking of World Order* (New York: Simon & Schuster, 2011 [1996]).
124. See Tilly, "Contentious Performances"; Tilly, "Identities, Boundaries"; Tilly and Tarrow, *Contentious Politics*.
125. Shadi Hamid, *Islamic Exceptionalism: How the Struggle Over Islam Is Reshaping the World* (New York: St. Martin's Press, 2016).
126. Mark Curnutte, "Churches Struggle with How to Confront Racism," *USA Today*, June12, 2018, 1A & 2A.
127. For a comparable discussion, see Connor, *Ethnonationalism*.
128. Kaufman, *Modern Hatred*, 16.
129. Walter A. McDougall, *The Tragedy of U.S. Foreign Policy* (New Haven, CT: Yale University Press, 2016).
130. Michael Hechter, *Containing Nationalism* (Oxford, UK: Oxford University Press, 2000), 97-101.
131. Moon, "Who Am I," 1136-1179.
132. Rodney Stark, *Sociology*, 9th Edition (Belmont, CA: Wadsworth, 2004), 405-406.
133. Martin Marty and Scott Appleby, *Fundamentalisms Observed: The Fundamentalism Project, Book 1* (Chicago, IL: University of Chicago Press, 1994), 1.
134. Rory McVeigh, *The Rise of the Ku Klux Klan: Right-wing Movements and National Politics* (Minneapolis, MN: University of Minnesota Press, 2009).
135. For similar discussions, see Shunsuke Uehara et al., "What Leads to Evocation of Moral Outrage? Exploring the Role of Personal Morality," *International Journal of Psychological Studies* 6, no. 1 (2015), 58-67; C. Daniel Batson et al., "Anger at Unfairness: Is It Moral Outrage?" *European Journal of Social Psychology* 37 (2007), 1272-1285; Erin M. O'Mara et al., "Will Moral Outrage Stand Up? Distinguishing Among Emotional Reactions to a Moral Violation," *European Journal of Social Psychology* 41, no. 2 (2011), 173-179; Debra Lieberman and Lance Linke, "The Effect of Social Category on Third Party Punishment," *Evolutionary Psychology* 5, no. 2 (2007), 289-305.
136. Tilly, *Contentious Performances*; Tilly, *Identities, Boundaries*; Tilly and Tarrow, *Contentious Politics*.

137. Lewis S. Feuer, *Ideology and the Ideologists* (New York: Harper & Row, 1975), 77-79.
138. Ibid., 191-196.
139. Volkan, *Blind Trust*, 68.
140. Wuthnow, *Boundless Faith*.
141. Willard Gaylin, *The Psychological Descent into Violence* (New York: Public Affairs, 2003).
142. Mark Juergensmeyer, "The Logic of Religious Violence," in *Inside Terrorist Organizations*, ed. David C. Rapport (Portland, OR: Frank Cass, 2001), 181-184.
143. Hamid, *Islamic Exceptionalism*.
144. Rick Gladstone, "Attacks in Canada and Belgium Reflect Fuzzy Definition of Terrorism," *New York Times*, June 1, 2018, A7.
145. David C. Rapoport, "Sacred Terror: A Contemporary Example from Islam," in *Origins of Terrorism: Psychologies, Ideologies, Theologies, States of Mind*, ed. Walter Reich (Washington D.C.: Woodrow Wilson Center Press, 1998), 103-104.
146. Rukmini Callimachi, "ISIS Enshrines a Theology of Rape," *New York Times*, August 14, 2015.
147. Gbenga Akingbule, "Nigerian Kidnapped Schoolgirls Forced into Islam, Marriages," *Business Week*, April 30, 2014.
148. Denise Spellberg, *Politics, Gender, and the Islamic Past: The Legacy of A'isha bint Abi Bakr* (New York: Columbia University Press, 1994); Jenny Cuffe, "Child Marriage and Divorce in Yemen," BBC, 2008, November 6.
149. Nawal al-Maghafi, "The Teenager Married Too Many Times to Count," BBC, October 4, 2019.
150. Gordon Lynch, *The Sacred in the Modern World: A Cultural Sociological Approach* (Oxford, UK: Oxford University Press, 2014).
151. Johnson, "I Genuinely Believed."
152. Hibbard, "Religion and State in India," 121-141.
153. Mark R. Mullins, "Japanese Responses to Imperialist Secularization: The Postwar Movement to Restore Shinto in the Public Sphere," in *Multiple Secularities Beyond the West: Religion and Modernity in the Global Age*, eds. Marian Burchardt et al. (Berlin: De Gruyter, 2015), 141-168.
154. Glen Carey, "Saudi King Counters Protests with Handout as Tension Mounts," Bloomberg News, March 11, 2011.
155. Brian Ross and Jill Rackmill,

"Secrets of the Saudi Royal Family," *20/20*, ABC News, October 15, 2004.

156. Karen F. Balkin (Ed.), *Extremist Groups* (Farmington Hills, MI: Greenhaven Press, 2005), 16.

157. For detailed documentation, see Andrew Walder, *China Under Mao: A Revolution Derailed* (Cambridge, MA: Harvard University Press, 2015).

158. Thomas Piketty, *Capital in the Twenty-First Century*, Translated by Arthur Goldhammer (Cambridge, MA: Belknap Press, 2017).

159. E.g., Ayn Rand, from Ralph Ketcham, *Individualism and Public Life: A Modern Dilemma* (New York: Basil Blackwell, 1987), 51.

160. E.g., Friedrich A. Hayek, *Individualism and Economic Order* (Chicago: University of Chicago Press, 1969), 31.

161. Alissa Quart, *Squeezed: Why Our Families Can't Afford America* (New York: HarperCollins, 2018).

162. Nolasco, "Former Child Bride."

163. Maija Liuhto, "The Schools of the Taliban," *The Diplomat*, November 3, 2016.

164. Diaa Hadid, "Pakistan Wants to Reform Madrassas. Experts Advise Fixing Public Education First," NPR News, January 10, 2019.

165. Azmat Abbas, from Hadid, "Pakistan Wants to Reform."

166. Javier C. Hernandez, "Reading, Writing and Revolution," *New York Times*, October 16, 2017, A4.

167. Te-Ping Chen, "China Tests a New Kind of Class Struggle," *Wall Street Journal*, September 25, 2017, A13.

168. Te-Ping Chen, "China Pupils Learn Xi Philosophy," *Wall Street Journal*, March 24–25, 2018, A12.

169. From Fareed Zakaria GPS, CNN, September 23, 2012; akin to "oppositional consciousness" by Morris, "A Retrospective on the Civil Rights Movement."

170. Eric Hoffer, *True Believer: Thoughts on the Nature of Mass Movements* (New York: Harper & Brothers, 1951), 93.

171. Volkan, *Blind Trust*, 132–133.

172. For related arguments, see Marc J. Hetherington and Elizabeth Suhay, "Authoritarianism, Threat, and Americans' Support for the War on Terror," *American Journal of Political Science* 55, no. 3 (2011), 546–560; Marc J. Hetherington and Jonathan D. Weiler, *Authoritarianism and Polarization in American Politics* (Cambridge, UK: Cambridge University Press, 2009), 109–130; Karen Stenner, *The Authoritarian Dynamic* (New York: Cambridge University Press, 2005).

173. Yaroslav Trofimov, "Teheran's Sway Undermined by Sunni-Shiite Split," *Wall Street Journal*, July 16, 2015, A6.

174. Bruce Cumings et al., *Inventing the Axis of Evil* (New York: New Press, 2004).

175. Ali Soufan, *Anatomy of Terror: From the Death of bin Laden to the Rise of the Islamic State* (New York: W. W. Norton, 2017), 296–298.

176. Tore Bjørgo, "Extreme Nationalism and Violent Discourses in Scandinavia: 'The Resistance,' 'Traitors,' and 'Foreign Invaders,'" in *Terror from the Extreme Right* (London: Frank Cass, 1995), 182–220.

177. Molly K. McKew, "Putin's Real Long Game," *Politico*, January 6, 2017.

178. Fareed Zakaria, Global GPS, CNN, March 18, 2018.

179. Nachman Ben-Yehuda, "The European Witchcraze," in *Social Deviance*, 3rd edition, eds. Ronald Farrell and Victoria Swigert (Belmont, CA: Wadsworth, 1988), 43.

180. Dan Baum, "Legalize It All: How to Win the War on Drugs," *Harper's Magazine*, April Issue, 2016.

181. Jeremy Diamond, "Trump: We Can't Continue to Allow China to Rape Our Country," CNN, May 2, 2016.

182. U.S. Government Office, *The 9/11 Commission Report*.

183. Volkan, *Blind Trust*, 107–108; Roger Giner-Sorolla et al., "Dehumanization, Demonization, and Morality Shifting: Path to Moral Certainty in Extremist Violence," in *Extremism and the Psychology of Uncertainty*, eds. Michael A. Hogg and Danielle L. Blaylock (West Sussex, UK: Wiley-Blackwell, 2011), Chapter 10.

184. William I. Brustein, *Roots of Hate: Anti-Semitism in Europe Before the Holocaust* (Cambridge, UK: Cambridge University Press, 2003).

185. Ehud Sprinzak, "The Psychopolitical Formation of Extreme Left Terrorism in a Democracy: The Case of the Weathermen," in *Origins of Terrorism: Psychologies, Ideologies, Theologies, States of Mind*, ed. Walter Reich (Washington D.C.: Woodrow Wilson Center Press, 1998), 82.

186. Arthur Allen, *The Fantastic Laboratory of Dr. Weigl* (New York: Norton Publisher, 2014).

187. Alexander L. Hinton, *Why Did They*

Kill? Cambodia in the Shadow of Genocide (Berkeley, CA: University of California Press, 2005), 226.

188. Zeke Turner, "Culture Clash in Arts Capital," *Wall Street Journal*, April 21, 2016, A9.

189. Brian Myers, *The Cleanest Race: How North Koreans See Themselves and Why It Matters* (New York: Melville House, 2011).

190. Here & Now, WBUR, August 20, 2019.

191. Volkan, *Blind Trust*, 132–133.

192. Associated Press, "Text: Bin Laden's Statement," *The Guardian*, October 7, 2001; PBS Newshour, July 1, 2014.

193. Benjamin C. Hett, *The Death of Democracy: Hitler's Rise to Power and the Downfall of the Weimar Republic* (New York: Henry Holt, 2018).

194. Heather MacDonald, *The War on Cops: How the New Attack on Law and Order Makes Everyone Less Safe* (New York: Encounter Books, 2016).

195. Fareed Zakaria, Fareed Zakaria GPS, CNN, April 14, 2019.

196. Clarence Page, "'War on Whites' a Feeble Attempt to Play the Victim," *Chicago Tribune* (Op-Ed), from *Dayton Daily News*, August 13, 2014, 2014, A9.

197. Kathleen Belew, *Bring the War Home: The White Power Movement and Paramilitary America* (Cambridge, MA: Harvard University Press, 2018).

198. David Greene, "Narrative Change Makes White Supremacy Groups More Dangerous, Expert Says," NPR News, June 24, 2015; Amy B. Wang, "White Supremacists Picked Fight with an Interracial Couple After Tennessee Rally, Police Say," *Washington Post*, October 29, 2017.

199. Meg Kinnard (Associated Press), "Official Says Shooting Suspect's Friend Held," *Dayton Daily News*, September 18, 2015, A4.

200. Ramsey Touchberry, "Republican Congressman Claimed: There Was a 'Racial War' in America Started by Blacks on Whites," Newsweek.com, July 20, 2018.

201. Nick Kostov, "Suspect Echoed French Writer," *Wall Street Journal*, March 16–17, 2019, A8.

202. Peter Slevin, "Battle on Teaching Evolution Sharpens," *Washington Post*, March 14, 2005.

203. Andrew Sullivan, "My Problem with Christianity," *Time*, May 15, 2006, 74; Slevin, "Battle on Teaching Evolution";

Rachel Zoll, "Evangelicals in U.S. Feel Alienated, Anxious," *Wall Street Journal*, June 17, 2016, A9.

204. John Leo, "Not a Religious Fight," *U.S. News & World Report*, May 2, 2005, 66.

205. Aris Folley, "Mike Pence Tells Liberty University Graduates to Prepare to be 'Shunned,' 'Ridiculed' for Being a Christian," *The Hill*, May 11, 2019.

206. James D. Hunter, *Culture Wars: The Struggle to Define America* (New York: Basic Books, 1991), 156; Viviane Seyranian, "Constructing Extremism Uncertainty Provocation and Reduction by Extremist Leaders," in *Extremism and the Psychology of Uncertainty*, eds. Michael A. Hogg and Danielle L. Blaylock (West Sussex, UK: Wiley-Blackwell, 2011), Chapter 14.

207. John Micklethwait and Adrian Wooldrige, *The Fourth Revolution: The Global Race to Reinvent the State* (London: The Penguin Press HC, 2014).

208. Naomi Klein, *The Shock Doctrine: The Rise of Disaster Capitalism* (New York: Picador, 2008); Naomi Klein, *No Is Not Enough: Resisting Trump's Shock Politics and Winning the World We Need* (Chicago, IL: Haymarket Books, 2017).

209. PBS, "Welcome to North Korea: A Glimpse at Life Within the Country," PBS Documentary, January 16, 2006.

210. David Folkenflik, "Radio Conspiracy Theorist Claims Ear of Trump, Pushes 'Pizzagate' Fictions," NPR News, December 6, 2016.

211. John Lofland, *Doomsday Cults: A Study of Conversion, Proselytization, and Maintenance of Faith* (Upper Saddle River, NJ: Prentice Hall, 1966).

212. Jeremy W. Peters and Katie Benner, "N.R.A.'s Web Voices Warn We're "at the Mercy of Evil," *New York Times*, February 22, 2018, A17.

213. Kristof, "America's History of Fear"; David von Drehle, "The Agitator," *Time*, September 28, 2009, 30–35; Allan M. Winkler, *The Politics of Propaganda: Office of War Information, 1942–1945* (New Haven, CT: Yale University Press, 1978).

214. Elaine T. May, *Fortress America: How We Embraced Fear and Abandoned Democracy* (New York: Basic Books, 2017), 13–57.

215. CNN, "Bush: Don't Wait for Mushroom Cloud," October 8, 2002; Bob Herbert, "A War Without Reason," *New York Times* (Op-Ed), October 18, 2004.

216. Glen Johnson, "Powell Targets Terror

Comment," *Boston Globe*, September 13, 2004.

217. Peter Baker, "Bush Official, in Book, Tells of Pressure on '04 Vote," *New York Times*, August 20, 2009.

218. Soufan, *Anatomy of Terror*.

219. Mujib Mashal and Jawad Sukhanyar, "Afghan Suicide Attack on Anti-Violence Clerics," *New York Times*, June 5, 2018, A9.

220. Andrew E. Kramer, "More Afghan Civilians Are Victims of Targeted Attacks, U.N. says," *New York Times*, February 16, 2018, A10.

221. Craig Nelson, "U.S. Report Points to Setbacks in Afghanistan," *Wall Street Journal*, May 2, 2018, A1 & A8.

222. David Zucchino, "For Afghan Civilians, 2018 Was the Deadliest in a Decade," *New York Times*, February 25, 2019, A7.

223. Max Fisher, "Why Attack Afghan Civilians? Chaos Rewards the Taliban," *New York Times*, January 29, 2018, A9.

224. Eric Bradner, "Donald Trump: 'Our Country's Going to Hell,'" CNN, February 28, 2016; Alex Altman, "No President Has Spread Fear like Donald Trump," *Time*, February 9, 2017.

225. Charles Homans, "Blind Trust," *New York Times Magazine*, July 10, 2018, 9–11.

226. Laura King, "CV Coup? As Outbreak Grows, Authoritarians Around the World Seize the Moment," *Los Angeles Times*, March 31, 2020; Michael Sullivan, "In Southeast Asia, Government Exploit Coronavirus Fears to Tighten Grip," NPR News, April 3, 2020; BBC World Service Newshour, April 2, 2020.

227. See Hunter, *Culture Wars*, 157; Haidt, *The Righteous Mind*, 219–256.

228. Howard Zinn, from Democracynow.org, "Howard Zinn on the Uses of History and the War on Terrorism," December 18, 2006.

229. Karen deYoung, "U.S. Trucking Funds Reach Taliban, Military-led Investigation Concludes," *Washington Post*, July 24, 2011; CBS Evening News, September 3, 2009.

230. Diego Gambetta, *The Sicilian Mafia: The Business of Private Protection* (Cambridge, MA: Harvard University Press, 1996); Varese, *The Russian Mafia*; Jason Beaubien, "El Salvador Fears Ties Between Cartels, Street Gangs," NPR News, June 1, 2011.

231. Jason Beaubien, "Business Booms on Mexican Border Despite Violence," NPR News, August 4, 2011.

232. Kelly McEvers, "Gangs Demand That San Salvador's Buses Stop Running ... But Why?" NPR News, July 29, 2015.

233. Robbie Wielan, "New Breed of Gangs Chokes Latin America," *Wall Street Journal*, November 3–4, 2018, A1 & A9.

234. Lorne Dawson, "When Prophecy Fails and Faith Persists: A Theoretical Overview," *Novo Religio* 3, no. 1 (1999), 64–67.

235. Charles Sarno et al., "Rationalizing Judgment Day: A Content Analysis of Harold Camping's Open Forum Program," *Sociology of Religion* 76, no. 2 (2015), 199–221.

236. Lofland, *Doomsday Cults*.

237. Barbara B. Hagerty, "Doomsday Redux: Prophet Says World Will End Friday," NPR News, October 18, 2011.

238. Sarah Childress (PBS), "The Battle Over Bunkerville," *Frontline*, May 16, 2019.

239. Carla D. Shirley, "'You Might Be a Redneck if...' Boundary Work Among Rural, Southern Whites," *Social Forces* 89, no. 1 (2010), 35–62.

240. PBS, "The Vietnam War," *Frontline*, Documentary series aired in September of 2017.

241. See Ronald W. Cox and Daniel Skidmore-Hess, *U.S. Politics and the Global Economy: Corporate Power, Conservative Shift* (Boulder, CO: Lynne Rienner, 1999); David Gibbs, *Political Economy of Third World Intervention* (Chicago, IL: University of Chicago Press, 1999); Alexandra Homolar, "Rebels Without a Conscience: The Evolution of the Rogue State Narrative in U.S. Security Policy," *European Journal of International Relations*, 17, no 4 (2010), 705–757; Chalmers Johnson, *Blowback: The Costs and Consequences of American Empire* (New York: Holt Paperbacks, 2004).

242. NPR News, May 31, 2017.

243. See Colin J. Beck and Emily Miner, "Who Gets Designated a Terrorist and Why?" *Social Forces* 91, no. 3 (2013), 837–872; Austin T. Turk, "Sociology of Terrorism," *Annual Review of Sociology* 30 (2004), 271–286; David Boyns and James D. Ballard, "Developing a Sociological Theory for the Empirical Understanding of Terrorism," *The American Sociologist* 35, no. 2 (2004), 5–25.

244. Anthony Kuhn, "In Buddhist-Majority Myanmar, Muslim Minority Gets Pushed to the Margins," NPR News, May 28, 2014.

245. Julie McCarthy, "In Peaceful Sri Lanka, Army Holds Thousands of Acres Seized in Civil War," NPR News, August 5, 2015.

246. NPR News, May 3, 2019; Frank Langfitt, "China's Pollution Crisis Inspires an Unsettling Art Exhibit," NPR News, August 23, 2014; Rob Schmitz, "China Detains Hundreds of Thousands of Muslims in 'Training Centers,'" NPR News, May 3, 2019.

247. See Ian Lee et al., "Israel Defends Gaza Crackdown as Palestinians Bury Their Dead," CNN, May 16, 2018; Rich Gladstone, "U.S. Vetoes U.N. Resolution on Gaza, Calling Measure Unfair to Israel," *New York Times*, June 2, 2018, A11; Nick Cumming-Bruce, "U.N. Panel Sees Crimes by Israel in Gaza Toll," *New York Times*, March 1, 2019, A9.

248. Aljazeera, "Nigeria to Label Shia Group a 'Terrorist Organization,'" July 27, 2019.

249. Tamara Qiblawi and Ruba Alhenawi, "Saudi Arabia Executes 37 People, Crucifying One, for Terror-related Crimes," CNN, April 23, 2019.

250. BBC World Service Newshour, April 14, 2020; Ali Kucukgocmen, "Turkey Plans Prisoner Release, Excluding Those Jailed on Post-Coup Terrorism Charges," Reuters, April 7, 2020.

251. According to Pew Research Center, "5 Facts about Illegal Immigration in the U.S.," July 24, 2015, Available at http://www.pewresearch.org/fact-tank/2015/07/24/5-facts-about-illegal-immigration-in-the-u-s/.

252. For example studies, see Christopher R. Weber et al., "Placing Racial Stereotypes in Context: Social Desirability and the Politics of Racial Hostility," *American Journal of Political Science* 58, no. 1 (2014), 63–78; Mark Peffley and Jon Hurwitz, "Persuasion and Resistance: Race and the Death Penalty in America," *American Journal of Political Science* 51, no. 4 (2007), 996–1012; Christopher M. Federico, "When Do Welfare Attitudes Become Racialized? The Paradoxical Effects of Education," *American Journal of Political Science* 48, no. 2 (2004), 374–391; Martin Gilens, *Why Americans Hate Welfare* (Chicago, IL: University of Chicago Press, 1999); Rebecca C. Hetey and Jennifer L. Eberhardt, "Racial Disparities in Incarceration Increase Acceptance of Punitive Policies," *Psychological Science* 25, no. 10 (2014), 1949–1954.

253. Ben-Yehuda, "The European Witch-craze"; Elliot P. Currie, "Crimes Without Criminals: Witchcraft and Its Control in Renaissance Europe," *Law and Society Review* 3, no. 1 (1968), 7–28; Gary F. Jensen, *The Path of the Devil: Early Modern Witch Hunts* (Lanham, MD: Rowman & Littlefield, 2007).

254. Hinton, *Why Did They Kill?*

255. See Linda Herrera and Asef Bayat, "Introduction: Being Young and Muslim in Neoliberal Times," in *Being Young and Muslim: New Cultural Politics in the Global South and North*, eds. Linda Herrera and Asef Bayat (New York: Oxford University Press, 2010), 3–26; Soufan, *Anatomy of Terror*; Charles Kurzman, *The Missing Martyrs: Why There Are So Few Muslim Terrorists* (New York: Oxford University Press, 2011); Malcolm Fairbrother, "Economists, Capitalists, and the Making of Globalization: North American Free Trade in Comparative-Historical Perspective," *American Journal of Sociology* 119, no. 5 (2014), 1324–1379; Carl Ernst and Richard Martin, *Rethinking Islamic Studies: From Orientalism to Cosmopolitanism* (Columbia, SC: University of South Carolina Press, 2010); John L. Esposito and Dalia Mogahed, *Who Speaks for Islam? What a Billion Muslims Really Think* (New York: Gallup Press, 2008); Steven Fish, *Are Muslims Distinctive: A Look at the Evidence* (New York: Oxford University Press, 2011); Huntington, *The Clash of Civilization*; Zakaria, "Why Do They Hate Us?"; Andrew J. Bacevich, *America's War for the Greater Middle East: A Military History* (New York: Random House, 2016).

256. Susan Page, "Poll Shows Divide Between Muslims, West," *USA Today*, June 22, 2006.

257. See Neeraj Kaushal, *Blaming Immigrants: Nationalism and the Economics of Global Movement* (New York: Columbia University Press, 2019); Kristof, "America's History of Fear."

258. Paul Schemm (Associated Press), "Iraqi Christians Giving Up," *Dayton Daily News*, May 15, 2009, A8.

259. Devon Maylie, "South Africa Backs Off Murder Charges," *Wall Street Journal*, September 2, 2012; CNN, "270 Miners Charged in Co-workers' Deaths," August 31, 2012.

260. Aya Batrawy (Associated Press), "Riots Erupt After Verdict," *Dayton Daily News*, January 27, 2013, A2.

261. Jonny Bell, "Hillsborough Inquests Conclude 96 People Killed Unlawfully and Fans Not to Blame for Disaster," *The Telegraph*, April 26, 2016.

262. PBS, "Ken State Shooting," PBS

Documentary, aired on September 24, 2017.

263. Jonathan Stieglitz et al., "Infidelity, Jealousy, and Wife Abuse Among Tsimane Forager-Farmers: Testing Evolutionary Hypotheses of Marital Conflict," *Evolutionary Human Behavior* 33, no. 5 (2012), 438–448.

264. BBC, "Stoning Victim 'Begged for Mercy,'" November 4, 2008; Mark Tran, "Australian Muslim Leader Compares Uncovered Women to Exposed Meat," *The Guardian*, October 26, 2006; *Time*, "World Briefing," November 6, 2006, p. 19.

265. Kai Schultz and Suhasini Raj, "Repeatedly Gang-raped at Age 11, and Then Blamed for It, in India," *New York Times*, July 29, 2018, A6.

266. Ted Thornhill, "Indian Woman Who Survived Shocking Gang-rape Attack Is Raped Again by the Same Five Men Who Are Out on Bail," *Daily Mail*, July 18, 2016.

267. BBC World Service Newshour, December 7, 2019.

268. Rebecca Kheel, "Report: Sexual Assault Victims Wrongfully Discharged from Military," *The Hill*, May 19, 2016; PBS, Retro-Report, October 16, 2019.

269. Dana Farrington, "Baylor Removes Ken Starr as President Over University's Response to Sex Assault Cases," NPR News, May 26, 2016.

270. Sylvia Poggioli, "After Years of Abuse by Priests, #NunsToo are Speaking Out," NPR News, March 18, 2019.

271. McClure, "The Amish Keep to Themselves."

Chapter 4

1. Brian Ross et al., "Chattanooga Shooter Researched Religious Justification for Violence: Official," ABC News, July 20, 2015; Frances M. Young, *Sacrifice and the Death of Christ* (Eugene, OR: Wipf & Stock, 2010 [1975]); Coptic Orthodox Church, "Martyrdom," Accessed 2015, Available at http://www.copticchurch.net/topics/patrology/schoolofalex2/chapter18.html.

2. Jerod Post et al., "The Terrorists in Their Own Words: Interviews with 35 Incarcerated Middle Eastern Terrorists," *Terrorism and Political Violence* 15, no. 1 (2003), 171–184; John Horgan, *The Psychology of Terrorism* (New York: Routledge, 2005), 92–94.

3. Jay Tolson, "Aiming for Apocalypse," *U.S. News & World Report*, May 22, 2006, 34–35.

4. *New York Times*, "At Militarist Rally, Turkey's President Casts Weeping Girl, 6, in the Role of Martyr," February 27, 2018, A4.

5. See Linda D. Molm et al., "Building Solidarity through Generalized Exchange: A Theory of Reciprocity," *American Journal of Sociology* 113, no. 1 (2007), 205–242; Ko Kuwabara and Oliver Sheldon, "Temporal Dynamics of Social Exchange and the Development of Solidarity: 'Testing the Waters' Versus 'Taking a Leap of Faith,'" *Social Forces* 91, no. 1 (2012), 253–273.

6. Afe Adogame and James V. Spickard, *Religion Crossing Boundaries: Transnational Religious and Social Dynamics in Africa and the New African Diaspora* (Leiden: Brill Press, 2010); Afe Adogame and Shobana Shankar, *Religion on the Move! New Dynamics of Religious Expansion in a Globalizing World* (Leiden: Brill Press, 2013); Robert Wuthnow, *Boundless Faith: The Global Outreach of American Churches* (Berkeley, CA: University of California Press, 2009).

7. Fareed Zakaria, "Why Do They Hate Us?" *Newsweek*, October 15, 2001.

8. See Nancy J. Davis and Robert V. Robinson, *Claiming Society for God: Religious Movements and Social Welfare* (Bloomington: Indiana University Press, 2012), 59; Krishnadev Calamur, "Muslim Brotherhood: A Force Throughout the Muslim World," NPR News, August 17, 2013; Fouad Ajami, "The Heartbreak of History," *U.S. News & World Report*, July 31, 2006, 41; Brian Murphy (Associated Press), "Europeans Face Tough Choices on Islam," Yahoo News, November 6, 2004; Mark Mazzetti, "Saudi Arabia Warns of Economic Fallout if Congress Passes 9/11 Bill," *New York Times*, April 15, 2016; Nicholas Bariyo, "Kenya Vows to Curb al-Shabaab Terrorists," *Wall Street Journal*, January 19–20, 2019, A8; Zakaria, "Why Do They Hate Us?"

9. Jason Beaubien, "El Salvador Fears Ties Between Cartels, Street Gangs," NPR News, June 1, 2011.

10. David M. Davies, "In Honduras, Gangs Tell Boys to Join or Be Killed," NPR News, July 5, 2014.

11. Kevin Sieff et al., "Now Joining the Fight Against CV: The World's Armed Rebels,

Drug Cartels, and Gangs," *Washington Post*, April 14, 2020.

12. BBC, "How Coronavirus Inspired a Gangland Truce in South Africa," April 8, 2020.

13. Amanda Woods, "The Mafia is Thriving During Italy's Coronavirus Lockdown," *New York Post*, April 20, 2020.

14. Stephen Trachtenberg, "Should Colleges Consider Legacies in the Admissions Process?" *Wall Street Journal*, June 25, 2012, R7.

15. Sean Gregory and Kayla Webley, "Penn State of Mind," *Time*, December 12, 2011, 48–51.

16. Nicole Hong and Melissa Korn, "Harvard Set to Spill Secrets of Getting In," *Wall Street Journal*, October 12, 2018, A1 & A9.

17. Melissa Korn, "Legacies May Slow Colleges' Diversity Push," *Wall Street Journal*, July 10, 2018.

18. Francis Fukuyama, *Trust: The Social Virtues and the Creation of Prosperity* (New York: Free Press, 1995), 317.

19. *Ibid.*, 187–188.

20. *Ibid.*, 189.

21. PBS, "The Dictator's Playbook: Saddam Hussein," PBS Documentary Series, aired on January 16, 2019.

22. William Brustein, *The Logic of Evil: The Social Origins of the Nazi Party, 1925–1933* (New Haven, CT: Yale University Press, 1996), 141.

23. Thomas Omestad, "Culture Clash in Denmark: The Close-knit Danes Find Their Liberal Ideals Tested by a Growing, Alienated Muslim Population," *U.S. News & World Report*, January 8, 2007, 40–45; Douglas Waller, "An American Imam," *Time*, November 21, 2005, 60–62.

24. Lewis S. Feuer, "Science and the Ethic of Protestant Asceticism: A Reply to Professor Robert K. Merton," *Research in Sociology of Knowledge, Sciences, and Art*, Vol. II (Stamford, CT: JAI Press, 1979), 1–23; Frank Langfitt, "China's Pollution Crisis Inspires an Unsettling Art Exhibit," NPR News, August 23, 2014; Matt Goffman, "The World," PRI, January 14, 2008.

25. Albert Aji (Associated Press), "Official: Ancient Tombs Destroyed," *Dayton Daily News*, September 5, 2015, A7.

26. Sean Coughlan, "Iraqi University Rebuilds After IS 'Dark Age,'" BBC, November 21, 2019.

27. BBC World Service Newshour, February 5, 2012.

28. BBC World Service Newshour, June 11, 2015.

29. BBC World Service Newshour, March 10, 2010.

30. From Walker Connor, *Ethnonationalism: The Quest for Understanding* (Princeton, New Jersey: Princeton University Press, 1994), 206.

31. From Stuart J. Kaufman, *Modern Hatreds: The Symbolic Politics of Ethnic War* (Ithaca, NY: Cornell University Press, 2001), 27–28.

32. *Ibid.*, 219.

33. Michael M. Phillips, "The Civil War's Last Pensioner," *Wall Street Journal*, May 10–11, 2014, A1 & 10.

34. See Manuel Castells, *Networks of Outrage and Hope: Social Movements in the Internet Age* (Malden, MA: Polity Press, 2012); Doug McAdam, *Political Process and the Development of Black Insurgency, 1930–1970* (Chicago, IL: University of Chicago Press, 1982).

35. See Randall Collins, *Sociological Insight: An Introduction to Non-Obvious Sociology* (New York: Oxford University Press, 1992), 25–26.

36. Kaufman, *Modern Hatreds*, 29.

37. See Lory Britt and David R. Heise, "From Shame to Pride in Identity Politics," in *Self, Identity, and Social Movements*, eds. S. Stryker et al. (Minneapolis, MN: University of Minnesota Press, 2000), 252–271; Timothy J. Owens et al., "Three Faces of Identity," *Annual Review of Sociology* 36 (2010), 477–499.

38. Lev M. Ryazanovskiy, "Slogans and Mottoes of the Third Reich and the Way Nazi Propaganda Used Them," *Journal of Historical, Philological and Cultural Studies* 3, no. 53 (2016), 128–133.

39. Jenna Johnson, "'Life is a campaign': After a Difficult First Month, Trump Returns to His Comfort Zone," *Washington Post*, February 18, 2017.

40. See Charles Tilly, *Identities, Boundaries, and Social Change* (Boulder, CO: Paradigm Publishers, 2005); Charles Tilly, *Contentious Performances* (Cambridge, UK: Cambridge University Press, 2008); Charles Tilly and Sidney Tarrow, *Contentious Politics* (Boulder, CO: Paradigm, 2007).

41. Vamik Volkan, *Blind Trust: Large Groups and Their Leaders in Times of Crisis and Terror* (Charlottesville, VA: Pitchstone Publishing, 2004), Chapter 3.

42. Jeffrey C. Alexander, "Cultural

Pragmatics: Social Performance Between Ritual and Strategy," in *Social Performance: Symbolic Action, Cultural Pragmatics, and Ritual*, eds. Jeffrey C. Alexander et al. (New York: Cambridge University Press, 2006).

43. Bernard Giesen, "Performing the Sacred: A Durkheimian Perspective on the Performative Turn in the Social Sciences," in *Social Performance: Symbolic Action, Cultural Pragmatics, and Ritual*, eds. Jeffrey C. Alexander et al. (New York: Cambridge University Press, 2006), 325–367.

44. See Castells, *Networks of Outrage and Hope*.

45. Gary A. Fine, *Tiny Publics: A Theory of Group Action and Culture* (New York: Russell Sage Foundation, 2012), 89–106.

46. Simon Dein, "Prophecy: Social Scientific Perspectives and the Lubavitch," in *Prophecy in the New Millennium: When Prophecies Persist*, eds. S. Harvey and S. Newcombe (Surrey, England: Ashgate, 2013), 25–42.

47. See Collins, *Sociological Insight*, 44–46; Randall Collins, *Interaction Ritual Chains* (Princeton NJ: Princeton University Press, 2004).

48. Durkheim's theory of ritual, see Emile Durkheim, *The Elementary Forms of Religious Life*, translated by Karen E. Fields (New York: The Free Press, 1995 [1912]).

49. Collins, *Interaction Ritual Chains*.

50. E.g., Anne Heider and R. Stephen Warner, "Bodies in Sync: Interaction Ritual Theory Applied to Sacred Harp Singing," *Sociology of Religion* 71, no. 1 (2010), 76–97; Joseph O. Baker, "Social Sources of the Spirit: Connecting Rational Choice Theory and Interactive Ritual Theories in the Study of Religion," *Sociology of Religion* 71, no. 4 (2010), 1–25; Jason Wollschleger, "Interaction Chains and Religious Participation," *Sociological Forum* 27, no. 4 (2012), 896–912; Scott Draper, "Effervescence and Solidarity in Religious Organizations," *Journal for the Scientific Study of Religion* 53, no. 2 (2014), 229–248.

51. Tilly, *Identities, Boundaries*; Tilly, *Contentious Performances*; Tilly and Tarrow, *Contentious Politics*.

52. Adam Swart (CEO of Crowdson-Demand), from "The World," Public Radio International (PRI), July 30, 2015.

53. Richard Jenkins, "Different Societies? Different Cultures? What are Human Collectivities?" in *Making Sense of Collectivity: Ethnicity, Nationalism and Globalisation*, eds. Sinisa Malesevic, and Mark Haugaard (London: Pluto Press, 2002), 21.

54. Durkheim, *The Elementary Forms of Religious Life*, 76–86.

55. Connor, *Ethnonationalism*, 204.

56. Kaufman, *Modern Hatreds*, 29–30.

57. Ibid., 230.

58. Collins, *Sociological Insight*, 44–46.

59. Jan E. Stets and Michael J. Carter "A Theory of the Self for the Sociology of Morality," *American Sociological Review* 77, no. 1 (2012), 120–140.

60. Volkan, *Blind Trust*, 102.

61. Stets and Carter, "A Theory of the Self," 120–140.

62. From Serge F. Kovaleski, "To Crush an Outlaw Biker Club, Prosecutors Invoke Trademark Law," *New York Times*, November 25, 2018, A21.

63. Associated Press, "Afghan Riots Over Quran-burning: 2 Days, 20 Dead," *USA Today*, April 2, 2011.

64. Lauren Frayer, "Spate of Lynchings Target Minorities, Especially Muslims, In India," NPR News, August 19, 2019; Aljazeera, "India: Mob Lynches Muslim Man Transporting Cows in Rajasthan," July 21, 2018.

65. BBC World Service Newshour, October 10, 2015.

66. For similar arguments, see David Ignatius, "Why Facts Don't Matter to Trump's Supporters," *Washington Post* (Op-Ed), August 4, 2016; Salena Zito, "Taking Trump Seriously, Not Literally," *The Atlantic*, September 23, 2016.

67. Jean H. Lee (Associated Press), "Mythmaking Begins for N Korea's Next Leader," Yahoo News, December 22, 2011; Philip Wen, "Tanks and Guns Help Build the Myth of Kim," *Wall Street Journal*, January 10, 2012.

68. Murphy, "Europeans Face Tough Choices."

69. BBC, "China's Cultural Revolution," September 10, 2013; AFP (Agent France Press), "Eight Stone Chairman Mao Statue Unveiled," *The Telegraph*, December 13, 2013; Yang Su, *Collective Killings in Rural China During the Cultural Revolution* (New York: Cambridge University Press, 2011); Kerry Brown and Simone van Nieuwenhuizen, *China and the New Maoists* (London: Zen Books, 2016).

70. Chun Han Wong, "China to Pass a Law Protecting Its Heroes," *Wall Street Journal*, April 27, 2018, A16.

71. Anna Arutunyan, "As U.S. Pulls Down Monuments, Russia Adds Them—for Stalin," *USA Today*, August 23, 2017, 1A & 2A.

72. Stephen Kotkin, *Stalin: Waiting for Hitler, 1929–1941* (London: Penguin Press, 2017).

73. Kotkin, *Stalin*; Anne Applebaum, *Red Famine: Stalin's War on Ukraine* (New York: Doubleday, 2017).

74. James Marson, "Rediscovered Stalin Statue Roils Russian City," *Wall Street Journal*, October 23, 2018, A16.

75. BBC World Service Newshour, April 22, 2020.

76. Rick Hampson, "Confederate Memorials Keep Popping Up," *USA Today*, August 8, 2018, 1A & 6A.

77. Zygmunt Bauman, *Liquid Modernity* (Cambridge, UK: Polity Press, 2000), 213.

78. From Madeleine Albright, *Fascism: A Warning* (New York: HarperCollins, 2018), 79.

79. Donald M. Taylor, *The Quest for Identity* (Westport, CT: Praeger, 2002), 123.

80. According to Charlie Winter, a senior researcher at the UK-based counter-extremism think-tank Quilliam, from Ruth Pollard, "Islamic State Propaganda: What the West Doesn't Understand," *The Sydney Morning Herald*, July 9, 2015.

81. Tim Arango, "ISIS Transforming into Functioning State That Uses Terror as Tool," *New York Times*, July 21, 2015.

82. Mary L. Kelley, "The Curious Deaths of Kremlin Critics," NPR News, August 30, 2016; Brian Knowlton, "Prewar Arms Stance Was Wrong, Expert Says," *New York Times*, January 29, 2004.

83. Tim Arango, "U.S. Is Planning to Cut Its Staff at Iraq Embassy by as Much as Half," *New York Times*, February 7, 2012; MSNBC, April 14, 2006.

84. Francesca Chambers, "We Can't Continue to Be Led by Stupid People," *Daily Mail*, June 4, 2015; Danielle Kurtzleben, "The Best Insults of Donald Trump's Latest Campaign Speech," NPR News, July 21, 2015.

85. CNN, November 17, 2015.

86. CNN, December 8, 2015.

87. PBS, "The Dictator's Playbook."

88. Hannah Ellis-Petersen and Benjamin Haas, "How North Korea Got Away with the Assassination of Kim Jung-nam," *The Guardian*, April 1, 2019.

89. Krista Johnson, "I genuinely believed I would be destroyed because my dad told me that constantly," *USA Today*, April 19, 2018, 1A & 4A.

90. Brandon Ambrosino, "'Someone's Gotta Tell the Freakin' Truth': Jerry Falwell's Aides Break Their Silence," *Politico*, September 9, 2019.

91. Steven Erlanger, "Globe's Autocrats Echo Trump's 'Fake News' Cry," *New York Times*, December 13, 2017, A1 & A19.

92. Marc Santora and Benjamin Novak, "Protests of 'Slave Law' Pose Challenge for Orban," *New York Times*, January 9, 2019, A10.

93. Luke V. Ploeg, "Lack of Education Leads to Lost Dreams and Low Income for Many Jehovah's Witnesses," NPR News, February 19, 2017.

94. Reporters without Borders, "After Russia Awarded 2014 Winter Olympics, Authorities Should Demonstrate a Real Will to Solve Murders of Journalists," July 10, 2007.

95. BBC World Service Newshour, October 10, 2006.

96. BBC World Service Newshour, October 7, 2018.

97. NPR News, October 14, 2015.

98. Craig Nelson et al., "Attacks Leave 10 Afghan Journalists Dead," *Wall Street Journal*, May 1, 2018, A6.

99. Samantha Schmidt, "So Many Journalists Have Been Killed in Mexico This Year That a Newspaper Is Shutting Down," *Washington Post*, April 3, 2017; Carrie Kahn, "Being a Journalist in Veracruz, Mexico, Is a Very Dangerous Profession," NPR News, April 4, 2016; Jose de Cordoba, "Drug War Takes Mexican Newsman's Life," *Wall Street Journal*, May 20–21, 2017, A8.

100. Associated Press, "Journalist Shot to Death in Mexico," *New York Times*, March 23, 2018, A13; Schmidt, "So Many Journalists Have Been Killed."

101. *Time*, "Briefing," December 15, 2008, 14.

102. Nick Cumming-Bruce, "U.N. Official Scolds Trump for Attacking News Media," *New York Times*, August 31, 2017, A17.

103. Gerald Holton, *Science and Anti-Science* (Cambridge, MA: Harvard University Press, 1993).

104. Gordon Gauchat, "Politicization of Science in the Public Sphere: A Study of Public Trust in the United States, 1974 to 2010," *American Sociological Review* 77, no. 2

(2012), 167–187; Chris Mooney, *The Republican War on Science* (New York: Basic Books, 2005).

105. John Heilprin (Associated Press), "White House Accused of Censoring Climate Research," *Dayton Daily News*, November 2, 2006, A20; Tom Hamburger, "White House Tries to Rein in Scientists," *Los Angeles Times*, June 28, 2004; Lisa Friedman, "Bipartisan Report Says Trump's Abuse Has Pushed Federal Science to a 'Crisis,'" *New York Times*, October 3, 2019.

106. Karen Tumulty and Mark Thompson, "The Political Science Test," *Time*, February 13, 2006, 37–38.

107. Lewis S. Feuer, *The Conflict of Generations: The Character and Significance of Student Movements* (New York: Basic Books, 1969), 139–142.

108. Nasser Karimi (Associated Press), "Iran Head Wants Liberal Teachers Ousted," *Washington Post*, September 5, 2006.

109. Thomas Grove, "Turkey President Reshapes Military After Coup," *Wall Street Journal*, February 24, 2017, A8.

110. Laura Secor, "Human Collateral," *New York Times Magazine*, July 10, 2018, 32–39.

111. Kaufman, *Modern Hatreds*, 218–219.

112. See Maxwell Tani, "'They Would Vote No Against the Ten Commandments': GOP Congressman Resigns from Conservative Group," *Business Insider*, March 27, 2017.

113. Cari S. Babitzke, "Looking for Compromise on Gun Control is Futile, but Not for the Reasons You Think," *Washington Post*, October 4, 2017.

114. PBS, "The Rise of ISIS," *Frontline*, aired on October 28, 2014; Ian Bremmer, "Iraq after ISIS," Gzero World, April 24, 2019.

115. Tom Bowman, "Retrospective: The 18-Year, and Counting, Afghan War," NPR News, September 20, 2019.

116. Mel Leonor, "Trump Proclaims 'We Are Not Going to Apologize for America,'" *Politico*, May 25, 2018.

117. Matthew C. Ogilvie, "Religion Is Easily Exploited by Extremist Groups," in *Extremist Groups*, ed. Karen F. Balkin (Farmington Hills, MI: Greenhaven Press, 2005), 20.

118. Christopher Way and Jessica L. Peeks, "Making It Personal: Regime Type and Nuclear Proliferation," *American Journal of Political Science* 58, no. 3 (2014), 705–719.

119. Santanu Choudhury, "Foreign-Investment Reform to Reshape India's Defense Industry," *Wall Street Journal*, June 27, 2014, B6.

120. Julie McCarthy, "How a Lack of Toilets Puts India's Women at Risk of Assault," NPR News, June 9, 2014.

121. Ujala Sehgal and Robert Johnson, "15 Facts About Military Spending That Will Blow Your Mind," *Business Insider*, October 14, 2011; Yuka Hayashi, "Japanese Prime Minister Abe Pushes to Extend Military's Role," *Wall Street Journal*, September 17, 2013, A10.

122. NPR News, August 13, 2018.

123. NPR News February 27, 2017; Jeffrey Sparshott and Ted Mann, "Budget Plan Slashes EPA, Boosts Defense," *Wall Street Journal*, March 16, 2017, A4.

124. Thomas Grove, "Russia's Missile Defense Challenges U.S. Air Power," *Wall Street Journal*, January 24, 2019, A1 & A10; Julian Borger and Martin Pengelly, "Trump Says U.S. Will Withdraw from Nuclear Arms Treaty with Russia," *The Guardian*, October 20, 2018.

125. On the Issues, "Presidential Candidate Mitt Romney, During 2012 Republican National Convention Speech," August 30, 2012, available at http://www.ontheissues.org/2012/Mitt_Romney_Homeland_Security.htm.

126. Leo Shane, "Trump's Security Speech Light on Military, Veterans," *Military Times*, September 16, 2015.

127. CNN, "'Shock and Awe' Campaign Underway in Iraq," March 22, 2003.

128. PBS, "Russian Roulette," *Frontline*, aired on February 23, 1999; Chuck Hansen, *U.S. Nuclear Weapons: The Secret History* (Arlington, TX: Aerofax, 1988).

129. Edith M. Lederer, "U.N. Says Congo Rebels Use Cannibalism," Associated Press, August 1, 2003.

130. News.com.au, "ISIS Fanatics Publicly Crucify Nine Men in Syria as Rival Militias in Iraq Prove Just as Brutal," June 30, 2014.

131. AFP (Agence France Presse), "Daesh Drowns, Decapitates 'Spies' in Brutal New Video," *Khaleej Times*, June 24, 2015; Jim Michaels, "Video Shows Young Boy Executing Alleged Spies," *USA Today*, January 14, 2015.

132. Paul Wood, "Face-to-Face with Abu Sakkar, Syria's 'Heart-eating Cannibal,'" BBC, July 5, 2013.

133. PBS, "Here & Now," WBUR, April 15, 2019.

134. PBS, "The Dictator's Playbook."

135. Jean E. Smith, *Bush* (New York: Simon & Schuster, 2016), 300–325.
136. BBC, "Six Killed in Attack on World Vision Office in Pakistan," March 10, 2010.
137. Jeffrey Goldberg, "Is It Time for the Jews to Leave Europe?" *The Atlantic,* April, 2015.
138. BBC, "Why Are the Kurds Always in the Firing Line?" The Inquiry, October 30, 2019.
139. *Time,* "A Life of Extremes," May 20, 2011, 46–47.
140. PBS, "The Rise of ISIS"; Smith, *Bush,* 472–498; Bremmer, "Iraq after ISIS."
141. Richard Leiby and Michele Langevine, "In Pakistan, a Legal System Under Scrutiny," *Washington Post,* May 29, 2012.
142. Muneeza Naqvi (Associated Press), "Indian Council Ordered Teen Raped for Brother's Alleged Sex Assault, Police Say," *New York Daily News,* July 11, 2014.
143. BBC World Service Newshour, November 8, 2018.
144. AFP (Agence France Presse), "Israel Demolishes Homes of Palestinian Tel Aviv Attackers," Yahoo News, August 4, 2016; Human Rights Watch, "Israel: Stop Punitive Home Demolitions," November 22, 2014, available at http://www.hrw.org/news/2014/11/21/israel-stop-punitive-home-demolitions.
145. Rosie Perper, "A Canadian Political Refugee Made Videos Criticizing Saudi Arabia—Now Saudi Authorities Have Arrested His Friends and Family," *San Francisco Gate,* August 23, 2018.
146. Tom LoBianco, "Donald Trump on Terrorists: 'Take Out Their Families,'" CNN, December 2, 2015.
147. David Zucchino and Farooq J. Mangal, "Taliban Target Afghan Soldiers' Families in Quest for Revenge," *New York Times,* July 11, 2019, A6.
148. Stephanie Busari et al., "Suspected Boko Haram Attack on a Funeral Leaves 65 Dead in Nigeria, Official Says," CNN, July 29, 2019.
149. CBS, "Islamic State Claims Responsibility for Bombing at Kabul Wedding that Killed 63," August 18, 2019.
150. Jay Tolson, "Imbalance of Power," *U.S. News & World Report,* February 6, 2006, 58–60.
151. Gordon Thomas and Max Morgan-Witts, *Ruin from the Air* (London: Hamilton, 1977), 353–354.
152. Margaret Coker and Falih Hassan, "14 Death Sentences in 2 Hours: Iraq Shows No Mercy to ISIS Suspects," *New York Times,* April 18, 2018, A6.
153. Foster Klug, "Myanmar Limiting Food to Reduce the Rohingya," Associated Press, February 11, 2018.
154. Glen Greenwald, "Iran Sanctions Now Causing Food Insecurity, Mass Suffering," *The Guardian,* October 7, 2012.
155. Joy Gordon, "Cool War: Economic Sanctions as a Weapon of Mass Destruction," *Harper Magazine,* November, 2002.
156. Global Policy Forum, "Iraq Sanctions: Humanitarian Implications and Options for the Future," August 6, 2002, available at https://www.globalpolicy.org/component/content/article/170-sanctions/41947.html.

Chapter 5

1. Daniel Immerwahr, *How to Hide an Empire: A History of the Greater United States* (New York: Farrar, Straus & Giroux, 2019).
2. E.g., ALEC and Progressive States Network; for related coverage of this issue, see Thomas B. Edsall, Sarah Cohen, and James V. Grimaldi, "Pioneers Fill War Chest, Then Capitalize," *Washington Post,* May 16, 2004, A01; Gens Grober, Ernesto Reuben, and Agnieszka Tymula, "Political Quid Pro Quo Agreements: An Experimental Study," *American Journal of Political Science* 57, no. 3 (2013), 582–597; David Benoit, "Activist Investors Ally on Lobbying," *Wall Street Journal,* May 19, 2016, C1 & C2; Harland Prechel and Theresa Morris, "The Effects of Organizational and Political Embeddedness on Financial Malfeasance in the Largest U.S. Corporations: Dependence, Incentives, and Opportunities," *American Sociological Review* 75, no. 3 (2010), 331–354.
3. Val Burris, "Interlocking Directorates and Political Cohesion among Corporate Elites," *American Journal of Sociology* 111, no. 1 (2005), 249–283.
4. Mark S. Mizruchi, "What Do Interlocks Do? An Analysis, Critique, and Assessment of Research on Interlocking Directorates," *Annual Review of Sociology* 22 (1996), 271–298.
5. See William K. Carroll, *The Making of a Transnational Capitalist Class: Corporate Power in the 21st Century* (New York: Zed Books, 2010); William I. Robinson, *Global*

Capitalism and the Crisis of Humanity (New York: Cambridge University Press, 2014); Leslie Sklair, *The Transnational Capitalist Class* (Malden, MA: Blackwell, 2001).

6. Paul Kiernan, "Mining Giants Hit by Brazil Suit," *Wall Street Journal*, May 5, 2016, B3.

7. Thomas Hager, *Ten Drugs: How Plants, Powders, and Pills Have Shaped the History of Medicine* (New York: Abrams Press, 2019).

8. Selena Simmons-Duffin, "AIDS Activists Take on the High Price of HIV Prevention Pill," NPR News, March 29, 2019.

9. Hager, *Ten Drugs*; CBS News, "Opioid Crisis: The Lawsuits That Could Bankrupt Manufacturers and Distributors," *60 Minutes*, December 16, 2018; CBS News, "Ex-DEA Agent: Opioid Crisis Fueled by Drug Industry and Congress," *60 Minutes*, October 15, 2017; Beth Macy, *Dopesick: Dealers, Doctors, and the Drug Company That Addicted America* (New York: Little, Brown & Co, 2018).

10. Bill Whitaker, CBS News, *60 Minutes*, aired on June 17, 2018.

11. Robert Langreth, "Drug Prices," *Bloomberg News*, February 5, 2019.

12. Peterson Center on Healthcare, "How Will the Rising Cost of Prescription Drugs Affect Medicare?" September 4, 2018.

13. NPR News, June 9, 2009; U.S. Department of Health and Human Services, "The Health Consequences of Smoking—50 Years of Progress: A Report of the Surgeon General," Centers for Disease Control and Prevention, 2014, available at http://www.cdc.gov/tobacco/data_statistics/sgr/50th-anniversary/index.htm.

14. Jan Hoffman, "Teenagers Can't Stop Vaping Nicotine: Experts Can't Help Much," *New York Times*, December 19, 2018, A1 & A24.

15. Matthew Perrone, "Concern Rises for Teens Addicted to Nicotine," Associated Press, January 18, 2019.

16. Jill L. Harrison, *Pesticide Drift and the Pursuit of Environmental Justice* (Cambridge, MA: MIT Press, 2011); Kiernan, "Mining Giants."

17. John Schwartz, "Lawmakers Seek Information on Funding for Climate Change Critics," *New York Times*, February 25, 2015; Stephen Beard, from Marketplace Morning Report, NPR, February 2, 2007; Associated Press, "Group: ExxonMobil Paid to Mislead Public," Yahoo News, January 3, 2007.

18. Harrison, *Pesticide Drift*; David Schlosberg, *Defining Environmental Justice: Theories, Movements, and Nature* (Oxford University Press, 2007).

19. Jessica Donati, "Report Puts Price Tag at About $2.8 Trillion," *Wall Street Journal*, May 17, 2018, A2.

20. Daniel Brown, "These Are the 20 Defense Companies Donating the Most Money to American Politicians," *Business Insider*, October 24, 2018; F. Brinkley Bruton, "The U.S. Wants the Yemen War to End. Will it Stop Selling Arms to Saudi Arabia?" NBC News, November 5, 2018; Jeffrey E. Stern, "Tracing a Tragedy in Yemen Back to an American Bomb Factory," *New York Times Magazine*, December 16, 2018, 40–47, 65.

21. Sarah El Sirgany and Tamara Qiblawi, "U.S., UK, France, and Iran May be Complicit in Yemen War Crimes, UN Says," CNN, September 3, 2019; Aljazeera, "Yemen: War Profiteers," August 2, 2019.

22. Dawne Moon, "Who Am I and Who Are We? Conflicting Narratives of Collective Selfhood in Stigmatized Groups," *American Journal of Sociology* 117, no. 5 (2012), 1336–1379.

23. See Sarah A. Soule, *Contention and Corporate Social Responsibility* (New York: Cambridge University Press, 2009).

24. Michael Hechter, *Containing Nationalism* (Oxford, UK: Oxford University Press, 2000).

25. Similar to "symbolic violence" by Mustafa Emirbayer and Matthew Desmond, *The Racial Order* (Chicago, IL: University of Chicago Press, 2015), 255–269.

26. For similar discussion, see Rogers Brubaker, *Grounds for Difference* (Cambridge, MA: Harvard University Press, 2015), 10–47.

27. Herbert Blumer, "Race Prejudice as a Sense of Group Position," *The Pacific Sociological Review* 1, no. 1 (1958), 3–7.

28. See also Eduardo Bonilla-Silva, "From Bi-racial to Tri-racial: Towards a New System of Racial Stratification in the USA," *Ethnic and Racial Studies* 27, no. 6 (2004), 931–950; Emirbayer and Desmond, *The Racial Order*.

29. Andrew V. Papachristos, "Murder by Structure: Dominance Relations and the Social Structure of Gang Homicide," *American Journal of Sociology* 115, no. 1 (2009), 74–128.

30. Dan Frosch and Nathan Koppel,

"Motorcycle Gangs Still Riding High," *Wall Street Journal*, May 20, 2015, A3.

31. Robert Faris and Diane Felmelee, "Status Struggles: Network Centrality and Gender Segregation in Same- and Cross-gender Aggression," *American Sociological Review*. 76, no. 1 (2011), 48–73; Nancy G. Guerra, K. Robert Williams, and Shelly Sadek, "Understanding Bullying and Victimization During Childhood and Adolescence: A Mixed Methods Study," *Child Development* 82 (2011), 295–310; Philip C. Rodkin, Allison M. Ryan, Rhonda Jamison, and Travis Wilson, "Social Goals, Social Behavior, and Social Status in Middle Childhood," *Developmental Psychology* 49, no. 6 (2003), 1139–1150; P. H. Hawley, Kathryn N. Stump, and Jacklyn Ratliff, "Sidestepping the Jingle Fallacy: Bullying, Aggression, and the Importance of Knowing the Difference," in *Bullying in North American Schools*, 2nd edition, eds. D. L. Espelage and S. Swearer (New York: Routledge, 2011), 101–115.

32. Debra Pepler et al., "Peer Processes in Bullying: Informing Prevention and Intervention Strategies," in *Handbook of Bullying in Schools: An International Perspective*, eds. S. R. Jimerson et al. (New York: Routledge, 2010), 469–479.

33. Beth Doll et al., "Classroom Ecologies that Support or Discourage Bullying," in *Bullying in American Schools: A Social-ecological Perspective on Prevention and Intervention*, eds. D. L. Espelage and S. M. Swearer (Mahwah, NJ: Erlbaum, 2004), 161–183; Anthony D. Pellegrini and Jeffrey D. Long, "Part of the Solution and Part of the Problem: The Role of Peers in Bullying, Dominance, and Victimization During the Transition from Primary School Through Secondary School," in *Bullying in American Schools: A Social-ecological Perspective on Prevention and Intervention*, eds. D. L. Espelage and S. M. Swearer (Mahwah, NJ: Erlbaum, 2004), 107–117.

34. Martha Crenshaw, "Theories of Terrorism: Instrumental and Organizational Approaches," in *Inside Terrorist Organizations*, ed. David C. Rapoport (Portland, OR: Frank Cass, 2001), 20.

35. Angie Chan, "Japan Executes 6 in Attacks by Cult," *New York Times*, July 27, 2018, A12.

36. Tore Bjørgo, "Extreme Nationalism and Violent Discourses in Scandinavia: 'The Resistance,' 'Traitors,' and 'Foreign Invaders,'" in *Terror from the Extreme Right* (London: Fank Cass, 1995), 182–220.

37. Jessica Stern, *Terror in the Name of God: Why Religious Militants Kill* (New York: Harper Perennial), 208.

38. Craig Smith and Don Van Natta, Jr., "Officials Fear Iraq's Lure for Muslims in Europe," *New York Times*, October 23, 2004; Brian Bennett and Michael Ware, "Behind the Enemy Lines," *Time*, December 15, 2003, 28–35; Robert Siegel, "Foreign Policy Experts Weigh in on U.S. Strategy Against the Islamic State," NPR News, May 28, 2015.

39. Sudhir A. Venkatesh, "The Social Organization of Street Gang Activity in an Urban Ghetto," *American Journal of Sociology* 103, no. 1 (1997), 82–111; Clifford R. Shaw and Henry D. McKay, *Juvenile Delinquency and Urban Areas* (Chicago, IL: University of Chicago Press, 1942); William J. Wilson, *The Truly Disadvantaged: The Inner City, the Underclass, and Public Policy* (Chicago, IL: University of Chicago Press, 1987).

40. See Robert J. Duran, *Gang Life in Two Cities: An Insider's Journey* (New York: Columbia University Press, 2013), 66–93; Venkatesh, "The Social Organization of Street Gang," 82–111; David S. Kirk and Andrew V. Papachristos, "Cultural Mechanisms and the Persistence of Neighborhood Violence," *American Journal of Sociology* 116, no. 4 (2011), 1190–1233.

41. George Knox, *An Introduction to Gangs* (Chicago, IL: New Chicago School Press, 2000), 70.

42. Ruth Alexander, "Can You Make Gangs Good?" BBC Inquiry, May 4, 2019; Jan Ransom and Al Baker, "Behind Teenager's Death: Machete-Wielding Gang in a Civil War," *New York Times*, July 19, 2018, A1 & A17.

43. BBC, "Brazil Jail Riot Leaves More Than 50 Dead," July 29, 2019.

44. Tamara Audi, "L.A. Gangs Seek Profit in Peace," *Wall Street Journal*, December 30, 2009, A3.

45. Carlton J. H. Hays, *Nationalism: A Religion* (New York: The Macmillan, 1960), 132–133.

46. Ibid., 163.

47. Smith and Van Natta, Jr., "Officials Fear Iraq's Lure."

48. Bennett and Ware, "Behind the Enemy Lines," 28–35.

49. Craig J. Calhoun, *The Roots of Radicalism: Tradition, the Public Sphere, and Early Nineteenth Century Social Movements*

(Chicago: University of Chicago Press, 2012), 82.

50. E.g., Charles Kurzman, *The Missing Martyrs: Why There Are So Few Muslim Terrorists* (New York: Oxford University Press, 2011); Carl Ernst and Richard Martin, "Introduction: Toward a Post-Orientalist Approach to Islamic Religious Studies," in *Rethinking Islamic Studies: From Orientalism to Cosmopolitanism*, eds. Carl Ernst and Richard Martin (Columbia, SC: University of South Carolina Press, 2010), 1–23; John L. Esposito and Dalia Mogahed, 2008. *Who Speaks for Islam? What a Billion Muslims Really Think* (New York: Gallup Press, 2008); Steven Fish, *Are Muslims Distinctive: A Look at the Evidence* (New York: Oxford University Press, 2011).

51. Peter Berger, *The Desecularization of the World: Resurgent Religion and World Politics* (Washington, DC: Ethics and Public Policy Center, 1999); Rodney Stark and Roger Finke, *Acts of Faith: Explaining the Human Side of Religion* (Berkeley, CA: University of California Press, 2000); David Martin, *A General Theory of Secularization* (Aldershot, UK: Gregg Revivals, 1993[1978]); Steve Bruce, *God Is Dead: Secularization in the West* (Oxford, UK: Blackwell, 2002).

52. See Samuel P. Huntington, *The Clash of Civilization and the Remaking of World Order* (New York: Simon & Schuster, 2011); Charles Kurzman, *The Missing Martyrs: Why There Are So Few Muslim Terrorists* (New York: Oxford University Press, 2011).

53. Carlotta Gall, "Plan to Raise 'Pious Generation' Divides Turkey," *New York Times*, June 19, 2018, A1 & A10.

54. See Linda D. Molm et al., "Building Solidarity Through Generalized Exchange: A Theory of Reciprocity," *American Journal of Sociology* 113, no. 1 (2007), 205–242; Ko Kuwabara and Oliver Sheldon, "Temporal Dynamics of Social Exchange and the Development of Solidarity: 'Testing the Waters' Versus 'Taking a Leap of Faith,'" *Social Forces* 91, no. 1 (2012), 253–273.

55. See Anthony Giddens, *The Consequences of Modernity* (Stanford, CA: Stanford University Press, 1990), 118; Hechter, *Containing Nationalism*, 20.

56. Hechter, *Containing Nationalism*, 20–21.

57. Julie McCarthy, "Why Do So Few People Pay Income Tax in India?" NPR News, March 22, 2017.

58. William Brustein, *The Logic of Evil: The Social Origins of the Nazi Party, 1925–1933* (New Haven, CT: Yale University Press, 1996), 141.

59. See Nancy J. Davis and Robert V. Robinson, *Claiming Society for God: Religious Movements and Social Welfare* (Bloomington, IN: Indiana University Press, 2012), 59; Krishnadev Calamur, "Muslim Brotherhood: A Force Throughout the Muslim World," NPR News, August 17, 2013; Fareed Zakaria, "Why Do They Hate Us?" *Newsweek*, October 15, 2001; Fouad Ajami, "The Heartbreak of History," *U.S. News & World Report*, July 31, 2006, 41; Dan Murphy (Associated Press), "Hamas's Approach to Jihad: Start 'tm young." Yahoo News, August 20, 2007; Mark Mazzetti, "Saudi Arabia Warns of Economic Fallout if Congress Passes 9/11 Bill," *New York Times*, April 15, 2016.

60. Tim Fernholz, "ISIS Made More Money Taxing Farms Than Stealing Oil or Kidnapping People," Quartz Media, April 5, 2018.

61. See Diego Gambetta, *The Sicilian Mafia: The Business of Private Protection* (Cambridge, MA: Harvard University Press, 1996); Federico Varese, *The Russian Mafia: Private Protection in a New Market Economy* (London: Oxford University Press, 2001).

62. See M. A. Thomas, *Govern Like Us: U.S. Expectations of Poor Countries* (New York: Columbia University Press, 2015).

63. Ibid., Chapter 8.

64. John Tierney, "Iraq's Family Bonds Complicate U.S. Efforts," *New York Times*, September 27, 2003.

65. Ari Shapiro, "South Koreans Bristle at Growing Dominance of Family-Run Conglomerates," NPR News, July 29, 2015.

66. Anthony Spaeth, "Clans on the Run," *Time*, April 14, 2004; Alastair Gale, "'Nut Rage' Reignites Backlash against South Korea's Family-run Conglomerates," *Wall Street Journal*, January 7, 2015.

67. Justin Scheck and Bradley Hope, "Airbus Deal Powered Saudi Royal Family's Wealth," *Wall Street Journal*, May 17, 2018, A1 & A12.

68. Mark Doyle, "Kenya's Diplomatic Push for Peace," BBC, January 2, 2008; Mark Doyle, "Kenya Stokes Tribalism Debate," BBC, January 4, 2008; Steve Inskeep and Gwen Thompkins, "Kenya's Post-Election Violence Kills Hundreds," NPR News, January 2, 2008.

69. Doyle, "Kenya Stokes Tribalism Debate."

70. Inskeep and Thompkins, "Kenya's Post Election Violence"; Doyle, "Kenya's Diplomatic Push for Peace."

71. Anthony D. Smith, *Nationalism and Modernism: A Critical Survey of Recent Theories of Nations and Nationalism* (London, UK: Routledge, 1999), 177; Andreas Wimmer and Yuval Feinstein, "The Rise of the Nation-State across the World, 1916 to 2001," *American Sociological Review* 75, no. 5 (2010), 764–790.

72. James Brandon, "Yemen Attempts to Rein in Outlaw Tribes," *The Christian Science Monitor*, January 24, 2006.

73. Nicholas Bariyo, "Congo Crisis Sends Millions into Exile," *Wall Street Journal*, June 22, 2017, A12.

74. For example cases, see Tresa Baldas, "Ex-Jehovah's Witnesses Break Silence on Shunning," *USA Today*, March 28, 2018, 6A; Stephanie Nolasco, "Former Child Bride Who Helped Take Down Cult Leader Warren Jeffs Speaks Out in New Documentary," Fox News, February 19, 2018; Krista Johnson, "'I genuinely believed I would be destroyed because my dad told me that constantly," *USA Today*, April 19, 2018, 1A & 4A; Elizabeth Llorente, "Insular Hasidic Jews Struggle to Preserve Customs as Legal and Social Pressures Build," Fox News, June 11, 2018; John A. Hostetler, *Amish Society*, 3rd ed. (Baltimore, MD: Johns Hopkins University, 1980).

75. Alexander A. Weinreb, "Characteristics of Women in Consanguineous Marriages in Egypt, 1988–2000," *European Journal of Population* 24, no. 2 (2008), 185–210; Ghazi Tadmouri et al., "Consanguinity and Reproductive Health Among Arabs," *Reproductive Health* 8 (2009), 6–17; Geoff Harkness and Rana Khaled, "Modern Traditionalism: Consanguineous Marriage in Qatar," *Journal of Marriage and Family* 76, no. 3 (2014), 587–603; Tierney, "Iraq's Family Bonds."

76. Baldas, "Ex-Jehovah's Witnesses."

77. Sarah McClure, "The Amish Keep to Themselves. And They're Hiding a Horrifying Secret," *Cosmopolitan*, January 14, 2020.

78. Marie Keenan, *Child Sexual Abuse and the Catholic Church: Gender, Power, and Organizational Culture* (New York: Oxford University Press, 2011).

79. BBC World Service Newshour, April 2, 2020.

80. Max Weber, "Open and Closed Relationships," in *Inequality and Society*, eds. Jeff Manza and Michael Sauder (New York: W. W. Norton, 2009 [1920]), 94–98.

81. Emily Shapiro, "Waco, Texas, Biker Shooting: A Look at the Gangs that may be Involved," ABC News, May 18, 2015.

82. Dan Frosch and Nathan Koppel, "Novel Move to Crimp Bikers," *Wall Street Journal*, June 1. 2015, A3.

83. U.S. Government Printing Office, *The 9/11 Commission Report: Final Report of the National Commission on Terrorist Attacks upon the United States* (Washington, D.C., 2004), 47–55.

84. See Robert Wuthnow, *Boundless Faith: The Global Outreach of American Churches* (Berkeley: University of California Press, 2009); Scott Hibbard, "Religion and State in India: Ambiguity, Chauvinism, and Tolerance," in *Religion and Regimes: Support, Separation, and Opposition*, eds. Mehran Tamadonfar and Ted G. Jelen (Lanham, MD: Lexington Books, 2013), 251; Afe Adogame and Shobana), *Religion on the Move! New Dynamics of Religious Expansion in a Globalizing World* (Leiden: Brill Press, 2013); Afe Adogame and James V. Spickard, *Religion Crossing Boundaries: Transnational Religious and Social Dynamics in Africa and the New African Diaspora* (Leiden: Brill Press, 2010).

85. Susan Olzak, *The Dynamics of Ethnic Competition and Conflict* (Stanford, CA: Stanford University Press, 1994).

86. Kimon de Greef, "South Africa Taxi Rivalry Spurs Killing of 11 Drivers," *New York Times*, July 23, 2018, A4.

87. David E. Sanger et al., "U.S. Scrambles to Outrun China in New Arms Race," *New York Times*, January 27, 2019, A1 & A11.

88. Weber, "Open and Closed Relationships," 94–98.

89. See *Ibid.*

90. Randall Collins, *The Credential Society: An Historical Sociology of Education and Stratification* (Cambridge, MA: Academic Press, 1979).

91. Thijs Bol and Kim A. Weeden, "Occupational Closure and Wage Inequality in Germany and the United Kingdom," *European Sociological Review* 31, no. 3 (2015), 354–369.

92. Stephanie Simon, "A License to Shampoo: Jobs Needing State Approval Rise," *Wall Street Journal*, February 7, 2011, A1 & 16.

93. Jeremy Fiel, "Closing Ranks: Closure, Status Competition, and School Segregation," *American Journal of Sociology* 121, no. 1 (2015), 126–70.

94. "Blockage of social mobility" theory; see Randall Collins, "Maturation of the State-Centered Theory of Revolution and Ideology," *Sociological Theory* 11, no. 1 (1993), 117–128.

95. Eric Hoffer, *The True Believers: Thoughts on the Nature of Mass Movements* (New York: Harper & Brothers, 1951).

96. Richard Cloward and Lloyd Ohlin, *Delinquency and Opportunity: A Theory of Delinquent Gangs* (New York: Free Press, 1966); Albert Cohen, *Delinquent Boys: The Culture of the Gang* (New York: Free Press, 1955); Shaw and McKay, *Juvenile Delinquency*; Malcolm Klein, *The American Street Gang: Its Nature, Prevalence, and Control* (New York: Oxford University Press, 1995).

97. Duran, *Gang Life in Two Cities*, 118–120, 147–170.

98. Ransom and Baker, "Behind Teenager's Death."

99. Elijah Anderson, *Code of the Street: Decency, Violence, and the Moral Life of the Inner City* (New York: W.W. Norton, 2000).

100. See Kirk and Papachristos, "Cultural Mechanism," 1190–1233; Robert J. Sampson and Dawn J. Bartusch, "Legal Cynicism and (Subcultural?) Tolerance of Deviance: The Neighborhood Context of Racial Differences," *Law and Society Review* 32, no. 4 (1998), 777–804.

101. See Ruth Horowitz, "Honor and Reputation in the Chicano Gang," in *The Meaning of Sociology: A Reader*, 5th edition, ed. Joel M. Charon (Moorhead MN: Moorhead State University Press, 1996), 59–66; Kirk and Papachristos, "Cultural Mechanism," 1190–1233; Sampson and Bartusch, "Legal Cynicism," 777–804.

102. John Hagan, Joshua Kaiser, and Anna Hanson, "The Theory of Legal Cynicism and Sunni Insurgent Violence in Post-Invasion Iraq," *American Sociological Review* 81, no. 2 (2016), 316–346.

103. Moon, "Who Am I"; Andreas Wimmer and Thomas Soehl, "Blocked Acculturation: Cultural Heterodoxy among Europe's Immigrants," *American Journal of Sociology* 120, no. 1 (2014), 146–186; Fouad Ajami, "Within the Gates," *U.S. News & World Report*, July 25, 2005, 24.

104. See Wimmer and Soehl, "Blocked Acculturation"; Ajami, "Within the Gates."

105. Zakaria, "Why Do They Hate Us?"; Walter Erich, "Understanding Terrorist Behavior: The Limits and Opportunities of Psychological Inquiry," in *Origins of Terrorism: Psychologies, Ideologies, Theologies, States of Mind*, ed. Walter Reich (Washington D.C.: Woodrow Wilson Center Press, 1998), 261–278.

106. Erich, "Understanding Terrorist Behavior," 278.

107. Charlie Winter and Jordan Bach-Lombardo, "Why ISIS Propaganda Works," *The Atlantic*, February 13, 2016.

108. Linda Gordon, *The Second Coming of the KKK: The Ku Klux Klan of the 1920s and the American Political Tradition* (New York: Liveright Publishing, 2017).

109. Maxwell Tani, "'They would vote no against the Ten Commandments': GOP Congressman Resigns from Conservative Group," *Business Insider*, March 27, 2017.

110. Rodney Stark and William Bainbridge, "Secularization, Revival, and Cult Formation," *Annual Review of the Social Science of Religion* 4 (1980), 85–119.

111. Martin Marty and Scott Appleby, *Fundamentalisms Observed: The Fundamentalism Project, Book 1* (Chicago, IL: University of Chicago Press, 1994).

112. Crenshaw, "Theories of Terrorism," 21–24.

113. Stern, "Terror in the Name of God," 28.

114. Ibid., 208.

115. Catherine Nixey, *The Darkening Age: The Christian Destruction of the Classical World* (New York: Houghton Mifflin Harcourt, 2018).

116. Romesh Ratnesar, "Face of Terror," *Time*, December 27-January 3, 2004–2005, 96–100.

117. Crenshaw, "Theories of Terrorism," 21–24.

118. William Crotty, "International Terrorism: Causes and Consequences for a Democratic Society," in *Democratic Development & Political Terrorism: The Global Perspective*, ed. William Crotty (Lebanon, NH: Northeastern University Press, 2005), 525.

119. Stern, "Terror in the Name of God," 28.

120. Ibid., 28–29.

121. Llorente, "Insular Hasidic Jews."

122. Baldas, "Ex-Jehovah's Witnesses"; Nolasco, "Former Child Bride"; Johnson, "I Genuinely Believed"; Llorente, "Insular Hasidic Jews."

Chapter 6

1. Similar to "uncertainty-identity theory" of Michael A. Hogg, "Self-identity, Social Identity, and the Solace of Extremism," in *Extremism and the Psychology of Uncertainty*, eds. Michael A. Hogg and Danielle L. Blaylock (West Sussex, UK: Wiley-Blackwell, 2011), Chapter 2; "parochial cooperation" of Joseph Henrich and Natalie Henrich, *Why Humans Cooperate: A Cultural and Evolutionary Explanation* (Oxford, UK: Oxford University Press, 2007), 175–204; For similar discussions, see also Michael J. Gilligan et al., "Civil War and Social Cohesion: Lab-in-the-Field Evidence from Nepal," *American Journal of Political Science* 58, no. 3 (2014), 604–619; Renee F. Lyons et al., "Coping as a Communal Process," *Journal of Social and Personal Relationships* 15, no. 5 (1998), 579–605; James W. Pennebaker and Kent D. Harber, "A Social Stage Model of Collective Coping: The Loma Prieta Earthquake and the Persian Gulf War," *Journal of Social Issues* 49, no. 4 (1993), 125–145; James D. Fearon et al., "Can Development Aid Contribute to Social Cohesion After Civil War? Evidence from a Field Experiment in Post-Conflict Liberia," *American Economic Review* 99, no. 2 (2009), 287–291; Sam Whitt and Rick K. Wilson, "The Dictator Game: Fairness and Equity in Postwar Bosnia," *American Journal of Political Science* 51, no. 3 (2007), 655–668; Michael G. Findley and Joseph K. Young, "Terrorism, Democracy, and Credible Commitments," *International Studies Quarterly* 55 (2011), 357–378.

2. Joanne Nagel, *American Indian Renewal: Red Power and the Resurgence of Identity and Culture* (Oxford, UK: Oxford University Press, 1995).

3. R. Matthew Montoya and Todd L. Pittinsky, "When Increased Group Identification Leads to Outgroup Liking and Cooperation: The Role of Trust," *The Journal of Social Psychology* 151, no. 6 (2011), 784–806.

4. Of Robert Jervis, from Stuart J. Kaufman, *Modern Hatreds: The Symbolic Politics of Ethnic War* (Ithaca, NY: Cornell University Press, 2001), 34; Also similar to "C-escalation" of Randall Collins, "C-Escalation and D-Escalation: A Theory of the Time-Dynamics of Conflict," *American Sociological Review* 77, no. 1 (2012), 1–20; For "intergroup threat theory," see Walter G. Stephan et al., "Intergroup Threat Theory," in *Handbook of Prejudice, Stereotyping, and Discrimination*, ed. T. D. Nelson (New York: Psychology Press, 2009), 43–59.

5. Daphana Canetti-Nisim et al., "A New Stress-Based Model of Political Extremism: Personal Exposure to Terrorism, Psychological Distress, and Exclusionist Political Attitudes," *Journal of Conflict Resolution* 53, no. 3 (2009), 363–389.

6. See Marc J. Hetherington and Elizabeth Suhay, "Authoritarianism, Threat, and Americans' Support for the War on Terror," *American Journal of Political Science* 55, no. 3 (2011), 546–560; Stanley Feldman, "Enforcing Social Conformity: A Theory of Authoritarianism," *Political Psychology* 24, no. 1 (2003), 41–74; Karen Stenner, *The Authoritarian Dynamic* (New York: Cambridge University Press, 2005); Reza Aslan, *Beyond Fundamentalism: Confronting Religious Extremism in the Age of Globalization* (New York: Random House, 2010); Marc J. Hetherington and Jonathan D. Weiler, *Authoritarianism and Polarization in American Politics* (New York: Cambridge University Press, 2009), 109–130.

7. Linda Herrera and Asef Bayat, "Introduction: Being Young and Muslim in Neoliberal Times," in *Being Young and Muslim: New Cultural Politics in the Global South and North*, eds. Linda Herrera and Asef Bayat (New York: Oxford University Press, 2010), 3–26.

8. Joan Williams, *White Working Class: Overcoming Class Cluelessness in America* (Boston, MA: Harvard Business Review Press, 2017).

9. Vamik Volkan, *Blind Trust: Large Groups and Their Leaders in Times of Crisis and Terror* (Charlottesville, VA: Pitchstone Publishing, 2004).

10. E.g., Feldman, "Enforcing Social Conformity"; Stenner, *The Authoritarian Dynamic*; Gilligan et al., "Civil War and Social Cohesion"; Lyons et al., "Coping as a Communal Process"; Pennebaker and Harber, "A Social Stage Model"; Fearon et al., "Can Development Aid Contribute"; Whitt and Wilson, "The Dictator Game"; Michael A. Hogg and Danielle L. Blaylock, "Preface" in *Extremism and the Psychology of Uncertainty*, eds. Michael A. Hogg and Danielle L. Blaylock (West Sussex, UK: Wiley-Blackwell, 2011); "prospect theory" of Jeffrey D. Berejikian, "Model Building with Prospect Theory: A Cognitive Approach to International Relations," *Political Psychology* 23, no. 4 (2002), 759–786.

11. Amy Chua, *Political Tribes: Group Instinct and the Fate of Nations* (New York: Penguin Press, 2018), 165–196.

12. Ronald Inglehart and Wayne E. Baker, "Modernization, Cultural Change, and the Persistence of Traditional Values," *American Sociological Review* 65, no. 1 (2000), 28.

13. Eric Sylvers, "Jobless Youth Rattle European Politics," *Wall Street Journal*, June 18, 2018, A1 & A10.

14. Steffen Mau and Christoph Burkhardt, "Migration and Welfare State Solidarity in Western Europe," *Journal of European Social Policy* 19, no. 3 (2009), 213–229; Cybelle Fox, "The Changing Color of Welfare? How Whites' Attitudes toward Latinos Influence Support for the Welfare State," *American Journal of Sociology* 110, no. 3 (2004), 580–625; Maureen A. Eger, "Even in Sweden: The Effect of Immigration on Support for Welfare State Spending," *European Sociological Review* 26, no. 2 (2010), 203–217; Alexander W. Schmidt-Catran and Dennis C. Spies, "Immigration and Welfare Support in Germany," *American Sociological Review* 81, no. 2 (2016), 242–261.

15. Wim Van Oorschot, "Public Perceptions of the Economic, Moral, Social and Migration Consequences of the Welfare State: An Empirical Analysis of Welfare State Legitimacy," *Journal of European Social Policy* 20, no. 1 (2010), 19–31.

16. Elisabetta Povoledo, "With Little Fanfare, 2 Italian Regions Prepare to Vote on Greater Autonomy," *New York Times*, October 18, 2017, A8.

17. Lauren Frayer, "Hindu Nationalism, the Growing Trend in India," NPR News, April 22, 2019.

18. E.g., "field theory" applied to groups; see Kurt Lewin, *Resolving Social Conflicts: Field Theory in Social Science* (Washington, D.C.: American Psychological Association, 1997); see also John L. Martin, "What Is Field Theory," *American Journal of Sociology* 109, no. 1 (2003), 1–49.

19. Gerhard Lenski and Patrick Nolan, "Trajectories of Development: A Test of Ecological-Evolutionary Theory," *Social Forces* 63, no. 1 (1984), 1–23.

20. Charles C. Mann, *The Wizard and the Prophet: Two Remarkable Scientists and Their Dueling Visions to Shape Tomorrow's World* (New York: Knopf, 2018).

21. Parallel arguments have been made by many historians and scholars, most recently by Michael Shermer, *The Moral Arc: How Science and Reason Lead Humanity toward Truth, Justice and Freedom* (New York: Henry Holt, 2015); Angus Deaton, *The Great Escape: Health, Wealth, and the Origins of Inequality* (Princeton, NJ: Princeton University Press, 2013); Steven Pinker, *The Better Angels of Our Nature: Why Violence Has Declined* (New York: Viking, 2011); Johan Norberg, *Progress: Ten Reasons to Look Forward to the Future* (London: Oneworld Publications, 2016); Peter Wagner, *Modernity as Experience and Interpretation: A New Sociology of Modernity* (Cambridge, UK: Polity, 2008).

22. For similar discussions, see Inglehart and Baker, "Modernization, Cultural Change"; Ronald Inglehart and Christian Welzel, *Modernization, Cultural Change, and Democracy: The Human Development Sequence* (New York: Cambridge University Press, 2005); Ronald Inglehart and Paul R. Abramson, "Economic Security and Value Change," *American Political Science Review* 88, no. 2 (1994), 336–354; Daniel Kahneman and Alan B. Krueger, "Developments in the Measurement of Subjective Well-being," *Journal of Economic Perspectives* 20, no. 2 (2006), 3–24; Richard A. Easterlin, "Feeding the Illusion of Growth and Happiness: A Reply to Hagerty and Veenhoven," *Social Indicators Research*, 75 (2006), 429–443.

23. E.g., Pippa Norris and Robnald Inglehart, *Sacred and Secular: Religion and Politics Worldwide* (Cambridge, UK: Cambridge University Press, 2004); Inglehart and Welzel, *Modernization, Cultural Change*; D. Alastair Hay, "An Investigation into the Swiftness and Intensity of Recent Secularization in Canada: Was Berger Right?" *Sociology of Religion* 75, no. 1 (2014), 136–162; Peter Beyer, "Religious Vitality in Canada: The Complementarity of Religious Market and Secularization Perspectives," *Journal for the Scientific Study of Religion* 36, no. 2 (1997), 272–288; Charles Taylor, *A Secular Age* (Cambridge, MA: The Belknap Press, 2007); Charles Taylor, *Dilemmas and Connections* (Cambridge, MA: Belknap Press, 2011); Michael Adams, *Fire and Ice: The United States, Canada and the Myth of Converging Values* (Toronto, Canada: Penguin, 2004).

24. See Mann, *The Wizard and the Prophet*; Norris and Inglehart, *Sacred and Secular*; Inglehart and Abramson, "Economic Security and Value Change."

25. Collins, "C-Escalation and D-Escalation."
26. Similar to "intergroup threat theory"; see Stephan et al., "Intergroup Threat Theory."
27. See Debbie Elliott, "New Orleans Struggles with Murder Rates and Trust," NPR News, July 6, 2012; Douglas Belkin, "Chicago Hunts for Answers to Gang Killings: Police Build Facebook-Like Database to Prevent Swift Cycles of Retaliation," Wall Street Journal, July 13, 2012, A3.
28. Christopher E Paine et al., "The Arsenals of the Nuclear Weapons Powers: An Overview," Natural Resources Defense Council (Canberra Commission Issue Paper), January 4, 1996.
29. Vu Trong Khanh and Jenny W. Hsu, "Anti-China Riots Rattle Vietnam," Wall Street Journal, May 16, 2014, A8.
30. Lolita C. Baldor (Associated Press), "U.S. Sending Military Equipment to 7 European Countries," USA Today, June 23, 2015.
31. E.g., "failed states" and "legitimation crisis"; see Jürgen Habermas, Legitimation Crisis (Boston, MA: Beacon Press, 1975).
32. Joseph Henrich et al., "War Increases Religiosity," Nature: Human Behavior 3, no. 2 (2019), 129–135.
33. Arab Human Development Report 2004, Available at www.undp.org/rbas/adhr.
34. Gabriel Gatehouse, "Can Somalia's Cheap Peacekeeping Defeat al-Shabaab?" BBC, June 11, 2012.
35. Damian Cave (of the New York Times), Newshour with Jim Lehrer, PBS, August 9, 2007.
36. Jason Beaubien, "El Salvador Fears Ties Between Cartels, Street Gangs," NPR News, June 1, 2011.
37. David M. Davies, "In Honduras, Gangs Tell Boys to Join or be Killed," NPR News, July 5, 2014.
38. Manny Fernandez and Mitchell Ferman, "Living Well at the Border, Creased by Drug Money," New York Times, February 19, 2019, A10.
39. Kevin Sieff et al., "Now Joining the Fight Against CV: The World's Armed Rebels, Drug Cartels, and Gangs," Washington Post, April 14, 2020.
40. BBC, "How Coronavirus Inspired a Gangland Truce in South Africa," April 8, 2020.
41. Amanda Woods, "The Mafia Is Thriving During Italy's Coronavirus Lockdown," New York Post, April 20, 2020.

42. Jennifer Merolla et al., "Authoritarianism, Need for Closure, and Conditions of Threat," in Extremism and the Psychology of Uncertainty, eds. Michael A. Hogg and Danielle L. Blaylock (West Sussex, UK: Wiley-Blackwell, 2011), Chapter 13.
43. Madeleine Albright, Fascism: A Warning (New York: HarperCollins, 2018).
44. Ernesto Londono and Manuela Andreoni, "Fighting Violence with Violence, Police Kill Nearly 5 People a Day in Brazil," New York Times, May 27, 2019, A5.
45. Timothy J. Lombardo, Blue-collar Conservatism: Frank Rizzo's Philadelphia and Populist Politics (Philadelphia, PA: University of Pennsylvania Press, 2018), 49–77.
46. Ali Soufan, Anatomy of Terror: From the Death of bin Laden to the Rise of the Islamic State (New York: W. W. Norton, 2017).
47. Max Fisher, "Israel, Riding Nationalist Tide, Puts Identity First. It Isn't Alone," New York Times, July 23, 2018, A1 & A7.
48. Mujib Mashal and Jawad Sukhanyar, "Afghan Suicide Attack on Anti-Violence Clerics," New York Times, June 5, 2018, A9.
49. Andrew E. Kramer, "More Afghan Civilians Are Victims of Targeted Attacks, U.N. says," New York Times, February 16, 2018, A10.
50. Craig Nelson, "U.S. Report Points to Setbacks in Afghanistan," Wall Street Journal, May 2, 2018, A1 & A8.
51. David Zucchino, "For Afghan Civilians, 2018 Was the Deadliest in a Decade," New York Times, February 25, 2019, A7.
52. Stuart Miller, "'Cartel Land': Drug Cartels and the Vigilantes Who Fight Them," Wall Street Journal, July 3, 2015, D4.
53. Golden Mitka, "My Neighbour Is a Rapist," BBC, July 16, 2018.
54. Kai Schultz and Suhasini Raj, "After Girl's Rape, India Recoils at 'the Depravity and Horror,'" New York Times, July 19, 2018, A4.
55. David Luhnow, "400 Murders a Day: The Crisis in Latin America," Wall Street Journal, September 20, 2018, A1 & A9.
56. Ibid., A1 & A9.
57. Kaufman, Modern Hatreds; Gaylin, Hatred.
58. Randall Collins, Violence: A Micro-Sociological Theory (Princeton, NJ: Princeton University Press, 2008), 19–20.
59. Albright, Fascism.
60. Kaufman, Modern Hatreds.

61. John Lukacs, *Democracy and Populism: Fear and Hatred* (New Haven, CT: Yale University Press, 2005).
62. Darren Mulloy, *American Extremism: History, Politics and the Militia Movement* (New York: Routledge, 2005).
63. Willard Gaylin, *Hatred: The Psychological Descent into Violence* (New York: Public Affairs, 2003).
64. Renee Ruble (Associated Press), "American Indians Resort to Banishment," Freerepublic.com, January 3, 2004.
65. Tresa Baldas, "Ex-Jehovah's Witnesses Break Silence on Shunning," *USA Today*, March 28, 2018, 6A.
66. Christina Flores, "FLDS People Reportedly Brace for Apocalypse on Wednesday," KUTV News, Salt Lake City. April 5, 2016.
67. Kaufman, *Modern Hatreds*, 207.
68. Paul Singer, "White Christians Decline in USA but Dominate GOP," *USA Today*, September 6, 2017, 5A.
69. See Ahmed, *Journey into Europe*, 249–304.
70. See Samuel P. Huntington, *The Clash of Civilization and the Remaking of World Order* (New York: Simon & Schuster, 2011); Charles Kurzman, *The Missing Martyrs: Why There Are So Few Muslim Terrorists* (New York: Oxford University Press, 2011); Benjamin Barber, *Jihad vs. McWorld: Terrorism's Challenge to Democracy* (New York: Ballantine Books, 1996).
71. For related coverage, see Kurzman, *The Missing Martyrs*; Carl Ernst and Richard Martin, "Introduction: Toward a Post-Orientalist Approach to Islamic Religious Studies," in *Rethinking Islamic Studies: From Orientalism to Cosmopolitanism*, eds. Carl Ernst and Richard Martin (Columbia, SC: University of South Carolina Press, 2010), 1–23; John L. Esposito and Dalia Mogahed, *Who Speaks for Islam? What a Billion Muslims Really Think* (New York: Gallup Press, 2008); Steven Fish, *Are Muslims Distinctive: A Look at the Evidence* (New York: Oxford University Press, 2011).
72. Tariq Modood, "Is There a Crisis of Secularism in Western Europe?" *Sociology of Religion* 73, no. 2 (2012), 143.
73. Chua, *Political Tribes*, 137–164.
74. Philip Dray, *At the Hands of Persons Unknown: The Lynching of Black America* (New York: Modern Library, 2003).
75. Linda Gordon, *The Second Coming of the KKK: The Ku Klux Klan of the 1920s and the American Political Tradition* (New York: Liveright Publishing, 2017).
76. E.g., "power-devaluation theory" of Roy McVeigh, *The Rise of the Ku Klux Klan: Right-wing Movements and National Politics* (Minneapolis, MN: University of Minnesota Press, 2009).
77. E.g., "superiority complex" by Alfred Adler, *Understanding Human Nature* (Eastford, CT: Martino Fine Books, 2010 [1927]).
78. Mona Mahmoud and Mike Lanchin, "Basra Militants Targeting Women," BBC, November 15, 2007; AFP (Agence France Presse), "Islamic State Executing 'Educated Women' in New Wave of Horror: UN," from NDTV.com, January 21, 2015; Soraya S. Nelson, "Despite Dangers, Afghan Girls Determined to Learn," NPR News, May 1, 2009.
79. Elaine Weiss, *The Woman's Hour: The Great Fight to Win the Vote* (New York: Viking, 2018).
80. Matthew Haag, "The Equal Rights Amendment Was Just Ratified by Illinois. What Does That Mean?" *New York Times*, May 31, 2018.
81. Pew Research Center, "The Narrowing, but Persistent, Gender Gap in Pay," FactTank News in the Numbers, March 22, 2019.
82. Rob Picheta and Kieron Michandani, "Only Six Countries Have Equal Rights for Men and Women, World Bank Finds," CNN, March 2, 2019.
83. Candace Smith, "Some White Trump Supporters Fear Becoming Minority," ABC News, November 2, 2016.
84. According to Heidi Beirich, director of the Southern Poverty Law Center's Intelligence Project, from Kelly Weill, "From El Paso to Christchurch, a Racist Lie Is Fueling Terrorist Attacks," *The Daily Beast*, August 5, 2019.
85. Martha C. Nussbaum, *The Monarchy of Fear: A Philosopher Looks at Our Political Crisis* (New York: Simon & Schuster, 2018), 97–134; Smith, "Some White Trump Supporters."
86. Christian Devenport et al., *Repression and Mobilization* (Minneapolis, MN: University of Minnesota Press, 2005).
87. William Crotty, "Democratization and Political Terrorism," in *Democratic Development & Political Terrorism: The Global Perspective*, ed. William Crotty (Lebanon, NH: Northeastern University Press, 2005), 10–11.
88. U.S. Government Printing Office, *The 9/11 Commission Report: Final Report of the*

National Commission on Terrorist Attacks upon the United States (Washington, D.C., 2004), 47–55.

89. Fareed Zakaria, Global Public Square (GPS), CNN, Podcast, April 21, 2014; Andrew J. Bacevich, *America's War for the Greater Middle East: A Military History* (New York: Random House, 2016).

90. Bobby Ghosh, "Why They Hate Each Other," *Time*, March 5, 2007, 28–40.

91. Ian McGregor et al., "Religious Zeal After Goal Frustration," in *Extremism and the Psychology of Uncertainty*, eds. Michael A. Hogg and Danielle L. Blaylock (West Sussex, UK: Wiley-Blackwell, 2011), Chapter 9.

92. Adam Kirsch, "Michel Houellebecq's Sexual Dystopia," *New York Times Review*, June 9, 2018, 17.

93. Catherine Porter, "Thousands March in Toronto After Van Attack," *New York Times*, April 30, 2018, A7; Amanda Taub, "On Social Media's Fringes, Growing Extremism Targets Women," *New York Times*, May 9, 2018.

94. See Bert Useem, "Breakdown Theories of Collective Action," *Annual Review of Sociology* 24 (1998), 215–238; Max Herman, *Fighting in the Streets: Ethnic Succession and Urban Unrest in Twentieth-Century Urban America* (New York: Peter Lang Publishing, 2005), 152; Susan Olzak and Suzanne Shanahan, "Deprivation and Race Riots: An Extension of Spileman's Analysis," *Social Forces* 74, no. 3 (1996), 945; Susan Olzak et al., "Poverty, Segregation, and Race Riots: 1960 to 1993," *American Sociological Review* 61, no. 4 (1996), 604.

95. Clark McPhail, "Civil Disorder Participation: A Critical Examination of Recent Research," *American Sociological Review* 36, no. 6 (1971), 1058–1073; Anthony Oberschall, "The Los Angeles Riot of August 1965," *Social Problems* 15, no. 3 (1968), 322–341; Nathan Caplan and Jeffery M. Paige, "A Study of Ghetto Rioters," *Scientific American* 219, no. 2 (1968), 15–21.

96. See Michael Hechter et al., "Grievances and the Genesis of Rebellion: Mutiny in the Royal Navy, 1740 to 1820," *American Sociological Review*. 81, no. 1 (2016), 165–189; Doug McAdam et al., *Comparative Perspectives on Social Movements* (New York: Cambridge, 1996); Marice Pinard, *Motivational Dimensions in Social Movements and Contentious Collective Action* (Montreal Canada: McGill-Queen's University Press, 2011); Robert Benford and David Snow, "Framing Processes and Social Movements," *Annual Review of Sociology* 26 (2000), 611–639; Andrew Walder, "Political Sociology and Social Movements," *Annual Review of Sociology* 35 (2009), 393–412.

97. See Hechter et al., "Grievances and the Genesis of Rebellion"; Lars-Erik Cederman et al., *Inequality, Grievances, and Civil War* (New York: Cambridge University Press, 2013).

98. Juta Kawalerowicz and Michael Biggs, "Anarchy in the UK: Economic Deprivation, Social Disorganization, and Political Grievances in the London Riot of 2011," *Social Forces* 94, no. 2 (2015), 673–698.

99. See Carles Boix, *Democracy and Redistribution* (Cambridge, UK: Cambridge University Press, 2003); Daron Acemoglu and James A. Robinson, *Economic Origins of Dictatorship and Democracy* (Cambridge, UK: Cambridge University Press, 2005); Graeme C. Blair et al., "Poverty and Support for Militant Politics: Evidence from Pakistan," *American Journal of Political Science* 57, no. 1 (2013), 30–48.

100. Dave Cullen, *Parkland: Birth of a Movement* (New York: Harper Collins, 2019); Collins, *Violence*, 413–430.

101. Kawalerowics and Biggs, "Anarchy in the UK"; Michael Keith, *Race, Riots, and Policing: Lore and Disorder in a Multi-Racist Society* (London: UCI Press, 1993); Wayne A. Santoro and Lisa Broidy, "Gendered Rioting: A General Strain Theoretical Approach," *Social Forces* 93, no. 1 (2014), 329–354.

102. Collins, *Violence*, 413–430.

103. Charles Russel and Bowman Miller, "Profile of a Terrorist," *Terrorism* 1, no. 1 (1977), 17–34.

104. Kawalerowicz and Biggs, "Anarchy in the UK."

105. Alan B. Krueger, *What Makes a Terrorist: Economics and the Roots of Terrorism* (Princeton, NJ: Princeton University Press, 2007); Petter Nesser, *Jihad in Europe—A Survey of the Motivations for Sunni Islamist Terrorism in Post-Millennium Europe* (Oslo, Norway: Norwegian Defense Research Establishment, 2004).

106. Mortimer B. Zuckerman, "Confronting the Threat," *U.S. News & World Report* (Op-Ed), August 1, 2005, 68.

107. Hannah Beech and Jason Gutierrez, "From Charming Couple to Recruiters for ISIS," *New York Times*, March 24, 2019, A6.

108. BBC World Service Newshour, April 24, 2019.

109. Morgan Winsor and Dragana Jovanovic, "ISIS Claims Responsibility for Sri Lanka Easter Bombings That Killed Over 300," ABC News, April 23, 2019; Beech and Gutierrez, "From Charming Couple."
110. Geoffrey Rohinson, from Clyde Haberman, "A 200-Year-Old Lesson on Mass Killings from Southeast Asia," *New York Times*, December 11, 2017, A18.
111. Volkan, *Blind Trust.*
112. Gideon Rachman, *Easternization: Asia's Rise and America's Decline* (New York, NY: Other Press, 2017).
113. See Orville Schell and John Delury, "A Rising China Needs a New National Story," *Wall Street Journal*, July 13–14, 2013, C3; Andrew Browne, "Mao Now," *Wall Street Journal*, May 14–15, 2016, C1.
114. Fareed Zakaria, Global Public Square (GPS), CNN, April 21, 2014.
115. See Stephen F. Cohen, *Soviet Fates and Lost Alternatives: From Stalinism to the New Cold War* (New York: Columbia University Press, 2011); Zakaria, GPS, April 21, 2014; Samantha Power, "A Question of Honor," *Time* (Op-Ed), August 25, 2008, 22; Paul R. Pillar, from Jonathan Marcus, "Russia and the West: Where Did It All Go Wrong?" BBC, October 17, 2016.
116. Associated Press, "Text: Bin Laden's Statement," *The Guardian*, October 7, 2001.
117. Jessica Stern, "Militant Groups: Beneath Bombast and Bombs, a Cauldron of Humiliation," *Los Angeles Times* (Op-Ed), June 6, 2004; Jessica Stern, *Terror in the Name of God: Why Religious Militants Kill* (New York: Harper Perennial, 2004), 32–62.
118. Ghristophe Guillur, *Twilight of the Elites: Prosperity, the Periphery, and the Future of France,* translated by Malcolm DeBevoise (New Haven, CT: Yale University Press, 2019).
119. BBC World Service Newshour, September 10, 2016.
120. BBC Inquiry, "How Has the U.S. Gun Lobby Been So Successful," January 26, 2016.
121. Tom Beyerlein and Valerie Lough, "Growing Culture: Militia Mentality," *Dayton Daily News*, April 4, 2010, A8; Joshua R. Miller, "Michigan Militia Group Preparing for Antichrist, Web Site Says," FOX News, March 29, 2010.
122. Gordon, *The Second Coming of the KKK.*
123. Mohammed Tawfeeq, "Iraq Protests Death Toll Rises to 300 with Nearly 15,000 Injured," CNN, November 9, 2019.
124. Pascal-Emmanuel Gobry, "The Failure of the French Elite," *Wall Street Journal*, February 23–24, 2019, C1 & C2.
125. See Bacevich, *America's War for the Greater Middle East.*
126. Malcolm Fairbrother, "Economists, Capitalists, and the Making of Globalization: North American Free Trade in Comparative-Historical Perspective," *American Journal of Sociology* 119, no. 5 (2014), 1324–1379.
127. Lise M. Howard, "U.S. Foreign Policy Habits in Ethnic Conflict," *International Studies Quarterly* 59, no. 4 (2015), 721–734; Amy Chua, *World on Fire: How Exporting Free Market Democracy Breeds Ethnic Hatred and Global Instability* (New York: Doubleday, 2003); Alvaro Valle, "Dancing with Monsters: The U.S. Response to the 2009 Honduran Coup," *Harvard Political Review*, April 13, 2015.
128. Fareed Zakaria, "Why do they Hate us?" *Newsweek*, October 15, 2001.
129. E.g., Howard, "U.S. Foreign Policy Habits"; Chua, *World on Fire*; Noam Chomsky and Edward S. Herman, *The Washington Connection and Third World Fascism* (Atlanta, GA: Black Rose Books, 1979); Zakaria, "Why Do They Hate Us?"; Bacevich, *America's War for the Greater Middle East.*
130. See Arthur S. Alderson and Francois Nielsen, "Globalization and the Great U-Turn: Income Inequality Trends in 16 OECD Countries," *American Journal of Sociology* 107, no. 5 (2002), 1244–1299; Alan Tonelson, *The Race to the Bottom: Why a Worldwide Worker Surplus and Uncontrolled Free Trade Are Sinking American Living Standards* (Boulder, CO: Westview Press, 2000); Adrian Wood, *North-South Trade, Employment, and Inequality: Changing Fortunes in a Skill-Driven World* (New York: Oxford University Press, 1994); Thomas W. Volscho and Nathan J. Kelly, "The Rise of the Super-Rich: Power Resources, Taxes, Financial Markets, and the Dynamics of the Top 1 Percent, 1949 to 2008," *American Sociological Review* 77, no. 5 (2012), 679–699; Christopher Kellmeyer and Florian Pichler, "Is Deindustrialization Causing High Unemployment in Affluent Countries? Evidence from 16 OECD Countries, 1970–2003," *Social Forces* 91, no. 3 (2013), 785–812.
131. E.g., Nathan M. Jensen and Guillermo Rosas, "Foreign Direct Investment and Income Inequality in Mexico, 1990–2000," *International Organization* 61, no. 3 (2007),

467–487; Phillip G. Cerny, "Globalization and the Erosion of Democracy," *European Journal of Political Research* 36, no. 1 (2003), 1–26; Yunus Kaya, "Globalization and Industrialization in 64 Developing Countries, 1980–2003," *Social Forces* 88, no. 3 (2010), 1153–1182.

132. Kevin D. Curwin and Matthew C. Mahutga, "Foreign Direct Investment and Economic Growth: New Evidence from Post-Socialist Transition Countries," *Social Forces* 92, no. 3 (2014), 1159–1187.

133. Graeme B. Robertson and Emmanuel Teitelbaum, "Foreign Direct Investment, Regime Type, and Labor Protest in Developing Countries," *American Journal of Political Science* 55, no. 3 (2011), 665–677.

134. E.g., neocolonialism and world systems theories; For comparable arguments, see Bacevich 2016; Chua, *World on Fire*; Chomsky and Herman, *The Washington Connection*; Zakaria, "Why Do They Hate Us?"; Bacevich, *America's War for the Greater Middle East*.

135. Paul Kiernan, "Mining Giants Hit by Brazil Suit," *Wall Street Journal*, May 5, 2016, B3.

136. According to 2011 United Nations Environmental Program Commission report; from "Pollution from Oil Industry Extensive," *Los Angeles Times*, August 5, 2011.

137. BBC, "Nigerian Attack Closes Oilfield," June 19, 2008; Sam Olukoya, "Africa's Rain of Fire," CBC Dispatches (podcast), September 1, 2008.

138. BBC World Service Newshour, October 30, 2019.

139. Johaan Hari, "You Are Being Lied to About Pirates," *Huffington Post*, May 25, 2011; Mohamed Abshir Waldo, "Analysis: Somalia Piracy Began in Response to Illegal Fishing and Toxic Dumping by Western Ships Off Somali Coast," Democracynow.org, April 14, 2009.

140. Jensen and Rosas, "Foreign Direct Investment."

141. For coverage of these issues, see Enrique D. Arias and Daniel M. Goldstein, "Violent Pluralism," in *Violent Democracies in Latin America*, eds. Enrique D. Arias and Daniel M. Goldstein (Durham, NC: Duke University Press, 2010), 1–34; Ronald W. Cox, *Power and Profits: U.S. Policy in Central America* (Lexington, KY: University of Kentucky Press, 1994); Ronald W. Cox and Daniel Skidmore-Hess, *U.S. Politics and the Global Economy: Corporate Power, Conservative Shift* (Boulder, CO: Lynne Rienner, 1999); Bruce Cumings et al., *Inventing the Axis of Evil: The Truth about North Korea, Iran, and Syria* (New York: The New Press, 2004); David Gibbs, *Political Economy of Third World Intervention* (Chicago, IL: University of Chicago Press, 1991); David Gibbs, "Pretexts in U.S. Foreign Policy: The War on Terrorism in Historical Perspective," *New Political Science* 26, no. 3 (2004), 293–321; Jerry Harris, *The Dialectics of Globalization: Economic and Political Conflict in a Transnational World* (Tyne, UK: Cambridge Scholars Publishing, 2006); Alexandra Homolar, "Rebels Without a Conscience: The Evolution of the Rogue State Narrative in U.S. Security Policy," *European Journal of International Relations* 17, no. 4 (2010), 705–727; Chalmers Johnson, *Blowback: The Costs and Consequences of American Empire* (New York: Holt Paperbacks, 2004); Chalmers Johnson, *The Sorrows of Empire: Militarism, Secrecy and the End of the Republic* (New York: Metropolitan Books, 2004); Chalmers Johnson, *Nemesis: The Last Days of the American Republic* (New York: Metropolitan Books, 2007); Associated Press, "A Look at the Operation Condor Conspiracy in South America," *New York Times*, May 27, 2016; BBC, "Operation Condor: Landmark Human Rights Trial Reaches Finale," May 27, 2016.

142. James Buchan, *Days of God: The Revolution in Iran and Its Consequences* (New York: Simon and Schuster, 2013), 257; Andrew Glass, "Eisenhower Approves Coup in Iran, August 19, 1963," Politico, August 19, 2018.

143. Roger Morris, "A Tyrant 40 Years in the Making," *New York Times*, March 14, 2003.

144. Stephen Zunes, "The U.S. Role in the Honduras Coup and Subsequent Violence," *Huffington Post*, June 19, 2016; Valle, "Dancing with Monsters."

145. Valle, "Dancing with Monsters."

146. Nick Cumming-Bruce, "Oil Industry May Be Tied to 'Astonishing Brutality' in South Sudan, Panel Says," *New York Times*, February 21, 2019, A4; Matina Stevis-Gridneff, "Oil Revenues Seen Fueling War, Atrocities," *Wall Street Journal*, February 21, 2019, A16.

147. Michael Mandelbaum, *Mission Failure: America and the World in the Post-Cold War Era* (Oxford, UK: Oxford University Press, 2016); Antonia Juhasz, "As the U.S.

Discusses Staying in Iraq for 50+ Years, the Bush Administration and Congressional Democrats Push for Iraq to Open Its Oil Fields to Foreign Oil Companies," Democracynow.org, June 6, 2007.

148. NPR News, November 12, 2006.

149. Juhasz, "As the U.S. Discusses Staying in Iraq"; BBC, "Iraq Contracts Won by Bush Donors," October 31, 2003; Democracynow.org, January 8, 2007.

150. BBC, "Iraq Contracts Won by Bush Donors."

151. Jake Tapper, "Iraq Windfall: Corporations Benefit from Costs of Iraq Reconstruction," ABC News, September 6, 2003; Sally Denton, *The Profiteers: Bechtel and the Men Who Built the World* (New York: Simon & Schuster, 2016).

152. Ronald W. Cox, "The Military-Industrial Complex and U.S. Military Spending after 9/11," *Class, Race and Corporate Power* 2, no. 2 (2014), Article 5.

153. *Ibid.*, 2–3.

154. Hope Yen (Associated Press), "9/11 Panel Disputes Iraq Link to Attacks," Yahoo News, June 16, 2004; Suzanne Goldenberg, "Bush: Saddam Was Not Responsible for 9/11," *The Guardian*, September 11, 2006; Jean E. Smith, *Bush* (New York: Simon & Schuster, 2016), 326–356.

155. Cox, "The Military-Industrial Complex."

156. Pierre Razoux, *The Iran-Iraq War*, translated by Nicholas Elliott (Cambridge, MA: Belknap Press, 2015); Tony Paterson, "Leaked Reports Says German and U.S. Firms Supplied Arms to Saddam," *The Independent*, December 18, 2002.

157. Thom Shanker, "U.S. Sold $40 Billion in Weapons in 2015, Topping Global Market," *New York Times*, December 27, 2016.

158. Jeffrey E. Stern, "Tracing a Tragedy in Yemen Back to an American Bomb Factory," *New York Times Magazine*, December 16, 2018, 40–47, 65; Declan Walsh and Eric Schmitt, "Arms Sales to Saudis Leave American Fingerprints on Yemen's Carnage," *New York Times*, December 25, 2018.

159. Alexia F. Campbell, "Trump Says Selling Weapons to Saudi Arabia Will Create a Lot of Jobs. That's Not True," VOX.com, November 20, 2018.

160. Jonathan Cristol, "Trump's Yemen Veto Sets State for Potential Supreme Court Confrontation," CNN, April 17, 2019.

161. BBC, "Yemen War: Trump Vetoes Bill to End U.S. Support for Saudi-led Coalition," April 17, 2019.

162. Term used by Emile Durkheim, *The Division of Labor in Society*, Translation by George Simpson (New York: Macmillan, 1964 [1933]).

163. From Gregory Baum, *Nationalism, Religion, and Ethics* (Quebec City, Canada: McGill-Queen's University Press, 2001), 33–34.

164. From *Ibid.*, 86–88.

165. Christopher A. Bail, *Terrified: How Anti-Muslim Fringe Organizations Became Mainstream* (Princeton, NJ: Princeton University Press, 2014); Michael Kinsley, "The Religious Superiority Complex," *Time*, November 3, 2003,106.

166. David Brooks, "Death of Multiculturalism a Boon to Dems," *Dayton Daily News* (Op-Ed), May 1, 2006, A15.

167. See Dawne Moon, "Who Am I and Who Are We. Conflicting Narratives of Collective Selfhood in Stigmatized Groups," *American Journal of Sociology* 117, no. 5 (2012), 1336–1379; Francis Stewart, *Horizontal Inequalities and Conflict: Understanding Group Violence in Multiethnic Societies* (New York: Palgrave MacMillan, 2008).

168. Elizabeth Long, *Book Clubs: Women and the Uses of Reading in Everyday Life* (Chicago, IL: University of Chicago Press, 2003).

169. Gary A. Fine, "Group Culture and the Interaction Order: Local Sociology on the Meso-Level," *Annual Review of Sociology* 38 (2012), 159–179.

170. Sebastian Junger, *War* (New York: Twelve Publisher, 2010); Sebastian Junger, *Tribe: On Homecoming and Belonging* (New York: Twelve Publisher, 2016).

171. PBS Newshour, March 19, 2007.

172. Robert J. Lifton, *Home from the War—Vietnam Veterans: Neither Victims nor Executioners* (New York: Simon & Schuster, 1973).

173. Martin Chulov, "ISIS: The Inside Story," *The Guardian*, December 11, 2014.

174. David Greene, "Time in a U.S.-run Detention Center Helped Islamic State Leadership," NPR News, December 12, 2014.

175. Noemie Bisserbe, "Europe's Prisons Fuel Spread of Radicalism," *Wall Street Journal*, August 1, 2016, A1 & A6.

176. Eleanor Beardsley, "Inside French Prisons, A Struggle to Combat Radicalization," NPR News, June 25, 2017.

177. Bisserbe, "Europe's Prisons Fuel."

178. BBC World Service Newshour, October 11, 2016; Denis MacEoin, "Prisons: Harvard for Radicals," Gatestone Institute, September 6, 2016; Raphael Rowe, "From Jail to Jihad? The Threat of Prison Radicalization," BBC, May 12, 2014; Sajid Iqbal and Noel Titheradge, "Prison Islam Course 'Could Turn Prisoners to Violence,'" BBC, June 2, 2016.

179. Soeren Kern, "Britain: Muslim Prison Population up 200%," Gatestone Institute, August 2, 2013; Rowe, "From Jail to Jihad?"

180. E.g., "severe initiation costs"; see Martha Crenshaw, "Theories of Terrorism: Instrumental and Organizational Approaches," in *Inside Terrorist Organizations*, ed. David C. Rapoport (Portland, OR: Frank Cass, 2001), 23.

181. Edward N. Muller and Mitchell A. Seligson, "Inequality and Insurgency," in *Development and Underdevelopment: The Political Economy of Global Inequality*, ed. Mitchell A. Seligson and John T. Passe-Smith (3rd Edition) (Boulder, CO: Lynne Rienner Publishers, 2003), 88–91; Edward N. Muller and Erich Weede, "Cross-national Variations in Political Violence: A Rational Action Approach," *Journal of Conflict Resolution* 34, no. 4 (1990), 624–651; Erich Weede and Edward N. Muller, "Rebellion, Violence and Revolution: A Rational Choice Perspective," *Journal of Peace Research* 35, no. 1 (1998), 43–59.

182. NPR News, October 22, 2019; Ahmed Rasheed and Ahmed Aboulenein, "Iraqi Security Forces Killed 149 Protesters, Most by Shots to Head, Chest: Government Inquiry," Reuters, October 22, 2019.

183. Associated Press, "Egypt Court Sentences 75 to Death over 2013 Sit-in," July 28, 2018.

184. Ben Hubbard and Karam Shoumali, "Scores of Syrian Prisoners Died in Custody, Families Are Told," *New York Times*, July 27, 2018, A1 & A9.

185. Frances Robles, "Protests in Nicaragua Leave at Least 15 Dead," *New York Times*, June 1, 2018, A9.

186. Willie Osterweil, "Countries Around World Are Revoking Freedom of Assembly," Aljazeera America, May 4, 2015.

187. Ibid.

188. See Theda Skocpol, *States and Social Revolutions* (New York: Cambridge University Press, 1979); Randall Collins, "Maturation of the State-Centered Theory of Revolution and Ideology," *Sociological Theory* 11, no. 1 (1993), 117–128.

189. According to the United Nations Security Council, from David Shariatmadari, "Is It Time to Stop Using the Word 'Terrorist'?" *The Guardian*, January 27, 2015.

190. Georg Simmel, *Conflict*, Translated by Kurt H. Wolff and Reinhard Bendix (New York: Free Press, 1955 [1908]), 141–142.

191. Peter M. Blau, *Inequality and Heterogeneity: A Primitive Theory of Social Structure* (New York, NY: The Free Press, 1977), 129.

192. Randall Collins and Scott Coltrane, *Sociology of Marriage and the Family: Gender, Love, and Property* (Chicago, IL: Nelson-Hall Publishers, 1995), 164.

193. Randall Collins, *Four Sociological Traditions* (Oxford, UK: Oxford University Press, 1994), 189–190.

194. John Sperling et al., *The Great Divide: Retro vs. Metro America* (Sausalito, CA: PoliPoint Press, 2005).

195. Cheryl Corley et al., "Barbershop: Former Members Talk About What Led Them to Join Gangs in Chicago," NPR News, January 8, 2017.

196. David Ignatius, "Friday News Roundup—International," Diane Rehm Show, NPR News, July 27, 2007.

197. Mark Doyle, "Kenya Stokes Tribalism Debate," BBC, January 4, 2008.

198. Kaufman, *Modern Hatreds*, 5.

199. David A. Snow and Robert D. Benford, "Ideology, Frame Resonance, and Participant Mobilization," *International Social Movement Research* 1, no. 1 (1988), 197–217.

200. Neil J. Smelser, *Theory of Collective Behavior* (New York: Free Press, 1962).

201. See Manuel Castells, *Networks of Outrage and Hope: Social Movements in the Internet Age* (Malden, MA: Polity, 2012); Doug McAdam, *Political Process and the Development of Black Insurgency, 1930–1970* (Chicago, IL: University of Chicago Press, 1982).

202. See John D. McCarthy and Mayer N. Zald, "Resource Mobilization and Social Movements: A Partial Theory," *American Journal of Sociology* 82, no. 6 (1977), 1212–1241; Benford and Snow, "Framing Processes and Social Movements"; Walder, "Political Sociology and Social Movements"; Crenshaw, "Theories of Terrorism," 21.

203. William I. Brustein, *Roots of Hate: Anti-Semitism in Europe Before the Holocaust* (Cambridge, UK: Cambridge University Press, 2003).

204. Soufan, *Anatomy of Terror*, 298.
205. Ibid., 296–297.

Chapter 7

1. Dawne Moon, "Who Am I and Who Are We: Conflicting Narratives of Collective Selfhood in Stigmatized Groups," *American Journal of Sociology* 117, no. 5 (2012), 1336–1379; Andreas Wimmer and Thomas Soehl, "Blocked Acculturation: Cultural Heterodoxy Among Europe's Immigrants," *American Journal of Sociology* 120, no. 1 (2014), 146–186; Fouad Ajami, "Within the Gates," *U.S. News & World Report*, July 25, 2005, 24; Farah Pandith, *How We Win: How Cutting-Edge Entrepreneurs, Political Visionaries, Enlightened Business Leaders, and Social Media Mavens Can Defeat the Extremist Threat* (New York: Custom House Books, 2019).

2. See Bert Klandermans, Jojanneke van der Toorn, and Jacquelien van Stekelenburg, "Embeddedness and Identity: How Immigrants Turn Grievances into Action," *American Sociological Review* 73, no. 6 (2008), 992–1012; Rahsaan Maxwell and Erik Bleich, "What Makes Muslims Feel French?" *Social Forces* 93, no. 1 (2014), 155–179; William Haller, Alejandro Portes, and Scott M. Lynch, "Dreams Fulfilled, Dreams Shattered: Determinants of Segmented Assimilation in the Second Generation," *Social Forces* 89, no. 3 (2011), 733–762; Antonio J. Rojas et al., "Accumulation Preference Profiles of Spaniards and Romanian Immigrants: The Role of Prejudice and Public and Private Acculturation Areas," *The Journal of Social Psychology* 154, no. 4 (2014), 339–351; Celine Teney, "Endorsement of Assimilationism Among Ethnic Minority and Majority Youth in a Multination-Multiethnic Context: The Case of Brussels," *European Sociological Review* 27, no. 2 (2011), 212–229.

3. Wimmer and Soehl, "Blocked Acculturation"; Maxwell and Bleich, "What Makes Muslims Feel French?"; Moon, "Who Am I and Who Are We"; Fareed Zakaria, "Why Do They Hate Us?" *Newsweek*, October 15, 2001; Pandith, *How We Win*.

4. Robert Siegel, "Foreign Policy Experts Weigh in on U.S. Strategy Against the Islamic State," NPR News, May 28, 2015.

5. Pandith, *How We Win*.

6. Martha L. Cottam and Richard W. Cottam, *Nationalism & Politics: The Political Behavior of Nation States* (Boulder, CO: Lynne Rienner, 2001), 264.

7. John Heilprin, "Bush Says Kyoto Will Mean Loss of Jobs," Associated Press, February 16, 2005.

8. Juan Forero, "Bush's Aid Cuts on Court Issue Roil Latin American Neighbors," *New York Times*, August 19, 2005.

9. BBC, "INF Nuclear Treaty: U.S. Pulls Out of Cold War-era Pack with Russia," August 2, 2019.

10. See Zakaria, "Why Do They Hate Us?"; Lise M. Howard, "U.S. Foreign Policy Habits in Ethnic Conflict," *International Studies Quarterly* 59, no. 4 (2015), 721–734.

11. For discussion of this issue, see Ronald W. Cox, *Power and Profits: U.S. Policy in Central America* (University of Kentucky Press, 1994); Ronald W. Cox and Daniel Skidmore-Hess, *U.S. Politics and the Global Economy: Corporate Power, Conservative Shift* (Boulder, CO: Lynne Rienner, 1999); Bruce Cumings et al., *Inventing the Axis of Evil* (New York: New Press, 2004); David Gibbs, *Political Economy of Third World Intervention* (University of Chicago Press, 1991); David Gibbs, "Pretexts in U.S. Foreign Policy: The War on Terrorism in Historical Perspective," *New Political Science* 26, no. 3 (2004), 293–321; Jerry Harris, *The Dialectics of Globalization: Economic and Political Conflict in a Transnational World* (Newcastle, UK: Cambridge Scholars Publishing, 2006); Alexandra Homolar, "Rebels Without a Conscience: The Evolution of the Rogue State Narrative in U.S. Security Policy," *European Journal of International Relations* 17, no. 4 (2010): 705–727; Chalmers Johnson, *Blowback: The Costs and Consequences of American Empire* (New York: Holt Paperbacks, 2004); Chalmers Johnson, *The Sorrows of Empire: Militarism, Secrecy and the End of the Republic* (New York: Metropolitan Books, 2004); Chalmers Johnson, *Nemesis: The Last Days of the American Republic* (New York: Metropolitan Books, 2007); Associated Press, "A Look at the Operation Condor Conspiracy in South America," *New York Times*, May 27, 2016; BBC, "Operation Condor: Landmark Human Rights Trial Reaches Finale," May 27, 2016.

12. Howard, "U.S. Foreign Policy Habits in Ethnic Conflicts."

13. David H. Kamens, *Beyond the Nation-State: The Reconstruction of*

Nationhood and Citizenship (Bingley, U.K.: Emerald Group, 2012), 29–33.

14. For related discourses, see Sophie Body-Gendrot, *Globalization, Fear and Insecurity: The Challenges for Cities North and South* (New York: Palgrave Macmillan, 2012).

15. Lauren Frayer, "For Some U.K. Farmers, Business Looks Better Without 'Brexit,'" NPR News, May 24, 2019.

16. Natascha Divac, "Some East German Towns See Migrants as Salvation," *Wall Street Journal*, May 25, 2016, A8.

17. Ines S. Martin, "Pope Calls Gender Theory a 'Global War' Against Family," Cruxnow.com, October 1, 2016.

18. See Pippa Norris and Ronald Inglehart, *Cosmopolitan Communications: Cultural Diversity in a Globalized World* (New York: Cambridge University Press, 2009); Body-Gendrot, *Globalization, Fear and Insecurity*; M. A. Khan, "Huntington's Prophecies," *The Post Chronicle* (Commentary), January 2, 2009.

19. Charles Kurzman, *The Missing Martyrs: Why There Are So Few Muslim Terrorists* (New York: Oxford University Press, 2011); Carl Ernst and Richard Martin, *Rethinking Islamic Studies: From Orientalism to Cosmopolitanism* (Columbia: University of South Carolina Press, 2010); John L. Esposito and Dalia Mogahed, *Who Speaks for Islam? What a Billion Muslims Really Think* (New York: Gallup Press, 2008); Steven Fish, *Are Muslims Distinctive: A Look at the Evidence* (New York: Oxford University Press, 2011); Andrew J. Bacevich, *America's War for the Greater Middle East: A Military History* (New York: Random House, 2016); Zakaria, "Why Do They Hate Us?"

20. Peter Berger, *The Desecularization of the World: Resurgent Religion and World Politics* (Washington, D.C.: Ethics and Public Policy Center, 1999).

21. Benjamin Barber, *Jihad vs. McWorld: Terrorism's Challenge to Democracy* (New York: Ballantine Books, 1996).

22. Samuel P. Huntington, *The Clash of Civilization and the Remaking of World Order* (New York: Simon & Schuster, 2011).

23. Tariq Modood, "Is There a Crisis of Secularism in Western Europe?" *Sociology of Religion* 73, no. 2 (2012), 130–149.

24. John Boli and George M. Thomas, "World Culture in the World Polity: A Century of International Non-governmental Organization," *American Sociological Review* 62, no. 2 (1997), 171–190.

25. Amy Chua, *World on Fire: How Exporting Free Market Democracy Breeds Ethnic Hatred and Global Instability* (New York: Doubleday, 2003).

26. Norris and Inglehart, *Cosmopolitan Communications*, 5, 19–21; David J. Frank et al., "The Nation-state and the Natural Environment Over the Twentieth Century," *American Sociological Review* 65, no. 1 (2000), 105.

27. Mortimer B. Zuckerman, "Europe's Two Worlds," *U.S. News & World Report* (Op-Ed), July 25, 2005, 60.

28. Gabrielle Steinhauser and Kjetil M. Hovland, "EU Bickering Pauses for Nobel," *Wall Street Journal*, December 11, 2012, A12; John-Thor Dahlburg, "After Anti-EU Parties Surge, What's Ahead?" Yahoo News, May 26, 2014.

29. Craig Calhoun, *Nations Matter: Culture, History and the Cosmopolitan Dream* (New York: Routledge, 2007); Mabel Berezin, *Illiberal Politics in Neoliberal Times* (Oxford: Cambridge University Press, 2009); Michael Skey, *National Belonging and Everyday Life: The Significance of Nationhood in an Uncertain World* (New York: Palgrave Macmillan, 2011); Cynthia Miller-Idriss, *Blood and Culture: Youth, Right-wing Extremism, and National Belonging in Contemporary Germany* (Durham, NC: Duke University Press, 2009).

30. BBC World Service Newshour, June 2, 2016; Jenny Gross, "'Brexit' Vote Splits British Political Duo," *Wall Street Journal*, June 11–12, 2016, A7.

31. Skey, *National Belonging and Everyday Life*, Chapter 3.

32. Robert P. Jones, *The End of White Christian America* (New York: Simon & Schuster, 2016).

33. For similar discussions, see Arthur S. Alderson and Francois Nielsen, "Globalization and the Great U-Turn: Income Inequality Trends in 16 OECD Countries," *American Journal of Sociology* 107, no. 5 (2002), 1244–1299; Alan Tonelson, *The Race to the Bottom: Why a Worldwide Worker Surplus and Uncontrolled Free Trade Are Sinking American Living Standards* (Boulder, CO: Westview Press, 2000); Adrian Wood, *North-South Trade, Employment, and Inequality: Changing Fortunes in a Skill-Driven World* (New York: Oxford University Press, 1994); Thomas W. Volscho and Nathan J. Kelly, "The Rise of the Super-Rich: Power Resources, Taxes, Financial markets, and the Dynamics of the Top 1 Percent,

1949 to 2008," *American Sociological Review* 77(2012), 679–699; Christopher Kollmeyer and Florian Pichler, "Is Deindustrialization Causing High Unemployment in Affluent Countries? Evidence from 16 OECD Countries, 1970–2003," *Social Forces* 91(2013), 785–812; Christopher Chase-Dunn, *Global Formation: Structures of the World-Economy* (Oxford, UK: Blackwell, 1989); Joseph E. Stiglitz, *Globalization and Its Discontents* (New York: W. W. Norton, 2002).

34. Kai Ryssdal, Marketplace (podcast), July 1, 2019.

35. John Kay, *Culture and Prosperity: The Truth About Markets—Why Some Nations Are Rich but Most Remain Poor* (New York: Harper Collins Publishers, 2004), 346.

36. E.g., Frank R. Baumgartner et al., *Lobbying and Policy Change: Who Wins, Who Loses, and Why* (Chicago: University of Chicago Press, 2009); Nathalie Giger and Heike Kluver, "Voting Against your Constituents? How Lobbying Affects Representation," *American Journal of Political Science* 60, no. 1 (2016), 190–205; Christine Mahony, *Brussels versus the Beltway: Advocacy in the U.S. and the European Union* (Washington D.C.: Georgetown University Press, 2008); Joseph E. Stiglitz, *The Price of Inequality: How Today's Divided Society Endangers Our Future* (New York: W. W. Norton, 2013), Chapter 2; Jane Mayer, *Dark Money: The Hidden History of the Billionaires Behind the Rise of the Radical Right* (New York: Random House, 2016).

37. Jason W. Yackee and Susan W. Yackee, "A Bias Towards Business? Assessing Interest Group Influence on the U.S. Bureaucracy," *Journal of Politics* 68, no. 1 (2006), 128–139; Stanford C. Gordon et al., "Consumption or Investment? On Motivations for Political Giving," *Journal of Politics* 69, no. 4 (2007), 1057–1072; Wendy L. Hansen et al., "The Logic of Private and Collective Action," *American Journal of Political Science* 49, no. 1 (2005), 150–167; Brian K. Richter et al., "Lobbying and Taxes," *American Journal of Political Science* 53, no. 4 (2009), 893–909.

38. Jens Grober et al., "Political Quid Pro Quo Agreements: An Experimental Study," *American Journal of Political Science* 57, no. 3 (2013), 582–597; Mayer, *Dark Money*.

39. Paul Kiernan, "Mining Giants Hit by Brazil Suit," *Wall Street Journal*, May 5, 2016, B3.

40. Thomas Hager, *Ten Drugs: How Plants, Powders, and Pills Have Shaped the History of Medicine* (New York: Abrams Press, 2019).

41. E.g., Carlyle group; see M. Asif Ismail, "Investing in War: The Carlyle Group Profits from Government and Conflict," The Center for Public Integrity, updated on May 19, 2014 (originally published on November 19, 2004); Richard Lardner (Associated Press), "Army Says No Thanks; Tanks Keep Coming," *Dayton Daily News*, April 29, 2013, A1; Donna Cassata (Associated Press), "House OKs $633B Defense Bill," *Dayton Daily News*, December 21, 2012, A4; Roxana Tiron (Bloomberg News), "Earmark Ban Fails to Stop Lawmakers Spending Requests," *Dayton Daily News*, July 27, 2012, A2; Pamela Haag, *The Gunning of America: Business and the Making of American Gun Culture* (New York: Basic Books, 2016); William D. Hartung, *Prophets of War: Lockheed Martin and the Making of the Military-Industrial Complex* (New York: Nation Books, 2012); William D. Hartung, "Obama Admin Helps Undermine U.N. Arms Treaty Talks While Touting Record-High Weapons Sales Abroad," Democracynow.org, August 2, 2012; Emily Alpert, "Power of Global Arms Treaty Hinges on Next Steps, Activists Say," *Los Angeles Times*, April 2, 2013.

42. For example cases, see Tom Dreibach, "Tobacco's 'Special Friend': What Internal Documents Say About Mitch McConnell,'" NPR News, June 17, 2019; Brody Mullins and John D. McKinnon, "Lobbying Blitz Hits Washington," *Wall Street Journal*, January 11, 2017, A6; Shalini Ramachandran et al., "Comcast's Lobbying Machine Faces Test in Washington," *Wall Street Journal*, January 23, 2015, A1 & A12; Alicia Mundy, "Drug Industry Signals Lobbying Shift," *Wall Street Journal*, February 1, 2010, A4; Karen Tumulty and Michael Scherer, "How Drug-Industry Lobbyists Won on Health-Care," *Time*, October 22, 2009; Elizabeth Williamson and Brody Mullins, "Firms Keep Lobbying as They Get TARP Cash," *Wall Street Journal*, January 23, 2009, A4.

43. Mullins and McKinnon, "Lobbying Blitz Hits Washington."

44. Nick Visser, "White House Rolls Back Regulations Meant to Avoid the Next Deepwater Horizon," AOL.com, May 3, 2019.

45. For a similar discussion, see Dionne Searcey, "In Anti-bribery Law, Some Fear

Inadvertent Chill on Business," *Wall Street Journal*, August 6, 2009.

46. Francis X. Rocca and Farnaz Fassihi, "Pope Urges U.N. to Fight Social Injustice," *Wall Street Journal*, September 26, 2015, A5.

47. Heidi Vogt and Francis X. Rocca, "Pope Decries 'New Forms of Colonialism,'" *Wall Street Journal*, November 28-29, 2015, A10.

48. Daron Acemoglu and James A. Robinson, *Why Nations Fail: The Origins of Power, Prosperity, and Poverty* (New York: Crown Business, 2013).

49. James M. Scott and Carie A. Steele, "Sponsoring Democracy: The United States and Democracy Aid to the Developing World, 1988-2001," *International Studies Quarterly* 55, no. 1 (2011), 47-69; Burcu Savun and Daniel C. Tirone, "Foreign Aid, Democratization, and Civil Conflict: How Does Democracy Aid Affect Civil Conflicts?" *American Journal of Political Science* 55, no. 2 (2011), 233-246.

50. For similar discussions, see Marc J. Hetherington, *Why Trust Matters: Declining Political Trust and the Demise of American Liberalism* (Princeton, NJ: Princeton University Press, 2005); Thomas J. Rudolph and Jillian Evans, "Political Trust, Ideology, and Public Support for Government Spending," *American Journal of Political Science* 49, no. 3 (2005), 660-671.

51. See Sudhir A. Venkatesh, "The Social Organization of Street Gang Activity in an Urban Ghetto," *American Journal of Sociology* 103, no. 1 (1997), 82-111; Clifford R. Shaw and Henry D. McKay, *Juvenile Delinquency and Urban Areas* (Chicago: University of Chicago Press, 1942); William J. Wilson, *The Truly Disadvantaged: The Inner City, the Underclass, and Public Policy* (Chicago, IL: University of Chicago Press, 1987); Robert J. Duran, *Gang Life in Two Cities: An Insider's Journey* (New York: Columbia University Press, 2014), 66-93; Venkatesh, "The Social Organization of Street Gang"; David S. Kirk and Andrew V. Papachristos, "Cultural Mechanisms and the Persistence of Neighborhood Violence," *American Journal of Sociology* 116, no. 4 (2011), 1190-1233.

52. Steven Pinker, *The Better Angels of our Nature: Why Violence has Declined* (New York, New York: Viking, 2011).

53. Pamela Constable from NPR News, "Pakistan's Insurgency Begins at Red Mosque," Morning Edition, July 19, 2011.

54. AFP (Agence France Presse), "Islamic State Executing 'Educated Women' in New Wave of Horror: UN," January 21, 2015.

55. For similar arguments, see Kamens, *Beyond the Nation-State*, 89-121, 305-310.

56. In 2018, according to National Conference of State Legislatures.

57. According to Center for American Progress, 2018.

58. For the 2017-2018 school year, according to CollegeBoard.org.

59. According to Census Bureau's ACS survey.

60. See Cottam and Cottam, *Nationalism & Politics*, 268-269.

61. Nathan Hodge and Eghsanullah Amiri, "Afghan Candidates Court Minorities," *Wall Street Journal*, March 8, 2014, A9.

62. PBS, "Reconstruction: America after Civil War," PBS Documentary, aired on April 9 & 16, 2019.

63. Steve Peoples (Associated Press), "Religious Conservatives Asked to Back GOP Plans," *Houston Chronicle*, June 15, 2013.

64. Edward N. Muller and Mitchell A. Seligson, "Inequality and Insurgency," in *Development and Underdevelopment: The Political Economy of Global Inequality*, eds. Mitchell A. Seligson and John T. Passe-Smith (3rd Edition) (Boulder, CO: Lynne Rienner Publishers, 2003), 88-89.

65. See Peter M. Blau, *Inequality and Heterogeneity: A Primitive Theory of Social Structure* (New York: Free Press, 1977), 326.

66. James Bryce from Yehoshua Arieli, "Individualism and National Identity," in *American Chameleon: Individualism in Trans-national Context*, eds. Richard O. Curry and Lawrence B. Goodheart (Kent, OH: The Kent State University Press, 1991), 168.

67. Paul Starr, *Freedom's Power: The True Force of Liberalism* (New York, NY: Basic Books, 2007), 155-159.

68. See Karl Polanyi, *The Great Transformation: The Political and Economic Origin of Our Time* (New York: Farrar & Rinehart, 1944); Yehoshua Arieli, *Individualism and Nationalism in American Ideology* (Baltimore, MD: Penguin Books, 1966), 287.

69. Bernard E. Harcourt, *The Illusion of Free Markets: Punishment and the Myth of Natural Order* (Cambridge, MA: Harvard University Press, 2011).

70. From Arieli, *Individualism and Nationalism*, 176-177.

71. *Ibid.*, 225-226.

72. Richard O. Curry and Lawrence B. Goodheart, "Individualism in Trans-national Context," in *American Chameleon: Individualism in Trans-National Context*, eds. Richard O. Curry and Lawrence B. Goodheart (Kent, OH: Kent State University, 1991), 30.

73. From Arieli, *Individualism and Nationalism*, 237.

74. See Kim Pernell-Gallagher, "Learning from Performance: Banks, Collateralized Debt Obligations, and the Credit Crisis," *Social Forces* 94, no 1 (2015), 31–59; Neil Fligstein and Alexander F. Roehrkasse, "The Causes of Fraud in the Financial Crisis of 2007 to 2009: Evidence from the Mortgage-backed Securities Industry," *American Sociological Review* 81, no. 4 (2016), 617–643.

75. Ben S. Bernanke, *The Courage to Act: A Memoir of a Crisis and Its Aftermath* (W. W. Norton, 2015).

76. Jonathan Swift, "Lest We Forget: Why We Had a Financial Crisis," *Forbes*, November 22, 2011.

77. Kamens, *Beyond the Nation-State*.

78. Matthews S. Levendusky, "Why Do Partisan Media Polarize Viewers?" *American Journal of Political Science* 57, no. 3 (2013), 611–623.

79. Kay, *Culture and Prosperity*, 349.

80. Tovia Smith, "Companies 'Named and Shamed' for Bad Behavior," NPR News, March 7, 2010.

81. Tim Bartley, "Institutional Emergence in an Era of Globalization: The Rise of Transnational Private Regulation of Labor and Environmental Conditions," *American Journal of Sociology* 113, no. 2 (2007), 297–351; Joshua W. Busby, *Moral Movements and Foreign Policy* (New York: Cambridge University Press, 2010); Timothy Werner, *Public Forces and Private Politics in American Big Business* (New York: Cambridge University Press, 2012).

82. Richard N. Haass, "The Isolationist Temptation," *Wall Street Journal*, August 5, 2016, C1 & C2.

83. See Steve Coll, *Private Empire: ExxonMobil and American Power* (New York: Penguin Books, 2013); Stiglitz, *Globalization and its Discontents*, 166–179.

84. For similar discussions, see Malcolm Fairbrother, "Economists, Capitalists, and the Making of Globalization: North American Free Trade in Comparative-Historical Perspective," *American Journal of Sociology* 119, no. 5 (2014), 1324–1379; Jeff Faux, "The Party of Davos," *The Nation*, February 13, 2006; Sarah A. Soule, *Contention and Corporate Social Responsibility* (New York: Cambridge University Press, 2009); Bartley, "Institutional Emergence"; Tagi Sagafi-Nejad, *The UN and Transnational Corporations: From Code of Conduct to Global Compact* (Bloomington, IN: Indiana University Press, 2008); David Rothkopf, "Command and Control: Fixing Capitalism Means Taking Power Back from Business," *Time*, January 30, 2012, 44–46.

85. From Zygmunt Bauman, *Liquid Modernity* (Cambridge: Polity Press, 2000), 192.

86. Fairbrother, "Economists, Capitalists, and the Making of Globalization."

87. BBC, "Full Text: Bin Laden Tape," April 15, 2004; Associated Press, "Text: Bin Laden's Statement," *The Guardian*, October 7, 2001.

88. For similar discussions, see Faux, "The Party of Davos"; Chua, *World on Fire*.

89. Mortimer B. Zuckerman, "In for the Grim Long Haul," *U.S. News & World Report* (Op-Ed), June 14, 2004, 84.

90. See Starr, *Freedom's Power*, 220.

91. Cottam and Cottam, *Nationalism & Politics*, 268–269.

92. See Adrian Goldsworthy, *Pax Romana: War, Peace and Conquest in the Roman World* (London: Weidenfeld & Nicolson, 2016).

93. See David Held, "Democracy, the Nation-state and the Global System," In *Political Theory Today*, ed. David Held (Cambridge, UK: Polity Press, 1991), 232–233.

94. Ibid., 233, 259.

95. James Goodman, "The European Union: Democracy Beyond the Nation State," in *The Transformation of Democracy*, ed. Anthony McGrew (Cambridge, UK: Polity Press, 1997), 171–200.

96. Richard Falk, *On Humane Governance: Toward a New Global Politics* (Cambridge, UK: Polity Press, 1995), 7.

97. Ibid., 120.

98. Emilie N. Hafner-Burton and Kiyoteru Tsutsui, "Human Rights in a Globalizing World: The Paradox of Empty Promises," *American Journal of Sociology* 110, no. 5 (2005), 1373–1411; Wade M. Cole and Francisco O. Ramirez, "Conditional Decoupling: Assessing the Impact of National Human Rights Institutions, 1981–2004," *American Sociological Review* 78, no. 4 (2013), 702–725.

99. Barbara Wejnert, "Diffusion, Development, and Democracy, 1800-1999," *American Sociological Review* 70, no. 1 (2005), 53-81; Magnus Torfason and Paul Ingram, "The Global Rise of Democracy: A Network Account," *American Sociological Review* 75, no. 3 (2010), 355-377.

100. David J. Frank, "Science, Nature, and the Globalization of the Environment, 1870-1990," *Social Forces* 76, no. 2 (1997), 409-437; Evan Schofer and Ann Hironaka, "The Effects of World Society on Environmental Protection Outcomes," *Social Forces* 84, no. 1 (2005), 25-47.

101. Francisco O. Ramirez et al., "The Changing Logic of Political Citizenship: Cross-National Acquisition of Women's Suffrage Rights, 1890 to 1990," *American Sociological Review* 62, no. 5 (1997), 735-745; Pamela Paxton et al., "The International Women's Movement and Women's Political Representation, 1893-2003," *American Sociological Review* 71, no. 6 (2006), 898-920.

102. E.g., Farnaz Fassihi, "U.S. Envoy Brings Tough Talk to U.N.," *Wall Street Journal*, January 28-29, 2017, A6; Andrew Moravcsik, "Negotiating the Single European Act: National Interests and Conventional Statecraft in the European Community," *International Organization* 45 (1991), 19-57; Andrew Moravcsik, *The Choice for Europe: Social Purposes and State Power from Messina to Maastricht* (Ithaca, NY: Cornell University Press, 1998).

103. Moravcsik, "Negotiating the Single European Act"; Moravcsik, *The Choice for Europe*.

104. E.g., Robert H. Wade, "The Rising Inequality of World Income Distribution," in *Development and Underdevelopment: The Political Economy of Global Inequality*, eds. Mitchell A. Seligson and John T. Passe-Smith, 3rd Edition (Boulder, CO: Lynne Rienner, 2003), 39; Sarah Babb, *Behind the Development Banks: Washington Politics, World Poverty, and the Wealth of Nations* (Chicago: University of Chicago Press, 2009); Elizabeth Smythe, "In Whose Interests? Transparency and Accountability in the Global Governance of Food: Agribusiness, the Codex Alimentarius, and the World Trade Organization," in *Corporate Power in Global Agrifood Governance*, eds. Jennifer Clapp and Doris Fuchs (Cambridge, MA: MIT Press, 2009), 93-124; Faux, "The Party of Davos."

105. Babb, *Behind the Development Banks*.

106. Stiglitz, *Globalization and Its Discontents*, 89-132, 193-213.

107. Busby, *Moral Movements and Foreign Policy*.

108. Alpert, "Power of Global Arms Treaty."

109. PRI's Market Place, December 5, 2019.

110. Brooke Singman, "Global Battle Erupts as Trump Pulls WHO Funding over Coronavirus Response," Fox News, April 15, 2020.

111. From Raymond A. Belliotti, *Seeking Identity: Individualism versus Community in an Ethnic Context* (Lawrence, KS: University Press of Kansas, 1995), 151.

112. See Kay, *Culture and Prosperity*, 347.

113. Ibid., 106.

114. Erich Weede and Edward N. Muller, "Consequences of Revolutions," *Rationality and Society* 9, no. 3 (1997), 327-350.

115. Mordechai Rotenberg, "Alienating-individualism and Reciprocal-individualism: A Cross-cultural Conceptualization," *Journal of Humanistic Psychology* 17, no. 4 (1997), 3-17.

116. See Robert N. Bellah et al., *Habits of the Heart: Individualism and Commitment in American Life* (New York: Harper & Row, 1985), 192.

117. Walter T. Davis, "Economic Individualism and Social Disorder: The Power of Submerged Ideology," *Second Order* 6, no. 2 (1977), 21-43.

118. From Stephen Engstrom, "The Concept of the Highest Good in Kant's Moral Philosophy," *Philosophy and Phenomenological Research* 51, no. 4 (1992), 747-780.

119. Curry and Goodheart, "Individualism in Trans-national Context," 3-4; Bellah et al., *Habits of the Heart*, 192.

120. From Steven Lukes, "Durkheim's Individualism and the Intellectuals," *Political Studies* 17 (1969), 23-24.

121. Ibid., 23-24.

122. Of Émile Durkheim, from Anthony Giddens, *Profiles and Critiques in Social Theory* (Berkeley, CA: University of California Press, 1982), 45, 72.

123. Jonathan Haidt, "Romney, Obama and the New Culture War Over Fairness," *Time*, October 8, 2012.

124. Ibid.

125. See Katherine S. Newman and Rourke L. O'Brien, *Taxing the Poor: Doing*

Damage to the Truly Disadvantaged (Berkeley, CA: University of California Press, 2011); Volscho and Kelly, "The Rise of the Super-Rich," 679–699; Shane Croucher, "Trump's 2017 Tax Cuts Helped Super-rich Pay Lower Rate Than Bottom 50 Percent: Economists," *Newsweek*, October 9, 2019.

126. Bellah et al., *Habits of the Heart*, 161.

127. Georg Simmel, *On Individuality and Social Forms*, ed. with an introduction by Donald N. Levine (Chicago, IL: University of Chicago Press, 1971 [1908]).

128. Ibid., 272.

129. Arieli, *Individualism and Nationalism*, 209.

130. Quoted in Nathan Sharansky, "Identity, Freedom, or Both?" *U.S. News & World Report*, June 30, 2008, 30.

131. E.g., Paul E. Sigmund, *The Selected Political Writings of John Locke* (New York: W. W. Norton, 2005); Walt Whitman, *Leaves of Grass: The Original 1855 Edition* (Mineola, NY: Dover Publications, 2007 [1855]); Robert E. Shalhope, "Individualism in the Early Republic," in *American Chameleon: Individualism in Trans-National Context*, eds. Richard O. Curry and Lawrence B. Goodheart (Kent, OH: Kent State University, 1991), 76; Curry and Goodheart, "Individualism in Trans-national Context"; Arieli, "Individualism and National Identity"; Amitai Etzioni, *Spirit of Community* (New York, NY: Crown Publisher, 1993); Amitai Etzioni, "The Responsive Community: A Communitarian Perspective," *American Sociological Review* 61, no. 1 (1996), 1–11.

132. Thomas S. Weisner, "Culture, Childhood, and Progress in Sub-Saharan Africa," in *Culture Matters: How Values Shape Human Progress*, eds. Laurence E. Harrison and Samuel P. Huntington (New York: Basic Books, 2001), 155; John W. Meyer, "Myths of Socialization and Personality," in *Reconstructing Individualism*, eds. T.C. Heller and E. Wellbery (Stanford, CA: Stanford University Press, 1986), 216; Wade M. Cole, "Human Rights as Myth and Ceremony? Reevaluating the Effectiveness of Human Rights Treaties, 1981–2007," *American Journal of Sociology* 117, no. 4 (2012), 1131–1171.

133. Arieli, *Individualism and Nationalism*, 315–316.

134. Jill L. Harrison, *Pesticide Drift and the Pursuit of Environmental Justice* (Cambridge, MA: MIT Press, 2011), 1–24.

135. Jim Hightower, "It's Up to You," Alternative Radio, April 30, 2020.

136. See Arieli, *Individualism and Nationalism*, 193; A. S. Waterman, "Individualism and Interdependence," *American Psychologist* 36, no. 7 (1981), 767–772.

137. Waterman, "Individualism and Interdependence," 767–768.

138. Irene T. Thomson, *Culture Wars and Enduring American Dilemmas* (Ann Arbor, MI: University of Michigan Press, 2010).

139. Chua, *World on Fire*.

140. Robert Reich, "Five Prerequisites for War Against the Islamic State," *Dayton Daily News* (Op-Ed), November 26, 2015, A22.

141. Ben Casselman, "Slowing Growth Stirs Recovery Fears," *Wall Street Journal*, April 28, 2012, A1 & A2; Jon Hilsenrath and Conor Dougherty, "Inside the Disappointing Comeback," *Wall Street Journal*, July 5, 2011, A6.

142. James Mackintosh, "15,000 Layoffs? How a Bust in China Became the West's Suffering," *Wall Street Journal*, April 1, 2016, C1.

143. CNN, May 19, 2020.

144. BBC World Service Newshour, March 25, 2020.

145. Anthony Giddens, *The Consequences of Modernity* (Stanford, CA: Stanford University Press, 1990), 169.

146. See Albert Bandura, "Mechanisms of Moral Engagement," In *Origins of Terrorism: Psychologies, Ideologies, Theologies, States of Mind*, ed. Walter Reich (Washington D.C.: Woodrow Wilson Center Press, 1998), 166; D. J. C. Carmichael, "Of Beasts, Gods, and Civilized Men: The Justification of Terrorism and of Counterterrorist Measures," *Terrorism* 6 (1982), 1–26; Audrey Cronin, *How Terrorism Ends: Understanding the Decline and Demise of Terrorist Campaigns* (Princeton, NJ: Princeton University Press, 2011).

147. See Martha Crenshaw, "Theories of Terrorism: Instrumental and Organizational Approaches," in *Inside Terrorist Organizations*, ed. David C. Rapoport (Portland, OR: Frank Cass, 2001), 13–31.

148. Human Rights Institute, "Accountability for 'Targeted Killings' and Drone Strikes," (Columbia Law School, 2014). Available at https://web.law.columbia.edu/human-rights-institute/counterterrorism/accountability-targeted-killings-drone-strikes.

149. Jonathan Mummolo, "Militarization Fails to Enhance Police Safety or Reduce Crime but May Harm Police Reputation," *PNAS (Proceedings of the National Academy of Sciences)* 115, no. 37 (2018), 9181–9186.

150. Jesse Pang, "Violence Spreads Across Hong Kong's New Territories in 24th Weekend of Unrest," Reuters, November 10, 2019.
151. Magia Bahari, from Fareed Zakaria GPS, CNN, December 8, 2019.
152. See Natalie Y. Moore, *The South Side: A Portrait of Chicago and American Segregation* (New York: St. Martin's Press, 2016); Duran, *Gang Life in Two Cities*, 66–93.
153. See Bacevich, *America's War for the Greater Middle East*.
154. Fairbrother, "Economists, Capitalists, and the Making of Globalization."
155. For further examination of these issues, see Enrique D. Arias and Daniel M. Goldstein, "Violent Pluralism," in *Violent Democracies in Latin America* (Durham, NC: Duke University Press, 2010); Cox, *Power and Profits*; Cox and Skidmore-Hess, *U.S. Politics and the Global Economy*; Cumings et al., *Inventing the Axis of Evil*; Gibbs, *Political Economy of Third World Intervention*; Gibbs, "Pretexts in U.S. Foreign Policy"; Harris, *The Dialectics of Globalization*; Homolar, "Rebels Without a Conscience"; Johnson, *Blowback*; Johnson, *The Sorrows of Empire*; Johnson, *Nemesis*; Howard, "U.S. Foreign Policy Habits in Ethnic Conflict"; Chua, *World on Fire*; Associated Press, "A Look at the Operation Condor"; BBC World Service Newshour, May 27, 2016.
156. Zakaria, "Why Do They Hate Us?"
157. For related discourses, see Howard, "U.S. Foreign Policy Habits in Ethnic Conflict"; Zakaria, "Why Do They Hate Us?"; Noam Chomsky and Edward S. Herman, *The Washington Connection and Third World Fascism* (Atlanta, GA: Black Rose Books, 1979).
158. See Eitan Y. Alimi et al., *The Dynamics of Radicalization: A Relational and Comparative Perspective* (New York, NY: Oxford University Press, 2004); Jessica Stern, "Militant Groups: Beneath Bombast and Bombs, a Cauldron of Humiliation," *Los Angeles Times* (Op-Ed), June 6, 2004.
159. Susan Page, "Poll Shows Divide Between Muslims, West," *USA Today*, June 22, 2006.
160. Sibylla Brodzinsky, "Colombia on the Brink of Peace: Why Is It Such a Hard Sell to Citizens?" *Christian Science Monitor*, June 23, 2016; Dan Molinski and Sara S. Munoz, "Colombia Widens Peace Talks Before Vote," *Wall Street Journal*, June 10, 2014, A8; Juan Forro and Sara S. Munoz, "Columbia, Guerrillas Reach Breakthrough," *Wall Street Journal*, September 24, 2015, A11.
161. Terrence Lyons, "Abiy's Nobel Achievements Are Real but Brittle," *Foreign Policy*, October 12, 2019.
162. Sewell Chan, "Nobel Peace Prize Is Awarded to National Dialogue Quartet in Tunisia," *New York Times*, October 9, 2015.
163. Nick Hawton, "Bosnia's Quiet Army Revolution Finds Fans," BBC, October 9, 2003.
164. Don Melvin (Cox News Service), "CARE Finds Ways to Bridge Ethnic Divide in Kosovo," *Dayton Daily News*, September 24, 2003, A5.
165. Michael Elliott, "The Real Reason Americans Bash the French," *Time*, September 29, 2004, 53.
166. BBC World Service Newshour, April 31, 2019.
167. Ruud Koopmans, "Explaining the Rise of Racist and Extreme Right Violence in Western Europe: Grievances or Opportunities," *European Journal of Political Research* 20 (1996), 185–216.
168. Ekkart Zimmermann, "Right-wing Extremism and Xenophobia in Germany: Escalation, Exaggeration, or What?" in *Right-wing Extremism in the Twenty-first Century*, eds. Peter H. Herkl and Leonard Weinberg (Portland, OR: Frank Cass, 2003), 220–250.
169. Michael Moran (Council on Foreign Relations), "Terrorist Groups and Political Legitimacy," *Backgrounder*, March 16, 2006.
170. Ibid.
171. Ruth Alexander, "Can You Make Gangs Good?" BBC Inquiry, May 4, 2019.
172. Crenshaw, "Theories of Terrorism," 25.
173. Sibylla Brodzinsky, "Colombia on the Brink of Peace: Why Is It Such a Hard Sell to Citizens?" *Christian Science Monitor*, June 23, 2016; Dan Molinski and Sara S. Munoz, "Colombia Widens Peace Talks Before Vote," *Wall Street Journal*, June 10, 2014, A8; Juan Forro and Sara S. Munoz, "Columbia, Guerrillas Reach Breakthrough," *Wall Street Journal*, September 24, 2015, A11.
174. Moran, "Terrorist Groups and Political Legitimacy."
175. Peter H. Merkl and Leonard Weinberg, "Introduction," in *Right-wing Extremism in the Twenty-first Century*, eds. Peter H. Merkl and Leonard Weinberg (Portland, OR: Frank Cass, 2003), 18.
176. David Leonhardt, "Capitalism Needs

Elizabeth Warren," *New York Times* (Op-Ed), March 17, 2019.

177. Paul Hannon, "Shrinking Middle Class Threatens Global Growth, Stability," *Wall Street Journal,* April 10, 2019; Liz Alderman, "The Middle Class Shrinks in Europe," *New York Times,* February 16, 2019, B1 & B4.

178. Salman Rushdie, "India and Pakistan's Code of Dishonor," *New York Times* (Op-Ed), July 10, 2005 (Section 4), 13; Thomas L. Friedman, "Foreign Policy: Take Steps to Promote Our Values, Emphasize What Works," *New York Times* (Op-Ed), May 28, 2004; Zakaria, "Why Do They Hate Us?"

Conclusion

1. Irwin Arieff, "World Leaders Warn Terror War Abuses Fuel Militants," *New York Times,* September 22, 2003.

Bibliography

Aberson, Christopher L., Michael Healy, and Victoria Romero. "Ingroup Bias and Self-esteem: A Meta-analysis." *Personality and Social Psychology Review* 4, no. 2 (2000): 157–173.
Acemoglu, Daron, and James A. Robinson. *Economic Origins of Dictatorship and Democracy.* Cambridge, UK: Cambridge University Press, 2005.
Acemoglu, Daron, and James A. Robinson. *Why Nations Fail: The Origins of Power, Prosperity, and Poverty.* New York: Crown Business, 2013.
Adams, Michael. *Fire and Ice: The United States, Canada and the Myth of Converging Values.* Toronto: Penguin 2004.
Adarves-Yorno, Inmaculada, Jolanda Jetten, Tom Postmes, and S. Alexander Haslam. "What Are We Fighting For? The Effects of Framing on Ingroup Identification and Allegiance." *The Journal of Social Psychology* 153, no. 1 (2013): 25–37.
Adler, Alfred. *Understanding Human Nature.* Eastford, CT: Martino Fine Books, 2010 [1927].
Adogame, Afe, and James V. Spickard. *Religion Crossing Boundaries: Transnational Religious and Social Dynamics in Africa and the New African Diaspora.* Leiden: Brill Press, 2010.
Adogame, Afe, and Shobana Shankar. *Religion on the Move! New Dynamics of Religious Expansion in a Globalizing World.* Leiden: Brill Press, 2013.
Adorno, T. W., Else Frenkel-Brunswik, Daniel J. Levinson, and R. Nevitt Sanford. *The Authoritarian Personality.* New York: Harper & Brothers, 1950.
Ahmed, Akbar. *Journey into Europe: Islam, Immigration, and Identity.* Washington, D.C.: Brookings Institution Press, 2018.
Albright, Madeleine. *Fascism: A Warning.* New York: HarperCollins, 2018.
Alderson, Arthur S., and Francois Nielsen. "Globalization and the Great U-Turn: Income Inequality Trends in 16 OECD Countries." *American Journal of Sociology* 107, no. 5 (2002): 1244–1299.
Alexander, Jeffrey C. "Cultural Pragmatics: Social Performance Between Ritual and Strategy." In *Social Performance: Symbolic Action, Cultural Pragmatics, and Ritual,* edited by Jeffrey C. Alexander, Bernhard Giesen, and Jason L. Mast. New York: Cambridge University Press, 2006.
Alimi, Eitan Y., Chares Demetriou, and Lorenzo Bosi. *The Dynamics of Radicalization: A Relational and Comparative Perspective.* New York: Oxford University Press, 2014.
Allen, Arthur. *The Fantastic Laboratory of Dr. Weigl.* New York: Norton, 2014.
Altemeyer, Bob. *Enemies of Freedom: Understanding Right-wing Authoritarianism.* San Francisco: Jossey-Bass, 1988.
Altemeyer, Bob. *The Authoritarian Spector.* Cambridge, MA: Harvard University Press, 1996.
Altemeyer, Bob. "The Other 'Authoritarian Personality.'" In *Advances in Experimental Social Psychology, Vol. 30,* edited by M. P. Zanna, 47–92. New York: Academic Press, 1998.
Anbinder, Tyler. *City of Dreams: The 400-Year Epic History of Immigrant New York.* New York: Houghton Mifflin Harcourt, 2016.
Anderson, Elijah. *Code of the Street: Decency, Violence, and the Moral Life of the Inner City.* New York: W.W. Norton, 2000.
Andreescu, Viviana, John Eagle Shutt, and Gennaro F. Vito. "The Violent South: Culture of

Honor, Social Disorganization, and Murder in Appalachia." *Criminal Justice Review* 36, no. 1 (2011): 76–103.
Appiah, Kwame A. *The Honor Code: How Moral Revolutions Happen.* New York: W. W. Norton, 2010.
Applebaum, Anne. *Red Famine: Stalin's War on Ukraine.* New York: Doubleday, 2017.
Apter, David. "Political Religion in the New Nations." In *Old Societies and New States*, edited by C. Geertz, 57–104. New York: Free Press, 1964.
Arai, Tatsushi. "When the Waters of Culture and Conflict Meet." In *Conflict Across Cultures: A Unique Experience of Bridging Differences*, edited by Michelle Lebaron and Venashri Pillay. Boston: Intercultural Press, 2006.
Arias, Enrique D., and Daniel M. Goldstein. "Violent Pluralism." In *Violent Democracies in Latin America*, edited by Enrique D. Arias and Daniel M. Goldstein, 1–34. Durham, NC: Duke University Press, 2010.
Arieli, Yehoshua. "Individualism and National Identity." In *American Chameleon: Individualism in Trans-national Context*, edited by Richard O. Curry and Lawrence B. Goodheart, 167–187. Kent, OH: The Kent State University Press, 1991.
Arieli, Yehoshua. *Individualism and Nationalism in American Ideology.* Baltimore: Penguin Books, 1966.
Aslan, Reza. *Beyond Fundamentalism: Confronting Religious Extremism in the Age of Globalization.* New York: Random House, 2010.
Babb, Sarah. *Behind the Development Banks: Washington Politics, World Poverty, and the Wealth of Nations.* Chicago: University of Chicago Press, 2009.
Bacevich, Andrew J. *America's War for the Greater Middle East: A Military History.* New York: Random House, 2016.
Bail, Christopher A. *Terrified: How Anti-Muslim Fringe Organizations Became Mainstream.* Princeton, NJ: Princeton University Press, 2014.
Baker, Joseph O. "Social Sources of the Spirit: Connecting Rational Choice Theory and Interactive Ritual Theories in the Study of Religion." *Sociology of Religion* 71, no. 4 (2010): 1–25.
Balch, Robert W., and David Taylor. "Making Sense of the Heaven's Gate Suicides." In *Cults, Religion and Violence*, 209–228. London: Cambridge University Press, 2002.
Balibar, Etienne. "Racism and Nationalism." In *Race, Nation, Class: Ambiguous Identities*, edited by E. Balibar and I. Wallerstein, 37–67. New York: Verso, 1991.
Balkin, Karen F., ed. *Extremist Groups.* Farmington Hills, MI: Greenhaven Press, 2005.
Bandura, Albert. "Mechanisms of Moral Engagement." In *Origins of Terrorism: Psychologies, Ideologies, Theologies, States of Mind*, edited by Walter Reich, 161–191. Washington, D.C.: Woodrow Wilson Center Press, 1998.
Bapat, Navin A., and Sean Zeigler. "Terrorism, Dynamic Commitment Problems, and Military Conflict." *American Journal of Political Science* 60, no. 2 (2016): 337–351.
Barber, Benjamin. *Jihad vs. McWorld: Terrorism's Challenge to Democracy.* New York: Ballantine Books, 1996.
Barker, Tom, and David Carter. "'Fluffing Up the Evidence and Covering Your Ass: Some Conceptual Notes on Police Lying." *Deviant Behavior* 11, no. 1 (1990): 61–73.
Barkun, Michael. *Religion and the Racist Right: The Origins of the Christian Identity Movement.* Chapel Hill: University of North Carolina Press, 1997.
Barth, Fredrik. "Introduction." In *Ethnic Groups and Boundaries: The Social Organization of Culture Difference*, edited by Fredrik Barth, 6–38. Long Grove, IL: Waveland Press, 1998.
Bartley, Tim. "Institutional Emergence in an Era of Globalization: The Rise of Transnational Private Regulation of Labor and Environmental Conditions." *American Journal of Sociology* 113, no. 2 (2007): 297–351.
Batson, C. Daniel, Christopher L. Kennedy, Lesley A. Nord, E. L. Stocks, D'Yani A. Fleming, Christian M. Marzette, and Tricia Zerger. "Anger at Unfairness: Is It Moral Outrage?" *European Journal of Social Psychology* 37 (2007): 1272–1285.
Batson, C. Daniel, Mary D. Chao, and Jeffrey M. Givens. "Pursuing Moral Outrage: Anger at Torture." *Journal of Experimental Social Psychology* 45, no. 1 (2009): 155–160.
Baum, Gregory. *Nationalism, Religion, and Ethics.* Quebec City, Canada: McGill-Queen's University Press, 2001.
Bauman, Zygmunt. "Cultural Variety or Variety of Cultures." In *Making Sense of Collectivity:*

Ethnicity, Nationalism and Globalisation, edited by Sinisa Malesevic and Mark Haugaard, 167–180. London: Pluto Press, 2002.
Bauman, Zygmunt. *Liquid Modernity.* Cambridge, UK: Polity Press, 2000.
Baumgartner, Frank R., Jeffrey M. Berry, Marie Hojnacki, David C. Kimball, and Beth Seech. *Lobbying and Policy Change: Who Wins, Who Loses, and Why.* Chicago: University of Chicago Press, 2009.
Beck, Colin J., and Emily Miner. "Who Gets Designated a Terrorist and Why?" *Social Forces* 91, no. 3 (2013): 837–872.
Belew, Kathleen. *Bring the War Home: The White Power Movement and Paramilitary America.* Cambridge, MA: Harvard University Press, 2018.
Belin, Célia. "Old Enmities or New Beginnings?" In *The Second Bush Presidency: Global Perspectives,* edited by Amit Gupta and Cherian Samuel, 83–105. New York: Dorling Kindersley, Pearson Longman, 2006.
Bellah, Robert N., Richard Maddsen, Rilliam M. Sullivan, Ann Swidler, and Steven M. Tipton. *Habits of the Heart: Individualism and Commitment in American Life.* New York: Harper & Row, 1985.
Belliotti, Raymond A. *Seeking Identity: Individualism versus Community in an Ethnic Context.* Lawrence: University Press of Kansas, 1995.
Ben-Yehuda, Nachman. "The European Witchcraze." In *Social Deviance,* 3rd edition, edited by Ronald Farrell and Victoria Swigert, 41–49. Belmont, CA: Wadsworth, 1988.
Benford, Robert, and David Snow. "Framing Processes and Social Movements." *Annual Review of Sociology* 26 (2000): 611–639.
Berdahl, Jennifer L. "The Sexual Harassment of Uppity Women." *Journal of Applied Psychology* 92, no. 2 (2007): 425–437.
Berejikian, Jeffrey D. "Model Building with Prospect Theory: A Cognitive Approach to International Relations." *Political Psychology.* 23, no. 4 (2002): 759–786.
Berezin, Mabel. *Illiberal Politics in Neoliberal Times.* Oxford: Cambridge University Press, 2009.
Berger, Peter. *The Desecularization of the World: Resurgent Religion and World Politics.* Washington, D.C.: Ethics and Public Policy Center, 1999.
Berman, Paul. *Terror and Liberalism.* New York: W. W. Norton, 2003.
Bernanke, Ben S. *The Courage to Act: A Memoir of a Crisis and Its Aftermath.* W. W. Norton, 2015.
Beyer, Peter. "Religious Vitality in Canada: The Complementarity of Religious Market and Secularization Perspectives." *Journal for the Scientific Study of Religion* 36, no. 2 (1997): 272–288.
Birdsall, Nancy, and Richard Sabot. "Inequality as a Constraint on Growth in Latin America." In *Development and Underdevelopment: The Political Economy of Global Inequality,* 3rd Edition, edited by Mitchell A. Seligson and John T. Passe-Smith, 449–456. Boulder, CO: Lynne Rienner Publishers, 2003.
Bjørgo, Tore. "Extreme Nationalism and Violent Discourses in Scandinavia: 'The Resistance,' 'Traitors,' and 'Foreign Invaders.'" In *Terror from the Extreme Right,* 182–220. London: Frank Cass, 1995.
Bjørgo, Tore. "Introduction." In *Terror from the Extreme Right.* 1–16. London: Frank Cass, 1995.
Blair, Graeme C., Christine Fair, Neil Malhotra, and Jacob N. Shapiro. "Poverty and Support for Militant Politics: Evidence from Pakistan." *American Journal of Political Science* 57, no. 1 (2013): 30–48.
Blau, Peter M. *Inequality and Heterogeneity: A Primitive Theory of Social Structure.* New York: Free Press, 1977.
Blumer, Herbert. "Race Prejudice as a Sense of Group Position." *The Pacific Sociological Review* 1, no. 1 (1958): 3–7.
Body-Gendrot, Sophie. *Globalization, Fear and Insecurity: The Challenges for Cities North and South.* New York: Palgrave Macmillan, 2012.
Boix, Carles. *Democracy and Redistribution.* Cambridge, UK: Cambridge University Press, 2003.
Bol, Thijs, and Kim A. Weeden. "Occupational Closure and Wage Inequality in Germany and the United Kingdom." *European Sociological Review* 31, no. 3 (2015): 354–369.
Boli, John, and George M. Thomas. "World Culture in the World Polity: A Century of International Non-governmental Organization." *American Sociological Review* 62, no. 2 (1997): 171–190.

Bonilla-Silva, Eduardo. "From Bi-racial to Tri-racial: Towards a New System of Racial Stratification in the USA." *Ethnic and Racial Studies* 27, no. 6 (2004): 931–950.
Boyns, David, and James D. Ballard. "Developing a Sociological Theory for the Empirical Understanding of Terrorism." *The American Sociologist* 35, no. 2 (2004): 5–25.
Branscombe, Nyla R., Naomi Ellemers, Russell Spears, and Bertjan Doosje. "The Context and Content of Social Identity Threat." In *Social Identity: Context, Commitment, Content*, edited by Naomi Ellemers, Russell Spears, and Bertjan Doosje, 35–58. Hoboken, NJ: Wiley-Blackwell, 1999.
Brenneman, Robert. *Homies and Hermanos: God and Gangs in Central America*. New York: Oxford University Press, 2011.
Brewer, Marilynn B. "The Psychology of Prejudice: Ingroup Love or Outgroup Hate?" *Journal of Social Issues* 55, no. 3 (1999): 429–444.
Britt, Lory, and David R. Heise. "From Shame to Pride in Identity Politics." In *Self, Identity, and Social Movements*, eds. S. Stryker, T.J. Owens, and R. W. White, 252–271. Minneapolis: University of Minnesota Press, 2000.
Broockman, David E. "Black Politicians Are More Intrinsically Motivated to Advance Blacks' Interests: A Field Experiment Manipulating Political Incentives." *American Journal of Political Science* 57, no. 3 (2013): 521–536.
Brooks, Clem and Jeff Manza. *Whose Rights? Counterterrorism and the Dark Side of American Public Opinion*. New York: Russell Sage Foundation, 2013.
Brown, Kerry, and Simone van Nieuwenhuizen. *China and the New Maoists*. London: Zen Books, 2016.
Brubaker, Rogers. *Grounds for Difference*. Cambridge, MA: Harvard University Press, 2015.
Bruce, Steve. *God Is Dead: Secularization in the West*. Oxford, UK: Blackwell, 2002.
Brunson, Rod K. "Police Don't Like Black People: African American Young Men's Accumulated Police Experiences." *Criminology and Public Policy* 6 (2007): 71–101.
Brustein, William. *The Logic of Evil: The Social Origins of the Nazi Party, 1925–1933*. New Haven, CT: Yale University Press, 1996.
Brustein, William I. *Roots of Hate: Anti-Semitism in Europe Before the Holocaust*. Cambridge, UK: Cambridge University Press, 2003.
Buchan, James. *Days of God: The Revolution in Iran and Its Consequences*. New York: Simon & Schuster, 2013.
Burger, Jerry M., Nicole Messian, Shebani Patel, Alicia del Prado, and Carmen Anderson. 2004. "What a Coincidence! The Effects of Incidental Similarity on Compliance." *Personality and Social Psychology Bulletin* 30 (2004): 35–43.
Burris, Val. "Interlocking Directorates and Political Cohesion Among Corporate Elites." *American Journal of Sociology* 111, no. 1 (2005): 249–283.
Busby, Joshua W. *Moral Movements and Foreign Policy*. New York: Cambridge University Press, 2010.
Byfield, Natalie P. *Savage Portrayals: Race, Media, and the Central Park Jogger Story*. Philadelphia, PA: Temple University Press, 2014.
Calhoun, Craig J. *Nations Matter: Culture, History and the Cosmopolitan Dream*. New York: Routledge, 2007.
Calhoun, Craig J. *The Roots of Radicalism: Tradition, the Public Sphere, and Early Nineteenth Century Social Movements*. Chicago: University of Chicago Press, 2012.
Campbell, David E. John C. Green, and Geoffrey C. Layman. "The Party Faithful: Partisan Images, Candidate Religion, and the Electoral Impact of Party Identification." *American Journal of Political Science* 55, no. 1 (2011): 42–58.
Canetti-Nisim, Daphna, Eran Halperin, Keren Sharvit, and Stevan E. Hobfoll. "A New Stress-Based Model of Political Extremism: Personal Exposure to Terrorism, Psychological Distress, and Exclusionist Political Attitudes." *Journal of Conflict Resolution* 53, no. 3 (2009): 363–389.
Caplan, Nathan, and Jeffery M. Paige. "A Study of Ghetto Rioters." *Scientific American* 219, no. 2 (1968): 15–21.
Carley, Kathleen M. "A Theory of Group Stability." *American Sociological Review* 56, no. 3 (1991): 331–354.
Carmichael, D. J. C. "Of Beasts, Gods, and Civilized Men: The Justification of Terrorism and of Counterterrorist Measures." *Terrorism* 6 (1982): 1–26.

Bibliography

Carroll, William K. *The Making of a Transnational Capitalist Class: Corporate Power in the 21st Century*. New York: Zed Books, 2010.
Castells, Manuel. *Networks of Outrage and Hope: Social Movements in the Internet Age*. Malden, MA: Polity Press, 2012.
Castro, Carl A., Sara Kintzle, Ashley C. Schuyler, Carrie L. Lucas, and Christopher H. Warner. "Sexual Assault in the Military." *Current Psychiatry Reports* 17, no. 7 (2015): 54–67.
Cederman, Lars-Erik, Kristian S. Gleditsch, and Halvard Buhaug. *Inequality, Grievances, and Civil War*. New York: Cambridge University Press, 2013.
Cerny, Phillip G. "Globalization and the Erosion of Democracy." *European Journal of Political Research* 36, no. 1 (2003): 1–26.
Chagnon, Napoleon. *Noble Savages: My Life Among Two Dangerous Tribes—the Yanomamo and the Anthropologists*. New York: Simon & Schuster, 2014.
Chase-Dunn, Christopher. *Global Formation: Structures of the World-Economy*. Oxford: Blackwell, 1989.
Chin, Gabriel J., and Scott Wells. "'The Blue Wall of Silence' as Evidence of Bias and Motive to Lie: A New Approach to Police Perjury." *University of Pittsburgh Law Review* 59 (1998): 233–299.
Chomsky, Noam, and Edward S. Herman. *The Washington Connection and Third World Fascism*. Atlanta: Black Rose Books, 1979.
Chua, Amy. *Political Tribes: Group Instinct and the Fate of Nations*. New York: Penguin Press, 2018.
Chua, Amy. *World on Fire: How Exporting Free Market Democracy Breeds Ethnic Hatred and Global Instability*. New York: Doubleday, 2003.
Clark, Robert P. "Patterns in the Lives of ETA Members." *Terrorism* 6, no. 3 (1988): 423–454.
Clarke, Sathianathan. *Competing Fundamentalisms: Violent Extremism in Christianity, Islam, and Hinduism*. New York: Routledge, 2017.
Cloward, Richard, and Lloyd Ohlin. *Delinquency and Opportunity: A Theory of Delinquent Gangs*. New York: Free Press, 1966.
Cohen, Albert. *Delinquent Boys: The Culture of the Gang*. New York: Free Press, 1955.
Cohen, Stephen F. *Soviet Fates and Lost Alternatives: From Stalinism to the New Cold War*. New York: Columbia University Press, 2011.
Cole, Wade M. "Human Rights as Myth and Ceremony? Reevaluating the Effectiveness of Human Rights Treaties, 1981–2007." *American Journal of Sociology* 117, no. 4 (2012): 1131–1171.
Cole, Wade M. and Francisco O. Ramirez. "Conditional Decoupling: Assessing the Impact of National Human Rights Institutions, 1981–2004." *American Sociological Review* 78, no. 4 (2013): 702–725.
Coll, Steve. *Private Empire: ExxonMobil and American Power*. New York: Penguin Books, 2013.
Collins, Patricia H. "The New Politics of Community." *American Sociological Review* 75, no. 1 (2010): 7–30.
Collins, Randall. "C-Escalation and D-Escalation: A Theory of the Time-Dynamics of Conflict." *American Sociological Review* 77, no. 1 (2012): 1–20.
Collins, Randall. *Four Sociological Traditions*. New York: Oxford University Press, 1994.
Collins, Randall. *Interaction Ritual Chains*. Princeton NJ: Princeton University Press, 2004.
Collins, Randall. "Maturation of the State-Centered Theory of Revolution and Ideology." *Sociological Theory* 11, no. 1 (1993): 117–128.
Collins, Randall. *Sociological Insight: An Introduction to Non-Obvious Sociology*. New York: Oxford University Press, 1992.
Collins, Randall. "The Contentious Social Interactionism of Charles Tilly." *Social Psychology Quarterly* 73, no. 1 (2010): 5–10.
Collins, Randall. *The Credential Society: An Historical Sociology of Education and Stratification*. Cambridge, MA: Academic Press, 1979.
Collins, Randall. *Violence: A Micro-Sociological Theory*. Princeton, NJ: Princeton University Press, 2008.
Collins, Randall, and Scott Coltrane. *Sociology of Marriage and the Family: Gender, Love, and Property*. Chicago: Nelson-Hall Publishers, 1995.
Connor, Walker. *Ethnonationalism: The Quest for Understanding*. Princeton, NJ: Princeton University Press, 1994.

Costa, Dora L., and Matthew E. Kahn. *Heroes and Cowards: The Social Face of War.* Princeton, NJ: Princeton University Press, 2008.
Cottam, Martha L., and Richard W. Cottam. *Nationalism & Politics: The Political Behavior of Nation States.* Boulder, CO: Lynne, Rienner, 2001.
Cottee, Simon. *The Apostates: When Muslims Leave Islam.* London: Hurst, 2015.
Cox, Ronald W. *Power and Profits: U.S. Policy in Central America.* Lexington: University Press of Kentucky, 1994.
Cox, Ronald W. "The Military-Industrial Complex and U.S. Military Spending after 9/11." *Class, Race and Corporate Power* 2, no. 2 (2014): Article 5.
Cox, Ronald W., and Daniel Skidmore-Hess. *U.S. Politics and the Global Economy: Corporate Power, Conservative Shift.* Boulder, CO: Lynne Rienner, 1999.
Cravalho, Mark A. "Toast on Ice: the Ethnopsychology of the Winter-over Experience in Antarctica." *Ethos* 24 (1996): 628–656.
Crenshaw, Martha. "Theories of Terrorism: Instrumental and Organizational Approaches." In *Inside Terrorist Organizations,* edited by David C. Rapoport, 13–31. Portland: Frank Cass, 2001.
Cronin, Audrey. *How Terrorism Ends: Understanding the Decline and Demise of Terrorist Campaigns.* Princeton, NJ: Princeton University Press, 2011.
Crotty, William. "Democratization and Political Terrorism." In *Democratic Development & Political Terrorism: The Global Perspective,* edited by William Crotty, 3–16. Boston: Northeastern University Press, 2005.
Crotty, William. "International Terrorism: Causes and Consequences for a Democratic Society." In *Democratic Development & Political Terrorism: The Global Perspective,* edited by William Crotty, 523–531. Boston: Northeastern University Press, 2005.
Cullen, Dave. *Parkland: Birth of a Movement.* New York: HarperCollins, 2019.
Cumings, Bruce, Ervand Abrahamian, and Moshe Maoz. *Inventing the Axis of Evil: The Truth about North Korea, Iran, and Syria.* New York: The New Press, 2004.
Currie, Elliot P. "Crimes Without Criminals: Witchcraft and Its Control in Renaissance Europe." *Law and Society Review* 3, no. 1 (1968): 7–28.
Curry, Richard O., and Lawrence B. Goodheart. "Individualism in Trans-national Context." In *American Chameleon: Individualism in Trans-National Context,* edited by Richard O. Curry and Lawrence B. Goodheart, 1–19. Kent, OH: Kent State University, 1991.
Curwin, Kevin D., and Matthew C. Mahutga. "Foreign Direct Investment and Economic Growth: New Evidence from Post-Socialist Transition Countries." *Social Forces* 92, no. 3 (2014): 1159–1187.
Cutler, Brian L. *Conviction of the Innocent: Lessons from Psychological Research.* Washington, D.C.: American Psychological Association, 2011.
Dallago, Francesca, Alberto Mirisola, and Michele Roccato. "Predicting Right-wing Authoritarianism via Personality and Dangerous World Beliefs: Direct, Indirect, and Interactive Effects." *The Journal of Social Psychology* 152, no. 1 (2012): 112–127.
Das, Aniruddha. "Sexual Harassment at Work in the United States." *Archives of Sexual Behavior* 38, no. 6 (2009): 909–921.
Davis, F. James. *Who Is Black?: One Nation's Definition.* State College: Penn State University Press, 1991.
Davis, Nancy J., and Robert V. Robinson. *Claiming Society for God: Religious Movements and Social Welfare.* Bloomington: Indiana University Press, 2012.
Davis, Walter T. "Economic Individualism and Social Disorder: The Power of Submerged Ideology." *Second Order* 6, no. 2 (1977): 21–43.
Dawson, Lorne. "When Prophecy Fails and Faith Persists: A Theoretical Overview." *Novo Religio* 3, no. 1 (1999): 60–82.
Deaton, Angus. *The Great Escape: Health, Wealth, and the Origins of Inequality.* Princeton, NJ: Princeton University Press, 2013.
De Coster, Stacy, Sarah B. Estes, and Charles W. Mueller. "Routine Activities and Sexual Harassment in the Workplace." *Work and Occupations* 26, no. 1 (1999): 21–49.
Dein, Simon. "Prophecy: Social Scientific Perspectives and the Lubavitch." In *Prophecy in the New Millenium: When Prophecies Persist,* edited by S. Harvey, and S. Newcombe, 25–42. Surrey, England: Ashgate, 2013.

Denton, Sally. *The Profiteers: Bechtel and the Men Who Built the World*. New York: Simon & Schuster, 2016.
Devenport, Christian, Hank Johnston, and Carol Mueller. *Repression and Mobilization*. Minneapolis: University of Minnesota Press, 2005.
Doll, Beth, Samuel Song, and Erin Siemers. "Classroom Ecologies That Support or Discourage Bullying." In *Bullying in American Schools: A Social-ecological Perspective on Prevention and Intervention*, edited by D. L. Espelage and S. M. Swearer, 161–183. Mahwah, NJ: Erlbaum, 2004.
Domanick, Joe. *Blue: The LAPD and the Battle to Redeem American Policing*. New York: Simon & Schuster, 2015.
Dowling, Julie A. *Mexican Americans and the Question of Race*. Austin: University of Texas Press, 2014.
Draper, Scott. "Effervescence and Solidarity in Religious Organizations." *Journal for the Scientific Study of Religion* 53, no. 2 (2014): 229–248.
Dray, Philip. *At the Hands of Persons Unknown: The Lynching of Black America*. New York: Modern Library, 2003.
Duckitt, John. "A Dual-process Cognitive-motivational Theory of Ideology and Prejudice." In *Advances in Experimental Social Psychology*, Vol. 33, edited by M. P. Zanna, 41–133. New York: Academic Press, 2001.
Duran, Robert J. *Gang Life in Two Cities: An Insider's Journey*. New York: Columbia University Press, 2013.
Durham, Martin. *White Rage: The Extreme Right and American Politics*. New York: Routledge, 2007.
Durkheim, Emile. *The Division of Labor in Society*, translated by George Simpson. New York: Macmillan, 1964 [1933].
Durkheim, Emile. *The Elementary Forms of Religious Life*, translated by Karen E. Fields. New York: The Free Press, 1995 [1912].
Easterbrook, Gregg. *It's Better Than It Looks: Reasons for Optimism in an Age of Fear*. New York: Public Affairs, 2018.
Easterlin, Richard A. "Feeding the Illusion of Growth and Happiness: A Reply to Hagerty and Veenhoven. *Social Indicators Research* 75 (2005): 429–443.
Edgell, Penny, Joseph Gerteis, and Douglas Hartmann. "Atheists as 'Other': Moral Boundaries and Cultural Membership in American Society." *American Sociological Review* 71, no. 2 (2006): 211–234.
Eger, Maureen A. "Even in Sweden: The Effect of Immigration on Support for Welfare State Spending." *European Sociological Review* 26, no. 2 (2010): 203–217.
Eisenstadt, Shmuel N. "The Construction of Collective Identities and the Continual Reconstruction of Primordiality." In *Making Sense of Collectivity: Ethnicity, Nationalism and Globalisation*, edited by Malesevic, Sinisa and Mark Haugaard, 33–87. London: Pluto Press, 2002.
Elisha, Omri. *Moral Ambition: Mobilization and Social Outreach in Evangelical Megachurches*. Berkeley: University of California Press, 2011.
Eller, Jack D., and Reed Coughlan. "The Poverty of Primordialism: The Demystification of Ethnic Attachments." *Ethnic and Racial Studies* 16, no. 2 (1993): 183–202.
Emirbayer, Mustafa, and Chad A. Goldberg. "Pragmatism, Bourdieu, and Collective Emotions in Contentious Politics." *Theory and Society* 34 (2005): 469–518.
Emirbayer, Mustafa, and Matthew Desmond. *The Racial Order*. Chicago: University of Chicago Press, 2015.
Engstrom, Stephen. "The Concept of the Highest Good in Kant's Moral Philosophy." *Philosophy and Phenomenological Research* 51, no. 4 (1992): 747–780.
Erich, Walter. "Understanding Terrorist Behavior: The Limits and Opportunities of Psychological Inquiry." In *Origins of Terrorism: Psychologies, Ideologies, Theologies, States of Mind*, edited by Walter Reich, 261–278. Washington, D.C.: Woodrow Wilson Center Press, 1998.
Eriksen, Thomas. *Ethnicity and Nationalism: Anthropological Perspectives*. London: Pluto Press, 1993.
Ernst, Carl, and Richard Martin. "Introduction: Toward a Post-Orientalist Approach to Islamic Religious Studies." In *Rethinking Islamic Studies: From Orientalism to Cosmopolitanism*,

edited by Carl Ernst and Richard Martin, 1–23. Columbia: University Press of South Carolina, 2010.

Esposito, John L., and Dalia Mogahed. *Who Speaks for Islam? What a Billion Muslims Really Think*. New York: Gallup Press, 2008.

Etounga-Manguelle, Daniel. "Does Africa Need a Cultural Adjustment Program?" In *Culture Matters: How Values Shape Human Progress*, edited by Laurence E. Harrison and Samuel P. Huntington, 65–77. New York: Basic Books, 2001.

Etzioni, Amitai. *Spirit of Community*. New York: Crown Publisher, 1993.

Etzioni, Amitai. "The Responsive Community: A Communitarian Perspective." *American Sociological Review* 61, no. 1 (1996): 1–11.

Fackler, Guido. "Music in Concentration Camps, 1933–1945," translated by Peter Logan. *Music & Politics* 1, no. 1 (2007): 1–25.

Fairbrother, Malcolm. "Economists, Capitalists, and the Making of Globalization: North American Free Trade in Comparative-Historical Perspective." *American Journal of Sociology* 119, no. 5 (2014): 1324–1379.

Falk, Richard. *On Humane Governance: Toward a New Global Politics*. Cambridge, UK: Polity Press, 1995.

Faris, Robert, and Diane Felmelee. "Status Struggles: Network Centrality and Gender Segregation in Same-and Cross-gender Aggression." *American Sociological Review* 76, no. 1 (2011): 48–73.

Fearon, James D., Macartan Humphrey, and Jeremy M. Weinstein. "Can Development Aid Contribute to Social Cohesion after Civil War? Evidence from a Field Experiment in Post-Conflict Liberia." *American Economic Review* 99, no. 2 (2009): 287–291.

Federico, Christopher M. "When Do Welfare Attitudes Become Racialized? The Paradoxical Effects of Education." *American Journal of Political Science* 48, no. 2 (2004): 374–391.

Feldman, Stanley. "Enforcing Social Conformity: A Theory of Authoritarianism." *Political Psychology* 24, no. 1 (2003): 41–74.

Feuer, Lewis S. *The Conflict of Generations: The Character and Significance of Student Movements*. New York: Basic Books, 1969.

Feuer, Lewis S. *Ideology and the Ideologists*. New York: Harper & Row, 1975.

Feuer, Lewis S. "Science and the Ethic of Protestant Asceticism: A Reply to Professor Robert K. Merton." *Research in Sociology of Knowledge, Sciences, and Art*. Vol. II, 1–23. Stamford, CT: JAI Press, 1979.

Fiel, Jeremy. "Closing Ranks: Closure, Status Competition, and School Segregation." *American Journal of Sociology* 121, no. 1 (2015): 126–170.

Findley, Michael G., and Joseph K. Young. "Terrorism, Democracy, and Credible Commitments." *International Studies Quarterly* 55 (2011): 357–378.

Fine, Gary A. "Group Culture and the Interaction Order: Local Sociology on the Meso-level." *Annual Review of Sociology* 38, no. 1 (2012): 159–179.

Fine, Gary A. *Tiny Publics: A Theory of Group Action and Culture*. New York: Russell Sage Foundation, 2012.

Fish, Steven. *Are Muslims Distinctive: A Look at the Evidence*. New York: Oxford University Press, 2011.

Fiske, Alan P., and Tage Shakti Rai. *Virtuous Violence: Hurting and Killing to Create, Sustain, End and Honor Social Relationships*. Cambridge, UK: Cambridge University Press, 2015.

Fligstein, Neil, and Alexander F. Roehrkasse. "The Causes of Fraud in the Financial Crisis of 2007 to 2009: Evidence from the Mortgage-backed Securities Industry." *American Sociological Review* 81, no. 4 (2016): 617–643.

Flores, Edward O. *God's Gangs: Barrrio Ministry, Masculinity, and Gang Recovery*. New York: New York University Press, 2014.

Fox, Cybelle. "The Changing Color of Welfare? How Whites' Attitudes Toward Latinos Influence Support for the Welfare State." *American Journal of Sociology* 110, no. 3 (2004): 580–625.

Fox, Jonathan. "Paradigm Lost: Huntington's Unfulfilled Clash of Civilizations Prediction into the 21st Century." *International Politics* 42, no. 4 (2005): 428–457.

Frank, David J. "Science, Nature, and the Globalization of the Environment, 1870–1990." *Social Forces* 76, no. 2 (1997): 409–437.

Frank, David J., Ann Hironaka, and Evan Schofer. "The Nation-state and the Natural

Environment over the Twentieth Century." *American Sociological Review* 65, no. 1 (2000): 96–116.
Friedman, Thomas L. *The World Is Flat: A Brief History of the Twenty-first Century.* New York: Farrar, Straus, & Giroux, 2006.
Fukuyama, Francis. *Trust: The Social Virtues and the Creation of Prosperity.* New York: Free Press, 1995.
Gambetta, Diego. *The Sicilian Mafia: The Business of Private Protection.* Cambridge, MA: Harvard University Press, 1996.
Gauchat, Gordon. "Politicization of Science in the Public Sphere: A Study of Public Trust in the United States, 1974 to 2010." *American Sociological Review* 77, no. 2 (2012): 167–187.
Gaylin, Willard. *Hatred: The Psychological Descent into Violence.* New York: Public Affairs, 2003.
Gentile, Emilio. "The Sacralisation of Politics: Definitions, Interpretations and Reflections on the Question of Secular Religion and Totalitarianism." *Totalitarian Movements and Political Religions* 1, no. 1 (2000): 18–55.
Gerber, Elisabeth R., Adam D. Henry, and Mark Lubell. "Political Homophily and Collaboration in Regional Planning Networks." *American Journal of Political Science* 57, no. 3 (2013): 598–610.
Gessen, Masha. *Tsarnaev Brothers: The Road to a Modern Tragedy.* New York: Riverhead Books, 2015.
Gibbs, David. *Political Economy of Third World Intervention.* Chicago: University of Chicago Press, 1991.
Gibbs, David. "Pretexts in U.S. Foreign Policy: The War on Terrorism in Historical Perspective." *New Political Science* 26, no. 3 (2004): 293–321.
Giddens, Anthony. *Profiles and Critiques in Social Theory.* Berkeley: University of California Press, 1982.
Giddens, Anthony. *The Consequences of Modernity.* Stanford, CA: Stanford University Press, 1990.
Giesen, Bernhard. "Performing the Sacred: A Durkheimian Perspective on the Performative Turn in the Social Sciences." In *Social Performance: Symbolic Action, Cultural Pragmatics, and Ritual,* edited by Jeffrey C. Alexander, Bernhard Giesen, and Jason L. Mast, 325–367. New York: Cambridge University Press, 2006.
Giger, Nathalie, and Heike Kluver. "Voting Against Your Constituents? How Lobbying Affects Representation." *American Journal of Political Science* 60, no. 1 (2016): 190–205.
Gilens, Martin. *Why Americans Hate Welfare.* Chicago: University of Chicago Press, 1999.
Gilligan, Michael J., Benjamin J. Pasquale, and Cyrus Samii. "Civil War and Social Cohesion: Lab-in-the-Field Evidence from Nepal." *American Journal of Political Science* 58, no. 3 (2014): 604–619.
Gillon, Steven M. *Separate and Unequal: The Kerner Commission and the Unraveling of American Liberalism.* New York: Basic Books, 2018.
Giner-Sorolla, Roger, Bernhard Leidner, and Emannuele Castano. "Dehumanization, Demonization, and Morality Shifting: Path to Moral Certainty in Extremist Violence." In *Extremism and the Psychology of Uncertainty,* edited by Michael A. Hogg and Danielle L. Blaylock, chapter 10. West Sussex, UK: Wiley-Blackwell, 2011.
Glenn, Evelyn N. "Constructing Citizenship: Exclusion, Subordination, and Resistance." *American Sociological Review* 76, no. 1 (2011): 1–24.
Goffman, Erving. *Frame Analysis: An Essay on the Organization of Experience.* Cambridge, MA: Harvard University Press, 1974.
Goldsworthy, Adrian. *Pax Romana: War, Peace and Conquest in the Roman World.* London: Weidenfeld & Nicolson, 2016.
Goodman, J. "The European Union: Democracy Beyond the Nation State." In *The Transformation of Democracy,* edited by A. McGrew. Cambridge, UK: Polity Press, 1997.
Gordon, Linda. *The Second Coming of the KKK: The Ku Klux Klan of the 1920s and the American Political Tradition.* New York: Liveright Publishing, 2017.
Gordon, Stanford C., Catherine Hafer, and Dimitri Landa. "Consumption or Investment? On Motivations for Political Giving." *Journal of Politics* 69, no. 4 (2007): 1057–1072.
Gottschalk, Marie. *The Problems and the Gallows: The Politics of Mass Incarceration in America.* New York: Cambridge University Press, 2006.

Grober, Jens, Ernesto Reuben, and Agnieszka Tymula. "Political Quid Pro Quo Agreements: An Experimental Study." *American Journal of Political Science* 57, no. 3 (2013): 582–597.

Gueguen, Nicolas, Angelique Martin, and Sebastien Meineri. 2011. "Similarity and Social Interaction: When Similarity Fosters Implicit Behavior Toward a Stranger." *The Journal of Social Psychology* 151, no. 6 (2011): 671–673.

Guerra, Nancy G., K. Robert Williams, and Shelly Sadek. "Understanding Bullying and Victimization During Childhood and Adolescence: A Mixed Methods Study." *Child Development* 82, no. 1 (2011): 295–310.

Guillur, Ghristophe. *Twilight of the Elites: Prosperity, the Periphery, and the Future of France*, translated by Malcolm DeBevoise. New Haven, CT: Yale University Press, 2019.

Guinn, Jeff. *Manson: The Life and Times of Charles Manson.* New York: Simon & Schuster, 2014.

Gurr, Ted Robert. "Terrorism in Democracies: Its Social and Political Bases." In *Origins of Terrorism: Psychologies, Ideologies, Theologies, States of Mind*, edited by Walter Reich, 86–102. Washington, D.C.: Woodrow Wilson Center Press, 1998.

Haag, Pamela. *The Gunning of America: Business and the Making of American Gun Culture.* New York: Basic Books, 2016.

Habermas, Jürgen. *Legitimation Crisis.* Boston: Beacon Press, 1975.

Hafner-Burton, Emilie N., and Kiyoteru Tsutsui. "Human Rights in a Globalizing World: The Paradox of Empty Promises." *American Journal of Sociology* 110, no. 5 (2005): 1373–1411.

Hagan, John, and Joshua Kaiser. "The Displaced and Dispossessed of Darfur: Explaining the Sources of a Continuing State-led Genocide." *British Journal of Sociology* 62, no. 1 (2011): 1–25.

Hagan, John, Joshua Kaiser, and Anna Hanson. "The Theory of Legal Cynicism and Sunni Insurgent Violence in Post-Invasion Iraq." *American Sociological Review* 81, no. 2 (2016): 316–346.

Hager, Thomas. *Ten Drugs: How Plants, Powders, and Pills Have Shaped the History of Medicine.* New York: Abrams Press, 2019.

Haidt, Jonathan. *The Righteous Mind: Why Good People Are Divided by Politics and Religion.* New York: Vintage, 2012.

Haleem, Irm. *The Essence of Islamist Extremism: Recognition through Violence, Freedom through Death.* New York: Routledge, 2014.

Hall, John R. "Mass Suicide and the Branch Davidians." In *Cults, Religion and Violence*, 149–169. Cambridge, UK: Cambridge University Press, 2002.

Haller, William, Alejandro Portes, and Scott M. Lynch. "Dreams Fulfilled, Dreams Shattered: Determinants of Segmented Assimilation in the Second Generation." *Social Forces* 89, no. 3 (2011): 733–762.

Hamid, Shadi. *Islamic Exceptionalism: How the Struggle Over Islam Is Reshaping the World.* New York: St. Martin's Press, 2016.

Hannerz, Ulf. *Soulside: Inquiries into Ghetto Culture and Community.* New York: Columbia University Press, 1969.

Hansen, Chuck. *U.S. Nuclear Weapons: The Secret History.* Arlington: Aerofax, 2013.

Hansen, Wendy L., Neil J. Mitchell, and Jeffrey M. Drope. "The Logic of Private and Collective Action." *American Journal of Political Science* 49, no. 1 (2005): 150–167.

Harcourt, Bernard E. *The Illusion of Free Markets: Punishment and the Myth of Natural Order.* Cambridge, MA: Harvard University Press, 2011.

Harkness, Geoff, and Rana Khaled. "Modern Traditionalism: Consanguineous Marriage in Qatar." *Journal of Marriage and Family* 76, no. 3 (2014): 587–603.

Harris, Jerry. *The Dialectics of Globalization: Economic and Political Conflict in a Transnational World.* Tyne, UK: Cambridge Scholars Publishing, 2006.

Harrison, Jill L. *Pesticide Drift and the Pursuit of Environmental Justice.* Cambridge, Mass: MIT Press, 2011.

Hartung, William D. *Prophets of War: Lockheed Martin and the Making of the Military-Industrial Complex.* New York: Nation Books, 2012.

Hawley, P. H., Kathryn N. Stump, and Jacklyn Ratliff. "Sidestepping the Jingle Fallacy: Bullying, Aggression, and the Importance of Knowing the Difference." In *Bullying in North American Schools*, 2nd edition, edited by D. L. Espelage and S. Swearer, 101–115. New York: Routledge, 2011.

Hay, D. Alastair. "An Investigation into the Swiftness and Intensity of Recent Secularization in Canada: Was Berger Right?" *Sociology of Religion* 75, no. 1 (2014): 136–162.

Hayek, Friedrich A. *Individualism and Economic Order.* Chicago: University of Chicago Press, 1969.
Hays, Carlton J. H. *Nationalism: A Religion.* New York: Macmillan, 1960.
Hechter, Michael. *Containing Nationalism.* Oxford, UK: Oxford University Press, 2000.
Hechter, Michael, Steven Pfaff, and Patrick Underwood. "Grievances and the Genesis of Rebellion: Mutiny in the Royal Navy, 1740 to 1820." *American Sociological Review* 81, no. 1 (2016): 165–189.
Hegghammer, Thomas. *Jihadi Culture: The Art and Social Practices of Militant Islamists.* Cambridge, UK: Cambridge University Press, 2017.
Heider, Anne, and R. Stephen Warner. "Bodies in Sync: Interaction Ritual Theory Applied to Sacred Harp Singing." *Sociology of Religion* 71, no. 1 (2010): 76–97.
Heise, David R. "Conditions for Empathic Solidarity." In *The Problem of Solidarity: Theories and Models,* edited by Patrick Doreian and Thomas J. Fararo, 197–212. London and New York: Routledge, 1998.
Held, David. "Democracy, the Nation-state and the Global System." In *Political Theory Today,* edited by David Held, 197–235. Cambridge, UK: Polity Press, 1991.
Helfstein, Scott. *Edges of Radicalization: Individuals, Networks and Ideas in Violent Extremism.* Combating Terrorism Center, U.S. Military Academy, CreateSpace Independent Publishing Platform, 2014.
Heller, Sara, Harold A. Pollack, Roseanna Ander, and Jens Ludwig. "Preventing Youth Violence and Dropout: A Randomized Field Experiment." Working Paper 19014, National Bureau of Economic Research, May, 2013.
Henderson, Errol A., and Richard Tucker. "Clear and Present Strangers: The Clash of Civilizations and International Conflict." *International Studies Quarterly* 45, no. 2 (2001): 317–338.
Henrich, Joseph, and Natalie Henrich. *Why Humans Cooperate: A Cultural and Evolutionary Explanation.* Oxford, UK: Oxford University Press, 2007.
Henrich, Joseph, Michal Bauer, Alessandra Cassar, Julie Cyhtilova, and Benjamin G. Purzycki. "War Increases Religiosity." *Nature: Human Behavior* 3, no. 2 (2019): 129–135.
Hensley, Christopher, Jeremy Wright, Richard Tewksbury, and Tammy Castle. "The Evolving Nature of Prison Argot and Sexual Hierarchies." *The Prison Journal* 83, no. 3 (2014): 289–300.
Herman, Max. *Fighting in the Streets: Ethnic Succession and Urban Unrest in Twentieth-Century Urban America.* New York: Peter Lang Publishing, 2005.
Herrera, Linda, and Asef Bayat. "Introduction: Being Young and Muslim in Neoliberal Times." In *Being Young and Muslim: New Cultural Politics in the Global South and North,* edited by Linda Herrera and Asef Bayat, 3–26. New York: Oxford University Press, 2010.
Hetey, Rebecca C. and Jennifer L. Eberhardt. "Racial Disparities in Incarceration Increase Acceptance of Punitive Policies." *Psychological Science* 25, no. 10 (2014): 1949–1954.
Hetherington, Marc J. *Why Trust Matters: Declining Political Trust and the Demise of American Liberalism.* Princeton, NJ: Princeton University Press, 2005.
Hetherington, Marc J., and Elizabeth Suhay. "Authoritarianism, Threat, and Americans' Support for the War on Terror." *American Journal of Political Science* 55, no. 3 (2011): 546–560.
Hetherington, Marc J., and Jonathan D. Weiler. *Authoritarianism and Polarization in American Politics.* New York: Cambridge University Press, 2009.
Hett, Benjamin C. *The Death of Democracy: Hitler's Rise to Power and the Downfall of the Weimar Republic.* New York: Henry Holt, 2018.
Hewstone, M., M. Rubin, and H. Willis. "Intergroup Bias." *Annual Review of Psychology* 53 (2002): 575–604.
Hibbard, Scott. "Religion and State in India: Ambiguity, Chauvinism, and Tolerance." In *Religion and Regimes: Support, Separation, and Opposition,* edited by Mehran Tamadonfar and Ted G. Jelen, 121–141. Lanham, MD: Lexington Books, 2013.
Hinton, Alexander L. *Why Did They Kill? Cambodia in the Shadow of Genocide.* Berkeley: University of California Press, 2005.
Hoffer, Eric. *The True Believers: Thoughts on the Nature of Mass Movements.* New York: Harper & Brothers, 1951.
Hogg, Michael A. "Self-identity, Social Identity, and the Solace of Extremism." In *Extremism and*

the Psychology of Uncertainty, edited by Michael A. Hogg and Danielle L. Blaylock, chapter 2. West Sussex, UK: Wiley-Blackwell, 2011.
Hogg, Michael A. and Danielle L. Blaylock. "Preface" In *Extremism and the Psychology of Uncertainty*, edited by Michael A. Hogg and Danielle L. Blaylock. West Sussex, UK: Wiley-Blackwell, 2011.
Holmes, Kim R. *The Closing of the Liberal Mind: How Groupthink and Intolerance Define the Left*. New York: Encounter Books, 2016.
Holton, Gerald. *Science and Anti-Science*. Cambridge, MA: Harvard University Press, 1993.
Homolar, Alexandra. "Rebels Without a Conscience: The Evolution of the Rogue State Narrative in U.S. Security Policy." *European Journal of International Relations* 17, no. 4 (2010): 705–727.
Horgan, John. *The Psychology of Terrorism*. New York: Routledge, 2005.
Horowitz, Ruth. "Honor and Reputation in the Chicano Gang." In *The Meaning of Sociology: A Reader*, 5th edition, edited by Joel M. Charon, 59–66. Moorhead, MN: Moorhead State University Press, 1996.
Hostetler, John A. *Amish Society*, 3rd ed., Baltimore: Johns Hopkins University, 1980.
Hostetler, John A. "The Amish: A Small Society." In *Seeing Ourselves: Classic, Contemporary, and Cross-cultural Readings in Sociology*, 7th Edition, edited by John J. Macionis and Nijole V. Benokraitis. Upper Saddle River, NJ: Prentice Hall, 2007.
Howard, Lise M. "U.S. Foreign Policy Habits in Ethnic Conflict." *International Studies Quarterly* 59, no. 4 (2015): 721–734.
Htun, Mala. "Culture, Institution, and Gender Inequality in Latin America." In *Culture Matters: How Values Shape Human Progress*, edited by Laurence E. Harrison and Samuel P. Huntington, 189–199. New York: Basic Books, 2001.
Hughey, Matthew W. *White Bound: Nationalist, Antiracists, and the Shared Meaning of Race*. Stanford, CA: Stanford University Press, 2012.
Hultin, Mia. "Some Take the Glass Escalator, Some Hit the Glass Ceiling?" *Work and Occupations* 30 (2003): 30–61.
Hunter, James D. *Change the World: The Irony, Tragedy, and Possibility of Christianity in the Late Modern World*. Oxford, UK: Oxford University Press, 2010.
Hunter, James D. *Culture Wars: The Struggle to Define America*. New York: Basic Books, 1991.
Huntington, Samuel P. *The Clash of Civilization and the Remaking of World Order*. New York: Simon & Schuster, 2011 [1996].
Hurst, Charles E., and David L. McConnell. *An Amish Paradox: Diversity and Change in the World's Largest Amish Community*. Baltimore: Johns Hopkins University Press, 2010.
Immerwahr, Daniel. *How to Hide an Empire: A History of the Greater United States*. New York: Farrar, Straus & Giroux, 2019.
Inglehart, Ronald, and Christian Welzel. *Modernization, Cultural Change, and Democracy: The Human Development Sequence*. New York: Cambridge University Press, 2005.
Inglehart, Ronald, and Paul R. Abramson. "Economic Security and Value Change." *American Political Science Review* 88, no. 2 (1994): 336–354.
Inglehart, Ronald, and Wayne E. Baker. "Modernization, Cultural Change, and the Persistence of Traditional Values." *American Sociological Review* 65, no. 1 (2000): 19–51.
Isaac, Larry, Steve McDonald, and Greg Lukasik. "Taking It from the Streets: How the Sixties Mass Movement Revitalized Unionization." *American Journal of Sociology* 112, no. 1 (2006): 46–98.
Iyengar, Shanto, and Sean J. Westwood. "Fear and Loathing across Party Lines: New Evidence on Group Polarization." *American Journal of Political Science* 59, no. 3 (2015): 690–707.
Iyengar, Shanto, Gaurav Sood, and Yphtach Lelkes. "Affect, Not Ideology: A Social Identity Perspective on Polarization." *Public Opinion Quarterly* 76, no. 3 (2012): 405–431.
Jenkins, Richard. "Different Societies? Different Cultures? What are Human Collectivities?" In *Making Sense of Collectivity: Ethnicity, Nationalism and Globalisation*, edited by Sinisa Malesevic and Mark Haugaard, 12–32. London: Pluto Press, 2002.
Jensen, Gary F. *The Path of the Devil: Early Modern Witch Hunts*. Landham, MD: Rowman & Littlefield, 2007.
Jensen, Nathan M., and Guillermo Rosas. "Foreign Direct Investment and Income Inequality in Mexico, 1990–2000." *International Organization* 61, no. 3 (2007): 467–487.

Johnson, Chalmers. *Blowback: The Costs and Consequences of American Empire.* New York: Holt Paperbacks, 2004.
Johnson, Chalmers. *The Sorrows of Empire: Militarism, Secrecy and the End of the Republic.* New York: Metropolitan Books, 2004.
Jones, Robert P. *The End of White Christian America.* New York: Simon & Schuster, 2016.
Juergensmeyer, Mark. "The Logic of Religious Violence." In *Inside Terrorist Organizations,* edited by David C. Rapport, 171–193. Portland: Frank Cass, 2001.
Junger, Sebastian. *Tribe: On Homecoming and Belonging.* New York: Twelve Publisher, 2016.
Junger, Sebastian. *War.* New York: Twelve Publisher, 2010.
Juvonen, Janna. "Bullying Among Young Adolescents: The Strong, the Weak and the Troubled." *Pediatrics* 112, no. 6 (2003): 1231–1237.
Kahneman, Daniel, and Alan B. Krueger. "Developments in the Measurement of Subjective Well-being." *Journal of Economic Perspectives* 20, no. 1 (2006): 3–24.
Kalkan, Kerem O., Geoffrey C. Layman, and John C. Green. "Will Americans Vote for Muslims? The Impact of Religious and Ethnic Identifiers on Candidate Support." Presented at the annual meeting of the American Political Science Association, Boston, MA, 2008.
Kamens, David H. *Beyond the Nation-State: The Reconstruction of Nationhood and Citizenship.* Bingley, UK: Emerald Group, 2012.
Kamrava, Mehran. "Repression, Fundamentalism, and Terrorism in the Middle East." In *Democratic Development & Political Terrorism: The Global Perspective,* edited by William Crotty, 167–193. Boston: Northeastern University Press, 2005.
Kane, Robert J. "Compromised Police Legitimacy as a Predictor of Violent Crime in Structurally Disadvantaged Communities." *Criminology* 43, no. 2 (2005): 469–498.
Kaplan, Jeffrey. *Radical Religion and Violence: Theory and Case Studies.* New York: Routledge, 2015.
Kaplan, Jeffrey. "Right-wing Violence in North America." In *Terror from the Extreme Right,* 44–95. London: Frank Cass, 1995.
Kargin, Vedat. *Peer Reporting of Unethical Police Behavior.* Philadelphia: LFB Scholarly Publishing, 2010.
Kaufman, Stuart J. *Modern Hatreds: The Symbolic Politics of Ethnic War.* Ithaca, NY: Cornell University Press, 2001.
Kaushal, Neeraj. *Blaming Immigrants: Nationalism and the Economics of Global Movement.* New York: Columbia University Press, 2019.
Kawalerowicz, Juta, and Michael Biggs. "Anarchy in the UK: Economic Deprivation, Social Disorganization, and Political Grievances in the London Riot of 2011." *Social Forces* 94, no. 2 (2015): 673–698.
Kay, John. *Culture and Prosperity: The Truth about Markets—Why Some Nations Are Rich but Most Remain Poor.* New York: HarperCollins Publishers, 2004.
Kaya, Yunus. "Globalization and Industrialization in 64 Developing Countries, 1980–2003." *Social Forces* 88, no. 3 (2010): 1153–1182.
Keenan, Marie. *Child Sexual Abuse and the Catholic Church: Gender, Power, and Organizational Culture.* New York: Oxford University Press, 2011.
Keith, Michael. *Race, Riots, and Policing: Lore and Disorder in a Multi-Racist Society.* London: UCl Press, 1993.
Kelner, Shaul. *Tours That Bind: Diaspora, Pilgrimage, and Israeli Birthright Tourism.* New York: New York University Press, 2010.
Ketcham, Ralph. *Individualism and Public Life: A Modern Dilemma.* New York: Basil Blackwell, 1987.
Khalilzad, Zalmay. *The Envoy: From Kabul to the White House, My Journey Through a Turbulent World.* New York: St. Martin's Press, 2016.
Kharkhordin, Oleg. *The Collective and the Individual in Russia: A Study of Practices.* Berkeley: University of California Press, 1999.
Kirk, David S., and Andrew V. Papachristos. "Cultural Mechanisms and the Persistence of Neighborhood Violence." *American Journal of Sociology* 116, no. 4 (2011): 1190–1233.
Klandermans, Bert. *The Social Psychology of Protest.* Oxford, UK: Blackwell, 1997.
Klandermans, Bert, and Marga M. De Weerd. "Group Identification and Political Protest." In

Self, Identity, and Social Movements, edited by Sheldon Stryker, Timothy J. Owens, and Robert W. White, 68–90. Minneapolis: University of Minnesota Press, 2000.

Klandermans, Bert, Jojanneke van der Toorn, and Jacquelien van Stekelenburg. "Embeddedness and Identity: How Immigrants Turn Grievances into Action." *American Sociological Review* 73, no. 6 (2008): 992–1012.

Klein, Malcolm. *The American Street Gang: Its Nature, Prevalence, and Control.* New York: Oxford University Press, 1995.

Klein, Naomi. *No Is Not Enough: Resisting Trump's Shock Politics and Winning the World We Need.* Chicago: Haymarket Books, 2017.

Klein, Naomi. *The Shock Doctrine: The Rise of Disaster Capitalism.* New York: Picador, 2008.

Klockars, Carl B., Sanja K. Ivkovic, and M. R. Haberfield. *Enhancing Police Integrity.* New York: Springer, 2006.

Knox, George. *An Introduction to Gangs.* Chicago: New Chicago School Press, 2000.

Kollmeyer, Christopher, and Florian Pichler. "Is Deindustrialization Causing High Unemployment in Affluent Countries? Evidence from 16 OECD Countries, 1970–2003." *Social Forces* 91, no. 3 (2013): 785–812.

Koopmans, Ruud. "Explaining the Rise of Racist and Extreme Right Violence in Western Europe: Grievances or Opportunities." *European Journal of Political Research* 20 (1996): 185–216.

Kossinets, Gueorgi, and Duncan J. Watts. "Origins of Homophily in an Evolving Social Network." *American Journal of Sociology* 115, no. 2 (2009): 405–450.

Kotkin, Stephen. *Stalin: Waiting for Hitler, 1929–1941.* New York: Penguin Press, 2017.

Koukoutsaki-Monnier, Angeliki. "Understanding National Identity: Between Culture and Institutions." *American Journal of Cultural Sociology* 3, no. 1 (2015): 65–88.

Kranish, Michael, and Marc Fisher. *Trump Revealed: An American Journey of Ambition, Ego, Money, and Power.* New York: Scribner's, 2016.

Krueger, Alan B. *What Makes a Terrorist: Economics and the Roots of Terrorism.* Princeton, NJ: Princeton University Press, 2007.

Kubrin, Charis E., and Ronald Weitzer. "Retaliatory Homicide: Concentrated Disadvantage and Neighborhood Culture." *Social Problems* 50, no. 2 (2003): 157–180.

Kurzman, Charles. *The Missing Martyrs: Why There Are So Few Muslim Terrorists.* New York: Oxford University Press, 2011.

Kuwabara, Ko, and Oliver Sheldon. "Temporal Dynamics of Social Exchange and the Development of Solidarity: 'Testing the Waters' versus 'Taking a Leap of Faith.'" *Social Forces* 91, no. 1 (2012): 253–273.

Lamont, Michele, and Mario L. Small. "How Culture Matters for the Understanding of Poverty: Enriching Our Understanding." In *The Colors of Poverty: Why Racial and Ethnic Disparities Persist,* edited by Ann C. Lin and David Harris, 76–102. New York: Russell Sage, 2008.

Lamont, Michele, and Virag Molnar. "The Study of Boundaries in the Social Sciences." *Annual Review of Sociology* 28, no. 1 (2002): 167–195.

Landa, Dimitri, and Dominik Duell. "Social Identity and Electoral Accountability." *American Journal of Political Science* 59, no. 3 (2015): 671–689.

Laraña, E., H. Johnston, J. R. Gusfield. *New Social Movements: From Ideology to Identity.* Philadelphia: Temple University Press, 1994.

Legewie, Joscha. "Terrorist Events and Attitudes Toward Immigrants: A Natural Experiment." *American Journal of Sociology* 118, no. 5 (2013): 1199–1245.

Lenski, Gerhard, and Patrick Nolan. "Trajectories of Development: A Test of Ecological-Evolutionary Theory." *Social Forces* 63, no. 1 (1984): 1–23.

Leo, Richard A. *Police Interrogation and American Justice.* Cambridge, MA: Harvard University Press, 2009.

Levendusky, Matthew S. "Why Do Partisan Media Polarize Viewers?" *American Journal of Political Science* 57, no. 3 (2013): 611–623.

Levitsky, Steven, and Daniel Ziblatt. *How Democracies Die.* New York: Crown Publishing, 2018.

Lewin, Kurt. *Resolving Social Conflicts: Field Theory in Social Science.* Washington, D.C.: American Psychological Association, 1997.

Lieberman, Debra, and Lance Linke. "The Effect of Social Category on Third Party Punishment." *Evolutionary Psychology* 5, no. 2 (2007): 289–305.
Lifton, Robert J. *Home from the War—Vietnam Veterans: Neither Victims nor Executioners*. New York: Simon & Schuster, 1973.
Lim, Chaeyoon, and Robert D. Putnam. "Religion, Social Networks, and Life Satisfaction." *American Sociological Review* 75, no. 6 (2010): 914–933.
Locke, John. *The Selected Political Writings of John Locke*. New York: W. W. Norton, 2005.
Lofland, John. *Doomsday Cults: A Study of Conversion, Proselytization, and Maintenance of Faith*. Upper Saddle River, N.J.: Prentice Hall, 1966.
Lombardo, Timothy J. *Blue-collar Conservatism: Frank Rizzo's Philadelphia and Populist Politics*. Philadelphia: University of Pennsylvania Press, 2018.
Long, Elizabeth. *Book Clubs: Women and the Uses of Reading in Everyday Life*. Chicago: University of Chicago Press, 2003.
Lonsway, Kimberly A., Rebecca Paynich, and Jennifer N. Hall. "Sexual Harassment in Law Enforcement." *Police Quarterly* 16, no. 2 (2013): 1177–1210.
Loveman, Mara. *National Colors: Racial Classification and the State in Latin America*. New York: Oxford University Press, 2014.
Luhrmann, Tanya, Howard Nusbaum, and Ronald Thisted. *When God Talks Back: Understanding the American Evangelical Relationship with God*. NY: Vintage Books, 2012.
Lukacs, John. *Democracy and Populism: Fear and Hatred*. New Haven, CT: Yale University Press, 2005.
Lukes, Steven. "Durkheim's Individualism and the Intellectuals." *Political Studies* 17 (1969): 14–30.
Lynch, Gordon. *The Sacred in the Modern World: A Cultural Sociological Approach*. Oxford, UK: Oxford University Press, 2014.
Lyons, Renee F., Kristin D. Mickelson, Michael J. L. Sullivan, and James C. Coyne. "Coping as a Communal Process." *Journal of Social and Personal Relationships* 15, no. 5 (1998): 579–605.
MacDonald, Heather. *The War on Cops: How the New Attack on Law and Order Makes Everyone Less Safe*. New York: Encounter Books, 2016.
Macy, Beth. *Dopesick: Dealers, Doctors, and the Drug Company That Addicted America*. New York: Little, Brown & Co, 2018.
Mahony, Christine. *Brussels versus the Beltway: Advocacy in the U.S. and the European Union*. Washington, D.C.: Georgetown University Press, 2008.
Mandelbaum, Michael. *Mission Failure: America and the World in the Post-Cold War Era*. Oxford, UK: Oxford University Press, 2016.
Mann, Charles C. *The Wizard and the Prophet: Two Remarkable Scientists and Their Dueling Visions to Shape Tomorrow's World*. New York: Alfred A. Knopf, 2018.
Martin, David. *A General Theory of Secularization*. New York: Harper & Row, 1993 [1978].
Martin, John Levi. "What Is Field Theory?" *American Journal of Sociology* 109, no. 1 (2003): 1–49.
Marty, Martin and Scott Appleby. *Fundamentalisms Observed: The Fundamentalism Project, Book 1*. Chicago: University of Chicago Press, 1994.
Mau, Steffen, and Christoph Burkhardt. "Migration and Welfare State Solidarity in Western Europe." *Journal of European Social Policy* 19, no. 3 (2009): 213–229.
Maxwell, Rahsaan, and Erik Bleich. "What Makes Muslims Feel French?" *Social Forces* 93, no. 1 (2014): 155–179.
May, Elaine T. *Fortress America: How We Embraced Fear and Abandoned Democracy*. New York: Basic Books, 2017.
Mayer, Jane. *Dark Money: The Hidden History of the Billionaires Behind the Rise of the Radical Right*. New York: Random House, 2016.
McAdam, Doug. "'Initiator' and 'Spin-off' Movements: Diffusion Processes in Protest Cycles." In *Repertoires and Cycles of Collective Action*, edited by M. Traugott, 217–239. Durham, NC: Duke University Press, 1995.
McAdam, Doug. "Micromobilization Contexts and Recruitments to Activism." *International Social Movement Research* 1 (1988): 125–154.
McAdam, Doug. *Political Process and the Development of Black Insurgency, 1930–1970*. Chicago: University of Chicago Press, 1982.

McAdam, Doug, John D. McCarthy, and Mayer N. Zald. *Comparative Perspectives on Social Movements.* New York: Cambridge, 1996.
McAdam, Doug, Sidney Tarrow, and Charles Tilly. *Dynamics of Contention.* Cambridge, UK: Cambridge University Press, 2001.
McCarthy, John D., and Mayer N. Zald. "Resource Mobilization and Social Movements: A Partial Theory." *American Journal of Sociology* 82, no. 6 (1977): 1212–1241.
McDermott, Monika L. "Religious Stereotyping and Voter Support for Evangelical Candidates." *Political Research Quarterly* 62, no. 2 (2009): 340–354.
McDougall, Walter A. *The Tragedy of U.S. Foreign Policy.* New Haven, CT: Yale University Press, 2016.
McFarland, Sam. *Prejudiced People: Individual Differences in Explicit Prejudice.* Bowling Green, KY: Western Kentucky University Press, 2001.
McGregor, Ian, Kylie Nash, and Mike Prentice. "Religious Zeal After Goal Frustration." In *Extremism and the Psychology of Uncertainty,* edited by Michael A. Hogg and Danielle L. Blaylock, chapter 9. West Sussex, UK: Wiley-Blackwell, 2011.
McKinnon, Andrew. "Elective Affinities of the Protestant Ethic: Weber and the Chemistry of Capitalism." *Sociological Theory* 28, no. 1 (2010): 108–126.
McPhail, Clark. "Civil Disorder Participation: A Critical Examination of Recent Research." *American Sociological Review* 36, no. 6 (1971): 1058–1073.
McPherson, Miller, Lynn Smith-Loving, and James M. Cook. "Birds of a Feather: Homophily in Social Networks." *Annual Review of Sociology* 27 (2001): 415–444.
McVeigh, Rory. *The Rise of the Ku Klux Klan: Right-wing Movements and National Politics.* Minneapolis: University of Minnesota Press, 2009.
Medwed, Daniel S. 2012. *Prosecution Complex: America's Race to Convict and Its Impact on the Innocent.* New York: New York University Press, 2012.
Meier, Barry. *Pain Killer: An Empire of Deceit and the Origins of America's Opioid Epidemic,* 2nd Edition. New York: Random House, 2018.
Meleagrou-Hitchens, Alexander, Seamus Hughes, and Bennett Clifford. *The Travelers: American Jihadists in Syria and Iraq.* Program on Extremism, George Washington University, 2018.
Melucci, Alberto. *Nomads of the Present: Social Movements and Individual Needs in Contemporary Society.* Philadelphia: Temple University Press, 1989.
Merkl, Peter H. and Leonard Weinberg. "Introduction." In *Right-wing Extremism in the Twenty-first Century,* edited by Peter H. Merkl and Leonard Weinberg, 1–19. Portland: Frank Cass, 2003.
Merolla, Jennifer, Jennifer Ramos, and Elizabeth Zechmeister. "Authoritarianism, Need for Closure, and Conditions of Threat." In *Extremism and the Psychology of Uncertainty,* edited by Michael A. Hogg and Danielle L. Blaylock, chapter 13. West Sussex, UK: Wiley-Blackwell, 2011.
Meyer, David, and Nancy Whittier. "Social Movement Spillover." *Social Problems* 41, no. 2 (1994): 277–298.
Meyer, John W. "Myths of Socialization and Personality." In *Reconstructing Individualism,* edited by T.C. Heller and E. Wellbery, 208–221. Stanford, CA: Stanford University Press, 1986.
Michael, George. *Confronting Right Wing Extremism and Terrorism in the U.S.* New York: Routledge, 2012.
Micklethwait, John, and Adrian Wooldrige. *The Fourth Revolution: The Global Race to Reinvent the State.* The Penguin Press HC, 2014.
Miller-Idriss, Cynthia. *Blood and Culture: Youth, Right-wing Extremism, and National Belonging in Contemporary Germany.* Durham, NC: Duke University Press, 2009.
Mische, Ann. "Cross-talk in Movements: Reconceiving the Culture-Network Link." In *Social Movements and Networks, Vol. 1,* edited by M. Diani and D. McAdam, 258–281. Oxford, UK: Oxford University Press, 2003.
Mitchell, Clair. "The Religious Content of Ethnic Identities." *Sociology* 40, no. 6 (2006): 1135–1152.
Mizruchi, Mark S. "What Do Interlocks Do? An Analysis, Critique, and Assessment of Research on Interlocking Directorates." *Annual Review of Sociology* 22 (1966): 271–298.
Modood, Tariq. "Is There a Crisis of Secularism in Western Europe?" *Sociology of Religion* 73, no. 2 (2012): 130–149.
Molm, Linda D., Jessica L. Collett, and David R. Chaefer. "Building Solidarity Through

Generalized Exchange: A Theory of Reciprocity." *American Journal of Sociology* 113, no. 1 (2007): 205–242.
Montoya, R. Matthew, and Todd L. Pittinsky. "When Increased Group Identification Leads to Outgroup Liking and Cooperation: The Role of Trust." *The Journal of Social Psychology* 151, no. 6 (2011): 784–806.
Moon, Dawne. "Who Am I and Who Are We. Conflicting Narratives of Collective Selfhood in Stigmatized Groups." *American Journal of Sociology* 117, no. 5 (2012): 1336–1379.
Mooney, Chris. *The Republican War on Science*. New York: Basic Books, 2005.
Moore, Natalie Y. *The South Side: A Portrait of Chicago and American Segregation: A Portrait of Chicago and American Segregation*. New York: St. Martin's Press, 2016.
Moravcsik, Andrew. *The Choice for Europe: Social Purposes and State Power from Messina to Maastricht*. Ithaca, NY: Cornell University Press, 1998.
Moravcsik, Andrew. "Negotiating the Single European Act: National Interests and Conventional Statecraft in the European Community." *International Organization* 45, no. 1 (1991): 19–57.
Morning, Ann. *The Nature of Race: How Scientists Think and Teach about Human Differences*. Berkeley and Los Angeles: University of California Press, 2011.
Moroz, Hall. *America at Sunset: The End of Pax Americana*. CreateSpace Independent Publishing, 2015.
Morris, Aldon D. "A Retrospective on the Civil Rights Movement: Political and Intellectual Landmarks." *Annual Review of Sociology* 25 (1999): 517–539.
Moskos, Peter. *Cop in the Hood: My Year Policing Baltimore's Eastern District*. Princeton, NJ: Princeton University Press, 2008.
Mount, Yascha. *The People vs. Democracy: Why Our Freedom Is in Danger and How to Save it*. Cambridge, MA: Harvard University Press, 2016.
Muller, Edward N., and Erich Weede. "Cross-national Variations in Political Violence: A Rational Action Approach." *Journal of Conflict Resolution* 34, no. 4 (1990): 624–651.
Muller, Edward N., and Mitchell A. Seligson. "Inequality and Insurgency." In *Development and Underdevelopment: The Political Economy of Global Inequality*, 3rd Edition, edited by Mitchell A. Seligson and John T. Passe-Smith, 85–117. Boulder, CO: Lynne Rienner, 2003.
Mullins, Mark R. "Japanese Responses to Imperialist Secularization: The Postwar Movement to Restore Shinto in the Public Sphere." In *Multiple Secularities Beyond the West: Religion and Modernity in the Global Age,* edited by Marian Burchardt, Monika Wohlrab-Sahr, and Matthias Middell, 141–168. Boston and Berlin: De Gruyter, 2015.
Mulloy, Darren. *American Extremism: History, Politics and the Militia Movement*. New York: Routledge, 2005.
Mummolo, Jonathan. "Militarization Fails to Enhance Police Safety or Reduce Crime but May Harm Police Reputation." *PNAS (Proceedings of the National Academy of Sciences of the U.S.A.)* 115, no. 37 (2018): 9181–9186.
Mungiu-Pippidi, Alina, and Denisa Mindruta. "Was Huntington Right? Testing Cultural Legacies and the Civilization Border." *International Politics.* 39, no. 2 (2002): 193–213.
Murphy, Craig N. "The Emergence of Global Governance." In *International Organization and Global Governance,* edited by Thomas G. Weiss and Rorden Wilkinson, 25–36. New York: Routledge, 2018.
Myers, Brian. *The Cleanest Race: How North Koreans See Themselves and Why It Matters*. New York: Melville House, 2011.
Nagel, Joane. *American Indian Renewal: Red Power and the Resurgence of Identity and Culture*. Oxford, UK: Oxford University Press, 1995.
Nagel, Joane. "Constructing Ethnicity." In *Majority and Minority: The Dynamics of Race and Ethnicity in American Life*, 6th Edition, edited by Norman R. Yetman, 57–71. Boston: Allyn & Bacon, 1999.
Nash, Kate. "The Cultural Turn in Sociology: Toward a Theory of Cultural Politics." *Sociology* 35, no. 1 (2001): 77–92.
Nesser, Petter. *Jihad in Europe—A Survey of the Motivations for Sunni Islamist Terrorism in Post-Millennium Europe*. Oslo, Norway: Norwegian Defense Research Establishment, 2004.
Newman, Katherine S., and Rourke L. O'Brien. *Taxing the Poor: Doing Damage to the Truly Disadvantaged*. Berkeley: University of California Press, 2011.

Nippert-Eng, Christena E. "Boundary Work: Sculpting Work and Home." In *Cultural Sociology*, edited by Lynette Spillman, 79–86. Oxford, UK: Oxford University Press, 2002.

Nisbett, Richard E., and Dov Cohen. *Culture of Honor: The Psychology of Violence in the South*. Boulder, CO: Westview Press, 1994.

Nixey, Catherine. *The Darkening Age: The Christian Destruction of the Classical World*. New York: Houghton Mifflin Harcourt, 2018.

Noblitt, James R. and Pamela S. Perskin. *Cult and Ritual Abuse: Its History, Anthropology, and Recent Discovery in Contemporary America*. Westport, CT: Praeger, 2000.

Norberg, Johan. *Progress: Ten Reasons to Look Forward to the Future*. London: Oneworld Publications, 2016.

Norris, Pippa, and Ronald Inglehart. *Cosmopolitan Communications: Cultural Diversity in a Globalized World*. New York: Cambridge University Press, 2009.

Norris, Pippa, and Ronald Inglehart. *Sacred and Secular: Religion and Politics Worldwide*. Cambridge, UK: Cambridge University Press, 2004.

Nussbaum, Martha C. *The Monarchy of Fear: A Philosopher Looks at Our Political Crisis*. New York: Simon & Schuster, 2018.

Oberschall, Anthony. *Social Conflict and Social Movements*. Englewood Cliffs, NJ: Prentice-Hall, 1973.

Oberschall, Anthony. "The Los Angeles Riot of August 1965." *Social Problems* 15, no. 3 (1968): 322–341.

O'Brien, Timothy L., and Shiri Noy. "Traditional, Modern, and Post-secular Perspectives on Science and Religion in the United States." *American Sociological Review* 80, no. 1 (2015): 92–115.

Ogbu, John. *Minority Education and Caste*. New York: Academic Press, 1978.

Ogilvie, Matthew C. "Religion Is Easily Exploited by Extremist Groups." In *Extremist Groups*, edited by Karen F. Balkin, 18–26. Farmington Hills, MI: Greenhaven Press, 2005.

Olzak, Susan. *The Dynamics of Ethnic Competition and Conflict*. Stanford: Stanford University Press, 1994.

Olzak, Susan, and Suzanne Shanahan. "Deprivation and Race Riots: An Extension of Spileman's Analysis." *Social Forces* 74, no. 3 (1996): 931–961.

Olzak, Susan, Suzanne Shanahan, and Elizabeth H. McEneaney. "Poverty, Segregation, and Race Riots: 1960 to 1993." *American Sociological Review* 61, no. 4 (1996): 590–613.

O'Mara, Erin M., Lydia E. Jackson, C. Daniel Batson, and Lowell Gaertner. "Will Moral Outrage Stand up? Distinguishing Among Emotional Reactions to a Moral Violation." *European Journal of Social Psychology* 41, no. 2 (2011): 173–179.

Omi, Michael, and Howard Winant. "Racial Formations." In *Rethinking the Color Line*, edited by Charles A. Gallagher, 21–27. New York: McGraw-Hill, 2007.

Ostrovsky, Arkady. *The Invention of Russia: From Gorbachev's Freedom to Putin's War*. New York: Viking, 2016.

Owens, Timothy J., Dawn T. Robinson, and Lynn Smith-Lovin. "Three Faces of Identity." *Annual Review of Sociology* 36 (2010): 477–499.

Page, Scott E. *The Difference: How the Power of Diversity Creates Better Groups, Firms, Schools and Societies*. Princeton, NJ: Princeton University Press, 2007.

Paine, Christopher F., Thomas B. Cochran, and Robert S. Norris. "The Arsenals of the Nuclear Weapons Powers: An Overview." Natural Resources Defense Council (Canberra Commission Issue Paper), January 4, 1996.

Pandith, Farah. *How We Win: How Cutting-Edge Entrepreneurs, Political Visionaries, Enlightened Business Leaders, and Social Media Mavens Can Defeat the Extremist Threat*. New York: Custom House Books, 2019.

Papachristos, Andrew V. "Murder by Structure: Dominance Relations and the Social Structure of Gang Homicide." *American Journal of Sociology* 115, no. 1 (2009): 74–128.

Park, Justin H., and Edward Isherwood. "Effects of Concerns about Pathogens on Conservatism and Anti-fat Prejudice: Are They Mediated by Moral Intuitions?" *Journal of Social Psychology* 151, no. 4 (2011): 301–394.

Paroline, Eugene A. "Taking Stock: Toward a Richer Understanding of Police Culture." *Journal of Criminal Justice* 31, no. 3 (2003): 199–214.

Paroline, Eugene A., and William Terrill. *Police Culture: Adapting to the Strains of the Job*. Durham, NC: Carolina Academic Press, 2013.

Paternoster, Raymond, Robert Brame, Ronet Bachman, and Lawrence W. Sherman. "Do Fair Procedure Matter? The Effect of Procedural Justice on Spouse Assault." *Law and Society Review* 31, no. 1 (1997): 163–204.
Patty, John W. "Signaling Through Obstruction." *American Journal of Political Science* 60, no. 1 (2016): 175–189.
Paxton, Pamela, Melanie M. Hughes, and Jennifer L. Green. "The International Women's Movement and Women's Political Representation, 1893–2003." *American Sociological Review* 71, no. 6 (2006): 898–920.
Peek, Lori. *Behind the Backlash: Muslim Americans After 9/11*. Philadelphia: Temple University Press, 2011.
Peffley, Mark, and Jon Hurwitz. "Persuasion and Resistance: Race and the Death Penalty in America." *American Journal of Political Science* 51, no. 4 (2007): 996–1012.
Pellegrini, Anthony D., and Jeffrey D. Long. "Part of the Solution and Part of the Problem: The Role of Peers in Bullying, Dominance, and Victimization during the Transition from Primary School Through Secondary School." In *Bullying in American Schools: A Social-ecological Perspective on Prevention and Intervention*, edited by D. L. Espelage and S. M. Swearer, 107–117. Mahwah, NJ: Erlbaum, 2004.
Pennebaker, James W., and Kent D. Harber. "A Social Stage Model of Collective Coping: The Loma Prieta Earthquake and the Persian Gulf War." *Journal of Social Issues* 49, no. 4 (1993): 125–145.
Pepler, Debra, Wendy Craig, and Paul O'Connell. "Peer Processes in Bullying: Informing Prevention and Intervention Strategies." In *Handbook of Bullying in Schools: An International Perspective*, edited by S. R. Jimerson, S. M. Swearer, and D. L. Espelage, 469–479. New York: Routledge, 2010.
Pernell-Gallagher, Kim. "Learning from Performance: Banks, Collateralized Debt Obligations, and the Credit Crisis." *Social Forces* 94, no. 1 (2015): 31–59.
Pfaff, John F. *Locked In: The True Causes of Mass Incarceration and How to Achieve Real Reform*. New York: Basic Books, 2017.
Pieterse, Jan N. "Ethnicities and Multiculturalism: Politics of Boundaries." In *Nationalism, Ethnicity and Minority Rights*, edited by S. May, T. Madood, and J. Squires, 27–49. London: Cambridge University Press, 2004.
Piketty, Thomas. *Capital in the Twenty-First Century*, translated by Arthur Goldhammer. Cambridge, MA: Belknap Press, 2017.
Pinard, Marice. *Motivational Dimensions in Social Movements and Contentious Collective Action*. Montreal, Canada: McGill-Queen's University Press, 2011.
Pinker, Steven. *Enlightenment Now: The Case for Reason, Science, Humanism, and Progress*. New York: Viking, 2018.
Pinker, Steven. *The Better Angels of Our Nature: Why Violence Has Declined*. New York: Viking, 2011.
Polanyi, Karl. *The Great Transformation: The Political and Economic Origin of Our Time*. New York: Farrar & Rinehart, 1944.
Polletta, Francesca, and James M. Jasper. "Collective Identity and Social Movements." *Annual Review of Sociology* 27, no. 1 (2001): 283–305.
Post, Jerod, Ehud Sprinzak, and Laurita Denny. "The Terrorists in Their Own Words: Interviews with 35 Incarcerated Middle Eastern Terrorists." *Terrorism and Political Violence* 15, no. 1 (2003): 171–184.
Pratto, Felicia, James Sidanius, Lisa M. Stallworth, and Bertram F. Malle. "Social Dominance Orientation: A Personality Variable Predicting Social and Political Attitudes." *Journal of Personality and Social Psychology* 67, no. 4 (1994): 741–763.
Prechel, Harland, and Theresa Morris. "The Effects of Organizational and Political Embeddedness on Financial Malfeasance in the Largest U.S. Corporations: Dependence, Incentives, and Opportunities." *American Sociological Review* 75, no. 3 (2010): 331–354.
Prewitt, Kenneth. *What Is Your Race? The Census and Our Flawed Efforts to Classify Americans*. Princeton, N.J.: Princeton University Press, 2013.
Quart, Alissa. *Squeezed: Why Our Families Can't Afford America*. New York: HarperCollins, 2018.
Rachman, Gideon. *Easternization: Asia's Rise and America's Decline*. New York: Other Press, 2017.

Ramirez, Francisco O., Yasemin Soysal, and Suzanne Shanahan. "The Changing Logic of Political Citizenship: Cross-National Acquisition of Women's Suffrage Rights, 1890 to 1990." *American Sociological Review* 62, no. 5 (1997): 735–745.

Rapoport, David C. "Sacred Terror: A Contemporary Example from Islam." In *Origins of Terrorism: Psychologies, Ideologies, Theologies, States of Mind*, edited by Walter Reich, 103–130. Washington, D.C.: Woodrow Wilson Center Press, 1998.

Razoux, Pierre. *The Iran-Iraq War*, translated by Nicholas Elliott. Cambridge, MA: Belknap Press, 2015.

Rex, John. "The Fundamentals of the Theory of Ethnicity." In *Making Sense of Collectivity: Ethnicity, Nationalism and Globalisation*, edited by Sinisa Malesevic and Mark Haugaard, 88–121. London: Pluto Press, 2002.

Riaz, Mohammad Khan. *Afghanistan and Pakistan: Conflict, Extremism, and Resistance to Modernity*. Baltimore: Johns Hopkins University Press, 2011.

Richter, Brian K., Krislert Samphantharak, and Jeffrey F. Timmons. "Lobbying and Taxes." *American Journal of Political Science* 53, no. 4 (2009): 893–909.

Ridley, Matt. *The Rational Optimists: How Prosperity Evolves*. New York: HarperCollins, 2010.

Riva, Paolo, Kipling D. Williams, Alex M. Torstrick, and Lorenzo Montali. "Orders to Shoot (a Camera): Effects of Ostracism on Obedience." *The Journal of Social Psychology* 154, no. 3 (2014): 208–216.

Robertson, Graeme B., and Emmanuel Teitelbaum. "Foreign Direct Investment, Regime Type, and Labor Protest in Developing Countries." *American Journal of Political Science* 55, no. 3 (2011): 665–677.

Robinson, William I. *Global Capitalism and the Crisis of Humanity*. New York: Cambridge University Press, 2014.

Rodkin, Philip C., Allison M. Ryan, Rhonda Jamison, and Travis Wilson. "Social Goals, Social Behavior, and Social Status in Middle Childhood." *Developmental Psychology* 49, no. 6 (2013): 1139–1150.

Rohlinger, Deana A., Jesse Klein, Tara M. Stamm, and Kyle Rogers. "Constructing Boundaries: Collective Identity in the Tea Party Movement." In *Border Politics: Social Movements, Collective Identities, and Globalization*, edited by Nancy A. Naples and Jennifer B. Mendez, 177–205. New York: New York University Press, 2014.

Rojas, Antonio J., Marisol Navas, Pablo Sayans-Jimenez, and Isabel Cuadrado. "Accumulation Preference Profiles of Spaniards and Romanian Immigrants: The Role of Prejudice and Public and Private Acculturation Areas." *The Journal of Social Psychology* 154, no. 4 (2014): 339–351.

Rosell, Ellen, Kathy Miller, and Karen Barber. "Firefighting Women and Sexual Harassment." *Psychology of Women Quarterly* 32 (2008): 362–376.

Rotenberg, Mordechai. "Alienating-individualism and Reciprocal-individualism: A Cross-cultural Conceptualization." *Journal of Humanistic Psychology* 17, no. 4 (1997): 3–17.

Rowatt, Wade C., Jordan LaBouff, Megan Johnson, Paul Froese, and Jo-Ann Tsang. "Associations Among Religiousness, Social Attitudes, and Prejudice in a National Random Sample of American Adults. *Psychology of Religion and Spirituality* 1, no. 1 (2009): 14–24.

Rudolph, Thomas J., and Jillian Evans. "Political Trust, Ideology, and Public Support for Government Spending." *American Journal of Political Science* 49, no. 3 (2005): 660–671.

Russel, Charles, and Bowman Miller. "Profile of a Terrorist." *Terrorism* 1, no. 1 (1977): 17–34.

Russel-Brown, Katheryn. *Protecting Our Own: Race, Crime, and African Americans*. Lanham, MD: Rowman & Littlefield, 2006.

Ryazanovskiy, Lev M. "Slogans and Mottos of the Third Reich and the Way Nazi Propaganda Used Them." *Journal of Historical, Philological and Cultural Studies* 3, no. 53 (2016): 128–133.

Sachs, Jeffrey D. *A New Foreign Policy: Beyond American Exceptionalism*. New York: Columbia University Press, 2018.

Sagafi-Nejad, Tagi. *The UN and Transnational Corporations: From Code of Conduct to Global Compact*. Bloomington: Indiana University Press, 2008.

Sampson, Robert J., and Dawn J. Bartusch. "Legal Cynicism and (Subcultural?) Tolerance of Deviance: The Neighborhood Context of Racial Differences." *Law and Society Review* 32, no. 4 (1998): 777–804.

Santoro, Wayne A., and Lisa Broidy. "Gendered Rioting: A General Strain Theoretical Approach." *Social Forces* 93, no. 1 (2014): 329–354.

Santos, Boaventura S., Joao A. Nunes, and Maria P. Meneses. "Introduction: Opening Up the Canon of Knowledge and Recognition of Difference." In *Another Knowledge Is Possible: Beyond Northern Epistemologies*, edited by B. S. Santos, vii–xvix. New York: Verso, 2007.

Saperstein, Aliya, and Andrew M. Penner. "Racial Fluidity and Inequality in the United States." *American Journal of Sociology* 118, no. 3 (2012): 676–727.

Sarno, Charles, Benjamin Shestakofsky, Helen Shoemaker, and Rebecca Aponte. "Rationalizing Judgment Day: A Content Analysis of Harold Camping's Open Forum Program." *Sociology of Religion* 76, no. 2 (2015): 199–221.

Savun, Burcu, and Daniel C. Tirone. "Foreign Aid, Democratization, and Civil Conflict: How Does Democracy Aid Affect Civil Conflicts?" *American Journal of Political Science* 55, no. 2 (2011): 233–246.

Schaller, Mark, Justin H. Park, and Jason Faulkner. "Prehistoric Dangers and Contemporary Prejudices." *European Review of Social Psychology* 14 (2003): 105–137.

Schenck, Bob. *Costly Grace: An Evangelical Minister's Rediscovery of Faith, Hope, and Love.* New York: Harper, 2018.

Schlosberg, David. *Defining Environmental Justice: Theories, Movements, and Nature.* London: Oxford University Press, 2007.

Schmidt-Catran, Alexander W., and Dennis C. Spies. "Immigration and Welfare Support in Germany." *American Sociological Review* 81, no. 2 (2016): 242–261.

Schofer, Evan, and Ann Hironaka. "The Effects of World Society on Environmental Protection Outcomes." *Social Forces* 84, no. 1 (2005): 25–47.

Scott, James M., and Carie A. Steele. "Sponsoring Democracy: The United States and Democracy Aid to the Developing World, 1988–2001." *International Studies Quarterly* 55, no. 1 (2011): 47–69.

Sebestyen, Victor. *Lenin: The Man, the Dictator, and the Master of Terror.* New York: Pantheon, 2017.

Seyranian, Viviane. "Constructing Extremism Uncertainty Provocation and Reduction by Extremist Leaders." In *Extremism and the Psychology of Uncertainty*, edited by Michael A. Hogg and Danielle L. Blaylock, chapter 14. West Sussex, UK: Wiley-Blackwell, 2011.

Shalhope, Robert E. "Individualism in the Early Republic." In *American Chameleon: Individualism in Trans-National Context*, edited by Richard O. Curry and Lawrence B. Goodheart, 66–86. Kent, OH: Kent State University, 1991.

Shapiro, Jacob N., and David A. Siegel. "Understanding in Terrorist Organizations." *International Studies Quarterly* 51, no. 2 (2007): 405–429.

Sharkey, Patrick. *Uneasy Peace: The Great Crime Decline, the Renewal of City Life, and the Next War on Violence.* New York: W. W. Norton, 2018.

Shaw, Clifford R., and Henry D. McKay. *Juvenile Delinquency and Urban Areas.* Chicago: University of Chicago Press, 1942.

Shermer, Michael. *The Moral Arc: How Science and Reason Lead Humanity Toward Truth, Justice and Freedom.* New York: Henry Holt, 2015.

Shirley, Carla D. "'You Might be a Redneck if…' Boundary Work Among Rural, Southern Whites." *Social Forces* 89, no. 1 (2010): 35–62.

Sibley, Chris G., and John Duckitt. "The Personality Bases of Ideology: A One-year Longitudinal Study." *Journal of Social Psychology* 150, no. 5 (2010): 540–559.

Sibley, Chris G., M. S. Wilson, and John Duckitt. "Effects of Dangerous and Competitive Worldviews on Right-Wing Authoritarianism and Social Dominance Orientation Over a Five-month Period." *Political Psychology* 28, no. 3 (2007): 357–371.

Siegel, Jason, William Crano, Eusebio Alvaro, Andrew Lac, David Rast, and Vennessa Kettering. "Dying to Be Popular: A Purposive Explanation of Adolescent Willingness to Endure Harm." In *Extremism and the Psychology of Uncertainty*, edited by Michael A. Hogg and Danielle L. Blaylock, chapter 7. West Sussex, UK: Wiley-Blackwell, 2011.

Simmel, Georg. *Conflict*, translated by Kurt H. Wolff and Reinhard Bendix. New York: Free Press, 1955 [1908].

Simmel, Georg. *On Individuality and Social Forms*, edited with an introduction by Donald N. Levine. Chicago: University of Chicago Press, 1971 [1908].

Skey, Michael. *National Belonging and Everyday Life: The Significance of Nationhood in an Uncertain World.* New York: Palgrave Macmillan, 2011.

Sklair, Leslie. *The Transnational Capitalist Class*. Malden, MA: Blackwell, 2001.
Skocpol, Theda. *States and Social Revolutions*. New York: Cambridge University Press, 1979.
Smelser, Neil J. *Theory of Collective Behavior*. New York: Free Press, 1962.
Smith, Anthony D. *Nationalism and Modernism: A Critical Survey of Recent Theories of Nations and Nationalism*. London: Routledge, 1999.
Smith, Jean E. *Bush*. New York: Simon & Schuster, 2016.
Smith, Jeffrey A., Miller McPherson, and Lynn Smith-Lovin. "Social Distance in the U.S.: Sex, Race, Religion, Age, and Education Homophily Among Confidants, 1985–2004." *American Sociological Review* 79, no. 3 (2014): 432–465.
Smythe, Elizabeth. "In Whose Interests? Transparency and Accountability in the Global Governance of Food: Agribusiness, the Codex Alimentarius, and the World Trade Organization." In *Corporate Power in Global Agrifood Governance*, edited by Jennifer Clapp and Doris Fuchs, 93–124. Cambridge, MA: MIT Press, 2009.
Snow, David A., and Robert D. Benford. "Ideology, Frame Resonance, and Participant Mobilization." *International Social Movement Research* 1, no. 1 (1988): 197–217.
Somers, Margaret. "The Narrative Constitution of Identity: A Relational and Network Approach." *Theory and Society* 23, no. 5 (1994): 605–649.
Soufan, Ali. *Anatomy of Terror: From the Death of bin Laden to the Rise of the Islamic State*. New York: W. W. Norton, 2017.
Soule, Sarah A. *Contention and Corporate Social Responsibility*. New York: Cambridge University Press, 2009.
Spellberg, Denise. *Politics, Gender, and the Islamic Past: The Legacy of A'isha bint Abi Bakr*. New York: Columbia University Press, 1994.
Spencer, Philip, and Howard Wollman. "Blood and Sacrifice: Politics versus Culture in the Construction of Nationalism." In *Naitonalism Old and New*, edited by Kevin J. Brehony and Naz Rassool, 87–124. London: Macmillan Press, 1999.
Sperling, John, Suzanne W. Helbum, Samuel George, John Morris, and Carl Hunt. *The Great Divide: Retro vs. Metro America*. Sausalito, CA: PoliPoint Press, 2005.
Sprinzak, Ehud. "The Psycho-political Formation of Extreme Left Terrorism in a Democracy: The Case of the Weathermen." In *Origins of Terrorism: Psychologies, Ideologies, Theologies, States of Mind*, edited by Walter Reich, 65–85. Washington, D.C.: Woodrow Wilson Center Press, 1998.
Stainback, Kevin, Thomas Ratliff, and Vincent J. Roscigno. "The Context of Workplace Sex Discrimination: Sex Composition, Workplace Culture, and Relative Power." *Social Forces* 89, no. 4 (2011): 1165–1188.
Stamper, Norm. *To Protect and Serve: How to Fix America's Police*. New York: Nation Books, 2016.
Stark, Rodney. *Sociology*, 9th Edition. Belmont, CA: Wadsworth, 2004.
Stark, Rodney, and Roger Finke. *Acts of Faith: Explaining the Human Side of Religion*. Berkeley: University of California Press, 2000.
Stark, Rodney, and William Bainbridge. "Secularization, Revival, and Cult Formation." *Annual Review of the Social Science of Religion* 4 (1980): 85–119.
Starr, Paul. *Freedom's Power: The True Force of Liberalism*. New York: Basic Books, 2007.
Stenner, Karen. *The Authoritarian Dynamic*. New York: Cambridge University Press, 2005.
Stephan, Walter G., Oscar Ybarra, and Kimberly R. Morrison. "Intergroup Threat Theory." In *Handbook of Prejudice, Stereotyping, and Discrimination*, edited by T. D. Nelson, 43–59. New York: Psychology Press, 2009.
Stern, Jessica. *Terror in the Name of God: Why Religious Militants Kill*. New York: Harper Perennial, 2004.
Stets, Jan E., and Michael J. Carter. "A Theory of the Self for the Sociology of Morality." *American Sociological Review* 77, no. 1 (2012): 120–140.
Stewart, Francis. *Horizontal Inequalities and Conflict: Understanding Group Violence in Multiethnic Societies*. New York: Palgrave Macmillan, 2008.
Stieglitz, Jonathan, Michael Gurven, Hillard Kaplan, and Jeffrey Winking. "Infidelity, Jealousy, and Wife Abuse Among Tsimane Forager-Farmers: Testing Evolutionary Hypotheses of Marital Conflict." *Evolutionary Human Behavior* 33, no. 5 (2012): 438–448.
Stiglitz, Joseph E. *Globalization and Its Discontents*. New York: W.W. Norton, 2003.

Stiglitz, Joseph E. *The Price of Inequality: How Today's Divided Society Endangers Our Future*. New York: W.W. Norton, 2013.

Su, Yang. *Collective Killings in Rural China During the Cultural Revolution*. New York: Cambridge University Press, 2011.

Suzuki, Munenori, Midori Ito, Mitsunori Ishida, Norihiro Nihei, and Masao Maruyama. "Individualizing Japan: Searching for Its Origin in First Modernity." *British Journal of Sociology* 61, no. 3 (2010): 513–538.

Swidler, Ann. "Culture in Action: Symbols and Strategies." *American Sociological Review* 51, no. 2 (1986): 273–286.

Taagepera, Rein. "Prospects for Democracy in Islamic Countries." In *Democratic Development & Political Terrorism: The Global Perspective*, edited by William Crotty, 93–101. Boston: Northeastern University Press, 2005.

Tadmouri, Ghazi, Pratibha Nair, Tasneem Obeid, Mahmoud Al Ali, Najib Al Kjaja, and Hanan A. Hamamy. "Consanguinity and Reproductive Health Among Arabs." *Reproductive Health* 8 (2009): 6–17.

Tajfel, Henry, and John C. Turner. "An Integrative Theory of Intergroup Conflict." In *The Social Psychology of Intergroup Relations*, edited by W. Austin and S. Worchel, 33–47. Monterey, CA: Books/Cole, 1979.

Taylor, Brian D. *The Code of Putinism*. London: Oxford University Press, 2017.

Taylor, Charles. *A Secular Age*. Cambridge, MA: The Belknap Press, 2007.

Taylor, Charles. *Dilemmas and Connections*. Cambridge, MA: Belknap Press, 2011.

Taylor, Donald M. *The Quest for Identity*. Westport, CT: Praeger, 2002.

Taylor, Verta, and Nancy. E. Whittier. "Collective Identity in Social Movement Communities: Lesbian Feminist Mobilization." In *Waves of Protest: Social Movements Since the Sixties*, edited by J. Freeman and V. Johnson, 169–194. Oxford, UK: Oxford Univ. Press, 1999.

Taylor, Verta, and Nella Van Dyke. "'Get Up. Stand Up': Tactical Repertoires of Social Movements." In *The Blackwell Companion to Social Movements*, edited by David A. Snow, Sarah A. Soule, and Hanspeter Kriesi, 262–293. Malden, MA: Blackwell. 2004.

Telles, Edward, and Tianna Paschel. "Who Is Black, White, or Mixed Race? How Skin Color, Status, and Nation Shape Racial Classification in Latin America." *American Journal of Sociology* 120, no. 3 (2014): 864–907.

Teney, Celine. "Endorsement of Assimilationism Among Ethnic Minority and Majority Youth in a Multination-Multiethnic Context: The Case of Brussels." *European Sociological Review* 27, no. 2 (2011): 212–229.

Thomas, Gordon, and Max Morgan-Witts. *Ruin from the Air*. London: Hamilton, 1977.

Thomas, M. A. *Govern Like Us: U.S. Expectations of Poor Countries*. New York: Columbia University Press, 2015.

Thomson, Irene T. *Culture Wars and Enduring American Dilemmas*. Ann Arbor: University of Michigan Press, 2010.

Thurman, Quint, and Andrew Giacomazzi. *Controversies in Policing*. New York: Routledge, 2016.

Tilly, Charles. *Contentious Performances*. Cambridge, UK: Cambridge University Press, 2008.

Tilly, Charles. *Identities, Boundaries, and Social Change*. Boulder, CO: Paradigm Publishers, 2005.

Tilly, Charles. "States and Nationalism in Europe, 1492–1992." *Theory and Society* 23, no. 1 (1994): 131–146.

Tilly, Charles, and Sidney Tarrow. *Contentious Politics*. Boulder, CO: Paradigm, 2007.

Toch, Hans. *Cop Watch: Spectators, Social Media, and Police Reform*. Washington, D.C.: American Psychological Association, 2012.

Tololyan, Khachig. "Cultural Narrative and the Motivation of the Terrorist." In *Inside Terrorist Organizations*, edited by David C. Rapoport, 217–233. Portland: Frank Cass, 2001.

Tonelson, Alan. *The Race to the Bottom: Why a Worldwide Worker Surplus and Uncontrolled Free Trade Are Sinking American Living Standards*. Boulder, CO: Westview Press, 2000.

Tooze, Adam. *Crashed: How a Decade of Financial Crises Changed the World*. New York: Viking, 2018.

Torfason, Magnus, and Paul Ingram. "The Global Rise of Democracy: A Network Account." *American Sociological Review* 75, no. 3 (2010): 355–377.

Trammell, Rebecca. *Enforcing the Convict Code: Violence and Prison Culture*. Boulder, CO: Lynne Rienner Publishers, 2012.

Treitler, Vilna B. *The Ethnic Project: Transforming Racial Fiction into Ethnic Factions*. Stanford, CA: Stanford University Press, 2013.
Turchie, Terry D., and Kathleen Puckett. *Hunting the American Terrorist: The FBI's War on Homegrown Terror*. Palisades, NY: History Publishing Co, 2007.
Turk, Austin T. "Sociology of Terrorism." *Annual Review of Sociology*. 30, no. 1 (2004): 271–286.
Tyler, Tom R. "Enhancing Police Legitimacy." *Annals of the American Academy of Political and Social Sciences* 593 (2004): 84–99.
Uehara, Shunsuke, Tomohiro Nakagawa, and Toru Tamura. "What Leads to Evocation of Moral Outrage? Exploring the Role of Personal Morality." *International Journal of Psychological Studies* 6, no. 1 (2015): 58–67.
Uggen, Christopher, Amy Blackstone. "Sexual Harassment as a Gendered Expression of Power." *American Sociological Review* 69, no. 1 (2004): 64–92.
U.S. Government Printing Office. *The 9/11 Commission Report: Final Report of the National Commission on Terrorist Attacks upon the United States*, 47–55. Washington, D.C., 2004.
Useem, Bert. "Breakdown Theories of Collective Action." *Annual Review of Sociology* 24 (1998): 215–238.
Valle, Alvaro. "Dancing with Monsters: The U.S. Response to the 2009 Honduran Coup." *Harvard Political Review*. April 13, 2015.
Van Hiel, Alain, and Barbara De Clercq. "Authoritarianism Is Good for You: Right-wing Authoritarianism as a Buffering Factor for Mental Distress." *European Journal of Personality* 23, no. 1 (2009): 33–50.
Van Oorschot, Wim. "Public Perceptions of the Economic, Moral, Social and Migration Consequences of the Welfare State: An Empirical Analysis of Welfare State Legitimacy." *Journal of European Social Policy* 20, no. 1 (2010): 19–31.
Varese, Federico. *The Russian Mafia: Private Protection in a New Market Economy*. London: Oxford University Press, 2001.
Venkatesh, Sudhir A. "The Social Organization of Street Gang Activity in an Urban Ghetto." *American Journal of Sociology* 103, no. 1 (1997): 82–111.
Vito, Gennaro F., Scott Wolfe, George E. Higgins, and William F. Walsh. "Police Integrity: Rankings of Scenarios on the Klockars Scale by 'Management Cops.'" *Criminal Justice Review* 36, no. 2 (2011): 152–164.
Voicu, Mălina. "Effect of Nationalism on Religiosity in 30 European Countries." *European Sociological Review* 28, no. 3 (2012): 333–343.
Volkan, Vamik D. *Blind Trust: Large Groups and Their Leaders in Times of Crisis and Terror*. Charlottesville, VA: Pitchstone Publishing, 2004.
Volkan, Vamik D. *Killing in the Name of Identity: A Study of Bloody Conflicts*. Charlottesville, VA: Pitchstone Publishing, 2006.
Volscho, Thomas W., and Nathan J. Kelly. "The Rise of the Super-Rich: Power Resources, Taxes, Financial Markets, and the Dynamics of the Top 1 Percent, 1949 to 2008." *American Sociological Review* 77, no. 5 (2012): 679–699.
Wade, Robert H. "The Rising Inequality of World Income Distribution." In *Development and Underdevelopment: The Political Economy of Global Inequality*, edited by Mitchell A. Seligson and John T. Passe-Smith (3rd Edition), 31–39. Boulder, CO: Lynne Rienner, 2003.
Wagner, Peter. *Modernity as Experience and Interpretation: A New Sociology of Modernity*. Cambridge, UK: Polity, 2008.
Walder, Andrew. *China Under Mao: A Revolution Derailed*. Cambridge, MA: Harvard University Press, 2015.
Walder, Andrew. "Political Sociology and Social Movements." *Annual Review of Sociology* 35 (2009): 393–412.
Walker, Michael L. "Race Making in a Penal Institution." *American Journal of Sociology* 121, no. 4 (2016): 1051–1078.
Walker, Robert S., and Drew H. Bailey. "Marrying Kin in Small-scale Societies." *American Journal of Human Biology* 26, no. 3 (2014): 384–388.
Walsh, Chris. *Cowardice: A Brief History*. Princeton, NJ: Princeton University Press, 2014.
Walzer, Michael. *The Revolution of the Saints: A Study in the Origins of Radical Politics*. Cambridge, MA: Harvard University Press, 1965.

Waterman, A. S. "Individualism and Interdependence." *American Psychologist* 36, no. 7 (1981): 762–773.
Way, Christopher, and Jessica L. P. Peeks. "Making It Personal: Regime Type and Nuclear Proliferation." *American Journal of Political Science* 58, no. 3 (2014): 705–719.
Weber, Christopher R., Howard Lavine, Leonie Huddy, and Christopher M. Federico. "Placing Racial Stereotypes in Context: Social Desirability and the Politics of Racial Hostility." *American Journal of Political Science* 58, no. 1 (2014): 63–78.
Weber, Max. "Open and Closed Relationships." In *Inequality and Society*, edited by Jeff Manza and Michael Sauder, 94–98. New York: W. W. Norton, 2009 [1920].
Weede, Erich, and Edward N. Muller. "Consequences of Revolutions." *Rationality and Society* 9, no. 3 (1997): 327–350.
Weede, Erich, and Edward N. Muller. "Rebellion, Violence and Revolution: A Rational Choice Perspective." *Journal of Peace Research* 35, no. 1 (1998): 43–59.
Weinreb, Alexander A. "Characteristics of Women in Consanguineous Marriages in Egypt, 1988–2000." *European Journal of Population* 24, no. 2 (2008): 185–210.
Weisner, Thomas S. "Culture, Childhood, and Progress in Sub-Saharan Africa." In *Culture Matters: How Values Shape Human Progress*, edited by Laurence E. Harrison and Samuel P. Huntington, 141–157. New York: Basic Books, 2001.
Weiss, Elaine. *The Woman's Hour: The Great Fight to Win the Vote*. New York: Viking, 2018.
Wejnert, Barbara. "Diffusion, Development, and Democracy, 1800–1999." *American Sociological Review* 70, no. 1 (2005): 53–81.
Werner, Timothy. *Public Forces and Private Politics in American Big Business*. New York: Cambridge University Press, 2012.
Whitman, Walt. *Leaves of Grass: The Original 1855 Edition*. Mineola, NY: Dover Publications, 2007 [1855].
Whitt, Sam, and Rick K. Wilson. "The Dictator Game: Fairness and Equity in Postwar Bosnia." *American Journal of Political Science* 51, no. 3 (2007): 655–668.
Wiertz, Dingeman. "Segregation in Civic Life: Ethnic Sorting and Mixing across Voluntary Associations." *American Sociological Review* 81, no. 4 (2016): 800–827.
Wilber, Del Quentin. *A Good Month for Murder: The Inside Story of a Homicide Squad*. New York: Henry Holt, 2016.
Williams, Christine. "The Glass Escalator: Hidden Advantages for Men in the Female' Professions." *Social Problems* 39, no. 3 (1992): 253–267.
Williams, Joan C. *White Working Class: Overcoming Class Cluelessness in America*. Boston: Harvard Business Review Press, 2017.
Wilson, William. J. *The Truly Disadvantaged: The Inner City, the Underclass, and Public Policy*. Chicago: University of Chicago Press, 1987.
Wimmer, Andreas. *Ethnic Boundary Making: Institutions, Power, Networks*. New York: Oxford University Press, 2013.
Wimmer, Andreas, and Kevin Lewis. "Beyond and Below Racial Homophily: ERG Models of a Friendship Network Documented on Facebook." *American Journal of Sociology* 116, no. 2 (2010): 583–642.
Wimmer, Andreas, and Thomas Soehl. "Blocked Acculturation: Cultural Heterodoxy Among Europe's Immigrants." *American Journal of Sociology* 120, no. 1 (2014): 146–186.
Wimmer, Andreas, and Yuval Feinstein. "The Rise of the Nation-State Across the World, 1916 to 2001." *American Sociological Review* 75, no. 5 (2010): 764–790.
Winkler, Allan M. *The Politics of Propaganda: Office of War Information, 1942–1945*. New Haven, CT: Yale University Press, 1978.
Wollschleger, Jason. "Interaction Chains and Religious Participation." *Sociological Forum* 27, no. 4 (2012): 896–912.
Wong, Cara J. *Boundaries of Obligation in American Politics: Geographic, National, and Racial Communities*. New York: Cambridge University Press, 2010.
Wood, Adrian. *North-South Trade, Employment, and Inequality: Changing Fortunes in a Skill-Driven World*. New York: Oxford University Press, 1994.
Wuthnow, Robert. *Boundless Faith: The Global Outreach of American Churches*. Berkeley: University of California Press, 2009.
Wuthnow, Robert. *Communities of Discourse: Ideology and Social Structure in the Reformation,*

the Enlightenment, and European Socialism. Cambridge, MA: Harvard University Press, 1989.
Xu, Xiaohong. "Belonging Before Believing: Group Ethos and Block Recruitment in the Making of Chinese Communism." *American Sociological Review* 78, no. 5 (2013): 773–796.
Yackee, Jason W., and Susan W. Yackee. "A Bias Towards Business? Assessing Interest Group Influence on the U.S. Bureaucracy." *Journal of Politics* 68, no. 1 (2006): 128–139.
Yancey, George. *Who Is White? Latinos, Asians, and the New Black/Nonblack Divide.* Boulder, CO: Lynn Rienner, 2003.
Yearley, Steven. "Understanding Science from the Perspective of the Sociology of Scientific Knowledge: An Overview." *Public Understanding of Science* 3 (1994): 245–258.
Young, Frances M. *Sacrifice and the Death of Christ.* Eugene, OR: Wipf & Stock, 2010 [1975].
Zakaria, Fareed. *The Future of Freedom: Illiberal Democracy at Home and Abroad.* New York: W.W. Norton, 2007.
Zald, Mayer N., and John D. McCarthy. *Social Movements in an Organizational Society.* New Brunswick, NJ: Transaction, 1987.
Zimmermann, Ekkart. "Right-wing Extremism and Xenophobia in Germany: Escalation, Exaggeration, or What?" In *Right-wing Extremism in the Twenty-first Century,* edited by Peter H. Herkl and Leonard Weinberg, 220–250. Portland: Frank Cass, 2003.

Index

absolutism 79-82
academia, role in deterring extremism 264
al-Qaeda 62, 69, 109, 127-128; bashing of moderates 114-115; creating enemies with anti-West ideologies 127; goal of uniting Muslims 128; punishing deserters and defectors 109; reasons for joining 62; returning to "pure days in Islam" 114; seeking revenge 69; use of brutality to out-frighten enemies 170
al-Shabaab 55-56
alternative opportunities for advancement 195-198; *see also* oppositional culture; "social misfits"
al-Zarqawi 31, 33, 104, 119, 199
"American dream" 124
Amish 41, 107, 111, 112, 113, 144, 186, 191, 199, 211, 212
anti-atheist bias 35-36
anti-blasphemy laws 66
anti-EU extremisms in Europe 39, 115, 203, 246
anti-globalization extremisms 14, 115, 186, 245-247; *see also* anti-immigrant nativism
anti-immigrant nativism 20, 88, 115
anti-moderate sentiments 32-33, 95-96, 109; for lacking loyalty 114; in al-Qaeda 114-115; in U.S. partisan politics 114; *see also* "Blue Dogs" and "RINOs"
anti-Semitism 20, 123, 129, 132, 171, 238
"anti-snitch" culture 46, 53, 57; *see also* in-group protectionism
anti-West extremisms 13, 55-56, 186, 216, 224, 266; activities of multinational corporations 266; al-Shabaab 55-56; attacks on NGOs and humanitarian aid groups 56; Boko Haram 55-56; exploitation of resources 216, 224; killing collaborators of the West 56; military intervention 216, 224; political interference 216; propping up corrupt dictators 224; Taliban 55-56; unconditional sponsorship for Israel 216; Western support for dictators 216, 224; *see also* economic colonialism
apocalyptic cults 132, 136
apology 167-168
apostasy, punishing 10, 49, 109, 199
Arab Spring 222-223, 287
authoritarian leaders 18, 24, 91-94, 162-166; attachment to 23-24, 91-93; biases of 164-166, 220; command of absolute obedience, submission, and loyalty 162-163; consolidation of power 164-166; demanding unchallenged power 162; ideological indoctrination and framing 163-164; oppressive means of social control 163-164; rise during economic crisis and under external threats 127, 208; rule by fear and threats 163; *see also* authoritarianism, authoritarian submission; illiberal democracies, persecution of journalists
authoritarian submission 91; cause of illiberal democracies 92-94; defending leaders against critics 92
authoritarianism 20, 90-94; among white working-class 89-90; hypersensitivity to status hierarchies 90; right-wing 82, 90; rise during economic crisis 209; rise under existential threats 203-204; source of extremism 90; source of prejudice against minorities 90; submission to superiors and bullying to inferiors 90; *see also* authoritarian leaders; authoritarian submission
autonomy seeking 190-191, 197-198

balancing of clashing group interests 240-242, 248-251, 260; corporate and public interests 248-251; integration of marginalized groups 241-242; globalizing

383

and parochializing forces 244–248; group and humanity interests 242–244
bin Laden, Osama 54, 69, 114, 128, 171, 238; as "Robin Hood" 216; role of humiliation 220; vindictiveness 69
"Birthright Israel" 104
Black Lives Matter protests 223
blaming 137–144; of the West by jihadist movements 142; of victims 50, 72, 143–144; *see also* scapegoating, rape victims
"blood in, blood out" 109–110
"Blue Dogs" and "RINOs" 31, 114, 138; *see also* anti-moderate sentiments
Boko Haram 55, 70, 122, 172–173
Bolshevik revolutionaries 95
bonded laborers *see* indentured servitude
border psychology 109; *see also* boundary maintenance
"born-again" Christians, as status elevation strategy 119
boundary expansion 25, 115–116, 191–192; Cold War as 115–116, 192; communist expansionism 115–116; in religious missionary groups 116, 192; jihadist movement 192; *see also* inclusive identities; "open groups"
boundary maintenance 25, 99, 108–117, 212; defending tradition 42; defining power differentials and "deservedness" of insiders 108; demanding purity in identity 113–114; "genocidal elimination" 109; isolation and segregation 112–113; removing undesired outsiders 109; trapping 111–112; *see also* anti-immigrant nativism; border psychology; boundary-crossers, punishing
boundary-crossers, punishing 109–111; *see also* apostasy; whistle-blowers; anti-immigrant nativism; "anti-snitch" culture
bullying 50, 76, 90, 110, 137, 177, 182
bunker mentality 14, 27, 202, 244; *see also* "parochializing"
business elites 177, 265

"cafeteria Catholics" 33, 114
Catholic Church: demanding doctrinal purity 33, 114; extremist elements in 8; "sacred duty" of covering up pedophile priests 46, 53, 92, 123
"certainty trap" 80
Charlie Hebdo 66, 159
child brides 122–123; *see also* "spiritual marriages"
Christian Identity Group 123, 168
Christian nationalists 43
Civil Rights movement 9, 218
"clash of civilization" 15; as an effort to create "higher-order" group identity 116–117
"closed groups" 194–195; *see also* "status group ties"; occupational closure
code of silence 45; "cop code" 46, 53
Cold War 15, 19, 115, 132, 205–206; expansionist goals 192; stockpiles of nuclear weapons 170
collective defense mechanism 22, 202
collective fear 210–215
collective punishment 25, 171–174; among revolutionary and rebel groups 57; attacks on NGOs and humanitarian aid groups 56; economic sanctions as 173–174; guilt by association 171; killing collaborators with the West 56; to maximize terrorizing and deterrent effects 172; political purging as 59; state-sponsored 173–174; terrorist attacks as 22, 171–172, 251; *see also* cultural inversion
collective rejection 23, 55–59, 250; anti-Muslim hysteria and Islamophobia 56; anti-West sentiments as 55, 216, 224
collective shame and blame 54–55; *see also* guilt by association
collective support system, with pooled resources 187–188
collective wounds/traumas 68, 231
communes and enclaves, religious and ethnic 111–112, 190–191, 211; *see also* Amish groups
communism, as a class-based ideology 123–124
communist movements 15, 58, 115–116, 123–124, 128, 142, 152; appealing to emotions 152; blaming critics and dissenters for their failure 142; collective rejection 58; use of enemies 128; expansionism 115–116
communitarian spirit 28, 278–282; enhancing self-interests through collective interests 278–279; recognizing interdependency and shared fates of collectivities 279–280; shared sacrifices and shared benefits 280–281
competitive extremist groups 13
compromise, refusal to 81–82, 166–167; as a sign of weakness 81, 167
Confucianism 123
"cop code" *see* code of silence
corporate extremisms 177–180, 248–251; abusing employees 177–178; among drug companies 178; as a source of extremist violence 250–251; environmental destruction 178–179; to crush competitors 177; to maximize profit 177; tobacco industries 179; *see also* war profiteering

corporate interests, taming 250–251; *see also* multinational corporations
counter-extremism strategies 2, 9, 18, 28; empowering moderates 291–292; true goals of "war on terror" 36
criminal justice system, distrust in 53, 57; *see also* legal cynicism
crony capitalism 177
cultural deterrents of extremism 271–281; communitarian spirit 278–282; humanistic individualism 274–277; moderate centrism and fair-mindedness 271–272; pragmatic centrism 271–274
cultural differentiation, to justify superior status 100
cultural frames 21, 22, 44
cultural inversion 56–57; *see also* oppositional culture
"cultural revolution," communist: a form of collective rejection 59; creating and demonizing enemies 128; persecution and purging of intellectuals 166
"cultural turn" 21
"culture wars" 17; as identity construction process 99

"death squads" 226–227, 285; corporate-sponsored 74; used to quell leftist movements in Latin America 226–227
dehumanization 129
democracies, liberal and inclusive 205, 241, 256–258; offering legitimate outlets for expressing grievances 257–258; peaceful resolution of conflicts 258; peaceful transfer of powers 256; promoting inclusiveness 257; respect for equal rights of every group 256–257
dependency relationship, paternalistic 111–112; *see also* "paternalistic system"
deprivation theory of collective actions 218
deprivation-compensation theory 205
determent, extremist aggressions 25; balancing of clashing groups' interests 240–242; cultural changes 271–281; institutional assistance 258–271; strategic changes 282–292; structural changes 252–258
devolution, need for 269
dichotomous world view 22, 30–32; believers vs. non-believers 31; of "good vs. evil" and "us vs. them" 22
dictators, U.S. support for 285–286
disloyalty, acts of 109–110
"do-it-yourself" Catholics *see* "cafeteria Catholics"
dominant extremisms 12, 89, 263; by dominant groups to maximize group-centric interests 177; exploitation of employees 177; militarized 229–230; motivated by fear of losing power 89; by multinational corporations 224–226; police abuse of power and prisoner abuse 177; state-sponsored 231
dominant extremist groups 89, 176–180; defending superiority in identity 176; fear of losing dominance 89; maximizing group-centric interests 177; in patriarchy, colonialism, monarchism, white supremacy groups, right-wing extremist groups, anti-immigrant nativist groups 176–177; preserving privileged status and status quo 176
doomsday cults *see* apocalyptic cults
double standards 50; in partisan politics 51
drug companies, wrongdoings by 86–87, 249
Durkheim, Emile: on use of symbols in religion 155, 157–158; theory of ritual 95, 154
"duty to avenge" 67–71; as generational duty 68; goals of al-Qaeda and ISIS/Daesh 69; retaliation justice 68; *see also* vindictiveness

economic colonialism: "domination without annexation" 176; source of grievances against the West 216
economic elites 224; *see also* plutocrats; transnational capitalist class (TCC)
economic sanctions 173–174
ELN 101, 216, 226, 287, 290; *see also* leftist groups
emotional gratification, seeking 96
emotions: appealing to 149–152; to encourage self-sacrifice 151; fixated emotions of hatred 95–96; to inspire bravery and courage 151; to invoke group solidarity 150–151; power of 95; to suppress rational reasoning 150; *see also* hatred
empathetic solidarity, invoking 98
"end-justifies-the-means" mindset 24, 83–84, 89; among politicians 84; in achieving group-centric goals 83; in maximizing corporate profits 84, 86–87; state-sponsored extremist acts 84; using child soldiers and teenage suicide bombers 84; of "visionary leaders" 83–84; war profiteering by weapons industries and defense contractors 86
enemies, use of 126–129
"enemization and demonization" strategy 11, 31, 126–127
environmental destruction 179, 248–250

ethnic cleansing, of Rohingya Muslims 94
ethno-nationalism: white nationalism in Europe 39; white supremacists in America 12, 20, 63, 119, 130–131, 215
evangelicals, Christian 20, 35, 61; seeking "nobler/higher" causes and meanings in life 97; "spiritual satisfaction" from "saving lost souls" 97; war on "people of faith" 131
"exceptionalism": American 36, 117, 118, 120; Islamic 117, 122
existential denial: causing identity crisis 62, 242; experienced by marginalized immigrants 62
existential security: deterring extremism 204–205, 251–253; threats to 26, 184, 200–210, 242, 246
extremist groups 5–11; appealing to "social misfits" 196; charity work 146, 188, 207–208; as "family substitute" 62; offering alternative opportunities for power, advancement, excitement 196; as "protection mechanism" 60; satisfying yearning for belonging and identity 196; seeking "nobler/higher" causes and meanings 97; types of 11–12; *see also* collective fear; existential security; fate-sharing experiences; isolation; grievances, group-felt, humiliation, group-felt; legitimation crisis;
extremist leaders: ability to encourage self-sacrifice 239; ability to procure resource and build organizational infrastructure 238; exaggerating external threats for personal gain 127; as instrumental medium 237–238

"failed states" 27, 184–185, 207–209
fairness: in distribution of resources 275; in systems 252–258; inclusive economic development 255; systemic and procedural 276; as rules of reciprocity 175
"faith-healing," 45
FARC 101, 216, 226, 287, 289, 290; *see also* leftist groups
far-right extremism, in Europe and America 203, 220, 223
fate-sharing experiences 27, 231–233; collective wounds and traumas 68
fear of extinction 14, 42, 186
fear, collective 210–215; America's history of 132–133; of "appearing weak" 166–167; of change 212–213; of extinction 13, 42, 186, 212; as impetus for radicalization 25–26; invoking to attain loyalty and dependency 133–134; of losing power and superiority 89, 214–215; of rejection 112,
211; stoking for financial gains 135–136; stoking to justify violence 135; *see also* fearmongering
fear-mongering 131–135; creating chaos to solicit support 209; creating group hysteria and collective panic 131–132; to elicit loyalty and solidarity 132; for financial gains 135; to justify use of violence 135; to silence critics 132; stoking fear by exaggerating threats 131–132; *see also* apocalyptic cults
financial crisis of 2008 *see* "Great Recession"
FLDS *see* Fundamentalist Church of Jesus Christ of Latter-Day Saints (FLDS)
forced assimilation 106–108
Freedom Caucus: refusal to negotiate compromises 167; seeking autonomy 197
free-market fundamentalism: as an ideology 124; *see also* supply-side economic theories
Fundamentalist Church of Jesus Christ of Latter-Day Saints (FLDS): ideological indoctrination 125; "spiritual marriage" with teenage girls 123; threat of rejection 211, trapping through isolation 112

gangs: attraction to "social misfits" 62, 196; ethnic 62; exit strategies 61–62; as family substitution 62; seeking alternative means of achieving status, success, and acceptance 195–196; seeking belonging and acceptance 61–62; social isolation 236; trapping members within 109
"global governance" 28
global injustice 266
globalization 244–248, 265–267; controversy over multiculturalism 245; dealing with immigrants 245; forcing economic cooperation 244; free-trade economic policies 245; positive and negative views 244–245; producing "winners" and "losers" 247; regulating 247–248, 265–267; sources of working-class grievances 247–248; as threat to cultural identity 244
goals, of extremists: building an autonomous entity 190–191; collective defense 184–186; creating alternative opportunities for advancement 195–198; expansion 191–195; group empowerment 175–199; hierarchical positioning 181–182; organizational survival 198–199; pooling resources 187–190; redemption 183–184
governmental regulation 262
"Great Recession" 86, 262
grievances, group-felt 26, 215–219, 284–

286; anti-West 216; cause of resistance extremism 215; controversy over role of grievances in collective actions 217–218; from oppression, abuse, injustice 215; *see also* sympathetic grievances; deprivation theory of collective actions
group competition theory 193
group empowerment 25; for dominance or resistance 175–179
group expansionism *see* boundary expansion
group fragmentation 202–203
group identities: constructing 98, 100–103; cultivating 98–105; invoking 103–104; maintaining 38–39, 98; marking of 103; as mobilization tool 24, 102–103; nurturing 104–105; as political process 99–100; in politics 99–100; in social hierarchy construction 99; significance of 38; sources of 5–6, 101; symbolic nature of 102
group power 94–96
group reputation, importance of defending 44–46; *see also* organizational cover-up
"groupthink" 40, 80
guilt by association 23, 54, 171, 288
gun-rights activism 82

Haditha massacre 71
Hamas 34–35, 139
hardline approaches, to conflict resolution 25–26, 166–171; consequences of 167–168; to defend group honor 166; "must win" mindsets 167; negotiating compromises as "signs of weakness" 167; to "out-frighten" enemies 166, 168; refusing to negotiate, compromise, and apologize 167–168; U.S. policies during Iraq and Afghan Wars 167; *see also* fear of "appearing weak"; militaristic jingoism; zero-sum worldview
Hasan, Nidal Malik 52, 63
Hasidic Jewish community: seeking group survival 199; trapping through isolation 113
hatred: source of extremism 95–96; toward moderates, mixed-identities, "sellouts," and "traitors" 32–34
hazing 74; in Russia 42–43
Heaven's Gate 61
herd mentality 82, 210–211
hierarchical positioning 181–182; *see also* bullying
hierarchical positioning tool 118–119
"higher/nobler" causes in life 24, 96–97, 145; *see also* "righteous crusaders"; single-issue fanatics/voters; "true believers"
Hinduism, justifying caste system and Indian nationalism 123

Holocaust: role of anti-Semitic hatred instilled by Nazis 129; role of extremist leader 238;
"home-grown" terrorists 184, 196, 219–220, 242
homogenizing pressure 40–41; enforcing uniformity with repressive means 106; maintaining purity in identity and ideology 106; *see also* forced assimilations
homophilic affinity 22, 38–40
Hong Kong riots 223
honor, defending group 23, 65–67
honor killing 44, 49, 66
humanistic individualism 28, 274–277; fairness 275–276; respect for human dignity and basic human rights 274–275; social justice on the global level 277; universalistic views and concerns 277; *see also* cultural deterrents of extremism
humiliation, group-felt 219–221
Hussein, Saddam 55, 70, 162, 163, 170, 171, 216, 227
"hypersensitivity to fear" 82–83
"hypo-descent" rule *see* "one-drop rule"

"identitarian" demagogues 12
identity crisis 62, 196, 242; *see also* existential denial
identity politics 80, 99–100
"identity verification process" 156–157; showing loyalty as 48
ideological indoctrination and dissemination 125–126
ideological echo chamber 127, 152, 238
ideologies, group-centric 12, 23, 25, 40, 96, 112, 120–126, 192, 237; class-based 123–124; communist 123–124; justifying injustices and violence 121; power of 120–122; sexist 176; using "freedom" as 125; using religion as 121–122; using tradition as 124–125
idioculture 19
illiberal democracies 92–94; *see also* authoritarian leaders, attachment to
Incel *see* "Involuntarily Celibate"
inclusion strategies: accepting extremist groups into society 289–292; peace deals with extremist/terrorist groups 289–290; political inclusion 289; "re-embedding" opportunities 290
inclusive identities 116; *see also* "clash of civilization"; pan-Islamism
indentured servitude 87
indigenization movements 14, 186, 213, 246
inequalities, extreme and unfair 2, 7, 27, 101, 222–223; reducing 254–256
in-group protectionism 51–53
injustice: created by dominant extremisms

221–223; as source of resistant extremism 15, 21, 26, 27, 222
institutional assistance, in deterring extremism 258–268; international governing bodies 265–268; media and academia 262–264; role of the state 259–262; *see also* determent, extremist aggressions
interdependency, from globalization 280–281; *see also* shared fates of collectivities
intergroup clashes 17, 88, 167
intergroup threat theory 18
International Criminal Court (ICC) 243
international governing bodies, need for 265–271; enforcing international rule of law and punishing violators 268; mediating conflicts and disputes among nations 267–268; promoting global democracy 268; regulating globalizing economies 265–267
international organizations: empowering 268–270; limitations of existing 270–271
intolerance of disloyalty 49–50
"Involuntarily Celibate" (Incel) 63, 217
Iraq and Afghan wars 15–16, 17–18, 229–230; hardline U.S. policies 167; refusal to negotiate with Baath Party and Taliban 167; to secure America's oil interests 229
Iraqi Christians, attacks on 55
ISIS/Daesh 63; appealing to "social misfits" 52, 196; "cradle" for young Muslims seeking excitement, enjoyment, and collective power 95; goals of 31; monopolizing loyalty 149; reasons for joining 62; seeking revenge 69; sympathetic grievances among joiners 219; trapping through isolation 112; use of simplism 161; using brutality to "out-frighten" enemies 170; using repressive sanctions to enforce uniformity 107; violence against moderates, deserters, defectors 33, 109
Islamic Movement of Nigeria (IMN) 140
Islamism/jihadism 55; anti-West sentiments 55; defending group honor 66–67; expansionistic goal 192; fomenting victimhood mentality 130; fueled by anti-West grievances 224, 266; global expansionist ideology 116; inspired by humiliation 220; seeking "indigenization," retribalization and "re-Islamization" of the Middle East 213
Islamist/jihadist extremist groups 14; anti-West ideological echo chamber 127; fighting against injustices committed by Western nations 222; global outreach effort 116; in-group protectionism 52; promoting tribalistic lifestyle 43; reasons for joining 127; role of extremist leaders 238
"Islamization of Europe" 213, 244; *see also* Islamophobia
Islamophobia 56
isolation 27, 50, 235–236; accentuating group identities and boundaries 236; encouraging group-centric mindsets 236; fostering group-centric mindsets 236; "mental insularity" 113, 236; trapping 112–113

Jehovah's Witnesses 49; paternalistic system 112; trapping by isolation 112–113
Jim Jones *see* People's Temple

Khmer Rouge genocide 96
Klu Klux Klan (KKK): claiming moral superiority 119; offering alternative route for power, success, and advancement 197

labeling 137–140; as hierarchical positioning process 137–138; to justify mistreatments 138–139; to persecute dissenters and critics 140; protesting minority groups as "terrorists" 139; religious and ethnic slurs and epithets 137; in U.S. politics 138
laissez-faire economic policies 261–262
law enforcement 45–46; abuse of power 64, 208–209
leftist groups: protesting against dominant extremisms 226–227; *see also* FARC; ELN
legal cynicism 53, 57, 196
"legitimation crisis" 206–210; economic crisis 208; from corrupt systems and inability to enforce rule of law 206; rise of extremist groups 206; *see also* authoritarianism; "failed states"
London riot 218–219
"lone-wolf" (individual) terrorists 12; ideological belonging 62–63
Lord's Resistance Army (LRA) 84
"losing face," fear of 63, 66
loyalty: cultivating and invoking 146–147; in exchange for protection 48; gangs' efforts to procure 146–147; as "identity verification process" 48; monopolizing loyalty 149; needed to induce sacrifice 48, 145; soliciting with social services 146
lynch mobs: 34, 73, 110, 157–158, 210, 213

marginalized groups, integration of 241; *see also* immigrant minority groups
martyrdom, glorifying 145–146
mass shooters 79
mass suicides 61

media, role in deterring extremism 262–264; exposing wrongdoing 263; oversight over established powers 263; preventing distortions of realities and truths 262; public shaming by 264; role in debunking 262
militaristic jingoism 168–169
military intervention: instigating military coups 226–227; to quell leftist movements 226; use of paramilitary "death squads" 226; U.S. role in Latin America 226
military-industrial complex 229–230
militia groups 190
moderate centrism *see* cultural deterrents of extremism
moderates 14–17; bashing of moderates by extremists 32–33, 114; clashing values with extremists 16–17; empowering to tame extremism 290–292
monarchism 43
Mongols, use of symbols 157
monopolization, as extremist goal: in corporate and business enterprises 194; of power, resources, and rewards 25, 193–194; *see also* "closed groups"; occupational closure
moral foundation of groups 40, 105–106
"moral panic/outrage," exaggerated display of 119
moral superiority 35–36; defending 36–37; formulating and cultivating 25, 117–118; "hierarchical positioning tool" 118–119; source of group power 118–119; to encourage willingness to sacrifice for groups 117; used to justify violence and injustice 119–120
Movement for the Emancipation of the Niger Delta (MEND) 225–226
MS-13: cultivating loyalty 147; defending group honor 65; punishing deserters and defectors 110; stoking fear to collect protection money 135
multinational corporations: America's role in protecting overseas 226; generating anti-West extremisms 224–225, 266; growing power of 265–266; infiltrating Africa 228; need for regulating 251–252; regulating of 252; U.S. role in Latin America 285; use of paramilitary "death squads" 74, 226–227, 285; without oversights and regulations 265; wrongdoing by 225–226, 249, 266
"myth of origin" 38–39

National Liberation Army (Columbia) *see* ELN
National Rifle Association (NRA) 124

nationalism: curtailing 242–244; in globalizing world 242; leading to isolationism, protectionism 242; protecting national honor 47–48; white nationalism in Europe 39
Nazi movement: appealing to emotions 152; blaming minority groups for failures 143; creating and demonizing enemies 128; fomenting victimhood mentality 130; Hitler's use of simplism 161; invoking loyalty 148; reasons for joining 62
neo-liberal economic theories 124
9/11 Commission Report 18, 116, 192, 216
9/11 terrorist attacks 5, American response 9, 15–16, 18–19, 37; "fate-sharing" event 231; rise of extremist mindsets among Americans 18, 31, 202
NRA *see* National Rifle Association

obstructionism, in partisan politics 11, 31, 57–58
occupational closure 194
Occupy Wall Street movement 223
"one-drop rule" 101
ontological security, from belonging 60
"open groups" 115, 192
oppositional consciousness 108; *see also* "us vs. them"
oppositional culture: among "social misfits" 196; creation of 57, 196
organizational cover-up 46–47
organizational survival 198–199; trapping members within 109, 111–112, 199
"out-frightening": importance of 166, 168–169; use of brutality 170
outlaw biker groups 61; importance of symbols 157; *see also* Mongols
"outsiders within" 114–115; *see also* anti-immigrant nativism

pack mentality *see* herd mentality
pan-Islamism 116, 128
parochialism 27, 43, 202, 245–246; *see also* anti-globalization extremism; "bunker mentality"
paternalistic system 111–112
patriarchy 6, 124–125; attacks on professional women and school girls 214–215; men's effort to preserve 176, 214; protected by traditions 43; using sexist ideologies 176; violence against women 214
patronage system 188–189
peace deals, with extremist groups 289–290; *see also* inclusion strategies
pedophiles 42; in Catholic Church 46, 53

People's Temple 61; *see also* mass suicides
persecution of journalists 164–165
personal responsibility, as an ideology 124
plutocrats 224
political parties, as extremist group 11, 31, 89–90
political purging 128, 165–166; as collective rejection 59
political tribalism 203
politics of fear *see* fear-mongering
pooling resources, for redistribution 187–188; *see also* patronage system
Pope Benedict XVI 33
Pope Francis 33; on corporate greed 251
populism: and authoritarianism 89–90; anti-establishment 17; role of humiliation 220; of Trump base 89–90, 221; of working-class 220
post-materialist values 205
pragmatic centrism 28, 272–274; *see also* cultural deterrents of extremism
preemptive attacks 23, 170–171
prejudice: against outsiders and minorities 203; and authoritarianism 90; rising under existential threats 203
prime shelter nostalgia/refuge 43, 61–62
pro-business policies 248–250, 280–281; damaging environment and injuring consumers 249; in favor of "rent-seeking" large corporations 248–250; *see also* profit-sharing schemes
profit-sharing schemes 249–250
projection, need for 34–35
protection money 134–135
purification ritual 96
purity in identity 113; in al-Qaeda 114; banning intergroup mingling and marriages 113–114; bashing of moderates 114–115; in Catholic Church 114; ideological purity 113; religious orthodoxy 114
Putin: demonizing the West 128; zero-sum view 88

race and ethnicity, socially-constructed aspects of 101; *see also* racial formation; status hierarchies, constructing
racial formation 101
rape, victim blaming 143–144; in the military 72; punished for accusing rape 50, 72
rackets *see* protection money
reactionary extremist groups 15, 22–23, 186–187; defending traditions 41–42, 186; "de-secularization" and "indigenization" 186; fear of change 212; motivated by fear of extinction 186, 212; nostalgia for the past 213; pursuing organizational survival 199; rejection of modernity 43, 186
redemptive extremist groups 13, 29, 72, 183–184, 218
"re-embedding" opportunities 289–290
regime change, policy of 227–228, 285
religion, used as ideology: 123–124; to justify injustice and violence 121–122; sacralizing" violence as "divine mission" 122; *see also* Christian Identity Group
religious fundamentalist groups 8, 14, 16–17, 19, 20, 32, 73, 82, 114, 125; defending traditions 41, 186; fear of extinction 212; fear of change 212; victimhood mentality 130–131; "war on people of faith" 131
resistant extremisms 2, 13, 66; as alternate means of achieving change 234; goals of 180–181; rebelling against dominant extremisms 221–222; root causes of 27; seeking fairness, equal rights, and justice 222; to change unfair social conditions 180
resource mobilization 27, 218
retaliatory justice 23
retribalization 13, 43, 213, 246
revenge-taking: in African tribes 68; against whistle-blowers 71–72; among American Indians 68; escalation of violence 70–71; gang retaliation murders 68–69; sectarian violence in Iraq 70; of the Taliban 70; in terrorist groups 69–70
"reverse colonization," of Europe 131
Revolutionary Armed Forces of Columbia *see* FARC
"righteous crusaders" 96
"righteous violence": committed for "noble causes" 119–120; role of ideology in justifying violence 120–121; with a sense of moral superiority 120
right-wing extremisms 19, 82; enemies of 127–128; goal of "saving America" from "corrupting" sources 183
"RINOs" *see* "Blue Dogs" and "RINOs"
rituals, collective 24, 153–155; arousing emotions 153; in politics and military 154; promoting group solidarity and power 153–154; in religious services 153–154; to stagecraft powerful image of leaders 155; *see also* Durkheim, Emile
Rohingya Muslims 94, 139
role of the state, in deterring extremism 259–262; balancing clashing interests and values 260; enforcing rule of law 259; promoting fair competition through regulation 260–262; protecting equal rights 259–260
Roof, Dylann 63

rule of law, democratic 251–253
Rwandan genocide 34, 72

sacrifice 145–146; *see also* martyrdom; suicide bombers
Sarbane-Oxley Law 71
Saudi royal families 189
"savior" image of leadership: 134
scapegoating 141–143
sectarian violence in Iraq: escalation after U.S.-led invasion of Iraq 55; as revenge-taking 70; role of grievances 216–217; symbolic boundaries between Shiite and Sunni 41
securities dilemmas 18, 202, 205–206
shared fates of collectivities 279–280; of globalized economy 28; of humanities 279
Shintoism 123
shunning 49, 63, 112; *see also* fear of rejection
simplism 160–162
single-issue fanatics/voters 96
social hierarchy in prisons 78
"social misfits" 62; alienated immigrants 196; attraction to extremist groups 195–196; seeking alternative source of achievement, protection, support system, and status-attainment 195–196
social performance theory 153
solidarity-in-kind 60; *see also* homophily
Somali pirates 226
special interest groups, corporate sector 248–250
"spiritual marriages" 123
state-sponsored extremist acts: genocides and ethnic cleansing 84; human rights violations 85–86; military invasion and annexation 85; using weapons of mass destruction 85; war crimes 84–86
"status group ties" 100, 177, 194
status hierarchies: bullying as "status achievement struggle" 182; constructing group identities to create 100–103; elevation of group status 24–25; *see also* hierarchical positioning
stereotyping 140–142; to accentuate group differences 141; effects of 141–142; as group "positioning tool" 141; to justify mistreatment 141; of minority groups 141; in U.S. politics 141
strategic changes, in dealing with extremist groups 282–292; deescalating extremist aggressions 283–284; fostering and empowering moderates and technocrats 290–291; inclusion of extremist groups into society 289–290; negotiating compromises with respectful diplomacy 286–288; promoting reconciliation 288–289; rectifying the root causes of grievances 284–286
"strongmen" autocracy 203; *see also* authoritarian leaders
structural changes, to deter extremism 251–258; enforcing democratic rule of law 251–252; liberal and inclusive democracies 256–258; reducing extreme and unfair inequalities 254–256
sub-prime loan scandal 86
"sui generis," groups as 38
suicide bombing, as martyrdom 145–146
supply-side economic theories 124; problems with 280–281; *see also* pro-business policies
symbolic leadership 91–92, 158–160; Catholic popes 158; leaders as representation of the group 158; monarchs 158; with "spiritual persona" 158; *see also* "symbolicizing"
symbolic politics/choice theory 156
"symbolicizing" past legendary heroes 159–160
symbols, use of 25, 155–160; as group identifiers 38, 103, 156; becoming "group in reification" 156; importance of defending 157–158; invoking sense of belonging 156; objects that epitomize the group 155–156
sympathetic grievances/indignation 27, 218–219; in Civil Rights movement 218; in London riot of 2011 218–219; vicarious indignation on behalf of the victims of injustice 218
"synthetic nationhood" 102

Taliban: ideological indoctrination 126; revenge-taking 70; school attacks 55; stoking fear to collect protection money 135
Tamil Tigers 139
TCC *see* transnational capitalist class
terrorism: moderates' rebuke of 16; rationales for 23; strategy used by military underdogs 234; terrorist attacks as collective rejection and punishment 23, 251; *see also* collective punishment; guilt by association
terrorist groups: joining to earn respect through violence 77; reason for joining 62; for redemptive goals 183; for revenge-taking 69
"too-big-to-fail" banks 86, 262
tradition: justifying unfair and unjust systems 125; patriarchy, monarchy, caste system 43, 124–125; source of

radicalization 41; as symbol of group identity 42; upholding 41–42; used as an ideology 124–125; used by privileged groups to maintain status quo 43–44, 125; *see also* fear of extinction
"traitors" and "sell-outs" 49
transgendered people, violence against 33
transnational capitalist class (TCC) 177, 224
"trapping" 111–112; *see also* dependency relationship
traumas, collectively-shared: 101
tribalism 190; yearning for tribalistic lifestyle 43; *see also* retribalization; prime shelter nostalgia/refuge
trickle-down wealth effect 124
Trinitarios 65
"true believers" 96
Trump, Donald: appealing to emotions 152; fear-mongering 134; labeling of opponents and critics 138; obsession with military prowess 169; strategy of simplism 162
Tsarnaev brothers 52, 63
"Turkey-bashing" in Germany 143

Uighurs 107, 139
unity, in-group 22, 25, 40–44, 105–107; source of courage and sacrifice 105; source of group power 105–106; *see also* homogenizing pressure; moral foundation of groups
"us vs. them" mindset 22–23, 30–34, 38, 40, 99, 102–103, 277; in American politics 31; use of group symbols to identify 103
utopian vision 24, 161

victimhood mentality 130–131
vigilante violence 209–210; *see also* legal cynicism; lynch mobs
vindictiveness 67–70; escalation of violence 68; in terrorist groups 69–70
violence 73–76; against homosexuals and transgendered 111; against women 73–74; corporate-sponsored 74; flaunting 78; as form of enjoyment, excitement, thrill 76, 96; institutional and state-sponsored 74; as performance 78; as "purification ritual" 96; "righteous" 121; role of ideologies in justifying 121–122; role of religion in justifying 122–123; as source of power, respect and "status symbol" 76–77; "spiritual" violence 122; "virtuous" rape 122

Wahhabism 116
war profiteering 86; from Iraq War, Iraq-Iran War, and Yemeni civil war 229–230; by U.S. weapons industries, oil companies, and defense contractors 86, 179–180, 229–230, 249
Weathermen 15
welfare states, in Europe 256
whistle blowers: retaliation against, by corporations and government agencies 71–72; as "traitors" 50
"white genocide" 131
white supremacist groups 12, 20; fear of extinction 212; fear of losing power, dominance 212; "great replacement" theory 215; nostalgia for the past 213; resentment over rise of minority population and their improving status 220–221; rise after election of president Obama 220; use of victimhood mentality 130
"witch craze" 128; as scapegoating 142
women's suffrage movement 9

xenophobia 35, 201, 203,

Yanomamo Indians 68
"Yellow Vest" protests 223

zero-sum view 24, 87–90, 202–203